SILVER IN AMERICA

SILVER IN AMERICA
1840–1940
A CENTURY OF SPLENDOR

CHARLES L. VENABLE

TOM JENKINS, LEAD PHOTOGRAPHER

BIOGRAPHICAL ENTRIES BY D. ALBERT SOEFFING

DALLAS MUSEUM OF ART

DISTRIBUTED BY

HARRY N. ABRAMS, INC.

PUBLISHERS

This book has been published in conjunction with the exhibition *Silver in America, 1840–1940: A Century of Splendor*, organized by the Dallas Museum of Art and held at the Dallas Museum of Art from 6 November 1994 to 29 January 1995; the Carnegie Museum of Art, Pittsburgh, from 12 March to 21 May 1995; the Milwaukee Art Museum from 13 June to 13 August 1995; and the Henry Francis du Pont Winterthur Museum, Winterthur, Delaware, from 9 September 1995 to 7 January 1996.

The exhibition and catalogue were made possible by grants from the National Endowment for the Humanities and the National Endowment for the Arts, federal agencies.

Additional support for the exhibition and catalogue came from The Andrew W. Mellon Foundation; The Edward and Betty Marcus Fund, established in their honor by Melba Davis Whatley; Gorham Silver; Lenox, Inc.; and Sotheby's. American Airlines was the official carrier for the exhibition. KDFW-TV was the exclusive television sponsor of the exhibition in Dallas.

Distributed in 1995 by Harry N. Abrams, Incorporated, New York
A Times Mirror Company

Gerald W. R. Ward, content editor
Patricia Draher, copy editor
Ed Marquand, designer
Tomarra LeRoy, design assistant

Produced by Marquand Books, Inc., Seattle

Printed and bound by C & C Offset Printing, Hong Kong

Library of Congress Cataloging-in-Publication Data
Venable, Charles L. (Charles Lane), 1960–
   Silver in America, 1840–1940 : a century of splendor / Charles L. Venable, author ; Tom Jenkins, lead photographer ; D. Albert Soeffing, biographical entries.
      p.   cm.
   "Published in conjunction with the exhibition 'Silver in America, 1840–1940: a century of splendor' held at the Dallas Museum of Art from 6 November 1994 to 29 January 1995. . . . " —T.p. verso.
   Includes bibliographical references and index.
   ISBN 0-8109-3199-0
   1. Silverware—United States—History—19th century—Exhibitions. 2. Silverware—United States—History—20th century—Exhibitions. I. Dallas Museum of Art. II. Title.
NK7234.V46   1994
739.2'3773'090340747642812—dc20

                                                                                                      94-16572
                                                                                                      CIP

Front jacket: Selection of flatware, Dallas Museum of Art, see ill. 6.1.
Back jacket: Cigar humidor, Dallas Museum of Art, see fig. 6.63.
Frontispiece: Coffeepot, Dallas Museum of Art, see fig. 5.6.
Page 6: Pitcher, Dallas Museum of Art, see fig. 2.5.
Page 8: *Isis* pattern fish set, Dallas Museum of Art, see fig. 3.26.
Page 10: Sewing implements, Dallas Museum of Art, see fig. 5.2.

CONTENTS

FOREWORD

In 1985, the Dallas Museum of Art established a decorative arts department to oversee the cataloguing and care of two recently acquired collections: The Wendy and Emery Reves Collection of European decorative arts and the Faith P. and Charles L. Bybee Collection of American furniture. The following year the Museum hired Charles L. Venable as curator of decorative arts and began devising an acquisition policy designed to both knit together its current holdings and take advantage of market opportunities. Since that time, the Museum has made steady and significant progress in several areas within European and American decorative arts. Its activities in the area of nineteenth- and early twentieth-century silver made in the United States have been especially noteworthy.

This field of specialization was chosen for several reasons. First, the aesthetic and technical quality of the best silverwork from this period was truly outstanding. Second, compared to colonial American silver, there were still many exceptional objects in private hands and on the art market that could potentially be acquired by a museum. And third, the ratio of quality to investment was high. With these facts in mind, in 1987 the DMA began to solicit gifts and to purchase silver made after 1840. This process was greatly furthered in 1989 when Margaret McDermott, through the Eugene and Margaret McDermott Fund, made possible the purchase at auction of several important objects from the Sam Wagstaff Collection. Dallas's acquisitions at that sale elicited enough publicity to attract the attention of numerous dealers and private collectors. As a result the DMA was offered many fine objects for its growing collection. Of special note has been the acquisition in 1991 of the Charles R. Masling and John E. Furen Collection, and of the Oberod Collection of *Martelé*. In 1992 and 1993 highlights of the Stephen Vaughan Collection came to the DMA, ensur-

ing that its holdings of American flatware were of the first rank. The Museum is extremely grateful to all the donors, dealers, and collectors who made these and other stellar acquisitions possible.

The organization of *Silver in America, 1840–1940: A Century of Splendor* grew directly out of this collecting activity. As new objects entered the collection, Charles Venable became acutely aware of how neglected was the study of this area of American art history. As a result he decided to focus on the phenomenal rise in production and consumption of silverware in the United States for his doctoral dissertation at Boston University. The research for that work, "Silver in America, 1840–1940: Production, Marketing, and Consumption," firmly convinced Venable that a major exhibition accompanied by a scholarly catalogue should be organized on this subject. Five years of work on Charles's part, as well as that of DMA staff photographer Tom Jenkins, have resulted in this volume and the exhibition it documents.

This project has benefited from the commitment and dedication of the DMA staff, and is fortunate to have attracted significant funding from a variety of sources. The National Endowment for the Humanities has been especially generous. Without its support this catalogue and exhibition would not have been possible. Similarly, the exhibition would have been much more difficult to organize in a timely fashion without the early commitments from the three other venues. We in Dallas are pleased that the visitors to our sister institutions in Pittsburgh, Milwaukee, and the Delaware Valley will find our efforts both intellectually stimulating and aesthetically pleasing.

Jay Gates
Director, Dallas Museum of Art

LENDERS TO THE EXHIBITION

The Art Institute of Chicago
David M. Campbell
The Carnegie Museum of Art, Pittsburgh
The Charles R. Masling and John E. Furen Collection
Chicago Historical Society
The Chrysler Museum, Norfolk, Virginia
Cranbrook Academy of Art Museum, Bloomfield Hills,
    Michigan
Dallas Museum of Art
Charles Folk
Denis Gallion and Daniel Morris/Historical Design
    Collection, New York
The Henry Clay Memorial Foundation, Lexington,
    Kentucky
High Museum of Art, Atlanta
William Hill Land and Cattle Company
Maryland Historical Society, Baltimore
The Masco Art Collection, Taylor, Michigan
The Meriden Historical Society, Meriden, Connecticut
The Metropolitan Museum of Art, New York
The Minneapolis Institute of Arts
The Mitchell Wolfson, Jr., Collection, The Wolfsonian
    Foundation, Miami Beach, Florida, and Genoa, Italy
Musée Bouilhet-Christofle, Paris

Museum of Art, Rhode Island School of Design, Providence
Museum of the City of New York
Museum of Fine Arts, Boston
Museum of Fine Arts, Houston
Museum of New Mexico, Palace of the Governors, Santa Fe
National Museum of American History, Smithsonian
    Institution, Washington, D.C.
New York Yacht Club
Norwest Corporation, Minneapolis
Philadelphia Museum of Art
The Preservation Society of Newport County, Rhode Island
Private Collections
Private Collection, courtesy Hoffman Gampetro Antiques
Private Collection, San Antonio
Mr. Jerome Rapoport and Ms. Susan Falk
Reed & Barton, Inc., Collection
Charles J. Robertson
D. Albert Soeffing
Mr. and Mrs. Alexander Speyer III
Sylvia and Charles Venable
Rusty Venable
Wadsworth Atheneum, Hartford
John R. Young

PREFACE
AND
ACKNOWLEDGMENTS

Five years ago when I began building a collection of nineteenth- and twentieth-century American silver for the Dallas Museum of Art, it was not in preparation for this book or exhibition. Rather, I simply felt that silver of this period was one of the few remaining areas that offered exceptionally high quality objects of great aesthetic distinction for relatively little money. As Dallas's collection grew, however, it became clear that a broad survey of the period and its accomplishments in silver was needed. Consequently, I decided to investigate the subject in the form of a doctoral dissertation for the American and New England Studies Program at Boston University. Following a year of initial research, it was obvious that enough primary source material existed to warrant pursuing the topic not just as a dissertation, but as a full-scale traveling exhibition. My hope is that readers and museum visitors will find the results rewarding. Certainly, points in my argument will require revision over time as more information comes to light. Whatever errors exist are totally mine; I can only hope my work at worst will be found wanting in detail and not in the broad overview that was my main intent. I also apologize for not being able to put the information on individual objects found in the back of the book below the appropriate images. Doing so would have forced the reduction in size of each illustration, which I felt was even more of a compromise. And imbedding extensive information on each object within the text would have made a coherent story line impossible due to constant digressions.

During the past five years, I have drawn upon the expertise of scores of individuals, without whose cooperation and help this book and exhibition would not have been possible. I am particularly indebted to D. Albert Soeffing for sharing so much of his vast knowledge with me. Stephen Vaughan, Samuel Hough, Elenita C. Chickering, and Charles H. Carpenter, Jr., have also been enormously helpful in answering my myriad questions. The staffs of numerous libraries and archives have led me to many important documents. I wish to thank Mark Brown at Brown University; Neville Thompson at Winterthur; Beatrice Morehouse at the Meriden Historical Society; and Annamarie Sandecki and Debbie Morgan at Tiffany's, as well as their predecessors Janet Zapata and Ruth Caccavale. James McMenamin at the Chilton Co. was instrumental in arranging for me to examine the firm's early issues of the *Jewelers' Circular-Keystone*. Fred Roy, Jr., at Gorham similarly

allowed me to review a wealth of material still held by the firm. Also, several people in the antique silver trade helped track down pieces I desired for the book and show. Jeanne Sloan of Christie's and Kevin Tierny of Sotheby's, as well as Ron Hoffman and Phyllis Tucker were especially helpful.

Following the initial research, I relied on the guidance of several persons to improve my dissertation, "Silver in America, 1840–1940: Production, Marketing, and Consumption" (1993). The efforts of professors Keith N. Morgan and Richard Candee of Boston University; Edward S. Cooke, Jr., of Yale; and Philip Scranton of Rutgers were most beneficial. Gerald W. R. Ward and Patricia Draher, who served as content and copy editors respectively, were especially important in turning the dissertation into a more readable book for public consumption. The staff of Marquand Books helped ensure that this volume is both clearly presented and beautiful.

Above all I need to thank the staff of the Dallas Museum of Art who worked to make this effort a success. Former director Richard R. Brettell approved and supported the original idea as something the DMA would undertake. Jay Gates, director; Clay Johnson, chief operating officer; and Susan Barnes, deputy director, have been enthusiastic about and supportive of *Silver in America*. Of those who have contributed directly to the book, thanks must go first to Tom Jenkins whose photography is some of the finest I have ever seen, and Virginia Fain whose efforts brought order to the project. Others who assisted in preparing the manuscript and illustrations include Gary Wooley, Kevin Comerford, Rita Paschal, Darin Marshall, Heather Hoyt, Allen Townsend, Cathy Zisk, Scott Hagar, Barbara Scott, and Marie Chiles. Staff members who worked to make the exhibition a success include Kim Bush, Karen Zelanka, Andrew Meredith, Anna McFarland, Debra Wittrup, Gail Davitt, Melissa Berry, George Speer, Meg Hanlon, John Dennis, Ginger Reeder, Queta Watson, Stone Savage, Roderick McSwain, Russell Sublette, Lawrence Bruton, David Miller, Ron Moody, Skip Alexander, Ron Jordan, Doug Velek, and Melissa Jolin.

In terms of financial support for the book and exhibition, I am indebted to Emily Summers, associate director of exhibition funding, and her assistant, Mary McLean, for coordinating our fund-raising efforts. Of those who have underwritten *Silver in America*, the National Endowment for the

Humanities and the National Endowment for the Arts, federal agencies, have been particularly generous, contributing to both the planning and implementation of the exhibition. Additional underwriting has been provided by the Andrew W. Mellon Foundation; the Edward and Betty Marcus Fund, established in their honor by Melba Davis Whatley; Gorham Silver; Lenox, Inc.; and Sotheby's. American Airlines is the official carrier of the exhibition, and KDFW-TV is the exclusive television sponsor of the exhibition in Dallas. The Dallas Museum of Art is extremely grateful for all of these contributions.

And finally I wish to think my wife, Sylvia, and daughter, Alexandra, for putting up with my absences and obsessions relating to this project during the past five years. Without their encouragement my efforts would have been much more difficult. I dedicate this book to them.

INTRODUCTION

In 1836 Edward Hazen in *Panorama of Professions and Trades* described the work of a silversmith as consisting primarily of hand labor. While noting the use of simple roller dies for making decorative borders and turning lathes for cleaning and burnishing vessels, Hazen said:

> In forming the body [of a vessel] . . . , the plate . . . is cut into a circular form, and placed on a block of soft wood with a concave face, where it is beaten with a convex hammer until it has been brought to a form much like that of a saucer. It is then placed upon an anvil, and beaten a while longer with a long-necked hammer with a round flattish face.[1]

Hazen's description is one that could have been made at almost any time since the Renaissance, and perhaps even since antiquity, for in many ways the silversmiths who worked in the United States during the early nineteenth century were little changed from their American and European forebears. During the first four decades of the century, most silversmiths worked in small artisan shops with fewer than six employees; produced objects by hand with only occasional aid from simple machinery; labored in a "familial" atmosphere where the master/owner worked alongside his journeymen and apprentices; served a local market of well-to-do clients; did little or no advertising; and produced objects that were derivative of English and French prototypes. In short, the typical silversmith working in this country before 1840 led a life closer to his eighteenth-century predecessors than to that of his late-nineteenth-century successors.[2] By 1890 silversmithing in America had changed so drastically that it is still hard to believe that such a revolution was accomplished in just fifty years.

The most dramatic aspects of this evolution occurred after 1840. Some significant developments did happen earlier, however. As Deborah Dependahl Waters has shown, there existed in urban centers such as Philadelphia and New York silversmiths whose ambition and capabilities pushed them beyond the traditional boundaries of their artisan counterparts and toward change. Rather than maintain a small shop, use only hand power, and serve a local market, these silversmith-entrepreneurs were "eager to expand by exploiting wider markets. . . . Such proprietors supervised production of consumer goods in quantity and retailed a portion of their wares to local customers but reserved the bulk for merchants and general store owners outside the metropolitan area."[3] Foremost among these urban-based entrepreneurs were men like Thomas Fletcher and Baldwin Gardiner (active 1808–1827) of Boston and Philadelphia and William Gale, Sr. (1799–1864), of New York. Desiring to expand both production capabilities and their markets, such silversmiths sought out or invented labor-saving devices and advertised their wares. For example, Fletcher (1787–1866) moved to Philadelphia in search of a more dynamic market and then traveled to England in 1815 to contact possible suppliers and observe production techniques using steam-power rolling mills and drop presses.[4] Also, interested in new technology, Gale greatly improved his production capabilities and eventually revolutionized the American flatware industry by inventing a roller die in the mid 1820s that would shape forks and spoons from blanks more efficiently than the primitive drop stamps, hand swages, and screw-presses then in use (ill. 1.1).[5] To increase sales as their production expanded due to better organization and improved tools, men such as these also advertised more than their artisan brothers. Fletcher and Gardiner, for example, capitalized on the publicity surrounding the silver urn commissioned from them for presentation to Captain Isaac Hull in 1812 by having the piece engraved on their trade cards and shown in advertisements as late as 1822.[6]

Rural metalworkers were less likely to modernize production and expand markets before 1840 in comparison to their urban counterparts. The leading exception, however, is Babbitt & Crossman, founded in Taunton, Massachusetts, in 1824. In this typical artisan shop, Isaac Babbitt (1799–1862) and William Crossman (b. 1794) worked side by side with the five to six men they employed in the production of pewter ware.[7] In running this small-scale firm, Babbitt and Crossman sought ways to improve and expand both production and markets. Babbitt made countless experiments with alloys in hopes of duplicating the English Britannia metal that was flooding the American market. In 1824 he succeeded. In 1826 the partners decided to abandon erratic water power and expand their business. That year they erected a two-story brick shop and purchased both a James rotary-valve steam engine and a new rolling mill capable of flattening the Britannia metal into smooth sheets. In 1833 Crossman invented, or at least improved, the technique of metal spinning (ill. 4.5). The patent granted him in 1834 notes:

> The ordinary mode used in making such ware is to raise, or stamp up, from the sheet metal, such parts, say one-half, of these vessels, as will relieve from the mould or die after stamping, and then to solder such parts together. By the process which I have adopted, I rub, or burnish up, the required vessels, from a single flat plate, or sheet.[8]

This technique of creating hollowware by bending a sheet of flat silver over a wooden form while both rotated on a spinning lathe revolutionized the metalware industry over the next two decades. Although they faced numerous financial difficulties in the trying economic times of the 1820s and 1830s, the development and application of innovative production processes, coupled with the introduction of electroplating technology in the 1840s, eventually transformed the small-scale firm of Babbitt & Crossman into the giant silverplate and sterling manufacturing company of Reed & Barton, employing several hundred workers.

The emergence of a few leading firms in both urban and rural settings was significant. Nevertheless, American silverware production was dominated by numerous small-scale producers located throughout the East before 1840. Often working seasonally to accommodate farming activities, most of these makers produced coin-silver spoons for local markets. Consequently, the development of U.S. silversmithing from the early decades of the nineteenth century, when such artisan shops dominated the trade, to a multimillion-dollar industry controlled by large corporations must be seen as an amazing achievement. However, it was not an isolated phenomenon in American business history. Other producers of luxury goods and custom machinery underwent parallel developments. The evolution of the piano industry, for example, was especially close to that of silverware. As Gary Kornblith and Craig Roell have shown, nineteenth-century leaders like Jonas Chickering in Boston, the Steinways in New York, and Baldwin in Cincinnati reorganized piano production using large numbers of specialized artisans and the division of labor.[9] Also, like silver producers, they sought a national market through intensive advertising and world's fair competition. And finally, the general pace of the piano industry's development was similar to that of silverware, with massive expansion of production occurring in the mid nineteenth century, the centralization of the trade in the hands of a few major concerns after the Civil War, and the ultimate stagnation of the market in the early twentieth century. This type of evolution—common in numerous labor-intensive, luxury trades—was in direct contrast to that of mass-produced consumer goods such as tobacco, matches, flour, and soap. As Alfred Chandler has explained, manufacturers of these goods, unlike those of silverware or pianos, completely standardized production, relied more on processing machinery than skilled labor, and produced millions of identical objects.[10]

In the case of silverware, the transition from small-scale producer to large manufacturer was not easy for many artisans. Dozens of silversmiths who preferred the traditional small shop in which they worked alongside their few employees and knew most of their customers personally, were eventually forced to work in the emerging large manufactories, become retail store owners or wholesale jobbers, or leave the trade altogether. Even the most aggressive of the early silversmiths did not anticipate the challenges of running large manufactories, which required sizable capital investment, the management of scores of men, world-class design teams, advertising campaigns, extensive international distribution networks, production efficiency, and detailed accounting. Furthermore, few could have guessed that, in spite of huge manufactories with their organized work routines and labor-saving equipment, large amounts of handwork requiring highly skilled silversmiths would be needed throughout the period.

The emergence of the United States as a world leader in silverware production, marketing, and consumption between 1840 and 1940 affected the lives of countless men and women. Not only did the industry provide jobs for thousands of workers, but it also created silverware for consumers who used it in both utilitarian and symbolic ways. The chapters that follow attempt to document the rise of the American silverware industry during these ten decades, as well as provide insight into the important role silver objects played in the daily lives of many consumers. To bring order to the enormous mass of data on this fascinating but often chaotic industry, the story is broken chronologically into three periods: 1840–75, 1875–1915, and 1885–1940. Although such divisions are to some extent arbitrary—history being a continuous flow, never starting and stopping so conveniently—these three divisions constitute temporal brackets around major developments in the silverware industry. Parts II and III overlap because many of the business and cultural changes that defined the nature of the early-twentieth-century silver industry began in the 1880s.

Within each of these three sections the information is organized into three further categories: production, marketing, and consumption. The one exception is Chapter 3, which focuses on design almost exclusively, leaving consumption in this early period to Chapter 6. This arrangement helps to bring clarity to the distinct but related processes that lay behind the creation and use of every silver object. While most aspects of the American silverware phenomenon fit neatly into one of these categories, design does not. Designing is both the first part of the production process and the end result of consumption. Thus it is the link between production and consumption that makes the entire process a circular one—managers trying to create demand through novel designs and consumers influencing product design as they accept or reject objects in the marketplace. Consequently, design is discussed throughout the text as necessary. In the 1860s and 1920s, for example, producers often tried to lead public taste by introducing novel shapes with innovative decoration. At other periods, they tended to respond to consumer preferences by designing conservative objects that did not aesthetically challenge potential buyers.

Hopefully this effort will shed light on an industry that has been generally neglected by scholars in comparison to other fields such as painting or furniture. Even with soaring auction prices for nineteenth- and twentieth-century American silver, relatively little work has been done in the field. Furthermore, most efforts have been of an antiquarian nature, seeking to determine where and when an object was made. Others, such as Graham Hood's *American Silver* (1971), give such cursory attention to the silver of this period in relation to earlier work that they suggest artifacts from this era are not worthy of study.

To be sure, some studies contain a wealth of information and have been vital to this effort. George Gibb's *The Whitesmiths of Taunton* (1943) is an amazing book which should be more widely read by collectors and scholars. It is one of the few works that rightly concentrate on economics and business practices to explain why objects often were created the way they were. However, it was a series of works in the 1960s and 1970s that drew attention to nineteenth-century silver. Dorothy T. Rainwater's *Encyclopedia of American Silver Manufacturers* (1966), and her and H. Ivan Rainwater's *American Silverplate* (1968), along with Katharine Morrison McClinton's *Collecting American Nineteenth Century Silver* (1968), were the first of this group. Next came Berry Tracy's landmark cata-

logue and exhibition at the Metropolitan Museum of Art, *19th-Century America* (1970). These were followed in quick succession by Noel D. Turner's *American Silver Flatware, 1837–1910* (1972); Edmund P. Hogan's *An American Heritage* (1977); Sharon S. Darling's *Chicago Metalsmiths* (1977); Mary Grace Carpenter and Charles Carpenter's *Tiffany Silver* (1978) and *Gorham Silver, 1831–1981* (1982); and *Silver in the Golden State* (1986), edited by Edward W. Morse. While all these studies have added greatly to our knowledge of specific aspects of American silver history, the works that have been most successful in placing silver within a cultural context are Barbara McLean Ward and Gerald W. R. Ward's *Silver in American Life* (1979) and David Warren, Katherine Howe, and Michael Brown's *Marks of Achievement* (1987).

As good as these studies are, however, not one addresses the American silverware industry as a whole with all of its many facets. Either they are monographs on a particular firm or region; deal with a single category like presentation silver; or concentrate primarily on eighteenth- and early-nineteenth-century material or styles. Given the significant difficulties in researching and writing about a huge industry that consisted of dozens of firms, produced millions of objects in myriad styles, and served diverse markets, it is little wonder that such an overview has not been attempted. While I hope that this effort in some ways comes near its lofty goal of providing such a resource, I hope even more that it will encourage others to delve further into the history of American silver.

NOTES

1. Hazen 1839, 261.

2. Waters 1981. This is an excellent study of the traditional nature of silversmithing in this country between 1788 and 1832 and how it was beginning to change under the leadership of a few silversmith-entrepreneurs.

3. *Ibid.*, 5.

4. For excellent discussions of Fletcher and Gardiner, see Waters 1981, 78–93, and Fennimore 1972.

5. "Silversmithing in America, Part IV: Dominick & Haff, New York," *JCK* 24:21 (22 June 1892):6.

6. Waters 1981, 79–80.

7. See Gibb 1943 for an excellent discussion of the history of Reed & Barton from 1824 to 1943.

8. *Ibid.*, 73.

9. Kornblith 1985 and Roell 1989.

10. For a discussion of these industries, see Chandler 1977.

Part 1

FOUNDATIONS LAID
1840–1875

Upon examining the manufactory of the New York firm of Dominick & Haff in 1892, a writer for the *Jewelers' Circular* stated:

> Silversmithing has become a craft of industry, retaining many of the traditions and essentials of pure art in whose realms it formerly resided. The student of industrial progress visiting the modern silversmith's factory will find much food for meditation. Before his mind's eye rises involuntarily an image of the shop in which the ancient solitary silversmith hammered the metal, and, manipulating it with a few simple tools, produced a work of art. Here in the modern factory he sees hundreds of men, divided into bodies each of whom performs an individual operation; the whirring of the shafting, the bussing of hundreds of wheels, the twanging of hammers, produces a conglomeration of noise which drowns the voice. The result of this animation is the production of articles, beautiful in form, exquisite in decoration, and artistic in treatment.[1]

What had occurred between the early and late nineteenth century to produce such changes? What processes worked to transform the "solitary" silversmith's shop into a place employing scores of workers performing specialized functions? And how in this modern factory setting was it still possible to produce "articles, beautiful in form, exquisite in decoration, and artistic in treatment" not unlike the "works of art" from an earlier time? Somehow the late-nineteenth-century factory setting with all of its structure and machinery had maintained silversmithing as a "craft of industry" complete with many of the craft's "traditions and essentials."

The answers to these questions are difficult at best. However, it seems clear that the great transformations noted by this observer had their beginnings in the 1840s. During this decade several pivotal things occurred that allowed silversmith entrepreneurs to exploit new methods of production, shop organization, and marketing. Even though they had experimented with these during the trying economic climate that followed the War of 1812, few changes had resulted. The fact that the country's economy improved dramatically in the 1840s and continued to expand until the Panic of 1873, however, meant that innovative practices could be exploited to great advantage.

Chapter 1

THE TARIFF OF 1842 AND THE REORGANIZATION OF PRODUCTION

Beginning in the 1810s the United States experienced a long period of economic stagnation that extended through the 1820s. While the situation improved somewhat in the early 1830s, the end of the decade saw the Panic of 1837 which initiated a severe economic contraction characterized by numerous business and bank failures and high unemployment, which lasted into the early 1840s. About 1843, however, the economy revived strongly. During the next three decades, the U.S. economy and especially the expanding industrial sector in the North grew almost continuously.[2] With an expanding economy, silversmiths who wished to enlarge their shops, hire more workers, and purchase new machinery found it easier to attract investment capital. Simultaneously, a growing economy meant that more people were employed and earning money with which they in turn could purchase luxury goods such as silverware.

Along with the improved economic climate, an increase in the ad valorem tax on imported silverware (along with other commodities including textiles, iron, glass, and porcelain) from 20 percent to 30 percent enacted by Congress in August 1842 greatly aided silver producers.[3] Contemporary commentators agreed that the increased tariff was critical to the foundation of large-scale silver manufacturing in this country. Looking back from 1871 a reporter for the *New York Daily Tribune* stated:

> The successful manufacture of plate in this country is a direct result of Protection. Until that was afforded, the industry languished and many houses which embarked on it failed. At length the case was presented to Henry Clay, and by his powerful aid a 40 percent duty on imported plate was levied. Thence forward this industry prospered and expanded, until, by the aid of American inventions and machinery, we now make the cheapest and best Silver Ware in the world.[4]

Although he exaggerated the amount of increase, the importance this observer placed on the 1842 tariff was warranted.

For some time before the tariff increase was enacted, American silversmiths had been pressuring Congress for protection. In 1841, for example, more than 500 silversmiths and precious-metals workers from New York City signed a petition that was presented in Washington calling for increased duties on imported plate. Fortunately for the silversmiths, Senator Henry Clay, the champion of "Home Protection," took up their cause and saw the increase on foreign silverware through Congress. To show their appreciation "the gold and silver artisans of the City of New York" presented Clay in 1845 with an elaborate urn surmounted by an American eagle (fig. 1.1). As D. Albert Soeffing has pointed out, "silversmiths were faithful until death; they formed a substantial and prominent portion of Clay's funeral procession when it was held in New York City on Saturday, July 3, 1852."[5]

The effect of the increased duty was quickly felt. In 1840, for example, the London silversmiths Storr & Mortimer established a branch in New York City, which they stocked with approximately $150,000 worth of silverware. Despite their fame and the high quality of their wares, however, the increased duty placed on imported silver in 1842 made it impossible for them to succeed in this country. Within a year of the tariff's implementation, Storr & Mortimer's American branch was out of business.[6] Furthermore, those items that were still imported cost substantially more. Consequently, American consumers were more likely to purchase domestic silver, which was cheaper or at least competitive in price and, by the late 1850s, of generally equal quality. The federal government continued to promote the consumption of domestically made items through tariff protection during the rest of the nineteenth and early twentieth centuries. In 1913 the duty on imported solid silver hollowware was increased to 50 percent ad valorem, in 1922 to 60 percent, and in 1930 to 65 percent.[7]

Another beneficial consequence of the Tariff of 1842 was a greatly expanded source of raw material: silver coins. Since the founding of the British North American colonies in the seventeenth century, the main source of silver bullion for metalsmiths was foreign coinage, especially Spanish-American coins, which circulated throughout the western hemisphere.[8] However, silver and gold coins of all types were always in short

FIG. 1.1. Covered urn. William Adams, New York, N.Y., 1845. Coin silver. Collection of the Henry Clay Memorial Foundation.

supply in the British colonies; hence most trade here was conducted by barter and credit. The passage of the Tariff of 1842 helped to change this situation. Because provisions in the tariff legislation required duty on imports to be paid in silver or gold specie, large quantities of bullion came into the country after passage. In just the first nine months following the implementation of the tariff, $22 million in coin flowed into the United States.[9] By 1844 the *Hartford Courant* was able to report that "10,000 American or Mexican half-dollars are melted in Boston every week (about $250,000 per year). New York and Philadelphia must use still more."[10] And indeed they did. An 1868 description of New York's Wall Street, where most precious-metal trading firms were located, noted that "large kegs of Mexican dollars are to be seen in the vaults or behind the counters of the dealers in bullion, as numerous as kegs of nails in a hardware store."[11] Many of the Mexican coins, as well as the metal for the domestic ones, had probably entered the country in payment of tariff duties.

Although some sterling objects were being made by the 1850s, silver coins continued to be the primary source of metal for silverware until the late 1860s, by which time most large producers had switched from making "coin" silver to sterling in order to compete more effectively with their highly regarded English counterparts.[12] Like coins, the source for sterling silver was usually Wall Street, where it was bought "in the form of small, rough, silver bricks" marked with the metal's quality.[13] Most of this high-grade silver also came from Mexican or Peruvian sources, as well as rich U.S. mines like the Comstock Lode, which was discovered in Nevada in 1859.

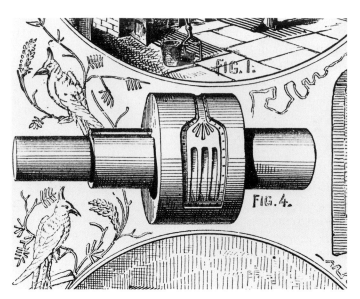

ILL. 1.1. Roller die.

PRODUCTION

Given the growing economy and an increasing supply of silver bullion, many American silversmiths decided to enhance their production capacity noticeably between 1840 and 1875. One of the chief means of achieving this goal was to acquire new tools and machinery. As pointed out by Deborah Dependahl Waters, it is difficult to know exactly what tools a "typical" silversmith used in the early nineteenth century. However, the estate inventory made upon the death of Philadelphia silversmith John Owen in 1828 is suggestive of what a shop generally contained. In his shop were "a rolling mill [for flattening silver into sheets], . . . a . . . turning lathe [for cleaning and polishing vessels], a draw bench and tongs, for the preparation of silver wire moldings, stakes, hammers, turning tools, flatware pounces, vices, files, scrapers, burnishers, chasing tools, used to ornament finished articles, shears, pliers, saws, steel and iron binding wire, forge tools, scotch and pumice stone for polishing, bellows, and a soldering lamp."[14] Beyond these basic tools, shops increasingly had, as noted by Edward Hazen in 1836, "engraved steel rollers" for the production of decorative borders, as well as iron drop stamps, which could press silver sheets into desired shapes.[15] Furthermore, by the 1850s, some firms increasingly were spinning up round vessels from sheet silver using the technique that Taunton metalworker William Crossman

had patented in 1834. As discussed below, for example, John Gorham introduced spinning into his Providence, Rhode Island, manufactory in the early 1850s.

Although patented in 1826, the roller dies invented by New York silversmith William Gale for pressing designs onto flatware blanks did not become widely used throughout the flatware industry until after the expiration of Gale's patent in 1840 (ill. 1.1).[16] One observer stated:

> William Gale will always be remembered in the history of silversmithing in America, as the inventor of the process of producing spoons and forks by means of rolls with the patterns sunk into them, instead of drops which in a crude and unsatisfactory condition had till then been the usual apparatus. Mr. Gale's invention was universally ad[o]pted by the silversmiths throughout America. By its application the cost of making spoons and forks was reduced to such a degree that the invention may be considered as having effected a revolution in this industry.[17]

However, while Gale's patent was in force, this technological advance gave his firm "a great advantage over coexisting competitors, and they controlled the trade in sterling flatware to a great extent in several sections of the United States."[18]

Technological innovations like Crossman's spinning techniques and Gale's roller dies were rare achievements; most advancements in silver production were brought about through more intensive use of older inventions like drop stamps. One new process, however, was indeed revolutionary—plating. Following numerous experiments, the firm of Elkington & Co. of Birmingham, England, secured a patent on the process of silverplating using electricity in 1840.[19] By means of an electrical current generated by a series of batteries, silver was deposited onto the surface of an object that was suspended in a solution containing dissolved silver. Prior to Elkington's process, British metalworkers had used the techniques of fused and French plating. In fused plating a "sandwich" of two silver sheets separated by a copper one is worked into the desired shape. In French plating thin sheets of silver leaf are burnished onto the surface of a base metal. The new technique of electroplating was a great improvement over these older methods and quickly replaced them.[20]

If Elkington & Co. tried to license its patent to an American manufacturer as it did in France with Orfèvrerie Christofle, it appears the firm was never successful in doing so. Rather, Americans seem simply to have experimented on their own using the bits of scientific and technical information they could pick up from contemporary journals or from English silverplate workers who emigrated to this country. One such immigrant was Thomas Shaw, who apprenticed at Elkington & Co. in the late 1840s or early 1850s, but was working for Gorham by 1865, where he helped initiate silverplating. With the financial backing of the famous New York retailer Charles L. Tiffany, he founded Thomas Shaw & Co. in Providence, Rhode Island, about 1868.[21]

J. O. Mead of Philadelphia was apparently the first to begin plating experiments in this country. In 1837 he journeyed to Europe and returned with a Smee battery with which to generate electricity. Within a few years Mead had developed a successful plating process.[22] In Connecticut other metalworkers were experimenting with electroplating as well. On 1 November 1842 the *Hartford Times* ran the following notice placed by Summer Smith (1811–1847):

Galvanism

The subscriber would respectfully announce to the public he has discovered the art of Gilding, Silvering, etc. by Galvanism; all orders left at the store of Horace Goodwin, 2d, 166 Main Street, will be promptly attended to. The superiority of this process consists in the fact, that any quantity of gold or silver can be put on to all kinds of metals, and will stand the test of acids or alkalies; the superiority of the articles thus covered will be seen at a glance.

N.B. Any person wishing information in this beautiful Art, can obtain it of the subscriber for a moderate compensation.[23]

How Smith learned electroplating is unknown. Upon his death, however, his estate noted that he owed the Franklin Institute in Philadelphia $10.[24] Dedicated to America's scientific and technical advancement, the institute was running articles on electroplating as early as 1840 in its *Journal*. In December 1841 the *Journal* published an essay entitled "Specification of a Patent granted to HENRY ELKINGTON, of Birmingham, in the county of Warwick, for his invention of Improvements in Covering, or Coating, of Certain Metals with Platina; and also Improvements in Gilding Certain Metals, and in Apparatus used in such Processes." Another article on "Elkington's Process of Electro-Plating and Gilding" appeared in March 1844.[25] It is

likely that Smith used such printed descriptions as the basis for his success.

Given that Smith was willing to teach his "beautiful Art" for a "moderate compensation," it is little wonder that Hartford and the surrounding towns had by the late 1840s numerous silverplaters at work. This ready supply of skilled silverplaters, along with the Britannia metalsmiths who worked in the area, provided an ideal pool of labor for entrepreneurs who wished to manufacture silverplated wares on a large scale. For example, Horace C. Wilcox (1824–1890) and his brother Dennis C. Wilcox (1829–1886), along with several other investors, founded the Meriden Britannia Co. in 1852. Struggling through the early 1850s, the firm eventually prospered and employed seventy-four people in its plating room in December 1856. Within a few years it had 320 workers. In 1852 Meriden Britannia Co.'s capital stock was $50,000; by 1879 it had increased to the huge sum of $1.1 million.[26] Besides Meriden Britannia, numerous other silverplate manufacturers of all sizes were established in the northeast, and especially in southern New England during the 1850s and 1860s. In 1859 the census of manufactures reported 128 establishments employing an average of 2,500 workers producing plated wares. Ten years later the number had grown to 203 firms with more than 4,200 workers.[27] During the 1840s and 1850s, the plating done by these early firms was often fragile and tended eventually to flake off. Nevertheless, some of their best products were exceptional, such as a revolving table caster in the Gothic revival taste patented by Roswell Gleason & Sons in 1857 (fig. 1.2).

Although new technology and processes like silverplating found their way into a growing number of silversmith shops in the mid nineteenth century, the majority of this equipment, including rolling mills and drop presses, was powered by hand, horse, or water before 1870. George Armitage, a Philadelphia silverplate manufacturer, was a rare exception indeed when by 1815 he had obtained a steam-powered rolling mill.[28] However, during the 1840 to 1875 period, an increasing number of aggressive American silver makers utilized steam power to drive their machines.

The steady rise in the use of steam power in silver workshops is evident in the census of manufactures, which the federal government compiled every ten years. In Philadelphia, for example, comparing the returns for 1850, 1860, and 1870 reveals that 13 percent of the silversmiths listed in 1850 used steam power, compared to 21 percent in 1860 and 34 percent in 1870.[29] While the overwhelming majority of shops in America still made silverware by hand, an increasing number of makers were turning to steam power to aid production.

Just as they increasingly strove to expand production through the use of machinery powered by horse, water, and sometimes steam, the most aggressive silverware makers attempted to raise production capacity by adding larger and larger numbers of workers. Before 1850 a shop with ten or more workers was uncommon and examples with twenty or more were rare. Again using census data for Philadelphia, one finds

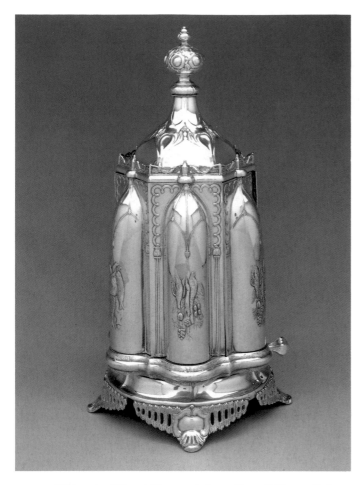

FIG. 1.2. Table caster. Edward Gleason, designer; Roswell Gleason & Sons, maker, Dorchester, Mass.; patented 1857. Silverplate, brass, and cut glass. Dallas Museum of Art.

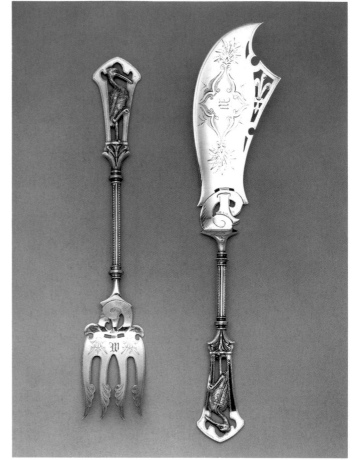

FIG. 1.3. Fish set. George B. Sharp, Philadelphia, Pa., ca. 1869–1873. Sterling silver. Dallas Museum of Art.

that of twenty-three producers listed in 1850 only eight (35 percent) employed ten or more male workers a year on average. Of these only Filley, Mead & Caldwell and William Wilson & Son employed twenty or more, having twenty-five and twenty-one male workers respectively. In 1860 eleven of the twenty-eight (39 percent) firms employed ten or more men yearly, with five of them having twenty or more male workers. The three firms of John D. Mead & Son, Meyer & Warne, and Bailey & Co. employed 100 men each, while William Wilson & Son had grown to forty-eight.

The data for 1870 reveals that Philadelphia's larger shops had grown smaller since 1860. Of the thirty-five makers listed, only eight (29 percent) worked more than ten men annually; only the shops of Krider & Biddle (thirty-five men) and George Sharp (forty-five men) employed more than twenty.[30] While disruptions caused by the Civil War may have had some effect, this shift during the 1860s likely occurred because of increased competition from other makers in southern New England, New York, and Ohio. In 1858, for example, Edwin T. Freedley noted that "a great deal of silver made in Philadelphia is retailed in New York as Parisian."[31] With the rise of companies such as the Gorham Mfg. Co., Meriden Britannia, and Reed & Barton in New England; a host of firms in New York including Wood & Hughes, J. R. Wendt & Co., and Tiffany & Co. in

the city, Willard & Hawley, Joseph Seymour, and Hotchkiss & Shreuder in Syracuse; Duhme & Co. in Cincinnati; and Kirk & Son in Baltimore, several of Philadelphia's largest makers found it more profitable to retail the products of others or to concentrate on jewelry making. For example, Bailey & Co., which was capitalized at $300,000 and employed 100 men, using only handpower to make both silverware and jewelry in 1860, had by 1870 acquired a steam engine but downsized its investment and labor force to $100,000 and ten men. Probably still manufacturing some of its own jewelry, Bailey & Co. now primarily retailed silverware.[32] Much of this silverware was produced by the former manufactory superintendent George Sharp, who in the mid 1860s reestablished his own shop and supplied Bailey until his firm failed in 1873 (fig. 1.3). This reduction in the number of silver manufacturers in Philadelphia in the 1860s reflected a national trend. In 1859 there were 106 firms employing 1,344 wage earners making solid silverware across the country. By 1869 the total had dropped to fifty-five establishments employing only 815 individuals.[33]

What had occurred was a consolidation of the industry in the hands of a few firms in New York City, the Syracuse area, southern New England, Cincinnati, and Baltimore. Even though the number of workers making solid silverware fell 40 percent in the 1860s nationwide, some producers augmented their labor forces. For example, Gorham in Rhode Island increased its work force from 14 in 1850, to 86 in 1857, and to 312 in 1865.[34] In Taunton, Massachusetts, Reed & Barton had 125 workers in 1860, but 425 in 1871.[35] Tiffany & Co. probably employed over 100 workers at its New York manufactory by 1870.[36] The rapid growth of such firms in the 1840 to 1875 period is the direct result of aggressive entrepreneurs who were willing to risk everything in pursuit of their visions of enterprises on a scale and complexity undreamed of by others.

JOHN GORHAM—SILVERSMITH-ENTREPRENEUR

In 1868 *Harper's New Monthly Magazine* stated:

> To speak of the progress in the United States of the various arts involved in the production of silver plate without giving prominence to the Gorham Manufacturing Company would be impossible, for that progress is essentially their work. Their establishment, too, is a representative one. What they have done in silver, other Americans have done and are doing in other materials. During the last thirty years the industry of the country has been emerging from the condition represented by the word *shop* to the height and amplitude indicated by the word *manufactory.*[37]

The dynamic leader who took Gorham from shop to manufactory was John Gorham (1820–1898, ill. 1.2). Son of the firm's founder, Jabez Gorham (1792–1869), John is the supreme example of a silversmith-entrepreneur. Trained in the jewelry and spoonmaking shop that his father founded in 1831 in Providence, Rhode Island, John Gorham was admitted to the business in 1841. Within only a few years his influence was being felt in dramatic ways.

For one so young to have the courage and vision to promote unparalleled expansion in the silverware field in the mid nineteenth century indicates a special type of person. A phrenological report that analyzed Gorham's character based upon the bumps on his head (or perhaps more on what he told the phrenologist in conversation) gives a fascinating picture of John Gorham. On 19 March 1863, John was told that he was ambitious and imaginative, and had great business acumen. The examiner stated: "You have a capacity for being a good mechanic; you would like to manufacture things of grace, stylish goods; you could be a merchant in many things and do more business than most men with the same amount of capital, because you would look after the business yourself and do more with the same help or the same with less help than others, and you are cautious in guarding against the losses which are so prevalent in business."[38] Although it is doubtful that the surface of Gorham's head actually revealed this information, the picture it draws of a highly motivated, energetic, and imaginative individual fits the list of John Gorham's achievements.

ILL. 1.2. John Gorham, ca. 1885.

The business that John Gorham joined in 1841 was small but successful. According to John, the shop, tools, and fixtures were valued at $1,400. Sitting on a 40-by-40-foot lot at 12 Steeple Street in Providence, "the premises . . . consisted of the basement, first floor, and one half the attic room. . . . In the basement was a Horse Power Machine, the horse traveling in a circle. The manufacturing was done in the first floor, the room being about 30 × 35 feet. The burnishing of the work was done in the attic." The firm employed about twelve to fourteen men and ten young women.

Besides gold chains, the primary products of the Gorham shop were "silver spoons & forks, silver & steel-topped thimbles, nursing tubes, and simple styles of Ladies Belt-Buckles, and silver combs." The company sold very little retail; rather it catered to New England peddlers as well as to a few retail firms in Boston and New York. According to John Gorham, the peddler trade was especially important since "few were the habitable parts of New England, which they did not penetrate."[39] By supplying these wholesale customers, the Gorhams generated annual sales between $10,000 (1842) and $35,000 (1846) during the 1840s.

Although J. Gorham & Son, as the firm was now called, was making money, by 1847 John was anxious to expand. As he notes:

ILL. 1.3. The Gorham Mfg. Co. plant on Steeple St., Providence, R.I., ca. 1885.

The difficulties of making silverware with jeweler's tools with inadequate room and power had been growing more and more apparent. The old shop had become overloaded; steam power was a necessity. It was evident that if progress was to be made and the business extended, there must be a revolution in the method of manufacturing; heavy rolls and presses must be had and lathes and tools of much greater magnitude. For some considerable time the plan had been maturing in my mind [by] which these necessities could be met.[40]

To alleviate their cramped working conditions, John suggested to his father that they lease a lot nearby and erect a substantial brick building complete with a fifty-horsepower steam engine. The structure could be divided and the unused spaces rented out until such time as they were needed to accommodate increased production. Except for some money invested by Jabez Gorham, $17,000 had to be borrowed to fund the expansion (ill. 1.3).[41]

While Jabez Gorham initially went along with his son's ideas, he soon became anxious about the great risks involved. John stated that "all seemed to be going on smoothly until early mid summer (1847) when my father began to fully realize the magnitude of the undertaking and became exceedingly nervous over the scheme." When neighbors expressed their concern about the safety of having a steam boiler in downtown Providence, it was too much for him. In early 1848 Jabez Gorham withdrew from the business.[42]

Now at the helm, John Gorham moved rapidly to "revolutionize" his firm. When his father pulled out he secured additional financing from the Providence financier Richmond

Bullock. In 1850 he took on his cousin Gorham Thurber as a partner in return for additional capital. With Thurber now managing part of the business and with added capital, John could, as he said, "give more attention & thoughts to the processes of manufacture, the improvement of our machinery and tools, and especially to the introduction of Hollow Ware as Dinner & Tea Services etc."[43]

John Gorham's first major attempt to produce hollowware occurred in 1851 when he orchestrated the creation of the *Chinese Service* (ill. 1.4). Believing that fancy hollowware like that made in New York, Philadelphia, and Boston was what would bring his firm recognition, Gorham "procured from a designer in New York the drawings of a tea service which [John] had had some time in mind." Similar to contemporary English and American examples in the rococo revival style, the service's design required extensive casting and repoussé work. Since the Gorham workshop had never executed such a complicated object, it was ill prepared, not having the proper tools or workmen. Gorham noted that "as it was our first effort in this direction it took an unusual[ly] long time to complete the service." Once the drawings were approved, wax models of all the applied parts to be used as casting patterns were made in New York. Using these models and the designs, the Gorham workmen painstakingly completed the service, which "was doubtless somewhat crude in comparison with later productions."

John Gorham wanted to see how elaborate hollowware would succeed in the marketplace, and the 1851 Rhode Island State Fair sponsored by the Domestic Society for the Encouragement of Rhode Island Industry offered him the opportunity to show his silverware line to a large number of potential customers and critics. The *Providence Journal*, which gave the

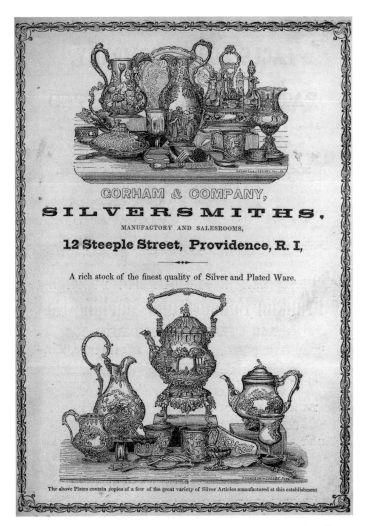

ILL. 1.4. Gorham Mfg. Co. advertisement, 1852. The kettle from the *Chinese Service* is shown at bottom.

firm's display a long and positive review, estimated that Gorham exhibited at least $10,000 worth of silverware and the same amount of goldware. The *Chinese Service* was the centerpiece of the display; "it attracted much attention" and was purchased for $700.[44]

John Gorham was encouraged despite the fact that the New York designer of the set sold the same designs to a New York City competitor.[45] He noted:

> In the early part of 1852 I spoke to Mr. Thurber of what had been revolving in my mind since the Exhibition at the Fair of our Chinese Tea Service. That to make our business a success much was to be done which had never to my knowledge been undertaken by any silversmiths in this country. That although we had made considerable progress in changing our small tools to improved ones, we were still working with a class of machines only suitable to jewelers. Heavy rolls & stamps must be introduced in their places of sufficient size & power for us to handle our silver as though it were putty. New processes & methods must be experimented upon and when found practical be put into use. Skilled workmen from abroad

must be obtained and in fact a thorough and radical change must be made in conducting the works . . . from the melting of the silver, supervising the workmen, and of the detailed care of orders through the factory.[46]

Gorham Thurber supported John, and "to accomplish these changes" they took on their cousin Lewis Dexter, Jr., as a partner who brought additional investment for expansion.

With this new partner to help with the day-to-day operations of the business and more money for tools and labor, John Gorham moved decisively. To gather information on manufacturing he traveled to the U.S. Mint in Philadelphia and the Federal Armory in Springfield, Massachusetts. Armed with letters of introduction, John Gorham then left for Europe on 1 May 1852. His diary of the trip records visits to numerous silver workshops and manufactories in London, Birmingham, Manchester, and Sheffield where he examined machinery and tools and talked to workers. While he was allowed to visit many shops, including those of Elkington & Co., Gorham's efforts were sometimes unsuccessful. At James Dixon & Son, for example, he "was treated very politely but couldn't get in the shop." Nevertheless, he did leave with their "styles and price books."[47]

Besides visiting larger shops, Gorham also talked to many individual specialists, including craftsmen and toolmakers. Furthermore, he spent extended amounts of time with two master craftsmen. Charles Martin was paid $50 by John for teaching him how to "cast molding of all kinds."[48] When he had completed his work with Martin, John made an arrangement with a plateworker and electrotypist named Franchi "to learn the art of precipitating metals."[49] Gorham also visited important public institutions such as the Royal Mint and the Royal Armory at Woolwich, and toured the exhibits of machinery and products that were still on display at the Crystal Palace after the official close of the 1851 London world's fair. Gorham visited the Crystal Palace again in 1860 and found it to be "Wonderful! Wonderful! Wonderful!"[50]

While he did try to entice some workmen to leave England for Providence, John Gorham's main objective while in England was to secure cutting-edge technology for his workshop, especially for the production of flatware. Until his trip to Europe, Gorham had used the inefficient process of making spoon bowls with a hand-held punch and die and decorating the handles by hammering them into a die upon which the pattern was cut. For patterns such as *Prince Albert*, Gorham sent partially finished blanks to New York where the flatware maker Michael Gibney ran them through his roller dies and returned them to Providence. John noted that "for this service we paid him a larger price per dozen than we charged ten years later for the whole work complete."[51]

Previous to his departure for England, Gorham had decided that it was necessary to acquire a powerful drop press, which would stamp decoration onto flatware handles automatically by pressing them between engraved dies. To obtain such a device, John went directly to James Nasmyth (1808–1890) who had invented the steam hammer. Gorham recalled that after explaining his desires, an astonished Nasmyth remarked that he had tried unsuccessfully to interest English manufacturers in such a press and would be pleased to build one for Gorham.[52] The press, which was to cost between £165 and £170 delivered, was probably in operation in Providence by 1853 or 1854.[53]

Along with the steam-powered drop press, John Gorham adopted other machines and processes during the 1850s and early 1860s. Describing this period, he said it "was a steady growth of the works of the Company in the number of employees, the addition of new & larger machines & various labor-saving machines & new devices for manufacturing."[54] About 1852, for example, the firm first experimented with spinning up forms on a turning lathe.[55] As noted earlier, this process was invented or at least perfected by William Crossman in 1834 in nearby Taunton, Massachusetts. In the eighteen years since its introduction, numerous workmen must have learned to spin metal from Crossman. The art of spinning probably spread with these men as they moved to other Britannia ware and silver workshops like Gorham. It is also possible that John Gorham traveled to Taunton to see spinning being done firsthand. But however the process was introduced, Gorham was successfully making spun silver bodies by the mid 1850s. In the early 1860s, Gorham experimented with and then introduced yet another important innovation—silverplating. Although he had visited plating facilities in 1852 while in England, he waited until 1863 to develop a line of silverplated wares. With the help of immigrant Thomas Shaw, Gorham was ready to introduce this new line in 1865. Gorham's plated articles were of exceptionally fine quality and aimed at the high end of the market. In 1868 *Harper's* commented that

> five years ago all the really serviceable plated ware—all that was good economy to buy for household use—was brought here from Sheffield and Birmingham. The importation of such ware has now ceased, and nothing is imported except the cheaper kinds, which are only cheap in the imagination of the purchaser. The Gorham plated ware blocks the way, making it impossible for the foreign article of equal merit to be imported at a profit.[56]

Plated ware proved to be profitable for Gorham, and the firm has continued to produce it throughout its history.

Another important technological innovation introduced at Gorham was the use of industrial photography, which began around 1856. Photography had only been perfected in the 1840s, yet by the early 1860s John Gorham had instituted an entire photographic department complete with a studio and laboratory, two photographers, a boy assistant, and a woman to mount the prints. The firm used two types of cameras: a Southworth camera for producing multiple small images on one glass negative and a stereoscopic camera.[57] The reasons for using photography were explained by a later French observer:

Each new piece of silver is immediately photographed in the factory, and the proofs, once printed, and the price set, are distributed to the traveling salesmen in order to be able, without the loss of an instant, to find out how [the design] is received by the public, receive the orders, and dedicate the amount of stock to manufacture, for the American, faithful to the old English principle, "Time is money," does not wish to lose in groping, a moment of precious time.[58]

Besides aiding the firm's marketing efforts, the practice of maintaining bound photographic albums of all its products gave Gorham designers a convenient visual index of the company's products so that they did not have to rely solely on drawings, as most firms did. Thirty years after its establishment, the department was handling more than 80,000 prints annually. To maintain control over the thousands of photographs produced for these purposes, the photographic department had to be exceptionally well organized. As one observer commented: "The most remarkable thing is the order which reigns here; all the negatives are numbered, entered in the register which is carefully kept; hundreds of photographs are printed and kept in portfolios ready to be sent out at the first demand."[59]

Besides adding new machines and processes during the 1850s and 1860s, John Gorham also sought out highly skilled foreign workmen who could train a native work force. The premier example of such an employee is George Wilkinson (1819–1894), whom Gorham hired as a designer in 1857. As discussed below, Wilkinson was exceptionally talented as both a designer and a workshop manager. Early successes with foreign-trained talent like George Wilkinson obviously encouraged John Gorham to seek out such men for leadership positions in every department of his factory. For example, when Wilkinson left Gorham briefly in 1860 to form a short-lived partnership in New York, John "went abroad for the second time, being particularly in want of a designer of high talent."[60] Armed with photographs of Gorham products, John visited the design school of the South Kensington Museum (now the Victoria & Albert) in London, as well as schools in Birmingham, Stoke-on-Trent, Manchester, and Sheffield. Not finding a suitable designer at any of them, he departed for Paris where he hired a designer named Thabard. (At present nothing is known of Thabard's work for Gorham.) Gorham also procured educational items to instruct future designers and craftsmen. He recalled that "in the [South Kensington Museum] I was able to make a nice collection of electrotypes and casts which I felt would be of great service and value in the future operations to the factory in educating American workers. Also made quite a collection of books, illustrations, samples of work in the line."[61] Beyond these he acquired some new research equipment, including a microscope.[62] Although Gorham had trouble finding a designer, he was extremely successful in hiring master chasers, modelers, engravers, and other workmen. He almost certainly did the same on his third trip to Europe in 1867, during which he probably attended the *Exposition Universelle* in Paris[63] and may well have met the French-trained designer Thomas J. Pairpoint (1847–1902), who was engaged in London at the time. Pairpoint was at work in Providence in 1868 shortly after John's return from Europe in November 1867.[64]

Three volumes of *Articles of Agreements* between the company and master workmen and apprentices reveal John Gorham's strategy for building a highly skilled work force, even though they record only a fraction of the employees who joined Gorham between 1865 and 1886. The first book records the hiring of fifty-eight mature workers between October 1865 and August 1871. Most of these joined Gorham in 1865, 1866, and 1871, and most were paid between $18 and $20 per week, although salaries ranged from $6 to $30. A wide variety of skills were represented, including silversmith, molder, chaser, engraver, polisher, figure and pattern cutter, embosser, stamper, designer, set maker, mounter, dresser, brazer, raiser and mangler, plasterworker, and plate chest maker and fitter. One worker was from Paris, thirty-one came from London, and twenty-six from Birmingham.[65] Volumes two and three record the hiring of eighty-seven apprentices and reveal a different story. Without a single exception in the case of those whose origins are noted, John Gorham hired local boys, most being from Rhode Island or the nearby Fall River, Massachusetts, area. Apprentices were hired for terms ranging from three to seven years at a pay scale of $3 to $8 a week, respectively. Most were engaged for three to four years.[66]

These records suggest that John Gorham succeeded in rapidly raising the level of skills in his manufactory by hiring foreign-trained, especially English, workmen who in turn passed on their knowledge and skills to American-born apprentices. Contemporary accounts confirm this observation. For example, in 1868 one remarked that

> from time to time, as their business has expanded, they have brought from foreign lands artisans and artists to exercise and (what is of much more importance) to communicate their skill and knowledge in the United States. About ninety-five foreigners in all have crossed the ocean in compliance with their invitation, most of whom have remained among us, and are still in the employment of this Company. Thus the various arts involved in the production of fine silver plate and plated ware are firmly planted here, and could not but flourish though the Providence Company were destroyed.[67]

Gorham itself publicized its talented work force. In 1868 an advertisement in *Harper's* boasted that "besides employing the best native silversmiths, the Gorham Manufacturing Company has procured the services of over one hundred of the best workmen and artists of Paris, Germany, and England, who have come to this country at the company's invitation, and have settled in Providence."[68]

While teaching apprentices the "arts" of silversmithing, foreign-trained workers must have also taught Americans how to function in the emerging manufactory setting. As in other firms, Gorham employees worked ten hours a day and were divided into distinct departments, depending on their specialty. For adult American workers trained in the less structured atmosphere of early-nineteenth-century silversmith shops, the regularity and fractured nature of work in a manufactory may have meant a difficult adjustment. However, many foreign workers (especially those who came from important metal-working centers like Sheffield and Birmingham) were used to the regimen of manufactory life and thus would have served as preconditioned behavioral models for young apprentices who had not been trained in the small-shop traditions. This system of importing key master craftsmen to teach native-born apprentices how to work and behave seems to have been followed to a great degree by other firms such as Tiffany & Co., which also employed a core group of foreign craftsmen.

The combination of better manufactory buildings, steam power, new and improved machinery and processes, good designs, and a highly skilled labor force was a dynamic one for Gorham. Output and sales rose dramatically between 1840 and 1870. In 1842 sales totaled $10,000. By 1853 they had risen to $50,000. Declining somewhat in 1861 and 1862 due to the Civil War, sales reached $414,750 in 1863 and in 1866 climbed to a new high of $1,093,000 (a near doubling when adjusted for inflation). One contemporary observer noted that "the war gave an amazing development to this business, as it did in all others ministering to pleasure or the sense of beauty. When the war began in 1861, the Gorham Company employed about one hundred and fifty men; and in 1864 this number had increased to four hundred, all engaged in making articles of solid silver."[69] Although he overestimated the number of employees in Gorham's plant in 1864, the magnitude of growth was nevertheless spectacular—from 14 workers in 1850 to 86 in 1857, 189 in 1864, and 312 in 1865. Under the leadership of John Gorham, the firm had grown from a small workshop to a large profitable manufactory. Its sales for the years 1861–70 totaled $6,240,000.[70]

In 1863 the firm abandoned its old partnership structure and applied to the state of Rhode Island for a charter of incorporation. Two years later the Gorham Mfg. Co. was founded, and three hundred shares valued at $1,000 each were issued. John Gorham (president) and Gorham Thurber (treasurer) each received one hundred thirteen shares, with C. C. Adams (agent) getting twenty-five shares, and J. F. Lawton (secretary) having five. George Wilkinson also acquired twenty shares. This new corporate structure facilitated the entrance and exit of stockholders should the need arise, and also introduced the possibility of a division between owners and managers that had not existed in the earlier partnerships. The older concept of the entrepreneur who chanced his money and energies, and, if successful, reaped the reward was becoming outmoded.[71] As a large stockholder John Gorham retained considerable control over the company, but this situation changed in the depression of the 1870s.

During the late 1860s, Gorham's adventuresome spirit led him to invest in the Thurber Mining Co., which speculated in western silver mines. After John had encouraged his friends and business associates to invest with him, his situation faltered in 1868. A credit reviewer for R. G. Dun & Co. reported in August of that year: "He was eng[aged] in Silver speculations & all was sunk. He prob[ably] lost but not enough to involve him at all. . . . He has some other outside speculations but not large—His 'Thurber' Mine speculation is believed by some to be a swindle & that he made money by it. His com[pany] is mk'g money & he must be good I think."[72] John Gorham, however, had lost money along with many of his associates. With the onset of economic depression in 1873 he was forced to transfer his shares back to the company in payment for debts. By 1875 he held no stock at all, and in 1878 the board of directors fired him as president and removed him from the board. John Gorham appeared at the 1878 annual stockholders' meeting and presented a letter outlining his service to the company, but was not reinstated. Presumably the board felt it could no longer be associated with a man who not only was in personal bankruptcy but was responsible for the loss of other people's money as well.[73] For the next two decades until his death in 1898, John Gorham lived a rather pitiful life. Broken both financially and spiritually, he had little to show for his remarkable efforts at Gorham during its rise from small shop to manufacturing giant in the 1850s and 1860s. Clearly things were changing in the American silver industry in the 1870s, as more and more firms moved to a corporate structure and hired professional managers who displaced the original silversmith-entrepreneurs.

CHARLES L. TIFFANY—MERCHANT-PROMOTER

While some men like John Gorham built silver manufactories during the 1840 to 1875 period through the use of their own mechanical inclinations and knowledge of metalworking, others organized large firms from a merchandising point of view. The supreme example of such a figure is Charles L. Tiffany (1812–1902), who by the early 1870s had made the name of Tiffany & Co. nationally known as a producer and retailer of silverware (ill. 1.5).

Charles L. Tiffany was born in Danielsonville, Connecticut, in 1812. As Charles Carpenter has explained, Tiffany's father was a successful cotton mill owner who opened a small country store in Danielsonville and placed Charles in charge. As his duties, Tiffany managed the store, kept the books, and went on buying trips to New York City. Realizing that New York held great promise for retailers, Charles decided to move to the city in 1837 to open a store. With a $1,000 loan from his father, Tiffany joined his friend John B. Young, who had preceded him to New York, and the two opened Tiffany & Young at 259 Broadway. Tiffany & Young prospered with its line of stationery and fancy goods in spite of the troubled economic times that accompanied the Panic of 1837.[74]

ILL. 1.5. Charles L. Tiffany, ca. 1890.

To fund their growing business, Tiffany and Young took on J. L. Ellis as a partner in 1841, and the firm's name was changed to Tiffany, Young & Ellis. With a new infusion of capital, John Young left the same year for the firm's first buying trip to Europe. The types of goods carried by Tiffany, Young & Ellis in the 1840s are documented by a small catalogue that the firm produced in 1845 and had reprinted the next year.[75] The firm carried few silver objects at this time, but the catalogue lists a wide variety of other merchandise including inlaid ebony and rosewood goods, French and Bohemian glass, Berlin ironwork, fancy stationery, umbrellas and whips, perfume and toilet articles, brushes and combs, Chinese and Indian goods, *papier-mâché* items, French furniture, jewelry, confectionery, and over 100 other "sundries."

Along with maintaining a varied and high-quality stock, another move that helped Tiffany's to succeed was requiring cash payments. This "cash and carry" policy was in force as early as 1845, when the firm printed on the cover of its catalogue that it invited "Cash Wholesale purchasers, who may suppose they will be asked higher prices in Broadway than elsewhere, . . . to test the truth of their supposition." The 1846 reprint goes even further. On its title page is noted that the firm's merchandise is "for sale at fixed prices for cash only." During the mid nineteenth century, many business transactions were still done by barter or on credit. This tradition was particularly dangerous for retailers like Tiffany, Young & Ellis who maintained large stocks of fashion-oriented and imported goods. If they allowed customers to use barter to purchase items, they

FIG. 1.4. Basket. Edward C. Moore, maker; Tiffany & Co., retailer, New York, N.Y.; ca. 1854–1855. Coin silver. Dallas Museum of Art.

then generally had to resell what they took in trade outside their own shop, since they specialized in new, foreign merchandise. Extending significant amounts of credit to either wholesale or retail customers was also problematical because it meant that incoming cash flow would be slow and erratic. In such a situation it was difficult to properly plan the acquisition of new stock, which had to be bought at specific times of the year in preparation for seasonal traffic, as at Christmas time. Tiffany, Young & Ellis's eschewing this practice must have aided them greatly in many aspects of their business, from simpler bookkeeping to obtaining bank loans.

Tiffany's opened a branch at 79 Rue Richelieu in Paris in 1850 to enhance its control over quality and make more economical purchases of stock, as well as to promote retail sales abroad. This move overseas was prompted by the addition of

G. T. D. Reed as a partner. Reed had been a partner in the successful Boston firm of Lincoln & Reed and brought $125,000 in capital to Tiffany's. Reed moved to Paris to manage the branch and do the firm's buying.[76] In 1868 a similar branch was opened at 29 Argyle Street in London, and in the early 1870s yet another one at 7 Rue Livrier in Geneva. This latter branch was primarily concerned with acquiring watches and clocks for the company. Eventually Tiffany's even opened a watch manufactory in Geneva.

In addition to G. T. D. Reed's joining as a partner, the structure of Tiffany's underwent considerable change in the 1850s and early 1860s to accommodate such aggressive expansion. In 1853 both Young and Ellis retired, having made enough from the firm to move to the country. Following their departure, the name of the firm was changed to Tiffany & Co., and two store clerks, H. R. Treadwell and William Branch, were admitted as partners. Neither of these men brought large sums to the firm, but they were willing to forgo set salaries for part of the profits. With Reed in Paris and Tiffany busy promoting the store, presumably they were needed to manage the New York headquarters. In 1856 Branch sold his share of Tiffany & Co. to the three remaining partners for $11,250.[77]

This expansion in store outlets and silver manufacturing required greater financial flexibility and large amounts of capital. During the late 1860s, both Tiffany and Reed continually poured their profits back into the firm. In 1865 R. G. Dun & Co. estimated the men had at least $1 million invested. In 1866 the credit reviewer revised the estimate upward to $2 million. In May 1868 Tiffany & Co. was incorporated with a total capital of $2 million divided into 20,000 shares of $100 each. Exactly why Reed and Tiffany chose to incorporate is unclear, since they personally held all the initial stock. Furthermore, they chose not to file annual corporate statements with the state of New York, thus failing to qualify themselves for limited financial and legal liability, something that had prompted many firms to incorporate. R. G. Dun & Co. speculated on the reason when it commented that "it is said that Chas. L. Tiffany intends to retire from bus[iness] and in order to dispose of the bus[iness] they thought it in their int[erest] to form an incorporated Co. to sell the shares in small or large lots so that they could dispose of a large part of their stock containing old fashioned goods." However, rather than selling out, Tiffany and Reed had increased the investment in the firm to $2.4 million by 1870. By 1874 the investment was estimated at $4 million.[78] Perhaps in reality Tiffany & Co. was incorporated so that if exceptionally large amounts of capital were needed in the future they could be obtained by selling shares owned by Reed and Tiffany to a new partner.

During the same period as they were expanding overseas and building investment capital, Tiffany's enhanced or added two important product lines that were to become their mainstay. First, in 1845 Tiffany & Co.'s small line of jewelry was greatly expanded, especially into diamonds.[79] Soon thereafter, according to George F. Heydt, the firm took advantage of the huge fall in diamond prices that occurred in the wake of the 1848 European revolutions. Diamonds having lost nearly half their value temporarily, Tiffany's decided to invest all its available capital in stones that could be brought back to America, held until the market recovered, and then sold for a large profit. The ultimate success of this scheme rapidly placed Tiffany's in the forefront of American jewelry dealers, a position they have maintained to the present.[80]

Although more gradual, Tiffany & Co.'s move into the silver line began simultaneously with its expansion into jewelry. Around 1847 the firm added silverware to its inventory. As with its other merchandise, the silver was made by various domestic and foreign producers and only retailed by Tiffany's. During this early period suppliers included Gorham, Gale &

ILL. 1.6. Edward C. Moore, ca. 1885.

Hayden, Wood & Hughes, Grosjean & Woodward, Henry Hebbard, John Polhamus, William Bogert, George Sharp, and John C. Moore, all of whom were capable of making exceptional silverware. However, they also sold to many of Tiffany & Co.'s competitors. It was probably for this reason that Charles Tiffany and his partners decided to take control of a silversmithy in 1851. In that year they arranged for John C. Moore (active 1827–ca. 1851), who sold wares to retailers across the country, to produce silver exclusively for them. As demonstrated by a rococo revival cake basket (fig. 1.4), Moore's silversmithy was one of New York City's finest. For the most part, Moore made hollowware for Tiffany's, which it sold along with flatware and other hollowware from various other sources.

Soon after making this arrangement with Tiffany's, John C. Moore retired, leaving his son Edward C. Moore (1827–1891, ill. 1.6) to run the shop. Edward was a talented designer and manager. In 1865 one observer described him as "an hon[est], indust[rious], straightforward man, close and shrewd in his bus[iness] transactions, prompt in his engagements and parties w[oul]d trust him for all he w[ould] ask for."[81] Under his direction both his workshop and Tiffany & Co.'s silver line prospered. In 1865 Moore noted that he "manuf[actures] Silverware for the trade [presumably Tiffany's] who supply the material [and he] owns the building of wh[ich] he occupies 4 lofts and the rest he lets out." The building, which had a small mortgage on it, was estimated to be worth $60,000 to $70,000; the tools and machinery it contained were worth $40,000.[82]

FIG. 1.5. Sugar sifter. Edward C. Moore, maker; Tiffany & Co., retailer, New York, N.Y.; ca. 1865.
Sterling silver and silvergilt. Dallas Museum of Art.

The silver that Moore produced in his four lofts became increasingly well made and interesting in design during the 1860s and early 1870s (fig. 1.5). Charles L. Tiffany must have been extremely pleased with Edward Moore's work. In 1868, following its incorporation, Tiffany & Co. purchased Moore's manufactory on Prince Street for $55,000 and sixty-one shares of Tiffany's stock. Moore was added to the staff as the general manager and designer for the company's silverware division. The following year he designed the firm's first flatware pattern, called *Tiffany*.[83]

Since the Prince Street manufactory did not produce silverplated wares in any quantity, Charles L. Tiffany made arrangements to obtain a secure source for such goods. Shortly after the company's incorporation, Tiffany's enticed the master silverplater Thomas Shaw to leave Gorham, where he had helped to establish its line of high quality plated ware. Tiffany's was well acquainted with Gorham's products, since it had served as one of that firm's primary retail outlets in New York. With Tiffany's financial backing, Shaw founded Thomas Shaw & Co. in Providence, with Charles L. Tiffany as treasurer. The firm

became Adams, Shaw & Co. in 1874 when C. C. Adams left Gorham to become a partner. Although the company made a line of sterling and plated wares for the trade, their top quality plated goods were sold through Tiffany's. This new source of plated ware supplanted other suppliers like Gorham that had sold plate to Tiffany & Co. in the mid 1860s.[84]

By obtaining exclusive contracts with and then control over silver producers, expanding its retailing and purchasing network overseas, and reorganizing its business structure to increase flexibility and capital investment, Tiffany & Co. positioned itself exceptionally well to take advantage of opportunities generated by rapid expansions in the U.S. economy during the 1860s and post-1873 depression. However, simply having exceptional merchandise on hand does not ensure that people will buy it, especially when a firm has only one domestic outlet, yet desires a national clientele. It was the genius of Charles L. Tiffany that not only overcame such potential problems but transformed them into advantages between 1840 and 1875.

1. *JCK* 24:21 (22 June 1892):6.

2. Gordon 1982, 50, notes that "net national product . . . appears to have grown by roughly 4 percent or more per year over this period, a significant speedup from the pre-1840 rate, and industrial output spurted to over 6 percent."

3. I am indebted to D. Albert Soeffing for his insights on the 1842 Tariff; see Soeffing 1991. For the tariff regulations, see *CR* 1842.

4. *N.Y. Daily Tribune*, 20 Nov. 1871. For a similar quotation, see Bolles 1879, 334–35.

5. Soeffing 1991, 8.

6. "Ornamental Art in America—Silverware," *JCK* 8:8 (Sept. 1877):128. The firm's three-year venture in New York was evidently never listed in the city directory.

7. *Silverware* 1940, 1 and 42.

8. For a discussion of the coins circulating in early America, see Ward 1979, 57–64.

9. Colton 1846, v. 2, p. 323. I am indebted to D. A. Soeffing for directing me to this source.

10. Quoted in Hogan 1977, 29.

11. *HNMM* 1868, 440.

12. To judge by surviving objects some sterling was being produced in the early 1850s in this country. Tiffany & Co. required that the silver it retailed be of the sterling standard in 1857. By the late 1860s most of the industry was on the sterling standard. Gorham officially switched in 1868. Between 1858 and 1860, Ball, Black & Co. was on a 950–1000 standard.

13. *HNMM* 1868, 439.

14. Waters 1981, 122.

15. Hazen 1839, 262.

16. Gale patented his invention on 7 Dec. 1826. I am indebted to D. A. Soeffing for providing me with a transcript of the patent.

17. *JCK* 24:21 (22 June 1892):6.

18. *Ibid.*

19. For a discussion of Elkington's early development, see Culme 1977, 116–17.

20. For a discussion on fused and French plating, see Bradbury 1912.

21. "The Adams & Shaw Co.," *JCK* 6:7 (Aug. 1876):99.

22. Gibb 1943, 126–27.

23. Snow 1935, 202.

24. *Ibid.*

25. *JFI* 2:6, 2nd s. (Dec. 1841):408–9, and "Elkington's Process of Electro-Plating and Guilding," *JFI* 7:3, 3rd s. (Mar. 1844):212–13. For other articles on plating, see 26:5 (Nov. 1840):343; 11:3, 2nd s. (Sept. 1841):213–15; 4:2, 3rd s. (Aug. 1842):143; 5:3, 3rd s. (Mar. 1843):141–43; 5:4, 3rd s. (Apr. 1843):272–75; and 6:5, 3rd s. (Nov. 1843):356–57.

26. For a discussion of the history of Meriden Britannia Co., see Hogan 1977, 15–28.

27. Figures derived from comparing tables 7 and 17 in *Silverware* 1940, 19 and 31. For a description of silverplating in a large manufactory, see *Scientific American* 1879.

28. Waters 1981, 82.

29. PHSHP 1976, 1850, 1860, and 1870 censuses. In 1850 there were 23 makers listed of whom 3 used steam power. Of the 28 makers in 1860, 6 employed steam and in 1870 12 of 35 used it.

30. *Ibid.*

31. Quoted in Waters 1981, 174.

32. PHSHP 1976, censuses for 1860 and 1870.

33. Figures from Census of Manufacturers tabulated in *Silverware* 1940, 32, table 17.

34. Historical 1950, chart.

35. Gibb 1943, 272.

36. Totals for the number of employees at Tiffany & Co.'s factory seem not to have survived for years before the 1880s. Parsell 1901, 40, shows that the company employed 321 men, women, and children in 1882.

37. *HNMM* 1868, 436.

38. Fowler 1863.

39. For a general overview of the rolls of Jabez and John Gorham, see Carpenter 1982, 19–65. For John Gorham's own account from which this information is taken, see Gorham 1893 and Gorham 1894.

40. Gorham 1894, 7.

41. Gorham 1893, 8–10.

42. For the bill of sale of J. Gorham & Son to John Gorham, see Carpenter 1982, 31. The information cited here is from Gorham 1893 as is most of the information used by Carpenter.

43. Gorham 1893, 7.

44. *Providence Journal*, 13 Sept. 1851, 2. For a reprint of the review, see Carpenter 1982, 43–44.

45. *HNMM* 1868, 438.

46. Gorham 1893, 15.

47. Gorham 1852, 21 May and 8 June, respectively.

48. *Ibid.*, 16 June.

49. *Ibid.*, 23 June.

50. Gorham 1860, 22 May.

51. Gorham 1893, 7.

52. *Ibid.*, 23–24. This passage is quoted in Carpenter 1982, 48.

53. Gorham 1852, 5 June.

54. Gorham 1893, 18.

55. *Ibid.*, 14.

56. *HNMM* 1868, 448.

57. The best description of Gorham's use of photography at this early date is found in Alden *vs.* Gorham 1867. This document records the legal action brought against Gorham by Augustus E. Alden. Alden, who owned the patent to the Southworth camera, claimed that the Gorham photographers used this type of camera to produce over 300 *cartes de visite* for customers and staff during 1864 and 1865 without paying royalties to Alden. Alden won and Gorham stopped producing *cartes de visite* and paid Alden for the use of the Southworth camera. I am grateful for Sam Hough for directing me to this source.

58. Krantz 1894, Silver Factories, 4–5.

59. *Ibid.*, 11.

60. Gorham 1893, 20.

61. *Ibid.*, 17.

62. For a summary of Gorham's 1860 trip to Europe, see Carpenter 1982, 59–60. The basis for this information is Gorham 1860 and Gorham 1893, 20–22.

63. Adding support to the supposition that Gorham attended the 1867 fair is the fact that the company purchased at that fair a device for regulating the amount of silver deposited on silverplated wares. The device is cited in *HNMM* 1868, 445.

64. The only known mention of John Gorham's trip to Europe from July to November of 1867 is in Alden *vs.* Gorham 1867, 40.

65. Articles 1865, v. 1 (1865).

66. *Ibid.*, v. 2–3 (1872).

67. *HNMM* 1868, 447.

68. *HNMM* 37:219 (Aug. 1868): n.p.

69. *AM* 1867, 732.

70. Employee figures and sales totals are taken from Historical 1950, chart.

71. For a discussion of the process, see Williamson 1944, 307.

72. R. G. Dun & Co., Rhode Island, v. 9, p. 439.

73. While the R. G. Dun & Co. credit reports provide insight into John Gorham's financial problems, the best secondary source is Carpenter 1982, 91–93.

74. The best single work on the history of Tiffany's is Carpenter 1978. All general information is taken from this source unless otherwise noted.

75. Carpenter 1978, 7, only notes the 1845 edition. However, among its collection of *Blue Books* the Tiffany & Co. Archives owns an 1846 printing of this book in which the new street number of 271 is inked in above "Broadway, corner of Chamber Street directly opposite the City Hall and for sale at fixed prices for cash only."

76. R. G. Dun & Co., New York, v. 318, p. 308.

77. For information of these partnerships, see R. G. Dun & Co., New York, v. 318, p. 308, and a bill of sale from Branch for his part of Tiffany & Co. dated 12 January 1856 (effective 1 May 1856) in Scrapbooks, v. 1.

78. R. G. Dun & Co., New York, v. 322, pp. 719 and 735.

79. *JCK* 8:8 (Sept. 1877):129.

80. Heydt 1893, 17. This story is recounted in Carpenter 1978, 8.

81. R. G. Dun & Co., New York, v. 426, p. 42.

82. *Ibid.*

83. The best secondary source for information on Tiffany & Co.'s move into silver production is Carpenter 1978, 8–15 and 26–27.

84. For information on Shaw and Tiffany, see *JCK* 6:7 (Aug. 1876):99, and Carpenter 1978, 214. For general information on Shaw, see Rainwater 1975, 11.

Chapter 2

THE RETAIL
AND
WHOLESALE TRADES

THE RETAIL TRADE: TIFFANY & CO. AND
BALL, BLACK & CO.

Unlike most silverware producers, including John Gorham, discussed below, Charles L. Tiffany ran a strictly retail trade by 1850. Rather than act as a middleman who purchased in large quantities and then resold items wholesale to retailers such as peddlers, jewelry store owners, and fancy goods dealers, or as a silver manufacturer who sold wares to middlemen who in turn distributed them, Tiffany restricted his marketing network to the New York, London, Paris, and Geneva stores.[1] Since the foreign operation was primarily for buying goods to export to America, the vast majority of silver and other merchandise handled by Tiffany & Co. was moved through the New York showroom.

For most retailers who wished to reach a national market, having a single American store would have seemed an insurmountable obstacle. Through good location, innovative advertising, and brilliant publicity, however, Charles L. Tiffany turned the restrictive nature of his single domestic outlet into an advantage. First, he made certain that his headquarters was always in a fashionable location and elegantly appointed. During the firm's entire history it has constantly upgraded its New York location. Opening in 1837 in a small store at 259 Broadway, Tiffany's had expanded into number 260 next door by 1845. In 1847 the store moved to larger quarters at 271 Broadway, opposite City Hall. Probably challenged by the firm of Ball, Tompkins & Black opening a grander showroom in 1848, Tiffany's moved into an even larger space at 550–552 Broadway in 1853 and then in 1870 to Union Square (ill. 2.1). As fashionable New Yorkers moved up Manhattan Island, so too did Tiffany & Co.

In 1869 a reporter described the soon-to-open Union Square store as "the most valuable business house in the city," costing "between $700,000 and $800,000."[2] Two years later a visitor compared its fashionable interiors to "the Museo Bourbonico, the Hotel Cluny and the South Kensington Museum," when he said that the sense of beauty was

abundantly gratified on every hand, as one strolls from show-case to show-case, and passes from story to story, making the ascent in the luxurious "lift" without fatigue and, indeed, without the idea of motion. The gems, the cabinets, the silverware, the rich ornaments in gold, the thousand little elegant utilities and inutilities, the porcelains, the statuary, are all so tastefully combined and arranged, so judiciously disposed and exhibited, that the visitor is never wearied or oppressed by the show.[3]

Observers were equally impressed by the displays that Tiffany & Co. placed in its store windows and felt "the exposition of these objects of art and vertu in our thoroughfares, where the great moving crowds may view them, as they hurry by, must exert in no limited degree an educative and refining influence upon the popular taste." Such exhibits could uplift the masses and allow them to escape momentarily their "anxieties of toil and poverty."[4] Along with its jewelry, Tiffany & Co.'s silverware inventory was remarked on regularly. In 1877, for example, one observer called the showroom a "palace of art . . . on any floor of which the finest four or five silver warerooms in Europe might be moved in bodily." The silverware was sold to meet simultaneously the "demands of extreme taste, of more showy luxury, and of solid simplicity."[5] Given such glowing reports, it is not difficult to understand why Tiffany & Co.'s new quarters were acclaimed as one of New York City's most important attractions.

Along with maintaining a fashionable showroom and well-appointed windows, Charles L. Tiffany drew people to his store through innovative advertising and publicity events. The 1845 Tiffany's catalogue, for example, tells the reader he need not feel intimidated about coming by, but rather can "examine the collection [as if at a museum] without . . . obligation." He will be handled with "politeness" and can visit whether on "business or pleasure." The showroom is hailed, correctly or not, as the biggest of its kind in the country, "if not the world." The merchandise is stressed as being "the largest, richest and

ILL. 2.1. Tiffany & Co. store on Union Square, New York, N.Y., ca. 1890.

FIG. 2.1. Transatlantic cable section. Tiffany & Co., New York, N.Y., ca. 1858. Steel and brass. D. Albert Soeffing Collection.

FIG. 2.2. General Winfield Scott Hancock sword hilt. Tiffany & Co., New York, N.Y., 1864. Sterling silver, silvergilt, and steel. Smithsonian Institution, National Museum of American History.

best collection," "from the best sources," "made to order," of "better quality," "newer and more select in style," and "elegant articles of taste." Nonetheless, prices are noted as low.[6]

The combination of high quality merchandise, excellent location, and good customer service, all publicized with hyperbole, is the foundation upon which the house of Tiffany was built. And Charles L. Tiffany made sure that none of these elements were ever neglected. In 1857, Tiffany's ran an ad that illustrated a splendid silver epergne and the firm's elegant building on Broadway, complete with well-dressed shoppers crowding the door and gazing into the show windows. Besides noting that its foreign connections gave it "extraordinary facilities for the selection of their general stock, and the execution of special orders," the text proclaimed that Tiffany & Co.'s "importations and manufactures in Gold and Silver, comprise a more extensive variety then any other house in the same line."[7] Advertisements such as this, which stressed variety, quality, beauty—and, increasingly, exclusivity—characterized Tiffany & Co.'s ambitious advertising throughout the last half of the nineteenth century.

Charles L. Tiffany was also skilled at manipulating the press to ensure that it ran glowing reports of his establishment.[8] For example, before Christmas each year, papers in New York and elsewhere frequently reported on Tiffany & Co.'s splendid inventory and thriving business. Typical of such reports is one from 1869:

Messers. Tiffany & Co., Nos. 550 and 552 Broadway, whose palatial establishment is among the wonders of New York, and whose superb specimens of American workmanship do so much credit to the skill and taste of our national designers and artisans, excel themselves in their array of rich and costly articles for the present year. Their magnificent stock, embracing values of $1,500,000, is displayed in combinations of splendor in the pieces themselves, without the aid of meretricious outside adornments, that would awaken the envy of the old time Caliphs of Baghdad.

Following a description of how crowded with "hurrying customers" the store is and what fabulous jewels are to be seen there, the article continues:

Among the most striking and splendid departments, is one devoted entirely to every description of silver ware, of the most delicate design and exquisite workmanship. Every *chef d'oeuvre* of modern art in this line, has there its finest specimen in the original, or its choicest counterpart, and the most thoroughly posted expert would tax his memory, in vain, to recollect any article that could not at once be shown him. In this unrivalled assortment, variety vies with beauty, utility, and costliness.[9]

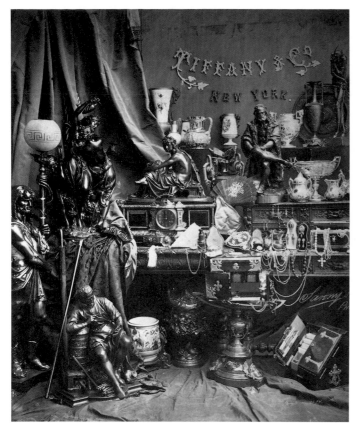

ILL. 2.2. Tiffany & Co. merchandise shown at the 1867 Paris world's fair.

officers during the Civil War (fig. 2.2). At the outbreak of the war, Tiffany had turned his store into a military supply depot "and tendered its facilities to the Government."[12] In recognition of this act, the firm received numerous commissions for fine swords, medals, and other military paraphernalia. Certainly profit was to be made from executing these patriotic commissions, but their primary value to Tiffany's, like Tom Thumb's carriage, was probably high profile publicity. Both the carriage and war items could be displayed in the firm's store windows, attracting the attention of passersby. In addition, given the popularity of figures like Tom Thumb and various Union generals, such objects assured good press coverage for Tiffany's.[13]

Perhaps most important of all the publicity events Tiffany's staged between 1840 and 1875 was its participation in the 1867 world's fair in Paris. True, the firm had sent a group of objects to the New York Crystal Palace Exhibition in 1853, but never to an international fair before 1867. Tiffany & Co. shipped to Paris a variety of silverware and jewelry, all of which was displayed in a single case. Nevertheless, surviving photographs and objects document the high quality and variety of objects (ill. 2.2). To the surprise of many observers, the New York house received an award for silverware. Favorable press from numerous sources followed. For example, in November 1867 the London *Art Journal* commented on the silver pieces exhibited by Tiffany's:

> They are designed and executed by American artists, and are not surpassed by any articles of the kind in the Exhibit. The designs are of the best order, introducing neither too much nor [too] little ornament, while they all bear evidence of good workmanship. The establishment of Messers. TIFFANY is the largest in the New World; it is of great importance, therefore, that they should minister to pure taste in America; they are doing so, if we may judge from their contribution. Our only regret is that they have not sent more; it is, however, something to show what America is producing and estimating. These "exhibits" hold their own beside the best of England and France.[14]

Tiffany's lost no time proclaiming that it had "received the only award ever made by a foreign country to American manufacturers of silver-ware." Advertisements including the above quotation from the *Art Journal* appeared in 1868 in the *Atlantic Monthly* in April, May, September, and October. Numerous American newspapers ran advertisements and articles that incorporated such excerpts. Because of the excellent publicity it received in return for its efforts and financial investment in participating in the 1867 fair, Tiffany & Co. never missed a major international exhibition between 1867 and World War I.

Charles L. Tiffany had by 1875 made the name of Tiffany & Co. synonymous with excellence in jewelry and silver through a combination of a well-located and elegantly appointed store, good customer service, extensive advertising, and publicity events. Achieving such high name recognition

When one compares articles that appeared over the years in many different newspapers, one is struck by the similarity among them in wording and subject. It is highly probable that Charles L. Tiffany encouraged such articles by sending out press releases or inviting reporters to view his firm's merchandise on guided tours.

Along with using advertising copy to capture potential customers' attention, Charles L. Tiffany orchestrated regular publicity events to keep his firm's name before the public. In 1858, for example, Tiffany arranged with Cyrus Field, who had just successfully completed the transatlantic telegraph cable between Great Britain and America, to purchase twenty miles of salvaged cable from an earlier attempt. To promote his scheme, Tiffany advertised in Frank Leslie's *Illustrated Newspaper* that "in order to place it within the reach of all classes, and that every family in the United States may possess a specimen of this wonderful mechanical curiosity," the firm would mount and sell 4-inch sections of the cable complete with "a copyrighted facsimile certificate" (fig. 2.1).[10] For the more affluent, Tiffany's created gold boxes and medals decorated with pieces of cable. One such box was presented to Cyrus Field by the City of New York.[11]

Other events designed to focus attention on Tiffany & Co. during this early period range from making in 1863 a wedding gift in the form of a miniature silver filigree carriage and horse for the famous midget, Tom Thumb, to the creation of numerous elaborate presentation swords for Union military

ILL. 2.3. Interior view of the Ball, Black & Co. store, 247 Broadway, New York, N.Y., in 1857.

on a national level, and to some extent an international one, enabled Tiffany to develop a national market for a single New York store. By the late 1860s, Tiffany's was an important stop for most wealthy Americans when they visited New York City. And as the country's sea and land transportation networks improved during the 1860s and 1870s, uniting the nation as never before, more and more wealthy Americans made the trip to Tiffany's. The firm's introduction in 1877 of its famous mail-order catalogues known as *Blue Books* further strengthened its share of the national market.

It cannot be denied that Charles L. Tiffany was a master at public relations and a talented organizer who associated himself with high quality producers. However, his firm was not the only manufacturing retailer that achieved success between 1840 and 1875 on a local and sometimes even a national scale. In Philadelphia there were the firms of John O. Mead & Sons, Bailey & Co., Meyer & Warne, and R. & W. Wilson & Son. Boston had Samuel T. Crosby and Jones, Ball & Poor (fig. 2.3). In Baltimore there was Samuel Kirk & Son, and in Cincinnati Duhme & Co. New York, the center of the silverware trade by 1860, had several important manufacturing retailers, including Albert Coles and Wm. Gale & Son.

Of all Tiffany & Co.'s competitors in New York, Ball, Black & Co. was its retailing arch rival during the 1850s and 1860s. Ball, Black & Co. had grown out of the shop of Frederick Marquand (1799–1882), who had begun as a retailer in New York in 1823. Following a series of partnerships, Ball, Black & Co. was founded in 1851 by Henry Ball, William D. Black, and Ebenezer Monroe, all former store clerks and managers.[15] From the start Ball, Black & Co. was immensely successful. Like Tiffany & Co., it sold a wide variety of imported and domestic

merchandise, including jewelry, silverware, watches, clocks, bronzes, statuary, paintings, dressing cases, work boxes, and fans. These wares were displayed in a fashionable showroom at 247 Broadway. Built by the former partnership of Ball, Tompkins & Black in 1848, this ornate emporium probably inspired Charles L. Tiffany to open a similarly ornate store in 1853. An interior view of Ball, Black & Co.'s showroom reveals a long gallery complete with a plasterwork ceiling, chandeliers, and seating furniture (ill. 2.3). Both sides of the main floor are lined with wall cases and glass freestanding vitrines. Hundreds of pieces of silver are shown displayed in the store. A sign hanging from the ceiling notes that there was another showroom upstairs. And yet, by the late 1850s, this elaborate showroom was felt to be lacking, and a grand marble building was opened by Ball, Black & Co. at 565–567 Broadway in 1860. Besides having the largest display windows in the country and a steam-powered elevator, this commercial "palace" had the first safe-deposit vault system in the United States in its basement for the storage of customers' valuables.

Ball, Black & Co., as did its rivals, prided itself on superior customer service, maintaining it at a high level by employing large sales and support staffs. The 1857 interior view of the firm's showroom documents this fact. No fewer than twelve sales clerks and a cashier are shown standing behind the counters. A company payroll ledger covering this early period reveals that the firm employed between 1863 and 1872 (when the firm was dissolved) from thirty to fifty-six clerks, cashiers, and doorboys at any given time. Furthermore, the names of clerks recorded prove that working in such a retail house was an excellent training ground for future store owners. For example, in 1863 Ball, Black & Co. employed Henry A. Spaulding, who

FIG. 2.3. Pitcher. Jones, Ball & Poor, Boston, Mass., ca. 1846. Coin silver. D. Albert Soeffing Collection.

eventually opened major retail stores under his own name in Paris and Chicago, as well as Robert C. Black, Courtland Starr, and Aaron V. Frost. Black was the son of senior partner William D. Black, while Starr and Frost were cashier-bookkeeper and silver department manager, respectively. Following Ball, Black & Co.'s dissolution between 1872 and 1874 due to the retirement of two senior partners and William Black's death, these three young men took over the remains of the firm as Black, Starr & Frost.[16]

Besides maintaining an impressive showroom, Ball, Black & Co., like Tiffany's, attracted upper-class customers by running illustrated advertisements which noted the exceptional quality of its merchandise. In an 1857 advertisement, for example, "B.B.& Co. invite[d] citizens and strangers to inspect their Stock, which is much the largest and most recherché in the United States, comprising every article in their line, which taste or refinement can call for." It also was noted that business had increased so dramatically in the early 1850s that the firm had "establish[ed] an Agent in each of the principal Cities of Europe, . . . thus enabling [the firm] to bring out every new and tasteful article without delay, and at the very lowest prices."[17] Although, like their rivals, they often exaggerated in their advertising, Ball, Black & Co. was extremely successful during the 1850s and probably surpassed Tiffany's in this period. R. G. Dun & Co.'s agent reported in 1854 that the firm had "a lar[ge] patronage, d[oin]g [the] most bus[iness] of any in the trade." The next year they were said to "make money every day."[18]

Like Tiffany's, Ball, Black & Co. used public displays and world's fairs for promotional purposes. It was the first American firm ever to exhibit silverware at an international exhibition. In 1851 the company sent to the London Crystal Palace exhibition an elaborate rococo revival tea service, made of solid gold from the Mariposa mine in California for Edward K. Collins. The set was illustrated in several books on the fair (ill. 2.4). Although in 1851 the English press mentioned only the fact that it was fabricated from California gold, one commentary stated later that the set was "remarkable for the elegance of the smaller pieces and the general excellence of the workmanship."[19] It appears from engravings that the set was made in John C. Moore's shop, which is known to have produced vessels covered in delicately chased grape vines of this character for Ball, Black & Co. as well as other retailers.[20]

Ball, Black & Co. again exhibited the *Collins Service* at the 1853 New York world's fair, but also showed a large assortment of other wares. Commenting on the patriotic quality of its exhibit in New York, one reporter said:

There is nothing in the whole palace more thoroughly American than this gorgeous, mineral and artistic display. All the gold, and much of the silver, came from the

mines of the occidental world. Every article was made here, by our own artists, under the immediate supervision of Messrs. Ball, Black & Co. . . . they . . . exhibit only what came from American soil, and what was elaborated by American genius. This imparts to their exposition the charm of the unique, and the enduring type of nationality. It commands the admiration and respect of foreigners, because it is free from the servility of imitation, and breathes the vital air of American freedom.[21]

Probably encouraged by Ball, Black & Co.'s participation in the London fair and aware of its preparation for the New York Crystal Palace, several rival silver retailers entered the 1853 competition as well. Tiffany's entered, among other items, an allegorical centerpiece depicting the four ancient elements of earth, air, water, and fire (fig. 2.4).[22] Bailey & Co. of Philadelphia contributed an ornate chinoiserie tea and coffee service,[23] while Jones, Ball & Co. of Boston sent "a very satisfactory series of the ordinary articles in silver for domestic use" as well as a presentation vase for Daniel Webster.[24] After the 1853 Crystal Palace exhibition, Ball, Black & Co. apparently never participated in any other international fairs, although some of its rivals did so, such as Tiffany's in 1867.

It is interesting to note that the most spectacular piece ever shown by Ball, Black & Co. at a fair, the *Collins Service*, was probably made by John C. Moore. His signing an

FIG. 2.4. Centerpiece. John C. Moore, maker; Tiffany & Co., retailer, New York, N.Y.; ca. 1851. Silver, silvergilt, and silverplated bronze. The Preservation Society of Newport County, Newport, R.I.

FIG. 2.6. Detail of salad set. Attributed to J. R. Wendt & Co. (or successor), maker; Ball, Black & Co., retailer, New York, N.Y.; ca. 1866–1873. Sterling silver and silvergilt. Dallas Museum of Art.

exclusive contract in 1851 to produce only for Tiffany's must have created problems for Ball, Black & Co., which suddenly found itself without a source for some of its most expensive silverware. However, in 1877 one commentator said that Ball, Black & Co. countered Tiffany & Co.'s move by "inducing John R. Wendt & Co. . . . to remove from Boston and establish their manufactory on the upper floors of [Ball, Black & Co.'s] . . . famous marble building on Broadway and Prince Street."[25] Although it was not actually in place until 1860, Ball, Black & Co.'s arrangement with the talented German immigrant John Wendt (1826–1908) must have made the firm more competitive because he was capable of exceptionally high quality work (figs. 2.5–6). As Tiffany's had discovered, the security of being able to control the source of one's merchandise, as well as tout its exclusiveness, was worth the extra investment of capital and energy. Wendt's close alliance with Ball, Black & Co. lasted until his retirement from the trade in 1871.

THE WHOLESALE TRADE: GORHAM AND OTHERS

Although a few firms, including Ball, Black & Co. in New York and Bailey & Co. of Philadelphia, at some points were, like Tiffany & Co., the exclusive retailers of their own or others products, the vast majority of silver producers sold their wares primarily through wholesale channels. The history of the Gorham Mfg. Co. is characteristic in many ways of this type of marketing.

Jabez Gorham initially sold the majority of his wares through the peddler network that covered most of New England. Once Gorham began producing rather expensive hollowware in the 1850s, however, the firm had to move from this primitive distribution system to a more sophisticated and reliable one. In the 1850s and 1860s, Gorham developed its own sales force, which, armed with volumes of photographs of wares and perhaps a few actual objects, covered the East and West Coasts and Midwest, taking orders from retail jewelry stores. A salesman's pocket notebook probably dating from the early 1860s gives one some idea of how extensive Gorham's wholesale trade was by this time. After listing hotels in which to stay, the author notes the names and addresses of seventy-one silverware dealers in his territory. Most were located in Boston (twenty-seven) and New York (fifteen). However, the list covers a wide geographic area, from Albany to Baltimore and from Manchester, New Hampshire, to Chicago. Towns in southern New England are particularly well represented. Among Gorham's customers were many well-known retailers, including Ball, Black & Co. and Tiffany's in New York, and Canfield Brothers & Co. in Baltimore.[26] Other salesmen would have traveled through the Midwest and California, which were particularly important markets for Gorham.[27]

FIG. 2.5. Pitcher. J. R. Wendt & Co., maker; Ball, Black & Co., retailer, New York, N.Y.; ca. 1866. Sterling silver. Dallas Museum of Art.

ILL. 2.5. View of silverware and jewelry district of lower Manhattan, ca. 1885.

ILL. 2.6. View of the Waltham Building, 1–5 Bond St., New York, N.Y., 1877.

Gorham also realized that it had to maintain a showroom in New York, since that was the market center to which most silverware retailers came to replenish their stock on annual buying trips (ill. 2.5). Consequently, Gorham opened a wholesale showroom at 4 Maiden Lane in 1859 and the very next year, in conjunction with G. & S. Owen, erected a building at 3–7 Maiden Lane to house its showroom. Gorham's business at this location in the heart of the jewelry and silvermaking district of lower Manhattan was substantial. One observer remarked that "on Christmas morning, 1864, there was left in the store in Maiden Lane . . . but seven dollar's worth of ware, out of an average stock of one hundred thousand dollars' worth."[28]

Gorham continued to sell solely to the wholesale trade until 1873. Until that time Tiffany & Co. had been one of Gorham's primary retail outlets in New York, especially for silverplate. Quantities of Gorham wares were also sold through Howard & Co. and Starr & Marcus (fig. 2.7).[29] However, when Tiffany's decided to stop marketing Gorham products, the Providence firm opened retail operations at its wholesale salesroom in the new Waltham Building at 1–5 Bond Street into which it had moved in 1871 (ill. 2.6). In 1876 it opened a retail showroom at the fashionable location of 37 Union Square, only to

alter these plans when the Waltham Building burned to the ground in March 1877. Gorham was forced to combine its wholesale and retail stock at the new Union Square location, using the basement and a refurbished stable behind the building for wholesale displays. But as one observer put it, "[the store] is too crowded for showing samples to dealers."[30] Consequently, the Union Square location was retained as a wholesale showroom, and the retail line was turned over to Theodore B. Starr, formerly of the retail firm Starr & Marcus. At Gorham's insistence, Starr moved to a more fashionable part of the city, where he opened an elegant jewelry and silverware store, which extended from 206 Fifth Avenue back to Broadway, just above Madison Square.[31] Complete with an "Art-Room" to display exceptional objects, Starr's store was divided into two floors: the first floor was for watches and silverware, the second for jewelry.[32] Theodore B. Starr continued to be the exclusive retail outlet for Gorham products in New York until the opening of an opulent Queen Anne–style combination retail and wholesale showroom at Nineteenth Street and Broadway in 1884 (ill. 5.1). The firm also launched branch wholesale showrooms in San Francisco (1879) and Chicago (1882) to increase the number of buyers who could examine its wares in person.

Because Gorham generally did not sell directly to the public before the early 1880s, its advertising was directed primarily to wholesale buyers during this early period through trade periodicals like city and advertising directories and almanacs. Most of Gorham's advertisements were rather plain, but an advertisement from 1852 pictures a variety of ornate wares (ill. 1.4).[33] However, even these visually exciting advertisements were for the trade only. Most specifically directed the reader to the wholesale showroom in New York "where a stock of goods [was] kept for the accommodation of the trade." In others, Gorham "invited the Trade to call and examine [its] stock." The typical, less elaborate Gorham advertising copy in-

FIG. 2.7. Tea and coffee set. George Wilkinson, designer; Gorham Mfg. Co., maker, Providence, R.I.;
Starr & Marcus, retailer, New York, N.Y.; designed 1868, made 1870–1871.
Sterling silver, ivory, and silvergilt. Dallas Museum of Art.

variably carries such notices, as do the regular ads the firm placed in trade journals like the *Jewelers' Circular* (founded 1870).[34]

Advertisements in popular periodicals encouraged name recognition and increased sales for Gorham retailers. For example, in 1867, 1868, and 1869, when articles on the Gorham silver manufactory appeared in the *Atlantic Monthly* and *Harper's New Monthly Magazine*, the company launched a series of notices in these popular periodicals to capitalize on the publicity.[35] Lasting several months, this series of ads attempted to heighten Gorham's name recognition and associate that name with high quality silver products which could be identified by their markings. The company's trademarks of a lion, anchor, and *G* for sterling and an anchor in a shield for plate were generally included in ad copy, as was the fact that in 1868 Gorham switched to the sterling standard. Although the public could not buy directly from the producer in this period, John Gorham realized that his sales would benefit if retail customers asked for Gorham silverware by name at jewelry stores across the country, and could verify Gorham products by checking the marks stamped on the bottom.

Gorham relied on the retailers of its products to properly display and market them to the public. While later in the century Gorham would devise numerous ways to help its retailers properly do this job, it appears that the firm generally did not concern itself with assisting retailers before the 1880s. Consequently, when Gorham products were displayed it was usually the retailer whose name was attached to the goods, not Gorham's. In the late 1860s, for example, when Gorham made an elaborate silverplated service for the new steamer *Japan*, it was displayed at Tiffany's, where it made a "truly superb appearance . . . , filling all the four windows."[36] Tiffany's displayed the service because it was retailed by them to the Pacific Mail Co., which owned the ship.

The maintenance of a wholesale showroom and the use of advertising directed primarily to the trade—which emphasized name recognition and quality, with limited concern for how retailers actually sold one's products—represented a marketing pattern followed by the vast majority of producers between 1840 and 1875 and often beyond. For example, almost the entire silverplate industry, including such giants as the Meriden Britannia Co. and Reed & Barton, sold primarily to the trade. Also, most makers of solid silverwares whose names are today well known by collectors were little known to the buying public during the nineteenth century. Important firms such as Augustus Rogers of Boston (fig. 2.8), William B. Durgin of Concord, New Hampshire, and Wood & Hughes of New York City appear to have sold almost exclusively to the wholesale trade. Concerning the important New York makers Dominick & Haff, for example, an observer noted that "it has never been the object of the firm to achieve an acquaintance with the customers; instead they have exerted their endeavors to acquire reputation and popularity with the retail houses, and in this they have been successful."[37] This attitude was put even more forcibly when it was remarked that "as the Whiting [Manufacturing] Company rigidly refrain from retailing and exhibiting, their more important class of works, for dinner-services,

center-pieces, and presentations, are known only as the property and products of their customers, the retailers who dispose of the goods."[38] While a few silverware makers, such as Gorham, established successful retail outlets in New York between 1870 and 1885, most did not until the 1890s or later. Rather, during this next phase, the majority of makers took advantage of advances in marketing, especially in the areas of advertising and transportation, to expand and make more efficient their wholesale marketing networks.

NOTES

1. In Scrapbooks, v. 3B, is a clipping from *JW* (2 Feb. 1887) which states that the firm was to open a West Coast branch in the J. C. Flood Building in San Francisco. Whether this happened is unknown at present.

2. "Architectural Improvements: Tiffany's New Store . . . ," *N.Y. Evening Post*, 7 Oct. 1869.

3. "Tiffany's as a School of Taste," *N.Y. Evening Post*, 19 Dec. 1871.

4. "Art in Store Windows," *N.Y. Dispatch*, 28 Nov. 1869.

5. *JCK* 8:8 (Sept. 1877):129.

6. Similar grandiose statements and lists of merchandise are made on early Tiffany's billheads. For examples, see Scrapbooks, v. 1.

7. Bigelow 1857, 16–17.

8. A 4" by 4" Tiffany's flyer (ca. 1868) is preserved in Scrapbooks, v. 1.

9. Quote taken from unidentified New York newspaper clipping dated 1869, which is in Scrapbooks, v. 1. Numerous similar holiday articles on Tiffany's are contained in this volume.

10. For a reproduction of the advertisement, see Carpenter 1978, 14.

11. For an article on and illustrations of the cable boxes and medals, see Frank Leslie's *Illustrated Newspaper*, 13 Aug. 1859. Ball, Black & Co. also sold cable souvenirs including paperweights.

12. "The Exhibitors. . . . Part 1. Tiffany and Co.," *JW* 8:6 (6 June 1889):32.

13. For a good discussion of Thumb's carriage and Tiffany & Co. swords, see Carpenter 1978, 22–23 and 154–64.

14. This quote from the *Art Journal* was repeatedly used in advertising by Tiffany's. It along with others is reprinted in numerous periodical and newspaper advertisements in 1867–69 as seen in clippings in Scrapbooks, v. 2A.

15. Financial and organizational information for this firm is contained in R. G. Dun & Co., New York, v. 318, p. 309; and v. 370, pp. 634, 638, 700a/54, and 700a/141.

16. Ball, Black & Co. 1863, v. 2, p. 108. For information on the formation of Black, Starr and Frost, see R. G. Dun & Co., New York, v. 370, p. 638.

17. Bigelow 1857, 138.

18. R. G. Dun & Co., New York, v. 318, p. 309.

19. *Official* 1851, v. 3, p. 177. For information on and other images of the *Collins Service*, see *Gleason's* 5:13 (24 Sept. 1853):213; *Household* 1862, opp. 482; Mayall 1851, opp. 1471; and *New York* 1854, 55.

20. For a similar kettle-on-stand, see Tracy 1970, 141.

21. *Gleason's* 5:13 (24 Sept. 1853):213.

22. For a contemporary illustration of the centerpiece, see Goodrich 1854, 45.

23. For an illustration of this set, see *Philadelphia* 1976, 337, and Goodrich 1854, 64.

24. *New York* 1854, 55, and Richards 1853, 154. For an extensive description and illustrations of Jones, Ball & Co.'s exhibit, see *Gleason's* 5:10 (3 Sept. 1853):153.

25. *JCK* 8:8 (Sept. 1877):130.

26. This 3" by 4.5" book belonged to a C. B. Y. Gorham and is in GA, Gorham Collection. While he has yet to be identified as a Gorham employee, the fact that his book descended in the Gorham family and is full of the names of silverware retailers leaves little doubt that he must have worked for the company. The dating is based on the street addresses listed for retailers. For example, Tiffany & Co. is listed at 550 Broadway, a building it occupied between 1853 and 1869.

27. For a discussion of Gorham wares in California, see Morse 1986, 4ff.

28. *AM* 1867, 732.

29. For advertisements by these retailers which list Gorham silverplate for sale, see *HNMM* 34:203 (Apr. 1867):n.p. and *AM* 18:110 (Dec. 1866):n.p.

30. *JCK* 8:8 (Sept. 1877):129.

31. Board 1868, 5 and 7, states that Starr & Marcus had tried to gain exclusive right to sell Gorham products in New York City back in 1869. Although an agreement was nearly reached, nothing was finalized. Pages 38 and 39 (1 June 1877) say that Starr and Marcus were given "the sole retail trade in New York City, provided that they move to 206 Fifth Ave. to a better part of town and do wholesale in Lower Manhattan." Evidently Marcus did not wish to do this, so Starr opened the new showroom alone. Marcus subsequently went to work for Tiffany's.

32. For a description of Starr's showroom, see "Chronograms," *JSW* 4:3 (Nov. 1877):41.

33. Another elaborate ad appears in Bigelow 1857, 410–11. A note in GA says the Perry ad also appeared in the *Illustrated American Advertiser*, published in Boston in 1856.

34. For a typical trade ad, see Carpenter 1982, 87. Other early Gorham ads appear in *The Pictorial Advertiser* (Boston, 1852) and *Rhode Island Almanac* (1852).

35. Ads, usually opposite the first page and printed on various colors of tissue paper, are in *AM* in Apr., May, June, Sept., and Dec. 1867 and June and Dec. 1868, and in *HNMM* in Apr. 1867; June, Aug., Sept., and Oct. 1868; and Feb. and May 1869. Other copy is in the *Eclectic Magazine Advertiser*, Dec. 1868.

36. *HNMM* 1868, 446.

37. *JCK* 24:21 (22 June 1892):7.

38. *JCK* 8:8 (Sept. 1877):130.

FIG. 2.8. Kettle-on-stand. Augustus Rogers, Boston, Mass., ca. 1850. Coin silver and ivory. Dallas Museum of Art.

INFLUENCES AND INNOVATION: DESIGN

Regardless of whether they were sold directly to retail customers or through a wholesale middleman, many of the objects produced in this country between 1840 and 1875 were of high quality workmanship and sometimes innovative in design. Particularly during the 1840s and 1850s, the men who designed the majority of American silver were probably master silversmiths who drew inspiration from foreign design sources. During this early phase, however, professional designers (as opposed to master craftsmen who occasionally designed objects) began to emerge in the American silver industry. Some were native born, while a substantial number were European immigrants. In 1848, for example, the New York firm of Ball, Tompkins & Black informed the public that it had recently hired "several experienced ARTISTS from ENGLAND, FRANCE and GERMANY, who, until the recent troubles in Europe [had] been in the employ of the most fashionable Jewellers in the capital cities of those countries."[1]

GEORGE WILKINSON AND FOREIGN INFLUENCES

George Wilkinson is the quintessential example of a foreign designer in America during this period (ill. 3.1).[2] Born in the metalworking center of Birmingham, England, Wilkinson trained at the Birmingham School of Design in the 1830s, served an apprenticeship, and went into business for himself in the 1840s. In 1854 he was brought to America by the Ames Co. of Chicopee, Massachusetts. Three years later John Gorham hired Wilkinson as his firm's chief designer. Because his pay rate was almost three times what his other designers earned, John Gorham must have valued Wilkinson's ability highly. Over forty years later one writer stated that Wilkinson "became to the metal industry of the United States during the period of its most rapid growth what Josiah Wedgewood [sic] was to the pottery industry of England during its rise, about a century earlier."[3]

With the exception of several months during 1860 when he went to New York to join in the short-lived firm of Rogers, Wendt & Wilkinson to make silver for Ball, Black & Co., Wilkinson remained at Gorham as head designer. Upon the firm's incorporation in 1865, he was granted twenty-five shares of

ILL. 3.1. George Wilkinson, 1892. Portrait by F. A. Heller.

stock and was elected to the Board of Directors. In 1870 he became general superintendent of the plant, a position he maintained until his death in 1894. During the 1870s Wilkinson's salary greatly increased. In 1873, for example, the board of directors voted to set his pay at $10,000 a year.[4] Although there is evidence that Wilkinson neglected his duties in the years shortly before his death,[5] he was indeed one of the most innovative and important silver designers ever to work in the industry.

Before Wilkinson's arrival at Gorham, its best products tended to be derivative of other rococo revival work being done in the United States. It is not surprising that Gorham was turning out objects which were close in style and form to other

FIG. 3.1. *Lady's* pattern serving spoon and fish set. Attributed to George Wilkinson, designer; Gorham Mfg. Co., maker, Providence, R.I.; designed 1868. Sterling silver. Dallas Museum of Art.

FIG. 3.2. Chafing dish. Attributed to George Wilkinson, designer; Gorham Mfg. Co., maker, Providence, R.I.; ca. 1865. Coin silver. High Museum of Art.

producers, because John Gorham is known to have commissioned designs from outside sources in the 1850s. He and his competitors probably had to rely on the same small group of designers for ideas due to the scarcity of such professionals. When Wilkinson arrived, however, an entirely new look was given to Gorham products. Past its prime as a fashionable style, the rococo revival was phased out and replaced by neoclassical concepts. Objects believed to have been designed by Wilkinson during the late 1860s, including flatware in the *Lady's* pattern and a chafing dish (figs. 3.1–2), exhibit a propensity for bold shapes decorated with cast or engraved neoclassical elements, juxtaposed with large areas of unornamented surface. Wilkinson's powerful designs proved both popular and influential and were unlike anything being made in Europe at the time. Because other designers and silversmiths could easily view Wilkinson's finished work when it was displayed for sale, and because he worked with John Wendt in 1860, making silver for Ball, Black & Co. in New York, Wilkinson's style spread rapidly throughout the industry. For example, a tea service probably made in the Wendt workshop for Ball, Black & Co. in the 1860s (fig. 3.3) shows a great affinity with Wilkinson. Although he was back at Gorham when these pieces were made, it is possible that he produced numerous models for Wendt that were later made up as needed. It is also likely that his working with young designers and other workmen in Wendt's shop allowed them to absorb the gist of Wilkinson's style, which they perpetuated throughout the 1860s.

The importance of this innovative neoclassical style is dramatically seen by comparing Wilkinson's designs with those of silverplate companies from the late 1860s and early 1870s.

For example, the more expensive items in the trade catalogues of the Meriden Britannia Co. from this period are almost all copied or adapted from Wilkinson-type objects manufactured either by Gorham or for Ball, Black & Co. (ill. 3.2).[6] Although still expensive (a six-piece tea service cost between $50 and $250), silverplated wares were cheaper than their solid silver counterparts. Thus they were affordable to a much larger number of consumers. As a result, Wilkinson-style objects were in use in many parts of the United States by 1870. Wilkinson's designs were so popular that Gorham had to warn customers against poor quality reproductions made by its rivals. In 1867, for example, one Gorham advertisement in *Atlantic Monthly* stated, "CAUTION. We call attention to the fact that imitations of our ELECTRO-PLATE . . . are extensively produced by American manufactories; also that there are English imitations in the market; both of inferior quality. These goods are offered for sale by many dealers, & are well calculated to deceive. Purchasers can only detect & avoid counterfeits by noting our trademarks."[7] The prolific number of copies or adaptations made of Gorham wares across the country and occasionally abroad, such as pitchers made by Koehler & Ritter of San Francisco and Elkington & Co. of England (fig. 3.4, ill. 3.3), attest to the truth of these comments.[8]

The success of George Wilkinson established a long tradition of hiring European designers at Gorham. In 1868 the French-trained Thomas Pairpoint left the English firm of Lambert & Rawlings to work for Gorham. A. J. Barrett, who had worked for the famous London silversmiths Hunt & Roskell, joined the firm around the same time. In 1873 the famous French designer F. Antoine Heller left Tiffany & Co., where he had

FIG. 3.3. Tea and coffee set. Attributed to J. R. Wendt & Co., maker; Ball, Black & Co., retailer, New York, N.Y.; ca. 1865–1871. Sterling silver and ivory. Dallas Museum of Art.

worked since coming to America in 1872, and went to Gorham. Tiffany's hired Heller back in 1879, but he returned to Gorham in 1881 and remained in its employ until his death in 1904.[9] And finally, in 1891 the English designer William C. Codman came to America to work in Providence.[10]

There were important exceptions to this tendency to procure design talent from abroad, however. Edward C. Moore, for example, was trained in his father's shop during the 1840s. Shortly after signing an exclusive agreement with Tiffany & Co. in 1851, John C. Moore retired, leaving Edward in charge. As Charles Carpenter has noted, a sketchbook made by Edward Moore in 1855 while he was in Paris visiting the international exposition indicates that he was enamored with the then-popular rococo revival style. Given that his father had become well known by making objects in this taste, it is little wonder that Edward practiced designing in the idiom and perpetuated it in actual objects upon his return. It was not until Edward Moore's imagination was stimulated by Middle Eastern and Asian art in the late 1860s and especially the early 1870s that he broke with tradition and developed his own style.

Besides bringing foreign designers to America and sending native-born ones to Europe to study, producers in this country had a variety of foreign-made silver to look at before 1875. A few foreign producers even opened retail outlets in New York to supply this rich market. While the 1842 tariff made the venture short lived, the famous English firm of Storr & Mortimer,

ILL. 3.2. Meriden Britannia Co. tea and coffee set design no. 01660, 1867.

for example, maintained a showroom in New York from 1840 to 1843.[11] Furthermore, major English metalware producers such as Elkington & Co. and James Dixon & Sons regularly sent trade catalogues to American retailers. In addition, retailers like Tiffany's and Ball, Black & Co. advertised widely that they sold high quality imported silverware in the 1850s. And finally, foreign design books and illustrated world's fair catalogues, which they purchased for their design libraries, enabled American producers to keep abreast of European developments in silver design.[12]

Influences and Innovation

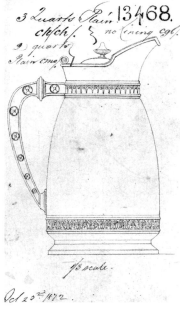

FIG. 3.4. Pitcher. Koehler & Ritter, San Francisco, Cal., ca. 1870–1875. Silver. Private Collection, San Antonio.

ILL. 3.3. Frederick Elkington & Co. tankard design no. 13,468, 1872.

Chapter 3

FIG. 3.5. Coffeepot with trivet from nine-piece tea and coffee set. Attributed to Gale, North & Dominick, maker; Ford & Tupper, retailer, New York, N.Y.; ca. 1869. Silver and ivory. Dallas Museum of Art.

ILL. 3.4. Frederick Elkington & Co. kettle-on-stand design no. 10,513, 1867.

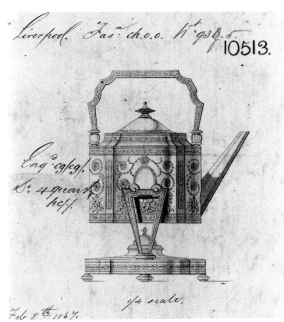

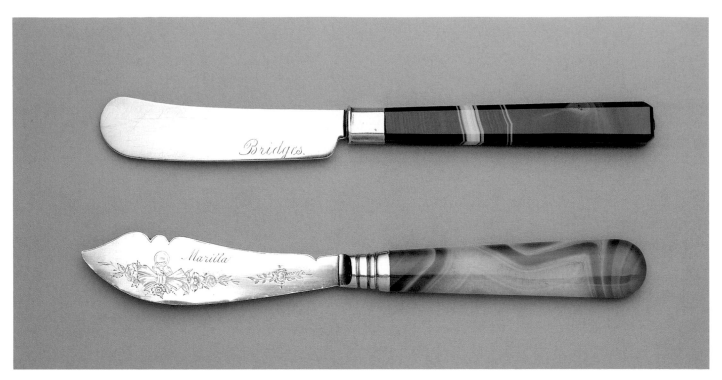

FIG. 3.6. Two butter knives. *TOP:* New York, N.Y., or New England, ca. 1850–1860.
BOTTOM: Tifft & Whiting, New York, N.Y., ca. 1850–1860. Silver and agate. D. Albert Soeffing Collection.

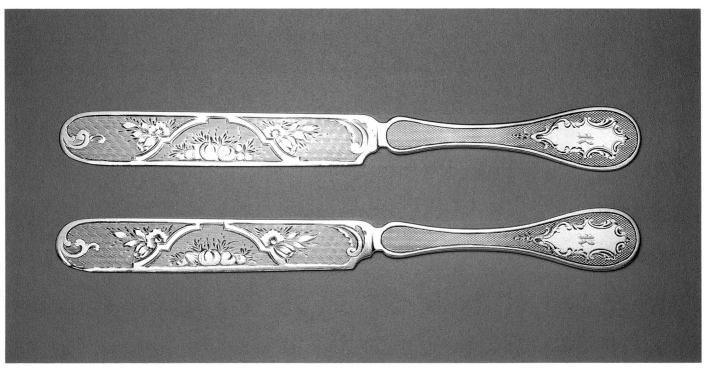

FIG. 3.7. Pair of dessert or fruit knives. Joseph Seymour & Co., Syracuse, N.Y., ca. 1865. Coin silver.
D. Albert Soeffing Collection. The background decoration is engine turned.

FIG. 3.8. Detail of *Cottage* pattern ice cream server. Joseph Seymour & Co., Syracuse, N.Y., ca. 1865. Coin silver. D. Albert Soeffing Collection.

Immigrant designers and metalworkers, imported silver and other objects, and foreign publications had a major impact on American silver design before 1875. Although technical skill, and thus quality, improved during the middle decades of the century, and although a few designers like George Wilkinson were producing innovative ware in the 1860s, most designs were derivative of conservative foreign work. This situation was especially true of hollowware in which some designs were exact or near copies of foreign work. For example, if one compares a coffeepot by Gale, North, & Dominick with contemporary designs by the English firm of Elkington & Co., one is struck by the similarities (fig. 3.5, ill. 3.4). Surprisingly, in the case of flatware foreign influence was less important. Certainly some makers copied designs like the classic British "King's" pattern or produced British-style knives with agate handles (fig. 3.6). In the flatware centers of Philadelphia, New York City, and Syracuse, producers were also making numerous die-stamped and engraved patterns by the 1860s which were vaguely based on French prototypes. In keeping with their continental counter-parts, such designs often featured geometric engine turning (fig. 3.7). Simultaneously, some makers were experimenting with innovative decorative schemes. In fact, before 1870, after which production became increasingly centralized in New York City and southern New England, regional styles of flatware decoration and shapes flourished. For example, Syracuse makers, who catered to the upstate and midwestern markets, specialized in flatware with engraved scenes on engine-turned grounds (fig. 3.8); many in Philadelphia produced flatware having elaborately cut-out handles and bright-cut decoration (fig. 3.9). Exactly why flatware design was so much more innovative than that of hollowware is difficult to explain. It may be that producers realized that consumers were more willing to experiment with unusual designs in flatware than in hollowware. The fact that many types of hollowware, like tea sets, often remain on display in the home, while flatware is stored away until needed, suggests that a consumer might be more

FIG. 3.9. Spoon. James Watts, maker; Butler, McCarty & Co., retailer, Philadelphia, Pa.; ca. 1868–1876. Coin silver. Dallas Museum of Art.

conservative when purchasing expensive hollowware. But regardless of the reason, the period before 1875 was a complex one in which many producers remained relatively conservative in the case of expensive hollowware, while experimenting on the design of less costly and more visible flatware.

THE GOTHIC AND ROCOCO REVIVALS

Neoclassicism, which was highly popular between 1780 and 1840 in this country, remained an underlying design force throughout the century. However, the most fashionable styles for silverware between 1840 and 1860 were those of the Gothic and rococo revivals.[13] The Gothic taste, which was revived in England and on the Continent during the late eighteenth and early nineteenth centuries, was based on a medieval European

FIG. 3.10. Pitcher and goblet. Zalmon Bostwick, New York, N.Y., ca. 1845.
Coin silver. High Museum of Art.

architectural style. Greatly advanced by designer/architects such as the Englishman Augustus W. N. Pugin (1812–1852) and the Frenchman Eugène Viollet-le-Duc (1814–1879), the Gothic revival was in use on both sides of the Atlantic by the 1830s and 1840s. American silverware in the style could be based directly on foreign prototypes, as with a pitcher by Zalmon Bostwick, or adapted from European architectural details, as with Gale & Hayden's *Gothic* pattern flatware (figs. 3.10–12). Other pieces, however, were much more original. For example, Roswell Gleason's mechanical table caster (fig. 1.2) incorporates Gothic arches into a complex, tentlike composition unknown in Europe. Although the popularity of Gothic revival silver peaked in the 1840s and 1850s, it remained, as it does today, a potent force in ecclesiastical design. The work of New York silversmith Francis W. Cooper illustrates the Gothic style's longevity. In the late 1860s, Cooper was still producing communion flagons which were based on English examples (fig. 3.13). When Gorham added an ecclesiastical line in the 1880s, many of its objects were of similar shape and carried related ornamentation.

Like Gothic revival designs, the curvilinear shapes and naturalistic ornamentation which became popular in the 1820s and reached a peak in the 1840s and 1850s in Europe and the United States were based on an earlier style. In silver, the rococo revival was initiated by shops like those of the famous English silversmith Paul Storr (1771–1844). In the 1820s and

FIG. 3.11. Pitcher. Charles Meigh Pottery, Hanley, Staffordshire, England; design registered 1842. Stoneware. Dallas Museum of Art.

FIG. 3.12. *Gothic* pattern dessert knife, sugar sifter, fork, and spoon. Gale & Hayden, New York, N.Y., patented 1847; knife dated 1852, fork 1853, and spoon 1848. Coin silver. Dallas Museum of Art.

FIG. 3.14. Tureen. Wm. Gale & Son, New York, N.Y., 1855. Silver and silverplate. Dallas Museum of Art.

1830s, Storr, along with other metalworkers, drew heavily for inspiration upon eighteenth-century rococo-style objects by masters like Englishman Paul de Lamerie (1688–1751) and the Frenchman Thomas Germain (1726–1791). Synthesizing this earlier work, nineteenth-century silversmiths produced a vigorous rococo revival idiom which applied naturalistic decoration to swelling, bulbous shapes.

The rococo revival was pervasive among American silversmiths, unlike the Gothic ornamentation which was used rather infrequently for secular silver. From Boston to New Orleans, objects were made in this curvilinear style and eagerly purchased by customers between 1840 and 1860. Characteristic of the high level of American work in this taste is a soup tureen from New York City (fig. 3.14). Made by Wm. Gale & Son, the decoration on this piece is well executed and suited to the object's shape. The side handles are made in the form of three-dimensional flower heads to complement the flatter flowers chased on the tureen's walls. The handles and finial are given extra definition

and a matte surface, which also contrasts with the rest of the composition through extremely fine chasing.

While rococo revival silver was made nationwide, Baltimore appreciated the style the most. Silversmiths in that city worked almost exclusively in the idiom into the twentieth century. By the 1870s, they had developed a regional rococo revival variant featuring masses of finely chased flowers. This type of ornament is today referred to as "Baltimore repoussé." Of all the practitioners, Samuel Kirk (1793–1872) was the most important. Founded in 1815, Kirk's firm rose to prominence during the second quarter of the nineteenth century and sold ware throughout the nation. However, Kirk's main market was the South, which continued to appreciate the rococo revival style of his products long after they had fallen from favor in other parts of the country. At its best, Kirk's work could be exceptionally fine. A pair of ewers produced in the 1830s or early 1840s, for example, are beautifully made, with chinoiserie scenes and cast birds and dogs on the handles (fig. 3.15).

FIG. 3.13. Flagon. Francis W. Cooper, New York, N.Y., ca. 1867. Silver and semiprecious stones.
The Carnegie Museum of Art.

FIG. 3.15. Pair of ewers. Samuel Kirk, Baltimore, Md., ca. 1835–1846. Coin silver. High Museum of Art.

FIG. 3.16. Coffee set. Samuel T. Crosby, Boston, Mass., ca. 1846. Coin silver and ivory.
Philadelphia Museum of Art.

NEOCLASSICISM

Even though the Gothic and rococo revival tastes were the most popular styles between 1840 and 1860, neoclassical concepts survived as an acceptable alternative. For example, a Boston tea set made in the 1840s demonstrates the survival of late-eighteenth-century neoclassical ideas through this period (fig. 3.16), especially in conservative centers like Boston. Beginning in the 1850s, neoclassicism was bolstered by American silver designers when they adopted an English figural style for some pieces. English silversmiths like Paul Storr began incorporating three-dimensional neoclassical figures into their work with frequency in the first two decades of the nineteenth century.[14] By the second quarter of the century, the use of figures on strongly vertical pieces such as centerpieces and compotes was fairly common. Some examples of figural objects are known to have been imported into this country. For example, in the 1870s Leland Stanford of San Francisco, California, had in his dining room a complete *Pompeian* dessert service by the English firm of Elkington & Co. (ill. 6.5, fig. 3.17). Having originally been designed for exhibition in the 1862 London world's fair, the centerpiece of the service is of large scale and features three standing female figures around its base.

Inspired by such imported examples and design books, some American makers produced related objects. William Bogert (d. 1881), for example, who worked both in Newburgh and New York City, produced objects with figures related to

Elkington's in their classical stance and drapery. A dinner bell by Bogert (fig. 6.12) probably depicts Ceres, the goddess of the harvest. In one hand she holds an orb, in the other sheaves of grain. Her feet rest upon an abundant earth supported by turtles. At Gorham, George Wilkinson incorporated a similar female figure into a fruit stand in the late 1860s (fig. 3.18). Tiffany & Co. continued the tradition in a table service made in 1873 for presentation to three diplomats who had helped the United States settle a dispute with Great Britain (fig. 3.19). The female figures that support the candelabra are not only exceptionally well cast and chased but especially sophisticated in their contrapposto stance, wet drapery, and overall visual power. Some firms also used partial figures and heads in rondels in their work. John Wendt, for example, often used classical medallions on his pieces (fig. 2.5). The important firm of Wood & Hughes, the largest producer of silverware in New York City in 1860, also incorporated figural elements into many of its compositions, including the handle of a pastry server in the form of a female herm, and a ladle and pitcher with medallions in high relief (figs. 3.20–22).[15]

At the same time as they were using figures derived from ancient Greek and Roman art, designers also delved into a more mysterious and exotic part of the classical past—Egyptian civilization. Some architects and designers, such as the Englishman Thomas Hope (1769–1831), had advocated the use of Egyptian shapes and motifs since the early nineteenth century,

FACING PAGE: FIG. 3.17. Detail of centerpiece from *Pompeian* pattern dessert service. Albert Wilms, designer; Frederick Elkington & Co., maker, London and Birmingham, England; designed ca. 1862, made 1876. Sterling silver, silverplate, silvergilt, glass, and wood. Dallas Museum of Art.

FIG. 3.18. Fruit stand. Attributed to George Wilkinson, designer; Gorham Mfg. Co., maker, Providence, R.I.; designed 1866. Silver. Dallas Museum of Art.

Influences and Innovation

FIG. 3.19. Punch bowl and pair of candelabra. Tiffany & Co., New York, N.Y., 1873.
Sterling silver and silvergilt. © 1991 The Art Institute of Chicago.

but it was the mid nineteenth century that witnessed a full-fledged Egyptian revival in the decorative arts. Due to such events as the digging of the Suez Canal (completed 1870) and the premiere in Cairo of Verdi's famous opera *Aida* in 1871, ancient Egyptian civilization received an unusual amount of attention between 1865 and 1875. The use of Egyptian motifs in American silver was exactly concurrent.

It is true that Europeans also worked in the Egyptian revival style (fig. 3.23), and foreign pattern books like Owen Jones's *The Grammar of Ornament* (1856) were available. However, American silversmiths do not seem to have copied or adapted foreign objects, or even their figural work, to the extent that they had with the Gothic and rococo revivals. In comparison to European examples in this taste, American objects tend to have bolder shapes which are not overwhelmed by Egyptian-inspired decoration (figs. 3.24–25). Some objects in the taste, especially flatware designed by Wilkinson for Gorham, have a decidedly modernist quality due to the use of wire handles with circular and rectangular attachments (figs. 3.26–27).

Exactly why some American silver designs, especially ones in the classical tastes of the ancient Mediterranean world, became less derivative during the 1860s and early 1870s is unclear. Some nineteenth-century commentators postulated that this advancement was partially due to the freedom that foreign-trained workmen and designers were allowed in the American workplace. In 1867 a Gorham ad in *Atlantic Monthly* stated that "the freedom of this country's institutions, which

leaves its imprint on men and things, has given some of its tone to this art. In American designs, the modern predominates, in European, the antique and medieval. The American designer in part gives the spirit of the living age; the dead past is revived by Europeans."[16] Seven years later another observer commenting on Gorham stated:

> They draw the most cultivated artists and the most skillful artificers in their line, often in one person, away from the old world by superior wages, higher social position, and better prospects for their families, and when here, they gradually Americanize them and make them capable of a hundred things they never could have turned to or aspired to at home. They bring the inheritance of an older and richer world to the quick and fertile genius of the new.[17]

Observers felt the same was true almost twenty years later.[18]

While a silversmith's life in Europe probably was more restrictive due to the presence of craft organizations and regulatory institutions such as London's Goldsmith's Hall, and of centuries-old silverworking traditions that were hard to move beyond both technically and aesthetically, it is difficult to document changes in silversmiths' behavior and thinking upon coming to this country. However, the work of immigrant George Wilkinson may lend support to the claim of greater artistic freedom in America. His work for Gorham from 1857 onwards is characterized by innovative new shapes and

FIG. 3.20. Detail of pastry server. Wood & Hughes, New York, N.Y., ca. 1860–1875. Sterling silver and silvergilt. Private Collection, San Antonio.

FIG. 3.21. Detail of ladle. Wood & Hughes, New York, N.Y., ca. 1860–1875. Coin silver. Charles J. Robertson Collection.

FACING PAGE: FIG. 3.22. Pitcher. Wood & Hughes, New York, N.Y., ca. 1865–1875. Coin silver. William Hill Land & Cattle Co. Collection.

FIG. 3.23. Candelabrum (one of a pair). Frederick Elkington & Co., London and Birmingham, England; designed 1872. Goldplated bronze. Dallas Museum of Art.

FIG. 3.24. Centerpiece. Dominick & Haff, maker, New York, N.Y.; Cowell & Hubbard Co., retailer, Cleveland, Ohio; ca. 1872–1875. Sterling silver and glass. © 1991 The Art Institute of Chicago.

applications of ornament, which bear little if any relation to his English training. Perhaps the willingness on the part of many Americans, like his employer John Gorham, to experiment in almost every facet of silver production did stimulate Wilkinson and some of his fellow immigrants to explore new avenues of design and production which would have never been traveled in the Old World.

Furthermore, in the 1860s and first years of the 1870s "sudden fortunes without number rushed to express themselves to the best of their ability in costly equipage and array,"[19] creating a prosperous economic climate in which many silver producers encouraged their designers to try out new ideas, rather than practice restraint, as tends to happen when profits are slim. Speaking in 1868 at the height of this prosperity about Gorham's new neoclassical designs, a reporter noted:

Ten years ago the Providence makers . . . dared not abandon the old forms endeared to the public by habit and by fashion. Many a time they were obliged to modify or lay aside a fine design only because the taste of the public was not "up to it"—it was too simple, too violent a departure from established patterns, or else it was "chased beyond the market." At present they find the public taste responsive to their own.[20]

Evidently the widespread accumulation of wealth which occurred in the late 1860s and early 1870s encouraged many consumers to become more adventuresome in their choice of silverware. Simultaneously, manufacturers who had been innovative primarily in the area of flatware finally felt secure enough financially to experiment with hollowware design as

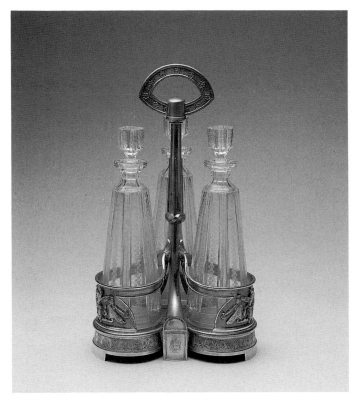

FIG. 3.25. Wine decanter set from the *Furber Service*. Attributed to George Wilkinson, designer; Gorham Mfg. Co., maker, Providence, R.I.; 1873. Sterling silver, silvergilt, and glass. Museum of Art, Rhode Island School of Design.

FIG. 3.27. Ladle. Attributed to George Wilkinson, designer; Gorham Mfg. Co., maker, Providence, R.I.; ca. 1870. Sterling silver and silvergilt. Dallas Museum of Art.

FIG. 3.26. *Isis* pattern fish set. Attributed to George Wilkinson, designer; Gorham Mfg. Co., maker, Providence, R.I.; William Wilson McGrew, retailer, Cincinnati, Ohio; designed 1871. Sterling silver and silvergilt. Dallas Museum of Art.

well. Whatever the reasons, by 1875 some American silver objects, especially those in the Wilkinson style, were technically advanced and innovative in design in comparison to their European counterparts. And as a result, Europeans began for the first time to take American silverware seriously as a potential rival in the international marketplace. Characteristic of this new awareness on the part of foreign observers is the fact that at the Paris world's fair of 1867, the English firm of Elkington & Co. offered to purchase Tiffany & Co.'s entire display. Not allowed to do this, Elkington's nevertheless did acquire several examples, at least some of which were copied (ill. 3.5). After almost two centuries of working in the shadow of Europe, entrepreneurial producers and aggressive retailers had by 1875 laid the foundations for an American silver industry that during the next quarter century would emerge as a world leader in production, marketing, and design.

ILL. 3.5. Frederick Elkington & Co. water jug design no. 527, 1868.

NOTES

1. *New York* 1848, 354.

2. The best discussions of Wilkinson are contained in Draper 1988, 1990, and 1991, and Carpenter 1982.

3. Quote from "Death of George Wilkinson." This clipping is from *MJ* [1894] and is in Scrapbook 1891. A bound sketchbook in the Gorham plant library is inscribed "William Wilkinson" (George's son). The silver designs depicted are obviously done by an English-trained designer and date from the 1840s or 1850s. It is possible that George Wilkinson brought the book with him to the U.S. and that William wrote his name in it when he inherited it from his father.

4. Board 1868, 13.

5. For excerpts from the diaries of William Crins which record this aspect of Wilkinson's life, see Carpenter 1982, 136–40.

6. For Wilkinson-inspired designs, see Meriden 1867, 9–11, 13, 14, and 50 (no. 79); and Meriden 1871, 12, 16, and 30 (no. 1404). Besides silverplate companies, solid silver makers also were inspired by Wilkinson. The author has seen, for example, tea sets by Wood & Hughes that are almost copies of Wilkinson-designed ones by Gorham.

7. *AM* 20:122 (Dec. 1867):rear cover.

8. For examples of Gorham-style silver made in California, see Morse 1986, 11–14.

9. "Career of Florent Antoine Heller," *JCK* 49:26 (25 Jan. 1905):18.

10. For fine discussions of Heller and Codman, see Carpenter 1982, 121–27 and 254–55.

11. *JCK* 8:8 (Sept. 1877):128. The author was also told by an French silver scholar that the French firm of Christofle once attempted to maintain a New York outlet but was unsuccessful. Thus far no documents or directory listings have been found to support this information.

12. Foreign design books and trade catalogues from French and English houses are in ISA and GA.

13. For an overview of the Gothic revival style, see Howe 1976.

14. For examples of early silver of this type, see Penzer 1954.

15. Soeffing 1987, 32, notes that in 1860 Wood & Hughes produced $300,000 worth of silverware, in comparison to Albert Coles who only made $70,000.

16. Ad inserted in inside front of *AM* 19:114 (Apr. 1867).

17. *Scribner's* 1874, 202.

18. For example, see "Silversmithing in America, Part II: Gorham Mfg. Co.— History and Development," *JCK* 24:19 (8 June 1892):3.

19. *JCK* 8:8 (Sept. 1877):129.

20. *HNMM* 1868, 448.

Part II

GLORY ACHIEVED

1875–1915

The period between 1875 and 1915 was a time of exceptional achievement for America's silver industry, as well as one of extraordinary change. During these years silver production and consumption reached new heights, and many foreign observers admitted that this country was the international leader in production. Some even felt that America had surpassed Europe in workmanship and quality of design, which were indeed often exceptional. Nevertheless, the very developments upon which these achievements were based also produced periodic crises (such as strikes) and intense competition. While glory was achieved in this period in terms of production and aesthetics, the seeds were sown for the many extraordinary changes which occurred within the industry between 1885 and 1940. Given the complexity of these events, the following analysis has been divided into two sections. Part II will deal with personalities, processes, and products which grew out of the antebellum period and came to dominate the industry between 1875 and 1915. Part III will explore those factors that, beginning around 1885, completely restructured and "reformed" the American silverware industry by 1940.

FIG. 1.

FIG. 6.

FIG. 4.

FIG. 5.

A.

A. FIG. 3. B.

FIG. 8.

FIG. 2.

FIG. 7.

Chapter 4

THE RISE OF THE MANUFACTORY
AND THE
DIVISION OF LABOR

One basic factor that affected all producers of silverware between 1875 and World War I was the price of raw silver. During the nineteenth century until 1872, the price of silver bullion was relatively stable. However, from 1872 until 1915 the price dropped continually, with few exceptions. During the course of these four decades, the metal lost more than 60 percent of its value. Furthermore, silver's deflation was greater than that of other commodities. In general, wholesale prices had decreased only 50 percent by 1897, after which they rose steadily while silver continued to drop until 1915. To a point this decline was welcomed, since more and more people could afford the less expensive silverware. On the other hand, if the drop in the price of silver was sharp enough or occurred quickly, the industry experienced a loss of value in its inventories of finished goods and raw material on hand. The price of silver eventually fell so low that during the late 1890s and early twentieth century, sterling silver production actually outpaced that of plated ware, creating great problems for silverplate producers.

Along with the falling price of silver, American silverware producers had to cope with a much more unstable business climate than had existed between 1840 and 1875. During this next phase of the industry's development, economic contractions occurred between 1873–79, 1882–85, 1893–97, 1907–8, and 1913–14. The business depression that began with the Panic of 1873 was in monetary terms second only in severity to the Great Depression of 1929–39.[1] Silverware is a luxury, not a necessity, and is therefore sensitive to even minor downturns in the economy; thus producers regularly had to adjust output to sudden contractions in sales between 1875 and 1915. In the case of large manufactories with dozens of machines and hundreds of employees, these adjustments often meant layoffs and low profit margins.

Following the rather heady economic years of the 1860s, the 1870s were indeed difficult for the silverware industry. For both sterling and silverplate makers, the decade was one of stagnation.[2] In the case of companies for which detailed data survives (Tiffany & Co., Gorham, and Reed & Barton), sales and production declined sharply in 1873–74. And with only a slight rebound in 1875 for some, production and sales continued to decrease until 1879.[3] Companies reacted to this contraction in various ways. Typically, auction sales were held to get rid of slow- or non-moving stock. While such sales did not bring in large sums, they cleared shelves of objects which were taking up space that could be used for items of different types that might sell better. And indeed, firms did try to anticipate what the public might purchase by adjusting the style of slow-moving products.[4] Furthermore, as sales dropped, plants and workshops reduced their work hours. Consequently, many workers either worked part-time, were laid off, or were even dismissed. Generally, the most skilled and difficult-to-replace employees were kept working as long as possible before their hours were cut. Thus if things improved, the company still would have its core work force intact.

When orders did pick up in the late 1870s, the change was quickly reported in the trade press. In January 1878 a correspondent from Providence wrote to the *Jeweler, Silversmith, and Watchmaker:*

> I am pleased to notify you that the spring trade has opened in our city in good earnest. Our manufactories are all running on full time at present, and I have heard of no failures to impede their progress, which makes things look very encouraging towards a fair run. Most of them have new styles for samples, and have received a good amount of orders from them already.
>
> There were an unusual number of representatives for the different branches of our industries upon the train en route for New York Monday night, bound out upon their usual spring trips through the Middle and Western States.[5]

But even though business was growing stronger, the trade press cautioned its readers not to move too quickly, especially where credit was concerned. Rather, producers and retailers had to have "backbone in business" and refrain from jeopardizing their cash flow through questionable credit risks.[6] Perhaps heeding

ILL. 4.1. Views of the Tiffany & Co. manufactory, 53 and 55 Prince St., New York, N.Y., 1877. The images are:
fig. 1, melting; fig. 2, rolling; fig. 3, flatware blanks; fig. 4, roller die; fig. 5, partially finished blank;
fig. 6, die stamping; fig. 7, polishing; and fig. 8, finished pitcher.

such advice, the silverware industry expanded production to fill the orders which were flowing in by 1879 and 1880.

The 1870s were stressful years in which silverware producers worked hard to refine the manufacturing process, thereby cutting their costs and increasing competitiveness. For example, Roger & Brothers, a silverplate maker in Waterbury, Connecticut, in part attributed their increase in business in the late 1870s "to the improvements which they have made the past season in their process of manufacturing."[7] However, refining the manufacturing process was a theme that permeated the entire silverware industry between 1875 and 1915, not just in the 1870s. In fact, it was the quarter century between 1885 and 1915 that saw some of the industry's greatest reorganization in the name of efficiency.

During the period up to 1875 machinery was increasingly brought to bear on silver production. Because almost all the basic silverworking machines, such as the rolling mill, die roller, drop press, and spinning lathe, were already in use by 1870, greater efficiency and economy of scale in this next phase was not achieved by inventing new labor-saving machinery. Naturally there were some improvements in the basic technology, but the most important changes were usually made in the areas of scale and power. For example, a larger and more powerful drop press for stamping out silver forms may have been added to a workshop, but it functioned in basically the same way as earlier presses.

THE RISE OF THE MANUFACTORY

Rather than invent new machines, the leaders of the industry primarily boosted production by increasing their work forces. In almost every silversmithy that achieved a significant level of production, more craftsmen were put to work during the last quarter of the nineteenth and early twentieth centuries than ever before. On average the number of employees per shop increased 25 percent in the 1860s, more than doubled in the 1870s, and doubled again by 1904.[8] In the larger shops this increase was truly amazing. Gorham had already begun this process, going from 14 employees in 1850 to 312 in 1865. Although the total number of workers at its Providence plant rose and fell in response to sales and seasonal production, the trend was steadily upward, with 526 laboring in 1882, 1,365 in 1892, and 1,966 in 1903. Reed & Barton followed suit, raising its number of employees from 425 in 1871 to 800 in 1887. Probably employing at least 100 craftsmen in the early 1870s, Tiffany & Co. averaged around 300 men, women, and boy workers in the 1880s and had increased this total to over 400 by 1910. Many other concerns grew dramatically during this period as well. By 1888, Duhme & Co. of Cincinnati employed 300. In 1890 it was estimated that the Meriden Britannia Co. had 1,200 workers; the Towle Mfg. Co. of Newburyport, Massachusetts, employed 200; the Rockford Silver Plate Co. of Rockford, Illinois, had 120 in its factory; and George W. Shiebler of New York City employed over 160. Three years later a Gorham inter-office memo sized up its competition as follows: the Whiting Mfg. Co. with 300 to 350 workers; Dominick & Haff with around 125 (other reports put this number at 200); and W. B. Durgin of Concord, New Hampshire, employing approximately 100.[9]

The reason why most silverware firms could increase output by simply increasing their number of employees was the fact that these manufactories did not mass-produce objects in a Fordian sense. Unlike standardized products such as pencils, paper clips, and even automobiles at the end of this period, most silverware was in some way customized. Even the cheapest silverplated goods (which came the closest to being mass-produced) could be individualized with dozens of different engraved monograms and decorations. Each design usually came in various sizes, with a choice of finish and base metal. As one moved up the price scale into elaborate plated wares and sterling objects, the variety of decoration, shapes, and finishes available became virtually infinite. In 1890, for example, it was estimated that the Meriden Britannia Co. was producing 4,000 different designs of silverplate, if all variations were taken into account.[10] Further complicating matters was the fact that many silver items were seasonal in nature and therefore only produced at specific times of the year. Consequently, when orders came in they generally were for small groups of items or single pieces, not thousands of identical ones.

The type of production that evolved to cope with this great diversity is known as batch production. As the historian Philip Scranton has explained, the creation of large numbers of custom or partially customized pieces of silverware required American producers to be extremely flexible in their organization.[11] Since few products were identical, both machine and worker had to be capable of changing operations and pace as demanded by an uneven flow of orders for a wide range of goods. Thus machines dedicated to the production of a specific item were seldom put to use or even invented, simply because they were not useful in batch production. Rather, a relatively small number of multipurpose devices were used in conjunction with a highly skilled and flexible work force. Both machines and workers were clustered, according to specialty, in different parts of a plant and were not positioned along a production line, since there was virtually no linear production.

With flexible, highly skilled workers arranged together near their equipment, the late-nineteenth-century silver manufactory represented the ultimate manifestation of a process that had been evolving in the silversmith's craft for hundreds of years. From the Middle Ages, and probably since antiquity, specialization in silversmithing had been increasing. In the great metalworking centers of Europe, including Antwerp, Augsburg, Paris, and London, an ever-growing number of craftsmen became specialists in branches of the trade, including casting, chasing, engraving, and repoussé work, as metal objects became ever more complicated. Consequently, by the early nineteenth century, the metalworking quarters that existed in

ILL. 4.2. Views of the Reed & Barton manufactory, Taunton, Mass., 1879. Views are of casting (top left); burnishing (top right); plating (center); satin finishing (lower left); and soldering (lower right).

all urban centers contained both general and specialized metalworkers who passed objects between them, depending on the demands of the order.

The large manufactories that emerged in the last half of the nineteenth century in some ways maintained this basic organization of the trade by grouping all the various specialty craftsmen within one manufactory. Now, rather than taking a teapot to a nearby engraver for decorating, a silversmith would simply take the pot to the engraving department. And within each of these specialized workshops, the cooperative and communal nature of an independent shop setting, complete with masters, journeymen, and apprentices, was to some extent preserved. The fact that most companies charged these individual departments separate rent based on the amount of floor space they occupied indicates how these various specialty shops were seen as distinct entities within the overall manufactory.

Therefore, by setting up a series of specialty workshops rather than a strict assembly line, companies could expand their production almost indefinitely by hiring more workers. For example, if orders for chased objects rose sharply, chasers could be added to the structure without disrupting the overall operation of the plant. The one great problem with such a system was that there were never enough skilled workers to add to and subtract from a work force at will. As a result, once a certain magnitude of work force was achieved, it tended to rise and fall in number gradually in all but the most severe economic times.

STAGES OF PRODUCTION

The typical silverware manufactory consisted of five basic divisions: design, preparation, forming, decorating, and finishing. Design departments usually resembled art studios complete with drafting tables and easels, art and natural specimen collections, and large libraries. In 1878 one visitor remarked on his tour of Reed & Barton's design department in Taunton:

The soft light streaming in from the half-curtained windows on casts and photographs, pencil-drawings and *bric-a-brac*, while on a side table a copy of the *Art Journal* lay open for ready reference. . . . we watched for some time . . . the designers, working slowly and patiently, putting on a bit of soft red wax here, carefully moulding it with the fingers, and then cutting it away again with the steel tool, until the shapeless lump of wax had grown into a perfect ornament. Another workman with ready pencil was tracing the pattern of [a] teapot upon paper, limning the gracefully-curved outlines carefully, and tracing the lines to be engraved clearly, pausing now and then to look for a line or a suggestion in a portfolio of foreign plates.[12]

The studio at Tiffany & Co.'s Prince Street manufactory in New York was very similar to Reed & Barton's (ill. 4.3). In 1887 it was described as follows:

Our first impression as we enter is that we have strayed into the Museum of Natural History. All around are well-preserved counterfeits of birds and smaller animals, as also gourds, ears of corn, grasses, &c., all of which have already served, or still serve, as studies. Running back the entire length of the long, light room are drawing-boards, at which sit busy designers, while about them hang plaster casts, models and electrotypes of designs which have graced work previously done.[13]

The collections of natural specimens, art reproductions, and books noted in these passages were, along with the talent of the designers, the life blood of each firm's design room. Consequently these collections were often extensive. For example, an inventory of Gorham's design room taken in 1871 lists in the design library well over 200 volumes, mostly foreign. Standard works like Owen Jones's *Grammar of Ornament* shared shelf space with rarities such as the sixteen-volume *Museo Barbonico* and Richardson's *Architectural Remains*. Numerous trade catalogues, including those from Orfèvrerie Christofle, Elkington & Co., and James Dixon & Son, lined the library's shelves. The rest of the room was filled with dozens of plaster casts and medallions; Wedgwood, parian, and majolica vessels; plaques and statuettes; bronzes and electrotypes; and shells. One observer described Gorham's design room and its importance as

an apartment which has the appearance of a library. It is indeed well stored with books, and with illustrated works of the costliest description. All beauty is akin. A designer may get from an arch of the Cologne Cathedral an idea for the handle of a mustard-spoon, and induce the spirit of a gorgeous mosque into the design for a caster. . . . Antique vases, the Elgin marbles, books of animals, birds, fishes, flowers, trees, portraits, pictures, statuary, architecture, and all other accumulations of grace and beauty, may be useful to those whose business it is to cover with grace and beauty the tables of mankind.[14]

These collections of books and inspirational artifacts continued to grow. In 1913 Gorham's extensive design library was appraised at the large sum of $10,000.[15]

Along with the final design, processed raw materials were needed before workmen could begin their duties. While smaller silverware firms often purchased their silver in the form of sheets, discs, wire, and strips ready for working, larger companies processed their own silver and other raw materials. By 1870 silver, typically as ingots, was purchased in New York from precious-metal traders.[16] Having been tested for quality by a company chemist, these ingots, or "pigs," were broken up with a hammer and placed in a furnace along with the correct proportion of base metal for melting (ill. 4.1). If sterling silver was being made, 7.5 percent of copper was added to the pure silver. Solder mixtures required less copper to ensure a lower melting point. Mixtures for base metals used in silverplate contained

ILL. 4.3. The design studio at Tiffany & Co. manufactory, 53 and 55 Prince St., New York, N.Y., ca. 1885.

no silver at all but were usually composed of various proportions of tin, copper, nickel, and antimony.

Once melted, the metal alloy was transferred to a cauldron and placed in a furnace where it was kept at about 500 degrees Fahrenheit until all the impurities, or "dross," were driven off or made to collect on the surface. The molten metal was then poured into molds and allowed to cool. The "plates" that were produced in these molds were typically about 7 inches long, 5 inches wide, and ¾ inch thick. In another room these plates were then run, sometimes repeatedly, through a flattening mill whose rollers reduced the thickness, or gauge, of the metal (ill. 4.1). Finally, the processed plates were cut into rectangles or discs depending on whether they were to be made into flatware or hollowware. All these processes required or produced heat, making the refining, rolling, and cutting rooms hot, sweaty environments. Nevertheless, one observer noted that "notwithstanding the character of the work done in this room, there was no noise and no dirt. The floor of flagstones was as clean and neat as the kitchen-floor of a good housewife."[17]

Another process necessary before work could begin on most silver objects was that of die making and hardening. Dies are rolls or blocks of steel into which patterns are "sunk," or cut with chisels, and then hardened. A pair of dies for hollowware fit together perfectly, the top one having a "male" version of the design which enters the "female" pattern of the bottom die. When finished, dies are fitted either into a roller or drop press. In both cases a strip, sheet, or disc of silver is placed over the bottom die, and the upper die is either rolled over it or pushed down onto its mate by means of a heavy weight, a hammer head, or steam power. The impact of the two die halves coming together forces the silver into the pattern cut on the dies, thus forming part or all of the desired silver object. In the case of pieces with complicated decoration, series of increasingly elaborate dies were produced for drop presses to avoid tearing the thin sheet of silver being pressed. In such a process the first die produces a crude impression of the design and each subsequent set of dies adds ever greater depth and detail to the impression. Often between stampings, the partially finished silver objects are annealed in an oven or with a torch to restore the silver's malleability before being struck by the next, more complicated, die.[18]

Because cutting precise patterns into hard steel blocks and rollers is extremely time-consuming and can only be done correctly by relatively few metalworkers, dies are costly tools and die cutting the most highly paid manual profession in the industry. In 1892 one observer commented upon visiting Gorham's plant:

> Not the least interesting feature of this preparatory room is the collection of dies, tools, and templates. They are not by any means the least valuable of its features; in fact, they make up a large proportion of the value of the entire plant. There are thousands of them, all marked, numbered and registered alphabetically, so that they can be put into active service at a minute's notice. They represent the labor of years, and possess an artistic value not to be calculated.[19]

A 1913 Gorham inventory supports these observations. In that year the firm's "Dies and Tools" were appraised at $2,418,253. While other types of hand and mechanical tools accounted for some of this total, the majority of it probably represented Gorham's large inventory of dies. Since the total valuation for the firm's entire plant, including the building and land, was less than

$4.5 million, its die collection was easily its most valuable asset.[20] Like Gorham, Tiffany's also invested heavily in dies. In 1901 its plant had about 10,000, all indexed and easily retrievable.[21]

Due to their high value, dies were kept by most manufacturers in secure vaults or safes, usually near the stamping rooms. In 1878 one visitor to Reed & Barton's Taunton, Massachusetts, plant noted that the dies "were . . . kept in a large fire and burglar proof vault, into which we were shown, and where, by the light which came through a small grating, we saw the [die] rollers ranged upon narrow shelves or frames, each die bearing a tag giving the number of its pattern."[22] By numbering the dies, their use within the plant could be tracked and their retrieval and prompt storage facilitated.

Procuring craftsmen who excelled at die cutting was always difficult. Consequently, firms guarded the die cutters they already had and were constantly on the lookout for new talent. A good example of how highly skilled die cutters were valued within the industry is the case of Florent Antoine Heller (1839–1904, ill. 4.4). Born and trained in France as a painter, designer, chaser, and die cutter, Heller came to America in 1873. Although Tiffany's lured him here, he began work for Gorham shortly after his arrival. However, Heller left for Tiffany's following the creation of objects for Gorham's display at the Centennial.[23] At Tiffany's he designed several successful flatware patterns, including *Olympian* in 1879. Shortly after his return to Paris in 1880, Heller was successfully recruited back to Gorham. Edward C. Moore, who desperately wanted to prevent the defection of this important artist, offered Heller $1,000 more than Gorham if he would return. Also, Tiffany's "proposed offering Mr. Heller $75 per week or $1.25 per hour payable as follows: $50 per week cash; $1200 at the expiration. For two years." Heller's rejection of this offer suggests that Gorham must have agreed to pay him $4,000 to $5,000 annually—a very high salary. Furthermore, it is known that Heller was allowed to work only eight hours per day at Gorham rather than the normal ten.[24] Working for Gorham until his death in 1904, Heller created numerous successful flat- and hollowware designs. His skill was such that French critics decried his loss to America. Shortly after his leaving France, one asked in the *Gazette des beaux arts*, "Now that Heller has gone to the United States, who in France can cut such perfect dies?"[25]

With the designs, processed raw materials, and dies in hand, work on most silver objects could begin in the various forming departments. One process in this area has already been mentioned, that of stamping and rolling. Stamping departments and die vaults were ideally located near one another. Often only those dies in active use were kept in the stamping room itself. The drop presses were regularly lined up together and were each operated by a single individual (ill. 4.1). The great and repeated downward force generated by a drop press meant that it was extremely dangerous to operate. John Gorham, for example, lost part of his hand in one. Furthermore, specially reinforced floors were needed to support these noisy machines. Consequently, stamping departments were often

ILL. 4.4. F. A. Heller in Gorham Mfg. Co. design studio, Elmwood manufactory, Providence, R.I., 1892.

located in basements where secure foundations existed and noise pollution could be minimized. In 1887 a visitor to Tiffany's stamping department said, "we descend into what apparently are the infernal regions, for the din from the enormous die-presses is something awful; swarthy, half-clad workmen dodge about, now in the half-darkness of the corners, anon in the fierce and ruddy glare of the melting pots."[26] When coupled with the fact that each sudden blow of a press could easily sever a hand or finger, while numbing the ears and shaking the body with vibrations, working in a press room was extremely unpleasant, especially when presses were grouped together. In 1892 Rogers & Brother of Waterbury, Connecticut, ran "eight drops, the hammers weighing from 570 to 975 pounds, the latter being perhaps the largest in the country used in making spoons and forks."[27] In the same year Gorham was operating twenty-four drop stamps that were "connected by massive cast-iron gallow-frames, which also carry the automatic driving mechanism. . . . It [was] said that the preparatory room as it stands could not be duplicated for $300,000" (ill. 7.6).[28]

Using dies and sheet silver in drop and roller presses, workers produced both decorative ornament, such as borders, and the bodies of vessels and flatware. Almost anything that was relatively flat or wider at the top than at the bottom, thus allowing the upper die to be extracted after stamping, could at least partially be formed on a drop press. For simple forms like flatware handles, trays, or plain bowls, pieces were near completion when they left the stamping room. For more complicated vessels like coffeepots and vases, however, stamping was only an initial step. In such cases the drop press simply began the forming process by taking the flat disc or sheet of silver and turning it into a bowl or truncated-cone shape. These "shells" would then go to the spinning room where they would be further processed. Small firms, which, unlike larger ones, had nei-

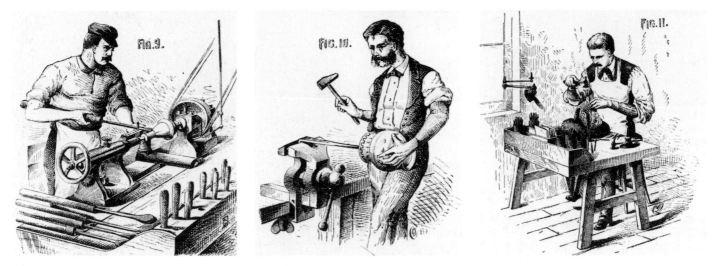

ILL. 4.5. Images of spinning, snarling (repoussé chasing), and chasing,
Tiffany & Co. Prince St. manufactory, 1877.

ther the financial resources to invest in big inventories of costly dies and presses, nor the sales volume to warrant such investment, could purchase prestamped shells from a supplier. Many, however, typically used the less complicated methods of spinning or hand raising to form their products.

As noted above, the technique of "spinning up" metal forms was first used in this country in the 1830s. By the 1870s the process had been perfected and was in use throughout the silver industry (fig. 4.1, ill. 4.5). In 1878 a visitor to Reed & Barton's spinning room described the production of a teapot:

> We were ushered into a long room, from whose ceiling was stretched a whirling network of belts and pulleys which turned the lathes occupying a long bench on one side of the room. . . . [W]e saw with interest that the shells [from the drop press] were placed upon a wooden mould, or chuck, . . . and set spinning at a tremendous rate. . . . [W]hile it was spinning dizzily around, a stick was used to press down the soft metal until it had assumed all of the curved lines of the steel chuck. . . . Then the lathe was stopped, and the chuck taken off. . . . The core or center piece was removed, and then the chuck fell into pieces or sections, which were readily removed from the interior of our teapot through its narrow neck.[29]

Developed in the 1870s, the sectional chuck as described here made spinning extremely useful and facilitated the process's rapid spread throughout the industry.[30] Although chucks were not nearly as expensive to produce as dies, the most progressive firms nevertheless took care of their investment. In these shops each chuck was numbered so that it could be retrieved easily and replaced in the storage room. Strict organization was necessary since firms owned numerous chucks. Tiffany & Co.'s Newark plant estimated that it had between 12,000 and 15,000 in 1901.[31]

Besides spinning up metal bodies, lathes were used in silver manufactories for other operations as well. For example,

in the spinning department a vessel's edges could be strengthened by rolling them over onto themselves or around a piece of wire. In the turning department lathes were used to shape solid metal, wooden, or ivory parts like knobs, insulators, and finials. This department was also responsible for cleaning excess solder from seams and cutting or trimming silver shells as needed. Finally, turners gave a high finish to each shell. "The turner takes off from it so fine a shaving with his lathe-tool that the metal drops around him like the finest frost of soft, glittering silver."[32]

Many parts of silver objects that could not be stamped or spun up were produced in the casting department. Items such as legs, finials, handles, and spouts (and occasionally entire objects) were cast here in either sand or metal molds (ill. 4.2, fig. 4.2). For custom pieces that were to be made only once, it was cheaper to fabricate parts with the age-old method of sand casting. In this process the desired parts were made to scale in wood, wax, or metal and then pressed down into special sand contained in boxes. When the patterns were removed they left their imprints in the sand, which could be filled with molten silver to produce part or all of an appendage. For production items, however, steel molds were made to facilitate the casting process. Consisting of two interlocking halves with the desired shape carved into them, the mold was closed and molten silver was poured into it. Once the outer layer of silver had hardened against the cooler steel, the still liquid silver in the center was poured out and the mold opened. The result was a one-piece spout or other part, which did not need to be soldered together from two halves. Like castings made in sand, those from steel molds still had to be hand finished through filing and polishing, and any casting flaws, such as air holes, had to be filled before the cast elements could be used.

With the stamped or spun bodies and cast elements completed, the parts were joined together in the soldering department (ill. 4.2). Here silver solder (or a base metal solder in the case of silverplate), which had a lower melting point than sterling, was used to attach appendages to the body. The blow-pipes

FACING PAGE: FIG. 4.1. Coffeepot. Meriden Britannia Co., Meriden, Conn., and Rogers Smith & Co., New Haven, Conn., makers, ca. 1871. Silverplate and ivory. Dallas Museum of Art. The pot's body was spun up over a chuck rotating on a lathe.

FIG. 4.2. Fish set. New York, N.Y., ca. 1865–1875. Sterling silver. Dallas Museum of Art. This set's handles were cast.

The Rise of the Manufactory

used in soldering created an unusual atmosphere in which to work. One observer noted that upon entering a making room his

> ears are greeted with a faint, far-off roar. . . . The rush of air from out the many little blow-pipes blends into that sound, which is like a blast of wind among far-off tree-tops. Here the shell is fastened on a frame, and the trimmings placed against it and soldered on. A compound blow-pipe is used, with air and illuminating gas forced through it. The air is carried up into these rooms from the first floor through a small tin pipe, into which it is forced by a simple valve and piston. The blow-pipe is attached to two small flexible rubber tubes, which feed it with the air and gas. The solder used is simply a little strip of white-metal, about the size of a straw. . . . [which] will melt more easily than the castings. The blow-pipe shoots out a tongue of blue flame against the solder, striking out a shower of yellow scintillations as it apparently devours the frail strip, and in a moment the joint is complete.[33]

Once assembled, plain objects could proceed directly to the finishing department and then on to be packed for shipment. Those that required chased, engraved, or applied decoration, of course, had to pass through those processes before being polished and packed. And in the case of plated wares, the newly assembled base-metal bodies had to be silverplated before proceeding further.

Although the majority of objects made by American silverware producers were relatively simple and thus could be processed in large part in the stamping, spinning, turning, and making departments, thousands of customized wares were almost entirely constructed by hand by highly trained silversmiths. Throughout the entire 1875 to 1915 period, observers frequently commented on the large amount of hand raising and decoration being done throughout the industry. In 1875, for example, one writer noted that "machinery is not used to any considerable extent in the manufacture of silver-work, if we except certain specialties, such as spoons and forks; and, even of these, many are still made by hand, although the ornaments on the handle are generally produced by stamping, or by letting the object pass between the rollers or dies in which the pattern is cut. But, in the production of silver designs of a high character, machinery performs only a small part."[34]

At the end of the century, the finer wares were still being made mostly by hand. In 1891 a visitor to the Gorham plant remarked that "the delicate hand touch is necessary to give [silver] a characteristic finish which stamps it as a work of art."[35] A decade later, Augustus Steward, chief instructor in gold- and silversmithing at the Central School of Arts and Crafts in London, found the frequency and high quality of fine silverworking in this country worth praising. He stated:

It is strange that one should have to admit it, but it is nevertheless true, that while America, youngest among nations, leads in a new style of design, she, at the same time, keeps very definitely to the old style of silversmithing. . . . It is true that machine methods are responsible for not a little of the American output, but, on the other hand, what makes an art craftsman feel satisfied with high class American silversmithing is the fact that he can see in it the thoughtfulness of the designer and the deftness of the craftsman.[36]

The American silversmiths whose work Steward so admired labored within almost every firm. Following drawings and wax or plaster models prepared in the design department and usually approved by the customer, company silversmiths worked up vessels using a series of hammers. The Gorham management noted that in this department "nearly all of the special or custom work is executed by those men. Trophies, elaborate centerpieces, or any special pieces are wrought by hand from the flat piece of silver to the finished masterpiece."[37] While certainly some smiths worked on the same object from start to finish as suggested by Gorham, most objects were the creation of more than one specialist. For example, a worker who specialized in raising would create the main body of a vessel using a series of hammers on a flat sheet of silver or a partially shaped shell from the stamping or spinning departments. If the object was to be decorated with chasing or engraving, as most expensive silverware was before 1915, however, it had to be given over to another worker.

Chasing rooms, as with most spaces in which much handwork was done, were well lit, with work benches placed before the windows. One description of a chasing room noted that it was "light and airy, with the sunlight tempered by shaded curtains, and the air filled with a gentle tick-tack, tick-tack, many times repeated, and suggesting the sound made by the rows of large clocks on the shelves of a clock-maker."[38] Chasing departments were also one of the few divisions in a silverware manufactory where women sometimes labored. Reed & Barton, for example, employed women almost exclusively to do its chasing in the late 1870s.[39] Chasing is divided into two types—flat and repoussé chasing. In flat chasing, the design is drawn on the object's surface using a paper pattern and lamp black or whiting and then heated so it will not smear. Pointed but blunt tools are then hammered along each line, thereby denting the surface with the desired pattern. In repoussé chasing, the design is drawn on as before, but the decoration is pushed out from the backside rather than dented down from above (fig. 4.3). To accomplish this, a curved steel tool called a snarling iron is used. A Gorham manual noted: "This iron is supported in a vise and the article to be chased is placed over the upturned point [ill. 4.5]. The part at which the ornament

FIG. 4.3. Pitcher. Tiffany & Co., New York, N.Y., 1893. Sterling silver. Dallas Museum of Art. The flowers were created through repoussé chasing.

ILL. 4.6. Gorham Mfg. Co. black coffee set and tray no. A 5535, by Nicholas Heinzelman, 1899.

is to stand out in relief is rested on the point and the iron is hammered. The vibration of the snarling iron bumps up the metal." Once this stage is completed, the vessel is removed and filled with hot pitch, which hardens when cool. The pitch fills in behind the newly raised areas, supporting them and preventing tears when work begins on the outside. "The ornament is then chased in the elevated section and any of the elevation not decorated is carefully pounded back, leaving the ornament in relief. Hundreds of tools, varying in size and shape, are employed by the chaser which are [often] fashioned by himself."[40] Although an expensive addition due to the amount of labor it required, chased decoration could be added to pieces that were not hand raised but spun or stamped up. This combination became more common between 1890 and 1920 as body shapes became increasingly standardized.

Chasing silver is an extremely difficult and time-consuming craft. Consequently, chasers were always in short supply and second only to die sinkers in receiving high wages, often as much as $40 or $50 per week. The fact that they were hard to replace meant that chasers, like die sinkers, had more power within a workshop than the average silverworker. When strikes occurred, for example, it was often the chasers who led the men out, as they did at many firms in 1887 and 1902. Furthermore, their talent often meant that they received special attention from manufacturers. The most extraordinary case is that of Nicholas Heinzelman (1837–1900, ill. 4.6). Born in Switzerland and trained as a chaser in New Orleans, Heinzelman was "discovered" by Edward Holbrook, the director of Gorham,

who recognized the craftsman's peculiar talent for flat chasing. Despite the fact that Heinzelman was unkempt, never became a formal employee, and was prone to disappear for long periods, Holbrook was fascinated by the quality of his naturalistic decoration. Consequently, Heinzelman was given a room by himself in the manufactory in which to work and was allowed to come and go at will. Nevertheless, he chased relatively few objects in his several years at Gorham. Because of his eccentric personal habits, low productivity, and the preferential treatment shown him, Heinzelman must have been resented by the rest of Gorham's chasers. And yet, his technical virtuosity so fascinated Holbrook that the firm published a book on Heinzelman eighteen years after the craftsman's death.[41] Although few men received the treatment Heinzelman did, companies nevertheless did try to protect and appease their most talented craftsmen.

Like chasing, engraving is primarily a hand process. In engraving, however, silver is actually dug out of the object rather than dented into it as in chasing (figs. 4.4–5). Engraving at Reed & Barton was described in 1878:

> In the engraving-rooms, which are in one of the detached buildings, the ware is placed upon a circular pad that revolves, and there the engravers, with their sharp, steel points, trace upon it the patterns or designs which are furnished them. With a firm hand and a true eye they spin the ware around on the pad, and trace vines and leaves, curling tendrils and intricate arabesques, in lines of light, while a delicate thread of metal falls away from the tool, showing that these lines are cut into the surface.[42]

When the vessel was finally polished, black oxidation was left in these channels so that they were clearly distinguishable from the shiny surface. Although not as common as engraving, a similar effect could be achieved by using acid. In a technique called acid etching, the areas of a design that were to remain shiny were marked off with varnish or lacquer. The object was then immersed in acid, which ate away the uncoated areas. When these etched areas were oxidized, the desired design stood out visually in relief (figs. 4.6–7).

Engine turning, or machine engraving, is another exception to hand engraving (ill. 4.7). This technique was most popular on American silver in the third quarter of the nineteenth century, especially on flatware and silverplated wares (figs. 3.7–8). In this process the vessel is attached to a machine, which moves the object from side to side and up and down according to a template. As the piece moves, it is pressed against a sharp, stationary diamond stylus, which scratches the desired geometric pattern into its surface. Similarly, simple monograms could be engraved on silver objects through the use of a pattern or jig that contained the desired letter. As an

FIG. 4.4. Fish set. James S. Vancourt, New York, N.Y., ca. 1852–1861. Coin silver. D. Albert Soeffing Collection. Except for the cut-out shape of the pieces, all the decoration was engraved.

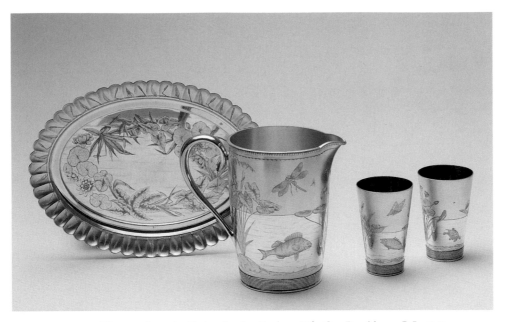

FIG. 4.5. Water set from the *Furber Service*. Gorham Mfg. Co., Providence, R.I., 1878.
Sterling silver and silvergilt. Museum of Art, Rhode Island School of Design.
The water imagery on this set was hand engraved.

operator traced a stylus along the pattern, a sharp tool attached to that stylus by means of a rod engraved the letter on the silver object, which was held fast in place. During the nineteenth century, however, this form of monogramming appears to have been seldom practiced. Rather, the hundreds of monogram styles available were simply engraved by hand, even in the case of entire sets of flatware.[43]

With their decoration completed, silver objects were next sent to the finishing department (ills. 4.1–2). If any of the decoration required highlights to be added so that it would stand out, this was done by a burnisher, who rubbed polished steel tools against the surface while holding the object, or, in some cases, while it rotated on a lathe. Next, all scratches, file traces, and hammer marks were removed through a process known as "bobbing." In bobbing, a walrus-hide buff impregnated with ground pumice stone and oil was worked against the silver's surface and edges until they were smooth. To remove the oil and pumice mixture, pieces were washed in a cleaning solution, and then any surfaces that were supposed to appear black were oxidized through submersion in boiling water and sodium sulphide.

Finally, silverware was ready to be polished (ill. 4.1). Generally, three finishes were available—French, bright, and butler. A French finish was given the silver by using pumice and oil to produce minute scratches, which gave the surface a gray, matte appearance. Both bright and butler finishes left the surface shiny; a butler finish was slightly more reflective. These two finishes were produced by using various polishing compounds to remove the tiny scratches that resulted from the bobbing process. Common polishing agents were jeweler's rouge (a mixture of iron oxide, lamp black, paraffin, stearic acid, and powdered talcum), whiting (calcium carbonate), and tripoli (a mixture of fat, vaseline, and volcanic dust).[44] Typically these compounds were used on a rotating polishing wheel into which

silverware was pushed. Commenting on Reed & Barton's polishing room, one observer noted that "the walls, floor, the ceiling even, . . . are of a murky, sanguinary hue. A row of ensanguined operatives are seen through a reddish mist standing in front of revolving disks, also of red. These are wheels made of cotton rags and filled with rouge, which make nearly four thousand revolutions per minute, and which give the final polish to the ware."[45] In spite of the fact that they performed some of the dirtiest work, constantly being covered with red jeweler's rouge, polishers as well as burnishers earned some of the lowest wages of all skilled workers in the industry. In 1869, for example, polishers in the state of Rhode Island made only half the pay of die sinkers. Burnishers were paid around 40 percent less than die sinkers, who averaged $26 a week.[46] While wages rose in the last decades of the century, the ratio between these workers remained relatively constant.

Although women were overwhelmingly outnumbered by their male counterparts, those who did work in the industry were primarily employed in finishing departments as burnishers and polishers. In the period, women's skin was thought to have a better texture than men's for the final rouge polishing of silver.[47] Tiffany's, which employed women as approximately 6 percent of its work force, did so mainly in the finishing department, as did Reed & Barton. And while both paid women a rate that was relatively high compared with other industries, they still earned on average about half that of male workers.[48] Besides those who worked as burnishers, polishers, and the few chasers and engravers, females could typically be found at jobs where delicate painting was required. Positions of this nature included enameling and masking silver for etching, gilding, and silver overlaying (fig. 4.8). And in Gorham's huge photographic department women worked to print and mount the 80,000 photographs produced each year. Finally, women also often worked in case-making departments producing the linings for

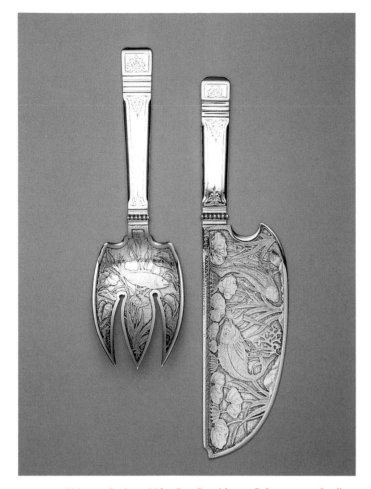

FIG. 4.6. Fish set. Gorham Mfg. Co., Providence, R.I., ca. 1885. Sterling silver. Private Collection, San Antonio. The elaborate decoration on the blade and tines was done by acid etching.

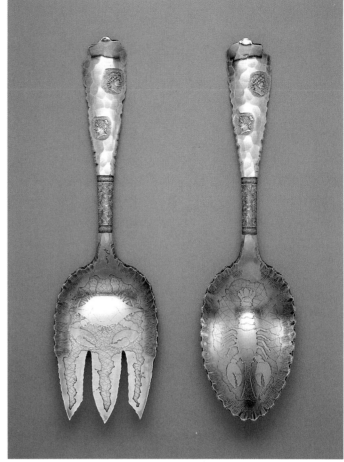

FIG. 4.7. Salad set. Wood & Hughes, maker, New York, N.Y.; A. B. Griswold & Co., retailer, New Orleans, La.; ca. 1885–1895. Sterling silver. Dallas Museum of Art. The lobster and crab were acid etched.

ILL. 4.7. Engine turning, ca. 1878.

cases and flannel bags for silver. For Gorham alone, women sewed 70,000 bags annually.[49]

The case-making and packing departments in which some women worked were the final stop in a plant for a silver object before it was shipped. If items such as flatware were simply to be replacement stock for a jewelry store, they were wrapped and packed in unassuming boxes and shipped. However, most pieces of hollowware and expensive flatware were fitted into rather elaborate presentation boxes before departing. Large firms like Gorham and Tiffany's kept on hand stocks of wood, leather, and fabric for making boxes and linings.[50] Even though many of the wooden parts were cut by power tools, box making required much hand labor. In 1892 it was reported that Gorham employed more than 100 male and female workers to produce the 100,000 boxes it required that year.[51] Contemporary photographs show rows of workers seated at benches in front of windows, each busy with a single box and silver article. Most boxes were covered in fabric or leather and lined with satin, but elaborate objects often required ornate cases of exotic woods with plush silk interiors (ills. 4.8–9, fig. 4.9). If a firm did not have the room or desire to maintain its own box-making department, boxes could be purchased from subcontractors. In 1877 Samuel C. Jackson in New York's silverware and jewelry district advertised that he could supply the trade with "Cases For Jewelry, Silver Ware, Trays, &c."[52]

The Rise of the Manufactory

ILL. 4.8. Woman working in Gorham Mfg. Co.'s box-making department, Elmwood manufactory, ca. 1892.

Besides furnishing cases, outside specialty suppliers could be called upon to furnish a host of products. For example, certain book dealers serviced the industry by providing technical expertise. Herman Bush of Mytongate Hull, England, advertised in 1877 in the American trade press that he sold "English, American, French and German PERIODICALS, and RECENTLY PUBLISHED HAND-BOOKS; FOR REFINERS, JEWELERS, WATCHMAKERS, ELECTRO-PLATERS AND LAPIDARIES. List sent free on application."[53] Like books and periodicals, raw or partially processed silver could be purchased through brokers, usually in New York City. At the other end of the spectrum, refiners purchased floor sweepings and other scrap for reprocessing. In 1892 the Chicago and Aurora Smelting and Refining Companies advertised that they accepted gold and silver sweepings for cleaning and re-smelting.[54] Similarly, a host of machine tool and die companies, such as the Mossberg & Granville Mfg. Co., advertised that they could supply the latest drop presses, lathes, and tools.[55] Occasionally, a supplier did such good work that a silver manufacturer sought to gain exclusive right to his products. In 1880, for example, Gorham successfully sought exclusive access to a new type of die developed by a Charles Mosser and assigned to the Smith Brothers Mfg. Co. Gorham had occasionally used this type of die before, the result of which was "a large saving in the actual cost of the finished goods."[56]

Even with the support of outside suppliers, the journey from silver ingot and paper design to polished surface and fitted box required amazing organization on the part of silverware producers. Scores of clerks had to keep track of orders and billing; drawings, dies, and chucks had to be numbered,

ILL. 4.9. View of Gorham Mfg. Co. products in their original boxes, 1879.

FIG. 4.8. Vase. La Pierre Mfg. Co., New York, N.Y., and Newark, N.J., ca. 1890–1910.
Glass with silver overlay. Philadelphia Museum of Art.

FIG. 4.9. Pastry or ice cream server in original box. J. E. Caldwell & Co., retailer,
Philadelphia, Pa., ca. 1880. Sterling silver. Dallas Museum of Art.

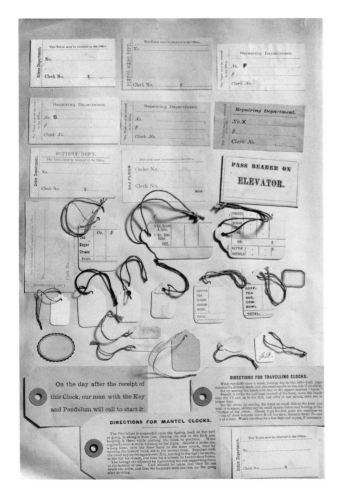

inventoried, and safely stored (ill. 4.10). Partially finished silver items had to be secured by removal to a vault each night,
and workers had to be watched so that objects and scrap metal
did not leave the premises.[57] And most important of all, production had to be orchestrated so that it resulted in the highest
quality merchandise at the lowest possible cost. Organizing a
manufactory was a difficult task at best, given the complicated
and multiple stages required for silverware production.

The Gorham Mfg. Co. opened a huge, modern manufactory outside Providence in 1890, and shortly thereafter a
handful of large producers like Tiffany followed suit. However, the compact shop where cramped conditions and relatively poor ventilation and lighting prevailed was typical of most
silverware producers throughout the nineteenth and early twentieth centuries. While the efficiency of these shops might be
improved by reorganizing the physical position of men and
tools within the old space or by restructuring the hierarchy
within the work force, only the largest and most profitable of
concerns could afford to totally redesign the working environment by building enormous and expensive manufacturing
plants in the last decade of the century.

ILL. 4.10. Selection of tags used to label and track stock as it moved through
the Tiffany & Co. manufactory and retail store.

1. For a discussion of business cycles in this period see Fels 1959, 107ff., and Williamson 1944, 745ff.

2. According to *Silverware* 1940, table 7, the value of silverware produced in America in 1869 was $10,487,000 and rose to only $11,114,000 in 1879, compared to $7,248 in 1859 and $17,938,000 in 1889.

3. Parsell 1901, 42, lists the number of silver ounces billed to the New York store from the plant, which reflects this drop from 103,900 ozs. in 1873 to 78,182 ozs. in 1878. Historical 1950 shows that sales dropped from $725,644 in 1873 to $531,602 in 1878. Gibb 1943, 206, shows that Reed & Barton's domestic sales dropped from approximately $690,000 in 1872 to $520,000 in 1875 and remained near there until 1879.

4. For an example of a Tiffany auction and Rogers & Brothers adjusting the style of their goods, see *JSW* 4:3 (Nov. 1877):40. An auction held by the Taunton Mfg. Co. is noted on page 39.

5. "Providence Letter," *JSW* 4:5 (Jan. 1878):76.

6. "Backbone in Business," *JCK* 8:8 (Sept. 1877):115.

7. *JSW* 4:3 (Nov. 1877):40.

8. A crude measure of growth in work force can be gained by dividing the number of wage earners reported by the Census of Manufacturers by the total number of establishments reporting for the U.S. The results by year are: 1859/16 workers; 1869/20; 1879/44; 1889/74; 1899/72; 1904/94; 1909/94; and 1914/89. Data taken from *Silverware* 1940, table 7.

9. The Gorham figures are taken from Historical 1950, chart. Tiffany & Co.'s come from Parsell 1901, 40. The total for Duhme is taken from Beckman 1975, 54. The 1890 totals are from "American Manufacturers of Silver and Silver Plated Goods, Part II," *JW* 9:20 (13 Mar. 1890):42 and 44, and "Part III," *JW* 9:21 (20 Mar. 1890):42 and 45. The Gorham memo, "Employees of the Gorham Mfg. Co.," is in GA, III. Personnel, 6. For similar figures from 1902, see "Strike in the Silver Trade," *JCK* 45:14 (5 Nov. 1902):53, and "Silversmiths Strike Ended," *JCK* 45:19 (10 Dec. 1902):28.

10. *JW* 9:20 (13 Mar. 1890):44.

11. For an excellent discussion of flexible production, see Scranton 1991.

12. Percy 1878, 484.

13. *JW* 4:23 (6 Oct. 1887):3019.

14. List of Assets, 1871, 34–44, GA, II. Corporate, f. For a description of Gorham design room, see *HNMM* 1868, 443. For a discussion of Tiffany's library and a selection of volumes included, see Carpenter 1978, 229–30.

15. Summary Volume 1913, 12.

16. For information on how silver ore was processed before it got to this stage, see "Smelting Ore in Colorado," *IIW* 18:909 (30 May 1877):156–57 and 461–61. For a general overview of silver as a useful metal, see Ward 1979, 3–9.

17. Quote and general description of these operations taken from a tour of the Reed & Barton works in Percy 1878, 484–86. For a brief description of this part of the Gorham works, see "Silversmithing in America. Part III. Gorham Mfg. Co.—Description of the Works," *JCK* 24:20 (15 June 1892):3, and for Tiffany's, see *NR* 1878, 24–25.

18. For a description of this process, see Percy 1878, 486.

19. *JCK* 24:20 (15 June 1892):6.

20. Summary Volume 1913, 12–13.

21. Parsell 1901, 6.

22. Percy 1878, 486.

23. "The Gorham Exhibit, Silverware," *JW* 8:8 (20 June 1889):38.

24. For a fine discussion of Heller and the above quotation, see Carpenter 1982, 121–40.

25. Quoted from an English translation printed in "The Gold and Silversmiths' Work at the Paris Exhibition," *JCK* 9:10 (Nov. 1878):180.

26. "Tiffany's. The World's Greatest Jewelry Store, From Cellar to Garret. Third Paper," *JW* 4:23 (6 Oct. 1887):3018.

27. "The Manufacture of Silverplated Ware. An Exposition of the Processes Employed with the Works of Rogers S. Bros., Waterbury, Conn.," *JCK* 24:17 (25 May 1892):42.

28. *JCK* 24:20 (15 June 1892):6.

29. Percy 1878, 487.

30. For information on the development of the sectional chuck at Reed & Barton, see Gibb 1943, 261.

31. Parsell 1901, 4.

32. Percy 1878, 487.

33. *Ibid.*, 489.

34. *AJ* 1875b, 372.

35. *JCK* 24:20 (15 June 1892):6.

36. Steward 1902, 35.

37. Gorham 1932, 86.

38. Percy 1878, 489.

39. *Ibid.*, 489.

40. Gorham 1932, 86.

41. Townsend 1918. Heinzelman's production was so low that he may have completed less than two dozen pieces.

42. Percy 1878, 489.

43. The use of hand engraving in such cases is supported through a close examination of monograms on sets of silver articles where the engraving is slightly different on each piece and not mechanical in appearance.

44. For informative descriptions of the various compounds and finishing methods used, see Gorham 1932, 87–88.

45. Percy 1878, 492.

46. Gibb 1943, 275.

47. Tomlinson 1858, 54.

48. The 6 percent figure for Tiffany's is taken from Parsell 1901, 40. The one-half pay figure is taken from Gibb 1943, 278.

49. For the best information on women in the silver industry, see Gorham 1892; "How Skilled Work Remunerates Women. In Silversmiths' Shops," *Harper's Bazaar* (18 Aug. 1883); and Stokes 1990.

50. For mentions of these supplies, see *JCK* 24:20 (15 June 1892):7–8, and *NR* 1878, 24.

51. Krantz 1894, Silver Factories, 10.

52. *JCK* 8:2 (Mar. 1877):facing 28.

53. *JSW* 3:1 (July 1877):12. For a price list of books of interest to "Jewelers, Silversmiths and Watchmakers," see *JSW* 3:2 (Aug. 1877):12. Both design and technical manuals are included.

54. *JCK* 24:5 (2 Mar. 1892):31.

55. *JCK* 45:27 (31 Dec. 1902):83.

56. Board 1868 (8 Mar. 1880):184.

57. For an example of a worker stealing silver bullion, see "Foreman of Gorham Mfg. Co. Arrested for Stealing Silver," *JCK* 45:11 (15 Oct. 1902):26. "Robbery of Manufacturers by their Workmen," *JCK* 11:9 (Oct. 1880):165–66, also warns of workers stealing.

AT HOME AND ABROAD: MARKETING

In 1869 all the solid silver and plated ware produced in the United States was valued by the Census of Manufactures at $10,487,000. By 1899 this figure had more than doubled to $26,114,000, and it subsequently rose to $42,229,000 in 1909.[1] Certainly some of the rise in value during the late 1890s and early twentieth century was due to inflation. The figures nevertheless reveal a massive growth in silverware production and sales between 1875 and 1915 despite the fall in raw silver prices.[2] When corrected for inflation, these figures reflect a fivefold increase in value between 1869 and 1899 and a further expansion of 20 percent during the next decade. To distribute this growing amount of silverware, manufacturers, wholesalers, and retailers honed their skills at promoting and selling their products.

EXPANDING DISTRIBUTION

The creation of a national network of middlemen, retailers, and salesmen between 1840 and 1875 provided a foundation upon which to build in the late nineteenth and early twentieth centuries. Several factors encouraged this expansion. First, between 1875 and 1900, the price of silver objects fell significantly due to a general decline in manufacturing costs, including raw materials and labor, and increased competition in the marketplace, which forced prices down. By expanding their sales forces, manufacturers sought to raise sales volume and thus maintain profits. Second, the phenomenal growth in America's railway system during the mid nineteenth century made it easier and cheaper to field more salesmen, who could cover wider territories faster. And finally, in 1881 the U.S. Supreme Court declared license fees for salesmen unconstitutional. Such county and state fees were often expensive and thus discouraged the use of salesmen. For example, Virginia charged a fee of $25 a year for the initial county where a salesman made a stop and $10 for each additional county.[3] With improved transportation and the abolition of fees, sales forces grew rapidly throughout the silverware and other industries in the late nineteenth century. In 1895, for example, the *Jewelers' Circular* reported that "more than 500,000 traveling salesmen are employed in the United States at the present time (in all lines of trade). . . . The salaries and commissions of these men equal $500,000,000, while their expenses, railroad fares, and hotel bills distribute another $500,000,000 into the nation's economy."[4] Reed & Barton was probably fairly typical of large silverware firms, employing seventeen salesmen in 1885.[5]

Salesmen, or drummers, as they were often called, had a reputation for being morally loose and professionally aggressive. An 1881 description of out-of-town salesmen cornering silverware dealers in New York reflects this stereotype. The writer said:

> It is reported and vouched for that one buyer, who contemplated leaving the hotel by an early train, on emerging from his room at 6 o'clock in the morning, found four Providence drummers fast asleep at the threshold of his door, each clasping a sample box in hand. Three of these persistent salesmen are reported to have followed to Coney Island a gentleman from the West, who, they thought, was about to elude them, and importuned him even while he was bathing in the surf.[6]

To combat this hustler image, firms whose sales were based on name recognition as much as product quality developed training programs for their sales forces and instituted codes of behavior. In 1908, for example, Gorham distributed to its salesmen a pocket-size booklet on how to handle silver properly. In it management stated that it would not tolerate salesmen leaving fingerprints on silver and the mishandling of goods in general. To avoid this problem, salesmen were directed to wear a silk handkerchief in their coat pocket with which to handle the silver. Proper treatment was supposed to reveal the value placed on cleanliness by the salesmen, and "the customer w[ould] be so impressed by his careful handling, as to feel a higher appreciation of the real beauty of the goods."[7]

Wanting one's salesmen to be respectable voices for the firm did not mean they should be unaggressive in obtaining orders. Entwining the concepts of respectability and forcefulness in selling, Gorham, for example, printed "Some Business Commandments." This booklet took a heavy-handed religious

FIG. 5.1. *Goelet Schooner Cup.* Whiting Mfg. Co., New York, N.Y., ca. 1891. Sterling silver. New York Yacht Club.

tone by following the form of the Ten Commandments. These instructions to salesmen list ten points, including:

> I. Thou shalt not wait for something to turn up, but thou shalt pull off thy coat and go to work that thou mayest prosper in thy affairs and make the word "failure" spell "success."

> II. Thou shalt not be content to go about looking like a bum, for thou shouldst know that thy personal appearance is better than a letter of recommendation.

> X. Thou shalt give every man a square deal. This is the last and great commandment, and there is no other like unto it. Upon this commandment hangs the law and the profits of the business world.

These commandments were supported by publications like "Our Creed," which mimics a catechism when it states: "We believe in the goods we are selling and in our ability to get results. . . . We believe in courtesy, in kindness, in generosity, in good cheer, in friendship and honest competition. We believe there is an order somewhere for every man ready to take one. We believe we're ready—right now!"[8]

An example of a dynamic salesman who was "ready—right now" is Horace C. Wilcox (d. 1890) of the Meriden Britannia Co. As part owner and head salesman for the company, Wilcox became legendary for his sales prowess. In 1887 the *Jewelers' Weekly* described his bravura style when it recalled how Wilcox once called upon a customer to find he had purchased stock of an inferior quality: "Mr. Wilcox swept the whole assortment from the case in a bruised and broken mass on the floor. 'You can't afford,' said he, 'to ruin your reputation with such trash. Send the company your bill and we will pay it. Now I want to sell you some reliable goods.'"[9] Along with selling a customer "some reliable goods," most salesmen were also expected to do credit checks and collect money owed the firm, as well as handle dealer complaints and explain how to use the manufacturer's promotional literature.[10]

Besides the hundreds of salesmen who crisscrossed the country selling wares for manufacturers, there were also scores of dealers, usually jewelry store owners, who made annual buying trips to wholesale showrooms located in New York City or elsewhere. Almost all of the most important sterling and plate manufacturers maintained showrooms in Manhattan, and several, like Gorham, Meriden Britannia, and Reed & Barton, had branch wholesale offices in Chicago and San Francisco and often had representatives in Detroit, Philadelphia, and Atlanta. Generally, the buyers who visited these showrooms were retailers who sold directly to the public or wholesalers who redistributed silverware to retailers in their territory. An example of such a wholesaler is Leonard Clower of New Orleans. His advertisements from the 1880s reveal that while he made some of his own items, he mainly wholesaled those of others along the Gulf Coast from his "Southern Jewelers' Supply House."[11] The southern market had been greatly curtailed by the Civil War but had recovered by the late 1870s and offered fertile ground for men like Clower because of the rapid growth of cities such as Houston, Galveston, New Orleans, Birmingham, Mobile, Memphis, and Atlanta.[12]

Dealers usually went to New York or some regional center at least once a year for several weeks. Probably having traveled by rail, upon arrival in New York they often registered at the office of periodicals like *Jewelers' Weekly*, leaving their name, place of residence, and hotel. This information was subsequently published in the next issue so that salesmen from various firms would know a particular dealer was in the city and where to find him. Consequently, samples or photographs could be brought to the hotel and reviewed more speedily. By the mid 1880s, issues of trade journals typically listed the names of dozens of "New Arrivals."[13] Also aiding dealers to find sources of merchandise were publications like the *Directory of Wholesale Dealers (Manufacturers & Jobbers) of Jewelry, Watches, Clocks, Diamonds & Precious Stones, Silver & Silver-Plated Ware-Etc. in the United States* that listed the names and addresses of hundreds of suppliers according to specialty.[14]

The many wholesale showrooms located in lower Manhattan, along Broadway, and increasingly uptown on Fifth Avenue were frequented by out-of-town dealers. The Waltham Building (1876, ill. 2.6), Hays Building, and Silversmith's Hall (1892, ills. 7.3, 7.10) are examples of structures in the jewelry and silverware district of lower Manhattan that contained the showrooms and/or workshops of several manufacturers under the same roof. Between 1875 and 1915, however, firms with significant retail trades within New York City left such multi-occupant buildings and established individual showrooms, if they had not done so already. Some, like Gorham, kept a wholesale office in buildings such as these, but also established spacious and elaborate showrooms further uptown. In 1876 Gorham had a retail store at 37 Union Square and a wholesale one in the Waltham Building downtown. The Waltham Building burned in 1877, frustrating Gorham's efforts to separate its retail and wholesale trade. However, in 1884 the firm reinstituted the plan by erecting a seven-story, brick Queen Anne–style building at Nineteenth Street and Broadway. In 1892 the downtown wholesale branch was removed to the new Hays Building.

Designed by New York architect Edward H. Kendall, the 1884 showroom was extremely elaborate and efficient (ill. 5.1). The interior was noted for its spaciousness, high ceilings, and large windows admitting abundant light. The ceiling was decorated and the walls were of polished cherry. Both the retail showroom on the first floor and the wholesale one on the second floor were furnished with mahogany and plate-glass wall and floor cases manufactured by B. and W. B. Smith. The offices and elevator were in the rear of the store, and the entire space was lit by an "Edison system of electric lighting, the plant having the capacity of 288 lamps." One observer commented, "Here can be found everything desired in the silver line, the stock embracing all the latest designs and rich goods, some of severely plain patterns and others elaborate in their ornamentation."[15]

ILL. 5.1. The Gorham Co. Building, Broadway and 19th St., New York, N.Y., built 1884.

ILL. 5.2. The Gorham Co. Building, Fifth Ave. and 36th St., New York, N.Y., built 1904.

By 1904, however, Gorham felt this building and its location had become outdated, and it commissioned Stanford White of the leading architectural firm of McKim, Mead & White to design a new building (ill. 5.2). Located further uptown on Fifth Avenue at Thirty-sixth Street near the New York Public Library, the structure was in the Renaissance style. The facade of the two-story-high ground floor was ornamented with Ionic columns from which sprang arches. The spaces between the arches were carved with figures representing art and industry. Much decoration was also lavished on the building's ceiling and exterior bronze doors and trim that had been cast at Gorham. By having one of America's foremost architects design its building in the Renaissance taste, Gorham sought to please America's fashionable elite and link itself and its products with the glorious artistic legacy of fifteenth-century Italy. This desire is evident in the frontispiece of its 1904 catalogue, which states: "With the added facilities that will come with the new building in Fifth Avenue and 36th Street, New York, a fine architectural creation after design by McKim, Mead & White, with the ripening skill of the Gorham silversmiths, devoted always to their traditions and their art, the company will continue its artistic development."[16]

Gorham also opened branches in San Francisco in 1879 and Chicago in 1882. While both the West Coast and Midwest markets were important, the Midwest one was vital to Gorham, since a large proportion of its orders came from that region.

To secure the firm's position in this market, Edward Holbrook, then Gorham's treasurer, purchased 31 percent of the stock of Spaulding & Co., one of Chicago's prestigious jewelry stores, in 1888. Blocks of stock the same size were also held by founder H. A. Spaulding and by L. J. Leiter. By Holbrook's buying into Spaulding & Co., Gorham obtained a major retail outlet in Chicago, as well as access to Spaulding's Paris store at 36 Avenue de l'Opéra. This relationship proved beneficial to Gorham, which moved large quantities of silverware through Spaulding & Co. and sometimes chose to introduce new product lines there. Its art nouveau line, *Martelé*, for example, was first offered for sale to the American public through the Chicago store, and judging from surviving pieces with retailer marks, a large proportion of all *Martelé* was sold in Chicago.[17]

Like Gorham, the Meriden Britannia Co. repeatedly upgraded its showrooms in the second half of the nineteenth century. In 1872 the firm left the cramped quarters at 199 Broadway that it had occupied since the early 1860s and relocated to the elaborate showroom at 550 Broadway that Tiffany & Co. had recently vacated. Only six years later, the firm moved to the more fashionable location of 46 East Fourteenth Street at Union Square near Tiffany & Co.'s and Gorham's showrooms. Surviving interior views show that the store was quite stylish, with Corinthian columns and chandeliers (ill. 5.3). For the display of goods it was fitted with over 300 feet of wall cases and more than twenty-five counter cases and tables. In 1867 a branch

ILL. 5.3. The Meriden Britannia Co. showroom, Union Square, New York, N.Y., ca. 1887.

showroom was opened in San Francisco, and in 1878 another was opened in Chicago. The Chicago store was claimed to be the largest west of the Alleghenies, though not as large as that in New York.[18]

The space that Meriden Britannia Co. occupied in 1872 was available because the ever-fashion-conscious Charles L. Tiffany had moved his salesroom further uptown to Union Square in 1870. Seventeen years later, its 78-by-140-foot space with high ceilings and ornamental pillars was still considered elegant.[19] By the turn of the century, however, Tiffany's decided once again to relocate uptown, since its elite clientele were moving in that direction. In 1906, it opened a spacious new building on Fifth Avenue and Thirty-seventh Street, one block from Gorham's showroom. Also designed by McKim, Mead & White, the structure was based on the Palazzo Grimani in Venice (ill. 5.4). *Architects' and Builders' Magazine* said of the interior:

> Gray, foggy tones—"gris-de-perle"—have been used almost exclusively. The coffered classical ceiling is supported by columns of purplish-gray Formosa marble, with composite capitals. . . . The artificial lighting is from silvered chandeliers. The walls are divided into panels of polished Terrazzo of a speckled texture. The elevators are the finest piece of steel work in this country and place our metal workers on a level with the great smiths and forgers of the German Renaissance.[20]

In short, Tiffany & Co.'s new building, like Gorham's, was a "Commercial Palace."

As evident from interior photographs, these new showrooms were, like their predecessors, heavily populated with sales clerks (ill. 5.5). Arrayed behind long U-shaped cases, large floor staffs promoted high quality customer service. Since Tiffany's,

ILL. 5.4. The Tiffany & Co. Building, Fifth Ave. and 37th St., New York, N.Y., built 1906.

unlike most of its competitors, only sold to retail customers through a single store in this country, it tried hard to hire salesmen who had contacts throughout the country. In 1886 the *Manufacturing Jeweler* of Providence wrote that one method employed by Tiffany's to work up a big business in all parts of the country was to engage salesmen who had once run fashionable jewelry stores in distant cities but had failed in business for some reason. According to the article, "The distance of New York from the inland city proved no hindrance; in fact, it was frequently a help, for the magic phrase 'from Tiffany's'

ILL. 5.5. Interior of the Tiffany & Co. Building, ca. 1906.

counterbalanced all consideration of distance, time and cost. If a wedding in high circles was to take place, the clerk who formerly lived in that city went down with a trunk full of goods, and generally came back with a pocket full of money."[21] Judging from other evidence, this claim was indeed true. For example, in 1878 Herman Marcus, who had been a partner in the well-known New York firm of Starr & Marcus, went to work for Tiffany's. In 1887 William T. Gale (not the same Gale discussed earlier), who had run his own store in Boston until recently, took "pleasure in informing you, his former patrons, that he is engaged in an agreement with Messrs. Tiffany & Co." The same year a Mr. C. H. Arms, "lately with the Gorham Manufacturing Co. of New York," became a salesman in Tiffany & Co.'s silver department.[22] By 1893 it was estimated that Tiffany's employed 120 salesmen in the New York store.[23]

New York's mercantile palaces became models for jewelry store design across the country between 1875 and 1915. More than simply purchasing goods, the dealers who visited these establishments on their semiannual buying trips returned home with ideas of how a fashionable store should look and how its employees should behave. By the mid 1870s, there were dozens of fine jewelry stores across America that in many ways resembled the great emporia of New York. For example, in 1877 T. Steele & Son opened a new store in the Miller Building in downtown Hartford, Connecticut (ill. 5.6). It was reported that

> the interior arrangements are on the latest New York and Boston plans, the cases for the goods being arranged in an oblong square, in the center of which the clerks stand. Along the side walls extend massive show-cases of black and French walnut, inlaid with ebony and holly. The

ILL. 5.6. Interior of the T. Steele & Son store, Hartford Conn., ca. 1877.

goods inside these cases are made more conspicuous by a cardinal red background of heavy reps, laid in box folds, and they are protected by large plate-glass fronts reaching from the floor to the top of the cases, which have elaborately carved ornaments as a finish.[24]

Besides fancy casework, the store also had elegant gas lighting fixtures and a blue, drab, and yellow encaustic tile floor. "The front windows [were] large, and so arranged as to give perfect ventilation and prevent 'sweating.'"

Ten years later the store of J. P. Stevens & Brothers in Atlanta carried on the tradition of drawing inspiration from New York. In 1887 one observer remarked:

> On entering the place the visitor's first impression is the wonderfully harmonious richness of the *tout ensemble*. The floor is covered with heavy linoleum quaintly designed in imitation of old English tiling, and the walls are decorated in French gray, cream and gilt, with a frieze of delicately tinted flowers and a dado of dead gold, with scarlet and dull red flowers in relief. The ceiling is a delicate study in pale blue, fretted gold and light cream tints, so arranged as to produce a perfect harmony with the side walls, and at the same time lend a light, airy effect to the whole room. From this ceiling hang six magnificent chandeliers of hammered copper, oxidized silver and fire-gilt, with globes of ground glass ornamented with frost-work patterns of singular beauty. These chandeliers are among the handsomest ever imported to the region south of Mason and Dixon's line.[25]

Along with the fashionable color scheme and lighting fixtures, Stevens & Brothers had elaborate cases lining the wall for the display of silver and ceramics.

At the end of the "art-goods" department the store copied the idea of an "art room" from New York retailers with its "Mikado" cabinet. Of it was said, "The cabinet is a beautiful combination of turquoise blue, and old imperial yellow, flanked by yellow curtains of raw silk. It is surmounted by a rich, imported Madras scarf, striped with gilt, red, yellow and blue, and draped from ebony and brass rods. Wherever the eye rests at this point it is met by some rare specimens of Satsuma, Nahgesaki or Cloisonne ware, and the effect of the elegant combination of color and tasteful arrangement is enchanting."[26] The creation of Mikado cabinets for displaying Asian or Asian-inspired objects or special "art rooms" for especially artistic pieces was widespread in the 1880s and 1890s. In 1895 the well-known Philadelphia firm of Bailey, Banks & Biddle was reported as having in its art room an elaborate display of silverware that "was embellished with most artistic surroundings in tapestries and silks, ferns, potted plants and cut flowers. Beautifully shaded candles and tapers shed a mellow light over the picture, and the crowds of fashionable people who thronged the handsome apartment during the week the exhibition lasted, testified to its artistic and intrinsically valuable merits."[27]

One reason why jewelry stores across the country came increasingly to resemble one another was that few relied on the services of architects or interior designers for plans. Rather, the fixtures and their placement in a store were usually worked out by the owner and the supplier of the cabinetwork. During the last quarter of the nineteenth century, the premier source for display cases and furniture for showrooms was B. & W. B. Smith at 220 West Twenty-ninth Street in New York City (ill. 5.7).

ILL. 5.7. B. & W. B. Smith advertisement, 1886.

By the mid 1880s the firm dominated the field, having supplied casework for almost all of New York's major showrooms. The Smiths' clients in the city included Whiting, Gorham, Derby Silver Co., Wilcox Silver Co., Simpson, Hall, Miller & Co., Reed & Barton, Meriden Silver Plating Co., Knowles, Rogers & Brother, Pairpoint Mfg. Co., Dominick & Haff, and Meriden Britannia, as well as a host of jewelry stores. The firm had also done work throughout America, from New Orleans to Albany and Memphis to Washington, D.C. Display furniture came in several quality grades and numerous variations could be achieved by arranging the individual units differently. However, the Smiths' basic concept was the same for big New York showrooms and small-town jewelry stores. In general, between 1875 and World War I, the display of silver and jewelry goods was carried out in a long rectangular space, with entryway and offices at the two narrow ends. The side walls of the interior were lined with tall multishelved wooden and glass cases that often had drawers in their bases. The center of the store contained a U- or O-shaped display case that wrapped around the central columns which supported the ceiling. This configuration maximized display space and security because it enabled salesmen to stand behind the merchandise while talking to customers. The tops of these cases were flat so that objects could be set on them when necessary.[28] Although the dark paneled ambience of the late nineteenth century is no longer in fashion, this basic arrangement of cases for a jewelry store still persists today in larger establishments.

Just as they followed New York's lead in interior furnishings and layout, jewelry stores around the country also emulated New York retailers' designs for show windows and other marketing devices. This type of advertising took on greater importance in the last decades of the nineteenth century under the pressure of growing competition from rival firms (especially department stores and mail-order houses).[29] Typically a jewelry store or silverware showroom had at least two sizable display windows each of which flanked the front door. Corner stores often had additional windows running down the side facade. If these windows were flush with the front door, the entry was often recessed so that the display windows appeared to project from the facade, making them more dramatic. Or windows could protrude from the building. In 1890 it was said of the Gorham showroom, "The matter of projecting the windows into the street to the extent the law allows, has been under advisement by the management for sometime and it is expected that the time is not far distant when the Gorham Co. will have the most prominent windows of all the jewelry and silverware stores on Broadway."[30]

The proper manner of dressing a display window was a topic that preoccupied the trade press for decades. Starting in the 1880s, countless articles were written on the subject.[31] The December 1890 issue of the *Jewelers' Circular* reflected the importance that was placed on show windows in an article entitled "Store and Window Decoration." It stated, "The most effective of all advertising for a retail business is artistic or attractive window display and store decoration. At no season of the year is it so important that the windows and interiors of stores should be attractive as the present, when the thoroughfares are crowded with holiday shoppers and sightseers."[32] From this article that critiques the windows of Rogers & Brother, Gorham, Meriden Britannia, Whiting, Reed & Barton, and Tiffany's, one learns what a typical store window for silverware looked like in the late nineteenth century. If space allowed, the floor of the window was usually fitted with a tiered plateau. To set off the silver, the window's linings and plateau were covered in plush, brightly colored fabric, green, blue, and yellow being common. Large silver objects like trophies, vases, hot-water urns, or candelabra were placed atop the plateau and around the perimeter of the window's floor. Smaller objects were then interspersed throughout the display. Sometimes unusual objects were included to catch people's attention. This particular writer suggested using imported mechanical dolls.[33] Judging from the numerous photographic entries sent to window dressing contests held by the trade press, it appears that store owners across the country heeded their advice and sought to improve the appearance of their show windows between 1880 and World War I.

Beyond window displays, many stores tried to draw attention to themselves in other ways. For example, between the late 1890s and 1915, cast-iron street clocks were erected outside scores of jewelry and silverware stores in New York and throughout the country. Owners hoped that when people stopped to check the time, they would pause and look at the objects on display in the windows. By the 1910s, however, civic reformers were condemning such clocks as impediments to pedestrians and dangerous to car doors and consequently had them removed. In 1908 city officials in Milwaukee went so far as to have the fire department destroy clocks outside jewelry stores at one o'clock in the morning.[34] Besides street clocks, some store owners chose to use electric lights to attract attention. In 1893 electricity was praised as the "chief agent in the window-dressing of the future, putting your store on constant display." Moving displays powered by electricity were sometimes employed in windows. To attract attention one store owner re-created the 1901 electrocution of President McKinley's assassin. When first unveiled, the spark-filled display was cheered by over 1,200 onlookers.[35]

SELLING ABROAD: THE FOREIGN MARKET

The efforts to build market share by constructing increasingly lavish showrooms with compelling window displays and other attention-getting devices were primarily directed at the domestic market. However, the larger manufacturing firms and a few of the retail stores did attempt to make inroads into foreign markets through similar means. As noted earlier, Tiffany & Co. established stores in Paris (1850), London (1868), and Geneva (ca. 1870–75). Although these facilities had originally been intended to act as buying offices for the New York store, retail departments evidently were added by the 1870s.[36] Other firms followed Tiffany & Co.'s lead in founding foreign branches. In 1889, for example, Gorham obtained an outlet in Paris on the fashionable Avenue de l'Opéra when Spaulding & Co. opened a store there. Also, in 1904 Gorham opened a branch in London under its own name. This office was established following a sales experiment in 1901–2 in which the company sent a representative to South Africa to see if Gorham silver had a market there. He was so successful that the London office was established as a base from which representatives could work. Through this system Gorham products were introduced to Holland, Italy, Belgium, Switzerland, Australia, India, South Africa, the Straits Settlements, Sumatra, Malta, Egypt, Java, China, and Ceylon. Because the British government required imported silver to be stamped as foreign, Gorham opened a manufacturing facility in Birmingham in 1909. Evidently the British and other markets that were served from London preferred silver bearing British hallmarks, and by actually producing silver in England, Gorham could have its silver marked in the typical British manner.[37]

Silverplate companies also sought out foreign customers by opening facilities abroad. Plate makers were especially enthusiastic about the prospect of foreign sales as a means of combating their loss of domestic market share. As the price of silver fell throughout the 1880s and 1890s, sterling wares became ever cheaper and consequently took over a large part of the silverplate market. Furthermore, foreign markets exhibited a different seasonal pattern from the domestic one, allowing factories to maintain a more constant volume of production throughout the year. Also, goods that were no longer fashionable in the United States were acceptable in some foreign markets, thus relieving firms of old, unsold stock.[38]

In 1878 the Meriden Britannia Co. opened an office and showroom at Holborn Viaduct in London. Although sales were made to British dealers in this branch, it primarily served the South American and Australian markets. In 1881 this London office was evidently moved to the 7 Cripplegate Building, Wood Street. Similarly, to service the Canadian market, Meriden Britannia built a manufacturing plant in Hamilton, Ontario, in 1879. Canadian import duties on American silverplate made its ware so expensive in Canada that the company hoped to be more competitive by actually producing wares there.[39]

Real success in the export area was limited, however. Certainly, a few firms including Tiffany's, Gorham, Meriden Britannia, and Reed & Barton emphasized the fact that they received commendations and titles from foreign royalty and boasted about sending silver abroad. But in reality, few if any made significant profits outside the domestic market.[40] The royal commissions that Gorham received from the Queen of Portugal were indeed few and far between, as were Tiffany & Co.'s appointments from the crowned heads of Europe. George Gibb's study of Reed & Barton's foreign sales reveals this situation with great clarity.

In the early 1870s Reed & Barton's primary foreign customers were Canadian. In 1874, the firm arranged for an agent to travel through the West Indies and South America and take orders for its wares. The effort proved unsuccessful because the leading French manufacturer, Orfèvrerie Christofle, already dominated the South American market for plated wares, holding exclusive contracts with the most reputable dealers and maintaining resident agents in the principal cities. The experiment mainly served to expose the many obstacles that blocked U.S. entrance to these markets. Especially noteworthy were differences in language, customs, and temperament, as well as practical problems concerning poor transportation between North and South America, damage in shipping, large import duties, crude monetary exchange facilities, and expectations of huge discounts. Nevertheless, Reed & Barton's sales force, under the leadership of George Brabrook, persisted, and by 1881 the company had 103 foreign customers scattered from Hong Kong to St. Petersburg, Stockholm to Melbourne. The bulk of foreign clients were located in South America and the West Indies. In 1874 foreign sales were only $13,764. By 1881 they had grown ninefold in real terms to $103,128. By 1887 sales had doubled again in real terms, reaching a peak of $174,916. After 1887, foreign sales declined steadily. In 1900, for example, Reed & Barton sold only $50,972 worth of silverware abroad. As part of overall sales, the foreign markets never accounted for a large part of Reed & Barton's business. At their peak in 1887 foreign sales made up about 14 percent of the total. Typically, however, the percentage was under 10 percent, as in 1900 when it was less than 7.[41]

Total exports of U.S. silverware mirrored those of Reed & Barton's, rising through the late 1870s and 1880s and then declining steadily into the early twentieth century. The vast majority of ware sold abroad was electroplated. In 1870 total foreign sales of American plated goods was only $29,679. In 1880 exports reached $292,563 and had grown to $587,163 in 1889, an increase of 60 percent in real terms. Nevertheless, even at the height of the export trade, the large sum for 1889 represented only 5 percent of U.S. silverplate production that year.[42] In 1902 the government study *Silver Plate and Plated Ware in Foreign Countries* revealed the slow death of the American export trade in silverware. Explaining America's lack of success, consuls around the world cited many of the same reasons that had stymied Reed & Barton in the 1870s. In general, the consuls noted that if U.S. manufacturers were going to improve foreign sales they had to invest in more foreign showrooms and resident salesmen. Several noted how little credit American firms gave foreign dealers. The Chilean consul, for example, stated, "American merchants give the least commercial advantages of any of the large exporting countries, usually demanding cash in exchange for bill of lading at New York, or thirty days' draft on receipt of goods, while English and German merchants give from three months to a year's credit, and are willing, as one merchant expressed it, 'to throw their goods into your hands and take their chances of getting their pay for them.'"[43]

In Scotland the main problem was that American products were too ornate for local tastes. A "prominent silversmith" in Edinburgh was quoted as follows when asked to review an American silverware trade catalogue:

> This is all superb work of its kind, some of it beautiful, no doubt about that; but from the Scotch point of view it is mostly thrown away. . . . [H]owever much artistic merit we craftsmen may be ready to concede to them. Generally speaking, in Scotland, at least in Edinburgh (for tastes differ somewhat in different cities), the preference is for the plain and rich. . . . I do not mean that all fancy ideas should be discarded; but elaboration in design and ornamentation does not suit us.[44]

American silverware was considered too ornate in many parts of the world, and where it was admired, as in Central and South America, it was often thought too thin, because it damaged easily in shipping. In the end, U.S. manufacturers found it uneconomical to make the changes necessary to cater to varied foreign markets, especially when this country's domestic market was so vast.[45]

Since trade catalogues were not exceptionally expensive and did not require large amounts of additional work, many silverware manufacturers did send copies abroad. A few even published foreign language editions, usually in Spanish or Portuguese for the Central and South American markets. For at least a short period, the primary trade journal for the industry, the *Jewelers' Circular*, published a Spanish version. The first Spanish edition came out in January 1875 and was sent to 2,500 dealers in Central and South America.[46] For the most part, however, the trade catalogues and journals sent abroad were simply the same as those designed for the domestic market. Nevertheless, foreign recipients were often extremely impressed by these publications and their wide distribution. In 1878 a writer for the British journal *The Jeweller and Metalworker* wrote that American silverplate seemed to be making some headway in Britain because of its good design and because American manufacturers freely distributed trade catalogues, maintained large sales forces, and advertised in trade periodicals. The writer concluded that British "manufacturers would find a little imitation of the wisdom of our cousins conducive to their interests at home and in the colonies."[47] Over the next ten years, the American trade catalogues admired by this observer became even more impressive.

ADVERTISING

The first silverware trade catalogues appeared in the late 1850s and 1860s and were standard throughout the business in the 1870s. By the mid 1880s, American silverware trade catalogues were being published by the hundreds at every level of the silverware trade. The most extensive and elaborate trade catalogues were printed by manufacturers. In 1886 one observer noted:

> American illustrated trade catalogues excel all others in the world. No other country produces any in comparison. With them, catalogue printing has become a wonderful and distinct business in itself. It is conceded by the most distinguished European critics that Americans have surpassed all other nations in printing, and have well-nigh done so in wood-engraving. The great silverware houses of [New York] publish more costly and gorgeous catalogues than any other line of trade. They usually issue one edition of 7,000 copies, because they have about that many customers. One house on Broadway paid $100,000 for its edition of 7,000 last year, while other silverware houses paid sums ranging from $35,000 to $50,000. Another house, besides publishing a trade catalogue, issues a handbook for its customers, at a cost of $6,000.[48]

What manufacturers produced with such huge investments was often exceptional indeed. For example, perhaps the two finest catalogues ever produced by the industry, and probably those that the writer claimed cost $100,000, were the 1885 Reed & Barton and 1886 Meriden Britannia Co. catalogues. Measuring 14 by 17 inches, Reed & Barton's publication contained almost 4,000 wood engravings and four lithographic color plates. The wood engravings took the firm's team of twenty-seven engravers three years of working full time to complete. With its almost 400 pages printed on heavy stock and its muslin-covered, gold and silver embossed cover, the tome weighed 16 pounds.[49] In response, the Meriden Britannia Co. produced an equally lavish catalogue. Measuring 12 by 16 inches, its 450 pages illustrated over 300 classes of wares in 3,200 wood

engravings. Supposedly, over 50 tons of paper were consumed in printing 30,000 copies, each weighing 13½ pounds.[50]

All the catalogues generally had the same purpose and similar formats, regardless of their elaboration. Most important, trade catalogues were not for the buying public; rather, they were sent to wholesalers and retailers who ordered goods at discount prices. However, since a jewelry store owner might allow his customers to look through a catalogue to pick out wares, manufacturers often printed the wholesale price list separately so it could be removed by the dealer and kept from customers. Thus retail customers did not know what the dealer had paid for a given item wholesale and therefore did not know what his profit margin was. These detached price lists were usually keyed into the catalogue through numbers representing each pattern and class of goods. Some companies, like Gorham, gave every catalogue a date letter so that the dealer would be certain which price list matched which catalogue. Once a wholesale customer had selected what he wished to order he either wrote or telegraphed the manufacturer. Some firms, including Reed & Barton and Meriden Britannia, devised systems to simplify ordering by telegraph. In them a word was assigned to every item in the catalogue. The orderer need only telegraph the correct words and quantities required, thus saving the cost of dozens of words per message. An example in Reed & Barton's 1885 catalogue demonstrates how ten words could be used instead of 100.[51] When the order was filled and a customer had his merchandise, he typically labeled each item with its wholesale cost for ready reference when dealing with a retail customer. Again to keep the customer guessing as to his own investment in a given object, these labels were usually in code. A typical example is that which Gorham used for both wholesale and retail pricing. In Gorham's code each number was given a corresponding letter or symbol, such as three being a T and all consecutively repeated numbers being denoted by an X. Thus TX.XX translated into $33.33. Such codes gave sales clerks instant recall as to their actual cost, which enabled them to better bargain with customers without having to look through a catalogue or price list.[52]

Almost without exception, the types of silverware illustrated in trade catalogues were the less expensive lines, consisting of relatively plain, stock objects. In its 1892 catalogue, for example, Gorham stated:

> Necessarily the most elaborate and costly pieces; those which would endure to our credit as works of the highest merit, are not here shown for the obvious reason that the compass of a catalogue, restricted to a single volume, confines us to the illustration of goods strictly within the category of commercial work. It must be apparent, however, even to the casual observer, that the efforts expended in the production of articles of exceptional merit have been the means of elevating the standard of all.[53]

At most, firms would include one or more illustrations of their most exceptional work to let dealers know that if a customer wanted a custom item it could be produced. Typical is Gorham's 1888 catalogue, which depicts several elaborate yachting trophies on its frontispiece, followed by the notice: "We are prepared to submit at reasonable notice designs with accompanying estimates of characteristic pieces for the various requisite purposes. . . . In ordering designs the amount to be expended should be named in order to avoid delay."[54] Like Gorham, many firms were ready to encourage potential sales of expensive custom pieces. In 1908 the Philadelphia retailer Bailey, Banks & Biddle, stated in its catalogue of trophies that customers could use the enclosed "photographic form" to request pictures of more elaborate silverware not illustrated. While the custom objects of which one received photographs would not be duplicated, they might serve as inspiration. Designs for custom orders could be obtained by using the "special order form."[55]

Tiffany & Co.'s famous pocket-size *Blue Books* served many of the same purposes as other manufacturers' catalogues. The firm did not begin publication of the *Blue Book* until 1877, after which time it became an annual publication until around 1920. Like catalogues from other makers, Tiffany's served to promote the quality of its wares by listing all the awards and commendations the firm had received at world's fairs and from royalty. Nevertheless, the book listed stock items that could be shipped immediately, not custom ones. To supply the latter, *Blue Books* stated that Tiffany's would gladly furnish drawings for custom objects or even photographs of stock ones to those who wished them. This was especially important, since *Blue Books* did not contain any illustrations, even though some were 500 pages long.[56]

Just as manufacturers used trade catalogues to promote sales of their wares, so too did middlemen and occasionally jewelry store owners. Typically, middlemen, or jobbers, as they were known, would purchase at discounted prices large quantities of goods from several manufacturers and then resell them to dealers who in turn passed the items on to retail customers. By the late 1870s and 1880s, these jobbers were causing problems in the trade with their catalogues because they were asking a manufacturer for $100 to $500 to underwrite the cost of publications which contained some of that manufacturer's ware. If he did not pay, the jobber dropped the maker's line. The trade press warned manufacturers about such schemes, but also told them not to try to deceive jobbers. Occasionally a manufacturer would sign an exclusive contract with a jobber and then illustrate the same items it sold that jobber in its general catalogue that went out to jewelry stores. Conflict occurred when the manufacturer and the jobber had the same jewelry store as clients.[57]

This surge in trade catalogue publishing was part of the huge increase in advertising that occurred in the silverware industry between 1875 and the early twentieth century. The combination of cheaper and more efficient printing techniques with the rise of popular and trade magazines and the development of professional advertising agencies during the late nine-

teenth century led to a dramatic rise in advertising at all levels of the trade. In 1919, for example, the high-end Pittsburgh retailers John M. Roberts & Son noted that while they had initially advertised solely with handbills during the mid nineteenth century, they now used a host of modern advertising devices, including newspaper ads, illuminated bulletin boards, and "day-light bulletin boards along the various railways entering Pittsburgh."[58]

Besides these devices, newspaper and magazine advertisements were commonly used throughout the industry by the 1870s. As early as 1876 Tiffany & Co. spent $3,696 on newspaper advertisements alone in December, the busiest month of the year. In all, the firm ran copy in forty-eight newspapers located in New York, New England, the Mid-Atlantic, and the Midwest.[59] The expenditure of advertising funds during the holiday season and other peak times was standard throughout the industry. For retailers like Tiffany's and other jewelry stores, the high points of the year's advertising and sales were May and June, the wedding season, and November and December, the Christmas season. Manufacturers concentrated their advertising budgets on a slightly earlier cycle of March–April and September–October to accommodate the time it took to make and ship goods for the retail high seasons.[60]

During the late nineteenth century, hundreds of magazines came into being through which manufacturers and retailers could address potential customers. Manufacturers who only sold wholesale generally restricted their advertisements to trade journals. The primary trade periodicals were *Watchmaker and Jeweler* (founded 1869); *Jewelers' Circular* (1870); *Jeweller* (1872); *American Watchmakers, Jewelers and Silversmiths Journal* (1872); *Manufacturing Jeweler* (1884); *Jewelers' Weekly* (1885); *Jewelers' Review* (1887); and *Keystone* (1899). Many of these journals were short-lived. However, *Jewelers' Circular, Weekly, Review,* and *Keystone* were successful. In 1900 the *Weekly* merged into the *Circular,* followed by the *Review* in 1902 and the *Keystone* in 1935, thus leaving only *Jewelers' Circular-Keystone* as the primary voice of the trade, as it is today.[61]

Advertising by manufacturers in these trade journals generally was of two forms. First, makers ran copy that stressed the high quality of their products in terms of workmanship and materials, while often warning dealers about other firms that produced lesser wares. The text from an 1890 Gorham advertisement in *Jewelers' Weekly* is classic:

> The recently completed works of the Company at Providence, R.I., are regarded as a model establishment for the making of Sterling Silverware, and their wares should be for sale in the stock of every first-class jeweler in the United States. If the trade would insist upon having this make of goods they would be sure of securing the best quality of ware made—925/1000 fine. There are other wares upon the market that when correctly assayed prove to be less than the standard. The GORHAM trade mark is never used on any other than English Sterling.[62]

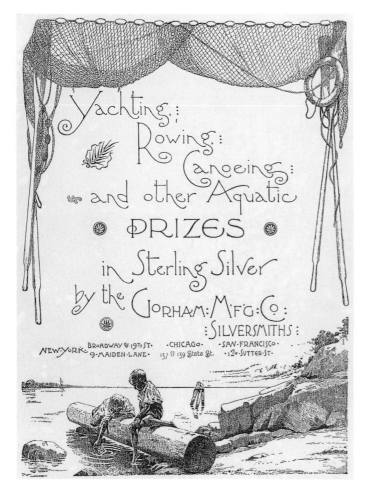

ILL. 5.8. Gorham Mfg. Co. advertisement, 1889.

which a single firm supplied every illustration. In the early twentieth century, articles began appearing in which the manufacturers may well have supplied the text as well. Sometimes companies paid for such "editorial-style" advertisements. However, it is often unclear whether or not this was the case. For example, Evelyn Marie Stuart's 1912 article, "The American Renaissance in Silversmithing," which appeared in the *Fine Arts Journal*, is illustrated solely with images "Courtesy The Gorham Company." Never mentioning the firm by name except in the illustration captions, it nevertheless quotes known Gorham employees. Consequently, the endorsement of Gorham's products is unmistakable.[65] More typical of manufacturers advertising in popular periodicals were ads that, while still stressing name recognition, emphasized the importance of silverware in daily life and to a family's history. In 1905, Reed & Barton stated in *House Beautiful*: "For Weddings, Silverware is essential. Nothing is more appropriate or more appreciated. Next to the ring, itself, it dominates all other gifts. It becomes the heirloom of the family. . . . The wedding gifts your grandparents received and your family heirlooms bear testimony to the lasting quality of REED & BARTON silverware. The standard for generations."[66]

Although it is difficult to measure how successful firms were in creating new demand for their products through advertising, in the case of some novelty goods or new forms, it was advertising that primarily convinced the public to purchase them. Throughout the history of silversmithing there have always been makers who specialized in small, novelty goods. In the late nineteenth and early twentieth centuries, numerous American firms, such as Daniel Low & Co. in Salem, Massachusetts, The Sterling Co. of Providence, Rhode Island, and Unger Brothers of Newark, New Jersey, made items like silver tea balls, glove buttoners, garters, match safes, scissors, nail files, baby rattles, penholders, and sewing equipment (fig. 5.2).[67] Most of these articles were traditional ones for which there was already an established market. However, when the Alvin Mfg. Co. decided to market silver-deposit ware or when Gorham introduced a new line of silver-mounted cut glass, they had to tell dealers and retail customers why such things were necessary or how theirs differed from those of others. Concerning its mounted glass, for example, Gorham noted: "While silver mounted glass has been produced for years, the combinations of effects seen in this line made by the Gorham Mfg. Co. are entirely new this season. Both in the methods of mounting the silver, and the designs of the mountings, this line is a radical change from anything heretofore manufactured."[68] Through advertising, companies were usually able to keep such lines active for several seasons until their novelty wore off with the public. No amount of advertising could move the public to purchase certain items, however. Gorham's *Shrapnel Shell* cocktail shaker, for example, seems never to have been accepted in spite of the interesting booklets printed up to introduce it (fig. 5.3). The buying public of 1915 was probably too worried about the war raging in Europe to want to mix its cocktails in

Besides this type of general advertising, which associated brand name with quality and status, manufacturers also concentrated on defining their specialties in the trade press. For example, a maker might repeatedly let dealers know through specialized ads that he made toilet ware, flatware, or trophies. Gorham, which made almost every line of goods, reminded retailers in many of its summertime advertisements that it excelled in trophies. Some of these ads simply relied on artwork to attract attention and suggest a romantic mood (ill. 5.8). Others, like that for the 17 July 1895 *Jewelers' Circular*, combined suggestive illustrations of sporting activities and elaborate prize trophies with prose. Included was the following information: "Unconventional PRIZE CUPS and objects emblematic of all field and aquatic pastimes have been prepared on an extensive scale. The manufacturer of these articles will be continued through the OUTING SEASON, with the constant introduction of new features."[63]

Sometimes this kind of specialized advertising could also be accomplished at little cost by providing woodcuts, engravings, and photographs of one's products to the popular and trade presses for inclusion in articles. For example, Whiting probably provided the images of the 1891 *Goelet Schooner Cup* that appeared in *Harper's Weekly* and *Jewelers' Circular* (fig. 5.1).[64] The apogee of this kind of advertising are articles in

FIG. 5.2. Tape measures, needle cases, thimble cases, shuttle, thread winder, scissors, darning egg, and emery. Various makers, United States, ca. 1890–1910. Sterling silver, silverplate, wood, and fabric. Dallas Museum of Art.

a shaker which was a "fac-simile in every detail of [an] Eighteen Pounder Shrapnel Shell."[69]

Occasionally manufacturers actually managed to change consumers' behavior with new products and advertising to the point that a novelty became a necessity. The silverplated tilting ice water pitcher is an excellent example of this process (fig. 5.4). Invented in 1854 by James Stimpson of Baltimore, the insulated pitcher soon became popular as a novelty. However, during the 1860s and 1870s, numerous silverplate manufacturers promoted such pitchers as convenient, healthy, and fashionable. Encouraged by temperance reform, they had become common throughout the United States and a standard form found in trade catalogues by the 1880s. Meriden Britannia alone, in its 1886 catalogue, illustrated fifty-seven varieties of ice water pitchers. It was only with the advent of refrigeration and local ice plants in the 1890s that these pitchers fell from favor.[70]

Similar circumstances surrounded the introduction of the ice tea spoon in the first decade of the twentieth century and its promotion by silverware companies in advertisements and with literature on "How to Make Ice Tea."[71] Perhaps the most spectacular instance of a piece of novelty flatware gaining public acceptance after substantial advertising is the souvenir spoon. According to contemporary sources, the first American example

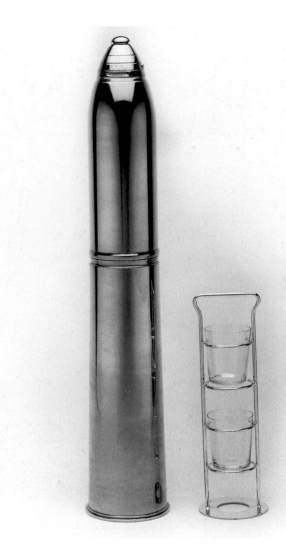

FIG. 5.3. Cocktail shaker. United States, ca. 1915. Silverplate, brass, copper, and glass. The Mitchell Wolfson, Jr., Collection. Although unmarked, this piece may be by Gorham.

was the *George Washington* spoon patented by the Washington, D.C., jewelry store, M. W. Galt Bros., around 1889. Following the success of that spoon, Daniel Low, the silver novelty purveyor from Salem, Massachusetts, went to Europe and formed a collection of unusual spoons. Inspired by these examples, he introduced the famous *Witch* spoon commemorating the Salem witch trials (fig. 5.5). Over 7,000 were sold the first year. By 1891 almost all flatware manufacturers were producing and advertising souvenir spoons. It was estimated that $500,000 annually was invested in the manufacture of these spoons, and an encyclopedia entitled *Souvenir Spoons of America* was needed to sort them all out. Commenting on the success of such spoons, *Jewelers' Circular* noted: "The breath of another fad pervades the atmosphere. The act of an unsatiated American public, ever seeking for variety, has something new to chatter about to interest or bore their intimates. Panoramic novelty has been turned, and the reign of souvenir spoons has begun from Maine to California."[72] More than almost any other

FIG. 5.4. Tilting ice water set. Meriden Britannia Co., Meriden, Conn., ca. 1872. Silverplate, ivory, and enamel. Dallas Museum of Art.

FIG. 5.5. *LEFT: George Washington* pattern souvenir spoon. Davis & Galt, maker, Philadelphia, Pa.;
M. W. Galt Bro. & Co., designer and retailer, Washington, D.C.; designed 1889. Sterling silver with
silvergilt. D. Albert Soeffing Collection. *RIGHT: Witch* pattern souvenir spoon. Seth Low, designer;
Gorham Mfg. Co., maker, Providence, R.I.; Daniel Low & Co., retailer, Salem, Mass.; designed 1891.
Sterling silver with silvergilt. Dallas Museum of Art.

novelty, the souvenir spoon has proven perennially popular with countless collectors active today.

Along with creating novelty products and building print campaigns around them, manufacturers as well as retailers used handouts, press releases, and exhibitions to advertise. Charles L. Tiffany, who was a master at attracting attention to his store, provides a good example of how these three techniques could be used to advantage. Around 1880 Tiffany & Co. began issuing attractive pocket calendars imprinted with its name. These free calendars kept the Tiffany name foremost in the mind of the customer. Other types of "give-away" printed matter distributed at Tiffany's included a small booklet entitled *American Art Appreciated: Tiffany & Co.* Printed in 1883, this book quotes newspapers from around the world praising Tiffany's products and lists the various crown heads who had appointed Tiffany's as one of their royal purveyors. This last point was further advertised with large 8-by-10-inch cards that listed these royal personages. Evidently, either these cards were sent to the press and customers, or a special press release was produced at the same time, for almost simultaneously, newspapers across the country ran stories on the appointment of Tiffany's as official jewelers to Europe's ruling houses. Tiffany & Co.'s own records show that at least seventy-three American and Canadian papers ran one or more notices about these appointments in 1883.[73] Like Tiffany's, many other firms gave away or mailed out free advertising material, especially trade cards.[74] Some manufacturers, usually those who made cheaper grades of silverplate, even offered premiums to customers who purchased goods in substantial quantities. In 1910, for example, the Royal Mfg. Co. of Detroit, Michigan, gave away children's toys and inexpensive jewelry to purchasers of its "celebrated Brazil silver goods."[75]

To further draw attention to themselves, firms took on the mantle of art museums, staging frequent exhibitions of their own products and foreign curiosities. In 1876 Tiffany & Co. put on exhibition in New York the silverware it had made for the Hotel Baldwin in San Francisco,[76] and in 1895 its store windows were the setting for a display of English yachting trophies "won by the *Vigilant* in foreign waters." At the same time, the Whiting showroom, located only a few blocks away, put together an exhibition of American-made yachting trophies. For those who appreciated fine silver, the proximity of the exhibits was rewarding. As one observer noted: "During the past fortnight the connoisseur or the student in silversmithing had an opportunity, were he in New York, to study the characteristics of the higher expressions of the art, as embodied by English and American craftsmen."[77] Besides using their windows and showrooms for museum-like exhibitions, makers and retailers also staged such events at hotels, as Gorham did at the Waldorf Astoria in 1897, or in parades, as Reed & Barton did in 1889.[78]

WORLD'S FAIRS

Of all the silver exhibitions held by manufacturers between 1870 and 1915, those presented at world's fairs were the most spectacular. A few American firms had participated in the international expositions held between 1851 in London and 1873 in Vienna, and a broader group had gained experience by exhibiting at domestic fairs held by organizations like the American Institute of New York, the Franklin Institute of Philadelphia, and the Massachusetts Charitable Mechanic Association of Boston. Reed & Barton, for example, showed in New York in 1838, 1867, and 1869, and in Boston in 1869 and 1874. Some firms also participated in continental fairs, such as the 1875 South American International Exposition in Santiago, Chile, where Reed & Barton was awarded a first premium. Later ones, including the 1881 International Cotton Exposition in Atlanta and the 1898 Trans-Mississippi and International Exhibition in Omaha, Nebraska, also attracted some American silverware producers like Meriden Britannia.[79]

It was the 1876 Centennial Exposition held in Philadelphia that first drew a significant number of this country's silverware producers into the international arena. American solid silver and silverplate manufacturers and retailers that exhibited in Philadelphia included Gorham, Tiffany's, J. E. Caldwell & Co., Robbins, Biddle & Co., Meriden Britannia, Reed & Barton, Bailey & Co., Simpson, Hall, Miller & Co., C. Rogers & Bros., Meriden Silver-Plate Co., Manning Bowman & Co., Mall, Elton & Co., Derby Silver Co., and Middletown Plate Co.[80] Why a particular firm chose to participate is difficult to ascertain. The simple fact that the fair was held in the United States made it logistically easier and much less costly to attend than it would have been overseas. Too, the patriotic aura surrounding the fair as a celebration of the 100th anniversary of the nation's founding must have encouraged American manufacturers to participate. Furthermore, the Centennial occurred in the depths of an economic depression. Consequently, many manufacturers probably felt that showing off their wares to more than eight million fairgoers might generate publicity and stimulate lagging sales. With many idle or underemployed workmen, firms had plenty of time to create pieces for the fair.

Whatever the motivation, exhibiting at the Centennial or any other fair was an expensive undertaking. Besides fees charged by the fair's promoters, firms had to build display cases and pavilions and pay staff to man them, along with making and shipping a wide range of expensive silverware for which there was no guaranteed purchaser. For example, Reed & Barton's 1876 exhibit pavilion with its 1,040 pieces of silverplate cost the company $15,000.[81] Meriden Britannia's pavilion probably cost a similar amount (ill. 5.9). At Gorham the cost of maintaining the sizable staff required to run its exhibit was large enough that the board of directors recommended renting a suite of rooms from a private Philadelphia family rather than paying for hotel accommodations.[82]

Furthermore, some firms chose not to produce all new silver for their displays. Rather, they included past work or took items from existing stock. For example, while Tiffany & Co. undoubtedly made up some new objects for exhibition, much was old. In fact, they entitled their exhibit *Loan Collection: A*

ILL. 5.9. The Meriden Britannia Co. pavilion at the 1876 Philadelphia world's fair.

Retrospective Exhibit of Silver Presentation and Commemorative Pieces, Presentation Swords, Yachting, Racing, Rowing, Shooting, and Rifle Cups, made by Tiffany & Co. During the Past 25 Years. The work ranged in date from 1848 to 1875, with only one piece being dated 1876 in the catalogue. A coffeepot loaned by the Cook family, for example, had been made in 1874 (fig. 5.6, ill. 5.10). By borrowing objects from their current owners, Tiffany's did not have to make new silverware, thus cutting its exhibition costs. Furthermore, the firm could emphasize how prestigious owning its silver was by associating itself with a list of well-known, wealthy lenders that included William Cullen Bryant and members of the Astor and Belmont families.[83]

Gorham and Reed & Barton contained their exhibition costs through similar means. While Gorham did invest heavily in making the *American Shield* and mammoth *Century Vase* (ill. 5.11), which weighed 2,000 troy ounces and stood over 4 feet high,[84] it borrowed back or took from stock most of the rest of its display objects.[85] For example, pieces from the dinner service it had been making for Colonel and Mrs. Henry J. Furber of Chicago since 1871 were included (fig. 6.1). Furthermore, Gorham cautioned fair visitors that "articles purchased from our exhibit can only be delivered after the close of the Exhibition in November, but duplicates may be had at the Company's Store, 37 Union Square, New York." This statement indicates that Gorham did not even ship substitute objects to the fair to fill in following a sale, but simply referred customers to the New York showroom, which maintained a large stock.

The firm did, however, hire the well-known New York decorating company of Herter Brothers to design its exhibition pavilion.[86] Reed & Barton seems to have done much the same. The company concentrated its efforts on the ornate *Progress Vase*, while taking most of the remainder of its display from stock (fig. 5.7).[87]

But no matter how firms tried to contain costs, participation in an international exposition was time consuming and expensive. What was it that made such investment worth the effort? First, exhibitors usually received large amounts of free publicity. For example, the Centennial fair was commemorated by dozens of books. Ones that wax eloquent about American silverware include *Treasures of Art, Industry and Manufacture Represented in the American Centennial Exhibition at Philadelphia, 1876; The Illustrated History of the Centennial Exhibition; The Great Centennial Exhibition;* and *Gems of the Centennial Exhibition.*[88] Popular magazines and trade journals also ran regular stories about the Centennial and its silverware displays. The *Art Journal* ran monthly articles on the fair from June 1876 to April 1877,[89] and major newspapers ran columns on the fair with great frequency. The *New York Times* published *The World's Exhibition* as well as specific columns on various exhibits. On 7 August 1876 it ran "The Silverware Display: England and America Competing," which concluded "that as regards silver for use, Gorham can take the highest place over all competitors in foreign lands" and noted that the German Commission was so impressed that it purchased several examples from the Providence firm.[90]

FIG. 5.6. Coffeepot. Attributed to Edward C. Moore, designer; Tiffany & Co., maker, New York, N.Y.; 1874. Sterling silver and ivory. Dallas Museum of Art.

ILL. 5.10. Part of the Tiffany & Co. exhibit at the 1876 Philadelphia world's fair.

ILL. 5.11. *Century Vase*, designed by George Wilkinson and Thomas Pairpoint for Gorham Mfg. Co., ca. 1876.

FIG. 5.7. *Progress Vase.* W. C. Beattie, designer; Reed & Barton, maker, Taunton, Mass.; ca. 1876. Sterling silver. Reed & Barton, Inc., Collection.

In the end, this type of publicity was perfect source material for manufacturers' own advertising. After the fair closed, for example, Gorham ran full-page advertisements that quoted positive critiques from the *Providence Journal, Boston Daily Advertiser, New York Evening Post,* and Birmingham, England's *Daily Post.*[91] Furthermore, since all exhibitors were given bronze medals, these could be reproduced in advertisements and trade catalogues to illustrate to potential customers one's prowess in the international arena. Reed & Barton, for example, reproduced all the medals it had won at past fairs, including Philadelphia, along with quotes from judges' reports. Images of its Centennial pavilion, the *Progress Vase,* and a tea service bought at the fair for the Emperor of Japan were also used.[92] And finally, exhibitors could capitalize on the excitement surrounding a fair by showing their displays one last time in their own showrooms before dispersing them. Both Gorham and Tiffany's mounted such "farewell" exhibitions in New York in November and December 1876.[93]

The next world's fair to which American manufacturers were invited was the *Exposition Universelle* held in Paris in 1878. The fact that the fair was overseas, however, meant that the costs involved in exhibiting were much greater than they had been in 1876. Furthermore, the United States was still in the grip of a severe depression, so funds for advertising must have been few. Concerning the Providence jewelry firms that were sending objects to Paris, one writer said: "They will undoubtedly exhibit a greater display of taste in their goods than they did at our Centennial Exposition, as they have had so much spare time to work them up."[94] For most companies, however, this "spare time" meant they had few orders and thus probably could not afford to exhibit in Paris. Furthermore, the U.S. Congress was unenthusiastic about the 1878 fair and refused for months to allocate financial aid to American exhibitors. In the end it did provide ships to transport American exhibits and a small amount of underwriting, but the sum allotted was nowhere near enough to enable most American manufacturers to exhibit. Consequently, relatively few participated. In the silverware category, only two firms represented the United States: a Mr. Thomas B. Oakley who showed "works of art in California gold and quartz" and Tiffany & Co.[95]

The reason behind Tiffany's participation probably rests on the ambition of Charles L. Tiffany. As noted earlier, he, more

FIG. 5.8. Punch bowl and ladle from the *Mackay Service*. Charles Grosjean, designer; Tiffany & Co., maker, New York, N.Y.; ca. 1878. Sterling silver and silvergilt. David M. Campbell Collection.

than almost any retailer in America, knew how important it was to be seen as a world-class purveyor of exceptional objects. And success in the art capital of the Western world would certainly bring acclaim to his house. Furthermore, Tiffany & Co., unlike other American firms, had a well-established Paris branch, which could coordinate the exhibition and provide French-speaking staff to man it. Yet even with these advantages, Tiffany & Co. did not invest in all new objects to send to Paris. Rather, it received loans once again from customers and produced electrotypes of some objects they could not borrow. Of the loans it obtained, that of the extensive Mackay dinner service elicited the most comment (fig. 5.8).[96] While the service was indeed new in 1878, it had already been paid for by the Mackay family and thus cost Tiffany's little to exhibit. The *Bryant Vase* was also exhibited, but in the form of an electrotype copy (fig. 6.24). Other electrotypes included were "exact reproductions in Gold of the Curium Treasures, Cesnola Collection and reproductions in all metals of Museum articles." Electrotypes were created by depositing a thick layer of silver or gold on the interior of a mold taken from the object one wished to copy. The metal was deposited using electricity in a process similar to electroplating. Since handwork was limited to touching up details on the copy, the cost of electrotypes was much less than that of wrought silverware. By displaying a large number of electrotypes, Tiffany & Co. was able to have an impressive display with less investment.[97]

Even though Tiffany & Co. was circumspect in how it used its funds for the Paris exposition, the firm nevertheless did make an exceptional group of new objects for its exhibit. Besides jewelry, Tiffany's showed silverware of various types, including: "Repousse work of high quality. Encrusted work. Chromatic decoration of silver. Damascened work of Steel, Gold, Silver, and Copper. Hammered Silver decorated with alloys of various metals and their patinas. Mixed or laminated metals, consisting of Gold, Silver, Copper, and their alloys."[98] It was this group of exotic metalwork that took Europe by storm and vaulted Tiffany's into the forefront of international silverwork (figs. 5.9, 6.45, 6.47).

Tiffany & Co. received the grand prize for artwork in silver in competition against such famous European silverware makers as Elkington of London, Odiot and Christofle of Paris, and Christensen of Copenhagen. Also, Edward C. Moore, its chief designer, was decorated with a gold medal, and Charles L. Tiffany was made a Chevalier of the French Legion of Honor. While Tiffany's imaginative mixed-metal silver was a revelation in itself, the decision of the international jury sent shock waves through the European silverware industry. The magnitude of the decision was made clear in an article entitled "An American Wedge" that appeared in the *International Review* (1878):

It was only when the display of American gold and silver work was discovered to the eyes of Europe that there

FIG. 5.9. Coffee set. Tiffany & Co., New York, N.Y., ca. 1878–1885.
Sterling silver, copper, and ivory. Private Collection.

Chapter 5

came to our Transatlantic cousins a full realizing sense that it was possible to take cognizance of American art work, and it was "because things seen are mightier than things heard" that the self-reliant Briton awoke to find that in at least one high industrial art he had found a new competitor. His mind was deeply stirred by the positive and prospective decline of an important national industry.[99]

A writer for the London *Spectator* summed up this feeling:

> It is a modern mistake to assume that the production of good silver-work demands neither special training nor high artistic power. It will not suffice to study old models, however excellent, unless fresh inspiration be gathered from nature, assimilated by the trained mind, and wrought out by the skilful hand into forms of fresh and seemly designs. . . . We confess we were surprised and ashamed to find at the Paris Exhibition that a New York firm, Tiffany & Co., had beaten the old Country and the Old World in domestic silver plate.[100]

Even the Japanese, from whose culture Tiffany's had derived much of its inspiration, were said to have "regarded with astonishment" these objects, and consequently the Japanese commissioner "purchased one of the most characteristic specimens for his government."[101] Other purchases were made by foreign agents for museums in Vienna, Berlin, Stuttgart, and Dublin. European silverware makers who acquired examples by Tiffany's included Sasikoff of St. Petersburg, Christofle of Paris, and Ehni of Stuttgart, as well as the English china and glass manufacturers Minton, R. W. Binns, and Webb & Sons. In addition, no fewer than sixty-five sales were made to European aristocracy, such as the Prince of Wales and nine members of the Rothschild family.[102]

The excitement surrounding Tiffany & Co.'s new creations prompted a variety of responses. For example, the British government, which was in the midst of Parliamentary hearings on Britain's silverware industry, saw the company's strong showing as additional proof that the United States was emerging as a world leader in the field and could one day threaten its own domestic industry. Trying to decide whether or not to abolish the system of hallmarking and taxing solid silverware sold in Great Britain, the committee heard testimony that its country's production of solid silver had dropped from 994,360 troy ounces in 1855 to 798,206 in 1877. The decline was said to be due to an increase in the use of silverplate, which was not taxed, and to a general decrease in the public's demand for sterling silverwares. Although it was heard that Great Britain imported little foreign silver, some witnesses felt the United States could soon change that. When asked "Do we not import any [silverware] from America?" a Mr. Orr Ewing responded, "A very small quantity at present, but that will be very greatly altered; people are beginning to wake up and to find that they can get much better things made in Rome, and America, and Munich."[103] Another witness startled the committee with the large size of some American firms when he commented on Gorham: "One manufacturer employing 800 workmen, works up more silver in one year than the whole of the British silversmiths put together."[104] Both the number of workers and amount of silver produced were exaggerations, but the witness made his point about the large size of some American manufacturers. Tiffany & Co.'s winning the grand prize in the middle of these proceedings only served to heighten the dilemma. If the government did away with the hallmarking rules, domestic producers could produce mixed metals and try to compete with Tiffany's and other Americans. However, if the regulations were dropped, the United States could export more ware to Britain. A Tiffany's employee was quoted as saying: "Tiffany & Co. are now about largely increasing their manufacture, and he has no doubt that if they are not prevented from importing by our system of hall-marking and the duty, they will very likely import largely into this country."[105] In the end no changes were made in the British hallmarking and duty system.

The British firm of Elkington & Co. was also worried about the rise of American silverware manufacturers and closely studied the Parisian exhibits of Tiffany's and others. C. J. Hammerton, the metalworker who carried out the investigation, recommended that Elkington refrain from entering the mixed-metal field because he felt it "should in a short time find, the market to a great extent glutted." Nevertheless, he thought aspects of Tiffany's silver worth close study. Hammerton said there was "much to be learned in the new fields thrown open to us, more especially in the matter of ground works by replacing the ordinary chasing by edging . . . or by combinations of metals, either left with their natural colors or bronzed as in the marbling of surfaces by Tiffany (which process I think I have mastered)." He also noted that the hammered surface used by Tiffany's was of "great character and suitable of adaptation to many objects, whether plain, embossed or etched in parts."[106]

The success of Tiffany & Co. in Paris encouraged several other large American silverware manufacturers to participate in the world's fairs that occurred between 1878 and 1915. Even the somewhat remote international exposition held in Sydney, Australia, in 1880 had four U.S. silverware exhibitors. All large producers of silverplate—the firms of Reed & Barton, Simpson, Hall, Miller & Co., Meriden Britannia Co., and Gorham—saw Australia as a huge potential market for silverplated goods.[107] For a retail manufacturer like Tiffany's, however, creating and shipping an exhibit to Australia was not cost effective, since the likelihood of selling large amounts of its expensive ware there was not great. The Paris world's fair of 1889 was a different matter.

The American firms that exhibited at the 1889 Paris exposition were Tiffany's, Gorham, and Meriden Britannia; along with two specialty makers, Leroy W. Fairchild & Co. of New York and Paris, and J. F. Fradley & Co. of New York. Fairchild & Co. was known for its gold and silver novelty goods such as pencil and cigarette cases, penholders, pocket knives, cigar cutters, and flasks. Fradley & Co. produced gold heads for walking canes.[108] Unlike these specialized makers, however, the other three exhibitors sent to Paris a wide range of silverware. For example, one visitor said of the Gorham display "that it is impossible to see a greater variety of silver articles in the Paris Exhibition" and that he "could go on almost indefinitely describing tea sets, punch bowls, tureens, pitchers, candelabra, flower vases, toilet sets, etc., all different in style and decoration."[109] These different styles included East Indian, Saracenic, Japanese, Louis XVI, and Grecian.[110]

A few objects shown by these manufacturers were not new, including Gorham's *Century Vase*, but most of the silverware appears to have been made especially for the exposition. Supported by strong profits generated by the economic boom of the late 1880s, Tiffany's, Gorham, and presumably Meriden Britannia created lavish, speculative work for Paris. As one observer asserted about Tiffany & Co.'s objects: "Many of the finer specimens have been produced at a cost far beyond the means of the average purchaser, and possibly some of them are beyond the range of custom of the average dealer."[111] For example, a seven-piece tea and coffee service lavishly chased with different American wildflowers supposedly had taken three years to make and had a retail price at the fair of $20,000.[112] Many other objects shown by Tiffany's and Gorham were so technically complicated that they too must have taken exceptionally long to complete. One writer described this outstanding quality on the part of American objects: "Each is a masterpiece of its class and each is as much a work of art as is a handsome painting by a master of the brush. Perfection is perhaps as nearly approached as the skill of the age renders possible in all the branches of art which have contributed to render this exhibit magnificent."[113]

When prizes were awarded for silverwork, four of the five American exhibitors received awards for excellence. The U.S. Commissioners' report to the fair concurred with these commendations: "The United States made in this class an exhibit which attracted deserved attention and admiration from the public as well as the jury, and showed how much can be accomplished where the restless search for new forms and effects is modified and directed by good taste."[114] Even the British *Reports of Artisans* stated that "in making comparisons of the [silver]work exhibited, it must be conceded that America is by far the finest," although it blunted its comments by noting that the designer/chasers who created the *Century Vase* for Gorham were English-trained and that British exhibitors sent to Paris only "their ordinary commercial work, and that for the most part of the poorest class."[115] And finally, a writer for *Jewelers' Weekly* noted how proud the American silverware industry in general was of this achievement: "Every jeweler, however sternly he competes with the prize winners in his own line, experienced a measure of satisfaction in the announcement that Tiffany & Co., the Leroy W. Fairchild Company, the Gorham Manufacturing Company and the Meriden Britannia Company had been crowned victors by la belle France."[116] Some of the exhibitors themselves were so proud of their work that they

ILL. 5.12. Facade of the American Section of Manufacturers, showing entrances to the Tiffany & Co. and Gorham Mfg. Co. displays at the 1893 World's Columbian Exposition.

offered examples of it to the newly established Musée des Arts Décoratifs in Paris. Gorham gave a selection of flatware that included examples designed between 1861 and 1889, and Tiffany's donated an enameled vase and bowl in the Persian style.[117]

The world's fairs following the one in Paris were in many ways very similar as far as the exhibits of American silverware manufacturers were concerned. During the next twenty-five years, U.S. firms participated in at least nine major expositions including Chicago (1893), Paris (1900), Buffalo (1901), Turin (1902), St. Louis (1904), Liège (1905), Milan (1906), Seattle (1909), and San Francisco (1915). Gorham, for example, showed at every one of these, and Tiffany & Co. went to Chicago, Paris, Buffalo, St. Louis, and San Francisco. Other companies who participated at given fairs included Whiting, Alvin, and Meriden Britannia.[118] The only major difference between these later expositions and those that had gone before was that American silverware displays and the pavilions that housed them were expanded, perhaps the most elaborate being built for Chicago in 1893 (ill. 5.12). The U.S. government would not underwrite the pavilion, so it was funded by three companies.

ILL. 5.13. The Gorham Co. pavilion at the 1915 Pan American Exposition, San Francisco.

ILL. 5.14. *Christopher Columbus*, by Frédéric Auguste Bartholdi, 1893.

The entrance to the American section in the center of the Manufactures Building was a tribute to the public spirit and enterprise of three New York firms, Tiffany & Co., Gorham Manufacturing Company and the Tiffany Glass and Decorating Company. They assumed the responsibility of erecting a pavilion which would worthily represent the United States when contrasted with those of England, Germany and France on the other three sections formed by the central aisles; an undertaking which the United States government would not perform, and which the Chicago management through lack of funds could not do.[119]

Designed by New York architect John DuFais, the neoclassical style of the building was described as "Colonial." A monumental Doric column crowned by an American eagle atop a terrestrial globe separated the entrances into the Tiffany's and Gorham sections. The interiors were large and quite elaborate. The Gorham space measured 3,770 square feet and was embellished with a paneled ceiling and lunettes decorated by the New York painter Charles F. Naegele. Between each lunette were medallions featuring the likenesses of great designers and silversmiths, including John Flaxman, Michelangelo, Albrecht Dürer, Peter Vischer, and Paul Revere. After Chicago, American firms continued to house their exhibitions in spacious and well-appointed pavilions at world's fairs through 1915 (ill. 5.13).

In terms of the quantity and quality of the silverware exhibited at these later expositions, the 1889 Paris world's fair had definitely set the standard. After Paris almost all the wares exhibited were especially made for international competition. This was certainly the case with Gorham and Tiffany's. For example, at the 1893 World's Columbian Exposition in Chicago,

Gorham made up scores of new pieces, including a 6-foot-high, 36,000 troy ounce, silver statue of Christopher Columbus sculpted by the famous French artist Frédéric Auguste Bartholdi (ill. 5.14). One French critic remarked, "This is one of the largest . . . casting[s] in silver that has ever been made. . . . The pose is noble, and the gesture of the great navigator is altogether that of the man of genius pointing the way which will open to the world a new path for human activity."[120] The rest of the opulent display highlighted the firm's skill in a wide variety of innovative silverworking techniques, which attracted much attention. These processes included chasing, enameling, oxidizing surfaces, and blowing glass into silver mounts.[121] Of the silverware made for the fair, much was costly. A tea and coffee service with lavishly chased American flowers covering its surface had a retail price of $4,000, for example. The *Nautilus Centerpiece* alone, designed by William C. Codman as a yachting trophy, took 360 silversmithing, 48.5 casting, and 410 chasing hours to make at a cost of $1,000 to the factory, over a year's salary for Gorham's most skilled metalworker (fig. 5.10).[122] This piece is a good example of the risk that silverware firms ran in investing in such costly objects for expositions, since sales were never guaranteed. This centerpiece appears to have remained in Gorham's stock for almost thirty years, until it was

FIG. 5.10. *Nautilus Centerpiece*. William C. Codman, designer; Gorham Mfg. Co., maker, Providence, R.I.; 1893. Sterling silver, silvergilt, shell, pearls, and semiprecious stones. Dallas Museum of Art.

FIG. 5.11. *Egyptian* pattern coffeepot. Tiffany & Co., New York, N.Y., 1893.
Sterling silver, enamel, ivory, and jade. The Carnegie Museum of Art.

finally sold in 1921 to the American Metal Co. as a birthday gift to its president, Ludwig Vogelstein. Similarly, the $25,000 *Century Vase*, the one old piece Gorham showed in Chicago, never sold and was melted down in the 1930s.

In spite of hardships caused by a severe recession, Tiffany & Co. also invested heavily in display objects for the 1893 fair.[123] One commentator estimated that the company's investment in both jewelry and silverware for Chicago was about $1,000,000. Much of this sum was undoubtedly for jewelry, including the $100,000 Tiffany's diamond, but a substantial portion went for silverware.[124] The Tiffany's exhibition catalogue for Chicago lists almost 500 pieces of silver and nearly 350 "silver fancy articles," including a toilet table of South American amaranth wood mounted with silver.[125] While the cost of typical exhibition items like a water pitcher decorated

with chrysanthemums or an enameled coffeepot was high (figs. 4.3, 5.11), that of truly amazing objects such as the *Magnolia Vase* (ill. 5.15) and the *American Flora Tea Set* was extreme. Heavily chased with native American flowers, the retail price for the tea set was $21,000.[126]

In the fairs that followed Chicago, the extraordinary quality of American work persisted. One need only to view a sampling of objects shown at fairs until 1915 to realize how exceptional these U.S. exhibitions must have been. In Paris in 1900, both Tiffany's and Gorham displayed pieces of solid silver furniture: an oval cheval glass by Tiffany and a dressing table by Gorham (fig. 9.6). The Gorham table and mirror took 2,297 man-hours to execute at a cost to the firm of $1,283 for labor alone. For San Francisco, Gorham made yet another table.[127] The general effect of regularly displaying silverwork of this qual-

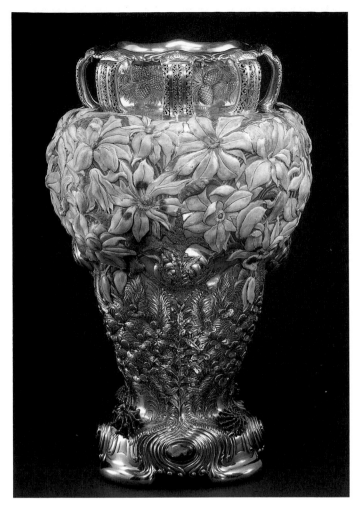

ILL. 5.15. *Magnolia Vase*, designed by John T. Curran for Tiffany & Co., 1893. © 1980 The Metropolitan Museum of Art.

Co.: "If we have sometimes blamed or criticized certain exaggerations which shock our European ideas, it is none the less certain that there is [in America] a great effort, for which one must praise those who direct this important house of silverware, which nothing can stop in this road of creative originality and manual perfection; and which remains worthy of the reputation it made in Europe at the Exposition of 1878 and 1889."[128]

Beyond the adulation of both their own countrymen and foreigners, exactly how much financial reward American firms generated from participating in international exhibits is impossible to know. Although the increase was not directly caused by successful competition in world's fairs, the volume of silver sales in this country did rise dramatically between 1878 and 1915. The value of silverware and silverplated wares produced in America soared from $17,938,000 in 1879 to $42,229,000 in 1914, then climbed to $87,424,000 in 1927. There were only two major declines, during the recessions of the mid 1890s and 1907–8.[129] Certainly inflation accounted for some of this increase, but in real terms the figures still reveal a doubling by 1914 and a tripling by 1927 in comparison to the 1879 amount. The production of Tiffany's and Gorham, who invested the most in international exhibitions during this period, mirrored this growth closely. In the 1878–79 fiscal year ending in April, the Tiffany & Co. silver shop sold the retail store $426,236 in silverware, the dollar total being the wholesale cost. By the 1906–7 year, the total had reached a high of $1,016,940 and then dropped back to $793,035 in 1913–14.[130] Gorham's combined retail and wholesale sales grew nearly tenfold in the period, increasing from $683,275 in 1879 to $6,192,812 in 1906.[131] Without question, world's fairs provided exposure to millions of potential customers and generated publicity both at home and abroad. In so doing they created a forum in which Americans could compete and win internationally, fueling the flames of the hot U.S. market, which generated such dramatic growth throughout the silverware industry between the 1870s and World War I.

ity was that U.S. firms, especially Tiffany's and Gorham, became world famous. In concluding his report on the American silverware exhibits at the 1893 fair and the U.S. industry in general, a French critic verbalized the attitude of many Europeans toward this country's best products when he said of Tiffany &

NOTES

1. *Silverware* 1940, 19, table 7.

2. For information on inflation and deflation in the nineteenth century, see Williamson 1944, 754.

3. For a good discussion of factors affecting salesmen, see "Peregrinating Beau Brummels," *JCK* 139:9, part 2 (June 1969): 24–34.

4. Quote from the August 1895 issue reprinted in *ibid.*, 28. For a humorous salute to the jewelry and silverware "drummer," see "The Jewelry Drummer," *JW* 5:4 (28 Nov. 1887):95.

5. Gibb 1943, table 10. Gibb's discussion of salesmen is a very good one.

6. Quote from an unidentified 1881 issue of *JCK* printed in *JCK* 139:9, part 2 (June 1969):28.

7. "To Our Salesmen" (Gorham, 27 May 1908):1–2. The copy used is in the design library of the Gorham plant in Providence.

8. Both documents are still in the design library of the Gorham plant in Providence. While undated, they appear to be from the 1905–15 period.

9. "A Chapter in the History of American Silver-Plated Ware," *JW* 4:12 (20 July 1887):1039.

10. For a discussion of the importance of salesmen, see Strasser 1989, 56–64 and 194–202.

11. *JW* 4:23 (6 Oct. 1887):2186.

12. For comments on the recovering southern market, see "The North and the South," *JCK* 9:4 (May 1878):61–62.

13. For a typical list, see *JW* 1:6 (9 Dec. 1885):274–75.

14. *Directory* 1884.

15. "The Gorham Manufacturing Co.'s New Building," *JCK* 15:5 (June 1884): 155–56.

16. Gorham 1904, D.

17. For a brief discussion of the relationship with Spaulding & Co., see Carpenter 1982, 237. An entry in Gorham's board minutes suggests that the company had even closer ties to the Chicago retailer. On 22 May 1890 (pp. 189–93)

in Board 1868 it is noted that the board agreed to sell Charles Grenville Peters of Boston a partial interest in Gorham for $3.6 million. Evidently Peters was also a stockholder in Spaulding & Co., perhaps having bought out one of the earlier stockholders. The nature of these connections is left unclear by the minutes.

18. "A Chapter in the History of American Silver-Plated Ware. First Paper," *JW* 4:12 (20 July 1887):1040–41. According to this source, the New York showroom sold retail to local New York customers, but wholesale to others.

19. For a description of the building in 1887, see "Tiffany's. The World's Greatest Jewelry Store, from Cellar to Garret. First Paper," *JW* 4:21 (27 Sept. 1887):1928; for one in 1874, see *Hotel Record* 1:1 (16 Sept. 1874):1–2. A clipping from this periodical survives in Scrapbooks, v. 2B, p. 255.

20. *ABM* 1906, 182.

21. Clipping from the Sept. 1886 issue in Scrapbooks, v. 3B.

22. Notices from these men survive in Scrapbooks, v. 3B.

23. Krantz 1894, Tiffany & Co., 3.

24. Steele 1877, 9–10.

25. "A Handsome Southern Store," *JW* 4:7 (15 June 1887):560.

26. *Ibid.*, 560–62.

27. "Bailey, Banks & Biddle Co.'s Display of Silverware," *JCK* 30:8 (27 Mar. 1895):16. The exhibit contained silverware by Bailey, Banks & Biddle; Whiting; Gorham; Dominick & Haff; Goodnow & Jenks; Wm. B. Durgin; and Ludwig, Redlich & Co.

28. For B. & W. B. Smith ads with views of many of their interiors, see *JW* 1:1 (4 Nov. 1885):37; 1:20 (17 Mar. 1886):978–79; 1:22 (31 Mar. 1886):1083–84; 1:26 (28 Apr. 1886):1343; 2:7 (16 June 1886):373–75; and *JCK* 30:1 (6 Feb. 1895):13. The most common variant of the standard floor plan was the elimination of the central U-shaped case and the addition of flat-topped cases along the sides in front of the wall cases.

29. For comments on competition from department stores, see "The Department Store Problem," *JCK* 30:3 (20 Feb. 1895):17.

30. "Store and Window Decoration," *JCK* 21:11 (Dec. 1890):34.

31. For typical ones, see "Artistic Window Dressing," *JW* 7:3 (15 Nov. 1888):57; and *JCK* 21:11 (Dec. 1890):33–36; "Store Keeping Department," *JCK* 50:1 (1 Feb. 1905):179; "Fourth Annual . . . Window Dressing Contest," *JCK* 50:3 (15 Feb. 1905):41; "Background Displays for Washington's Birthday and Easter," *JCK* 78:1 (5 Feb. 1919):453; and "Show Window Display Cards and Signs," *JCK* 78:2 (12 Feb. 1919):99–100.

32. *JCK* 21:11 (Dec. 1890):33.

33. *Ibid.*, 33–35.

34. For a discussion of this clock phenomenon, see "The Jewelry Store Look," *JCK* 139:9, part 2 (June 1969):106–7.

35. *Ibid.*, 111–12.

36. An undated newspaper story in Scrapbooks, v. 2A, notes the additions of retail departments. The clipping appears to be from the 1870s.

37. Notes on the British branch found in GA, I. Historical, 7. Plant.

38. Gibb 1943, 240.

39. *JW* 4:12 (20 July 1887):1041, and Hogan 1977, 26.

40. Hogan 1977, 26. *JW* 4:12 (20 July 1887):1041 notes that Meriden Britannia "has received titles from the royal families of both Spain and Portugal."

41. Gibb 1943, 225–47.

42. Figures taken from Gibb 1943, 236. *Silverware* 1940, table 25, shows American silverplated products valued at $11,503,000 for 1889.

43. *Silver* 1902, 335.

44. *Ibid.*, 279–80.

45. For various comments on the American export trade, see "America: Sending Silverware Abroad," *JCK* 5:11 (15 Dec. 1874):186; "Our Export Trade," 10:10 (Nov. 1879):195; "Epergnes," *JSW* 4:3 (Nov. 1877):34; "American

Houses," *JM* 3:95 (15 Oct. 1877):158; 3:96 (1 Nov. 1877):vii; and "American Electro-Plate," 3:114 (1 Aug. 1878):310.

46. "Jeweler's Circular," *JCK* 5:12 (12 Jan. 1875):211. For an example of a trade catalogue with ordering instructions in Spanish, see Reed & Barton 1885.

47. "American Electro-Plate," *JM* 3:112 (1 July 1878):295.

48. "Trade Catalogues," *JCK* 17:8 (Sept. 1886):271.

49. For information on the history of Reed & Barton's catalogues, see Gibb 1943, 204–5.

50. Hogan 1977, 25. Gorham continued the tradition of printing large elegant trade catalogues from the 1880s through the early twentieth century, although they were not as lavish. For information on Gorham's catalogues, see *JCK* (12 Oct. 1892). A clipping of this notice is in Scrapbook 1891.

51. Reed & Barton 1885, n.p. For information on Meriden Britannia's system, see Hogan 1977, 23–24.

52. Gorham's entire code was: 1=I; 2=W; 3=T; 4=□; 5=∧; 6=S; 7=L; 8=∇; 9=Ø; 10=E; 0=E; and all repeats=X. I am indebted to Stephen Vaughan for this information. Usually these codes were used on paper labels and tags that occasionally survive on original boxes. For a discussion of such codes, see Strasser 1989, 74.

53. Gorham 1892, preface.

54. Gorham 1888, frontispiece and following page. A similar frontispiece is in Gorham 1886.

55. Bailey 1908, 6. According to Tufts 1899, preface, James W. Tufts Co. was even willing to have a salesman come by with large photographs of each piece in its catalogue if one wished to see them better.

56. The TA has copies of almost all the firm's *Blue Books*. Especially informative ones include those for 1878 and 1917. For ads telling people to write for their free copy, see *HB* 18:4 (Sept. 1905):3 and 18:6 (Nov. 1905):3.

57. "Artful Dodgers," *JCK* 10:6 (July 1879):102 and 11:3 (Apr. 1880).

58. "Merchandizing Methods in the Days of Old and Now," *JCK* 78:1 (5 Feb. 1919):431.

59. This information is found in "Statement of Advertising during the Month of December 1876," Scrapbooks, v. 2A.

60. These patterns appear to have been constant throughout the entire 1840 to 1940 period. For a modern breakdown of when retail jewelry store owners advertise, see "Spreading the Word," *JCK* 139:9, part 2 (June 1969):44.

61. For a history of the *JCK*, see "A Golden Anniversary," *JCK* 78:1 (5 Feb. 1919):161–73.

62. *JW* 10:14 (3 July 1890):4.

63. *JCK* 20:6 (July 1889):18 and 30:23 (17 July 1895):16.

64. "The Paine Testimonial," *HW* 32:1628 (3 Mar. 1888):151 and "A Masterpiece in Art—Silversmithing," *JCK* 23:20 (16 Dec. 1891):3. For other examples of this practice, see "Boston's Labor Day Regatta Trophies," *JW* 8:19 (4 Sept. 1889):49–50; "American Silversmithing in its Highest Expression," *JCK* 30:10 (10 Apr. 1895):3; and "The German Renaissance Style in Silversmithing," 30:26 *JCK* (31 July 1895):3.

65. Stuart 1912.

66. *HB* 18:5 (Oct. 1905):47.

67. For ads for these two firms listing these wares, see *JCK* 19:9 (Oct. 1888):4 and *HB* 18:6 (Nov. 1905):65.

68. "Novelties for the Holiday Trade," *JCK* 23:14 (4 Nov. 1891):11. For an Alvin ad, see *JCK* 50:2 (8 Feb. 1905):2.

69. A copy of the promotional booklet is in GA, X. Advertising, 2 (1915).

70. Venable 1987.

71. For a Wallace & Sons ad for ice tea spoons, see *JCK* 78:11 (16 Apr. 1919):146.

72. "Souvenir Spoons, Part I," *JCK* 22:8 (25 Mar. 1891):1. For more on these spoons, see almost any issue between March and *JCK* 23:17 (25 Nov. 1891):41.

73. Examples of calendars from 1880 through the 1890s, copies of the booklet and card noting Tiffany & Co.'s appointment, and the list of newspapers that reported it are in Scrapbooks, v. 3B, pp. 210–14.

74. For an illustration of a Reed & Barton trade card from 1884, see Gibb 1943, 216.

75. Royal 1910, 104.

76. "A Splendid Display of Silverware," N.Y. Express, 25 Nov. 1876.

77. "American and English Silversmithing," JCK 30:8 (27 Mar. 1895):17.

78. For a description of the Waldorf exhibition, see "Rare and Unique Exhibit of Works in Hand Wrought Silver," JCK 35:16 (17 Nov. 1897):16. A Gorham notice for this exhibition in the east room of the Waldorf is in the collection of Phyllis Tucker, Houston, Texas. For an image of Reed & Barton's parade wagon, see Gibb 1943, opp. 216.

79. The vase is described in Reed & Barton 1875. Hogan 1977 notes that Meriden Britannia showed at these domestic fairs.

80. Souvenir 1877 contains information on the Connecticut silverplate firms that participated.

81. "Splendor at the Fairs," JCK 139:9 part 2 (June 1969):142.

82. Board 1868 (11 Mar. 1876):23.

83. Tiffany 1876. For a description of Tiffany & Co.'s exhibit, see JSW 1:6 (Oct. 1876):6.

84. The American Shield was designed by F. A. Heller. For an image, see JW 8:8 (20 June 1889):38. For information on the Century Vase and an image, see Carpenter 1982, 77–79.

85. For comments about Gorham's stock items, see "Jewelry and Silver at the Centennial," JCK 8:6 (July 1876):93.

86. Gorham 1876. Information on the pavilion will be in Katherine S. Howe and Alice C. Frelinghuysen's Herter Brothers: Furniture and Interiors for a Gilded Age (forthcoming, 1994).

87. For a description of Reed & Barton's display, see Norton 1877, 303.

88. Norton 1877, McCabe 1877, Sandhurst 1876, and Gems 1877.

89. For an example, see AJ 1876.

90. "The Silverware Display. England and America Competing," N.Y. Times, 7 Aug. 1876. For an article entitled "Artistic Silverwork," see 27 Sept. 1876.

91. JCK 8:6 (July 1877):n.p.

92. Reed & Barton 1877.

93. For information on Tiffany & Co.'s exhibit, see Newark Daily Adviser, 24 Nov. 1876. An invitation to Gorham's survives in Scrapbooks, v. 2B.

94. "Providence Letter," JSW 4:8 (Apr. 1878):109.

95. For an account of Congress's actions, see "Our Success in Paris," JCK 9:10 (Nov. 1878):title page. For a list of American participants, see Reports 1880, v. 1, p. 366.

96. For period comments on the service at the fair, see Carpenter 1978, 58–60.

97. For a list of the type of objects shown by Tiffany's, see Pickering 1878, 109, and Illustrated 1878, 130.

98. Pickering 1878, 109.

99. Taylor 1879a, 170.

100. Spectator, London, 21 Sept. 1878, quoted in ibid., 171.

101. Taylor 1879a, 174.

102. A clipping containing a list of purchasers from the Continental Gazette, 26 Sept. 1878, survives in Scrapbooks, v. 3A.

103. British 1971, 82.

104. Ibid., 71.

105. Ibid., 362.

106. "The Exposition of Paris, 1878: A Comparison of Elkington's Exhibits at Paris, 1878, With Those of Other Nations." This document survives in the EA, v. 8, p. 229.

107. JCK 10:6 (July 1879):103.

108. Official 1889, 126–27.

109. "Glimpses of the Exposition," JCK 20:6 (July 1889):29.

110. For descriptions of the objects by Tiffany's and Gorham, see "Glimpses of the Exposition," JCK 20:5 (June 1889):25–26; 20:6 (July 1889):28–32; and "Tiffany Exhibit," JW 8:5 (30 May 1889):43–50; "The Gorham Exhibit. Part I," JW 8:7 (13 June 1889):26–29; and "The Gorham Exhibit. Part II," JW 8:8 (20 June 1889):35–39.

111. JW 8:5 (30 May 1889):44.

112. Ibid., 45–46.

113. Ibid., 44.

114. Reports 1891, 314.

115. Reports 1889, 594–95.

116. "The Exposition Awards," JW 8:24 (10 Oct. 1889):cover story.

117. Nineteen pieces of the Gorham flatware and both the objects by Tiffany's are still in the museum's collection. Their accession numbers are: 6024–44 and 5827–28. For a contemporary account of the Gorham donation, see "A Rich Present by the Gorham Co.," JCK 21:23 (Apr. 1890):58.

118. Whiting exhibited in Chicago (1893); Alvin did so in Buffalo (1901); and Meriden Britannia showed in San Francisco (1915).

119. Krantz 1894, 85.

120. Ibid., Gorham, 2.

121. An article commenting on such articles appeared in the Springfield Republican, 3 Sept. 1893. A clipping of this article survives in Scrapbook 1891.

122. Letter, Hough to Venable, 20 Oct. 1990.

123. A marginal note for the year 1893 in Parsell 1901, 30, states, "Chicago Exbn. further reason for falling off." Evidently the effort and money required to prepare for the fair aggravated Tiffany's falling profits in the silver shop that year.

124. Krantz 1894, 85.

125. Tiffany 1893.

126. For a description of Tiffany & Co.'s exhibit, see Heydt 1893, Krantz 1894, and Tiffany 1893, 7.

127. For an image of the Tiffany's silver cheval glass, see Report 1901, v. 5, opp. p. 618. For a detailed account of the Gorham dressing table, see Hough 1990. For the 1915 table, which is now in the collection of the Rhode Island School of Design, see RISD 1985, 327.

128. Krantz 1894, 16–17.

129. Silverware 1940, 19, table 7.

130. Parsell 1901, 30.

131. Historical 1950, chart.

Chapter 6

CONSUMPTION AND DESIGN

Between 1875 and 1915 the consumption of silverware rose dramatically. Because relatively little American-made silver was exported, the near quadrupling of production that occurred over these four decades was consumed by the domestic market. This massive increase in the use of silver articles in the United States elicited comment by both American and foreign observers. For example, in the 1878 Parliamentary hearings on hallmarking, British officials who were worried about the decline in British sterling silverware production repeatedly asked witnesses questions such as "Are you prepared to give me an opinion as to the cause why this trade should be so prosperous in America, and so stagnant in this country?"[1] Some witnesses responded vaguely that America "is comparatively a new country," or incorrectly claimed that the United States exported most of its wares.[2] Others were more insightful. One witness who had spoken to a Tiffany's representative on the matter said, "The growth of the last 20 or 30 years has arisen by the home demand; before that time comparatively little silver was used in the United States, and most of that was imported from England, but that importation from England has now entirely ceased. He told me, moreover, that the use of silver was very great, notwithstanding the increased use of electro-plate."[3] Another witness gave an often-heard foreign response, "The Americans are ostentatious people, who are likely to go in for expensive articles in gold and silver in proportion to their increasing prosperity."[4]

Americans were also commenting on the growing pervasiveness of silver in their society by the 1870s. For example, after stating that silverware was often used by farmers and mechanics in this country, a writer for *Scribner's Monthly* said in 1874 that "Plated tea services, castors, salvers, pitchers, ladles, cake and fruit baskets, etc. are too common to be noticed. . . . [H]ardly any comfortable young couple now begin housekeeping without a fair show of genuine table silver, as far at least as spoons, forks, butter, fruit, pie and fish-knives, napkin-rings, and such trifles."[5] Since contemporary trade catalogues reveal that a simple silverplated table service consisting of four five-piece place settings, two platters, and a tureen cost between

$50 and $60 dollars, or around 10 percent of a working-class family's annual income, one must assume that this writer overstated the pervasiveness of silverware in working-class households, especially rural ones. His perception that Americans were acquiring more silverware than ever before was correct, however.

Why Americans purchased increasing amounts of silverware during the late nineteenth century remains a complicated question. Certainly the fact that a growing proportion of citizens at all but the lowest levels of society could now afford to buy sterling or plated wares is key to any explanation. On the whole, economic conditions of this period worked in concert to make silverware more affordable. First, between 1870 and 1900, per capita income increased from $170 to $210. When coupled with the fact that the same period was deflationary, the result was a real average annual increase of approximately 2.4 percent.[6] Second, the late nineteenth century saw a steady decline in the price of silver bullion, increasing competition between silverware manufacturers, and perfection of the process of silverplating. Together these factors drove the price of silver products down. The combination of consumers with greater discretionary income and lower-priced objects created a growing demand for silverware.

Simply because a consumer can afford a particular item does not, however, mean that he will purchase it. Consequently, the explanation for this increase in silverware consumption must also be sought within American culture, not just within its growing late-nineteenth-century economy. Certainly, the ownership of silver objects has for millennia been associated with high social status. Thus, as *Scribner's* noted, when American farmers and mechanics, and the middle class as a whole, could finally afford silver objects, it is not surprising that many of them chose to acquire pieces just as America's elite had been doing since the seventeenth century. But beyond the thrill of partaking in a traditionally upper-class activity, average Americans, along with the country's wealthiest citizens, were encouraged to acquire silver objects by the positive moral and artistic associations that silver was given in the nineteenth century.

ILL. 6.1. Selection of flatware representing the wide variety of forms and designs made in the United States between 1860 and 1890. Dallas Museum of Art.

FIG. 6.1. Part of Gorham Mfg. Co.'s *Furber Service* on exhibition in 1992 at the Museum of Art, Rhode Island School of Design.

SILVER IN THE NINETEENTH-CENTURY HOME

From midcentury on, the female-dominated home increasingly became the refuge of America's moral virtue. Catharine Beecher, in her *Treatise on Domestic Economy* (1841) and *The American Woman's Home* (1869), held up the home as the center of family life and childhood education and as a safe haven from the pressures of an increasingly crowded and industrialized country. As Harvey Green has noted, "The home was to be the opposite of the man's world; rather than an environment that bespoke commerce and trade, it was a miniature universe of culture and education for family and visitors."[7] The dining room was consistently cited as one of the most important arenas for family life and social interaction with appropriate outsiders. In 1886, for example, the importance of this room and its dining rituals was stated by one writer:

> If the truth must be known, all affectations and pretense aside, the dinner, the world over, is the symbol of a people's civilization. A coarse and meanly cooked and raggedly served dinner expresses the thought and perhaps the spiritual perception of a nation or family. A well-cooked and a prettily-served dinner will indicate the refinement and taste of a nation or family.[8]

Given their critical role in educating and civilizing, middle- and upper-class dining rooms were usually well appointed with rugs, light fixtures, sideboards, chairs, and a table. Furthermore, many homes had two eating spaces, one near the kitchen for informal family meals and another, larger room for more formal dining. The latter was generally separated from the kitchen, being on a different floor or in another part of the house to protect the dining environment from kitchen noises and smells. In less wealthy households this was often achieved by using a folding screen between the kitchen and dining room.

And even in the case of poorer families, which could not afford a separate dining room, formal meals were often eaten in the best room of the house, usually the parlor.[9]

American silverware benefited from the dining room's prominent place in nineteenth-century American middle- and upper-class culture. In 1874 one observer noted: "The beauty of the ordinary American table, with its snowy damask and china, sparkling cut-glass, and lustrous utensils of silver, all deposited in the tasteful symmetry native to the American housewife, is a power, and one that goes too near the springs of moral as well as aesthetic culture to be lightly esteemed by the most serious observer."[10] In 1916 the silver manufacturer R. Wallace & Sons reflected the longevity of this belief when it told potential customers that silver hollow- and flatware were more than utility or luxury—they were necessities.

> The family silver has always occupied a place of honor by its appreciated usefulness, beauty and lastingness. It is the symbol of refinement, of culture, and of good breeding. It comes first in the list of wedding gifts. It is the last possession poverty will give up. Home without it is unthinkable.[11]

The heightened role of dining rituals and their accoutrements was, in many ways, made possible by the generally expanding economy that existed from the 1860s to the 1920s. During the Civil War and the early 1870s, more Americans than ever before amassed fortunes unparalleled in size during the antebellum period. As *nouveaux riches* pushed their way into America's social elite during the 1870s and 1880s through marriage and money, entertaining and the accompanying need for silverware reached unprecedented heights. Even the French, who had set the standard for fine dining, were amazed by American opulence. In 1882, for example, a Paris chef wrote in

Cuisine artistique of "the Americans, those robust gourmets who, newly arrived in the arena, have nevertheless made remarkable progress, in cooking as well as gastronomy. But the luxuries of the table in that country of voracious appetites have assumed such extraordinary proportions as to make one involuntarily think of the famous excesses of the feasts of Ancient Rome."[12] For the highest level of society this was indeed an accurate description, as it had in fact been for some time. In 1874 *Scribner's* published an article entitled "The Silver Age," which described an idealized dinner given in one of New York's finest homes (fig. 6.1). The imaginary table is 36 by 6 feet with place for twenty-four guests and is bedecked with "jewelry of silver." In the center stands a "magnificent silver *epergne*, overtopped with calla lilies" that rests "as if floated, on the dazzling surface of a silver sea, or more literally a burnished 'plateau'" (fig. 6.29). Two large seven-light candelabra are on either side of the centerpiece and the twenty-four spaces along the table's edge are marked off "by the sparkling cluster of glasses, spoon, fork, and knife like a mirror, with the curved corniform part that almost holds itself in your hand." At the appointed hour the guests are

marshaled to their places—millionaires, ambassadors, generals, admirals, authors, and the President of the United States; no less distinguished company, surely, could support so princely an equipage. They have a moment to admire the display, for the indescribable beauty of the new style of tureens . . . down to the iridescent oxides and gold on the dainty little butterflies just flitting over the edges of the silver salt-cellars, and the fanciful form of the chased pepper-bottles and salad castors ranged within reach of every hand. . . . All at once, at the secret signal of their chief, the well-trained and well-dressed attendants execute their manual of arms, as if moved by one set of muscles; the covers of the first course vanish over their heads . . . and in another moment the silver salver comes floating down before each guest with a mirror in which the rims of soup and silver blend undefinable.

But what soup, or nectar of Jove, is worthy to rest in that elysium of art which we profane with the name of tureen! The white glory of its interplay sheen and shade, lit up again with dewy sparkle of cut foliage festooned to either side, then surprised by a delicate molding of gold, and reflected back on itself from the mirror-like plateau or tray beneath, with rim of pale gold bas-relief that catches and blends the chaster luster with its own in a silver-golden halo—ah, Solomon! thou wouldst never have likened the setting of a perfect apropos to apples of gold in pictures of silver, if thou couldst have seen this silver picture wreathed in golden haze.

The scene continues with course after course served on "symbolical works of art" that reflect their function, such as bread plates adorned with "landscapes of golden grain, with Ceres

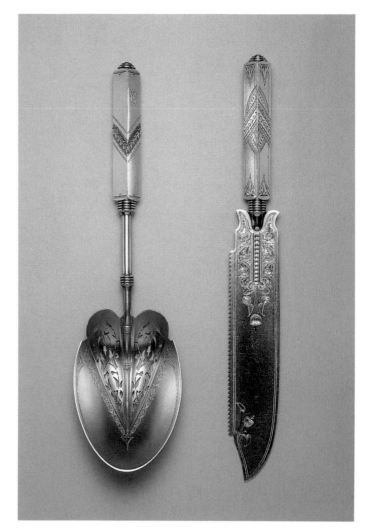

FIG. 6.2. Ice spoon and cake knife. Gorham Mfg. Co., Providence, R.I., ca. 1870. Sterling silver and silvergilt. Dallas Museum of Art.

and her reapers, circling around the silver lakes, filled by reflection, to their depth, with snowy slices." There are vegetable bowls, butter dishes, water pitchers, and containers for "crushed ice rimmed with pendent icicles of frost-silver, and their bases piled with rugged Arctic scenery, in blocks and bergs and polar bears" (fig. 6.69). For the main course, the table was reset with "glittering nautical models; each another silver picture, reflected in its silver sea; disclosing a mighty salmon at full-length repose in the hold of each vessel. A broad aquatic leaf, with a mermaid handle clinging to its stem, divides the red-golden flesh, and aided by a barbed trident, distributes it to the plates. The small boat or tender alongside supplies sauce, dipped with an enameled and iridescent shell." For the last stage of the meal the guests withdraw, and the table is stripped and reset for the dessert course in which "ice-cream towers on massive silver stands sculptured with more Arctic scenery" and compotes for cakes and bonbons stand in wait. Specialized flatware is required—"knife-edge ice-cream spoons" and a "cake-knife which has a fine saw back to its splendid blade, to divide the frosting without fracture" (fig. 6.2). In conclusion, fruit taken from "a sort of fairy barge" (fig. 6.3) and nuts accompanied by silver nut picks are passed around.[13]

FIG. 6.3. Fruit or nut bowl (one of a pair) from the *Furber Service*. Gorham Mfg. Co., Providence, R.I., 1871. Sterling silver with silvergilt. Museum of Art, Rhode Island School of Design.

FIG. 6.4. Salad set. Gorham Mfg. Co., Providence, R.I., ca. 1880. Sterling silver and silvergilt. Dallas Museum of Art.

The author stated, "I shall not pretend sumptuous living is the right use of money in a world so full as this is of evils that money can aid to remove." But he conceded that for those who wanted such opulence "it is just as well to have works of art that can delight and refine the taste, if nothing more."[14] Some advice-givers, however, believed that such spectacles should never take place. Two of America's most famous advisors on domestic economy, Sarah Hale and Catharine Beecher, for example, cautioned at midcentury against opulent displays. "In giving dinners, avoid ostentation, which will not only be very expensive, but will make your guests uncomfortable," wrote Hale. She further warned, "To ensure a well-dressed dinner, provide enough, and beware of the common practice of having too much. The table had better appear rather bare than crowded with dishes not wanted."[15] Given the popularity of their books, some people must have agreed with them, or at least found their advice useful as a rationalization for not entertaining in ways they could not afford. By the 1870s, however, increasing numbers of Americans were rejecting this early advice in favor of more lavish dining rituals, complete with greater amounts of silverware.

As the dinner party idealized in *Scribner's* suggests, by the 1870s many of America's wealthiest individuals were rivaling, if not surpassing, their European counterparts. For example, between 1871 and 1879 Henry Jewett Furber (1840–1918), the young president of Universal Life Insurance Company of New York and Chicago, and his wife Elvira Irwine Furber commissioned from Gorham an extraordinary 740-piece dinner service (fig. 6.1).[16] Similarly, Marie Louise and John W. Mackay ordered from Tiffany's a 1,250-piece service for which they supplied their own silver, having become millionaires from the famed Comstock Lode (fig. 5.8).[17] If one did not wish to purchase an entire service at once, one could acquire large amounts of china, glassware, and silver over an extended period of time, as did Mary Jane Morgan, widow of shipping magnate Charles Morgan. The year following her death in 1885, her collection of dining equipage was sold at auction at New York's American Art Gallery. The silverware was said mainly to have been custom ordered from Tiffany's and Gorham, having had "special designs prepared by the manufacturers and improved by Mrs. Morgan before work was begun upon them." One observer noted:

There were again at this display examples of pretty much everything that a person of the most extravagant taste could think of to place upon a dinner table, either for practical service or a mere ornamentation; and there was the greatest profusion of everything, fanciful knives and forks in numerous patterns and quantities; spoons by the score; fish knives in elegant elaborate designs and rich in ornamentation; beautifully decorated vases, berry and fruit dishes in artistic designs and showing the highest degree of skilled workmanship; candelabra of varied patterns; some massive and rich, while others were light

ILL. 6.2. Candelabra on stands by Tiffany & Co., 1884. Private Collection.

and delicate as in most work on glass. Then there were dishes in almost every variety, showing beautiful combinations of various precious metals not infrequently associated with glass of different colors. Then there were silver candelabra standing fully six feet high and with many branching arms to hold wax candles [ill. 6.2].[18]

Bidding for Morgan's silver was lively, with retail firms like Tiffany's and its rival, Howard & Co., buying numbers of objects. Nevertheless, the trade noted that the sale recouped only about half of what Mrs. Morgan originally paid for the objects, approximately $65,000.[19]

Obviously the Furbers, Mackays, and Mrs. Morgan are extreme examples. Few Americans ever had the opportunity to dine with such persons, much less own such silver articles. Nevertheless, this elite class set the standard for opulence and refinement in dining between 1875 and 1915. And countless members of this country's less wealthy upper class and expanding middle class heard from friends or read about these social

FIG. 6.5. Ice cream server. Gorham Mfg. Co., Providence, R.I., 1870. Sterling silver. Dallas Museum of Art.

trendsetters in periodicals like *Scribner's Monthly Magazine* or the *Ladies' Home Journal*. In 1891, for example, the *Journal* published "How Delmonico Sets a Table." The author noted that although a dinner "is perhaps one of the chief pleasures of life . . . all people cannot have rare foods, served on gold or silver plates . . . and for the lack of these . . . must make up in less expensive ways. And one of the most important is a well set and attractive board, snowy napery, polished glass and china, and brightly burnished silverware, if you possess it."[20] Thus through written and verbal descriptions, many Americans who were experiencing real growth in discretionary income could dream about the avant-garde and in doing so learn ways in which they too could partake of the revolution in diet and dining that swept the United States following the Civil War.

The "Dining Room Revolution" had several basic components that worked to increase demand for silverware after midcentury. First, as transportation, growing, and processing methods improved, numerous new foods were introduced into the American diet. Items that precipitated new silver flat- or hollowware forms were oysters (which appeared with frequency in the 1840s), asparagus (1850s), celery (1860s), and sardines (1860s). An increasing appreciation of fresh green salads by Americans during the second half of the nineteenth century resulted in salad servers and lettuce forks (fig. 6.4). The fact that greens were perishable and expensive meant that salads had high status as a luxury food. Hence many of their associated serving utensils were elaborately decorated. The same was true of many desserts. Ice cream, for example, appeared in the United States during the 1860s and quickly grew in popularity. By the 1870s, one could purchase ice cream hatchets and spoons for cutting the frozen blocks, as well as specialized individual spoons and forks with cutting edges (figs. 6.5, 6.51). Because it was expensive, requiring sugar, ice, and lots of labor to make, ice cream was highly regarded and many utensils associated with it are extremely beautiful. Even more common desserts like cakes and pastries were costly enough to have their status reflected in elaborate flatware, cake knives and pastry servers often being elaborately engraved (figs. 4.9, 6.2). Even the now-ubiquitous orange was unusual enough to warrant a splendid fruit knife (fig. 6.46).[21]

Other foods that were already part of the American diet maintained their status as luxury items because of their high cost and perishability. Butter was such a food. Even after the early 1860s, when it first was produced by factory methods, butter remained expensive and thus was used sparingly at the table. Consequently, individual butter pats were often employed to apportion butter to each guest (fig. 6.6).[22] Even though it was common, tea was also a product that remained expensive throughout the late nineteenth century. Small tea sets were made for a single drinker at breakfast (fig. 6.7). Taking high tea with friends became a daily ritual for many, and its accompanying equipage was a symbol of feminine hospitality, the hostess distributing a warm, comforting drink as well as

FIG. 6.6. Butter pats from the *Furber Service*. Gorham Mfg. Co., Providence, R.I., 1879.
Sterling silver and silvergilt. Museum of Art, Rhode Island School of Design.

FIG. 6.7. Tea set. Whiting Mfg. Co., New York, N.Y., ca. 1880–1890. Sterling silver. Dallas Museum of Art.

expensive pastry or crackers to family and guests. At its most lavish, special "tea" flatware was used at these gatherings (fig. 6.8). In 1884 *The Ladies' Home Journal* noted: "The tea-table is as a flower of this growth that we call home. It is like the 'round table' where the knights come together. Or it is the shore where the drift from the waves that surged through the day, is deposited. Foolish things and useless things, and true and precious things are stranded there."[23] Given their use in a ritual felt to provide a refuge from life's "drift" and their strong association with feminine domesticity, tea wares were important in nineteenth-century life and hence were often quite elaborate. A tea caddy by Gorham, for example, not only has elaborate bright-cut engraving, but features jewelry-like bangles depicting Medusa, which jingle when in motion, thus drawing attention to the tea ceremony (fig. 6.9). Coffee, like tea, was a popular drink in America, this country consuming almost four times more coffee than tea by 1850. Strong black, or "Turkish," coffee typically had assumed the honored position as the last course of a formal dinner by the 1870s. Given this importance, it too required an appropriate silver vessel, and elongated "Turkish" coffeepots were made in large numbers during the final three decades of the century (fig. 6.10).[24] The

same was true for hot chocolate. Having been drunk in America during the eighteenth century, it remained expensive and fashionable during the nineteenth, resulting in the production of silver and porcelain chocolate pots (fig. 6.11).

The second major change in nineteenth-century dining rituals that increased silverware consumption was the introduction of *service à la russe*. Before the 1870s, most Americans served their meals in the traditional English fashion in which the main "course" and side dishes were placed on the table at the beginning of the meal, and guests passed food around, helping themselves. Certainly many households continued to eat in this fashion, especially for informal family meals. However, Americans increasingly adopted the new Russian form of service during the 1860s and 1870s. In 1879 the etiquette guide *Our Deportment* described the new style: "The latest and most satisfactory plan for serving dinner is dinner *à la Russe* . . . all the food being placed on a side table, and servants do the carving and waiting. This style gives an opportunity for more profuse ornamentation of the table, which as the meal progresses, does not become encumbered with partially empty dishes and platters."[25] Freeing the table for ornament was critical to the rise in silver consumption because it allowed a hostess to make

FIG. 6.8. Tea flatware. Gorham Mfg. Co., Providence, R.I., ca. 1879.
Sterling silver and silvergilt. Dallas Museum of Art.

Chapter 6

FACING PAGE: FIG. 6.9. Tea caddy. George Wilkinson, designer; Gorham Mfg. Co., maker, Providence, R.I.; designed 1861. Coin silver. Dallas Museum of Art.

FIG. 6.10. Coffeepot and tray. Gorham Mfg. Co., Providence, R.I., designed 1889, made 1891. Sterling silver and ivory. Minneapolis Institute of Arts.

ILL. 6.3. Diagram of *service à la russe*, 1862.

much greater use of items like centerpieces, candelabra, and vases (ill. 6.3). Furthermore, this type of service dramatized each course by serving it individually rather than simply placing it on a crowded table. With less to distract the diner, more attention could be paid not only to the food of a specific course, but to its serving utensils and vessels as well.

And finally, *service à la russe* required a larger staff of servants. Through nonverbal signals or the ringing of a bell (fig. 6.12), the hostess of a dinner made sure that "Dish after dish [came] round, as if by magic."[26] In reality, however, the "magic" in these rituals was the hands and minds of servants who cooked, carved, served, and cleared food, and washed, polished, and stored silver in upper-class households. By 1880 one-quarter of all urban households had at least one servant who could help prepare and execute a meal. Other support staff could be hired for the evening if needed.[27] In 1891 *The Ladies' Home Journal* advised that for a dinner of eight, two men were needed. For parties of fourteen to eighteen, four were required and for larger parties, six to eight had to be on hand.[28] Although most American families could neither afford servants nor all the expensive dining equipage, a significant portion of the middle class could afford to serve meals *à la russe* and purchase the silverware and other items needed to make the technique successful, if only in some simplified fashion in which the host and hostess and their older children did much of the work.

The amount of silver owned by the average American family between 1875 and 1915 is difficult to know. Numerous advice books and trade catalogues give one an insight into what was thought of as the ideal amount. Furthermore, documents such as lists of wedding gifts serve as a check on the validity of such sources, which record only what people were told to do, not what they actually did. In 1845 the American edition of the Englishman Thomas Webster's *Encyclopedia of Domestic Economy* listed the following items as

the usual articles in silver required to furnish a table: dishes and covers, table knives and forks, dessert knives

FIG. 6.12. Bell. William Bogert & Co., New York, N.Y., ca. 1866–1875. Sterling silver. Dallas Museum of Art, lent by The Charles R. Masling and John E. Furen Collection.

and forks, table spoons, gravy spoons, soup ladles, salt spoons with gilt bowls, fish slice, trays and waiters, bread baskets, cake baskets, decanter stands, decanter labels, liquor and bottle stands, cruet frames, asparagus tongs, cheese scoops, knife rests, nut crackers, grape scissors, tea urns, coffee urns, tea pots, coffee filters, sugar basins, cream ewers, sugar tongs, teaspoons, toast racks, butter coolers, snuffer trays, [and] candlesticks.[29]

Most if not all of these items remained in favor throughout the century, and other silver articles were added as the dining ritual became more complicated and new foods were introduced. In 1891 a writer for *Demorest's Family Magazine* noted in an article on "A Course Dinner" other items like bonbon dishes, centerpieces, candelabra, and butter pats. But by far

FIG. 6.11. Chocolate pot. John T. Vansant Mfg. Co., maker; Simons, Bro. & Co., retailer, Philadelphia, Pa.; ca. 1881–1884. Sterling silver and ivory. Mr. and Mrs. Alexander C. Speyer III Collection.

the largest increase was in flatware. Whereas the 1845 writer suggested that one have table and dessert knives, forks, and spoons, as well as a few serving pieces, by 1891 one could have "dinner" knives, forks and spoons, "entree" knives, forks and spoons, fish forks and knives, butter knives, fruit knives, oyster forks, salad forks, ice cream forks, soup spoons, coffee spoons, and nut picks, as well as additional flatware including a crumber (ill. 6.1).[30] Since all these articles and more were available in relatively inexpensive silverplate, many Americans were able to obtain significant amounts of flatware even if they could not afford complete sets. Furthermore, inexpensive silverplate was often given away as premiums by a host of retailers and publishers, including those of *The Ladies' Home Journal*.[31] And for many members of the middle class, the fall in the price of silverware that occurred during the late nineteenth and early twentieth centuries enabled them to acquire sterling flat- and hollowware.[32]

The development and proliferation in the United States of specialized flatware forms and patterns was one of the most striking phenomena in American silverware between 1850 and 1915. True, both American and some foreign firms, like Elkington & Co. in England, were by the mid nineteenth century making specialized flatware, including fish sets, individual "asparagus eaters," lobster crackers and scoops, tart servers, nut picks, ice hammers, sardine tongs, and bread forks (fig. 6.13).[33] However, American makers quickly overtook and passed their European counterparts by adding cheese, macaroni, tomato, and cucumber servers; pudding, berry, oyster, olive, orange, grapefruit, ice, ice cream, and ice tea spoons; cake, ice cream, and jelly knives; pickle, terrapin, lettuce, lemon, fruit, lobster, and mango forks; and picks for butter, nuts, and seafood, as well as a host of others (figs. 6.14–16). By the late nineteenth century, many flatware manufactures maintained patterns each containing over 100 different forms. A 1926 analysis of U.S. flatware patterns found that while some lines had as few as 59 distinct elements, some contained as many as 148. Surveying only major patterns, the *Jewelers' Circular's* series on "The Spoon Patterns of American Silversmiths" took seventeen installments to complete in 1895.[34] Even as late as the decade between 1914 and 1924, the nine manufacturers that made up the Sterling Silversmiths' Guild (discussed below), introduced 108 new patterns.[35] By 1937 the *Jewelers' Circular-Keystone Sterling Silver Flatware Index* listed 1,300 flatware patterns, of which 908 were still available—and this compilation did not even include silverplate patterns, which were even more numerous![36]

The range of American flatware fascinated Europeans. In 1886, A. St. Johnston, in commenting on an illustration of some Gorham flatware in London's *Magazine of Art*, commented:

It is certain that had we in England the chance of buying spoons and forks as beautiful as those engraved [here], at

the same price that we pay at present for the hideous articles procurable here, we should do so. But what choice have we? If we go to one of the first London silversmiths and ask for spoons and forks, we are met at once with the smiling query. "Yes, Sir; fiddle or old English?" Fiddle or old English! If we decline both those chaste designs we are assured that there is still a large selection of patterns remaining. The "Lily," the "Beaded," "King's Pattern," and "Queen's Pattern." There perforce, our choice must end. . . . Mark the difference, in this one article, between the supine conservatism of the English manufacturers and the alertness and constant progress of the American maker. For instance, the company whose forks we present would not be satisfied unless it produced every year or two new patterns, nearly all of which are beautiful, and of which they will produce a complete service of all articles for table use from a salt-spoon to a soup ladle.[37]

Seven years later, in 1893, a French observer was surprised at this country's "remarkable fertility in the variety of its patterns for table services." In commenting on flatware patterns designed by F. A. Heller, he said, "We have no idea of the richness of ornamentation of these services, and of the amount of talent expended by him in the engraving of the dies which he has made on the other side of the Atlantic." The same critic, however, was appalled at how the names of American patterns were not reflective of their ornament: "*Rouen, Cluny, Fontainebleau, Versailles, St. Cloud,* are all the names chosen by [Gorham] for patterns whose style recalls in nothing the brilliant epochs to which they make allusion."[38]

Americans were evidently unconcerned about how closely the decoration related to the names of patterns, for they consumed millions of pieces of flatware during the late nineteenth and early twentieth centuries. The quantities sold were so large that flatware constituted the bulk of production throughout the industry. Although the proportions may have been lower in the late nineteenth century, the importance of flatware was reflected in a 1937 study in which 55 percent of all sterling and 70 percent of silverplate made in America was flatware.[39] Why Americans needed such large quantities and wide variety of flatware in comparison to Europeans, who survived with much less, is an intriguing question.

Certainly the wish to draw attention to high-status foods, as a fine frame does to a painting, generated consumer demand for flatware. However, subtler dynamics were also at work. As part of a growing desire for greater order and hierarchy in an increasingly chaotic, industrialized society, Americans became extraordinarily particular and fastidious about the consumption of food. By the last quarter of the nineteenth century, for example, table etiquette reached its apex and more efficient flatware played a vital part in this development. First, the skills necessary to consume a host of foods ranging from oysters and

FIG. 6.13. Fish set. Albert Coles, New York, N.Y., ca. 1865. Coin silver. D. Albert Soeffing Collection.

FIG. 6.14. *Bird* pattern macaroni server. B. D. Beiderhase & Co., New York, N.Y., patented 1872. Sterling silver and silvergilt. Private Collection, San
Antonio.

FIG. 6.15. *Hizen* pattern berry spoon. Gorham Mfg. Co.,
Providence, R.I., ca. 1880. Sterling silver and silvergilt.
Dallas Museum of Art.

FIG. 6.16. Lobster pick. Frank W. Smith
Co., Gardner, Mass., ca. 1910–1930. Sterling silver. Dallas Museum of Art.

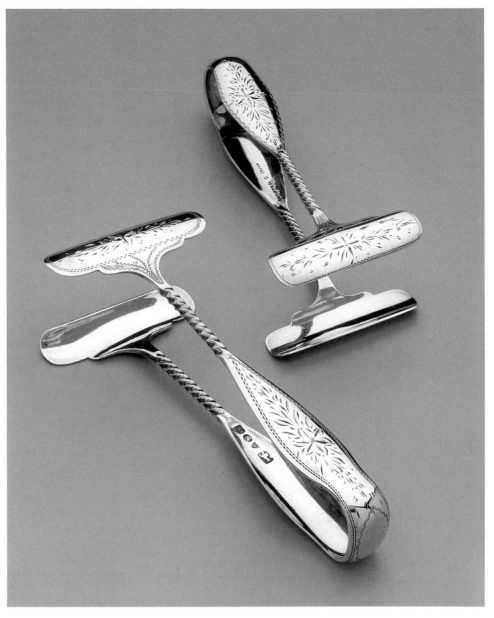

FIG. 6.17. Pair of asparagus tongs. Bailey & Co., Philadelphia, Pa., ca. 1865–1868.
Sterling silver. Dallas Museum of Art.

asparagus to oranges and walnuts were diverse and complicated, and the ability to execute properly such maneuvers was a sign that one rightly belonged within an elevated class. Furthermore, this complicated code of nonverbal table protocol functioned as a system of control for both the initiated and the outsider. As John F. Kasson has noted, "By cultivating practices of refined dining, social conservatives presented an alternative model of social incorporation and growth. According to this model, diners might properly enjoy abundance and, if their means allowed, even luxury, but the appetites were satisfied in a quiet and orderly way, and the cool control of intellect never faltered for an instant."[40] Likewise, etiquette rules formed a hurdle that outsiders had to overcome before they could hope for admittance to a higher social class. Flatware aided in this process by rigidly ordering the act of ingesting food. Using specialized eating tools, diners refrained from touching foods with their hands,

while eating with great neatness and grace. Those who could not properly peel an orange with a fruit knife, sever a raw oyster from its shell with an oyster fork, or manipulate asparagus spears with individual asparagus "eaters" risked social ostracism, for their clumsy actions revealed them as unrefined and disordered (fig. 6.17).

When used in sets, flatware also enhanced the users' sense of social order by serving as a physical manifestation of idealized community. As Susan Williams has explained, the growing use of sets of flatware as well as tea and coffee services, in which each piece was of the same pattern, was part of an overall trend towards matched sets of all kinds, including china and glassware, that accelerated after 1850.[41] Producers undoubtedly encouraged the purchase of sets because it increased sales, but this phenomenon also reflected a desire on the part of consumers to preserve symbolically a sense of community among

FIG. 6.18. Napkin ring. United States, ca. 1865. Silver. D. Albert Soeffing Collection.

friends and family while still maximizing privacy. While every-one ate with utensils alike in appearance, none were shared. Furthermore, it was commonly recommended to acquire enough silver so that one need not wash silverware during the meal.[42] Setting out all the required flatware for the dinner at once certainly made logistics easier, and it also avoided the unpleasant thought of not getting the same fork or spoon back after washing. Silver napkin rings, which were owned by many Americans for informal dining, also served to alleviate this fear. Highly ordered objects, napkin rings are typically identified by number, engraved name, or distinctive ornamentation (fig. 6.18). The ability to distinguish one's own ring meant that one was reusing one's own napkin. Since most families did not own the entire boxed sets of flatware that became available in the 1860s, problems in keeping track of what pieces were used by whom could arise. Many Americans had larger quantities of certain items like medium-size forks and teaspoons to alleviate such concerns. Producers realized that such forms were espe-cially useful, since they could perform several functions during the same dinner or be used when entertaining large numbers of guests. Consequently, sets of dessert forks or spoons were often sold alone, and after 1897 standard knives, forks, and spoons were typically sold in boxes of one dozen, rather than by weight as previously.[43] But even if an individual had only a single piece of silverware, that one object could serve as an important symbolic link to another world. Grant McCracken has explained that "consumer goods are bridges to . . . hopes and ideals" and how consumers purchase single objects "to take possession of a small concrete part of the style of life to which they aspire."[44] Thus through the purchase of an ornamented fish slice or set of silverplated demitasse spoons, the owner

could vicariously participate in a more opulent and ordered world than the one he actually inhabited.

Along with its nonverbal roles in American society, spe-cialized flatware simply performed its physical tasks more effi-ciently. Nineteenth-century flatware design was responsive to customers' needs in dealing with an increasingly wide array of food in the neatest possible manner.[45] Consider the pastry fork. In 1864 Eliza Leslie noted a new fashion:

> It's an affectation of ultra-fashion to eat pie with a fork, and has a very awkward and inconvenient look. Cut it up first with your knife and fork both; then proceed to eat it with care, the fork in your hand. Much of this deter-mined fork-exercise may be considered foolish. But it is fashionable.[46]

Manufacturers were quick to solve this design problem. In 1869 Reed & Barton patented the first "cutting fork," which elimi-nated the need for a knife at all. The widespread manufacture and use of pastry forks by the 1880s reflect their efficiency in executing the task of cutting up a slice of pie, conveying the pieces to the mouth, and picking up any remaining crumbs of crust. To optimize the fork's ability to do these jobs, one out-side tine was widened and given a cutting edge, and the tines were pointed to aid in picking up flakes.[47] Similar adaptations were made to other implements to increase their efficiency: cake knives were elongated to extend through a cake without get-ting one's hands in the icing, and the serrated blades parted the frosting without marring it. Sardine forks were short and wide to fit the scale of the prey and pierced to allow the smelly oil to flow away. Butter picks, on the other hand, had small, sharp tines to spear and hold the butter fast until it could be depos-

FIG. 6.19. Butter pick and sardine server. George W. Shiebler, New York, N.Y., ca. 1880–1890. Sterling silver and silvergilt. Dallas Museum of Art.

ited on one's plate or butter pat (fig. 6.19). Olive spoons were long and thin to fit through the narrow-necked jars in which olives were packed and had drain holes to get rid of the juice. Ice tea spoons were similarly elongated to accommodate the tall glasses in which the beverage was served. In short, the myriad shapes seen in American flatware of this period are virtually all the product of serious design and engineering decisions on the part of manufacturers.

In 1906 Reed & Barton proclaimed in *House Beautiful:* "NO GIFT to the bride, save the wedding ring itself, can supersede the chest of silverware. It is the one essential gift, the foundation of the 'family silver'—the heirloom of the future."[48] Although the manufacturer knew that the flatware pictured in the chest were efficient tools for eating and guardians of the social order, neither point was mentioned in its sales pitch. Rather, Reed & Barton chose to emphasize the ability of silver, and all objects, to unite the past with the future through the present. Even though the silverware pictured in the advertisement was brand new, the text in calling it an "heirloom of the future" transmuted the present into the past and conjured up images of the bride and groom's descendants admiring the beloved "family silver." Furthermore, it equated the new silver with heirlooms the family might already have. In so doing, a family's dead were united with its unborn through the material possessions of its living. These images were powerful ones. They work because all objects, while they physically exist only in the present, live spiritually in the mind of the viewer, where time and space are as malleable as silver.[49]

This power of objects to bridge time makes them ideal carriers of the hopes and dreams of a family or an entire people. Consequently, the passage of ideals and values from generation to generation is a seminal act, in which silverware has an important role. Silver is an ideal medium for gift giving. High in status as a precious metal and able to carry symbolic ornament, silverware has been presented to individuals and groups and passed from generation to generation for millennia as "icons of continuity."[50]

Between 1840 and 1940, silverware was often given to mark rites of passage. At birth, infants, themselves symbols of the future of their lineage, were commonly presented with silver mugs, rattles, flatware, and porringers. Offspring of wealthy families could even receive entire sets of children's silver fitted into its own chest (fig. 6.20). Similarly, for weddings silverware was the most highly valued gift (fig. 6.21). Depending on the wealth of the families being joined, gifts could range from a few silverplated spoons to elaborately ornamented creations of great expense. Throughout the ebb and flow of life, silver could also be given to mark milestones such as graduation, a sports victory, or anniversary. And at death, silver objects were typically passed to the next generation, gifts from the dead to the living. Even the gift of an object as simple as a thimble could manifest the love of the giver (fig. 6.22).

The gift, as Lewis Hyde has told us, creates bonds between people.[51] The grandparents who lovingly present their new grandchild with a silver teething ring or engraved mug do more than give the child a useful object, just as the parents who purchase silverware for their child upon the occasion of her wedding give more than something to aid her physically in her new life. The husband who presented his wife with a fish set for St. Valentine's Day strengthened the bonds of marriage (fig. 6.23), and after the funeral of her husband, the widow passes on to her

FIG. 6.20. Child's table service. Tiffany & Co., New York, N.Y., 1905.
Sterling silver and ivory. The Chrysler Museum.

FIG. 6.21. Cake plate. Shreve & Co., San Francisco, Cal., ca. 1911. Sterling silver. Dallas Museum of Art. This plate was given as a wedding present.

daughter more than a silverplated tea set. In each case the giver has selected an object that embodies his or her own values and hopes for the future. The engraved inscription on the child's mug keeps the memory of the giver alive long after he is dead, while the physical presence of a silver mug helping to nourish generations of a family continually calls forth dreams of a bright and secure future, thereby comforting the giver. The flatware chosen by a mother for her daughter tries to instill the tastes and expectations of the parent into the child, whether she desires them or not; while the family heirloom passed on in old age makes eternal the history and mythology of a family.

In 1889 the *Jewelers' Weekly* ran a cartoon showing two scenes.[52] In one a soon-to-be bride lies asleep, dreaming of a table stacked with a wide variety of elegant but useful gifts. Below she is seen gazing upon a table covered with silver cake baskets. The caption to the first reads: "Such a beautiful variety of handsome presents! Almost everything we want for housekeeping!" The second says, "Dear me! Do they expect us to live on cake?" To anyone who has ever been married, the image humorously conjures up memories of wedding gifts that they considered ridiculous, if not hideous, and could not imagine why someone ever sent them. What the girl in the cartoon did not realize, as we usually do not at the time of our marriages, is that the gifts are extensions of the givers, not embodiments of the receiver. Rather than expecting the newlyweds "to live on cake," the gift of a silver cake basket symbolized the giver's hope that the couple would always be able to have cake when they wanted it and the prosperous life that accompanies such a refined and costly food.

The humorous image of a young woman confronting a sea of unwanted cake baskets also suggests silver's role in establishing women's identity within the family. As Barbara McLean Ward has demonstrated for eighteenth-century American society, silverware, along with several other types of goods, was clearly identified with women and "the importance of the matrilineal line's contribution to the household of the marital couple, and the influence of objects displaying a connection to the wife's lineage in the preservation of complex kin relationships."[53] Legal and cultural changes had occurred by the mid nineteenth century that enabled women to inherit and own land and other property, which in the eighteenth century was reserved for males. Nevertheless, nineteenth-century America were a male-dominated society in which women's roles still centered around the home and family. In this context, silver continued to help establish a woman's identity as both homemaker and representative of the maternal line. Certainly there were exceptions that were specifically male, such as cigar humidors and smoking sets, but the vast majority of silverware was designed for and consumed by women. Women were the primary purchasers of everything from baby mugs to dressing sets. Furthermore, forms like tea and coffee sets continued as icons of femininity and a woman's role as nourisher as well as social representative of her family. While a man might join in drinking tea, women always served it, controlling the ceremony. Similarly, at weddings, rituals often commemorated with silverware, women generally purchased the gifts with the bride in mind. And it was the bride, her mother, and female friends of the bride who planned gift-giving parties before the wedding, arranged displays of the gifts

FIG. 6.22. Thimble in original box. United States; W. F. Robbins, retailer, Skowhegan, Maine; ca. 1875–1920. Silver and velvet. This example retains the original note that accompanied its presentation. It reads: "To my dear Mary whom I love the most of any girl." Dallas Museum of Art.

FIG. 6.23. Fish set. Bailey & Co., Philadelphia, Pa., ca. 1860. Sterling silver.
Private Collection, San Antonio. This set was a Valentine's Day present.

ILL. 6.4. *The Bridesmaids' Dinner*, New York, N.Y., 1905.

at home before the nuptials, and wrote thank you notes afterwards. The importance of silverware in embodying women's identity in such rituals and life in general is seen in a view of a bridesmaids' dinner given by Mrs. Eben Wright for Miss Julia Lorillard Edgar and her friends on the occasion of her wedding in 1905 (ill. 6.4). It is no coincidence that while the women ritually join together in support of one of their own, silverware surrounds the participants. Proudly displayed, the silver simultaneously embodies the desire of the giver for the bride to take her proper place as a wife and mother, and to keep the traditions, memories, and social standing of her family intact for the next generation.

SILVER AS ART

Among the many things that a piece of silver can embody is the concept of beauty. In the initial act of creation, the designer's personal ideas regarding beauty are imparted to the object, while the final act of consumption either validates or rejects that concept. Nineteenth- and early twentieth-century silverware producers and consumers understood the medium's ability to be beautiful, even considered as art. In 1878, while discussing sil-

verware, one commentator declared that "disregard of ornament as a source of enjoyment is generally an indication of mental weakness or want of culture; and as extremes meet, it is common to observe the lavish use of decorative agents and total disuse of them, alike by persons who are timid and vulgar."[54] Even the preface to Gorham's 1889 catalogue stated:

> It has been the theory of the Gorham Company that all articles within its sphere of manufacture, however commonplace or humble, could be made beautiful as well as useful; and it has aimed to advance American civilization by observing, in all its work or product, that perfect harmony between purpose, proportion, and ornamentation, which satisfies at once the mind and the eye, and which, by combining the spirit of truth with the spirit of beauty, at once educates and refines.[55]

As with Gorham's statement, comments on the purpose of silverware commonly focused on the metal's ability to embody highly refined aesthetics, which could "at once educate and refine." In fact, one of the single most important developments affecting the role of silver objects in American life dur-

ILL. 6.5. Dining room of the Leland Stanford house, San Francisco, Cal., 1874–1876.

ing this period was their recognition as art whose importance went well beyond overt utility. From the late 1860s on, most writings on American silverware stressed its artistic qualities. For example, in the early 1870s one writer stated about Gorham silver of the previous decade, "There is no hazard in saying that the Gorham Company and the brilliant cluster of artists it includes, have made this a memorable decade to the future historian of art."[56] Not only did he invoke the relatively new discipline of art history and refer to silversmiths and designers as artists in this passage, but throughout the article he compares modern work and workers with famous masterpieces and silversmiths from the past. A portrait of the great Renaissance sculptor and metalsmith Benvenuto Cellini (1500–1571), for example, opened the article.

The placement of American silverwork within this grand artistic tradition became standard over the course of the next half century. And Cellini emerged as the icon of the U.S. silver industry.[57] In 1878 New York's *International Review* published "Silver in Art," which associated the artistic nature of American silverwork with that of sixteenth-century Italy:

From the days of the restless Benvenuto Cellini until now, no process of presenting designs in metals has been so much esteemed as the *repoussé*, as the reason is manifest, for none is so clearly the work of man's mind and hand. The artist chaser can send into the pliant metal his very thought, and by the cunning of his hand render it palpable forever. The extreme ductility of silver renders

it highly susceptible to treatment by the *repoussé* process, and it is possible to produce the most delicately finished and expressive *repoussé* pictures.[58]

Even in the early twentieth century, the imbedding of American work within a grand international artistic tradition embodied by figures like Cellini was a potent idea. In 1901, for example, Gorham introduced two flatware patterns called *Florence* and *Florentine* and another in 1915 called *Cellini* in hopes of profiting from the positive associations the buying public made between silverware and high art. In her 1912 promotional article for Gorham entitled "The American Renaissance in Silversmithing," Evelyn Marie Stuart told her readers:

To Florence in the fourteenth [*sic*] century we look for the most exquisite examples of silver which the world has yet seen, and in Benvenuto Cellini we find the great master of silversmithing. Florentine is a name to conjure with. It suggests to the mind beauty, grace, elegance, and luxury delicately refined, and these are indeed characteristic of [a] style of silverware, a style having its source in the works of the early silversmiths of Florence.[59]

While some firms had used similar imagery in the 1840s and 1850s, "artistically" named flatware became common between 1860 and 1915, including patterns like *Cellini, Florence, Florentine, Italian, Angelo, Antique Athemion, Corinthian, Doric, Grecian, Ionic, Medici, Olympian, Pompeii, Raphael, Renaissance, Roma, Tuscan,* and *Venetian.*[60]

The belief that silverwork was an art form ran much deeper in the American psyche than a simple association with an older artistic tradition, however. The vocabulary of the art world and the environment of the museum came to pervade the consumption and production of silver. Usually when silver objects were purchased, their standing as *objets d'art* was heightened by their being fitted into plush presentation cases not unlike treasure chests. At the highest level these containers could be most elaborate. In 1876, for example, one reviewer said of Gorham's silver cases: "These chests . . . are among the most beautiful things in this line to be seen. The most perfect taste in display in the contrasting color of the satin linings, and in the finish of the exteriors, which are in oak, Eastlake style, French walnut, sealskin, etc."[61] Once at home, flatware was generally left in its chest and removed only when needed. Larger hollowware objects and candlesticks, however, were often put on "exhibition" so family and visitors could see them (ills. 6.4–5). Sideboards, for example, were often covered with a mass of silverware, while objects like card receivers, dressing sets, and vases populated the rest of the house.

In showrooms and jewelry stores the "artistic" nature of silverware was carried further. As noted earlier, many of these stores maintained "art rooms" and displayed silverware in glass vitrines and display windows. For world's fairs, large producers spent sizable amounts of money in creating especially elaborate objects and in designing museum-like exhibitions complete with catalogues. In return they were awarded medals by juries, as if participating in a salon for painting and sculpture. Furthermore, world's fairs helped firms gain sufficient stature to warrant the attention of authors and journalists. In the late nineteenth and early twentieth centuries, a significant number of articles on silverware appeared in *Art Journal, Magazine of Art, Connoisseur, Fine Arts Journal, International Studio,* and other periodicals. Titles such as "Silver in Art," "American Art-Work in Silver," and "Artistic Silverware" were common.

In advertising, the association of silverware with high art and culture was often overt. During the late nineteenth and early twentieth centuries, trade catalogues and other publicity material became increasingly "artistic." In 1881 Meriden Britannia Co. published a catalogue that contained romantic and painterly images of silverplated objects in association with drawings of landscapes depicting the appropriate season for particular objects. For example, a coffee and tea service is shown with a scene of winter (ill. 6.6). The preface reads: "Only artists of long experience and established talent are employed in the department of design which combined with unsurpassed facilities for manufacturing enables us to produce articles even for the most common use in a style strictly conforming to the highest rules of art."[62] These sentiments were restated by firms and newspaper reporters constantly over the next thirty years. In its 1904 catalogue, the cover of which was decorated with a beautiful figural frieze, Gorham reprinted reviews of its display at the recent St. Louis world's fair. The lead paragraph reads:

ILL. 6.6. *Winter*, from a Meriden Britannia Co. trade catalogue, 1881.

The Gorham Company have again shown by their exhibits that their work is the standard of measuring what America is doing in combining art with craftsmanship. And this union of the two is deeply interesting in showing what can be done under the stimulating conditions of freedom. For the Gorham Company has always encouraged full expression of the artist spirit and the designs shown in its exhibits in St. Louis, as were those at Chicago, Buffalo, and Paris, are creations, not copies.[63]

In his 1895 advertising George W. Shiebler even went so far as to run full-page ads that carried no copy whatsoever, excepting his firm's name and address. The piece relied totally on an image of a variety of silverware "artistically" arranged at the bottom of the page. Evidently no words were potent enough to describe the value and beauty of Shiebler silver.[64]

One result of this strong connection between silverware and art was that the silverware manufactory or workshop increasingly took on the aura of an artist's atelier. Producers found this imagery appealing, and thus they began to speak of their designers and craftsmen as artists and of their finest products as masterpieces. In a small elegant catalogue printed for the 1893 World's Columbian Exposition in Chicago, for example, Meriden Britannia Co. combined seductive drawings of its displayed products with an exotic typeface to create the desired artistic mood. The firm asserted: "The constant endeavor of our artist-designers is to give even the simplest article a high artistic character; while skilled artisans, by careful and exact workmanship, add all the desirable qualities of durability." The catalogue concluded, "We supply ornamental and useful pieces for the drawing room, the dining-room, the boudoir, the library; everywhere objects of tasteful form, rich with lustrous silver and embellished with decorations complying with the highest canons of ancient and modern art."[65] In 1910 Gorham similarly elevated its craftsmen to the level of artist in an advertisement in *House Beautiful* entitled "Revival of the Silver Age":

> The ancient Silversmith was half brother to the Alchemist. His magic touch transformed the metal into beautiful shapes and forms which found their way into the shrines of art lovers and the palaces of kings.
>
> Side by side with the Sculptor who produced the Venus and the Painter who gave the world a Madonna the ancient Silversmith held high place in the realm of art.
>
> Today his ancient and honorable craft is preserved and exemplified at its best in the beautiful creations offered by The Gorham Company through the best jewelers.[66]

The following year, the Pittsburgh retailer, Grogan & Co., printed a colorful and artistically rendered booklet called *The Search for Beauty: Art*. Intended to promote Gorham's *Martelé* silver line, both its illustrations and text praise this handmade silverware as the latest achievement in the age-old tradition of fine silverworking. Below an illustration depicting a working chaser surrounded by fellow silversmiths from past epochs, the copy proclaims:

> We are the heirs of thousands of years of striving, blessed and surrounded by things beautiful; it will be well for us if we remember, as we look upon some creation of art, that *this* represents, not one man's effort, not yet the labor of one year or of one century. But here, in every work, there is something that has been handed down the ages — something from the faraway dreamer of Babylon, or a touch of mystic Egypt, or a design from the Greek who first hammered metals into lyric poems.
>
> All people who lifted up their souls to create contribute to this, our heritage of spiritual beauty. By the light of such labor, upward through centuries of struggles, ignorance, blind persecution, and wars, man has risen. The history of his soul is written in the beautiful things he has created.[67]

Thus, if one believed what Grogan & Co. said, one could participate in this great tradition of artists and noble creations by purchasing a piece of fine silverware, especially an example of *Martelé*. The text drove home this point when it concluded, "And if the greatest work one can achieve is the creation of beauty, perhaps the second greatest achievement is to attain appreciation of beauty. It is well to realize that true ownership rests not in mere possession, but in appreciation."

The fact that silverworkers came to be seen increasingly as artists meant that many of their finest creations were viewed as major artistic masterpieces. The best example of a single object assuming the mantle of high art is the *Bryant Vase* (fig. 6.24). On the occasion of his birthday in November 1874, a group of his admirers told the famous American poet William Cullen Bryant (1794–1878) that they planned to commission a presentation vase in his honor. Following a call for designs, five proposals were seriously considered. Among the competing designers and their respective firms were James T. Pairpoint of Gorham, Charles Osborne of Whiting, and Charles Witteck, who provided competition designs for both Starr & Marcus and Black, Starr & Frost. Tiffany & Co.'s winning entry was designed by the English-trained James H. Whitehouse (1833–1902), who was the head of the chasing department. Following more than a year's worth of work by Tiffany & Co.'s finest chaser, Eugene J. Soligny, the vase was presented to Bryant in June 1876, after which it was sent to Philadelphia for exhibition in the Tiffany's display. At the 1878 Paris world's fair, Tiffany's exhibited an electrotyped replica of the vase.[68]

The excitement that surrounded the creation of this testimonial to William Cullen Bryant was extraordinary.[69] The national subscription campaign, the design competition, and the unveiling were all widely covered by both popular and professional presses. As late as 1890 articles were still being written on the *Bryant Vase*. Beyond lengthy descriptions of the vase's iconography, which referred to America and Bryant's poetic opus, authors typically waxed eloquent about the vase's embodiment of high art and its meaning to the nation. In 1876 the Rev. Dr. Samuel Osgood, writing for *Harper's New Monthly Magazine*, associated the *Bryant Vase* with the works of the Renaissance masters Cellini, Ghiberti, Brunelleschi, and Donatello, "in which the metal bears to the work very much the relation that the canvas bears to the painter's masterpiece." He concluded that the country could be justly proud of this great accomplishment which "combine[s] Greek culture with Christian faith, and lifts this tribute to a man into a monument of the life of the age and of the mind of the nation."[70] A year later the *Jeweler, Silversmith and Watchmaker* stated the trade's appreciation for the work's technical perfection when in an article called "Art in Metals" it noted that the vase was equal to and in many ways surpassed the finest work of contemporary European artisans, including Morel-Ladeuil, Antoine Vecht (1799–1868), or Désiré Attarge (ca. 1820–1878).[71] Such comments left few doubts in the minds of American producers and consumers alike that the silverworkers of this country were worthy standard-bearers of a long and glorious tradition of artistic silversmithing and that their finest achievements not only belonged in the nation's homes, where they could educate and refine its citizens, but in its burgeoning art museums in New York (1870), Boston (1876), and Philadelphia (1876).[72] In 1877 the *Bryant Vase* was the first piece of American silver to enter the collection of the recently founded Metropolitan Museum of Art.

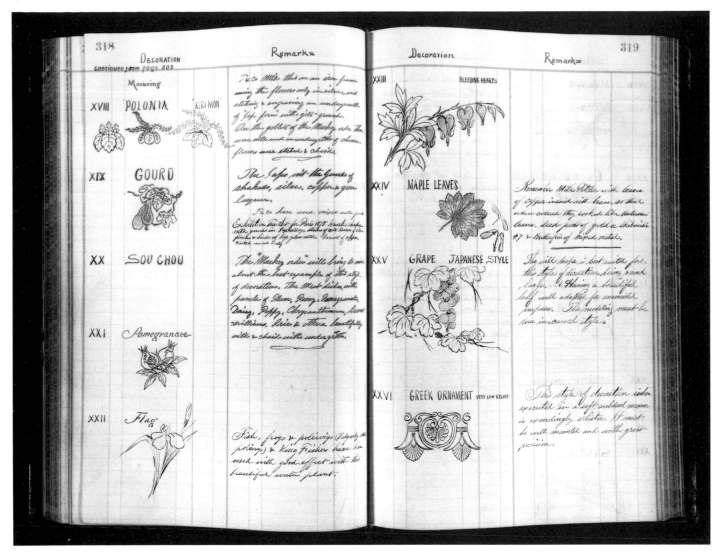

ILL. 6.7. Pages from a Gorham Mfg. Co. technical notebook, ca. 1877–1878.

To ensure that they could maintain the level of artistic design and technical expertise that the production of *objets d'art* demanded, manufacturers tried hard to attract and maintain the most talented designers and master craftsmen possible. Before 1875 entrepreneurs like John Gorham had successfully wooed skilled workmen and a few designers from Europe, especially England. Once here, these skilled foreigners trained American-born workmen who formed the majority of craftsmen employed in the industry by the late nineteenth century. The importance of attracting the finest craftsmen is illustrated by the case of Frederick A. Jordan. Although as yet little is known about him, research by Samuel Hough indicates that he worked as a chaser in Tiffany & Co.'s Prince Street manufactory in the 1870s where he learned an enormous amount concerning the recent foray of Tiffany's into Japanese design and the use of mixed metals. In 1878 he was hired away by Gorham. In Providence he provided his new employer with a wealth of information about its rival's progress, as evidenced by his annotations in a Gorham technical notebook (ill. 6.7).[73] Because workers like Jordan possessed such extensive and valuable knowledge when fully trained, manufacturers tried unceasingly to educate and retain their own employees. Simultaneously, they sought to lure gifted employees away from their competitors.

To guarantee a steady supply of qualified workers, some larger firms developed instructional programs for designers and craftsmen that went beyond the standard apprenticeship system. Tiffany & Co., for example, was lauded by the press for the thorough course of study it offered apprentices. To hone its trainees' skills, Tiffany's held competitions and offered cash awards to those producing the finest designs and examples of chasing, repoussé, raising, and other technical skills.[74] With its fine design and technical library and excellent teachers, like designers Edward C. Moore and Charles T. Grosjean, the so-called "Tiffany School" produced some outstanding talents, including the American-born designers John T. Curran and Paulding Farnham

FIG. 6.24. *Bryant Vase.* James H. Whitehouse, designer; Tiffany & Co., maker, New York, N.Y.; 1875–1876. Sterling silver and gold. © 1989 The Metropolitan Museum of Art.

(1859–1927). Curran is best known for the flatware patterns he designed for Tiffany's and the *Magnolia Vase*, which he designed for the 1889 Paris Exposition (ill. 5.15).[75] Farnham designed many of the firm's most lavish jewelry and silver creations between 1885 and his departure in 1908 (fig. 6.66). In 1893 a French observer reported that Tiffany & Co. employed twelve designers under the direction of Paulding Farnham.[76]

Native-born craftsmen and artists who were trained within the industry, as well as older artists, were a great source of pride for American manufacturers and the trade press. In 1881, for example, a writer for the *Jewelers' Circular* commented:

> The very best workmen in the business, men possessing the rarest skills and the most comprehensive knowledge of art, are Americans, born in this country, educated in our workshop, and developing their latent talents in strict obedience to the spirit of Yankee progressivism that is irresistible. Some of the most elaborate work with which this generation is familiar is the product of men who have never been outside this country and whose whole training has been in American workshops.[77]

While the apprentice system did produce a large number of workers for the silverware industry, others, especially designers, were educated in technical schools founded in the second half of the nineteenth century. The most important of these institutions were New York City's National Academy of Design (founded 1826), Art School of the Cooper Union (1857), Art Students League (1875), and Pratt Institute (1886), as well as the Cincinnati School of Design (1869), the Rhode Island School of Design (1877), and the Newark Technical School (1885). An example of a designer who was academically trained in the United States before entering the silver trade is Charles Osborne (1848–1920, ill. 6.8). Following studies at the National Academy of Design, Osborne went to work for Whiting in 1871 at a starting annual salary of $1,800.[78] Osborne's work was impressive from the start. For example, a fork and cheese scoop from the 1870s attest to the high quality achieved by Whiting under Osborne's design leadership (fig. 6.25). Concerning his unsuccessful attempt to gain the *Bryant Vase* commission, Osborne's brother, who was a Whiting salesman, wrote to him:

> Am also <u>very</u> sorry you [were] disappointed in the matter of the "Bryant." You deserved it and I think would have had it if the thing had been fairly decided: at all events the attempt has given you a big name among the principal houses, many of whom declare yours to be the best design by far—It has also raised you very much in the estimation of our house. Mr. B[uckley] told Joe Reach to-day that "there is not a house in the country able to hire you from them." How is that for high? When you next make arrangements with them don't you forget this and put your figure high enough.[79]

As noted, Osborne was well respected within the industry, and several firms vied for his talent. On 2 November 1878, for ex-

ILL. 6.8. Charles Osborne at work, ca. 1900.

ample, H. Blanchard Dominick of Dominick & Haff wrote Osborne, saying they "would be glad to see [him] at [their] office to talk over some matters of business." In the event that Osborne felt that location was too obvious, Dominick and Haff would meet him at an alternative place. Dominick was unsuccessful, but Tiffany & Co. did entice Osborne away from Whiting just two weeks later. On 15 November 1878, Osborne resigned from Whiting, writing:

> I have long felt that I was making no real progress in my art work; and that I would be glad if I could find an opening, a place, where I could have a larger field for what talent I do possess. I felt that what I knew was superficial and that I needed to go to school—for many things were to be learned that I was not in the way of learning—that I needed more solid basis in my art education and that I should properly be under a master—who could guide and instruct me so as to make me more able & thorough for the rest of my life.
>
> I became acquainted with Mr. Moore of Tiffany & Co. and recognized in him a man whom I believe has in him all the qualities I desire in a master.
>
> I broached the subject to him, and explained my wishes. He has been good enough to think favorable on the matter—and the result is that I have found an engagement with him for a period of three years. I could have gone from you to other places—but would not. I

FIG. 6.25. Serving fork and scoop. Whiting Mfg. Co., New York, N.Y., ca. 1875–1880. Sterling silver. Dallas Museum of Art.

(ill. 9.2). It also reveals that Whiting, unlike bigger firms like Gorham and Tiffany's, produced exceptional handmade silverware in relatively small quantities. Ranging from a high of forty-five (October 1884) to a low of nine (January 1885) pieces, the monthly average for the shop was twenty-eight over the course of the two years from March 1884 to March 1886. In any given month a wide range of work was in process simultaneously, from trophies and tureens to buckles and purse corners.[82]

Regardless of its standing as a middle-size producer, Whiting gained a fine reputation under Charles Osborne's design leadership. In 1893 an official French governmental report on silversmithing in America ranked Whiting third in both taste and production behind Tiffany's and Gorham. Noting that while Osborne's style was "a mixture of Hindoo, Japanese, and Chinese" and that it owed much to Edward C. Moore, the report was most enthusiastic about Osborne's flatware designs for Whiting, especially *Ivory* (patented 1891), which it said had "an air of originality and great richness" (fig. 6.27). Concerning flatware in general it states:

> Whiting possesses one of the most interesting and numerous collections of table ware—tea spoons, and all the small useful objects which constitute small silverware. This silversmith is very original in his creations, and it is a pleasure to examine the diversity of his models, the variety of their decoration, where one finds arrangements full of taste, inspired by a serious study of nature.[83]

Charles Osborne's talents were evidently also appreciated by Whiting's management, because by 1892 he was superintendent, and by 1905, he had become a vice-president in the firm. In 1915, however, he left Whiting to become vice-president and head of design at the Sweetser Co., which produced small silver items. He remained there until he died in 1920 after an accident.[84]

While the apprentice system and design schools supplied a large part of those working in the American silverware field, many foreign-trained workers were still recruited throughout the industry. A few of these men were Americans who had gone to Europe to study. For example, Albert A. Southwick, who was designing for Tiffany & Co. in 1906, had sailed to Europe at age twenty-one, following some practical experience at engraving and die cutting in this country. In Berlin he studied steel engraving, after which he traveled to Dresden, Vienna, and Paris. In 1898 he took an examination at the Ecole des Beaux Arts and studied metalworking in the studios of Julian, Constant, and Laurens.[85]

Most foreign-trained workers in the American silverware industry were not natives, however. Both the designer and chaser of the *Bryant Vase* were foreign. James Horton Whitehouse had trained in England at Elkington & Co. with the famous designer/chaser Leonard Morel-Ladeuil before becoming head of Tiffany's engraving department around 1858. Similarly, Eugene J. Soligny, the French master chaser who executed Whitehouse's design, worked for Tiffany & Co. from the late 1860s until his

feel however that I cannot afford to let this opportunity for higher development pass by.[80]

Evidently based on nothing more than a "verbal understanding," Charles Osborne worked for Tiffany & Co. for the next nine years.

In January 1888, however, Whiting wooed Osborne back as head designer by offering him a four-year contract in which he would receive fifty shares of company stock annually along with his salary.[81] Due to Osborne's return, Whiting's design aesthetic became ever closer to that of Tiffany & Co. during the late nineteenth and early twentieth centuries. However, surviving objects indicate that Whiting was already working in the Tiffany's style before Osborne returned (fig. 6.26). A workshop ledger that contains dated miniature drawings of presumably all custom-order hollowware produced between 1884 and 1898 further documents Tiffany & Co.'s influence on Whiting

FIG. 6.26. *Goelet Schooner Prize.* Whiting Mfg. Co., New York, N.Y., ca. 1882. Sterling silver, enamel, and glass. © 1994 The Metropolitan Museum of Art, lent by Samuel Schwartz.

FIG. 6.27. *Ivory* pattern jelly server. Charles Osborne, designer; Whiting Mfg. Co., maker, New York, N.Y.; designed 1890. Sterling silver, silvergilt, and ivory. Dallas Museum of Art.

ILL. 6.9. William Christmas Codman, ca. 1895.

death in 1901. Tiffany's was also responsible for bringing the master die sinker and designer F. Antoine Heller from Paris to New York in 1873, although he did not work for the firm until 1877–80. Beyond Tiffany's, foreign-trained designers existed throughout the entire industry. Around 1874, for example, Reed & Barton brought W. C. Beattie from England to be its first professional designer. In 1889 Beattie was succeeded by another English-trained designer, A. F. Jackson, who remained with the firm until around 1900. According to George Gibb, a similar situation existed at the Meriden Britannia Co.[86]

Gorham also employed a series of foreign-trained designers. The first was the Englishman George Wilkinson, who worked in Providence from 1854 to 1891. Others at Gorham included Thomas J. Pairpoint (d. 1902) and F. A. Heller. Pairpoint was with the firm from 1868 to 1877. For the next three years he worked for the Meriden Britannia Co. before co-founding the Pairpoint Mfg. Co. in New Bedford, Massachusetts, in 1880.[87] Heller began work for Gorham and remained in its employ until 1876. Following an engagement at Tiffany's, he returned to Gorham in 1880 and stayed with that firm until his death in 1904.[88] In 1891, Gorham hired an Englishman who would be its chief designer for the next quarter century—William Christmas Codman (1839–1921, ill. 6.9).

As Charles Carpenter has explained, William Codman had worked as an ecclesiastical designer for the English firm of Elkington & Co. before coming to America.[89] Objects he designed for these companies were widely appreciated and purchased by parishes from Ottawa to Delhi. Gorham added an ecclesiastical fixtures department in 1885, prompting management to look for a designer with experience in the field. After his arrival, Codman spent the first two years working on objects for Gorham's display at the 1893 World's Columbian Exposition in Chicago. The richness and academic nature of much of the silver Codman designed for the fair is reflected in the *Nautilus Centerpiece* (fig. 5.10). Patterned after Renaissance Italian and German prototypes, the work is very much in the academic taste popularized by the Ecole des Beaux Arts in Paris.

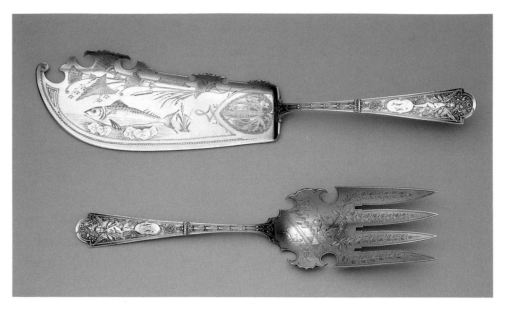

FIG. 6.28. *Cupid* pattern fish set. Morgan Morgans, Jr., New York, N.Y., patented 1878.
Sterling silver and silvergilt. D. Albert Soeffing Collection.

The combination of the classical reference to the birth of Venus, who rose from the sea, and the work's rich materials of silver, gold, shell, pearls, and a variety of semiprecious stones are in keeping with the beaux-arts tradition. Codman was a versatile designer, and his most famous contribution to American silver was Gorham's *Martelé* line, which he initiated in 1896 in conjunction with the company's president, William Holbrook.[90] As discussed below, this line of handwrought goods was based on the philosophy of the arts and crafts movement, which was spreading throughout Europe and America in the 1890s. Popular through the first decade of the new century, *Martelé* was falling from favor by 1909. In 1914, at the age of seventy-five, William C. Codman left Gorham and returned to England, where he died in 1921.

Codman retired just as his greatest achievement, the *Martelé* line, was fading from popularity. Nevertheless, his contribution to Gorham and the American silverware industry in general was substantial. As Charles Carpenter has explained, Codman designed no fewer than fifty-five flatware patterns for the company, including *Chantilly* (1895), reportedly the most popular pattern ever made. Furthermore, he was responsible for most of the objects that Gorham displayed at the world's fairs in Chicago, Paris, Turin, and St. Louis. With such achievements, it leaves little doubt that William C. Codman was in large part responsible for the continued acclaim that Gorham received at home and abroad between 1891 and 1914.

Besides educating native designers and craftsmen and hiring the finest possible workers from abroad, American silverware manufacturers often protected the technical and artistic contributions of these individuals through patents. For example, flatware patterns, which were the lifeblood of the industry, were sometimes patented. Beginning in the mid 1840s numerous silversmiths, including William Gale, Michael Gibney, Philo B. Gilbert, Morgan Morgans, Jr., John Polhamus, George Sharp,

John R. Wendt, and George Wilkinson, sought protection for their flatware by obtaining design patents (fig. 6.28).[91] D. Albert Soeffing estimates that of the 500 to 700 different flatware patterns produced in this country between 1840 and 1875, approximately 15 to 20 percent were patented. The tradition continued into the late nineteenth and early twentieth centuries with prolific designers like Moore, Grosjean, Heller, Codman, and Osborne patenting patterns.[92] Besides flatware patterns, hollowware designs as well as technical processes and devices were sometimes patented.

It was not uncommon for rival firms to infringe on another's patents as competition intensified during the second half of the nineteenth century. If the trespass could not be worked out privately, legal battles often resulted. Dominick & Haff, for example, seems to have been particularly aggressive in protecting its design patents. In 1890 it ran full-page notices in the *Jewelers' Circular* stating that designs for the illustrated flatware had been sustained in federal court. In conclusion the firm warned: "It is our purpose to protect our rights to all our patents and to prosecute rigorously all persons who may be found making or selling goods—whether spoons, or other articles—that carry an imitation of our patent assigned."[93] In 1903 Dominick & Haff again ran full-page copy in the trade press entitled "WARNING!" that told rivals to stop producing copies of its patented art nouveau candlestick.[94]

Like designs, technical knowledge was often protected legally. As the research of D. Albert Soeffing has shown, for example, Tiffany & Co. went to great lengths to protect the patent it had been assigned in 1872 for putting a "satin finish" on sterling wares through the use of rotating brushes. While it could do nothing about the use of "satin finish" on plated wares, which was protected by earlier patents it did not control, Tiffany's successfully litigated against other large firms who did not pay royalties during the late nineteenth century.[95] In 1905

ILL. 6.10. *Helicon Vase*, by Leonard Morel-Ladeuil for Frederick Elkington & Co., 1871.

Gorham found itself in a similar situation. It had developed and patented a new material for making casting molds from plaster of Paris and nonmelting fibers, such as asbestos, as well as on particular uses of rubber patterns to construct intricate molds. Tiffany's and Whiting took out licenses to use the new materials, but other firms did not. Consequently, Gorham sued the Mauser Mfg. Co., Dominick & Haff, and Graff, Washbourne & Dunn, as well as one Joseph G. Weyer of Providence.[96]

STYLISTIC DEVELOPMENTS: NEOCLASSICISM

The designs that were created by artists and craftsmen and occasionally patented throughout the industry between 1875 and 1915 covered a broad spectrum. Beginning with publications like Owen Jones's *Grammar of Ornament* (1856), art historians, anthropologists, archaeologists, and designers catalogued the art and artifacts of ancient and modern, known and exotic cultures from around the world during the second half of the nineteenth century. Simultaneously, innovations in printing leading to the proliferation of books and periodicals, improvements in transportation that made travel easier, and the establishment of art museums and world's fairs as exhibition forums all promoted the exchange of this artistic and historical information on an international scale as never before. The result was that by the 1880s American designers and craftsmen had access to the same design and technical publications as their European counterparts. Furthermore, the illustration first by woodcut and then by photogravure of contemporary silver objects from around the globe meant that visual comparisons could be made relatively easily.

Americans flourished in this new environment, finding inspiration for silverware in myriad cultures and epochs. For-

eign observers were quick to note how free this country's designers and craftsmen seemed to be in comparison to many of their transatlantic counterparts. In the British *Magazine of Art* in 1886, A. St. Johnston suggested that the reason why American silverwork was more adventuresome and thus more innovative than the English was because the silversmiths of Great Britain were bound by their long and often glorious tradition of fine metalworking. With all its Guild Hall rules, including strict purity standards that did not permit innovations like mixed metals, and overwhelming adherence to the styles of the late seventeenth and eighteenth centuries, Britain discouraged originality in metalworking.[97] The American Horace Townsend captured the spirit of St. Johnston's remarks in a speech entitled "American Silverwork" that he read before London's Society of Arts in 1893.

> Roughly speaking, we may say that the silverwork of England is a tradition, and that of America a discovery. . . . As in their architecture so in their subsidiary arts, the Americans seem unconsciously to assimilate, in a degree unknown to nations fettered by the bonds of tradition, all that is good in the art work of other peoples, and at the same time to impart to the conglomeration thus obtained a distinct flavor of their own individuality. . . . But in England there exists, among trade silverworkers, as I have already hinted, a more than slavish adherence to tradition and a slothfulness of mind, as it were, which no other craft can parallel.[98]

A comparison of British and U.S. silver objects from the late nineteenth century supports the hypothesis of St. Johnston and

FIG. 6.29. *Neptune Epergne* and plateau from the *Furber Service.* Attributed to Thomas Pairpoint, designer; Gorham Mfg. Co., maker, Providence, R.I.; 1872 and 1876. Sterling silver, silvergilt, and glass. Museum of Art, Rhode Island School of Design.

Townsend. Most British silverware from this period is directly inspired by or copied from earlier London-made prototypes. Those that are innovative in design, materials, or technique are definitely the exception.

George Wilkinson dominated American silver design of the 1860s. Although his influence waned in the 1870s, objects in the Wilkinson style continued to be made on a limited scale during the last decades of the century. On the whole, however, the classical impulse in American silver moved away from Wilkinson's ideas towards Renaissance and baroque concepts. At the highest level, this shift is seen in display pieces created in the 1870s for international expositions. As mentioned above, both Gorham and Reed & Barton created monumental vases

as centerpieces for their exhibits at the 1876 Philadelphia Centennial fair. The *Century Vase* and the *Progress Vase* (ill. 5.11, fig. 5.7) were similar in composition. The affinity resulted from the fact that both were patterned after Elkington's *Helicon Vase* (ill. 6.10), which was first exhibited at the 1872 Industrial Exhibition in London and then again at the 1873 Vienna world's fair. The creator of the vase was the Frenchman Leonard Morel-Ladeuil (1820–1888). Famous as a chaser/sculptor before leaving France, Morel-Ladeuil came to England to work for Elkington in 1859 and continued in their employ until his death.[99] Characteristic of the heavy, figurative style of silverware that had developed in France and England in the 1840 to 1875 period, Morel-Ladeuil's composition illustrates the "Triumph of

FIG. 6.30. *Dewey Loving Cup.* William C. Codman, designer; Gorham Mfg. Co., maker, Providence, R.I.; 1899. Sterling silver, silvergilt, enamel, and wood. Collection of the Chicago Historical Society.

Music and Poetry." Described as in the Italian Renaissance style, the composition consists of a tall, central, two-handled vase flanked by a pair of recumbent figures. The work rests on a plateau. Cast and chased with exceptional skill over the course of six years, the *Helicon Vase* was widely illustrated following the 1873 fair. According to one observer, the jury in Vienna "declared it to be at once the most important as well as the most beautiful production in metal of modern times."[100] Given such lavish praise, it is not surprising that by the time the vase came to Philadelphia in 1876, several firms who hoped to rival Elkington as major silver producers had created similar vases. At least three versions were shown at the Centennial, one by the Danish firm of Christenson & Co. and the two American examples. All three copied Morel-Ladeuil's composition of a plateau supporting a central vase flanked by figural groups.

The designers of the American vases were George Wilkinson and Thomas Pairpoint at Gorham and W. C. Beattie at Reed & Barton. Because they had left England relatively recently, Pairpoint and Beattie would have had intimate knowledge of the heavy, figural style embodied by Ladeuil's vase. Unfortunately, however, their adaptations coincided with the decline of this monumental style, resulting in mixed reviews from critics. A writer for the *New York Times* in 1876 reflected this feeling: "The Helicon vase is the great object of universal admiration, and has doubtless been described again and again. For my part I think it, with the exception of the *repoussé* work on the small body of the vase, a soulless and conventional bit of work." A month later he continued, "It is in every respect a magnificent specimen of *repoussé* work and damascening. Morel, the artist, is undoubtedly a great *repoussé* worker, a master of technique, but unfortunately he is not a great designer, and his work, wonderful as it is in execution, is altogether unsatisfactory in design and effect."[101] Predictably, this writer believed the figures on the *Century Vase* to be poorly modeled and the overall composition lacking. The chasing was, however, "equal, if not superior, to anything in the Exhibition."[102] Although some observers still admired the *Century Vase* in later years,[103] Gorham's inclusion of the piece in its 1889 and 1893 world's fair exhibits became increasingly criticized, indicating the fall from favor of the work's retardataire style. In his 1893 official report, for example, a French critic chose simply to quote the judgment that his countryman M. L. Falize had made on the vase when it was in Paris four years earlier:

> That which betrays inexperience, and which marks a lack of taste among these silversmiths, is the importance which they attach to the huge piece which they call the Century Vase. . . . It is a sort of a trophy, on which is erected a pyramidical group of badly modeled allegorical figures — badly arranged, and which reveal all the inexperience of the sculptor and decorator.[104]

American designers seldom chose to imitate so closely their European counterparts following the production of the *Century* and *Progress* vases. However, they did continue to work in the classical taste. In some cases these designs accommodated classical decorative motifs in their ancient or Renaissance forms to innovative body forms; or they enriched traditional forms with interesting ornament. A fine example of the former process is the *Neptune Epergne* of 1876, which was designed for Gorham by Thomas J. Pairpoint as part of the massive dining service ordered by Colonel and Mrs. Henry Jewett Furber (fig. 6.29). Although the overall composition is slightly reminiscent of the *Helicon Vase*, being pyramidal and placed on a plateau, it is on the whole quite innovative. For example, the pair of lower baskets are navette-shaped and cantilever out from the central shaft, and the upper ones thrust out into space on scrolls. Adding further excitement to the work is the figure of Aurora, who seems to hover above the composition. The work is enlivened with color through a sophisticated use of gilt elements that contrast with silver areas.

More typical than such eccentric uses of neoclassicism were objects that derived both their form and decoration from classical and Renaissance prototypes. The *Dewey Loving Cup*, for example, takes from the antique its urn form as well as the decorative elements of eagle, dolphin, wreath, shell, acanthus leaf, and winged figure of victory (fig. 6.30).[105] A wine cooler by Tiffany & Co. is even closer to its ancient sources (fig. 6.31). The vessel's shape is based directly on classical ceramic wine *kraters* made in southern Italy. Typical of these ceramic prototypes are the bold handles scrolling up around the lip. Furthermore, the details of fluting, dentils, and grape vines are all found on ancient metalwork, although not necessarily in this configuration. A similar situation exists with a water jug on stand made by Samuel Kirk & Son (fig. 6.32). In this case inspiration for both form and decoration was found in Renaissance metalwork featuring grotesque-style scrollwork of classical elements. In the Baltimore example, classical dolphins and acanthus leaves abound and a herm-like figure peers from beneath the spout.

Overall, the classical impulse was probably the most persistent of all in American silver design. Having its roots in early-eighteenth-century British America and flourishing from 1790 to 1840, this style dominated once again in the 1860s and early 1870s. For the rest of the century under discussion, it remained one of the most important styles among the many available to silverware designers. Nevertheless, the silverware that brought international attention to this country was more exotic in nature.

THE MORESQUE AND RELATED STYLES

Throughout the entire 1875 to 1915 period, American designers and craftsmen sought out myriad techniques, forms, and ornament to incorporate into their own work. In 1893 an

FIG. 6.31. Wine cooler. Tiffany & Co., New York, N.Y., 1900. Sterling silver and copper.
© 1992 The Art Institute of Chicago.

FIG. 6.33. Teapot from a three-piece set. Edward C. Moore, maker; Tiffany & Co., retailer, New York, N.Y.; 1867. Sterling silver, ivory, and silvergilt. Philadelphia Museum of Art.

American observer commented on this artistic quest before the Society of Arts in London:

> Here in England we are content, not so much to endeavor to revivify a corpse, as to hospitably entreat, and to be perfectly satisfied with the presence at our feasts of the mere mummy of an art. To travel out of the path beaten by the hammers, of the ruts cut by the gravers of two centuries ago, seems to the English smith not only useless, but positively vicious. . . . In America, on the contrary, he is ever on the lookout, not only among the archaeological dust-heaps of the centuries, but in the world of science of to-day, and the almost newly-discovered world of still living Oriental art.[106]

In fact, by the time these remarks were made, American silver-workers had been finding inspiration in Asian art as well as the related arts of the Near East, India, and Russia, for a full quarter century. The earliest work of this type was done by Tiffany & Co. under the direction of its designer Edward C. Moore, who had traveled in Europe and had an extensive knowledge of world art history. In the late 1860s he began experimenting with designs that Tiffany's records call moresque. Based on the intricate, interlacing scrollwork found throughout the applied arts of the Islamic world, this early moresque style was used only for surface decoration, the basic body forms remaining untouched. The first example of it to be widely seen and reproduced in the press was a tea set exhibited at the 1867 Paris world's fair (fig. 6.33).

FIG. 6.32. Water jug and stand. Samuel Kirk & Son, Baltimore, Md., 1879. Silver. The Maryland Historical Society.

FIG. 6.34. Coffee set. Tiffany & Co., New York, N.Y., 1902–1903. Sterling silver, silvergilt,
enamel, ivory, and pearls. The Masco Art Collection.

During the 1870s Moore's use of the style broadened, developing into what became known variously as the Persian, Saracenic, or East Indian style. Certainly other designers eventually worked in the idiom, but Moore's efforts were rightly recognized as the driving force behind the fashion. In 1893, for example, a French observer noted the importance to American design of Moore as well as the style:

A man of taste and invention, Mr. Moore had traveled much; he had seen and had seen it intelligently. He had brought back from his travels most complete collections of dies, photographs, authentic specimens of the Arts of Persia, India, China and Japan. He had appropriated their ideas, their methods of decoration, and from all this he drew a new expression, suiting exactly the taste of cultivated women who wished novelties; he baptized with the name "Moresque Style," a style which was neither Egyptian, nor Hindoo, nor Japanese, but an individual and personal conception of Oriental Art, which the name of "American style" would suit much better today.[107]

Two decades before these words were written, Moore's work in the style was primarily confined to influences from the Near East. A coffeepot from 1874, for example, shows how close Moore could stay to foreign prototypes without losing any creative vitality (fig. 5.6). The attenuated shape of the pot is directly based on Near Eastern brass examples, while the decoration is derived from Near Eastern and Indian sources. In fact, when this "Turkish" coffeepot was included in Tiffany's exhibition at the 1876 Philadelphia world's fair, the Turkish department had on display a pot of similar form, and the Indian department had two water bottles with similar bulbous shapes and domed tops. One also had a spiral-fluted and collared neck, like Moore's.[108]

The moresque style reached its height of popularity in the 1870s and 1880s, but remained in fashion well into the twentieth century. Tiffany & Co., for example, executed a gilt coffee set decorated with pearls and green enamel in the style in 1902 (fig. 6.34). Between 1880 and World War I, the most popular variants of the taste appear to have been the "Saracenic" or

FIG. 6.35. *Four-Elephant Fruit Stand.* Gorham Mfg. Co., Providence, R.I., 1881.
Sterling silver and silvergilt. The Masco Art Collection.

"East Indian." Compared to designs from the Near East, objects in these styles tend to have much denser patterning and often incorporate decorative elements like textiles and elephants. An exceptional example is an 1881 fruit stand by Gorham. In keeping with the East Indian theme, the vessel takes the form of a textile-draped litter supported by four elaborate elephants (fig. 6.35). The 1889 Paris world's fair appears to have been the apex of the style's popularity, for both Tiffany's and Gorham exhibited large numbers of objects described as "Saracenic" or "East Indian." Nevertheless, objects continued to be made in this exotic taste until World War I.[109] In 1910 Tiffany & Co. created an extraordinary silver and ivory flagon complete with a parade of elephants around the base (fig. 6.36). Although the overt use of Near Eastern and East Indian design elements passed from fashion in the early twentieth century, more conservative variants remained popular. Tiffany's line of flat- and hollowware decorated with "Indian chrysanthemums," which was introduced in the 1880s, for example, remained in fashion

with the buying public through the early twentieth century. The flatware pattern *Chrysanthemum*, which had been designed in 1880, was not discontinued until 1934.[110]

The intricate and dense ornament that characterized the moresque style and its variants between 1875 and 1915 was related to those of other cultures, which were also used on silverware by many U.S. producers. For example, wares bearing interlacing motifs native to Scandinavia, Ireland, and New Zealand are known, including a covered beaker by Tiffany & Co. that is decorated with Teutonic or Celtic motifs (fig. 6.37).[111] More important than these influences, however, was that of Russia.

THE RUSSIAN TASTE
It is known that some Russian-made silverware was imported into the United States during the second half of the nineteenth century. In 1891 Tiffany & Co. staged an entire exhibit of Russian silver.[112] Furthermore, the existence of pieces like a trompe

Consumption and Design

FACING PAGE: FIG. 6.36. Flagon. Tiffany & Co., New York, N.Y., 1910. Sterling silver, silvergilt, ivory, and semiprecious stones. Private Collection, courtesy Hoffman Gampetro Antiques.

FIG. 6.37. Covered beaker. Tiffany & Co., New York, N.Y., ca. 1878. Sterling silver and moonstones. The Carnegie Museum of Art.

Fig. 6.38. Beer pitcher. Bailey & Co., Philadelphia, Pa., ca. 1860–1868.
Sterling silver. Dallas Museum of Art.

l'oeil ice-water set by Meriden Britannia and a beer pitcher by Bailey & Co. reveals that Russian influence was being felt in this country in the 1860s and early 1870s (figs. 5.4, 6.38). Nevertheless, most Russian-inspired American work dates from the last quarter of the nineteenth century and appears to have been stimulated by the Russian exhibits sent to world's fairs during these decades. At the 1876 Philadelphia exhibition Americans were fascinated by the Russian examples of chasing that imitated wood and textiles, as well as pieces with enameling and niello work. A contemporary wrote:

> Russia presented to the attention of the Judges an admirable and profuse display of fascinating examples of her manufactures in gold and silver, in fine bronze, and in articles made of Russian ornamental stones. There were many novelties in their court that were a revelation to an American. The remarkable silver-ware simply displayed by Sazikoff and others, both from St. Petersburg and

Moscow, in specimens of repoussé and chiseled effects, and the peculiar representations of linen and damask in this metal, with the radiant beauty of the gem-like enameling upon gold and silver and gilded silver utensils in Greek, Byzantine, and Asian taste, were such marvelous illustrations of the capabilities and truly artistic fancy of Russian artisans as would have awakened the enthusiasm of a Benvenuto Cellini and that of the historical Palissy, the famed enameler of Limoges. There was much of ingenious and pleasing caprice in the novelties in silver and in the gold jewelry and niello-work that were suggestive to the American workers in the precious metals.[113]

The examples of Russian silver that imitated textiles prompted several firms in this country, as well as England and France, to work in a similar trompe l'oeil style.[114] Although other firms, including Whiting, are known to have made silverware with textile-type decoration (fig. 6.39), the most prolific producer

FIG. 6.39. Coffeepot. Whiting Mfg. Co., New York, N.Y., ca. 1883.
Sterling silver, ivory, and silvergilt. Dallas Museum of Art.

FIG. 6.40. Tray. Attributed to Kennard & Jenks, maker, Boston, Mass.; Bailey, Banks & Biddle, retailer, Philadelphia, Pa.; ca. 1878–1880. Sterling silver. Mr. and Mrs. Alexander C. Speyer III Collection.

was Gorham. During the late 1870s and 1880s, the firm made a series of incredible objects inspired by Russian work that simulated cloth, straw, and dented surfaces. Initially, Gorham appears to have used the Boston firm of Kennard & Jenks as a specialty subcontractor for such wares before purchasing and moving the Boston firm's production facilities to Providence in 1880 (fig. 6.40).[115]

The Russian specialty of niello work was also used by some American makers, as it was in Europe, for objects in various styles.[116] Niello work involves inlaying an alloy or base metal like copper into the body of the silver object, which had been prepared with an indentation of the proper shape. Judging from the rarity of surviving American examples and research done by Ruth Caccavale, niello work was popular for only a brief time in this country. Tiffany & Co., for example, began doing niello decoration around 1874. Caccavale shows that during

their first year of production in 1875–76, over 150 designs for niello work were executed. In 1876 Tiffany's showed several examples at the Centennial that were well received (fig. 6.41). A writer for the *New York Times* said of such pieces: "A novel feature of the display is a treatment of silver with rich colors produced by a peculiar process of incrustation. A large plate of silver in the style of Henry II and colored with copper niello and gold, in the way mentioned, attracts much attention."[117] Probably due to such publicity, the production of objects with niello work remained strong through 1876. During 1877 and 1878, though, few designs were executed for such work, indicating that its novelty had worn off with the public.[118] Nevertheless, Tiffany & Co. did send examples of its niello work to Paris in 1878, where it also received good reviews. One observer, commenting on the firm's "many novel methods of ornamentation" said, "Conspicuous among these are silver articles

FIG. 6.41. Pitcher. Tiffany & Co., New York, N.Y., 1875. Sterling silver and copper. Museum of Fine Arts, Boston.

FIG. 6.42. Pair of vases. Jomi Eisuke, Kyoto, Japan, ca. 1885. Bronze, copper, silver, and the Japanese alloys *shakudo, shibuichi,* and *sentoku.* Dallas Museum of Art.

inlaid with niello, somewhat after the manner of *champlevé* enamel, and similar to the beautiful Russian work which excited such admiration at the International Exhibition of our Centennial Year."[119] Apparently Gorham also was doing some type of niello work in the late 1870s, because it advertised in 1879 that "pleasing effects of color engraving . . . maintains its popularity." This technique probably involved inlaying engraved lines with some colored metal or possibly enamel.[120]

THE JAPANESE STYLE

While American silver in the moresque and Russian styles was certainly noticed by foreign observers and competitors, the silverware that truly brought international fame to American producers was in the Japanese taste. America's achievements in this area were so impressive that some foreign critics claimed that it was the result of Japanese metalworkers emigrating to this country to work for Tiffany & Co. True, a few Japanese craftsmen were brought to America to work in some fields, the most notable being Kataro Shirayamadani (1865–1948), who was hired in 1887 by the Rookwood Pottery in Cincinnati, Ohio. However, no trace of Japanese workers in the American silverware industry has been found. Even the detailed records of Tiffany's and Gorham, the two firms that led the nation in Japanese-inspired silverwork, give no support to the belief that Japanese workers were employed by either company. In fact, following Tiffany & Co.'s success with Japanese-

inspired mixed-metal objects at the 1878 Paris fair, a Japanese newspaper said of the firm's wares, "They have very beautiful works of our *Mokume* metal which is, I am told, fruit of their hard study and work of many years."[121] Furthermore, no evidence has been found indicating that any U.S. producer ever sent unfinished wares to Japan for decorating, as did some London firms, including Streeter & Co. and Daniel John & Charles Houle.[122] Rather, American silverware producers were inspired to make Japanese-style objects by other sources, including Japanese fine and decorative arts. As early as 1848 Tiffany's could announce that it had "an extensive importation of Japanese Goods, probably the most extensive and magnificent collection ever seen out of Japan."[123] And following Admiral Matthew Perry's opening Japan to Western trading in 1854, such goods flooded into Europe and the United States.[124] During the late 1850s and 1860s these prints, lacquerwares, textiles, porcelains, and metal objects began to have a dramatic impact on much Western design (fig. 6.42).

The first artistic reaction to these Japanese imports occurred in Paris. Beginning in 1856 with Felix Bracquemond's chance discovery of pages from the sketchbook of the great Japanese artist Katsushika Hokusai, the *Manga*, an ever widening circle of artists and designers was influenced by Japanese design. The number of people working in this style greatly increased in response to the exhibit that the Japanese government sent to the Paris world's fair in 1867. Yet even before then

FIG. 6.43. Tea kettle. Tiffany & Co., New York, N.Y., ca. 1879.
Sterling silver and ivory. Dallas Museum of Art.

FIG. 6.44. Tray. Gorham Mfg. Co., Providence, R.I., 1881. Sterling silver. Dallas Museum of Art.

some metalwork designers were producing objects in the idiom. The most important of these was Emile-Auguste Reiber (1826–1893) who designed Japanese-, as well as Chinese-, Indian-, and Middle Eastern–inspired wares in bronze, copper, and silver for Orfèvrerie Christofle from 1866 onward. Avant-garde in design, many of these objects were also innovative in their use of cloisonné decoration and polychrome patinas that simulated Japanese surfaces through the use of acid baths, oxidizing, and silverplating.[125] In 1878 a writer for the French periodical *Gazette des beaux arts* called Reiber "the high priest of Japanism" and said of his importance in introducing Asian-style metalworking to the West: "Reiber has caught the true key, he keeps to the happy mien in this art which is still a mystery to be handled with care."[126] Some American firms were certainly aware of Reiber's work for Christofle. Tiffany & Co. would have seen his designs in the form of silver-encrusted and cloisonné-decorated bronze wares at both the 1867 Paris and 1873 Vienna world's fairs, since the New York firm also exhibited at both.[127] John Gorham, who appears to have attended the 1867 exhibition, probably saw Reiber's work firsthand as well. Furthermore, large firms like Tiffany's, Gorham, and Meriden Britannia often had subscriptions to French art periodicals like the *Gazette des beaux arts* and *Revue des arts décoratifs*, which regularly reviewed exhibitions of such work.

The fact that Tiffany & Co.'s first significant designs for silver in the Japanese taste, done around 1871, resemble those of French firms like Christofle, in that they are rather stiff westernizations of Japanese motifs, suggests that the company's designer, Edward C. Moore, may well have been inspired as much by French work as by Japanese originals.[128] But Moore quickly moved off in innovative directions. This was in part accomplished by studying authentic Japanese metalwork and items in other media. Along with what could be seen in private collections in cities like New York and Boston, American silversmiths and designers had the opportunity to examine or at least read about objects sent by Japan to the world's fairs between 1862 and 1878.[129] Tiffany & Co. was regularly importing Japanese items for sale by 1869, and in 1877 held an auction of almost 2,000 Japanese objects in various media. This last group had been collected for the firm by the famous English designer Christopher Dresser (1834–1904), who had come to America during the Philadelphia Centennial. Although most of the imported objects were sold, some were retained by Tiffany's and Moore for their design collections.[130]

Moreover, the amount of primary and secondary printed sources on Japanese fine and applied art available to Americans was rather substantial. Both Gorham's and Tiffany & Co.'s design libraries had a significant number of Japanese art books, including volumes from Hokusai's influential *Manga*. At least one of six volumes entered Gorham's library in 1871 and other works may have been acquired in the 1860s. Also in the libraries of American firms were secondary works concerning Japanese art in English and French. Typical of the range of these books were Meriden Britannia's copy of the *Art-Worker* (1878),

ILL. 6.11. Ceramic plate by the Japanese potter Hizen, ca. 1875.

which illustrated numerous Japanese motifs, and Gorham's imprint of Louis Gonse's *L'Art japonaise* (1883).[131] And finally, to gain a better knowledge of Japanese art, some American designers actually traveled there, as Gorham's George Wilkinson did in 1880. Using the sources of early Franco-Chinese designs, actual Asian objects, and printed material, as well as occasionally visiting Japan itself, Americans were able to produce many exceptional silver objects in the Japanese taste.

The ornament on American objects in this style generally is of two types. The first and simplest is the application of Japanese-inspired motifs through engraving or chasing. A fine example of this work is a tea kettle made by Tiffany & Co. around 1879 (fig. 6.43). Here not only the figures and plant forms are probably derived from a work like the *Manga*, but the vessel's shape is Asian. The Y-shaped legs are reminiscent of supports found on Ming dynasty Chinese furniture, and the pot's form is close to Japanese porcelain examples fitted with bamboo or reed handles of similar squared profile. By using chasing and repoussé, or even die stamping, flat ornament of this type could be made three-dimensional. For example, in 1881 Gorham made a tray which was directly copied from a ceramic plate that had recently been published in *Keramic Art of Japan* (ill. 6.11, fig. 6.44). Finally, American producers could cast near copies from Japanese originals. For example, Gorham produced a line of fruit knives and dessert flatware with cast bronze handles that were copied from the handles of Japanese knives called *kodzuka* (fig. 6.46).

Americans used various techniques to add color to their silverware, as is characteristic of much Japanese work. First, one could solder on ornament that had been cast or electrotyped. Color was obtained when these appliqués were of a

FIG. 6.45. Punch bowl. Tiffany & Co., New York, N.Y., 1881.
Sterling silver and silvergilt. Dallas Museum of Art.

contrasting metal like copper or gold or an alloy. To obtain stronger contrast, or simply create an interesting surface, the body of the vessel could be darkened through intentional oxidizing or textured with hammer marks (fig. 6.45, ill. 6.12). Firms including Gorham, Whiting, and Dominick & Haff used hammered surfaces, but a silversmith at Tiffany's was the first to use them in this way in America around 1876. This decorative technique was so admired that Tiffany & Co. felt it received the *grand prix* in 1878 for its hammered surfaces rather than its use of mixed metals.[132] To achieve still greater contrast between body and appliqué, the body or flatware blank could be made of a metal other than silver, such as iron, steel, copper, bronze, or dark, oxidized silver; or even executed in something other than metal, like ivory or wood, onto which silver appliqués were mounted (figs. 6.47–48). Gorham was especially successful in producing wares which had bodies of something other than silver, such as a line of red copper objects introduced in 1881 (fig. 6.49). The ultimate in adding color to silverware was achieved by enameling large areas of the surface, resulting in painterly effects (fig. 6.50).

The most complicated means of producing polychrome silverware was to forge together various metals and alloys of different colors. The most basic form of this technique is seen on the handle of an ice cream slice by Gorham (fig. 6.51). In this case particles of copper and gold were evidently sprinkled

ILL. 6.12. Tiffany & Co. hammering and mounting design for punch bowl no. 6,310, 1881. Courtesy Dallas Museum of Art.

FIG. 6.46. Set of twelve fruit knives. Gorham Mfg. Co., Providence, R.I., ca. 1880.
Silver, bronze, and gilding. Dallas Museum of Art.

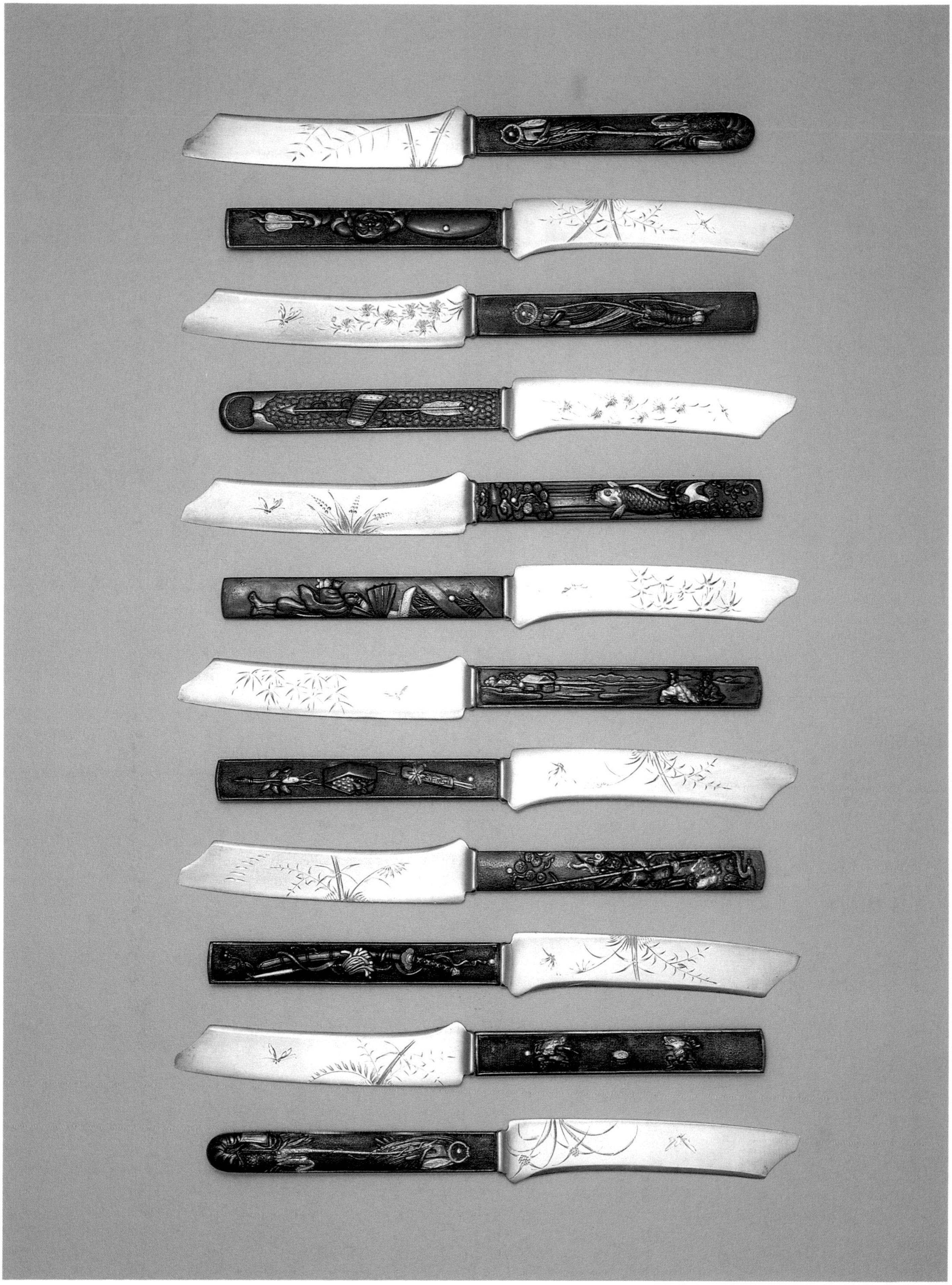

FIG. 6.47. Vase. Tiffany & Co., New York, N.Y., ca. 1877. Steel, sterling silver, and copper. Dallas Museum of Art.

FIG. 6.48. Salad set. Whiting Mfg. Co., New York, N.Y., ca. 1880–1885. Sterling silver, silvergilt, and wood. Dallas Museum of Art.

FIG. 6.49. Tray. Gorham Mfg. Co., Providence, R.I., 1883. Copper and silver. Dallas Museum of Art.

over the silver blank before it was run through a roller press. The intense force of the press fused the metals together and flattened out the colored metals into irregular dots. Much more difficult was the true production of *mokume*, which means "wood-grained metal." Examples of it were exhibited by the Japanese at the Philadelphia fair and fascinated American metalworkers.[133] Certainly Edward C. Moore was intrigued, for Tiffany & Co. was the first to discover how to reproduce this Japanese metal mixture, although documents at Gorham indicated that it too could produce *mokume* and other Japanese alloys early on.[134] The production of *mokume* involves fusing together metals and alloys of different colors and then folding the multilayered "sandwich" back upon itself. The whole is then flattened and the process repeated until the desired degree of "grain" is achieved. Tiffany & Co. had successfully reproduced *mokume* by 1877.[135] It eventually mastered the technique to the extent that it could produce objects almost entirely of *mokume* by the early 1880s. Some pieces, such as a mantel clock (fig. 6.52),

were so complicated that they were constructed from different types of *mokume*.

During the late nineteenth century, technical manuals and lectures explained how to make *mokume* and a host of other Japanese alloys. An excellent example of such a work is W. Chandler Roberts-Austen's *The Colours of Metals and Alloys: A Lecture*, which was first read in Birmingham in 1886 and then published in London the next year.[136] As is the case for this work, however, all examples seen by the author postdate Tiffany & Co.'s use of Japanese metal mixtures. Consequently, its achievements, like those of other firms, were probably the result of experimentation. This view is supported by Tiffany & Co.'s own comments in 1881, which stated that "as early as 1877, we had obtained Moka-Meia [*sic*], after costly experiments."[137] Also, a notation made by a former Tiffany's employee in an unpublished Gorham technical manual supports this assertion. Commenting on a piece Tiffany's made in August 1878 he said: "Remember copper vase made for Paris order—the solder was

FIG. 6.51. *Cairo* pattern ice cream slice. Gorham Mfg. Co., Providence, R.I., ca. 1884.
Sterling silver, silvergilt, copper, gold, and other metals. Dallas Museum of Art.

full of holes and these were filled with plugs of brass (encrusted) and silver (fine) which, when finished, instead of repulsive, on the contrary, rendered the effect more beautiful than had been sought for. The shading around the leaves etc. added to the effect of making them the most successful of anything produced up to that date."[138] While this process of trial and error must have resulted in many failures along the way, in the end it achieved spectacular results.

The Japanese-inspired objects that Tiffany & Co. sent to the Paris world's fair of 1878 and later those it and Gorham exhibited there in 1889 truly astounded their European and Japanese rivals. Not only did Tiffany's receive the *grand prix* for metalwork in 1878, but it received enormous press and literary coverage both abroad and at home. For example, a reviewer of its exhibit in the *Gazette des beaux arts* notes how "Tiffany astounds us" when he says that Mr. Tiffany

> has adopted the features found in broad and free designs, such as foliage plants, birds and fishes, and has above all mastered the secret alloys. He has imitated to perfection

mokonwi [*sic*] . . . and *sibouili*, a gray alloy. Russian *niello*, fine copper, gold and silver complete—this novel palette of the goldsmith with which this American artist achieves varied effects, which are not affected in constancy of color by chemical reagents or continued use. This is a new departure, nor is it the only one. Tiffany has applied these decorations to practical, sensible and simple designs. He has retouched silver surfaces with light, but regular strokes, imitating contours with the die-hammer instead of the lathe. The result is exceedingly pleasing to the eye, while the beholder is not afraid to put his fingers on the polished surface, no longer hard and cold, while pores and wrinkles of skin, fibers of foliage, and the bloom and grain of fruit are wonderfully reproduced, and connoisseurs must . . . admire the charming novelty which is only a return to primitive methods.[139]

Other observers in Europe and America also compared Tiffany & Co.'s multimetal ware to metallic paintings. The American Edwin C. Taylor, for example, said in 1879:

FIG. 6.50. Vase. Tiffany & Co., New York, N.Y., 1893. Sterling silver, gold, and enamel.
Mr. Jerome Rapoport and Ms. Susan Falk Collection.

FIG. 6.52. Clock. Tiffany & Co., New York, N.Y., ca. 1880. Sterling silver and *mokume*. Private Collection, courtesy Hoffman Gampetro Antiques.

FACING PAGE: FIG. 6.53. Coffeepot. Orfèvrerie Christofle, Paris, France, ca. 1880. Silver, ivory, and other metals. Musée Bouilhet-Christofle, Paris.

FIG. 6.54. Cup and saucer. Orfèvrerie Christofle, Paris, France, ca. 1880. Silver and other metals.
Mr. and Mrs. Alexander C. Speyer III Collection.

FIG. 6.55. Tray. Pavel Ovchinnikov, Moscow, Russia, 1884. Silver and other metals.
Mr. and Mrs. Alexander C. Speyer III Collection.

FIG. 6.56. Tête-à-tête set. James W. Tufts Co., Boston, Mass., ca. 1885.
Silverplate and ivory. Wadsworth Atheneum.

The introduction of a new metal or alloy susceptible of assuming almost any color gives to the silversmith a palette only less varied than belongs to the painter and makes it possible to emulate not only the forms of nature in this class of decoration, but the many hues as well. These developments mark what may well be styled an American Renaissance, and the present decade of years is likely to stand out boldly in the history of industrial art in this century.[140]

Although Taylor (who worked for Tiffany's) was biased, others also admired the work. For example, similar praise was forthcoming at the 1889 Paris fair as well. Especially noteworthy in this exhibition was a 32-inch-tall *mokume* vase said to be "the most remarkable triumph of Tiffany & Co." because of the great difficulty involved in its production. Valued at $5,000, the *mokume* body was made from twenty-four layers of various metals.[141]

With such unanimous and unexpected acclaim following Tiffany & Co.'s triumph in 1878, it is not surprising that competitors or nationalist critics were quick to point out their achievements in the areas of Japanese-influenced design and metallurgy. The most noted of these claims concerned Orfèvrerie Christofle. In 1881 the French critic Eugene Fontenay implied, in Tiffany & Co.'s opinion, that Christofle was the first in the West to use *mokume* and that the hammered surface was only a passing fad. Tiffany responded by saying that although the French firm may now be making the material and others are copying the textured surface, it "claim[s] the right to have been the first to produce this thoroughly hammered

ILL. 6.13. The Sterling Co. advertisement, 1888.

FIG. 6.57. Tureen. George Gill, designer; Reed & Barton, maker, Taunton, Mass.; designed ca. 1873.
Silverplate. Dallas Museum of Art.

silver with polychrome drawing in relief as well as Moka-Meia [*sic*]."[142] Shortly thereafter Orfèvrerie Christofle responded about the question of *mokume:*

> We had no pretensions of remaking makoume [*sic*], whose origin is Japanese and which you have imitated with a rare perfection. The name of "forged metals" given by us to pieces made by our procedures indicated our claim that we had found a new manufacturing procedure not being mistaken nor wanting to be mistaken for Japanese makoume and still less for American imitations. . . . Concerning the second claim that you make concerning hammered silverwork in polychrome relief, our response is very simple: You first exhibited work only dating back to 1878. Ours have been seen in Vienna in 1873 and in Paris at the Expositions of the Central Union of 1874 and 1876.

> . . . We owe it to the truth, however, to state that our efforts were limited to making silverware from decorative copper, ornamented with silver and gold reliefs, while you have presented silver articles for everyday use, decorated with reliefs of brass, silver and gold. As have we, so you have felt the necessity of breaking the uniformity of silver production by work executed by hand. We have used, in order to imitate the Japanese, various production techniques obtained from the chasing tool and the hammer; but you have more readily increased the production of hammered work, from hence this term of hammered silver with which you have labeled your works. It is evident that these two types of silverwork were inspired by the same sources and borrowed their attractive elements from Japanese art.[143]

FIG. 6.58. Stand. Charles Parker Co. and Meriden Britannia Co., Meriden, Conn., ca. 1885.
Brass, marble, silverplate, and other metallic platings. Dallas Museum of Art.

Chapter 6

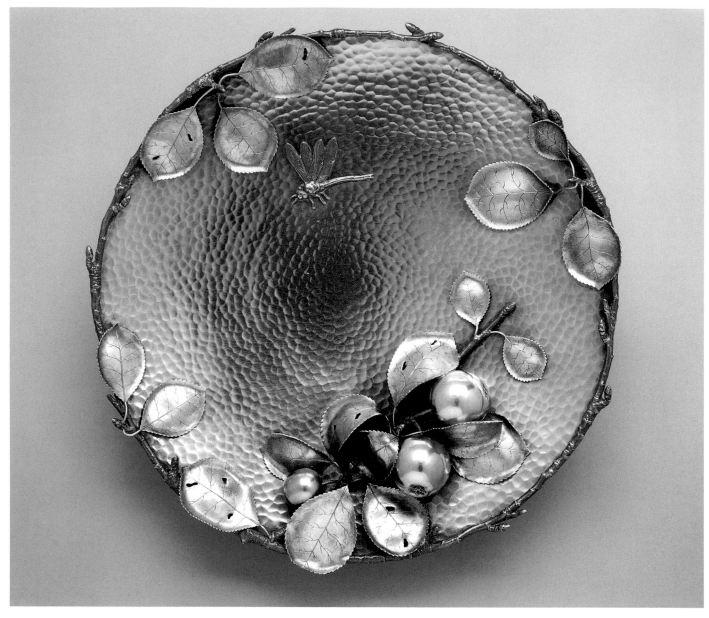

FIG. 6.59. Fruit plate. Gorham Mfg. Co., Providence, R.I., 1881.
Sterling silver, silvergilt, and copper. Dallas Museum of Art.

FIG. 6.60. *Narragansett* pattern berry spoon. Gorham Mfg. Co., Providence, R.I., designed 1884. Sterling silver and silvergilt. Dallas Museum of Art.

It was probably accurate that Orfèvrerie Christofle had used hammered copper bodies with silver and gold appliqués before Tiffany & Co., which only began producing hammered silverware in late 1876. What may really explain Tiffany & Co.'s sensitivity was the fact that Christofle had introduced a line of hammered solid silver wares decorated with applied ornament. Unlike all its other avant-garde work in the Japanese taste, this particular group of objects was obviously patterned on Tiffany & Co. examples, especially in the light, airy quality of the designs (figs. 6.53–54). The line was well received by the French critics, but appears not to have been extremely successful, judging from the rarity of the work today.[144] At least one other European firm produced a limited amount of silver in the Tiffany-Japanesque style in the early 1880s. The Moscow workshop of Pavel Ovchinnikov (1853–ca. 1917) copied a significant number of Tiffany & Co. models with appliqués and textured or patinated surfaces (fig. 6.55).

The reasons behind Tiffany & Co.'s rapid advance into the area of Japanese-style design and metallurgy are speculative at this point. Certainly, the simple fact that Japanese art with its strong emphasis on naturalism and clarity of composition was introduced to the West just as the rococo and Greek revivals were losing their vitality must have made the new style almost irresistible to sophisticated designers like Edward C. Moore and Charles Osborne. It should also be noted that just as Japanese influences appeared on the scene, the American silverware industry was plunged into one of the worst recessions ever.

The Panic of 1873 brought economic disaster to the country, resulting in a 16 percent decline in Tiffany & Co.'s silver sales the first year and a continuing slide each fiscal year except for 1874–75, until by early 1878 sales were down a full third from April 1873.[145] Although interest in Japanese-inspired objects was certainly not created by the depression of the 1870s, its quick acceptance in consumer-oriented industries like silverware manufacturing was probably promoted by managers' and designers' desperate need to find something new and innovative to attract customers. In light of this tense economic climate, it must have made perfect sense for someone like Edward C. Moore to direct his energy and talent to the rapid expansion of Japanese-style designs during 1873 and 1874, followed by a great surge in Japanesque, as well as all design activity, in 1875. Furthermore, 1875 saw the introduction of niello inlaying at Tiffany's. Hammered surfaces were begun in 1876; the *mokume* technique was perfected in 1877; and other colored alloys followed shortly thereafter. And finally, in 1878 the firm poured its energy into making a good showing at the Paris world's fair. The rapid nature of these extraordinary achievements suggests that, more than the appreciation of Japanese art as the driving force, perhaps economic factors were of equal if not greater importance from the producers' point of view. But whatever the reasons behind the adoption of Japanese design, Tiffany's and its rival American producers created many extraordinary objects in the style during the two decades beginning in the early 1870s.

FIG. 6.61. Dish and spoon. Wood & Hughes, New York, N.Y., ca. 1880–1890 (dish); Gorham Mfg. Co., Providence, R.I., ca. 1885–1890 (spoon). Sterling silver and silvergilt. Dallas Museum of Art.

As appears often to be the case, the silverplate industry only adopted the Japanese style after it had been popularized by solid silver producers. During the mid 1880s, those who could afford expensive sterling objects began purchasing silverware in other styles, evidently having become bored with the Japanese taste. For example, by 1884 an anonymous Tiffany & Co. employee felt compelled to note by that year's ledger entry for the silver workshop that Japanese-style "Mounted Work [was] dying out fast."[146] However, just as solid silver producers began looking for alternative styles, silverplate producers fully adopted the Japanese idiom. As William Hosley has pointed out, at firms such as Simpson, Hall, Miller & Co. of Wallingford, Connecticut, relatively little Japanese-style silverplate was manufactured in the late 1870s, although production soared in the 1880s and early 1890s.[147] Since the countless objects produced in the Japanese taste by America's silverplate companies during this period were generally less expensive than their sterling counterparts, many more middle-class households could afford to purchase them (fig. 6.56). Similarly, more Americans could see Japanese motifs in the silverware industry's advertising in the 1880s than in the previous decade (ill. 6.13).

Objects made in silverplate and related base metals may have occasionally followed Japanese prototypes in their forms, but most did not. Typical were items that mixed Japanese mo-

tifs with other forms of ornament or applied it to non-Japanese shapes. For example, in 1873 Reed & Barton introduced a line of hollowware that combined Japanesque diaper work and natural elements with Mideastern imagery (fig. 6.57). The Charles Parker Co. of Meriden, Connecticut, which produced a wide range of "artistic furniture" in brass and plated metals did the same with a polychromed stand (fig. 6.58). Made around 1885 from cast elements possibly supplied by the Meriden Britannia Co., the piece combines Japanese motifs such as song birds and cherry blossoms with European-style images of a dancing girl and thistles.

Of all the legacies of Japanese art to American metalwork, bringing natural motifs to the forefront of design was the most important. In 1878 the *Jewelers' Circular* captured the Japanese reverence for nature in its article "The Influence of Oriental and Particularly of Japanese Art on the Present Modes of Ornamentation":

One important point in Japanese ornamentation is the careful though subtle reproduction of nature. A celebrated painter in Paris used to tell his pupils that to know how to draw was of little use, to know how to paint was not of the greatest importance, but that what was required to be an artist was to *know how to see.* There lies the

FIG. 6.62. *Venetian* pattern nut bowl. Simpson, Hall, Miller & Co., Meriden, Conn., ca. 1887.
Silverplate. Meriden Historical Society, Inc.

whole secret, and the Japanese seem to "know how to see" better than any other school of decorators.[148]

Inspired by Japanese naturalism, American firms into the 1890s produced silverware that relied totally on natural forms for its decoration (and sometimes shape). Gorham, perhaps more than others, excelled at naturalistic trompe l'oeil work. Fine examples include a fruit plate dating from 1881 (fig. 6.59). Some of the firm's most startling creations in this vein were flatware designs from the 1880s, such as its "bamboo and shell" salad servers and a *Narragansett* pattern berry spoon (figs. 6.4, 6.60). In both hollow- and flatware Gorham's forms are startlingly close to their natural prototypes, the leaves on the plate hav-

ing worm holes, the bamboo handles growth rings, and the seashells sand. Besides Gorham, firms such as George Shiebler, Wood & Hughes, and Simpson, Hall, Miller & Co. produced naturalistic silverwork of high quality (figs. 6.19, 6.61–62). By the mid 1890s the spirit of Japanese art and design had faded from American metalwork, however, having been supplanted by nationalism, which manifested itself in various forms of silver design.

THE AMERICAN STYLE

Between the Civil War and 1915, the United States changed enormously. The war was a watershed that unleashed or accelerated processes that changed the country forever. The balance of population and power shifted decidedly in favor of metropolises like New York City and Chicago. Settled by immigrants from around the world and crisscrossed by railroads, the western frontier was officially pronounced closed in 1890 and by 1912 all the western territories had been organized into states. Increasingly, the mythic spaces of America were domesticated by the plow and barbed wire or set aside as endangered park land. Simultaneously, the nation's Native peoples were relegated to reservations, surviving in the American psyche as mythic images estranged from reality. Beyond its borders, the country acquired imperialist outposts like Hawaii, the Philippines, Samoa, Panama, and Puerto Rico. By World War I, the United States had developed into a wealthy industrialized country that was recognized internationally as a world power.

The great changes that reshaped America during the late nineteenth century had an effect on silverware design, as they had on all artistic expression. Whereas before the Civil War producers and consumers readily accepted European styles like the Gothic and rococo revival, postwar Americans were less willing to do so. Having had their mythic image of the New World as paradise shattered by a bloody civil war, Americans sampled exotic cultures, including those of the Middle East, India, Russia, and Japan, while groping toward a new cultural identity of their own. In silver design, the forging of a new America worked itself out in two ways. First, a few objects were made that were overtly American in symbolism and nationalistic in spirit. Second, a huge body of silverware was produced in the art nouveau, arts and crafts, and colonial revival tastes, all of which were seen as "American" in some way.

Overt American symbols such as the Native American or the eagle had been used on American silverwork before. However, the first important body of such pieces was made for the 1876 world's fair. The Philadelphia exposition celebrated the centenary of American independence, and consequently objects nationalistic in nature were especially appropriate. Hence, Reed & Barton lavished time and money on its *Progress Vase* (fig. 5.7), and Gorham produced the *Century Vase* (ill. 5.11). While these objects were American in theme, their overall design was completely within the European academic tradition. A similar situation existed with three elaborate tea and coffee services that Tiffany's and Gorham produced for the 1889 and 1893 world's fairs. Generally called *American Flora* services, these sets were decorated with flowers found in this country. In each case the overall style was decidedly Middle Eastern, however, with elaborately chased work covering the entire surface of the vessels.[149]

A writer for *Jewelers' Weekly* hoped in 1889 that a still "more thorough Americanism" would develop in silver design. However, he thought it sufficient simply to substitute Native American imagery in place of those from other cultures. Thus he asked:

Why are not the impudent prairie dog, the graceful squirrel, the wily fox, the beautiful salmon and speckled trout, the delicate wood flowers seen in so many parts of the

ILL. 6.14. *Indian Chief*, by Meriden Britannia Co., designed ca. 1876. Courtesy Meriden Historical Society, Inc.

continent, the peculiar foliage and flower of the magnolia and the poplar, the rude implements of both peace and war characteristic of the aboriginal inhabitants of our country, and hundreds of other equally adaptable subjects chosen for the designs of table services and jewelry? What could be more graceful than a coffeepot with a tiny chipmunk or a slender weasel for a spout, or even of one shaped like a fox, the tail of which might be a handle and an extended paw or even the muzzle the spout?[150]

Between 1875 and 1915 almost all the objects that sought to be "American" in style followed this formula.

Apparently the first objects to approach a more uniquely American aesthetic through Native American imagery were made in the 1870s. Meriden Britannia, for example, displayed at the 1876 Philadelphia Centennial the silverplated sculptures *Buffalo Hunt*, *Indian Chief*, and *Indian Squaw* (ill. 6.14).[151] Nearby, Tiffany & Co. showed a pair of related candelabra in the "North American" style (ill. 5.10). When exhibited in 1876 and again in 1878 in Paris they received positive reviews. *Harper's Weekly* described the pair as "adorned with Indian emblems, including the canoe, which is being propelled by a dusky warrior, whose natural complexion is faithfully represented by the metal of which he is composed. . . . Original in design and boldly executed, the artist has introduced a style of ornamentation but little used, yet which possesses certain elements of strength and beauty, and gains additional power from

FIG. 6.63. Cigar humidor. Robert Francis Hunter, artist; Tiffany & Co., maker, New York, N.Y.; 1889.
Sterling silver. Dallas Museum of Art.

FACING PAGE: FIG. 6.64. Pitcher. Gorham Mfg. Co., Providence, R.I., 1885. Sterling silver. Museum of Fine Arts, Boston.

FIG. 6.65. *Pueblo* pattern vase. Tiffany & Co., New York, N.Y., 1893. Sterling silver, copper, enamel, and rubies. William Hill Land & Cattle Co. Collection.

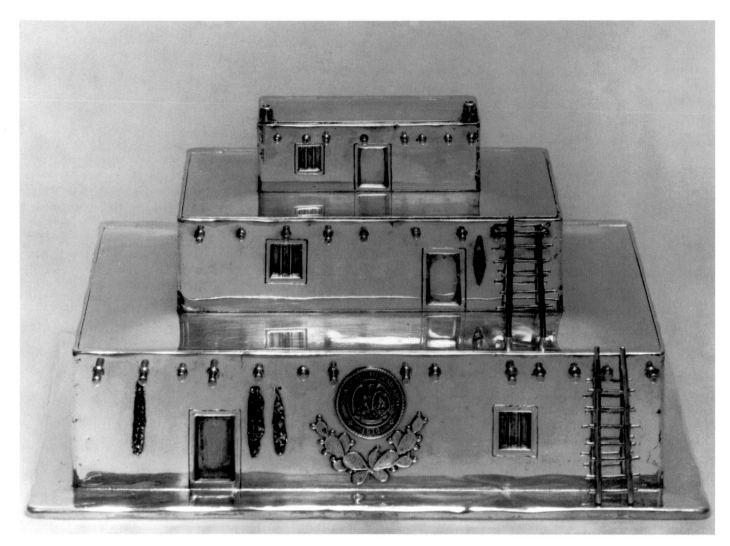

FIG. 6.67. Cigar humidor from the *U.S.S. New Mexico Service*. Tiffany & Co., New York, N.Y., 1918.
Sterling silver and enamel. Palace of the Governors, Museum of New Mexico.

being so distinctively American."[152] In 1878 the candelabra's "North American" style was found even more exciting, being "as pure a nationality as the everlasting Pyramids, and when developed in coming years it will insure a style of decoration as distinctive and as rich in artistic effectiveness as that of Egypt, Greece, or Japan."[153]

Unfortunately or not, a uniquely American "school" of silverware design never materialized. For the most part, the few objects with obvious American themes made in the final years of the nineteenth and the early twentieth centuries continued to take the form of traditional shapes covered with Native American imagery. The Belmont-Rothschild humidor is a fine example of such an object (fig. 6.63), being a rectangular box embellished with a buffalo finial and American sporting scenes. Conversely, silverware in the aesthetic that applies unusual decoration to original shapes is exceedingly rare, and with few exceptions, such as Gorham's snake-shaped pitcher (fig. 6.64), was limited to the work of Tiffany & Co., including a series of southwest-style vases (figs. 6.65–66). The earliest known example of this type was made for the 1893 Chicago Exposition, while the others were created for the 1900 Paris and 1901 Buffalo fairs. In both cases Native American decorative motifs were applied in metal inlays, niello work, and repoussé. While the decoration is suggestive of southwestern ceramics and weaving, no prototypes were slavishly copied. For example, the use of rattlesnake handles studded with New Mexican turquoise is not found on tribal work. Like the rest of the decoration, however, the underlying shape is based on indigenous basketry. The same is true of Tiffany & Co.'s design for a humidor from the *U.S.S. New Mexico Service* that takes the form of an Indian pueblo (fig. 6.67).

Although many Tiffany & Co.'s pieces are successful in terms of design and were admired in the period, few other firms seem to have designed objects in an overt "American" aesthetic. One rare exception is the obscure coppersmith Joseph Heinrich. In his New York and Paris workshops, Heinrich

FIG. 6.66. Vase. Paulding Farnham, designer; Tiffany & Co., maker, New York, N.Y.; 1900.
Sterling silver, copper, and turquoise. High Museum of Art.

FIG. 6.68. Bowl and tray from a punch set. Attributed to Joseph Heinrich, maker, New York, N.Y., and Paris, France; Shreve, Crump & Low Co., retailer, Boston, Mass.; ca. 1900–1915. Copper, silver, silvergilt, bone, and stone. © 1994 The Metropolitan Museum of Art, lent by Gloria Manney.

used copper trimmed with silver for a wide variety of interesting wares, including some in the "American" style. His punch sets with Indian faces, "birch bark," and real arrowheads are perhaps the best examples of his work in this manner (fig. 6.68).

Interestingly, several firms did produce highly creative objects in the "Arctic" or "Glacial" taste. Especially noteworthy are Gorham's designs from the early 1870s (fig. 6.69). Some of the enthusiasm for such wares undoubtedly had to do with the growing popularity of using ice and ice cream in dining and the publicity surrounding America's purchase of Alaska in 1867. However, they also may have embodied a growing sense of crisis concerning the nation's cultural identity. Certainly this ambivalence, which was in part responsible for the creation of silver objects of an obvious "American" nature, served to reinforce the romantic vision of the United States as paradise just as that mythic image was slipping away. Similarly, silverware clothed in Arctic imagery may have comforted contemporary viewers. For in the wake of the Civil War and the closing of the West, some Americans felt that the nation had to find a new mythic national identity and could only do so by turning spiritually north towards the last unexplored frontier, the Arctic.[154]

The quest for a new "Americanism" was a difficult one that sent seekers in many directions, not just north. In the applied arts numerous individuals called for a truly American style, but few, if any, knew what such a style should comprise beyond the application of Native American imagery. John Baynes's lecture "A Plea for an American Style in Industrial Art," which he delivered in 1892 to the New York Institute of Artist-Artisans, was typical. He noted

that you can furnish your house in the Colonial style, Empire style, Queen Anne style, Louis XVI style, Fourteenth Century, the Arabian or Turkish style, Byzantine, Assyrian, Egyptian or Babylonian, in the Persian, Japanese, Chinese, or it may be in the style of the Glacial period. In fact, you may procure the art of every century but the Nineteenth, the art of every country but your own.[155]

Lamenting this situation and assuring his audience that Americans are just as creative as those "of the Greek or of the Latin races," Baynes predicted that a truly American style would emerge, one which "shall be inspired by the spirits of the pioneers who conquered a continent in 100 years. They shall rise

Chapter 6

FIG. 6.69. Ice bowl and spoon. Gorham Mfg. Co., maker, Providence, R.I.; Galt Bros. & Co., retailer, Washington, D.C.; designed 1870, made 1871. Sterling silver. Dallas Museum of Art.

from the camping-grounds of pioneers and hunters, from the mining camp, and from the gulch, and in the cañon."[156] Unfortunately, the speaker had no suggestions as to what form an American style should take or how it should relate to the ornamental styles of other cultures.

For better or for worse, a truly American style based solely on ornament and forms native to this country never developed. Rather, nationalist impulses in design were channeled into the colonial revival movement that gained momentum in the late nineteenth century. Furthermore, under the pressures of new forces at work in both industry and home, the context that had created an enormous sea of specialized and often artistic silverware changed dramatically. The years between 1885 and 1940 witnessed the development of various reform aesthetics, a massive consolidation within the industry, the introduction of war work, and the worst depression in American history. On the home front, life and its trappings were simplified, with fewer servants and less elaboration.

NOTES

1. *British* 1971, 104.

2. *Ibid.*, 82.

3. *Ibid.*, 362.

4. *Ibid.*, 104.

5. *Scribner's* 1874, 198.

6. Gordon 1982, 52, and Williamson 1944, 745.

7. Green 1983, 93. For another discussion of this process, see Hayden 1982, 55ff.

8. Collier 1886, 71.

9. For a good discussion of the nineteenth-century dining room, see Williams 1985, chapter 3.

10. *Scribner's* 1874, 198.

11. Fales 1916, 4.

12. Quote from Urbain-Duboisin in Levenstein 1988, 17.

13. *Scribner's* 1874, 206–9.

14. *Ibid.*, 209.

15. Quote from Sarah J. Hale in Levenstein 1988, 13.

16. For examples from the service, see Carpenter 1982, 69–75.

17. For information on the *Mackay Service*, see Carpenter 1978, 56–67.

18. "Growth of Art Appreciation," *JCK* 17:3 (Apr. 1886):71.

19. A list of the principal pieces with auction prices is in "Sale of the Silverware of the Morgan Collection," *JCK* 17:1 (Feb. 1886):90. The value of these items was $32,125. If it is true that this figure represents half of the total value, $65,000 is an acceptable estimate since not everything was listed.

20. Coates 1891, 10.

21. For an excellent discussion of the status of various foods and their associated flatware, see Williams 1985, 109–29.

22. Ibid., 117–21.

23. "Around the Tea-Table," *LHJ* 2:1 (Dec. 1884):2.

24. Williams 1985, 128. For a discussion of nineteenth-century tea rituals, see Grover 1987, 3–14.

25. John H. Young, *Our Deportment* (1883):113; quoted in Williams 1985, 152. A good description of "A Course Dinner" is in *Demorest's Family Magazine* (ca. Dec. 1891). A copy of the article by this name survives in Scrapbook 1891.

26. Contemporary comment cited in Schlesinger 1946, 42.

27. Williams 1985, 153. Twenty-five percent of urban households represents approximately 7 to 8 percent of all households in the country. A larger number of families would have hired help for special occasions.

28. Coates 1891, 10.

29. Webster 1845, 338.

30. Taken from copy of "A Course Dinner" in *Demorest's Family Magazine* (ca. Dec. 1891) in Scrapbook 1891.

31. For a list of premiums available in return for new subscriptions, see *LHJ* 9:1 (Dec. 1891):43 and "Premium Supplement."

32. For a silverplate trade catalogue that combats the increased popularity of sterling, see Meriden 1907.

33. Elkington 1840, no. 4, 74–80.

34. The series begins in *JCK* 30:10 (10 Apr. 1895):19–20, and ends 30:26 (31 July 1895):5–6.

35. *Elimination* 1926, 3, and "Program of the Silver Conference at Washington," *JCK* 92:5 (3 Mar. 1926):83.

36. "When Spoons Sold by the Ounce," *JCK* 139:9, part 2 (June 1969):156.

37. St. Johnston 1886, 14. For a similar comment, see "The Artistic and Commercial Developments of the Silversmith's Craft," *JCK* 50:1 (1 Feb. 1905):61.

38. Krantz 1894, 4–5.

39. *Silverware* 1940, 1.

40. Grover 1987, 129.

41. O'Connor 1988, 34, and Williams 1985, 76ff.

42. For such a recommendation, see "High Tea," *LHJ* 5:5 (Apr. 1887):2.

43. "When Spoons Sold by the Ounce," *JCK* 139:9, part 2 (June 1969):158–59. For a depiction of a typical package of a dozen spoons complete with label illustrating world's fair medals, see Meriden 1910, n.p.

44. McCracken 1988, 104 and 111.

45. Petroski 1992, chapters 1 and 8.

46. Eliza Leslie, *The Ladies' Guide to True Politeness and Perfect Manners; or Miss Leslie's Behavior Book* (1864):128; quoted in Williams 1985, 42.

47. Petroski 1992, 148.

48. *HB* 19:6 (May 1906):43.

49. For a discussion of objects as family and cultural bridges, see McCracken 1988, 44ff.

50. For a discussion of American presentation silver, see Warren 1987. For a discussion of objects acting as "icon of continuity," see Csiksezentmihalyi 1981, 214ff.

51. Hyde 1979, chapter 4.

52. *JW* 8:18 (29 Aug. 1889):45.

53. Ward 1987, 76. Also see Ward 1986.

54. Taylor 1878, 244.

55. Gorham 1889, n.p. For other comments on silver's ability to refine, see *AJ* 1875b, 371.

56. Gorham 1889, 201.

57. Comments on images of Cellini occur throughout the literature. For a typical article, see "Benvenuto Cellini," *JW* 5:15 (9 Feb. 1888):58–60.

58. Taylor 1878, 243.

59. Stuart 1912, 573–75.

60. For a survey of American flatware patterns between 1837 and 1910, see Turner 1972.

61. "Jewelry and Silver at the Centennial," *JCK* 8:6 (July 1876):93.

62. Meriden 1881, 14.

63. Gorham 1904, n.p.

64. *JCK* 10:15 (15 May 1895):18.

65. Meriden 1893, n.p.

66. *HB* 27:6 (May 1910):xx.

67. Grogan 1911, n.p.

68. For images of the other designs, see *AJ* 1875a. For comment on Soligny and the vase, see Safford 1990.

69. For additional articles on the vase, see "The Bryant Vase," *JSW* 2:6 (May 1877):8, and "The Bryant Vase," *JW* 10:19 (7 Aug. 1890):1.

70. Osgood 1876, 252. For an excerpt of Osgood's dedication speech, see Carpenter 1978, 34.

71. "Art in Metals," *JSW* 4:1 (Sept. 1877):1.

72. The *Bryant Vase* was the first piece of American silver to enter the Metropolitan's collection. Boston acquired a Tiffany & Co. pitcher in 1876 at the Centennial (fig. 6.42). Philadelphia was founded as a museum of applied art and began collecting as well soon after its founding.

73. Research in the Gorham employee records by Samuel Hough suggests that Frederick Jordan, who came to Gorham in 1878, made the annotations in the technical handbook, GA, I. Historical 13. For a discussion of the diary, see Carpenter 1982, 107. The diary's author is as yet unknown.

74. "Art In Industry," *N.Y. Times*, 13 July 1874. For more information on this system, see *NR* 1878, 24.

75. See Carpenter 1978, 41 and 99.

76. Krantz 1894, Tiffany & Co., 6. For information on Farnham, see Zapata 1991a and 1991b and *IS* 1906.

77. "Our Workers in Gold and Silver," *JCK* 12:7 (Aug. 1881):162.

78. According to Osborne Collection 91x23.44, it increased to $2,000 the second year and $2,300 the third.

79. Osborne Collection 91x23.32. Dated 9 Mar. 1875, the letter's author is named Harry and appears to be Charles's brother.

80. *Ibid.*, 91x23.40.

81. *Ibid.*, 91x23.47.

82. *Evening Chronicle* (North Attleborough, Mass.), 7 Mar. 1905, notes that Osborne and an Edwin C. French both attended the National Academy and Art Students League before designing for Whiting. Nothing is known of French's work for the firm, although he evidently became famous as a book-plate engraver. For other information on Osborne, see *JCK* 5:4 (15 May 1874):162. The ledger is Whiting 1884.

83. Krantz 1894, Whiting, 1–2.

84. For a brief obituary on Osborne, see "New York Notes," *JCK* 80:9 (23 Mar. 1920):109. It notes his move to Sweetser in 1915 and his accident. Osborne's leaving Whiting may have resulted from Whiting's switching to war production in 1915 which would have left him with little to design. He is buried in Woodlawn Cemetery, Fairview plot, Bronx, New York. One year after his death, the Sweetser Co. went out of business.

85. *Craftsman* 1906. Little is known of Southwick. However, Purtell 1971, 176–77, notes that he managed Tiffany & Co.'s Paris branch in the 1930s and 1940s.

86. Gibb 1943, 251 and 254.

87. For the best overview of Pairpoint's life, see Rainwater 1975, 122–23.

88. I am indebted to Sam Hough for verifying the years Heller worked at Gorham. Hough believes that the designer A. J. Barrett who has been noted as working for Gorham around 1870 never actually existed. He can find no trace of him in the archives. Letter, Hough to Venable, 28 Jan. 1993.

89. Carpenter 1978, 203ff.

90. *Ibid.*, 221ff.

91. For a survey of patented medallion flatware for this period, see Soeffing 1988.

92. For information on Tiffany & Co. and Gorham patents, see Carpenter 1978, 97–100, and Carpenter 1982, 126–27, respectively.

93. *JCK* 21:3 (18 Apr. 1890):29.

94. *JCK* 45:24 (14 Jan. 1903):29.

95. Soeffing is currently working on an article about "satin finish."

96. "Suits by Gorham. . . . ," *JCK* 50:1 (1 Feb. 1905):111.

97. St. Johnston 1886, 13ff.

98. Townsend 1893, 27.

99. "Morel Ladeuil and his Work," *JW* 9:21 (20 Mar. 1890):37–38, and Wardle 1963, 147–51.

100. "The Centennial," *HW* 20:1029 (16 Sept. 1876):753. This article contains a complete description of the vase.

101. "The Silver Display. England and America Competing," *N.Y. Times*, 7 Aug. 1876, and "The World's Exhibition: Artistic Silver Work," 27 Sept. 1876.

102. "The Silver Display. England and America Competing," *N.Y. Times*, 7 Aug. 1876.

103. For a positive review of the vase at the 1889 fair, see *Reports* 1889, 593–94.

104. Krantz 1894, Gorham, 12.

105. "Vast Throng in Broadway Admiring the Journal's Loving Cup," *N.Y. Journal*, 28 Sept. 1899.

106. Townsend 1893, 27.

107. Krantz 1894, Tiffany, 4.

108. See *Gems* 1877, 42, and Sandhurst 1876, 200.

109. For a description of the exhibits, see *JW* 8:5 (30 May 1889):43–50 and 8:7 (13 June 1889):26–29.

110. Notices 1932, v. 1, p. 36. The pattern was dropped on 4 Sept. 1934 along with *Florentine*.

111. For an example with Maori imagery, see Carpenter 1978, 201.

112. *JCK* 23:17 (25 Nov. 1891) lead article.

113. "Russia," *JCK* 8:8 (Sept. 1876):124. For another description of the Russian display, see *JCK* 8:6 (July 1876):96.

114. For a version by Orfèvrerie Christofle, see *Christofle* 1991:36. Elkington 1840, v. 1, n. 5901 shows one from 1875. The author has seen English ones from ca. 1910. For an enthusiastic review of Russian ware of this type at the Centennial, see "The Centennial: The Russian Exhibit," *HW* 20:1034 (21 Oct. 1876):855. Page 853 of this article illustrates objects from the Russian exhibit.

115. For images of Gorham objects, see Carpenter 1982, 117–18. Several objects are known which bear marks from both Kennard & Jenks and Gorham. For one, see Christie's (Wagstaff-6748), 20 Jan. 1989, lot 209. See *JCK* 11:6 (July 1880):120, for information on the buyout. Board 1868, 71, states that on 3 Aug. 1880 Gorham paid E. B. Kennard $50,925 for the firm of Kennard & Jenks.

116. For a description of niello work by Elkington, see "British Department," *JSW* 1:3 (June 1876):15. For a brief description of how to do niello work, see "Niello Work," *JCK* 11:9 (Oct. 1880):184.

117. "The World's Exhibition: Artistic Silver Work," *N.Y. Times*, 27 Sept. 1876.

118. Caccavale 1990, 14–15.

119. Taylor 1878, 241.

120. *JCK* 10:8 (Sept. 1879):xi.

121. This quote is taken from an unidentified Japanese newspaper clipping ca. 1879 found in Scrapbooks, v. 3A.

122. For a description of Edwin W. Streeter's wares, see "Japanese Artists Employed on English Silver Ware," *JM* 5:153 (15 Aug. 1880):176, reprinted in Culme 1977, 437. For an image of such a set by John & Houle, see Culme 1977, 183. Ruth Caccavale, Charles Carpenter, and the author have found no trace of workers on their numerous and thorough searches of the Tiffany & Co. Archives. The author, Samuel Hough, and Charles Carpenter have found no evidence that Gorham ever employed a Japanese craftsman either. Apparently the first such claim to appear in print was Falize 1883, 359. This source has been cited repeatedly as proof of these workers' existence as recently as Burke 1986, 256. Nevertheless, to date there exists no evidence supporting the claim.

123. *New York* 1848, 356.

124. Hosley 1990.

125. For an overview of Reiber and Christofle's development in this area, see Weisberg 1975, 143ff., and *Japonisme* 1988, 68. The use of silverplating to create unusual patinas is noted in Darcel 1867, 430.

126. Falize 1878, 230. English translation appears in "The Gold and Silversmith's Work at the Paris Exposition," *JCK* 9:10 (Nov. 1878):180, and "The Gold and Silversmith's Work at the Paris Exposition, from a French Point of View," *JM* 3:95 (15 Dec. 1878):379.

127. For an image of Christofle wares from 1867, see Mesnard 1867, v. 1, p. 109.

128. A good example of this early design is the flatware pattern *Japanese* (now called *Audubon*) which was designed in 1871. For an illustration of several pieces, see Hosley 1990, 128.

129. For examples of the types of things available in American private collections, see Burke 1986, 255–60. For a sample of the types of items Japan showed at world's fairs, see Finn 1976, Hosley 1990, and *Japonisme* 1988.

130. For information on Tiffany & Co.'s Japanese imports and Moore's collection, see Carpenter 1978, 182–85, Burke 1986, 255–60, and Caccavale 1990.

131. For information on Japanese literary sources at Gorham, see Carpenter 1982, 95; and for Tiffany's, see *Metropolitan* 1907, 105–6. The remnants of Meriden Britannia's library is in ISA.

132. Carpenter 1982, 106–7. Tiffany's notes the importance of its hammered surfaces in [Letter to the Editor], *RAD* 1 (1880–1881):539.

133. Japanese Commission 1876, describes *mokume* on pp. 50 and 89–92.

134. Technical 1877, 107–10.

135. *RAD* 1 (1880–1881):538.

136. For other examples, see "Metalwork," *JCK* 8:11 (Dec. 1877):187–88; "Art in Metal," *JSW* 4:1 (Sept. 1877):1–2; "Japanese Castings," *JSW* 4:8 (Apr. 1878):110, and "Japanese Copper Castings," *JSW* 4:10 (June 1878):140.

137. *RAD* 1 (1880–1881):538.

138. Technical 1877, 309.

139. Falize 1878, 231–33. English translation taken from *JCK* 9:10 (Nov. 1878):180.

140. Taylor 1879b, 405. Similar comments are contained in an article entitled "American Orfevrerie" in an unidentified English-language newspaper from 13 Mar. 1879 in Scrapbooks, 3A. It discusses objects at Tiffany & Co.'s new Paris location at 36 Avenue de l'Opera.

141. For a description, see *JW* 7:5 (30 May 1889):47. The vase was not sold and was eventually cut down for a lamp by the Edward C. Moore family. They later gave the remaining central fragment to the Cooper-Hewitt Museum where it remains.

142. *RAD* 1 (1880–1881):539.

143. [Letter to the Editor], *RAD* 2 (1881–1882):28–29.

144. For examples, see Vinchon 1880, 433; Bouilhet 1912, 3:199; and *Christofle* 1991.

145. Parsell 1901, 30.

146. *Ibid.*, 30.

147. Hosley 1990, 135.

148. "The Influence of Oriental and Particularly of Japanese Art on the Present Modes of Ornamentation," *JCK* 9:4 (May 1878):65–66. Reprinted in *JM* 3:118 (1 Oct. 1878):342–43 and *Silver* 23:5 (Sept.–Oct. 1990):16–17.

149. For images of these sets, see *JW* 8:5 (30 May 1889):45; *Manufacturing Jeweler* [?] (28 June 1893):860 (clipping in Scrapbook 1891); and Heydt 1893, 12.

150. *JW* 8:8 (20 June 1889):1.

151. For an image of the *Buffalo Hunt*, see Hogan 1977, 112.

152. *HW* 20:1036 (4 Nov. 1876):855. Tiffany 1876, 27, no. 128, incorrectly lists the *Dauntless* as the *Sappho*. For another brief description, see "Exhibits of Tiffany & Co., New York," *JSW* 1:6 (Oct. 1876):6.

153. Unidentified clipping quoted in Carpenter 1978, 206–7.

154. Between 1861 and 1890, images of the frozen North appear rather regularly in the fine and decorative arts, as well as in literature. Eleanor Jones Harvey of the Dallas Museum of Art is currently researching this phenomenon.

155. Printed in *JCK* 24:6 (9 Mar. 1892):38.

156. *Ibid.*

Part III

RESTRUCTURE AND REFORM

1885–1940

Although many continuities characterized the period between 1885 and 1940, this era also ushered in profound changes within the American silverware industry. As had happened in the 1870s, the industry was shaken by dwindling profits as well as labor unrest. To combat such problems many new, more efficient manufactories were constructed and labor hierarchies changed. Furthermore, dozens of corporate mergers and liquidations occurred during this period, and war work was instituted during two world wars. To distribute their wares, firms intensified advertising and professionalized their practices, putting advertising departments and agencies on the payroll. Design too was affected in that it became increasingly directed by marketing needs. Art nouveau, arts and crafts, colonial revival, and modernist aesthetics, all seen as "American" styles in some ways, dominated the market. Production and consumption peaked in the late 1920s, but the Great Depression of the 1930s and changing consumer habits brought stagnation from which the industry never fully recovered. By 1940 technical and aesthetic development that had placed the United States in the forefront of silversmithing had come to an end. Whereas the future would bring many challenges and achievements, the glories of this century of splendor survived only as memories and as unfashionable and, until recently, often despised silver objects.

Chapter 7

THE DRIVE FOR EFFICIENCY: PRODUCTION

For those silverware makers who had relatively small work forces and thus modest production, the late nineteenth and early twentieth centuries did not necessarily bring extraordinary change. With limited capital to invest in new factories, technology, and reorganization, most small firms continued to produce silver objects as they had throughout the nineteenth century. Workers still performed much hand labor in cramped, poorly lit spaces. For firms that employed more than 100 silversmiths, however, this period was one of great change.

Between 1882–85, 1893–97, 1907–8, and 1913–14, the United States suffered economic recessions. Correspondingly, sales of luxury products like silverware remained flat or declined during these periods.[1] Further complicating the situation was the continuing fall in the price of silver. By the 1890s, sterling silver items had become so inexpensive due to the fall in bullion prices that they rivaled silverplate. For the years between 1899 and World War I, sterling production actually surpassed that of plated wares. The inroads sterling made into the plate market were so substantial that some plate manufacturers went out of business or added sterling lines, as did Reed & Barton in 1889. The number of plate producers during these years dropped from sixty-eight in 1889 to fifty-eight in 1909, while the total of those making sterling wares increased from fifty-four in 1889 to 125 in 1909. Due largely to the increase in the price of silver bullion, which began in 1915, however, sterling production was again surpassed by that of silverplate by the end of World War I.[2]

The more than twofold increase in the number of sterling producers and the pressure that the falling price of silver put on plate makers resulted in intense competition within the silverware industry as a whole. Further aggravating the situation was the fact that the late nineteenth century was a time of steady deflation. In spite of some increased production costs (fuel and purchased electricity, for example), which rose from the late 1880s through the First World War,[3] persistent deflation throughout the economy meant that makers could not easily pass on such increases to consumers, since prices overall were low. The result of this increasingly difficult economic situation was that managers came to believe that reforming, and in some cases massive restructuring, their firms was vital if they were to survive. In many ways the strikes of 1886–87 signaled the need for change.

THE STRIKES OF 1886 AND 1887 AND THEIR AFTERMATH

Since the Civil War, the organized labor movement had been growing slowly in the United States and silverworkers were not insulated from this larger trend. During the early 1880s, many workers in the industry joined America's foremost labor union, the Knights of Labor. Founded in 1869, the Knights attracted members slowly during the 1870s, but following a successful strike in 1885 against the Missouri Pacific Railway, in which the owners were forced to restore slashed wages, the union grew rapidly. By 1886 it claimed a membership of over 700,000 workers in a variety of industries, including that of silverware.

The 1880s were a trying decade for the U.S. silverware industry. A severe recession between 1882 and 1886 resulted in lower sales and profits and, as a result, a drop in production and the number of workers employed.[4] Simultaneously, the decade witnessed a rapid increase in labor unrest as workers attempted to counteract the wage reductions, layoffs, and dismissals that desperate managers had instituted. In 1886 the number of strikes and lockouts in industrial America reached epidemic proportions. A total of 1,572 such events occurred, involving an estimated 610,024 workers and 11,562 establishments.[5] As they watched more and more of their own labor force join the Knights of Labor, the owners and managers of America's silverware manufactories became increasingly anxious. In July 1886 the pro-management trade journal *Jewelers' Circular* printed "The Independence of Skilled Workmen."

> The man who is master of a good trade is also master of his fortune. At least, this is true if he has [strength] to preserve his independence and not pledge himself body and soul to some trade organization controlled by reckless and irresponsible leaders, who have nothing to lose

ILL. 7.1. The Tiffany & Co. Prince St. manufactory, New York, N.Y., ca. 1878.

by trade disturbances but everything to gain. . . . But no working men can study the events of the late strikes, and the disturbances of the public peace that accompanied them without being convinced that the organization that ordered them [the Knights of Labor] were not conducted in the interest of the workmen but, on the contrary, are calculated to foster enmity between employers and employees that should not exist and to impress the public with the idea that mechanics and laboring men of the country do not know their own minds, but are ready at any moment to set a law at defiance and encourage a reign of anarchy and bloodshed.[6]

The very next month the same magazine published another indictment against unions in "The Labor Troubles": "The sooner each individual workman determines to stand up for individuality and his right and to abjure labor organizations, or at least such as are not suited to his own particular [trade], the better it will be for them."[7]

Management had reason to be worried. Earlier that year a strike had occurred at the Derby Silver Co. in Birmingham, Connecticut, and in June the president of Gorham was presented with a petition signed by 275 employees asking that the work week be reduced from sixty to fifty-five hours, and that Saturday become a "half holiday." The board's response is recorded in its minutes as follows: "The Board of Directors in reference to a Petition signed by 2/5 [ths] of our employees asking to have Sat. afternoon for a holiday with full week's pay . . . declined to accede to the request largely for the reason that it was as well believed inspired by some organization in the city of N. Y. which has no position or standing to justify them such an interference with our relations to our employees."[8] At about the same time the first major strike hit the industry, when over half of Tiffany & Co.'s silverworkers walked out of the Prince Street manufactory.

It was apparently early fall when members of the Knights of Labor struck Tiffany's. By mid-October 1886 when the strike was settled, more than 150 men and twenty-six apprentices (65 percent of the entire work force) had joined the effort. According to contemporary accounts, the strike was called to force Tiffany & Co.'s management to concede to an advance in wages of about 7 percent and the abolition of the piecework system.[9] Wages at the Prince Street manufactory may well have been cut the year before in an effort to compensate for a severe fall in profits caused by the recession. But even if they had not, average wages throughout the industry had been falling gradually since 1870 and would continue to do so until the turn of the century.[10]

In the fiscal year 1884–85, the profit from Tiffany & Co.'s silver workshop was less than 50 percent that of only three years before. Even though the 1885–86 fiscal year proved more rewarding, with profits rising to 63 percent of their 1881–82 level, management must have been under great pressure to reduce costs in the silver shop. Cutting overhead meant that one's products could be sold more cheaply and thus more competitively in the marketplace. And if prices were raised on goods, lower overhead would simply increase a company's profits. Evidently Tiffany & Co.'s managerial staff felt that instituting piecework at the plant would help correct this poor situation by making production more efficient and consequently more profitable. Rather than pay a silversmith or chaser a set hourly wage regardless of what he worked on, under the piecework system he was paid by the "piece." Now the foreman would review the design for an object, determine the difficulty of executing the design, and size up the talent of the craftsman who was to do the work. The foreman would "rate" the finished object by assigning it a set number of hours within which the craftsman was to complete the work. In the eyes of management the piecework system was a useful one, since it increased competition among all workers in a particular specialty department. The faster, more talented ones would set the pace for the entire room and earn the most, while less productive workers had to improve their skills or receive lower wages. A writer for the New York Times clothed the piecework system in the veil of patriotism when he commented:

The aspect of the question which unfortunately does not seem to be regarded at all is the inalienable right of every person to work as long as he pleases and to earn as big wages as he can get. . . . This right of liberty of the individual will assert itself some day. Sooner or later the man with greater needs will demand an opportunity of honesty laboring to supply them, and the man with an ambition to be more than a mechanic all his days will assert his right to work overtime so that he may increase his savings. The skilled workman will insist on being paid at a higher rate than the dullard, and the hard-working man will claim a greater compensation than the drone. Demands like this must succeed in the end because they are just. Then, when once a premium is put, as it should be, upon skill and industry, will come a clash. The unions will be obliged to recede from the position they are now insisting upon, and, if they resist they will break up.[11]

Unions, and many workers in general, however, hated the piecework system. They felt that it destroyed the camaraderie of shops by pitting workers against each other and was degrading to highly skilled craftsmen because it treated them like machines. The day after the New York Times stated management's point of view, the German-language Union Printer blasted it with labor's position:

A piece worker . . . relegates himself to triple servitude by accomplishing more than three times as much for his exploiter than the Negro slave for his, and freely allows his health and life expectancy to be shortened without enjoying the sure prospect of gaining his independence through his savings and without his "boss" having to provide for him when he has become an invalid—which the Southern slaveowner was required to do. For the "boss" uses the piece work in order to learn how much the most skillful and industrious slave can accomplish in a day, and then he requires that the majority of less skillful workers accomplish as much or be satisfied with less pay, according to the number of wares delivered. The "boss" is only entitled to the average quality of the performance of his worker, even according to capitalistic ideas; since he pays on the average no more in earnings than is necessary to the lifetime of the same according to their way of life. However, through the piecework system he sets out to get as much work out of each worker in 20 years as the worker can accomplish in 30 without becoming an invalid. This system, which is declared as just by the entire capitalistic press, is therefore injustice itself.[12]

Evidently a majority of Tiffany's silverworkers sympathized with this latter view and were willing to strike in order to end piecework.

The workers' choice of early fall for a strike was well calculated. With Christmas being the annual peak for silver sales, fall is the busiest time of the year for a silverware factory. By leaving their workbenches at the beginning of the high season, workers placed management in a difficult position. Furthermore, when Tiffany & Co. attempted to wait out the strikers by having orders executed by other firms, union organizers warned manufacturers that they would also be struck if they aided Tiffany's. Prevented from filling its mounting orders, Tiffany's conceded to its workers' demands in mid-October by abolishing the piece system and advancing wages two dollars a week.[13] The next year silverworkers would not be so fortunate.

Buoyed by the success of the Tiffany's silversmiths, membership in the Knights of Labor must have grown substantially throughout the silverware industry in the late fall of 1886 and early spring of 1887. Naturally, this situation worried managers. In February the *Jewelers' Circular* noted that "the only thing that causes uneasiness among manufacturers or throws any doubt upon the business prospects of the coming season is the attitude of the working men."[14] Rather than stand by helplessly and watch their workers unionize, industry leaders including Tiffany's, Dominick & Haff, Shiebler, Wood & Hughes, Gorham, and Whiting joined to oppose the Knights of Labor. A Tiffany's spokesman stated management's position:

We had men with us who had been in our employ for 30 years. They had received good wages and we had never had any trouble with them. They went out with the utmost reluctance. That we knew perfectly well. But they went out. That was the important fact. It was made perfectly evident that the Knights of Labor controlled our employees to a greater extent then we. Now, we are business men and have our capital invested. We cannot afford to let any body conduct our affairs but ourselves. And we propose to control. If we cannot we will close our doors. That is all there is of it.[15]

Management was put to the test in March 1887. In that month twenty-two of twenty-six chasers went out on strike at Whit-

ing in protest of the firm's handling of the apprenticeship system. "Owing to an excess of work to be done and a scarcity of journeymen," Whiting was hiring more and more apprentices, while guaranteeing them less and less.[16] In the recent past, the firm had abandoned the tradition of indenturing apprentices for set periods with legal contracts between the firm and parents. Now they simply made verbal contracts with a child's guardian concerning pay, with no set number of years for an apprenticeship. This change must have been alarming to the silverworkers at Whiting because it cut at the roots of traditional craft practices, which they valued and understood. Without written contracts that clearly stated rates of pay and length of indenture, apprentices had few legal rights and were at the mercy of the company to train and pay them properly. It was the increase in the number of apprentices that was specifically cited as the cause of the strike. The Knights of Labor, to which many of the Whiting employees belonged, had set a ratio of one apprentice for every four journeymen in a shop. Whiting's hiring of another thirteen apprentices for the chasing shop exceeded this limit. When management refused to dismiss the new apprentices, the Knights ordered a strike.

Negotiations between managers and workers at Whiting proved unsuccessful. The strikers prevented the firm from having its work done at smaller workshops by threatening other producers. Finally, Whiting "gave notice to every man in its employ who was in any way contributing to the support of the strikers that his services were no longer needed." Between 80 and 90 men were fired, leaving more than 100 at work. Upon discovering that unionized workers throughout the industry were helping the Whiting strikers financially, the companies that had joined together to oppose the union threw their support behind Whiting's management. Not only did they refuse to hire any of the fired Whiting men, but, more important, they posted the following notice in their factories:

A strike is now existing in the factory of the Whiting Manufacturing Company on account of their refusal to discharge apprentices with whom they have agreements, and limiting their number and term of service. This strike being ordered by an outside labor organization, and supported by those employed in other factories, is an attempt of such organization to dictate the conduct of our business. We therefore give notice that our works will be closed on Wednesday, April 20, at 6 P.M. against all members of any organization contributing to the support of the strike.

Notice, therefore, that all members belonging to labor organizations may consider themselves discharged.[17]

Because large numbers of silverworkers were members of the Knights of Labor, the core of the solid silverware industry shut down as a result of the lockout. At Dominick & Haff 105 of 140 employees were members. Some 230 out of 300 of Tiffany's workers were unionized. At Shiebler 23 of approximately 60 employed were Knights, while an undetermined number of its

70 or so workers left Wood & Hughes. Although Gorham counted only about 100 Knights among its approximately 850 workers, it felt that this was "a good time to meet [the situation], because the trade [was] well stocked" and "if we permit[ed] it to develop it w[ould] constantly become more annoying and burdensome."[18] By acting in concert, these firms locked out approximately 1,200 workers overnight.

Under pressure from the lockout, which lasted from 21 April to 29 June 1887, the owners and managers of competing silverware companies were forced ever closer together. By June they had formally organized themselves into the Manufacturers' Association and had elected as president Edward C. Moore of Tiffany's and Leroy B. Haff of Dominick & Haff as secretary. Soon after the initial lockout, the original members pooled resources and established a $50,000 fund to help members weather the disruption in production and defeat the Knights of Labor. Furthermore, the Manufacturers' Association grew in size to about a dozen members. Besides the six original participants, other firms who joined included the Towle Mfg. Co. of Newburyport, Massachusetts, Hamilton & Diesinger of Philadelphia, W. B. Durgin of Concord, New Hampshire, and J. B. & S. M. Knowles of Providence.

Purportedly locked-out silverworkers in New York City "spent most of their time at their Fourteenth and Bowery Streets headquarters 'talking up' the project of a co-operative shop, on the same plan as the Solidarity Watch Case Company of Brooklyn."[19] But they really had no hope of winning the battle with management. Within days of being locked out, men broke ranks and began to return to work, having renounced the Knights of Labor. The greatest blow to the cause came only a week after the lockout began, when Gorham's unionized workers voted to disband their local chapter of the Knights and return to work. After firing several union leaders, Gorham took down its posted notices and endorsed the Silversmiths' Mutual Benefit Association as an organization its men could join if they desired. Gorham's peaceful solution to the situation no doubt strengthened other firms' resolve not to give in to union demands.

Given that many of their fellow workers had already returned to work, that the manufacturers were often successfully filling positions, and that only in a few cases were manufacturers actually suffering,[20] the remaining unionized silverworkers asked the New York State Board of Arbitration to investigate the dispute. Under recently amended state law, the board had the authority to call witnesses and investigate, but could not legally compel workers or manufacturers to do anything. Management felt that the board's work was as much of an interference in their business as the demands of the Knights of Labor. Consequently, they not only lambasted the board in the trade press, but refused to cooperate whenever possible. For example, when worker representatives and manufacturers were first subpoenaed to appear before the board on 1 June 1887, several manufacturers sent letters saying they would not arbitrate matters and refused to appear.[21] After likely being threatened with

contempt of court, the various owners or their representatives, along with their lawyers, appeared before the board the next week to face George W. Dunn of the Knights of Labor and several other worker representatives. Although the investigation by the Board of Arbitration solved nothing, it did make clear the paternalistic view that manufacturers had towards their workers. In his testimony, Henry B. Dominick stated that "he believed in workmen being the servants of their employers and not of the Knights of Labor." Mr. C. E. Buckley of Whiting said "that maybe some ignorant workmen could join [a union], but that for the high class ones [like silversmiths] it was a breach of trust with their employers."[22] In the end, the manufacturers would accept nothing short of their workers' loyalty to their employers and renunciation of the Knights of Labor.

By the end of June 1887 the lockout was over. The chasers, who had been the first to strike, back in March, were the last to return to their benches. Having won such a complete victory over labor, many manufacturers moved quickly to consolidate their control. For example, some demanded that their employees sign a document denouncing the Knights of Labor.[23] Other actions were taken within the industry to both reestablish control and combat shrinking profit margins that had begun in the early 1880s. The survival of internal documents gives a rare glimpse into this process at work in Tiffany & Co.'s plant.

In February 1888, Charles Grosjean (b. 1841) died.[24] Evidently Grosjean in his role as superintendent of Tiffany & Co.'s Prince Street works was seen as too close to his men and too traditional for a management that had recently suffered through two labor disputes and was worried about cutting production costs. Almost immediately following his death, the firm instituted sweeping changes in the manufactory which strengthened management's control. Internal explanatory notes to the manufactory's ledger state:

> Soon after Mr. Grosjean's death . . . reforms were inaugurated & changes in methods instituted that were as far reaching in effect as radical in nature: the "speculative" modeling, making & chasing of Stock Bronze Patterns & Steel-Dies that might never be used . . . was at once & forever stopped, and a score & more of mostly high priced men were either put at something else or let go; workmen were distinctly given to understand that their pay henceforth would depend solely upon the positive and comparative record of speed & quality to be kept in each dept; Apprentices by a system of ratings . . . that it lay entirely with themselves to determine what their pay would be after [their] term of service had expired. Time limitations on work, a revival of piece work, annual bonuses to Foremen as incentives to endeavor . . . and other devices followed to meet the falling prices that about this time commenced.[25]

Tiffany & Co.'s control over its labor force was indeed strengthened through such policies. In October 1888, shortly after these policies were implemented, most of the men at work in the

Prince Street manufactory allowed themselves to be enrolled as members in the Jewelers' Harrison & Morton Association, which pledged "to promote as far as possible the interest of these candidates." Given that an official copy of the membership list was kept among Tiffany & Co.'s office records, it is highly likely that management felt the election of Republican Benjamin Harrison to the presidency was in the firm's best interest and asked their workers to support the ticket. With 182 of approximately 207 male workers signing, compliance was almost unanimous.[26]

Workers at Tiffany's, and probably workers throughout the industry, felt the need to show deference to their employer following the disastrous lockout and subsequent "reforms," as documented by a thank you note from 1889. On 2 May of that year the entire retail and manufacturing staffs of Tiffany's (almost 350 individuals) personally signed the following statement: "We the undersigned employees of Tiffany & Co. do tender our hearty thanks for the great kindness and consideration shown by inviting us and our families to witness the grand Washington Inauguration Centennial Parade, and also for the desire shown for our comfort and pleasure so successfully attained."[27] Undoubtedly the workers were genuinely thankful for being allowed off work for the parade, but the overall tone is one of subordination to a paternalistic superior.

Although a paternalistic view on the part of owners and managers had its negative aspects, it also gave rise to policies and programs that benefited workers. This was especially true during the late 1890s and early twentieth century when it became increasingly clear that tightening control over workers was not increasing production in many cases. The simple fact that the industry's finest products required the painstaking labor of highly talented and well-paid craftsmen meant that such workers could never be totally dominated, much less eliminated, for they alone held the secrets of hand production. Similarly, in the case of systems such as piecework, it was craftsmen in their roles as foremen and producers who determined the proper "time rating" for the creation of an object, not business managers. As a result the substantial rise in production that managers expected from the system often did not occur. As they learned these lessons, manufacturers drew upon their paternal feelings toward their employees for new avenues to explore in search of higher profits.

The beginnings of this shift can be seen in the outcome of the 1902 silversmiths' strike. During the 1890s, union membership had reasserted itself. At the height of seasonal production for the 1902 holiday sales, 500 members of the silversmiths' union went out on strike in New York City and Brooklyn in demand of a nine-hour workday. Once again the shops of Shiebler, Whiting, and Dominick & Haff were affected, as well as several smaller producers like the Mauser Mfg. Co. and Graff, Washbourne & Dunn. While some men from Gorham's Manhattan workshop (active 1892–1921) went on strike, none did in Providence. However, within days of the strike's beginning, 300 workers walked out of Tiffany & Co.'s Forest Hill plant in

Newark. In all, approximately 800 of the estimated 3,000 silverworkers in the New York area struck.[28]

The manufacturers consulted one another as to what course of action should be taken. However, the outcome was not a unified one as it had been in 1887. Several firms conceded to the workers' demands almost immediately, including Whiting and Mauser in New York and the Newark firms of Lebkuecher & Co. and Merrill & Co. After the new nine-hour day had been in effect for a while, Mr. Kolb, treasurer of the Mauser Mfg. Co., stated, "The men are now satisfied and happy . . . and it does not make any difference to us whether other factories run nine hours or 10. We feel that we are getting as much work now out of the men as we ever did before."[29] Even some of those who publicly stood firm against the workers' demands realized that it might be necessary and even productive to seriously discuss their employees' views. The president of Tiffany's, Charles T. Cook, for example, stated publicly "that he would close his Forest Hill plant rather than concede anything to the strikers."[30] Privately, however, he was not so rigid. In a letter dated 15 January 1903 to Cook, J. M. Parsell, Tiffany & Co.'s plant superintendent, rages against the nine-hour day, saying Tiffany's should work with other manufacturers to "forestall and make [it] next to impossible of success for years to come." However, Cook, unlike his predecessors who made severe changes following the 1887 lockout, is quoted as having commented that the nine-hour day "might not prove as remote as heretofore believed and that if so its serious consideration could not much longer be deferred."[31] Having begun work at Tiffany's in the 1840s as a delivery boy and risen to the rank of president by 1902, Cook represented a different type of leader from those of the 1880s. He evidently believed that if workers' demands were unavoidable, then management had to make the best it could out of the situation. And perhaps being one of the first to implement such a change would boost worker morale and preserve production near its current levels under the ten-hour-day system, as had been the case in the Mauser and Whiting plants. Three years later in 1906, Cook instituted the nine-hour workday. Furthermore, he periodically called in accounting and management experts to see if his new practices were working.[32]

Although Gorham, like Tiffany's, had resisted the strikers in 1902, its management was obviously becoming more attuned to the advantages of working with, rather than struggling against, its employees. In 1905, for example, it gave all its many employees the nine-hour day by adopting the Saturday "half-holiday," which they had first requested in 1886.

NEW MANUFACTURING PLANTS

Beyond efforts to gain greater control over their labor forces and boost production through new policies, including the piecework system, more powerful foremen, and eventually employee benefits, many sizable firms erected efficient, modern manufactories in the late nineteenth and early twentieth centuries. This building and reorganization activity, like the changes in labor policies, was greatly stimulated by the shock of the

1886 and 1887 strikes. Many new plants, especially in the sterling silver sector, were erected shortly thereafter. Furthermore, in these facilities it was easier to watch and regulate workers' activities, thus making it more difficult for them to unite against management. Also, the removal of plants and workers to suburbs like Forest Hill, New Jersey, and Elmwood, Rhode Island, meant that manufacturers were not constantly surrounded by "uncontrollable" workers from other workshops who might again "infect" their own staffs.

Before the late 1880s, most manufactories consisted of a group of buildings joined together or located near each other (ill. 1.3). As staffs grew, space in basements and attics was first occupied, then neighboring buildings were taken over or additional ones built. In city settings, silver workshops were little different from other urban, nonresidential architecture. Usually built of brick or stone with wooden framing elements and floors, urban silverware manufactories placed great importance on quality of light. Consequently, they incorporated windows wherever possible so that workers could see well (ill. 7.1). The ceilings were typically a maze of belts, drive shafts, cables, and pipes. Working conditions were usually crowded and close, laborers standing within a foot or so of each other. In short, the average urban silverware manufactory was before 1890 a labyrinth of fragmented spaces, bustling bodies, and unfinished silver objects.

During the 1870s and 1880s, however, a few attempts were made to provide better urban workspaces. The Waltham Building of 1871 (ill. 2.6), for example, was a great improvement for urban silverworkers when it opened on Bond Street in lower Manhattan. Upon completion, the five-story, mansard-roofed structure was quickly occupied by fourteen silverware and jewelry firms. Gorham took over a large part of the ground floor for a wholesale showroom, while Adams & Shaw did the same on the second floor. Dominick & Haff, along with others, moved their factories onto the premises. The Waltham Building however, proved unsafe. In March 1877 a fire began on the third floor, quickly engulfing the entire building, which was finished entirely in pine. The tenants lost virtually all their stock and equipment.[33]

Although similar in being a well-lit, brick-cased building in an urban setting, George W. Shiebler's new manufactory in Brooklyn (1889) was built with more concern for safety (ill. 7.2). An advertisement said:

> It is five stories high, with basement, and is 64 × 85 ft. in dimensions, with separate extension for boiler and engine-room. It is built on the New England plan of factory construction, which insures the highest degree of safety and solidity, the floors especially, being laid in a manner to resist, steadily, all the strain that can be put on them. The staircase, elevator shaft, plumbing, etc., are all outside of the main building walls. The boiler and engine-room, as also the stamping room, are only one story in height, so that unobstructed light is assured on

ILL. 7.2. The George W. Shiebler manufactory, Underhill and St. Mark's Ave., Brooklyn, N.Y., 1889.

all sides. There are also fire-proof vaults of 6 × 7 feet 8 in. on each floor, and the first, third, fourth, and fifth floors are to rent from May 1st. The owner occupying the basement and second floor. Floors may be subdivided. A Corliss engine of 100 horse power supplies the power. It is accessible from the city by three separate street car lines from Fulton Ferry or the Bridge, as well as by the Elevated Railroad, taking twenty to twenty-five minutes.[34]

By 1892 the firm had taken over the third floor, where it installed seventy-five working silversmiths, jewelers, spinners, and machinists, including a number of girls doing saw piercing. A vault on each floor provided security for finished and incomplete silverwork at night. The second floor was said to contain "the offices, designing room, die-sinking room, the chasing department, the gilding department and the finishers. . . . In the gilding room, only women are employed, often as many as 25 being at work during the busy season."[35] Shortly after the completion of the Shiebler Building, similar structures appeared in Manhattan. In 1892, for example, the Hays Building at 21 & 23 Maiden Lane and Silversmith's Hall at 860 Broadway contained the showrooms and workshops of more than two dozen silverware, watch, and jewelry firms (ills. 7.3, 7.10). The eight-story Hays Building was especially modern, having a central light well to increase the amount of light to each floor and a support structure of iron and stone which was thought to be virtually fireproof.[36]

Unlike their urban counterparts, firms based in small towns or on the outskirts of cities often had enough space to employ classic New England mill architecture. Developed originally for textile mills in weaving centers like Waltham and

ILL. 7.3. The Hays Building, 21 and 23 Maiden Ln., New York, N.Y., built 1892.

Lowell, Massachusetts, the typical mill structure was a three- or four-story masonry building of rectangular shape. Usually such mills had enclosed but exterior stairwells, and sometimes a cupola or end tower for a bell. Perimeter windows, as well as dormers, lit the interior. The floors rested on beams supported by relatively wide spaced wooden (later iron) piers. Thus the long, rectangular spaces could be subdivided at will with simple, non-load-bearing partitions. Power derived from a stream or steam engine was distributed via a shaft-and-belt system usually mounted on the ceiling.

Silverplate companies appear to have been the first in the industry to exploit this specialized architectural form. For example, images of the two buildings constructed by the Meriden Britannia Co. in Meriden, Connecticut, in 1856 and 1863 clearly depict mill-type structures. By simply adding more and more of these "mills," Meriden Britannia's manufactory had become a truly mammoth complex by 1882 (ill. 7.4). Images of the site depict smokestacks, indicating the presence of smelters and boilers, a railway spurline for easy transport of goods and raw materials, and hundreds of windows ensuring ample light. To supplement the natural light, electric lighting was added in 1885.[37] Along with Meriden Britannia, numerous other silverplate manufacturers also had amassed large mill-type manufac-

turing complexes by the early 1880s. For example, an image from 1879 of the Middletown Plate Co. of Middletown, Connecticut, shows two parallel, three-story "mills" with dormer windows lighting the attics. Among the many firms whose factories were built around "mill" structures were Reed & Barton, Taunton, Massachusetts; Towle Mfg. Co., Newburyport, Massachusetts; Pairpoint Mfg. Co., New Bedford, Massachusetts; Simpson, Hall, Miller & Co., Wallingford, Connecticut; and R. Wallace & Sons, also of Wallingford.[38]

The erection of new buildings in both urban and rural settings during the 1870s and 1880s was at least partially an attempt to improve production efficiency. As Alan Trachtenberg has pointed out, "Unsettled economic conditions made manufacturers obsessed with efficiency, with the breaking of bottlenecks, the logistics of work flow, the standardization of parts, measurements, and human effort."[39] Like their counterparts in other industries, the top management of many of the largest silverware firms sought physical modernization as a way to weather future economic downturns similar to those they had just experienced or were experiencing between 1873–79, 1882–85, and 1893–97. Opening new manufacturing plants four years apart from one another, Gorham and Tiffany's set the standard for state-of-the-art production facilities.[40]

Undoubtedly impressed by how much more efficiently production could be carried out in the well-lit, open spaces of these "mill-type" buildings, and in search of ways to better control their workers following the 1887 strike, Gorham's Board of Directors voted in mid 1888 to construct a new manufactory outside the city center. The old plant was located in crowded, downtown Providence on Steeple Street (ill. 1.3). It consisted of the building that John Gorham had constructed in the 1840s, as well as neighboring structures which had been taken over in the ensuing forty years. Already by 1874, one visitor remarked that the Steeple Street plant was an "endless labyrinth . . . of buildings" in which you could walk "for half a day, and to complete exhaustion" and only see half the works.[41] The new plant was radically different (ill. 7.5).

Purchased in 1887, the site chosen for the facility was a thirteen-acre tract of wooded land in the Providence suburb of Elmwood. Situated on a pond and near the New York, Providence, and Boston Railroad, the location was well suited to a sprawling manufactory covering almost six acres in area. The building complex was designed by F. P. Sheldon, a mill engineer from Providence, and Gorham plant superintendent and designer George Wilkinson, and was completed in 1890. The main core consisted of two long "mill-type" buildings connected to form an H. Additional buildings filled the central spaces of the H. There were other structures on the property as well. To enhance the plant's fireproofing, the walls were constructed 2 feet thick with fireproof floors and doors. An 18-by-24-foot fireproof vault was built into the center of the building, and all staircases were in exterior wells, sealed off from the manufactory by fire doors, and constructed of iron and fireproof material. Furthermore, a separate fire department building was

ILL. 7.4. The Meriden Britannia Co. manufactory, Meriden, Conn., ca. 1882.

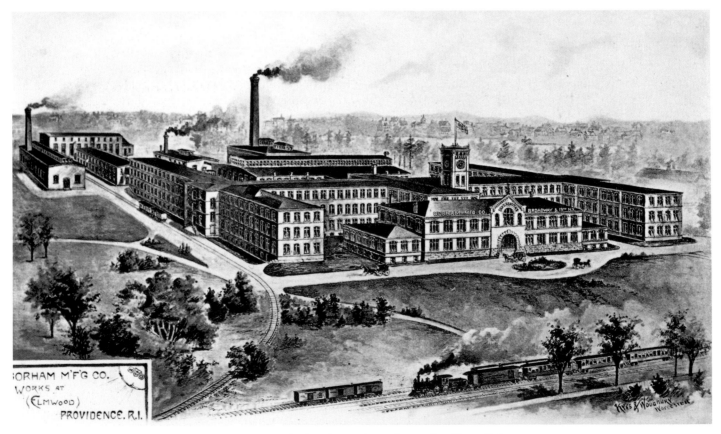

ILL. 7.5. The Gorham Mfg. Co. Elmwood manufactory, Providence, R.I., ca. 1890.

Chapter 7

ILL. 7.6. Drop presses in Gorham Mfg. Co. preparatory room, Elmwood manufactory,
Providence, R.I., ca. 1890.

erected behind the main structure. The need for such precautions had become evident in February 1888 when a fire started by a furnace in the basement of the old manufactory caused $12,000 in damage. Ten years earlier, a fire in the photography department had resulted in $20,000 in losses.[42]

The Elmwood plant had additional design features which were ideal for metalworking. For example, the preparatory department was powered by a Corliss, 400-horse-power engine supplied by six tubular boilers in the adjacent engine room. The preparatory department itself measured 205 by 80 feet and was housed in a one-story structure that filled in the upper half of the H-shaped plan. It had 12-foot-deep foundations constructed of 102 blocks of granite to support heavy machinery, like drop presses (ill. 7.6).[43] Among the machinery housed in the preparatory department and a few other nearby rooms were rolling mills, wire- and tube-drawing machines, and a die-sinking press.[44]

Appropriately, the walls of the building were pierced by scores of windows to assure proper lighting for all the various processes. The windows and workbenches were placed so that only two workers had to share each window. Also, the areas where lathes were used were designed to minimize dust. In commenting on the turning and polishing departments, a French observer noted:

The absence of belts in a workshop where lathes have a considerable speed, removes all chance of accidents, and further diminishes the stirring of dust which is not disturbed by the movement of belts. To complete the prudent and hygienic measures, a powerful ventilator draws in all the dust by means of a tube which runs along the bench of the lathe, and is furnished with a large funnel fixed in front of each workman. This also aids at the same time to renew the air, which is distributed to all parts of the room by blowing machines which bring pure air from the outside.[45]

The same observer said that besides removing dust from the air, "They have also taken all the precautions for a well studied hygienic system. The entire manufactory is kept, in Winter, at an equal temperature by steam heated air, which is distributed by ventilators. In Summer the shops are supplied with fresh air by these same ventilators."[46]

For all intents and purposes, the new Gorham manufactory was designed to be an independent operation. A commentator on the works said in 1892, "Some idea of the completeness of the establishment can be gained from the knowledge that it has its own independent water supply, its own fire department, electric light plant, machine and black-

ILL. 7.7. The Tiffany & Co. Forest Hill manufactory, Newark, N.J., ca. 1915.

smith's shops, its own photographic outfit, and a complete plant for making the artistic cases in which silverware is shown."[47] However, being self-contained was not what made Gorham's Elmwood plant so revolutionary, for it had had many of these specialized departments for years. Rather, it was the logical way in which these various parts were organized with respect to one another that was so different. For example, in the preparatory department, all the various stamps, presses, rollers, and cutters were placed together so that silver could flow quickly from one machine to the next as it was worked. Immediately adjacent to this large room were areas for melting metal and annealing it, both operations being necessary to the functioning of the preparatory department. Likewise, the turning and spinning departments were placed next to one another on the second floor. This proximity meant that pieces which had been spun and were ready to be trimmed or cleaned up in the turning department needed only to go next door. Similarly, the various finishing processes of burnishing, coloring, and polishing were all done near each other on the third floor. The advantages of such a layout can be seen even more clearly in the case of Tiffany's new Forest Hill works, which opened in 1894, for which rich contemporary analyses survive (ill. 7.7).

Tiffany & Co.'s original manufactory was located on Prince Street in lower Manhattan (ill. 7.1). Since 1851, when John C. Moore began producing sterling items exclusively for Tiffany's, most of the firm's sterling silverware had been made in this building. In 1868 the firm acquired title to the manufactory and its equipment when it bought out Moore. Like Gorham's original works in Providence, Tiffany & Co.'s was a brick building in a crowded, urban environment. Five stories

high and measuring 100 by 100 feet, the structure was bursting at the seams with equipment and an average of 300 workers by the 1880s.[48] In 1893 one observer noted the following large machinery in the plant: "2 large Stamping Presses; 1 Hydraulic Press; 18 Lathes for [spun?] work; 40 Polishing Lathes; 5 Drop Hammers, of which one is of 2000 lbs.; 3 large Band Rollers; 1 small Band Roller; 1 Planing Machine; 1 Vise-file; 1 Cutting Machine; 1 Piercing Machine; [and] 6 Lathes." Many of these machines were said to be "huddled closely together."[49] Furthermore, having relatively small rooms and windows primarily along the street facade meant that many workers had to stand in the middle of poorly lit cluttered spaces. A tour through the manufactory in 1887 by a reporter for *Jewelers' Weekly* clearly gives an impression of the Prince Street works as being a tangled maze with "corners" containing entire departments and numerous flights of stairs piercing through the mass of workers and equipment.[50]

Given such conditions and the fact that its archrival, Gorham, had just completed a modern factory, Tiffany's decided to build a new plant in the early 1890s. The firm's choice of a site outside Newark, New Jersey, was probably determined by the fact that it offered plenty of land upon which to erect a mill-type structure; was close to Manhattan; had a tradition of fine metalworking and hence an appropriate labor pool; would remove workers from the "corrupting" influences of urban-based labor organizations; and was already the location of Tiffany & Co.'s silverplate works. The firm of Adams & Shaw, which had begun in the 1860s in Providence with the aid of Charles L. Tiffany, moved its plant to Newark in 1877, where it occupied a three-story brick building and employed around eighty hands.[51] In 1879, Adams & Shaw was sold to Dominick & Haff. However, it appears that Tiffany & Co. purchased the manufactory building and retained the services of Shaw to oversee its plate production. In 1893 the Newark facility was described as being "located in an old building, and its equipment is superannuated."[52] Soon after the new Forest Hill works opened, however, the plating works moved into the new space. Thomas Shaw remained as superintendent of the plating department until he retired in 1898. Finally, in 1909, the plating division was completely absorbed into the silverware department.[53]

Thus, with firsthand knowledge of the Newark area and a desire to leave the crowded urban environment of New York City, Tiffany & Co. purchased a site in the suburban area of Forest Hill and began construction of a large new manufactory "built in imitation of those at Providence, and in rivalry with the Gorham factory."[54] Completed in 1894, the masonry structure was rectangular in plan, with an open courtyard in the center of which was a large vault. The mill-type building was two stories in height, except for the circular, four-story tower that marked the main entrance. Like its Gorham counterpart, this plant was planned down to the smallest detail. Surviving floor plans (ills. 7.8–9) note the placement of everything, including benches, stools, annealing ovens, and equipment. The plans also indicate exactly which spaces and fixtures were fireproof and which were not.

The great improvement of the new manufactory over the old is revealed in a document from 1901, which records general comments about the new building, as well as specific ones by each departmental foreman. "Special Features" of the plant included three different water sources to supply boilers, drinking water, and other needs. Drinking water came from an 800-foot-deep artesian well on the property. Also noteworthy were the steam call whistle; thirty fireproof compartments containing fire-fighting equipment; departmental fire- and burglarproof vaults; twenty-five clocks controlled by a master clock; twenty-five telephones; steam heating; oil-fired melting and annealing ovens; electric power and lighting; in-house smelting and refining plant for waste metal including floor sweepings and hand washings; all piping under the building in subways; and exceptional light and ventilation. Like Gorham's Elmwood plant, Tiffany & Co.'s was practically self-sufficient with such facilities, as well as its own "machinists, blacksmiths, plumber and pipe fitters, carpenters, painters, wheelwrights, and beltmaker."[55]

John T. Curran, design-room foreman, felt the best aspects of his new space were new storage areas and indexing systems for working drawings, metal patterns, and the library. Curran also admired the new secure and well-lit rooms in the tower for nude modeling and another for photographing and modeling. Finally, he applauded the location of the designing room between the silver shop and the engraving, die-sinking, and chasing workshops. This new location saved much time in moving between departments.[56]

Daniel Webster, foreman of the silversmiths who executed large-scale work, felt there were several especially sig-

nificant improvements, including a dumb waiter connection between stampers and molders; direct access to stock and spinning rooms; increased stocks of tools, which reduced the need to borrow from other departments; gas and air supplies for each worker; the department office located to allow a good view of the workers; improved ventilation and sanitation; and a "Separate Room for Gauges and Patterns scheduled and indexed—heretofore scattered all over rooms & no index—[representing] a very great saving of time—no hopeless hunting and making duplicates as before."[57]

The spinning department, supervised by one F. Peterson, also was greatly improved. Noteworthy features included a "Chuck Room Annex with Chucks so arranged and indexed, can go at once without hesitation to any one of the 12 to 15,000 of them, saving fully one man's labor per day"; an isolated area for lathes used in gold- and silverwork so that waste metal did not commingle; and racks and storage areas for tools that were "formerly scattered all over room."[58]

And finally, Henry Triebel, who was foreman for die sinkers and engravers, noted that new die-sinking machines and a sand blaster had been added to the department, as well as a new grindstone, forge, and lathe that did not have to be shared with other departments. Best of all, however, was the location of the well-lit department next to the design studio, rather than two floors away as before.[59]

As these testimonials reveal, Tiffany & Co.'s new Forest Hill works was indeed a great improvement over its original New York City facility. Where the insufficient space and poor organization in the old plant resulted in the clumsy handling of expensive items like drawings, patterns, tools, dies, and chucks, the ample space of the new one allowed for thorough storage and tracking. Furthermore, the plentiful light and ventilation at Forest Hill, and especially the logical placement of interdependent specialty workshops near one another must have greatly enhanced both the laboring conditions and efficiency of the 300 to 400 workers.

In commenting upon these new silverware manufactories, contemporary observers often noted how much they improved the lives of the workers. Speaking of Gorham's Elmwood plant, a writer said in 1890 that the company has "given every attention to the comfort and healthfulness of its working men and women, having employed the most advanced methods for heating and ventilation. . . . making the factory one of the most attractive and comfortable workshops in any branch of business in the United States."[60] Since healthy, happy employees are more productive, it is undoubtedly true that the company management and building planners did indeed care about the welfare and attitudes of workers. More than aiming to make workers' lives more pleasant, however, the organization and structure of these factories enhanced management's control over their employees.

Simply by improving lighting and making rooms less crowded in their new plants, management and their foremen could better watch workers. The need for workers to periodically walk to remote areas of the building for parts or to deliver

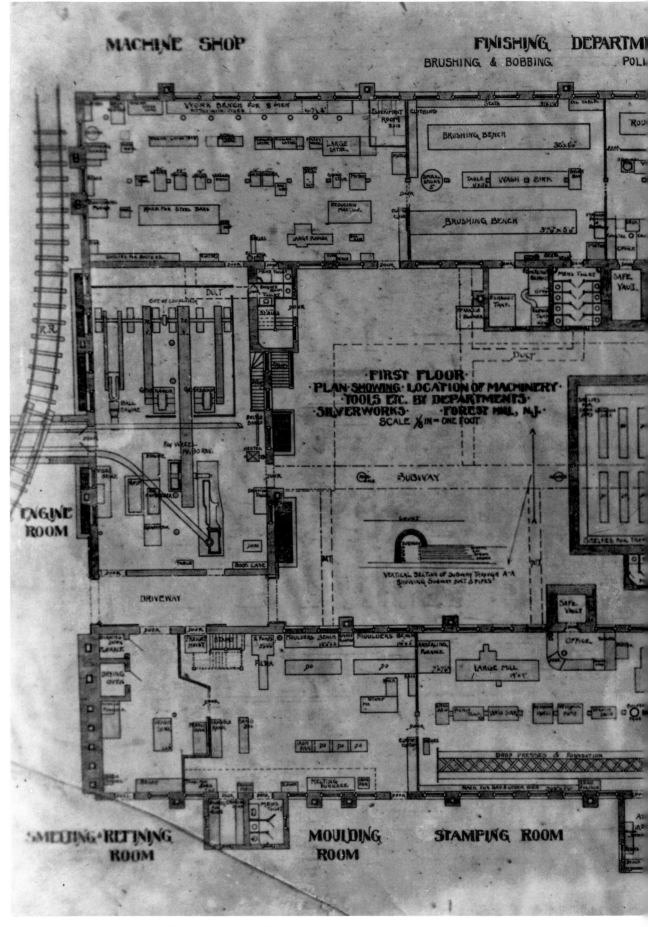

ILL. 7.8. First-floor layout of the Tiffany & Co. Forest Hill manufactory, Newark, N.J., ca. 1901.

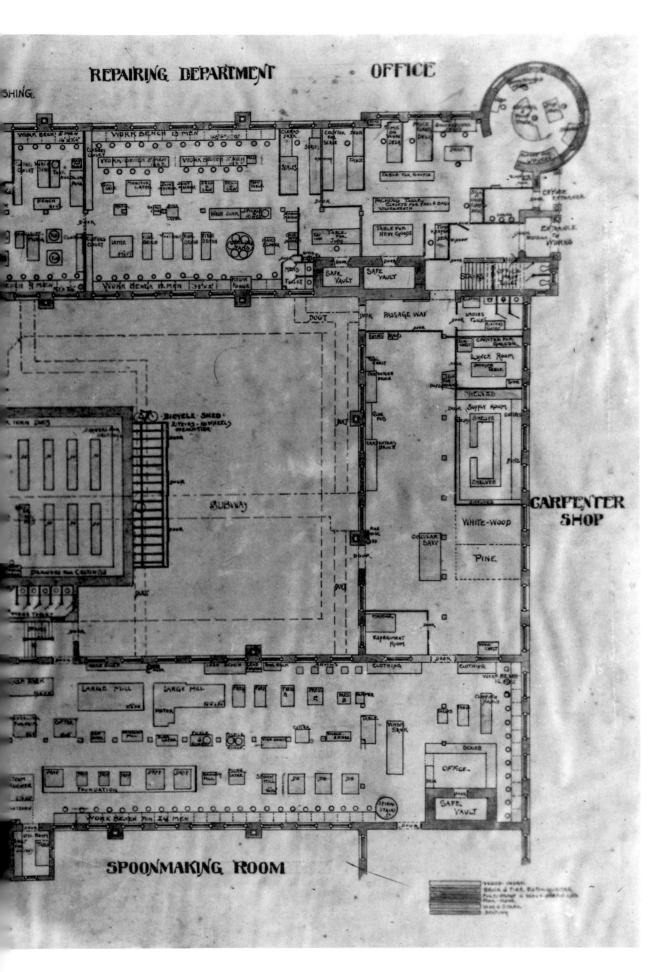

REPAIRING DEPARTMENT

OFFICE

CARPENTER SHOP

SPOONMAKING ROOM

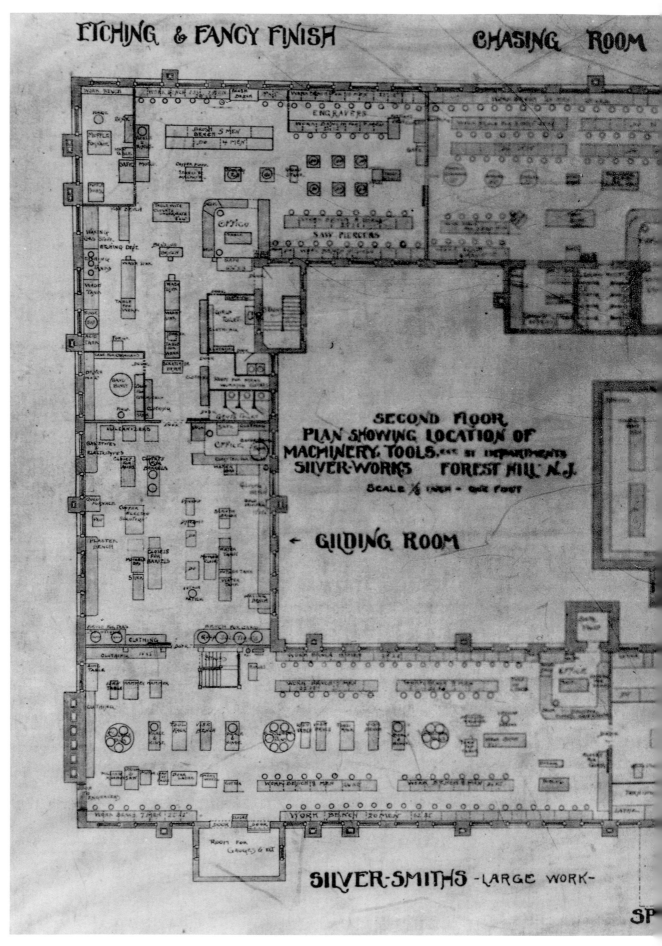

ILL. 7.9. Second-floor layout of the Tiffany & Co. Forest Hill manufactory, Newark, N.J., ca. 1901.

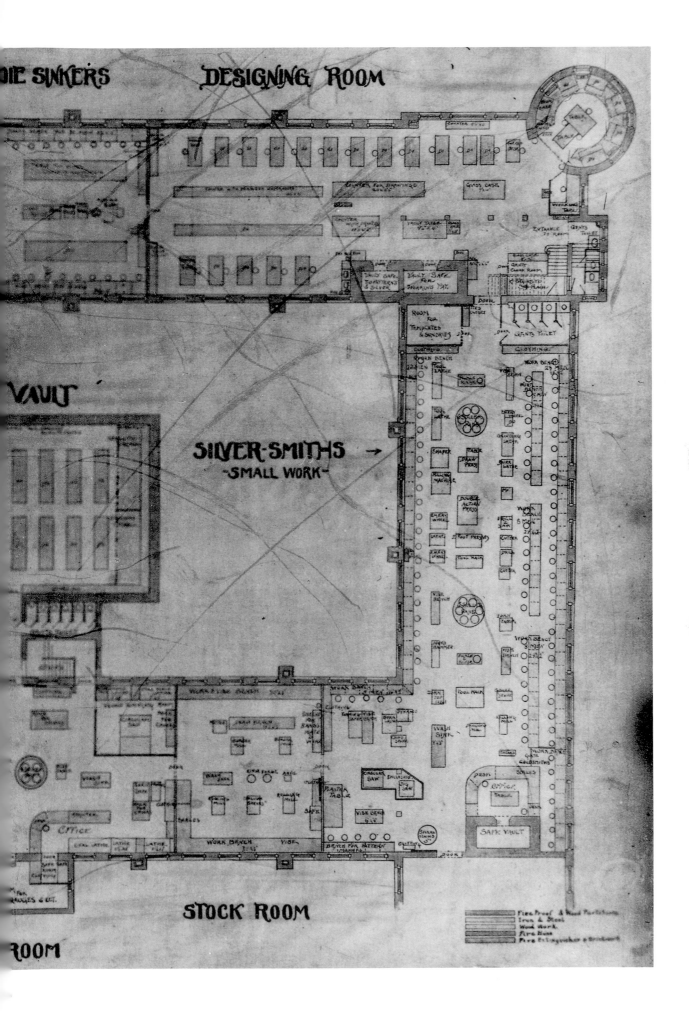

DIE SINKERS   DESIGNING ROOM

VAULT

SILVER-SMITHS →
~SMALL WORK~

STOCK ROOM

ROOM

objects was greatly reduced by organizing the space so that related departments were near one another. Similarly, the indexing and improved controls over tools and patterns meant that employees could find theirs more easily and thus did not have to visit other departments to borrow things. The result of such improvements was that workers "wasted" less time away from their benches. More efficient placement of toilets, lockers, showers, and lunch rooms also "saved" time.

Time itself was increasingly viewed as a precious commodity like silver. By the 1860s and early 1870s, firms had increased their efforts to control how their employees spent their hours at work. Companies based in more rural areas often installed bells whose tolling regulated the workday. Increasingly, more elaborate timekeeping was implemented. For example, by 1870 Gorham was using a system of small books in which departmental foremen recorded employees' "short time" (any time less than the standard ten hours). Each page recorded the room number, the "check" number that identified the employee, and his arrival and departure times. Each page was perforated so that the foreman could retain a copy of the information, while a signed duplicate was sent to the timekeeper's office where the tardy employee's pay would be docked.[61] Soon such manual systems gave way to mechanical ones like that at work in Tiffany & Co.'s Prince Street manufactory in 1887. On a tour of the building a visitor commented on a "timeboard" in the hall containing brass "checks" bearing numbers for each employee. Using this early version of a time clock, Tiffany's could more accurately keep track of hours actually worked by its employees.[62] When designing the Forest Hill plant in 1894, Tiffany's management enhanced timekeeping even further by installing "25 Clocks in Departments and one on the Tower electrically connected with [a] controlling clock in [the] office." It even went so far as to place a steam call whistle over the works' middle wing that was "operated by electrical push button" from the main office. The whistle "saved" time by improving communications: "The number of blasts indicating whether Manager, Master Mechanic, Electrician, Pipe Fitter, Oiler, Painter or Carpenter is wanted and to communicate at once by nearest telephone with [the] office."[63]

Besides seeking to regulate their workers through increasingly sophisticated timekeeping and communication devices, managers of silverware manufactories attempted to mold workers' behavior through work rules. All working environments, both large and small, have standards of behavior that are unwritten and often unspoken. These codes, which include proper dress and language for a given work environment, are usually communicated and enforced simply through the examples of fellow workers and superiors. Even more specific rules concerning the work routine might never be written down in some manufactories, especially the smaller, more personal ones. In crowded work environments, however, where upper management may have known all the foremen but certainly did not personally know scores of employees, written rules were thought essential.

Tiffany & Co., for example, not only wrote down work rules, but printed them up in large type and posted them around the manufactory. A placard from 1897 announced in giant letters, "TIFFANY & CO. / FOREST HILL WORKS / RULES." It then went on to list sixteen principal rules including:

1. HOURS OF WORK are from 7 A.M. to 12 noon; and from 12.30 to 5.30 P.M. except that on Saturday, work will end at 4.30 P.M.

4. OVERTIME until 9.30 will be paid an advance of 25 per cent.; after 9.30 P.M., 50 per cent. advance.

5. THOSE WHO ARE PAID overtime have no vacation allowed. No overtime allowed for Holidays.

8. EMPLOYEES are not allowed to visit rooms other than the ones in which they are employed at any time, except for some special reason connected with their work, sanctioned by their Foreman.

10. IT IS EXPECTED that workmen will see their friends elsewhere, and that calls during working hours will be those of necessity only.

11. WASHING UP, or other preparations for leaving before the Whistle blows, will not be allowed.

14. READING OF newspapers or books in Department rooms or Water Closets, will not be allowed during working hours.[64]

Like Tiffany's, Gorham also found such rules necessary in managing hundreds of workers. A pocket-size copy of its *Rules and Regulations* from 1910 lists fifteen points, most of which are very similar to Tiffany & Co.'s rules. Several of them concern the proper means of checking in and out from work, such as rule 7: "Any employee detected in depositing checks not his own will be immediately discharged"; and rule 8: "The sounding of the electric bells will be the signal for commencing and stopping work. Preparations to begin work must be made BEFORE, and preparations to quit must be made AFTER the signal is given."[65] Rules varying little from Tiffany & Co.'s and Gorham's were also in place at Reed & Barton as early as 1880.[66]

As managers attempted to increase efficiency by tightening controls over their work forces and redesigning their manufactories, the role of the foreman became pivotal. Throughout the history of metalworking, in almost every silversmithy that had more than one or two employees, a master craftsman was in charge. In small establishments, this figure might be the owner. However, as workshops increased dramatically in size during the nineteenth century, the foreman emerged as a mediator between workers and owners. As a master craftsman and trainer of apprentices, the foreman had strong personal ties to the men and women with whom he worked. Nevertheless, being better paid than those under him and responsible directly to upper management meant that he owed greater allegiance to those in the corporate hierarchy than to the average worker. Increasingly from the 1870s onward, managers tried to exploit the foreman, positioned between the worlds of labor and management, to do their bidding on the shop floor.

The growing responsibility of foremen in the workplace during the late nineteenth century can be seen in the lists of work rules that were specifically codified for foremen. At its Forest Hill works, Tiffany's posted the following *Rules for Foremen*:

> THOSE IN CHARGE OF DEPARTMENTS must be in their places at the hours of commencing and leaving work, or must send word as soon as possible if unable to be present.
>
> THEY ARE to confine themselves and their subordinates to their own Departments, and see that good order, proper warmth, ventilation and cleanliness is maintained.
>
> IT SHALL BE their particular duty to pass upon every piece of work before leaving their respective departments, and to see that it conforms in every respect to requirements of working pattern and order.
>
> AS THE FACTORY RULES are designed to promote the comfort and welfare of the workmen, as well as to maintain the general good order of the works, the foremen will see that the rules are strictly observed, and to that end will solicit the co-operation of their more intelligent and well disposed men.
>
> THE STOCK being in their charge they will be held to account for the same, and must exert themselves to lessen the Waste.
>
> SOLD ORDERS must always have the time they are to be finished specified on the ticket, and must be done promptly on time; if there should be any doubt the office must be immediately notified.
>
> IN CASE OF A HURRIED ORDER, each room through which it is passed must be notified.
>
> THEY WILL NOTIFY THE OFFICE at 11.30 A.M. and at 5.00 P.M. what workmen are absent, and at all times see that none but their own workmen are present and at work, in their rooms.[67]

The foreman's importance was also proclaimed in other types of signs that were posted around a factory. A Tiffany's sign stated that "Employees having bundles or packages to take away from factory, must report to their foreman before doing so, and have the same checked."[68]

The position of foreman in the increasingly organized environment of the late-nineteenth-century silverware manufactory was a difficult one. Often these men were senior workers who had become master craftsmen in their specialty through apprenticeship and work during the 1840s, 1850s, and 1860s. Therefore, they had matured at an earlier point in the industry's development, when work routines were more akin to the craft practices of the late eighteenth and early nineteenth centuries. The fact that firms found it necessary constantly to remind their employees that straying from one's own workroom to visit fellow workers or borrow tools, coming in late or leaving early, or being visited by friends or family during working hours was prohibited indicates that this more tolerant and less rigid view of working was still a potent force in the final decades of the century. Consequently, as managers pushed foremen to keep better watch over their men, report problem workers, maintain neat workrooms by organizing tools and workers, and, above all, drive their men to produce more faster, some foremen found themselves torn between older craft traditions and the modern desire for efficiency—between the men with whom they labored and the management to whom they reported. A good example of such a situation is that of Eugene J. Soligny (d. 1901).

Soligny was a French-trained master chaser who apparently emigrated to the United States in the early 1860s. By the mid 1870s he was working for Tiffany & Co., where he was employed on some of the firm's greatest commissions, including the *Bryant Vase* and the *Comanche Cup* (figs. 6.24, 7.1). Soligny was considered by Tiffany's as their finest chaser and was paid accordingly. His average wage of eighty-three cents an hour was three times that of any other chaser.[69] By the early 1890s, however, Soligny had been appointed foreman of the chasing department. In this capacity he was expected not only to execute exceptional work himself but to exercise control over his fellow chasers, pushing them to produce more in less time. On 1 June 1893, Tiffany's management instituted an incentive program to encourage Soligny and his fellow foremen in the form of a "Foreman's Contingent Bonus." Management stated that the purpose of the bonuses was to

> furnish an incentive to make [the foremen's] increase conditional on individual effort and make it so that the record must show. . . . They will then be made co-workers with Tiffany & Co. and in a certain sense sharers in their profit. 'Twill make them more vigilant over men and material, knowing that every case of excessive time on work will not only be recorded against them, but that every unnecessary dollar paid to men or expended that they can prevent militates against the value of the papers they hold.[70]

Under the terms of the bonus contract that Soligny signed, Tiffany and Co. would pay him $200 if during fiscal year 1893–94 he had successfully driven his men to produce more during the year while reducing waste. Specifically, he received the bonus if the plant's balance sheet for the chasing department showed an increase of 1 or more percent over the average of the four previous years, provided that management found "no just cause for complaint" in Soligny, "particularly where it concerned his men spending excessive time on an object."[71] Although E. J. Soligny entered into this agreement with Tiffany's management, he obviously found the conditions difficult to meet. Tiffany's paid him $100 in June 1894 and

FIG. 7.1. *Comanche Cup*. Tiffany & Co., New York, N.Y., 1873. Sterling silver. The Masco Art Collection.

voided the agreement because of "unfulfilled conditions by Mr. Soligny." Soligny had undoubtedly discovered that pushing highly skilled and proud craftsmen like chasers to work faster without lessening quality was often a thankless task—the chasers perhaps seeing him as a kind of managerial spy and taskmaster who earned significantly more then they, while management viewed him as too close to his men to drive them effectively and to report their shortcomings.

Management seldom reversed policies that increased its control over labor and thus production; however, it did become less confrontational in its attitude towards workers in the early twentieth century. Important policies concerning healthcare, pensions, and general morale were implemented at many firms. Gorham's efforts were exceptional in this area. In 1899 it built the "Casino" on its grounds to serve as a community center for workers. The Casino functioned as a lunch room where staff received food at cost; contained a library and reading room; included storage for bicycles; and had "one of the finest bowling alleys to be found in New England." Separate dining, rest, and recreation rooms in the Casino were set aside for female employees.[72] A pension plan of half pay for retirees was adopted in 1903.[73] Beyond these enduring changes, Gorham also instituted frequent company gatherings designed to promote a family atmosphere. Between 1900 and World War I, dozens of group activities, including beach parties, clambakes, sport events, and day trips, were organized. Many of these had elaborate programs and souvenirs printed to commemorate the events. To honor the heads of manufactory departments, fancy dinners were given by management in the Casino, while long-time employees were rewarded with membership in the Quarter Century Club (founded 1920).[74] Although problems between labor and management at Gorham and throughout the industry never disappeared altogether, and occasionally erupted into open conflict, many silverware manufacturers had come to believe by World War I that working with their employees was generally more effective in solving problems than not.

CORPORATE RESTRUCTURING

Many important silverware firms had incorporated long before the strikes of the mid 1880s. The forerunner of Reed & Barton, the Taunton Britannia Mfg. Co., had done so in 1833, with Meriden Britannia (1852), Gorham (1865), Whiting (1866), Tiffany's (1868), Towle (1882), Alvin (1886), Dominick & Haff (1889), Shiebler (1892), and many others following suit. By 1900 virtually the entire industry was incorporated. As Susan Strasser has noted, two fundamental legal changes that occurred in the 1880s and 1890s greatly enhanced this form of business organization. First, in a series of court cases beginning in 1886, the Supreme Court gave the corporation the legal rights of a person with none of a person's legal accountability. Although a corporation could be fined, its officers could not be sent to jail in most cases. Second, the Court, as well as the states, gave protection to new types of corporate assets. "Property" came to include not only physical items like land and buildings, but intangibles including market access, goodwill, and earning power. Furthermore, Delaware and New Jersey passed laws allowing corporations to own real estate in other states and stock in other corporations. "By the turn of the century, the corporate form was flexible enough to permit both owners and managers to pursue a variety of strategies. The new laws made the limited-purpose charter a thing of the past, promoted the separation of management from ownership and encouraged the growth of genuinely national enterprises."[75]

Between 1890 and 1910, these legal developments led to the formation of holding companies that controlled large segments of the silverware industry. Before these consolidations took place, however, various managers within the industry were already experimenting with ways to work with their competitors to oppose organized labor and to stabilize prices. Some trade organizations had been formed quite early, such as the Silver Plated Ware Manufacturers Association, which was created in 1876 to combat problems resulting from the 1870s depression.[76] Also, the 1887 strike led to the creation of the Manufacturers' Association to which several important firms belonged. This association, having successfully worked to defeat the Knights of Labor, continued as a voluntary organization geared to the promotion of management's desires. Over time such groups became more structured and eventually emerged as formal organizations like the Manufacturing Jewelers' and Silversmiths' Association (founded 1903) and the Sterling Silverware Manufacturers' Association (founded 1919). These organizations provided a forum for discussing policies that would affect the entire industry.

In addition to such efforts, managers from several firms joined together to form the Silversmith's Co., which was incorporated in New York State in December 1892 (ill. 7.10). Uniting the firms of Gorham, Whiting, Dominick & Haff, Shiebler, and Towle, the Silversmith's Co., was a holding company initially capitalized at $12 million and authorized to issue stock for another $8 million. With liberal bylaws, the Silversmith's Co. was a flexible instrument through which member companies could work together to gain greater power and profits.[77]

According to its own documents and the national and trade press, the purpose for creating the Silversmith's Co. was to secure "a uniformity of methods among the different Companies engaged in the trade, especially as regards the quality of the material used."[78] It was likened to London's Goldsmiths Co., which assayed solid silverwares, assuring their sterling standard. To regulate the sterling standard, the Silversmith's Co. stated: "The work of firms not in the organization will be assayed from time to time and if the silver used is found to be below the standard of 925–1000 it will be promptly advertised. In this way we hope to protect ourselves and the public."[79]

Calls for federal and state laws enforcing the honest marking of silverware had started in the late 1870s and intensified throughout the 1880s. Eventually, in 1906, the movement succeeded in getting Congress to pass the National Stamping Act, which outlawed the misrepresentation of silverware by requiring accurate marking or "stamping." Unfortunately, the law had no power of enforcement, and thus regulation fell to the states. While some states did pass stamping laws, few were strongly enforced, and consequently only a handful of convictions for fraud were handed down between 1906 and 1914, after which the issue disappeared beneath the shadow of war.[80]

Internal documents indicate that the Silversmith's Co. was indeed interested in furthering the cause of the honest stamping crusade. In 1894, for example, Towle's vice-president L. D. Cole suggested to Edward Holbrook of Gorham that the organization have bills introduced into the legislatures of New York, Rhode Island, and Massachusetts which would define the "meaning of the word 'sterling'."[81] Believing that the Silversmith's Co. might succeed in establishing the names and trademarks of its member companies as the most trustworthy in the industry, some outsiders publicly opposed its organization. In December 1892, for example, a letter from "A Fair Race" to the *Jewelers' Review* stated:

> I suppose that all of the unfortunate manufacturers who are not armed with this self-established incorporated trade mark [make] spurious goods. Just think for one moment of some of the names that would come under the head—Tiffany & Co., Reed & Barton and a long list of smaller houses that have honorable men at the head. Are the public to be educated to the belief that their wares are not 925–1000 fine, because they are not of the chosen few?[82]

In general, however, comments in the trade press were positive concerning the Silversmith's Co., but not because it was trying to achieve honest marking. Rather, outside firms were hopeful that the organization could stabilize silverware prices,

ILL. 7.10. Silversmith's Hall, 860 Broadway, New York, N.Y., built 1892.

which had reached dangerously low levels by the early 1890s. The *Jewelers' Review* reported that "if the object of the combination was to raise prices then that would have a healthy effect upon silverware interests. Silver goods . . . are represented as being at their lowest possible salable rates. Competition has not only lowered profits—legitimate not excessive profits—that on many lines of goods there is no gain at all."[83] Slim profit margins were evidently especially true for flatware since several commentators, including one from Wood & Hughes, hoped the Silversmith's Co. could raise its price.

Publicly, however, spokesmen for the new company denied that price management was its goal. The *New York Times* quoted them as saying that "there is no intention of forming a 'trust' in the sense of a combination for the raising or the maintaining of prices."[84] Despite such denials, the Silversmith's Co. was indeed created to stabilize prices. Internal correspondence survives indicating that a "manufacturers agreement" existed as early as 1891 which set prices on flatware in relation to the ever-falling price of silver bullion. Furthermore, in July 1892

representatives from Whiting reported to Gorham that they had "made some effort to obtain the views of the larger retail city houses," including Tiffany's, Theodore B. Starr, and Black, Starr & Frost. Finding that $1.60 per ounce was the favored price for "ordinary stamped patterns" and $1.50 was being charged for plain patterns and from $1.75 to $2.00 per ounce for elaborate ones, Whiting set its prices at the same levels.[85] Because pricing by weight provided a critical means to simplify price regulation in a trade where flatware was sold in hundreds of different patterns, the Silversmith's Co. moved quickly to standardize the process of price regulation by weight.[86] Within a few months, a "price" committee was in operation and attempting to respond to the sudden fluctuation in the price of silver caused by the Panic of 1893. In June the committee sent letters to nineteen major silverware producers asking for their cooperation in setting prices. By August it was clear, however, that some firms, including several represented on the committee itself, would not work in concert as a cartel to fix prices and "that each of the manufacturers [would] have to act

ILL. 7.11. Edward Holbrook, ca. 1910.

independently." Within a week of this statement, Gorham, by far the largest of the producers, gave notice that it had set the prices of sterling at $1.00 per ounce.[87]

The Silversmith's Co. proved a vehicle through which talented individuals, tools, and processes were shared. In December 1893, for example, Towle notified Gorham that it was short of good designs and that if Gorham or any of the other sister companies had designs for which they would like dies cut, Towle was willing to do the work. Three months later, Towle told Gorham that the changes George Wilkinson had made to the designs it had sent to Gorham "certainly appear to be improvements" and that it would probably cut dies for two of the patterns. Towle was also getting Gorham's opinions on the dies it was cutting and on the proofs those dies produced. Occasionally, Gorham must have made dies for the other firms as well, since in 1893 Towle "was to send [Gorham] drawings of a Tea set, from which [Gorham] was to consider the expediency of making bronze dies."[88] Given the high cost

in hard times of maintaining designers and die sinkers, as well as cutting dies, sharing such talent must have been more efficient than doing everything oneself. The Silversmith's Co. appears to have encouraged this type of personnel and technical cross-fertilization by starting a small workshop in December 1892, when it purchased the plant of Strong & Elder at 19–21 East Thirteenth Street in Manhattan. Superintended by a John Mason, the shop was moved to the Cable Building at Twenty-fifth and Lexington in 1895.[89] Presumably, this establishment provided a space where workers from the partner companies could come together and discuss ideas and processes, as well as produce silverware.

Although much study is still needed, it seems that the purpose of the Silversmith's Co. changed under the pressure of the financial Panic of 1893. Some of the member companies, much less nonmembers, clearly refused to act together to set prices within the industry. Recognizing the implausibility of achieving its original intent, the dynamic entrepreneur Edward

Holbrook (1849–1919. ill. 7.11) took over the Silversmith's Co. and used it as a tool for securing control of several silverware manufacturers. Holbrook was a pivotal figure in the history of the American silverware industry during the late nineteenth and early twentieth centuries. He joined Gorham in 1870 and became the firm's New York agent in 1876. Evidently his business acumen was appreciated by Gorham management because Holbrook was elected a company director in 1882, was named treasurer in 1888, and assumed the presidency in 1894 at age forty-five. He remained president for the next quarter century.

Holbrook's drive and ambition paralleled that of John Gorham, who had built up the company in the 1850s and 1860s, for in his obituary Holbrook was said to have been "the Napoleon of the silverware industry."[90] Unlike John Gorham, whose expertise was technical in nature, Holbrook was a professional manager who excelled at business organization and advertising. Consequently it was he who pushed the company to exhibit at world's fairs, beginning with the Centennial in 1876, and to erect the elaborate, Queen Anne–style, New York showroom in 1884, and the efficient Elmwood plant in 1890. Further, Holbrook masterminded the creation of the Silversmith's Co.[91]

Evidently, in the mid 1890s, when he found it impossible to get its member companies to cooperate, Holbrook began to take financial control of the Silversmith's Co. Presumably, Holbrook, who had profited greatly from Gorham, simply began buying Silversmith's Co. stock until he held a controlling interest. Perhaps the stock held by associates of Towle and Dominick & Haff was some of the first purchased, because those firms seem to have disassociated themselves from the Silversmith's Co. relatively quickly. Once Holbrook controlled the firm he used it as a holding company for the acquisition of other concerns.

The first company Holbrook acquired appears to have been Shiebler, which suffered greatly from the recession of the mid 1890s. Following unsuccessful proposals to combine with Gorham in 1892, Holbrook evidently purchased a controlling interest of Shiebler stock that had been issued in January of that year, merged the firm into the Silversmith's Co. sometime in the mid 1890s, and had eliminated the Shiebler brand name altogether in 1910 following Shiebler's retirement.[92] Although the William B. Kerr Company of Newark, New Jersey, which specialized in silver toilet ware and novelties, was not a founding party in the Silversmith's Co., Holbrook worked through the Silversmith's Co. to purchase the firm sometime before 1907.

The first decade of the new century was pivotal for Holbrook. In 1907 he launched a corporate raid on the major silverware producer Reed & Barton. Working through a holding company called the Silverware Stocks Co., which may have been established especially for this purpose, Holbrook acquired nearly a half-interest in Reed & Barton by purchasing shares from disgruntled stockholders. William Dowse, Reed & Barton's dynamic treasurer and major stockholder, managed to block Holbrook's efforts by miring them in the courts. In 1910 the courts ruled against Holbrook, and as a result he sold his now-useless stock to Dowse.[93] Failing to acquire Reed & Barton, Holbrook was more successful with Gorham.

In 1905 Holbrook had been president of Gorham for eleven years. Apparently by this time he not only owned a majority of the stock in the Silversmith's Co. but was in complete control of Gorham. From this powerful position, Holbrook orchestrated the purchase by Gorham of large interests in both Whiting and Durgin in 1905 and their sale the very next year to his Silversmith's Co. Thus through his own personal holdings of stock and those held by Silversmith's, Holbrook controlled a large segment of the sterling silverware industry in this country by 1907. To solidify this achievement, the directors of the Silverware Stocks Co. and the Silversmith's Co. agreed to merge on 28 February 1907.[94] During the years before his death in 1919, Holbrook strengthened his position still further. By 1922 the Silversmith's Co. held virtually all of Gorham's common stock, with the Holbrook estate and heirs personally owning the small amount of remaining common stock and 19 percent of Gorham's preferred stock. His estate also owned the vast majority of stock in the Silversmith's Co., as well as a large portion of its subsidiaries' stock.[95]

Under Holbrook's dynamic leadership, Gorham and the other firms controlled by the Silversmith's Co. appear to have prospered. In 1917, for example, Gorham's sales had risen to over $7 million, Durgin's to $1,242,000, Whiting's to $933,000 and to Kerr's $438,000.[96] Furthermore, Holbrook had expanded his empire by acquiring the Mount Vernon Co. Silversmiths, Inc. Purchased in 1914, this firm was especially important because it controlled the silverware makers Hays & MacFarland of New York City, Mauser Mfg. Co. of Mt. Vernon, New York, and Roger Williams Co. of Providence, Rhode Island. By the time of his death in 1919, therefore, Edward Holbrook controlled roughly 20 percent of all silverware production and perhaps as much as 40 percent of sterling production in the United States.[97] Without Holbrook at the helm and under great pressure from the severe post–World War I recession, however, the Silversmith's Co. faltered and was liquidated in 1924.

Although the rise of Edward Holbrook was exceptional and deserves further scholarly attention, the creation of large holding companies within the silverware industry was not unique to him. As Edmund Hogan has pointed out,[98] consolidations were especially prevalent in the silverplate section of the industry during the 1890s and 1910s. For example, in 1898 seventeen silverplate producers joined together to create the International Silver Co., which was said to control 70 percent of this segment of the silverware industry. This consolidation was the result of heavy losses suffered in the 1890s due to the recession and the inroads that sterling was making into the silverplate market as silver prices fell. In both 1894 and 1896, for example, the huge Meriden Britannia Co. lost money, as did Meriden Silver Plate Co., Wilcox Silver Plate Co., Holmes & Edwards, and Simpson, Hall, Miller & Co. in 1896. It was hoped that by joining forces, greater efficiency, and thus higher profits, could be generated by eliminating duplication and by gaining advantages of economy of scale. Toward this end, many product lines, sales forces and showrooms were combined, while others were eliminated completely. Despite these efforts, profits did not rise substantially. Consequently, International's stock prices fell dramatically. Preferred stock, which had opened at $90 in 1899, stood at $34 by 1900, while common stock went from $36 in 1899 to $5.50 a year later. In fact, dividends were not paid on common stock until 1926.[99]

Besides poor financial returns, International Silver also was plagued with other problems during the early twentieth century. In 1902, while in weak financial condition, it was confronted with a hostile takeover bid from the United States Silver Corporation. A dummy corporation controlled by investors who had acquired a majority of International's stock, United States Silver forced International to pay out several million dollars to retain the status quo. Furthermore, between 1900 and 1907, a disgruntled former member of International's board of directors, William H. Watrous, carried on a troublesome publicity campaign in which he portrayed International as the evil "Silver Trust." International Silver weathered these storms, but the years between 1900 and 1940 were difficult ones, substantial profits apparently being made only in the late 1920s.

While many firms either chose to merge or were forced to, some others managed to survive and eventually prosper on their own during the late 1890s and early twentieth century. George Gibb's exceptional analysis of Reed & Barton, for example, shows how that firm operated at a loss between 1891 and 1898 due to the general economic recession and antiquated management techniques, including overinvestment in inventory and borrowing to finance it.[100] However, the election as president in 1901 of Harvard-educated lawyer and financier William Dowse (1852–1928) changed this situation and brought modernization to Reed & Barton. Soon after his arrival, Dowse hired efficiency experts and auditors, purchased modern machinery, and reorganized production in order to cut production costs. Certainly profits were slim in some years, being less than 2 percent of sales in 1907, 1908, 1911, 1914, and 1915. Nevertheless, Dowse's administration showed an annual profit from 1902 to 1923, when he retired.[101] Under Reed & Barton's next president, the Harvard-trained banker Sinclair Weeks, Dowse's son-in-law, modernization was pushed still further in finance, production, and marketing. As a result, sales and profits between 1924 and 1929 were higher than ever in the company's history. Although the Depression brought operating losses from 1930 to 1932, Reed & Barton's situation gradually improved through the rest of the 1930s until World War II brought war production contracts and stabilized profits.[102]

Like Reed & Barton, Tiffany & Co. was a firm that avoided merger and managed to survive. As discussed above, it opened a modern manufacturing facility in 1894 at Forest Hill, New Jersey. However, the severe recession that began in 1893 made it difficult for the firm to take full advantage of its new capabilities because silver shop sales dropped to an average of $600,000 from 1894 to 1899, down from their 1890–93 average of nearly

$750,000. Nevertheless, an increase in net profits to total sales from 19.2 to 20.9 percent over the same period may have been the result of increased efficiency at the new plant and economy-wide deflation that occurred before 1898. Between 1900 and 1907 sales recovered, averaging over $850,000, with profits averaging nearly 24 percent. During the 1907–8 recession, sales fell from a high of over $1 million in the fiscal year 1906–7 to $715,463, with profits of less than 10 percent by the start of 1909. In an attempt to better understand the reasons behind this drop in profits, financial specialists were called in to examine the silver shop's procedures and accounts. Beginning with the entry for 1909, the shop's ledger notes that "Profits [were] determined by Experts after charging the factory with Depreciation on Building and tools and regarding all dies & patterns as expenses."[103] While sales recovered to an average of $864,331 between 1910 and 1914, profits averaged only 11.3 percent. Even in 1917, when sales went over $1 million, probably as the result of war work, profits were less than 10 percent.[104] One reason for such slim profit margins was undoubtedly the 30 percent rise in inflation that occurred in the 1910s.

Exactly why the Tiffany & Co. silver shop found it so difficult to make a substantial profit from silver products after the economy recovered from the 1907–8 recession is not entirely clear. Certainly, the "experts" brought in 1909 may have instituted a new accounting system that took more of the factory's overhead into account, thereby reducing profits shown on the books. These lower profits may also have been the result of the inflation that grew economy-wide after 1898. Having geared itself to the deflationary economy that had existed since the Civil War, Tiffany's, and the silverware industry as a whole, had significantly lowered prices on its products by the 1890s in order to stay competitive. With the onset of inflation, however, the company may have found it difficult to raise those prices in advance of increasing overhead. Exactly what would have caused such a situation is unclear. But perhaps the prestige of silverware was being eroded by new luxury goods like automobiles, radios, and electric appliances, thus lessening demand for silver and discouraging price increases needed to keep pace with inflation. The shift to less elaborate and formal lifestyles in the first decades of the twentieth century would also have worked to reduce demand and keep prices down.

FROM WAR TO WAR, 1915–1940

The United States' entry into World War I in 1917 brought sudden changes to the silverware industry. As men left for the service, the labor of those remaining became more valuable. In some cases the sudden increase in pay for those doing munitions work touched off labor disputes. In September 1915, for example, the Silver Workers Union at International Silver Co. demanded that all workers be given a 25 percent raise in pay and the eight-hour workday. The demands were made because International had increased pay and instituted three eight-hour shifts in its munitions plants, while maintaining the ten-hour workday and old pay rate in its silverware operations.

Management rejected the demands, and approximately 3,000 workers went on strike. Because the strike impaired the manufacturing of war materials, including gas masks, rifle and pistol magazines, knives, and mess kits, the federal government tried to arbitrate, but had little success. International offered a 10 percent wage raise and a fifty-five hour week, but workers rejected the offer. Violence erupted at one plant, resulting in minor injuries and the arrest of numbers of employees. With negotiations stalled, International filed for an injunction against the union to stop it from preventing workers from returning to work if they wished. After it was granted in January 1916, many employees returned to work. Although the strike was not officially called off until January 1919, the workers appear to have gained no more than they had already accomplished early in the strike, a 10 percent wage increase and a fifty-five hour week.[105]

Beyond increasing the cost of labor and sparking some labor unrest, the war meant that promising young apprentices departed for overseas, many never to return to the industry. The conflict also brought higher taxes, further inflation, and a scarcity of certain metals, especially base metal used in silverplate. In addition, the price of silver bullion, which had fallen steadily since 1870, rose dramatically during the war. Between 1915 and 1919 the value of silver increased 55 percent and remained above prewar levels until the late 1920s.[106] Nevertheless, some manufacturers saw the war as an opportunity to profit from the production of munitions and related goods, such as surgical implements, which Tiffany's produced.[107] While many firms like International Silver dedicated only a portion of their facilities to war production,[108] others, like Gorham, invested heavily in the field.

Soon after the beginning of the war in 1914, Gorham volunteered its services to the Allied governments and began taking contracts for bullet cartridges. Their experience in working metals made firms like Gorham ideal suppliers of armaments. In 1915 Gorham built and equipped a new plant for cartridge production and in 1918 erected two more munitions manufactories. One of the latter employed nearly 2,000 women and was the only facility in the country producing hand grenades, with a capacity of 100,000 per day. The other factory made naval shell cartridges. Over the course of the war, Gorham produced munitions for Serbia, France, Russia, Switzerland, the Netherlands, Denmark, Great Britain, Norway, Portugal, Greece, China, and the United States.[109] However, in the end, Gorham's expansion into munitions proved disastrous. Looking back from 1966, a company officer summed up the firm's experience when he said, "World War I dropped a bomb on us with unprofitable contracts, topped off by noncollectible debt of the Russian government."[110]

By the end of the war, Gorham and the Silversmith's Co., which controlled it, were in serious trouble. In 1919 their capable leader, Edward Holbrook, died, throwing the companies' management into chaos. The summer of 1920 found the Silversmith's Co. nearly insolvent, and a reorganization was proposed in which Gorham, by far the largest of its subsidiaries, would buy out the parent holding company. The goal was to eliminate Silversmith's altogether and merge the other firms with Gorham. "Greater manufacturing efficiency [was] to be achieved by eliminating duplication of plants and products."[111] Reorganization and refinancing, however, were slow and did not formally occur until 1924–26. Before these changes could be accomplished, the situation worsened. The sharp recession of 1920–21 hurt Gorham and the entire silverware industry. Sales declined for both sterling and plate, and prices had to be reduced from 10 to 25 percent industry-wide.[112] Furthermore, a strike affecting several manufacturers occurred in January 1921. In December of the previous year, many producers, in an attempt to reduce costs, lengthened the work week to forty-eight hours from forty-four, without increasing wages. Supposedly, this was done to prevent layoffs. Not surprisingly, several hundred silverworkers in New York City refused to accept the change and struck. Although the outcome at other companies is unknown, Gorham's reaction was swift. Apparently the only facility of the firm that was affected was the "City Shop," which had been started by the Silversmith's Co. in 1892 in Manhattan. Three months after the strike started, Gorham stopped all manufacturing in the shop, fired the strikers, and moved the hollowware dies to Whiting and the ones for toilet ware to Kerr. To care for those men who did not strike, a small repair shop was opened in a portion of the old space. This last operation was still active in 1938.[113]

Gorham's troubles went far beyond the loss of its small city shop, however. For the fiscal year ending 31 January 1921, it posted a net loss of over $1.5 million. Durgin and Whiting also lost money. The next fiscal year showed a loss of $167,297, with Whiting and Kerr losing approximately $78,000 and $102,000, respectively.[114] Furthermore, in 1922 the firm elected as president Franklin L. Taylor, who unfortunately instituted a disastrous new marketing scheme that alienated many of the firm's best customers. By 1924, when Gorham actually took control of the defunct Silversmith's Co., massive reorganization of production and marketing was necessary. To achieve this, Aldred & Co. of New York was called in to analyze every aspect of Gorham and the subsidiaries it had acquired from Silversmith's. Noting that silverware was still primarily produced by hand and that Gorham had a large work force (1,320 at the Providence plant in 1924) capable of such work, the study suggested examining ways to eliminate as much hand labor as possible by using machines. Also, it recommended that piecework, which was not used anywhere in the Gorham system, be tried for certain processes. It proposed making fewer patterns, "but those popular," and doing larger production runs rather than the small batches typical of the silverware industry. Studies were recommended to determine whether Gorham could subcontract out the work of its printing, photography, and case-making departments, rather than do the work in-house. In addition, reductions in staff were recommended in the construction and maintenance departments, and lower-paid workers were suggested for clerical staff. Furthermore, it was proposed that lower-paid girls might be used for most of the polishing and finishing, which was being done by men and consumed two-fifths of all productive labor at the Gorham plant. Durgin was evidently already employing many girls in this manner.[115]

However, Gorham's main problem in terms of production was its underutilized facilities. In 1917 a comparative cost analysis of the various factories then owned by the Silversmith's Co. showed Gorham's Providence plant as the most cost effective, followed closely by Durgin.[116] The new accounting system that was inaugurated in 1924, however, was far more sophisticated than the old means of computing costs and revealed that Gorham's plant actually produced the lowest return on its investment. When judged against the huge investment in the massive Elmwood plant and its equipment, Gorham was averaging a mere 1 percent return on investment. Whiting was doing somewhat better, with a 7 percent return, and Kerr and Durgin had a much healthier rate of 12 percent.[117] Complicating the situation still further was the fact that inflation was primarily responsible for the large sales figures of Gorham and its subsidiaries between 1916 and 1922. Gorham sales alone ranged from highs of $7 million in the fiscal year ending January 1917 to $9 million in fiscal 1919–20. Yet, as Aldred & Co. pointed out, when adjusted for inflation, sales were down 25 percent in real terms from their prewar levels of around $6 million annually. This meant that although more dollars were coming in, the actual quantity of objects sold was probably less. This fact aggravated the Gorham system's problem of underutilized manufacturing capacity still further.[118]

Under the leadership of a capable new president, Edmund C. Mayo, who arrived in 1924, Gorham rectified many of these production problems by consolidating or eliminating manufacturing facilities. The Mt. Vernon Co. and its subsidiaries were closed completely in 1924, and their dies and records transferred to Providence. Although their brand names were retained, the other firms were also consolidated at Gorham: Whiting moved from Bridgeport, Connecticut, in 1924; Kerr came from Newark, New Jersey, in 1927; and Durgin in Concord, New Hampshire, followed in 1931. At the same time, much of the marketing network was also reorganized. Besides consolidating manufacturing at the underutilized Elmwood plant, Edmund C. Mayo is said to have made production more efficient by taking power away from foremen.[119] Since the 1880s, these men had come to play important roles in the decision-making process concerning labor and production policies. As more and more of those decisions were affected by market research and outside specialists during the 1920s, foremen increasingly came to be seen as impediments to progress. At Reed & Barton, for example, foremen were no longer allowed to hire workers or set their rate of pay. These functions were taken over by the newly created personnel departments.[120] This transformation was not limited to Gorham and Reed & Barton, but was industry-wide.

By 1926 Gorham's reorganization was sufficiently complete and the firm profitable enough to buy out the estate and heirs of Edward Holbrook, who still controlled the company. During the remainder of the 1920s, Gorham paid off its debts and returned to profitability, thus placing itself in a relatively secure position to weather the Great Depression of the 1930s. While few of its rivals experienced the extreme transformations in corporate structure and production that Gorham did, the decade following World War I was a time of modernization and consolidation for many. As noted above, Reed & Barton updated itself during the period and profited throughout the decade, as did International Silver. Beyond individual efforts, the silverware industry as a whole attempted to increase efficiency. In 1919, for example, the Sterling Silverware Manufacturers' Association distributed booklets on a "Standardized Cost Accounting System for the Sterling Silverware Industry" and in 1920 announced that it had arranged "with [the] Research Department of the Geo. Batten Co. for a Full Survey Covering the Manufacture, Distribution and Consumer Demand for Silver."[121] Interested in increasing efficiency in American industry, the Federal Government focused its "Elimination of Waste" program on sterling flatware in 1926, recommending a drastic reduction in the number of weights, patterns, and forms of flatware produced throughout the industry. And after a pattern had been discontinued five years, it was not to be supplied again. Significantly, the chairman of the study was Gorham's president, Edmund C. Mayo.[122] Through such cooperative efforts and self-analyses, many firms were able to cut production costs enough to profit from record sales of sterling and plated wares in the late 1920s. In 1923 the value of all silverware produced in the United States reached a new high of over $81 million. In 1927 it peaked at nearly $87.5 million, declining only slightly by 1929 to almost $86 million.[123] Even taking inflation into account, the late 1920s were a prosperous time for most silverware producers.

With the crash of October 1929 and the ensuing depression, prosperity evaporated for the silverware industry. As consumers stopped buying luxury goods, sales plummeted and manufactories had to cut production and begin laying off workers. On 24 December 1930, Edmund C. Mayo sent Gorham's hundreds of employees a Christmas card with the following message:

> This has been a difficult year for us all, difficult for those who have had to make sacrifices by accepting short-time, and difficult for those who have had the anxiety of steering a course that will keep our company intact for our security.
>
> I am grateful for the uncomplaining manner in which you have met the situation with the loyalty and devotion, the service your attitude has shown.
>
> To be the leader of such a body of men and women is indeed a privilege.

I wish you all a merry Christmas and sincerely hope that the new year will open up visions of returning prosperity which will bring happiness to you and yours.[124]

Unfortunately, the new year brought only worsening economic conditions. By the end of 1931 the total value of American-made silverware had dropped 47 percent to approximately $46 million. Two years later the figure was down to $34.3 million. Only when the economy began to improve in the late 1930s did sales begin to rise. This ameliorating situation is reflected in figures for 1937, when the total value of silverware made in America reached $56.7 million, which represented only a small improvement over 1931 sales when adjusted for inflation. Furthermore, in just three years from 1929 to 1933, the number of sterling and plate manufacturers in this country fell from 179 to 126, rising to just 135 by 1937.[125]

An executive memo book dating from 1932 to the mid 1940s which survives in the Tiffany Archives provides insight into how such a firm reacted to the Depression. Because it manufactured and sold large amounts of jewelry, Tiffany's was especially hard hit. The Revenue Act of 1932, for example, placed an additional 10 percent tax on jewelry and articles mounted with precious stones and ivory. Rather than raise prices, Tiffany's decided to absorb the tax.[126] By December of that year "disappointing sales necessitate[d] a further decrease in overhead," and in January 1933 workers were laid off without pay for various periods, depending on what category of worker they were.[127]

On 14 April officers and directors, who had been exempt from the January layoffs, were now required to take two-week vacations during the summer and one further week off without pay. On 1 August staff was informed that Tiffany & Co. had joined the American National Retail Jewelers' Association and agreed to comply with its "Tentative Code of Fair Competition for the Retail Jewelry Industry." These guidelines were written as part of the National Recovery Act (NRA). Designed to stabilize the silverware and jewelry trades, the NRA rules asked manufacturers to increase wages and reduce work hours even though business was poor, in an attempt to stimulate the economy and prevent further unemployment.[128] However, Tiffany's management stated on 9 August that it was "still employing a very great many more persons than have been necessary, or are now necessary, to conduct the business" and that it could "point with pride to the fact that on August 1, 1933 there were only 22.7 [percent] fewer persons employed by them in New York than on August 1, 1929 and this moderate decrease includes those vacancies caused by death and resignation." Although layoffs were discontinued during the fall peak season, they were reinstituted in April 1934. And on 29 December of that year Tiffany's announced that although it had followed the NRA regulations during the past two years, the firm was so unprofitable that greater staff reductions were necessary for 1935. Further layoffs and dismissals were announced on 6 April 1938 and 17 April 1939.

Besides reducing production costs by cutting staff and hours, Tiffany's "Notices" reveal many other measures enacted to increase profits and lessen costs. For example, orders were encouraged for discontinued flatware patterns, provided an extra "set-up" fee was paid (13 October 1932); plated ware production was discontinued (29 November 1933) and cheaper English plate was sold (23 January 1935); only rough sketches were made for custom or new silverware because of the high cost of preparing finished designs (21 March 1935); the amount paid by the firm to employees while on jury duty was reduced (22 April 1936); health care coverage was reduced (5 April 1937); and custom orders for plated ware ceased being taken (25 September 1937). Other cost-cutting measures were adopted in the retail store. But in spite of such tactics, Tiffany & Co. was still in poor financial condition in 1940. That year $3.6 million had to be taken from reserve cash simply to stay open. In 1941 Tiffany & Co.'s capitalization was $4.8 million, exactly what it had been in 1919. As Joseph Purtell has stated, "If Tiffany's policies did not change rapidly, it would soon be bankrupt."[129]

Luckily for Tiffany's and for many other silverware producers, World War II brought lucrative munitions contracts. By late 1941 Tiffany & Co.'s Forest Hill manufactory was converting to war production, and the next January the company announced that silverware production would be limited "to the best selling, popular priced and simpler objects" and orders for discontinued flatware patterns would no longer be accepted.[130] On 29 July 1942 the firm announced that the War Production Board had issued Order M-199 restricting the use of silver for silverware production. Because its factory was running at full capacity, producing precision parts for anti-aircraft guns and fitting blocks for airplanes,[131] and because silver bullion was nearly impossible to purchase, Tiffany's suspended silverware production at its plant on 15 November 1942.[132] Although limited production was resumed in mid 1943 when the government allowed some domestically mined silver to be sold and used for silverware, production was very limited throughout the rest of the war, and by June 1944 silver objects were being rationed in the New York store.[133]

Most silverware manufacturers followed Tiffany & Co.'s pattern during World War II. At Gorham the entire bronze division was converted to war work, and by 1943 there were only about 160 employees producing silverware. Hollowware production was cut 70 percent and sterling flatware was limited to six-piece place settings in the thirteen most popular patterns. Toilet and ecclesiastical wares were virtually eliminated. And as early as 1 June 1942, silver was being rationed to Gorham's customers. Over thirty types of war material were manufactured by the firm, including steel cartridge cases, tank bearings, torpedo components, and small-arms parts.[134] The story was similar at Reed & Barton, which during 1940 and 1941 converted to war production. By mid 1941 the firm almost totally discontinued its commercial lines of ware and sold its samples. Soon 600 men and 300 women were at work making tableware for the Army and Navy and precision, steel surgical instruments.[135]

However, it was at International Silver that the transformation was perhaps most amazing. There, virtually 100 percent of its huge manufacturing capacity was devoted to war production. In all, International handled 447 prime war contracts and 1,450 separate subcontracts and invested nearly $750,000 in specialized munitions tools and equipment. The firm produced a wide range of materials, from surgical instruments and Army buckles to shell cartridges and incendiary oil bombs. Quantities were staggering, including nearly 173 million cartridge brass strips, 176 million shell case discs, and 217 million metallic links for machine guns. And although the making of silverplate was discontinued on 15 April 1942, a small amount of sterling was produced throughout the war in spite of the heavy volume of war work.[136]

By the end of the war, all of the firms mentioned above, as well as many others in the industry, had received the "Army-Navy 'E' Award" for excellence in manufacturing for the war effort. Given the custom-made, hand-processed, low volume nature of so much of the U.S. silverware industry's peacetime production, receiving these awards was truly a miraculous achievement. For even in the 1930s, the majority of silverware produced in this country required much hand labor in its creation and was made in relatively small batches. Consequently, to shift to the high volume production of thousands if not millions, of identical objects must have been difficult for workers who were used to a slower, more craft-oriented work routine. It is also ironic that in the end this transformation was made in two brief years, since countless managers, accountants, and efficiency experts had been trying to accomplish the same task for over half a century. But the industry had proven to be a stubborn one that did not yield easily to modernization and only did so during war time, at the expense of the original product.

NOTES

1. For production figures that reflect this trend, see Parsell 1901, 31; Historical 1950, chart; and Gibb 1943, 225 and 332.

2. *Silverware* 1940, tables 17 and 25. For silver prices during the period under discussion, see Jastram 1981, table 20.

3. Rise reflected in *Silverware* 1940, tables 17 and 25.

4. Tiffany's and Gorham records show the biggest falling off in production, sales, and work force occurring in the years 1883–85.

5. Peterson 1937, 29.

6. "The Independence of Skilled Workmen," *JCK* 17:6 (July 1886):169–70.

7. "The Labor Troubles," *JCK* 17:7 (Aug. 1886):208.

8. Board 1868 (12 June 1886):139.

9. *JW* (13 Oct. 1886), clipping from Scrapbooks, v. 3B.

10. Comparative wage rates were obtained by dividing the average number of workers in the industry as reported by the Census of Manufacturers by the total amount of wages paid in the industry. After 1900 wages continued to rise and skyrocketed after 1919. Data from *Silverware* 1940, tables 17 and 25. The same pattern was true for both sterling and silverplate makers.

11. "A Menace to Trade Unions," *N.Y. Times*, 8 Nov. 1886.

12. "Stückarbeit," *Deutsch-Amerikanische Union Printer—Typographia*, 9 Nov. 1886. Translated by Sylvia and Charles Venable.

13. For information on the strike, see *N.Y. Times*, 9, 15, and 16 Oct. 1886; *Mail and Express*, 14 Oct. 1886; and *N.Y. World*, 28 Oct. 1886. Clippings from these papers are in Scrapbooks, v. 3B.

14. "Dissatisfied Working Men," *JCK* 18:1 (Feb. 1887):3.

15. "The Silversmith's Fight," *N.Y. Times*, 21 Apr. 1887.

16. "The Strike of the Silversmiths," *JCK* 18:4 (May 1887):138. For more information, see "Determined to Rule in Their Factories," *N.Y. Times*, 21 Apr. 1887.

17. "Determined to Rule in Their Factories," *N.Y. Times*, 21 Apr. 1887.

18. *Ibid.* "Workingmen Coming to their Senses," *JCK* 18:4 (May 1887):148, states probably incorrectly that "nearly all" of Gorham's workers were Knights.

19. Clipping from "Silver Manufacturers Still Ahead," *Jewelers' News* (30 Apr. 1887) in Scrapbooks, v. 3B. For a view that takes such a cooperative company seriously, see "Silversmiths," *N.Y. Times*, 27 Apr. 1887.

20. Evidently firms like Dominick & Haff that specialized in chased goods were hurting the most because chasers were difficult to find in good times, much less during a lockout. Furthermore, the chasers were generally the last to return to work. For information on Dominick & Haff, see "The Beginning of the End," *JW* 4:7 (15 June 1887):544–46.

21. C. L. Tiffany's subpoena and a copy of the letter he sent survive in Scrapbooks, v. 3B, 68–69. Letters to the board are quoted in "Arbitration for the Silversmiths," *JW* 4:5 (1 June 1887):374. For managements' opinion of the board, see "The Strike of the Silversmiths," *JCK* 18:6 (July 1887):183, and 18:8 (Sept. 1887):259.

22. "The Silver Trade Law Court Under Scrutiny," *JW* 4:6 (8 June 1887):451–52.

23. For discussions of the end of the lockout, see "Free Shops at Last," *JW* 4:8 (22 June 1887):269 and "Among the Manufacturers," *JW* 4:9 (29 June 1887):732 and 738.

24. For biographical information on Grosjean, see Carpenter 1978, 98–99.

25. Parsell 1901, 31. Corresponding "Rules of Apprentices' Ratings" on page 36 states the weekly wages apprentices were paid during each year of their apprenticeship and their rating in relationship to the journeymen and masters in the department: year 1, $1.5 weekly pay, $8 rating; 2, $4, $12; 3, $5, $14; 4, $6, $16; 5, $7, $18; and 6, $8, $20. In Nov. 1906 the weekly wage the first year was changed to $4. An explanation of the rating system states: "The significance of the term rating and figuring as here applied can best be conveyed by the following instance: Mr. Spengler has an order for 50 competiers, #11230, six of these he gives to an apprentice in his fifth [year] whose pay is $7.00 per week and whose rating is $18.00 per week; the balance of the order is distributed among $16.00 and $18.00 men. On referring to book kept in this room for that purpose (during the last ten or twelve years) he finds the previous cost and fixes time limit accordingly, and to the boy the same as $18.00 men. In other words, the rating determines the time allowance, as our advanced apprentices and fully as good and many of them better than the average journeyman. The time allowance by rating is seldom exceeded excepting cases where old piece work prices are used." Page 50 of this documents notes that on 1 Nov. 1900 incentive bonuses for apprentices were instituted. However, they were seldom successful.

26. The Harrison & Morton membership list dated 2 Oct. 1888 is in Scrapbooks, v. 4A.

27. The Washington Parade note of 2 May 1889 survives in Scrapbooks, v. 4A.

28. For information on the 1902 strike, see "Strike in Silver Trade," *JCK* 45:14 (5 Nov. 1902):53; "The Strike of the Silversmiths," *JCK* 45:15 (12 Nov. 1902):57; "The Strike of the Silversmiths in New York," *JCK* 45:17 (26 Nov. 1902):52; "Silversmiths Strike Ended," *JCK* 45:19 (10 Dec. 1902):28; and "Striking Silversmiths at Tiffany and Co. Factory Ask to Return to Work," *JCK* 45:21 (24 Dec. 1902):26. At this point, Gorham's city shop belonged to the Silversmith's Co. discussed below.

29. *JCK* 45:19 (10 Dec. 1902):28.

30. *JCK* 45:15 (12 Nov. 1902):57.

31. Parsell 1901, 79.

32. *Ibid.*, 30. For 1909, for example, a notation reads: "Profits determined by Experts after charging the factory with Depreciation on Building, stock, machinery and regarding all dies & patterns as expenses."

33. "Destruction of the Waltham Building in Bond Street," *JCK* 8:2 (Mar. 1877):19.

34. *JCK* 20:2 (Mar. 1889):31.

35. "Silversmithing in America. Part XI, George W. Shiebler Co.," *JCK* 25:7 (14 Sept. 1892):8. Reprinted in *Silver* 29:1 (Jan.–Feb. 1986):31.

36. "Silversmith's Hall," *JCK* 24:12 (20 Apr. 1892):20–21; and "The Hays Building," *JCK* 24:13 (27 Apr. 1892):20–21. The Silversmith's Hall was owned by the Silversmith's Co. discussed below.

37. What is published about Meriden Britannia's plant is in Hogan 1977, 16–27. At the time of this research the ISA was not sufficiently organized to determine what, if anything, survived describing the plant.

38. For view of these factories, see Middletown 1879, frontis; Gibb 1943, 197; and in the series "American Manufacturers of Silver and Silver Plated Goods. Part I," *JW* 9:19 (6 Mar. 1890):37–43; "Part II," 9:20 (13 Mar. 1890):42–46; "Part III," 9:21 (20 Mar. 1890):41–45; and "Part IV," 9:22 (27 Mar. 1890):35–43. The last series of articles also show several examples of urban-based companies that could not use "mill-type" structures.

39. Trachtenberg 1982, 56.

40. Some firms followed these precedents closely. For example, the new factory of William B. Durgin Co. in Concord, N.H., followed the H-shaped plan developed by Gorham. For an image of the Durgin plant, see *JCK* 50:7 (15 Mar. 1905):22.

41. *Scribner's* 1874, 202–3.

42. "The Gorham Works Afire," *JW* 5:16 (14 Feb. 1888):36.

43. For a description of the plant, see *JW* 7:19 (8 Mar. 1889):54–56; "Factory of the Gorham Mfg. Company, Providence, R.I.," *JCK* 20:3 (Apr. 1889):25–26; *JCK* 24:19 (8 June 1892):7–8; and "Gorham Manufacturing: New Works at Elmwood," *Providence Sunday Journal*, 24 Feb. 1889.

44. Krantz 1894, Silver Factories, 4. Specifically included were: "Four rolling mills for rolling and smoothing sheets; other rolling mills for plain border roll; 1 wire drawing machine; 4 rolling mills of small diameter, for the preparation of spoon and fork blanks; 16 presses for shaping and curving; 24 stamp hammers in rows, one beside the other, varying from 500 to 1000 kilos., and having behind them all the collection of necessary dies; 6 double movement American presses for tube drawing; 2 small border rolls; 1 very large lathe used to stamp lightly patterns in relief on pieces of a circular form; [and] 1 hydraulic press for die-sinking."

45. *Ibid.*, 8.

46. *Ibid.*, 11–13.

47. *JCK* 24:19 (8 June 1892):7.

48. Carpenter 1978, 227, states that the Prince Street works employed around 500 workers in the 1870s and 1880s. However, Tiffany & Co.'s own figures for the 1882 to 1910 period show a range from 270 in 1886 to 434 in 1910. Before the Newark plant opened in 1894 the total never exceeded 360 (1892). These figures are from Parsell 1901, 40. Krantz 1894, Tiffany, 6, states, "We counted at the time of our visit [1893], 150 mounters, 60 engravers, 16 turners, 40 polishers."

49. Krantz 1894, Tiffany, 6–7.

50. *JW* 4:23 (6 Oct. 1887):3017–23.

51. *Ibid.*, 3023. An Adams & Shaw cash book at TA from the 1870s records (May 1875) that Tiffany & Co.'s Prince Street works supplied German silver, ornamental castings, and sterling silver sheets and circles for spinning and stamping. Therefore, Adams & Shaw (Thomas Shaw & Co. before 1876) was not only buying parts and semiprocessed silver from outside, but also making some sterling wares and not just plate.

52. Krantz 1894, Tiffany, 8.

53. For information on Adam & Shaw's relationship with Tiffany & Co., see Carpenter 1978, 214–16, and Parsell 1901, 60–61. The Tiffany & Co. Archives also retains one account ledger from Adams & Shaw. General information is in Rainwater 1975, 11–12 and 43.

54. Krantz 1894, Tiffany, 8.

55. Parsell 1901, 17–18.

56. *Ibid.*, 2.

57. *Ibid.*, 3.

58. *Ibid.*, 4.

59. *Ibid.*, 5.

60. *JW* 9:19 (6 Mar. 1890):37.

61. An example of one of these time books dated May 1870 survives in GA, III. Personnel, 6.

62. *JW* 4:23 (6 Oct. 1887):3021.

63. Parsell 1901, 17.

64. Tiffany Rules 1897. There are three sets of rules: the one for general employees quoted here, and others for foremen and watchmen.

65. Gorham Rules 1910.

66. For a copy of these rules, see Gibb 1943, 282.

67. Tiffany Rules 1897.

68. *Ibid.*

69. For information on Soligny, see Safford 1990.

70. Parsell 1901, 49.

71. *Ibid.*, 48.

72. "New York Jewelers of a Half Century Ago: Gorham Mfg. Co.," *JCK* 78:1 (5 Feb. 1919):367.

73. *Ibid.*

74. For a description of such a dinner, see "Gorham Mfg. Co. Gives Sixth Annual Dinner to Heads of Factory Departments," *JCK* 50:3 (15 Feb. 1905): 34–35. For examples of events and their printed matter, see GA, III. Personnel, 6. Working Conditions.

75. Strasser 1989, 25.

76. Gibb 1943, 194–95.

77. "The Silversmiths' Co. Incorporated. . . . ," *JCK* 25:20 (14 Dec. 1892):22. The holding company's purpose was to "manufacture, deal in and contract for sale, purchase and exchange of gold and silverware, plated-ware, crockery, metal ware, cutlery, leather ware, wooden ware, silks, tools and machinery. It [would] do business as principal, agent on commission and as consignee. It [might] allow the firms whose property it acquire[ed] to do business on almost any terms the directors [might] deem beneficial."

78. Taken from a typed manuscript, possibly a draft press release in GA, I. Historical, 9. Divisions, a. Corporate, 2. Silversmith's Co.

79. Unidentified newspaper clipping in Scrapbook 1891.

80. For an overview of the history of the honest stamping movement, see "The Fight for Honest Marking," *JCK* 139:9, part 2 (June 1969):178ff.

81. Letter, Cole to Holbrook, 26 Jan. 1894, GA, I. Historical, 9. Divisions, a. Corporate, 2. Silversmith's Co.

82. Unidentified clipping of "Opposed to the Combine" from *JR* in GA, I.

Historical, 9. Divisions, a. Corporate, 2. Silversmith's Co. The clipping is dated internally 9 Dec. [1892].

83. Unidentified clipping from the *JR* probably dating to Dec. 1892, in Scrapbook 1891.

84. Unidentified clipping entitled "Big Combine Formed" from *N.Y. Times* probably dating to Nov. or Dec. 1892 and in Scrapbook 1891.

85. Letter, Towle to Gorham, 6 Sept. 1892, and Whiting to Gorham, 22 July 1992, GA, I. Historical, 9. Divisions, a. Corporate, 2. Silversmith's Co.

86. Letter, Cole to Holbrook, 10 Mar. 1893, in GA, I. Historical, 9. Divisions, a. Corporate, 2. Silversmith's Co. documents that in March 1893, L. D. Cole wrote Edward Holbrook that in pricing several new patterns of butter spreaders Towle had introduced, he originally wanted to charge $15.00 per dozen but found that both Frank M. Whiting Co. and W. B. Durgin made similar ones that sold for $12.00 a dozen. Consequently, he priced Towle's at $12.00 because he felt "compelled to hit those heads, at least so far as making prices just as low as theirs, every time I see them." Nevertheless, he concluded, "I presume it will not be long now before the prices of all new goods will be submitted for the decision of a committee for that purpose, which, of course, is as it should be."

87. Holbrook letters dated 29 June and 1 Aug. 1893 and printed notice of Gorham's price dated 7 Aug. 1893, all in GA, I. Historical, 9. Divisions, a. Corporate, 1. 1893 Silver Cartel.

88. All letters from Towle to Gorham dated 30 Dec. 1892, 10 Mar. 1893 and 23 Mar. 1893, in GA, I. Historical, 9. Divisions, a. Corporate, 2. Silversmith's Co.

89. The only known information on this shop is contained in an inter-office memo to H. C. Hoyt of Gorham dated 3 Aug. 1938, GA, I. Historical, 7. New York Office, e. This document states that the shop was begun in 1892 by the Gorham Mfg. Co. of New York and was taken over by the Silversmith's Co. in 1907 when that firm took over Gorham. However, the Gorham Mfg. Co. (later the Gorham Co. of New York) was not founded until 1898. Therefore, it is highly likely that this New York City shop was begun initially by the Silversmith's Co., which itself started in Dec. 1892. In 1904 the shop was moved to 225 W. 36th St. and in 1918 to 454 Sixth Ave. and by 1920 was at 140 Sixth Ave. Following the 1921 strike, it was downsized and turned into a repair shop, which was operating as late as 1938. Appraisal book from Oct. 1920 for the factory and notes on disposal of most of its machinery in 1924 are in GA, II. Corporate, 3. Financial, f. Appraisals & Inventories.

90. Unidentified Holbrook obituary in Scrapbook 1891. It is probably from *JCK*.

91. For a list of Silversmith's Co.'s directors, see *JCK* 25:20 (14 Dec. 1892):22. Although he was not yet president of Gorham when Silversmith's was incorporated in 1892 and does not appear to have served initially as one of Silversmith's corporate officers, correspondence preserved in the Gorham archives leaves little doubt as to who was in charge.

92. Rainwater 1975, 154.

93. For an account of Holbrook's take-over bid, see Gibb 1943, 311–14.

94. For information about this merger, see GA, II. Corporate, 2. Secretary.

95. Aldred 1923, 7.

96. *Ibid.*, 7.

97. These estimates were derived by comparing the sales figures for Gorham and its affiliated companies in Aldred 1923, 7, with those for the industry as a whole in *Silverware* 1940, 19 and 32.

98. Hogan 1977, chapter 3.

99. *Ibid.*, 46.

100. Gibb 1943, 292–94 and chapter 14.

101. *Ibid.*, chapters 15 and 16.

102. *Ibid.*, chapter 17.

103. Parsell 1901, 30.

104. *Ibid.* All are fiscal years, which run from 1 May to 30 April. Therefore figures given for, say, 1900 are in reality for 1 May 1899 to 30 April 1900.

105. All information taken from Hogan 1977, 53–54.

106. Jastram 1981, table 20.

107. A drawing for surgical tools survives in TA.

108. Hogan 1977, 58

109. Gorham 1932, 6–7.

110. Getman 1966.

111. "Gorham Silver Concern Reorganized," *JCK* 80:22 (30 June 1920):93.

112. "Silver Comes Down," *JCK* 81:23 (5 Jan. 1921):99.

113. "New York Notes," *JCK* 82:4 (23 Feb. 1921):105 and Memo to H. C. Hoyt, 3 Aug. 1938, GA, I. Historical, 7. New York Office, e.

114. Aldred 1923, profit-loss statement, 1915–1922. Located in "Comments," n.p.

115. Aldred 1923 contains numerous other suggestions.

116. Manager's Notebook, GA, IV. Acquired Companies, 8. Kerr. Comparing the companies on the costs of producing the same compote, they ranked as follows: Gorham $70.22 (selling price), Durgin $71.12, Kerr $78.67, Silversmith's Co.'s City Shop $80.02, Mauser $80.71, Roger Williams Co. $82.65, and Whiting $85.33.

117. Aldred 1923, 10.

118. *Ibid.*, 7.

119. Getman 1966.

120. Gibb 1943, 366–67.

121. The booklet by this title is dated 1 Nov. 1919. For information on survey, see "Survey of the Silverware Industry Now Being Made," *JCK* 81:20 (8 Dec. 1920):83. At present, the findings of this survey are not known.

122. *Elimination* 1926.

123. *Silverware* 1940, table 7.

124. Example survives in GA, III. Personnel, 6. Working Conditions.

125. *Silverware* 1940, table 7.

126. Notices 1932, 1 (20 June 1932).

127. Notices 1932, 1 (13 Dec. 1932).

128. On 10 Aug. 1933, Edmund Mayo of Gorham issued a notice to his employees outlining Gorham's participation in the NRA and explaining that one need not be a member of a union to benefit from it. For a copy, see GA, III. Personnel, 7. Union.

129. Purtell 1971, 177.

130. Notices 1932, 1 (27 Jan. 1942).

131. Purtell 1971, 177.

132. Notices 1932, 1 (19 Nov. 1942).

133. Notices 1932, 1 (17 Apr. 1943) and (7 June 1944).

134. Carpenter 1982, 265.

135. Gibb 1943, 377.

136. Hogan 1977, 58–61.

Chapter 8

BOOSTING SALES AND CUTTING COSTS: MARKETING

THE MATURATION OF ADVERTISING

During the last years of the nineteenth century and first four decades of the twentieth, most of the marketing networks and techniques that were developed earlier continued to be used. While peddlers and some jobbers faded away, the extensive system of retail jewelry stores and salesmen that had evolved after the Civil War remained the primary basis of silverware distribution and sales. Trade catalogues became so common that some publishers, such as the Barta Press of Boston,[1] specialized in those for the silverware industry. Much emphasis was still placed upon window displays, although their use was increasingly guided by marketing research. A 1932 Gorham sales manual, for example, noted that "it has been estimated that the windows of any store, if properly used, are worth <u>at least one-half the rental of the entire store</u>, regardless of its size, its location or the type of merchandise it handles." It then proceeded to outline the proper use of "The Twelve Most Important Points of Display": power of attraction, color harmony, sales power of display, merchandise exhibited, arrangement, balance, lighting, uncrowded appearance, cleanliness, timeliness, originality, and window cards.[2]

Similarly, emphasis continued to be placed on advertisements in periodicals and newspapers. Most of this print advertising stressed name recognition, product quality, silverware as art, and its importance in daily life, as it had before.[3] Unlike printed advertising, however, participation in world's fairs lessened after 1915. For example, no Americans exhibited at the critically important *Exposition Internationale des Arts Decoratifs et Industriels Modernes* held in Paris in 1925. And at the 1939 New York world's fair Tiffany's, Cartier, and Black, Starr & Frost-Gorham (the successor to Gorham's New York showroom) placed their small exhibits next to one another in the House of Jewels, rather than invest in pavilions containing dozens of expensive objects (ill. 8.1).[4]

More important, however, than shifting attitudes towards world's fairs were the changes in the scale and sophistication of marketing that occurred throughout the industry. Under the pressure of falling prices between 1890 and World War I,

ILL. 8.1. Tiffany & Co. exhibit in the House of Jewels, 1939 New York world's fair.

manufacturers worked hard to sell more goods. Consequently many of them not only intensified their advertising efforts but modernized them as well. Reed & Barton's development in this area seems typical. In 1902 William M. Flagg was hired and an advertising department created under his management. In 1909 the services of the Morse International Agency of New York were obtained. Working together, these entities developed and coordinated Reed & Barton's advertising campaigns, which were directed at both New York City and the rest of the country.[5] The establishment of advertising departments and the engagement of agencies occurred at most large manufactories during the first decade of the twentieth century. Their primary impact on print advertising was twofold. First, these professionals launched well-coordinated campaigns, which usually lasted for several months. Secondly, they developed extensive lines of promotional pamphlets and marketing aids for distribution to retailers.

Gorham's efforts in these areas were exceptional. In 1907, for example, it launched a nationwide sales effort, which it

FIG. 8.1. *Martelé* dessert plate and *Grape* pattern salt dish and pepper shaker. William C. Codman, designer; Gorham Mfg. Co., maker, Providence, R.I.; 1905. Silver. Dallas Museum of Art.

introduced to dealers through a booklet entitled "An Advertising Campaign, The Benefits of Which You Share." On the opening page Gorham stated how it felt "extensive, national advertising" would "create a large and steady increase in the demand for Gorham productions, as a broader knowledge of a good commodity is invariably followed by increased sales. So much is assured." Besides espousing this relatively new concept of creating demand through advertising, the campaign was designed "to direct that demand to its dealers."[6] By not printing its address on the copy and by emphasizing "the fact that Gorham goods are to be had only of the best dealers in each locality," Gorham hoped to prevent complaints from those of its dealers who felt the company was already in competition with them because the firm maintained a New York retail showroom.

The campaign was to commence in September, with copy appearing "in such widely read magazines as *Century, McClures, Everybody's, Scribner's, Munsey's, Review of Reviews, Ladies Home Journal* [and] *Outlook*." It was estimated that through these periodicals "17,000,000 of the most well-to-do population in this country will read month after month about Gorham silver and Gorham dealers." The advertisements would appear as part of a series, each stressing a different aspect of the trade, such as "flatware, hollow ware, and novelties, special attention being given to silver for the household, the wedding gift and the Christmas gift." And finally, dealers were urged to order a substantial quantity of Gorham goods since "Your benefit from our advertising will consequently depend on your readiness to provide the goods demanded."[7]

In 1910 and 1911 a similar campaign was conducted, part of which included elegant and expensive monthly advertisements in *House Beautiful*. In the text of each advertisement, a different aspect of Gorham's silverware and its importance to the consumer was stressed. In May 1910 the firm associated its products with the great artistic epochs in European history. The next month, Gorham proclaimed silverware the quintessential wedding gift and a sound investment. However, it concluded the advertising copy with the art theme when it said, "The ownership of a piece of Gorham Silverware will mean as much to future generations as the ownership of an 'Old master' means to the Art lover of today." In August the copy linked the Gorham name with that of the world's richest families, like the Rothschilds, Lloyds, Krupps, and Pullmans. December brought text telling how perfect Gorham silverware was for holiday gifts, and February 1911 again associated silver with art by connecting the Gorham name with "The Silver of Louis Quatorze." Overall, the long series of elegantly designed advertisements stressed Gorham's name, trademark, and products as symbols of exclusiveness, art, power, tradition, and affection.[8]

Gorham also perfected the use of trade pamphlets and marketing ephemera to a greater degree than most. Perhaps the finest example of such a program was "The Gorham Mark." Instituted by Gorham's sales division around 1918, this program educated retailers about advertising in general and about Gorham products in particular. The preface of "The Gorham Mark" catalogue, which was mailed to dealers carrying the firm's products, states that "it is the first piece in a campaign to cooperate more extensively with dealers in making their local advertising more productive." The catalogue "contains illustrations of about two hundred booklets, folders, midgets, show cards, newspapers, electros, lantern slides, mats, doilies and signs, which are supplied without charge to dealers." Gorham hoped dealers would use this material liberally in customer mailings, interior displays, and show windows, thereby increasing sales of Gorham "hollow ware, flatware and toilet ware."[9]

Some manufacturers went so far as to publish their own magazines. A good example is *The Community Jeweler*, first sent to retail dealers in 1934. In 1902 Oneida Silversmiths of Sherrill, New York, had introduced a line of silverplated flatware called *Community Plate*. The new periodical was the late phase of a massive, national advertising campaign, which had helped make this line a great success since the first decade of the century.[10] Through *The Community Jeweler* Oneida informed dealers about a host of ways they could work together to increase silverware sales during the depths of the Depression. For example, in introducing a national sales campaign entitled "Community Plate Silver Parade" in April 1934, Oneida made clear the need for close cooperation between the manufacturer and the retailer if they were going to succeed:

> This is an age of competition between industries. The fight for the consumer's dollar is keener than it ever was before. Few people can afford to buy all the niceties of life they'd like to have. Hence the man who has radios to sell, but who fails to feature them aggressively, will probably see his potential customers going to the neighboring auto dealer, the furrier, the furniture man or one of a dozen other places. So it is with silver. Regardless of the universal appeal of proper table appointments, it is never safe to rely on this alone to produce all of the sales that should be made—and made promptly. An occasional special impetus—a special drive—is required to supply the winning punch—to spell the difference between a line that is only fair and one that is outstanding from the viewpoint of dealer and manufacturer alike.[11]

To "supply the winning punch," Oneida's sales campaign would run from 12 May to 9 June 1934 and consist of "National advertising in the most effective periodicals, radio broadcasting over 100 stations and numerous dealer helps in the form of literature, special display pieces and newspaper mats."[12] Dealers were encouraged to participate and take full advantage of the campaign through articles in *The Community Jeweler* that explained the best way to use each component of the sales drive.

Most advertising efforts had both retail and wholesale components, but some were specifically directed towards the retail customer. For example, in 1918, when consumers had become more conservative in their purchases because of the war, Gorham published a series of pamphlets to combat this attitude. In one entitled *Are You Practicing False Patriotism?* Gorham asked potential customers, "Is it not the truest form of patriotism to keep the wheels of commerce revolving—to keep the fires burning under the factory furnaces—to buy and sell and loan and borrow and in every other legitimate way keep money in circulation more than ever before?"[13] In *Are Your Economics on Straight?* Gorham again encouraged people to spend money on silverware, equating the purchase of silver with the development of great civilizations and strong, wealthy nations.[14]

Between 1885 and 1940, manufacturers and the trade press tried hard to persuade dealers not to reduce prices. During the deflationary 1890s and the recessions around 1907 and 1921, and throughout the Great Depression of the 1930s, dealers found it difficult to stay competitive without reducing prices. This pressure increased in this period due to the rise of new forms of retailers, including the department store, chain store, and mail-order company. Even when inflation commenced in the early twentieth century, the cost of marketing and distribution increased more rapidly than the price of silver, thereby hurting retailers and manufacturers who could not raise prices fast enough to cover their rising expenses.[15] As early as 1885 the *Jewelers' Weekly* cautioned retailers that "it is a primary rule in commerce that moderate sales at a high standard of prices are preferable to large sales at a depressed standard."[16] In the post–World War I recession, price cutting became such a problem that some firms launched advertising campaigns against the practice. In 1919, for example, Gorham ran copy in *Jewelers' Circular* announcing, "GORHAM Cuts the Gordian Knot." The text said:

> Perhaps the greatest problem facing Retail Jewelers today is that of price. Gorham Prices, like Gorham Silverware, maintain a general standard undisputed and unparalleled. Character of workmanship, beauty of design and variety of distinctive patterns all contribute to make the Gorham productions proverbial. Add to this a scale of prices ranged to meet the individual preference and the Gordian Knot of the Jewelers' difficulties is cut a Stroke.[17]

In a pamphlet entitled *Get Together*, Gorham put its case more forcefully by telling dealers to work together to set prices. The text concluded: "So, get together. Establish prices that give a fair profit. Nobody can dispute that you are entitled to this much. Remember that 'All your strength is in your union, / All your danger in discord; / Therefore be at peace henceforward, / And as brothers live together.'"[18] Eleven years later, in 1930, Gorham again felt compelled to try to stabilize prices. In an "Announcement to our Customers" the firm told retailers that cutting prices was an "economic evil" which "disorganized and demoralized the business not only of the manufacturer, but also of his other distributors." Consequently Gorham had decided "that to the full extent permitted by law it [would] pre-

vent price-cutters from using for their own selfish purpose the just popularity which its products [had] gained." It would achieve this goal by simply not selling silverware to retailers who were known to be price-cutters.[19] While it is difficult to know whether silverware dealers heeded such advice in light of the intense pressure they were under to stay competitive, it is clear that falling prices and increased competition had a major impact on the marketing efforts of manufacturers.

To cope with this difficult situation, various manufacturers became more specialized in terms of their primary markets. Many silverplate producers, for example, fought hard to win contracts from department stores and the transportation industry (ill. 8.2). Beginning in 1890 Meriden Britannia (after 1898 part of International Silver) kept a sizable portion of its manufacturing facilities busy supplying the huge retailer Sears, Roebuck & Co.[20] Like department stores, shipping and railway lines and hotels also consumed large amounts of silverplate. Although they did not totally abandon these markets, high-end producers like Tiffany's and Gorham became less active in them in comparison to others during the early twentieth century.[21] However, for companies that targeted these markets, the orders for commercial silverplate could be large. When R. Wallace & Sons of Wallingford, Connecticut, for example, refitted the dining rooms of the ocean liner S.S. *Leviathan* for the United States Lines in 1923, "over 60,000 pieces of silverware [made] up the silver service—50,000 of Flatware and 10,000 of Hollow Ware." This one order required nearly 10 tons of metal, 650 feet of nickel rod, and 1.5 tons of nickel-silver wire. Furthermore, it kept between 200 and 250 workers occupied for several months.[22]

Rather than strive for these high-volume, lower-quality markets, other makers chose to pursue the elite, luxury market more intensely. Gorham's efforts between the mid 1890s and 1940 are excellent examples of this type of market positioning. For example, the firm's assembling of a special group of workmen in 1896 under William C. Codman to develop *Martelé* and related art nouveau lines was central to this effort (figs. 8.1–2). Since Gorham had to invest capital in the research and development of this new product for four years before a single piece was sold to the public, *Martelé* was priced and marketed as the most luxuriant of silverwares. In 1905, for example, Gorham ran a series of advertisements for *Martelé* in the upscale magazine *Country Life in America*. The February issue stated that "These exquisite pieces—each an individual creation, never to be duplicated—are hand-wrought by craftsmen who are encouraged to realize the highest ideals of their art unhampered by the ordinary commercial consideration of expense." In November potential customers were told: "The ever-increasing fashionable predilection for Martelé Silver, one of the Gorham Company's exclusive products, is more reasonable than many of fashion's dictates. Not only is Martelé wrought entirely by hand, but at every stage of its fashioning it is controlled by the same artist

ILL. 8.2. International Silver Co.'s advertisement for *20th Century* pattern silverware, 1938.

whose creative ability conceived the design."[23] By positioning *Martelé* as an elitist product, Gorham hoped both to attract customers who could afford its high cost and thus make the labor-intensive line profitable, and to give additional cachet to the firm's other products through name association.

However, for companies like Gorham that actually manufactured a wide range of silverware, being seen primarily as a producer of expensive wares could be problematic. In the case of Gorham, the firm found it difficult to associate its name with high-end lines like *Martelé* and lower classes of goods like electroplate simultaneously without confusing the public. By the early 1920s, this situation was severe. On the one hand, Gorham needed to produce domestic and institutional electroplate because its huge plant capacity was so underutilized. Furthermore, silverplated wares for hotels, restaurants, cafeterias, and hospitals acted as "burden carriers" in off-seasons when little other work was available. And yet, producing silverplate was seldom profitable for Gorham by the 1920s. A 1923 study showed that its electroplated hollowware had a mere 8 percent profit built into its sale, as opposed to 17 percent for sterling. Similarly, electroplated flatware had a profit margin of 18 percent, while sterling had 29.[24] Given these relatively slim profit margins, Gorham was at a distinct disadvantage when competing with specialized manufacturers of electroplate who could undercut its prices and advertise more widely without fear of jeopardiz-

ing an upscale image. Nevertheless, Gorham decided to continue producing silverplate because its plant needed the work. The company did consider marketing it under another name, however. In the end, a compromise was made and the name was retained, although sterling was emphasized with the slogan: "If sterling cannot be afforded, the next best is 'Gorham Plate.'"[25] Eventually, however, silverplate production was de-emphasized, and in 1946 the hotel ware division was sold to International Silver.

As already noted, pressures such as those surrounding silverplate advertising and sales, along with a disastrous experience with munitions work during World War I, combined to cripple Gorham by 1921. In that year costs so far exceeded profits that the firm was effectively bankrupt. To revive the company, Franklin L. Taylor (d. 1931) as vice-president, and after March 1921 as president, launched a radical new marketing policy. Since the late nineteenth century, the firm's products had been distributed nationally through upscale jewelry stores, which were given exclusive or semi-exclusive rights to sell Gorham products or specific patterns in a particular local market. Advertising encouraged customers to go to these stores and ask for Gorham silverware by name. Only in New York City did the firm sell retail. In January 1921, however, Taylor called together representatives from rival manufacturers and the trade press to announce a new "open-door policy" of distribution by which any retailer who wished to sell Gorham products could do so, including department stores.[26] Also, Gorham itself began to sell its wares directly to the public through regional showrooms in San Francisco (founded 1879 and moved to Oakland in 1906), Chicago (1882), Boston (before 1912), Atlanta (1922), and Philadelphia (date unknown).[27] It was hoped that this new policy would increase silver purchases while reducing the costs of distribution and sales, "which were in many cases found to be excessive."[28]

Framed as a step towards democratizing the ownership of silverware, the new plan was marketed with editorial-style articles like "Sterling Silver for Everybody: How the Cost of Sterling Silverware to the Public is being Reduced," which appeared in *The Outlook*. In this advertisement Gorham told the public: "It took a revolution to free the American colonies from the monarchical grip; and it is likewise requiring a revolution to release the Sterling silver trade from aristocratic traditions. But this latter revolution is a friendly one, and dealers are gladly co-operating and are reviving in their communities a new appreciation of the singular merits of Sterling silver."[29]

Franklin Taylor's "revolution," however, proved disastrous for Gorham. By 1923 many of the company's best customers had been alienated by the new policy and other producers had cut into Gorham's market share of the high-end trade. Evidently Towle was especially successful in taking over Gorham accounts. A later Gorham president recalled how that firm was able "to move in and mop up" in the wake of Taylor's plan and how "this marked the beginning of [Towle's] growth as a friend of the fine jeweler."[30]

FIG. 8.2. Serving spoon. William C. Codman, designer; Gorham Mfg. Co., maker, Providence, R.I.; ca. 1895–1900. Sterling silver and silvergilt. Dallas Museum of Art.

In a comprehensive analysis of Gorham and its subsidiaries done in 1923, Aldred & Co. noted the "severe shaking" that the company had undergone. It concluded that "The trade feels that your people and policies have been dictatorial. This feeling is apparently the root of their attitude. Other reasons are: (a) objection to your selling to department stores; (b) discontinuance of allowing monopoly in a locality for a given pattern; [and] (c) objection to your being in competition with your customers, through retail stores."[31] Following Taylor's resignation in May 1923, Gorham moved to correct these problems. It discontinued distribution to department stores, with the exception of Marshall Field & Co. in Chicago and John Wanamaker in Philadelphia, where profits were evidently adequate.[32] In 1928 Gorham purchased the Alvin Silver Co. and moved it to Providence. Although the silverware was actually made in the Gorham plant, the Alvin name and sales force were retained "in order to enter the competitive department store

field without impairing the high reputation of the Gorham Company."[33] Furthermore, some branch stores and offices were consolidated and closed during the next two decades. Philadelphia was merged with the New York office in 1926. The Boston showroom was moved to Providence in 1927. Atlanta was closed altogether in 1930, as was San Francisco in 1941.[34] To some degree Gorham also reinstituted exclusive distribution rights for local retailers. And finally, Aldred & Co. recommended "strongly that a new spirit be injected into every person in [Gorham's] organization and that from now on, everything consistently possible be done to gain the warm and affectionate friendship of [its] customers, upon whom [Gorham's] success, in large measure, depends."[35]

Following Aldred's report, Gorham quickly moved away from the image of "Sterling Silverware for Everybody" and back to an elitist one. In 1924, for example, it launched the "Gorham Baby Campaign" in which it styled itself "Silversmiths to the

Nursery." National in scope, advertising copy was placed in thirty-nine newspapers across the country, as well as thirteen magazines including *Vogue, House & Garden, Arts & Decoration,* and *Town & Country.* As with all of Gorham's major campaigns, dealers received multifaceted display packages containing such clever devices as pink and blue price cards and brochures with fairy tale–type illustrations. The copy stressed the ability of silverware to symbolize one generation's love and aspirations for the next and silver's purported power to encourage fine table manners. Promotional material sent to dealers confided:

The secret is this—

Every parent is interested in giving his child the best that he can afford. The surest way to a parent's heart is through the children. OUR SILVER IS MADE ESPECIALLY FOR THEM—DECORATED WITH THEIR OWN PET STORIES AND ANIMALS AND ADJUSTED TO FIT LITTLE HANDS AND MOUTHS SO AS TO MAKE THE ACQUIREMENT OF TABLE MANNERS AS EASY AS POSSIBLE.

Every Quality Baby Silver purchase makes friends for quality grown-up silver and jewelry—both in the children's future purchases—and with their parents NOW. Your store becomes their jewelry and silver home.

TABLE MANNERS FOR GROWN-UPS—WE KNOW ALL ABOUT THOSE—but don't forget—MANNERS BEGIN WITH THE FIRST BABY SPOON.

WHAT ARE YOU DOING ABOUT IT <u>NOW</u>?

To deliver these messages to potential customers, display devices and advertising copy included statements like: "Your true affection for baby friends is best expressed by a gift of sterling"; "What a symbol of true affection—a gift of sterling—a gift of babyhood to endure through life"; "Babies fortunate enough to have sterling silver cups do not have to be coaxed to 'drink every drop'"; and "A child should behave mannerly at table—At least as far as she is able."[36]

Gorham's positioning of itself as a luxury producer was typical of most companies that made sterling before 1940. However, even silverplate makers employed elitist images in varying degrees, depending on the market they wished to reach. In 1930 a silverplate manufacturer explained the range of symbols he preferred in the advertising trade journal *Printer's Ink Monthly:* "modernistic illustrations and male servants to appeal to the most exclusive sophisticates; maids and more conservative art for 'quietly prosperous' Mary Smith; suburban chintz curtains, bright peasant ware, and no maid for Mary Jones with her nice little house and garden; and movie-star testimonials for Mary White."[37] The opposite ends of this symbolic spectrum can be seen in the celebrities chosen as representatives by International and Oneida in the early 1930s. About 1930, International Silver's sterling division targeted relatively sophisticated consumers when it hired New York's famous arbiter of "good" taste, Elsie de Wolfe (ill. 8.3), to endorse its wares. The "prominent hostess and authority on interior deco-

ILL. 8.3. Elsie de Wolfe, ca. 1929.

ration" lent her name to the publication *Correct Table Silver,* which was billed as "the most helpful booklet on silver in all the world."[38] Illustrated with a photograph of an elegantly dressed de Wolfe, the basic message of this twenty-five-cent guide was that readers should keep buying silver during the Depression, although they needed to plan its acquisition more seriously than had generally been done in the past.[39] Unlike International, however, Oneida targeted middle-class customers when it ran tabloid-type photographs of Hollywood movie stars with views of their dining rooms in its magazine *Community Jeweler.* In April 1935 one caption read: "The furnishings are just about what you would expect in the home of the Paramount player, Sylvia Sidney—dignified yet having a quiet beauty of undeniable appeal. Note how effectively the softly gleaming silver contrasts with the wood paneling."[40] Through association with famous individuals like Elsie de Wolfe and Sylvia Sidney, manufacturers hoped consumers of varying means would purchase their products as symbolic bridges between the reality of the buyer's life and the more desirable, perhaps mythic, lifestyle of the product endorser.

The pinnacle of elitist advertising was reached by Gorham in its 1929 campaign. Designed to promote the sale of sterling flatware for wedding gifts, the campaign featured "Prominent American Brides and the silver patterns they have chosen" in booklets and magazine copy. Illustrated with photographs of elegantly dressed brides from wealthy families around the coun-

ILL. 8.4. Gorham Mfg. Co.'s "Smartest Brides" advertisement, 1929.

try alongside their respective Gorham flatware patterns, one booklet opened:

> Silver to every bride is the symbol of the beauty and the quality she dreams for their own home. Though the pieces be few, the mere buds of an ideal, or splendidly complete—she knows that their artistry . . . purity . . . grace . . . give a picture crystal clear of taste and standards. . . . To the distinguished Gorham silversmiths patrician brides turn spontaneously, generation after generation, for that perfection, that superb finesse and style in silver, which interprets their desires.[41]

In the May 1929 issue of *Vanity Fair*, a Gorham advertisement describing "One of Washington's smartest Brides" went even further in its depiction of the "good" life (ill. 8.4).[42] While some readers may have found such heavyhanded examples of elitist advertising appealing, others did not. The writer Sinclair Lewis, for example, blasted Gorham for comments like these in the trade periodical *Advertising & Selling*. He said:

> I am not a bride—I don't seem ever likely to be—so I do not get quite so much personal inspiration out of the Gorham silver advertisement in May *Vanity Fair*. But for a bride that must be an awfully thrilling lowdown on how to be snobbish. It stands there that "Her distinguished connections in Baltimore and Washington[. . .]"

I wish I had distinguished connections in Baltimore! I don't know anybody there except Henry Mencken, and I'll bet he doesn't know a thing about silverware. . . .

But what I want to know is a little more about her graciously consenting to reveal her personal decision.

How graciously was it? And who got her to consent?

It means a lot to all of us.

Who wrung from her the secret? I can imagine the reporter, a sturdy honest fellow . . . bursting in on her and demanding, "Mrs. Parker, for the love of Mike, for the sake of thousands of fellow brides—especially for the daughter of Mike Piztka of Scranton, who is going to marry Leo Polcetti—will you give up that reserve which great ladies once used to have in Baltimore, and graciously, or pretty graciously, tell the world one of your very personal decisions as an important young hostess—the selection of your silver?"

Thank heaven, those stuffy old days of which Mrs. Edith Wharton wrote "The Age of Innocence" are gone! At last we plebes are admitted, per full-page advertisements, to the society of the select![43]

What effect critics like Lewis had on Gorham's advertising strategy is difficult to know. Within months of his comments, the nation was in economic chaos and Gorham was forced to change its image in order to stay competitive in a shrinking market. Certainly some makers still employed elitist imagery in their advertising, but the appeals were seldom so overt as that of Gorham's "American Brides" campaign.

Within less than a year of the October 1929 stock market crash, Gorham dramatically changed its advertising. Regardless of the fact that for the vast majority of Americans its products were still costly luxuries, Gorham tried to transform its image from that of purveyor to wealthy brides to one of an efficient, modern producer of moderately priced silverware. In the spring 1930 issues of national magazines like *Vogue* and *Vanity Fair*, full-page advertisements appeared proclaiming "The Silver you would rather have can be yours because Gorham sterling is not expensive" and "Gorham Sterling is not as expensive as many people imagine. 76 pieces of Gorham . . . complete service for eight . . . cost only $236.00." One advertisement stated that "The tradition of Gorham Sterling has often led women to assume that it must be costly. They have felt that because Gorham Sterling was designed by rarely gifted artists who imparted to the precious metal such unsurpassing beauty, they, themselves, would never be able to afford it. The most amazing thing about Gorham Sterling is its very moderate cost."[44] To symbolize this image of high technical and artistic quality at a moderate price, Gorham commissioned one of America's leading photographers, Edward Steichen (1879–1973), to do a series of photographs of its flatware in an avant-garde style (ill. 8.5). Through his selection of uncomplicated objects and a regimented placement, Steichen gave the

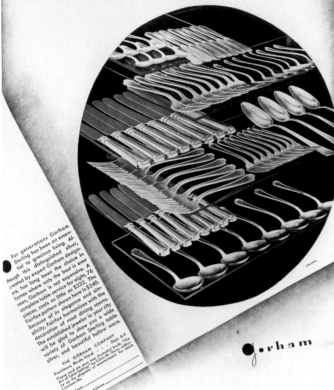

ILL. 8.5. Gorham Mfg. Co.'s "Without Being Extravagant . . ." advertisement, 1930.

ILL. 8.6. International Silver Co.'s *Silhouette* advertisement, 1929.

silver a "slick" modernist look, which simultaneously conveys a sense of fashionability and efficiency—exactly the image Gorham thought it needed in the midst of trying economic times.

Many silverware producers turned to the modernist aesthetic in the late 1920s and early 1930s in hopes of increasing sales. Although America did not participate in the 1925 Paris *Exposition Internationale*, many designers and consumers were nevertheless influenced by the art deco objects shown there and in subsequent exhibitions in the United States.[45] Several producers instituted lines of simplified, modernist-looking silverware beginning in the late 1920s. In marketing, the style was used to give a fresh appearance to advertising layouts. For example, International Silver used the aesthetic in introducing its new, streamlined flatware pattern *Silhouette* in 1929 (ill. 8.6). Citing Paris as the center of haute couture and the art deco style, International told readers that owning *Silhouette* pattern silverplate would identify them as being part of the vital Paris fashion scene. The text was graphically illustrated by depicting a fashionably dressed woman surrounded by elegant consumer goods, including a hat, purse, shoe, necklace, and, of course, *Silhouette* pattern flatware.

Some producers also redesigned the packaging of their wares both to make them seem more fashionable and to encourage purchases of entire flatware sets. This was especially true in the case of silverplate, which increasingly was marketed

in distinctive chests and boxes during the late 1920s and 1930s. In 1929, for example, R. Wallace & Sons announced to the trade that it was now offering sets of flatware in attractively designed chests. In keeping with modernist aesthetics, the boxes had streamlined gold trim and a slick, black glass top engraved with a starburst motif. R. Wallace & Sons said of the container: "BLACK AND GOLD . . . always attractive, always in style. That's the color scheme of this new chest for Wallace Silver Plate. Sunburst, as this creation is called, has a black glass cover with a miniature sun of the new 'moderne' gold, and edging of the same color . . . the kind of thing women are demanding nowadays."[46]

Oneida seems to have tried especially hard in the area of innovative packaging. In 1934, for example, the firm unveiled art deco–style "De Luxe Gift Boxes" (fig. 8.3). Designed to hold flatware, the containers were black with bright red, green, or ivory colored lids and were made of a new material—plastic. Introduced in the depths of the Depression, the boxes were intended to be reusable. Oneida noted:

Free from advertising (the label under the lid may easily be removed) they will add a colorful touch to thousands of bedrooms and living rooms during the coming year. Not only will they suggest gifts of Community Plate

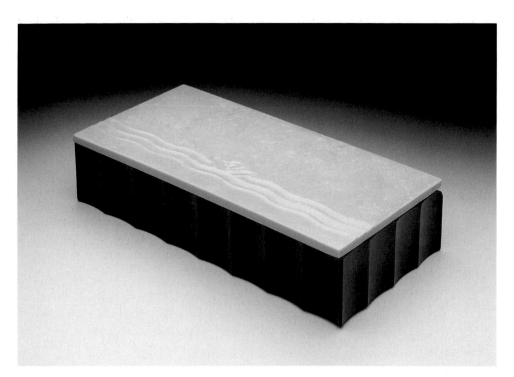

FIG. 8.3. *De Luxe Gift Box.* Oneida Ltd., Oneida, N.Y., designed 1934. Plastic. Rusty Venable Collection.

when displayed in your store — but, used as costume jewelry or cigarette containers in the home they will serve as a constant reminder of the gift value of this well-known silverware.[47]

Two years later, in 1936, Oneida experimented again with plastic packaging when it introduced "Crystal Cases" (ill. 8.7). Sent free to retailers with the purchase of a three-piece tea set or other large hollowware item, these cases were intended for use on display counters in jewelry stores. They consisted of a cardboard base into which was fitted a clear plastic vitrine top. Oneida encouraged their use when it said that "Crystal Cases not only prevent Dirt and Tarnish, but also provide a brilliant, sparkling, eyecatching display for the fastest selling pieces."[48]

Some retailers also believed that modernist stores and window displays could attract customers. During the late 1920s, for example, many jewelry store owners chose to update the facades and interiors of their establishments. Three firms that specialized in such work were Kawneer Mfg. Co. of Niles, Michigan; Finn, Iffland & Co. of New York, Scranton, and Philadelphia; and the Michigan Store Fixture Co. of Detroit and New York. In September 1929 the Michigan Store Fixture Co. proclaimed that it was "America's Largest Builders of Jewelry Stores" and had "30 STORES NOW UNDER WAY!" (ill. 8.8).[49] As part of its "dominant modernistic" scheme, Michigan, as with its rivals, created stores that were much cleaner in line and arrangement in comparison to late-nineteenth-century interiors. Typical were the use of marble surfaces and geometric ornamentation on plaster, wood, cast metal, and etched-glass architectural components. Similarly, window displays became less cluttered, more rigid in their arrangement of goods, and allied with "modern" art through the use of "artistic" signage and sometimes even abstract background material (ill. 8.9).[50]

ILL. 8.7. Oneida's "Crystal Cases" advertisement, 1936.

ILL. 8.8. Michigan Store Fixture Co.'s "30 Stores Now Under Way!" advertisement, 1929.

Many of the changes in distribution, advertising, packaging, and showroom design that occurred during the 1920s and 1930s were encouraged by an ever-growing amount of market and financial research which was done within the industry during these decades. In its simplest forms, this analysis consisted of asking one's employees for input on how to improve. In March 1935, for example, Tiffany & Co. issued a memo requesting from its retail sales force suggestions on how to increase business and cut costs. It may well have been comments from these employees during the Depression that resulted in cost-cutting measures like reducing store hours and operating only the front, "customer," elevator (eliminating use of the "staff" one). Salesmen could also have been responsible for a memo that reminded everyone to tell any customer who mentioned traveling to Europe that they should stop at the company's Paris branch.[51] More than simply asking for suggestions, by 1941 Tiffany's was requiring salesmen to fill out marketing surveys in which customers were to indicate if they had seen particular advertisements.[52] Furthermore, since most managers and salesmen in the silverware trade were male, some of the more progressive concerns hired women to gain greater insight into the female market, which dominated the industry. Tiffany's did this in 1935 when it engaged a Miss Elizabeth Darden "[f]or the presentation from a feminine point of view of suggestions as to fashions, style and in general what women want."[53] Gorham also hired women, such as Grace Robinson,

to work in its showrooms, where they demonstrated the proper use of silverware and undoubtedly advised the male-dominated firm on how to appeal to the opposite sex (ill. 8.10).

Another interesting marketing idea that could have been suggested by a salesman was to promote certain silverware forms as being multifunctional rather than highly specific in use, which had been the nineteenth-century view. In a 1932 Gorham sales manual, for example, salesmen were told that they should suggest various ways that any given piece of hollowware could be used. Silver baskets were noted as being appropriate for flowers, ferns, fruit, and centerpieces. Furthermore, they were said to be suitable in the dining room, living room, hall, on console tables, and combined with compotes and candlesticks. The same manual also contained extensive lists of silver objects appropriate as gifts for particular categories of people. Under "Suitable Christmas Gifts for Men" were listed traveling set, toilet set, belt buckles, military brushes, traveling whisk broom, flasks, cigarette cases, cigar boxes, clocks, cocktail sets, trays and cups, bottle opener, cork screw, desk ware, spectacle cases, library sets, match boxes, ash trays, razors, shaving sets, and shoe horns.[54]

At the other end of the research spectrum from these relatively simple ideas were marketing and financial studies that were highly complicated and "scientific" in nature. The analysis of Gorham done in 1923 by the New York firm of Aldred & Co. is a perfect example of such research. This document indicates that by the early 1920s Gorham was already tracking its sales sufficiently well that they could be tabulated geographically by state and by regional sales branch, as well as by individual customers.[55] The study documented that between 1919 and January 1923 Gorham's efforts to gain more retail customers had succeeded, increasing by 50 percent, to a total of around 2,000. In spite of this large number, however, over a third of Gorham's and its affiliates' output was taken by only 20 percent of the customers. And their purchases were on the decline. On the whole, average shipments to each customer dropped by half over the three years studied, the net result being flat sales and increased marketing and distribution costs.[56]

Similarly, such studies could tell manufacturers much about stock turnover and rates of returned merchandise. The Gorham analysis revealed that the firm had far too much of its capital invested in finished stock in its own showrooms and plants. It was estimated that $2 million was tied up in hollowware alone throughout the Gorham distribution system.[57] In such cases a producer could try to cut its large inventories and improve the temporal relationship between demand and production. If successful, the result was greater financial flexibility for the firm. Similar analysis could also be used to combat the "trade evil" of returned goods. Silverware manufacturers hated returned merchandise because it was often out of fashion or damaged when it came back. Statistical information on the rate of return enabled producers to take corrective measures before the situation got out of hand. In 1923, for example, Aldred & Co. recommended that returns be made only through district

ILL. 8.9. Gorham Co. demonstration window display, ca. 1928.

offices and accepted only with their approval. This way the sales-man who knew the returnee personally could make immediate inquiries and attempt to correct the situation before the actual objects were shipped back to the plant and reentered stock.[58]

Self-analysis could also reveal problems with demand and production cycles, as well as those concerning showrooms. Plagued, as were its rivals, by wide seasonal swings in demand, Gorham and its subsidiaries made half their annual sales dur-ing the period from September to the end of December. To help correct this imbalance, Aldred & Co. recommended developing products that could be marketed as especially "appropriate for events occurring in each month of the year—birthdays, weddings, wedding and other anniversaries, refur-nishing, etc.—with perhaps 'specials' for each month."[59] And finally, systematic study could pinpoint retail outlets that were performing poorly. For example, the 1923 report noted that Gorham's elaborate Fifth Avenue store represented an invest-ment of over $1.5 million and sometimes carried a stock of sil-verware worth $2 million. But since the outlet did over half its business around Christmas, the rest of the year was very slow, with "the people visiting [the] store each day hardly number-ing a baker's dozen." Furthermore, "the relations of sales to inventories, by lines, [were] in many cases almost ridiculous," while the number of clerical employees was far too high. To correct such problems, recommendations for greater inventory control, increased advertising, and reductions in overall size were made.[60] Shortly after these suggestions were submitted, the store was moved uptown to Fifth Avenue and Forty-sev-enth Street in hopes of gaining more customers. Still perform-ing below expectations, the store was sold to Black, Starr &

Frost who renamed it Black, Starr & Frost-Gorham, Inc., in 1929 (fig. 8.4). In 1930 the outlet was moved up a block to Forty-eighth Street and merged into the Black, Starr & Frost show-room. The name was later changed to Black, Starr & Gorham.

While the Aldred & Co. study of Gorham is a particu-larly rich example, this type of systematic self-analysis and adjustment occurred throughout the industry during the early twentieth century. George Gibb, for example, has documented the process at Reed & Barton. Soon after the turn of the cen-tury, Reed & Barton's management modernized the firm's ac-counting and costing procedures so as to better reflect the actual operations of the company and thus enable it to pinpoint ways to reduce overhead. Furthermore, Reed & Barton overhauled its sales force and in 1902 established a subsidiary called the Reed & Barton Co. of New York to handle retail sales in the city. This move was patterned after Gorham, which in 1898 in New York State had chartered the Gorham Mfg. Co. of New York (after 1906 called the Gorham Co.) to handle its retail sales and those of its affiliated companies. Like the Gorham Co., the Reed & Barton counterpart erected an impressive building on Fifth Avenue in 1905. But as with Gorham, the new accounting methods revealed that operating such an es-tablishment at a profit was difficult. The first year the store lost nearly $20,000. For more than a decade, results were poor, and in 1918 Reed & Barton purchased the fashionable jewelry store of Theodore B. Starr at 576 Fifth Avenue. The retail show-room was moved to this new location, and the New York cor-poration merged with Starr. However, because profits remained meager, in 1924 Reed & Barton abandoned its retail operation altogether in New York City, and the assets of Theodore B.

ILL. 8.10. A Gorham Co. employee, Mrs. Grace Robinson, demonstrating table setting
at the New York or Boston store, ca. 1925.

Starr were liquidated. Luckily, Reed & Barton's national distribution network did not suffer the same fate. Only the Philadelphia office, as at Gorham, was consolidated with New York.
However, the Chicago office grew and regional distribution
centers were founded in San Francisco, St. Louis, and Dallas.[61]

Oneida, unlike Gorham or Reed & Barton, saw its movement into retailing as a scientific experiment designed to benefit jewelry store owners nationwide. In early 1933 the firm "took
over in its entirety . . . the operation of a typical established
retail silverware department in a typical store in a typical city of
over 200,000 population." Claiming a 74 percent increase in
sales within a year, Oneida told retailers they could achieve
similar results by following these principles:

1. STOCK HIGH-PRICED MERCHANDISE IN GOOD
QUANTITIES.

2. PUT SELLING EMPHASIS ON POPULAR MEDIUM-
PRICED GOODS.

3. TIE UP WITH SPECIAL PRICE PROMOTION ON POP-
ULAR BRANDS.

4. FEATURE ITEMS OF "NEWS" INTEREST [i.e. new patterns and novelties].

5. RESERVE THE BEST DISPLAY SPACE FOR SPECIAL
PROMOTIONS.

6. ADVERTISE! ADVERTISE! ADVERTISE![62]

To encourage dealers to heed its advice, Oneida regularly published articles on the progress of its "retail experimental station"
in its magazine, *Community Jeweler*, during the mid 1930s.

Besides such individual attempts at research and reform,
similar efforts were made on a broader scale. The history of the
Sterling Silverware Manufacturers' Association is an example
of such a process. Having originally come together in 1917 as
the government sanctioned "War Industry Board" of the silverware industry, many member manufacturers felt it would
be useful to preserve this forum for solving problems after the
war's conclusion. Consequently, in 1919 the Sterling Silverware
Manufacturers' Association was founded and Harry A. Macfarland of the Mt. Vernon Co. (a Gorham-affiliated company)
was elected president. From the start it was obvious that many
of the industry's most pressing problems were in the areas of

FIG. 8.4. Part of a coffee set. Black, Starr & Frost-Gorham, Inc., retailer, New York, N.Y., 1936.
14 karat gold, ivory, and porcelain. Museum of the City of New York.

marketing and distribution, so the association chose to concentrate on these. For example, it worked toward standardization of forms and documents for billing, the wide variety of which confused retailers, and established guidelines for "suggested retail prices." To help in these efforts, the association commissioned the George Batten Co. in 1921 to conduct a national survey of the industry and its sales outlets. The survey was intended to "investigate the market from the standpoint of the consumer" on a national scale. It was also meant to analyze the industry itself, and to that end "investigators [were] instructed to thoroughly and impartially investigate and analyze the manufacturing, administrative and sales method of sterling silverware manufacturers."[63] The findings of this particular study are not known, but the effort must have helped convince the Association that the "prime objective to which it could direct its energies was the development of the general consumer market and the hiring of the best talent available for conducting effective national advertising and producing sales promotional dealers helps." By 1926 this reorientation toward the retail customer was complete and, accordingly, the organization changed its name to the Sterling Silversmiths Guild of America,

which was felt to have more public appeal. Although the guild employed many means to increase the consumption of silverware—including advertising in national magazines, holding public lectures, distributing sales aids to dealers, directing publicity to consumers, and even hiring a publicity agent—its major accomplishment was the creation of a credit purchase plan.[64]

Instituted in 1929, the program was entitled the Sterling Silversmiths Guild Purchase Plan. The scheme tried to increase sales by making it possible for customers to purchase silverware on credit or "out of income," as it was called. To do this, the guild arranged for the national lender, Commercial Credit Companies, to make loans to customers for the purchase of silver items that they could not afford if they had to pay cash. As an International Silver advertisement explained to dealers:

> Briefly the plan provides that jewelers may sell sterling, over the amount of $100, for a down payment of 25% of the piece. The purchaser signs the agreement to pay the balance, plus the carrying charge, in ten monthly installments. The Commercial Credit Company [*sic*], the largest finance organization in the world, will buy this paper

in $500 lots and advance to the jeweler, immediately, 90% of the price. The remaining 10% is retained by the jeweler from the last payment."[65]

The same advertisement noted that potential customers were being informed about this new purchase plan in copy appearing in *Good Housekeeping, Vogue, Vanity Fair, House & Garden, Harper's Bazaar, House Beautiful,* and *American Home.*

It is hard to judge how successful the purchase plan and all the accompanying self-analysis, reform, and advertising were during the first four decades of the twentieth century. Certainly the late 1920s was a boom period for the silverware industry, with the number of concerns making sterling and plated ware reaching a post–Civil War peak of 183 in 1925. Likewise, the value of products created by the industry climbed to a high of over $87 million in 1927. But the onset of the Great Depression changed everything. By 1933 the value of the industry's products had plummeted more than 50 percent and remained more than a third below 1927 levels in 1937.[66] In spite of all the financial and marketing studies done in the 1930s and all the advertising appeals made to dealers and the public, producers were unable to overcome the severe economic problems and important cultural changes which progressively devalued the role of silver in American society. It took World War II with its lucrative government contracts to revive the industry financially.

NOTES

1. Barta 1925.

2. Gorham 1932, 67–68.

3. For an Alvin ad linking art with its silverware, see *JCK* 78:12 (23 Apr. 1919):2. For a trade catalogue discussing the importance of silver trophies in life, see Wallace 1921, 1. For an ad on the quality of Gorham products, see *JCK* 78:1 (2 May 1919):368; and for one on Oneida silverplate, see *CJ* 4 (Nov. 1937):6–8. For an International Silver ad with a romantic theme, see *JCK* 78:5 (5 Mar. 1919):66.

4. For information on the fair, see TA, Box 4, New York World's Fair, 1939–40.

5. Gibb 1943, 330–31.

6. For a fine discussion of both techniques and philosophies in advertising of this period, see Strasser 1989.

7. The copy of "An Advertising Campaign" examined is in the design library at the Gorham plant, Providence, R.I. It is dated August 1907.

8. For the examples cited here, see *HB* 27:6 (May 1910):xx; 28:1 (June 1910): xiv; 3 (Aug. 1910):x; 5 (Oct. 1910):xvii; 29:1 (Dec. 1910):xviii; and 3 (Feb. 1911):xviii.

9. *Gorham Mark* 1918, n.p.

10. For general information on Oneida, see Rainwater 1975, 121.

11. "Community Plate Silver Parade. What-Why-When?," *CJ* 1 (Apr. 1934):9.

12. *Ibid.*

13. Pelletier 1918a, 1.

14. Pelletier 1918b, 1. This text is very ethnocentric with numerous racist comments about Asians.

15. For a discussion on how increased marketing costs and these new types of stores hurt traditional retailers, see "The Evolution of Advertising," *JCK* 78:1 (5 Feb. 1919):469–71.

16. "Jobbers and Retailers," *JW* 1:3 (18 Nov. 1885):117.

17. *JCK* 78:2 (12 Feb. 1919):80.

18. A copy of *Get Together*, bound among other pamphlets from ca. 1918–19, is in the design library, Gorham plant, Providence, R.I.

19. "Announcement" dated 24 July 1930 and located in GA, IX. Sales, 2.

20. Nelson 1946, 285.

21. Gorham's hotel division, for example, was finally sold to International Silver in 1946.

22. A Wallace brochure on the *Leviathan* survives in the ISA in the 1923 trade catalogue file.

23. *Country Life in America* 9 (Feb. 1905):398 and (Nov. 1905):32.

24. Aldred 1923, 18.

25. *Ibid.*, "Comments," 2.

26. "Outlines New Policies of the Gorham Interests," *JCK* 81:25 (19 Jan. 1921):87–89.

27. For information on and lists of the managers of these branches, see Historical 1950.

28. Fuessle 1929, [8].

29. *Ibid.*, [3–5].

30. Getman 1966, 1.

31. Aldred 1923, 6.

32. *Ibid.*, 6, and "Comments," [1].

33. Gorham 1932, 8.

34. Historical 1950, "District Offices."

35. Aldred 1923, 6.

36. For a campaign packet containing these quotes, see GA, IX. Sales. For similar advertising for Community Plate, see *JCK* 99:8 (19 Sept. 1929):back cover.

37. Quoted in Marchand 1985, 65.

38. *JCK* 99:7 (12 Sept. 1929):34

39. de Wolfe 1929.

40. "You've Seen Them Dine in REEL Life . . . ," *CJ* 2 (Apr. 1935):13. For other examples, see "Community Camera Clickings," *CJ* 3 (Apr. 1936):10–11.

41. Gorham 1929. The first three sets of ellipses do not represent omissions, but exist in the quoted text.

42. *VF* 32:3 (May 1929):101

43. Quoted from a reprint of "Sinclair Lewis Looks at Advertising" in *Advertising & Selling* 13:17 (15 May 1929) found in GA, X. Advertising, 2. Company and Image Promotion 1929.

44. *VF* 33:5 (Mar. 1930):163; 34:1 (Apr. 1930):83; and 34:3 (May 1930):87.

45. For information of such exhibitions shown at the Metropolitan Museum of Art in New York, see Miller 1990, 13–20.

46. *Ibid.*, 191.

47. "A New Sales Weapon That is a Repeater," *CJ* 1 (Apr. 1934):23.

48. *CJ* 3 (Oct. 1936):2.

49. *JCK* 99:7 (12 Sept. 1929):25. For a Finn, Iffland & Co. ad, see 99:6 (5 Sept. 1929):67. For one by Kawneer, see 78:1 (5 Feb. 1919):420. For images and information on store interiors in general, see "Making the Store Front an Advertising Factor," 78:1 (5 Feb. 1919):443–49 and "Getting More Fall Business by More Effort," 99:7 (12 Sept. 1929):45.

50. For other images of modernist windows, see *JCK* 99:7 (12 Sept. 1929): 42–44. For an article on proper use of windows, see "Make 'em Stop and Want to Buy," 99:6 (26 Sept. 1929):62–63.

51. Notices 1932, v. 1 (20 July 1937):89; (14 June 1938):107; and (11 Oct. 1938):n.p.

52. *Ibid.*, v. 1 (21 Mar. 1935):52 and v. 2 ([?] 1941):5.

53. *Ibid.*, v. 1 (9 July 1935):54.

54. Gorham 1932, 120 and 130.

55. Aldred 1923, "Sales by States" chart notes that for the fiscal year ending 31 Jan. 1923, 68 percent of sales for Gorham and its affiliates occurred in the following states: N.Y. (20 percent), Pa. (9 percent); Cal. (8 percent); Ill., Mass., and Ohio (6 percent each); N.J. (4 percent); and Mich., Ga., and Tex. (3 percent each).

56. *Ibid.*, 8 and 9.

57. *Ibid.*, 11.

58. *Ibid.*, 19. Although Gorham management disputed the figures as abnormal, if not incorrect, Aldred & Co. estimates for its rate of return were Gorham (4.6 percent); Durgin (2.8 percent); Whiting (5.4 percent); and Kerr (7.1 percent).

59. *Ibid.*, 14.

60. *Ibid.*, 24–25.

61. Gibb 1943, 316–20.

62. "What Does a Manufacturer Know About Retailing?," *CJ* 1 (June 1934):6–7 and 18.

63. *JCK* 81:20 (8 Dec. 1920):83.

64. All basic information about the Sterling Silverware Manufacturers Association and its evolution is taken from "Thumbnail Sketch of Highlights in the History of the Sterling Silversmiths Guild of America." This unpublished manuscript was provided by Robert M. Johnston of the Sterling Silversmiths Guild of America, 312A Wyndhurst Ave., Baltimore, Md., 21210. The members of the Guild were Gorham, International, J. F. Fradley & Co., Frank M. Smith Co., Redlich & Co., Reed & Barton, Dominick & Haff, Alvin, Frank M. Whiting, Rogers, Lunt & Bowlen, Towle, and R. Wallace & Sons.

65. *JCK* 99:7 (12 Sept. 1929):35. Booklets (*Guild* 1929) also were sent to dealers.

66. *Silverware* 1940, 19, table 7.

Chapter 9

ART AND COMMERCE: DESIGN

The waning years of the nineteenth century and the first four decades of the twentieth were an extremely interesting period in terms of silverware design. In an effort to reach as many customers as possible, the industry almost simultaneously created objects in the conservative beaux-arts and colonial revival styles, as well as in the more avant-garde tastes of art nouveau, arts and crafts, and, by the late 1920s, the modernist mode. In her 1912 article "The American Renaissance in Silversmithing," Evelyn Marie Stuart illustrated side-by-side contemporary Gorham silverware in the beaux-arts, colonial revival, and art nouveau styles.[1] Most previous analyses of this period, however, have concentrated on aesthetic and philosophical considerations of the reformist styles only, with little attention being given to the more conservative tastes. Furthermore, research on the silverware of this era has been done primarily from an aesthetic point of view, with almost no consideration of the role of economics in commercial design. Although it is true that certain producers and consumers held strong moral and aesthetic convictions during these years which drove them toward a particular style, it is also important to recognize that for the vast majority of silver makers, silverware was seen as a consumer good to be sold for profit, not an item created for sheer artistic enjoyment or moral uplift. Between 1885 and 1940, design became the servant to and occasionally a slave of the marketplace as perhaps never before in the history of metalsmithing.

The 1890s had been a difficult decade for the silverware industry because of increased competition and low profits. Furthermore, many firms like Gorham and Tiffany's had invested heavily in new, more efficient manufactories, which they found difficult to operate effectively due to the extremely seasonal nature of the trade. The situation improved somewhat in the 1910s, but World War I brought recession in its wake, as did the 1929 stock market crash. Thus throughout much of the period under consideration, silverware producers were forced to try to improve their operations until they consistently created objects that both met the demands of a large audience and generated the profits expected by investors.

The shift away from more costly, labor-intensive wares to cheaper, simpler ones occurred gradually between 1885 and 1940. Nevertheless, throughout the entire period, exceptional handmade objects were produced for the highest end of the market. For customers who could afford expensive chased decoration, for example, silver in the opulent beaux-arts taste was still being made painstakingly by hand into the 1930s. And until World War I, luxury-class goods in the "American" and moresque styles were available. However, these were styles that in many ways embodied the temperament of another age—one which yearned for elaboration and variety rather than simplification and versatility. Conversely, the arts and crafts, colonial revival, and modernist tastes were reformist in nature. Thus they were in some ways better suited to the dramatic cultural shifts, such as the dependence on fewer servants and a renewed appreciation of unadorned objects, that affected the silverware industry between 1885 and 1940.

THE ART NOUVEAU STYLE

Of the styles produced during this period, the one that best bridged the more opulent and patterned world of the mid nineteenth century and the reductionist age of the early twentieth was art nouveau. Developed and popularized in Europe between 1880 and World War I, the art nouveau style was characterized by undulating lines and swirling ornament. In its appreciation of pattern and complicated forms, the style was a continuation of earlier nineteenth-century traditions. Simultaneously, however, it was a "new art," a reform style that was not derived from some exotic or long-dead culture, but a contemporary reaction against revivalism. Some manufacturers even introduced patterns with names like *Modern Art* and *New Art* (fig. 9.1). Furthermore, the objects produced in this taste were, for the most part, visually simpler than their immediate predecessors and thus embodied change. In Europe the new style made important contributions to continental design in virtually all media, including architecture. Its effects in the United States were restricted primarily to graphic, ceramic, jewelry, and silver design.[2]

FIG. 9.1. *New Art* pattern salad set. William B. Durgin Co., maker, Concord, N.H.; Shreve, Crump & Low Co., retailer, Boston, Mass.; designed 1904. Sterling silver. Dallas Museum of Art.

FIG. 9.3. Chafing dish. Joseph Heinrich, maker, New York, N.Y., and Paris, France; Cowell & Hubbard Co., retailer, Cleveland, Ohio; ca. 1900–1915. Copper, silver, and wood. Dallas Museum of Art.

Inspired by European periodicals, trade catalogues, and imported objects, a relatively large number of American silver firms were working in the art nouveau style by 1900, including sizable concerns like Tiffany's, Reed & Barton, and Durgin (fig. 9.2), as well as small ones, including Joseph Heinrich's shop (fig. 9.3). In the 1910s, the Newark firm Unger Brothers and its designer Philemon Dickinson produced a wide range of relatively inexpensive die-stamped silverware in the art nouveau taste, the forms of which often undulated in concert with the decoration (fig. 9.4).[3] Although these and other wares compared well to their European counterparts, it is difficult to ascertain how the producers felt about their work because so little supporting documentation survives.

The case is different with Gorham. Under the leadership of its new, English-trained designer, William C. Codman, and its energetic president, Edward Holbrook, Gorham developed one of the most acclaimed lines of art nouveau silverware in the world. As noted earlier, Gorham hoped the new *Martelé* line would solidify its position as a luxury-goods producer and would add cachet to its less costly products through name association. However, *Martelé* was extremely difficult to produce. Unlike the detailed designs that were generally prepared throughout the industry, *Martelé* drawings by Codman and his fellow Gorham designers were often impressionistic and sometimes showed no ornament at all. Consequently the designer and silversmith had to work together closely during the

creation of an object, adjusting the decorative scheme as needed. To train additional craftsmen capable of such work, a special "school" within the manufactory was established in 1896. The decision to produce such labor-intensive wares was a major one on the part of Gorham's management because it required substantial investment over four years before a single object was sold. Enough examples had been completed to stage an exhibit in New York in 1897; however, the new line was not commercially introduced until the 1900 Paris world's fair. It is not surprising that Gorham chose Paris as the site of the line's international unveiling, given that *Martelé* simultaneously embodied the somewhat contradictory concepts of a distinctive national school and avant-garde foreign design. Shown in the American section of the exposition, Gorham could present *Martelé* both as a patriotic contribution to the glory of the United States, and simultaneously try to please the French critics. Gorham must have felt that Parisian fairgoers and critics would be especially receptive to its styling since they lived in the European center of art nouveau. From a marketing standpoint, positive reviews in the recognized art capital of the Western world would make the expensive objects more appealing to fashion-conscious customers in the United States.

To ensure success, Gorham's chief designer, William C. Codman, and the firm's best silversmiths created exceptional examples of *Martelé* to send to Paris. The highest possible artistic and technical quality was achieved by producing entire

FIG. 9.2. Decanter. William B. Durgin Co., Concord, N.H., and T. G. Hawkes & Co., Corning, N.Y., ca. 1900. Sterling silver, silvergilt, and cut glass. Norwest Corporation, Minneapolis.

FIG. 9.4. Ash tray and cigarette case. Unger Brothers, Newark, N.J., ca. 1900–1910.
Sterling silver. Dallas Museum of Art.

series of objects of a particular form, from which only a few were selected for shipment to France. For example, a pair of vases ornamented with irises and tulips was made in 1899 as part of a group considered for inclusion in the fair (fig. 9.5). The fact that these particular vases do not seem to have been chosen, in spite of their outstanding quality, indicates that those items exhibited in 1900 were the absolute best Gorham was capable of producing. As a tour de force for its display, the firm created a solid silver dressing table and stool that revealed the extraordinary level of artistic and technical virtuosity achieved by Gorham (fig. 9.6). Consuming over 2,300 hours of skilled labor and 1,253 ounces of silver, the table had a retail price of $8,800; the stool cost an additional $960.[4] Despite the sizable financial investment such objects represented, Gorham was probably satisfied with the results of the fair. Not only did Gorham sell the table upon its return to America, but the firm was awarded the *grand prix* for metalwork, being placed above Tiffany & Co. Furthermore, Gorham's president, Edward Holbrook, was made a Chevalier of the French Legion of Honor, and William C. Codman was awarded a gold medal for his designs.

The French critics were extremely impressed by the *Martelé* line. One exclaimed: "It is marvelous that while the taste of New Yorkers differs from ours in so many ways, the Gorham Manufacturing Co. has succeeded so grandly in satisfying us without dissatisfying its clientele."[5] Achieving this delicate balance was indeed laudable and had been accomplished by keeping up with current styles, adopting the basic design tenets of European art nouveau without losing sight of the American buying public's often conservative predilections. For example, rather than design the dressing table as a composition of swirling forms that appeared to grow out of the ground as a Frenchman might have done, Gorham gave it a conservative colonial revival form, complete with cabriole legs and ball-and-claw feet. By trying to "read" customer's desires, Gorham hoped *Martelé* would be a huge commercial success. However, the market was already becoming saturated by 1905.

Besides its high cost, part of the reason the *Martelé* line was eventually rejected by consumers may stem from the fact that in the first decade of the century the number of domestic servants in the country steadily declined from the peak of 1910.[6] The dwindling supply of servants meant that it was more diffi-

FIG. 9.5. Pair of *Martelé* vases. William C. Codman, designer; Gorham Mfg. Co., maker, Providence, R.I.; 1899. Silver. Dallas Museum of Art.

Art and Commerce

FIG. 9.7. *Martelé* pitcher. William C. Codman, designer; Gorham Mfg. Co., maker, Providence, R.I.;
Spaulding & Co., retailer, Chicago, Ill.; 1909. Silver. Dallas Museum of Art.

cult to maintain the bric-a-brac-filled houses and complicated dining rituals developed in the previous century. As a consequence, when selecting silverware consumers were increasingly likely to choose pieces that were simple in design and therefore easy to clean. Furthermore, they may well have chosen fewer large objects like vases and centerpieces because such pieces typically sat out in the open where they tarnished quickly. Given that *Martelé* was made in large forms with intricate surfaces, it must have been at a disadvantage when judged against plainer arts and crafts and colonial revival–style pieces. To meet this trend, Gorham simplified *Martelé* designs around 1909 (fig. 9.7). Nevertheless, sales continued to decline, although a

few pieces were made as late as the 1930s. But even if *Martelé* failed to generate sufficient profits to offset Gorham's large investment in the line's production, its extraordinary quality was nevertheless successful in generating positive publicity and reinforced Gorham's image as a producer of exceptional, high-end goods during the first decade of the twentieth century.

The firm's adoption of the art nouveau taste was more than simply an attempt to garner publicity, however. The development of *Martelé* was directly inspired by contemporary British reformist ideology.[7] Gorham employee Horace Townsend clearly stated this point in his essay of 1898, "An Artistic Experiment." In it he cites the English art theorist John Ruskin

FIG. 9.6. *Martelé* dressing table and stool. William C. Codman, designer; Gorham Mfg. Co.,
maker, Providence, R.I.; 1899–1900. Silver, glass, fabric, and ivory.
Private Collection, courtesy Hoffman Gampetro Antiques.

(1819–1900) as the founder of the reform movement that stressed "Truth and Beauty" as the principles that should underlie all creations. Gorham felt its new silverware line embodied Ruskin's ideas because it was almost totally handmade and because the designer and silversmiths worked closely together in the creation of each piece. Consequently, the hammer marks on each object represented the thoughts and skill of the maker, unlike the hammer marks of cheaper wares which were simply stamped onto the surface mechanically or added by hand as a decorative finish to machine-made pieces. To reflect this relationship between maker and object, Gorham named the line *Martelé*, a French word meaning "hammered."

While Gorham freely stated *Martelé*'s links to the English reform movement and contemporary continental design, the firm also promoted the line as the embodiment of a "Golden Age" in the evolution of American silver.[8] When describing its importance, Gorham writers repeatedly claimed *Martelé* represented the attainment of a new level in artistic metalworking for this country. For example, in an 1899 article in *Brush and Pencil*, "Martelé, A New Distinctive School: American Renaissance in Silversmithing," Henry C. Tilden explained:

> The spirit which dominated Cellini and the old masters seems here to have been revived and in this American Renaissance in silversmithing we may well take pride. . . . No piece or design is ever reproduced and the art lover must recognize in these distinguished productions a happy return to the principles of earlier days and hail with delight the advent of American silversmithing as a living art in design as well as in technical execution.[9]

In 1912 Evelyn Marie Stuart claimed in the *Fine Arts Journal* that Gorham had initiated "The American Renaissance In Silversmithing." Describing *Martelé*'s place in the history of silver styles, she wrote: "Here indeed is a new school, a distinctive type, a fresh beauty as novel and as characteristically our own as our Rookwood pottery or Tiffany glass." In conclusion she asked expectantly, "What may we not hope further from such a workshop in such a country and in such an age?"[10]

THE ARTS AND CRAFTS MOVEMENT

The age in which Stuart wrote witnessed a major shift in silverware design. In fact, by the time her articles appeared in 1912, *Martelé* was considered too elaborate and was rapidly declining in popularity. As Wendy Kaplan, Leslie Bowman, and others have explained, around the turn of the century reformers sought to strip away the ornament and complexity of the mid nineteenth century, thereby elevating form to the top of the aesthetic hierarchy. Instead of opulence and technical virtuosity, chasteness and structural simplicity were championed. For Americans, the primary source for this ideology was Great Britain. Progressing from the writings of A. W. N. Pugin (1812–1852) and Sir Thomas Carlyle (1795–1881) to those of John Ruskin and William Morris (1834–1896), the British reform movement was at the peak of its power between 1880 and 1910.[11] The goal of much of its highly moralistic rhetoric was to change society's attitudes toward the worker who was being "enslaved" by industrialism and its perfection of the factory system. The highly influential Ruskin, for example, blamed factories, with their division of labor and increasing reliance on machinery, for transforming craftsmen into automata who performed mindless, repetitive tasks. To reverse this process, Ruskin called for the reintroduction of hand labor and the production of objects whose creation reunited the designer and maker in a single individual. For Ruskin, objects should be honest in material and straightforward in design. Ornament was proper only insofar as it emphasized structure or suggested inspiration from nature.[12]

The arts and crafts movement, as this reforming impulse was called, found fertile ground in the United States and rapidly spread through intellectual channels across the country between 1895 and 1910. Although reformist design ideas had been at work in America since the 1870s, the moralizing nature of arts and crafts ideology was something different, and succeeded best in the context of small workshops and societies of like-minded individuals. The first such organizations appeared in America in 1897. The Boston Society of Arts and Crafts and the Chicago Arts and Crafts Society were inspired by the Arts and Crafts Society of London, which had been founded in 1888. Eventually, similar societies were established from coast to coast, including those in Detroit, Minneapolis, and Southern California. To promote reform, these organizations sponsored educational programs, which included lectures by such notables as the English silver designer C. R. Ashbee (1863–1942), who visited America frequently.[13] They also held many exhibitions and opened retail outlets through which member craftsmen could market their wares. Because many supporters of arts and crafts societies were wealthy intellectuals, membership could initiate contacts between craftsmen and potential patrons which might result in future silverware commissions.[14]

Beyond marketing and educating the public to appreciate their members' wares, such organizations offered moral support to both the foreign-born silversmith who had been trained in a traditional small shop and the native who had consciously opted to leave the manufactory. The prominence of such individuals in the history of arts and crafts silversmithing is astounding. In the vibrant reformist center of Boston, for example, central figures in the movement included Swedish-trained Frans J. R. Gyllenberg (b. 1883); Finnish-trained Karl E. Leinonen (1866–1957); Mary Catherine Knight (b. 1876), who had been a designer for Gorham; George Gebelein (1878–1945), who had worked for Shiebler, Tiffany's, and Durgin; and Arthur Stone (1847–1938), who had been trained in Sheffield before coming to America, where he worked at Durgin and the Frank W. Smith Silver Co. Foreign or manufacturing backgrounds were also characteristic of many arts and crafts silversmiths working in other parts of the country. Clemens Friedell

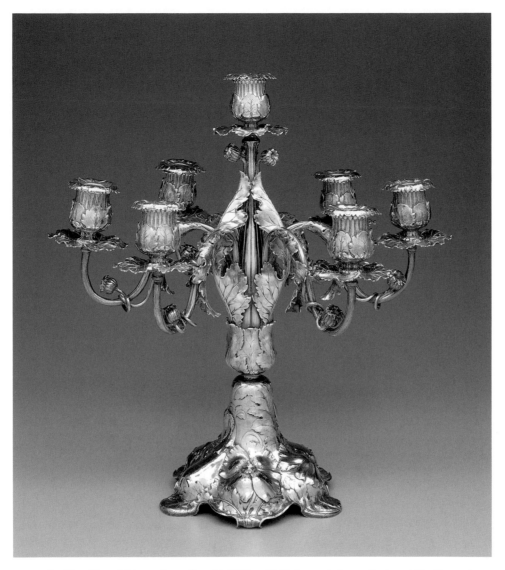

FIG. 9.8. *Martelé* candelabrum (one of a pair). William C. Codman, designer; Gorham Mfg. Co., maker, Providence, R.I.; 1905. Silver. Dallas Museum of Art.

(1872–1963), for example, was trained in Vienna and then worked for Gorham as a master chaser before going to Pasadena, California, where he opened his own shop.[15] Presumably, such craftspeople wished to avoid work in silverware manufactories altogether or had been disillusioned by their experiences there. As noted above, the years around the turn of the century when many of these individuals worked in manufactories were trying ones during which managers pressured designers and workers to work faster and produce more. Having worked in several manufactories, for example, Arthur Stone said that what he really wanted was "to work without stress in a little shop of his own."[16] If a silversmith's goal, like Stone's, was to be his own boss or to work in the more intimate, personal environment of a small shop, arts and crafts societies and related institutions like museum art schools could often help him make the transition.

But despite whatever emotional and financial support such institutions could give a silversmith, and all the rhetoric about exalting the skill and originality of the craftsman, the aesthetics that the arts and crafts movement espoused worked to deskill many craftsmen. With the exception of amateurs who were inspired by the reform movement to attempt metalworking for the first time, most professional silversmiths were not challenged to excel in technique because unornamented, simple shapes did not require them to. In most cases a silversmith could execute arts and crafts designs if he was competent in the basic skills of raising, soldering, and planishing. Certainly these techniques require talent, but they are not as difficult as chasing, fine engraving, or repoussé work, to say nothing of the use of complicated mixed metals. For craftsmen who in a manufactory setting received lower pay doing forming, soldering, or finishing work—because they were not skilled enough to earn higher wages as chasers or engravers—working outside the manufactory executing relatively simple wares must have been an improvement. And even for highly talented craftsmen like Arthur Stone, simply working in the less hurried atmosphere

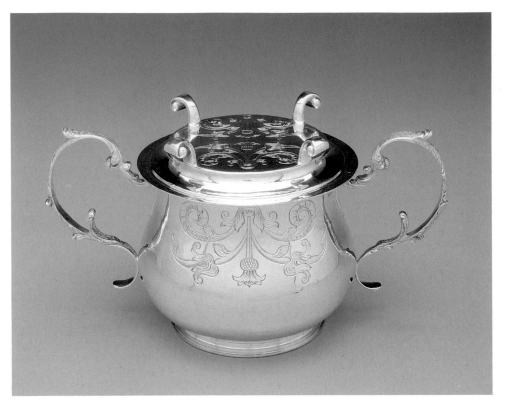

FIG. 9.9. Covered cup. George Christian Gebelein, Boston, Mass., ca. 1915–1930.
Sterling silver. Dallas Museum of Art.

of a small shop was worth sacrificing the opportunity to work on the wide array of goods that the typical manufactory had in production at any given time. For some exceptionally talented silverworkers, however, the transition from making elaborate objects to simpler ones was not always easy.

The life of Clemens Friedell is a good example of such a case. Born in Louisiana in 1872, Friedell moved to his parents' native Vienna when he was three. He served his apprenticeship in Austria before returning to the United States in 1892. After living in San Antonio for a while, he began work at Gorham in 1901. There he was employed as a master chaser making *Martelé*. An exceptional pair of candelabra documents Friedell's great skill (fig. 9.8). Made in 1905, the pieces required 247 hours at a labor cost of $123.50 for chasing alone.[17] Evidently anxious to be his own designer and work outside the manufactory, Friedell left Gorham in 1907 to open his own shop. However, the depression surrounding the Panic of 1907 forced him out of business. Following brief stays in San Antonio and Los Angeles, Friedell moved to Pasadena, California, in 1911 where he maintained a financially successful shop until his death in 1963. Friedell's exceptional skill as a master chaser, however, was not sustained by either the arts and crafts movement or the marketplace. By the mid 1910s, ornamentation in the art nouveau taste had fallen from favor and had been replaced by the unornamented forms and simple shapes promoted by reformers. Furthermore, the need to have a broad-based clientele to provide sufficient work for a silversmithy probably pushed Clemens Friedell to introduce cheaper, simpler lines of

silverware that the middle class could afford. In 1960, Friedell looked back over his long career and lamented that "great silver artists" no longer could compete in the marketplace. "Nowadays," he said, "they tell you to get it out as fast and as cheaply as possible. No artist can work that way."[18]

George Gebelein made a similar transition in his work. Apprenticed in the Boston silver workshop of Goodnow & Jenks in 1893, Gebelein went to New York in 1897, where he worked for Shiebler before securing a position at Tiffany & Co.'s Forest Hill plant. Judging from the fact that he was able to complete the difficult task of cutting and fitting an elaborate design in silver overlay onto a glass bowl as an initial test of his skill, and later worked on some of the opulent silverware Tiffany's sent to the 1900 and 1901 world's fairs, George Gebelein was a highly skilled silversmith capable of executing extremely complicated work. In 1900 he left Tiffany's for Durgin in Concord, New Hampshire, where he remained until 1903. That year he joined the Handicraft Shop, which was affiliated with the Boston Society of Arts and Crafts. There he worked with others until 1909, when he was able to open his own smithy. Although the Gebelein workshop occasionally produced more elaborate objects, it is best known for replicas or adaptations of relatively unornamented seventeenth- and eighteenth-century American silverware. Given his skill, it is hard to believe that he found most of these pieces terribly challenging from a technical point of view. Furthermore, the fact that many were near, if not exact, copies of earlier objects meant that Gebelein's abilities as a designer were not encouraged (fig. 9.9). Of course it is possible

FIG. 9.10. Pitcher. Tiffany & Co., New York, N.Y., 1909. Sterling silver.
William Hill Land & Cattle Co. Collection.

FIG. 9.11. Pitcher. Derby Silver Co., Derby, Conn., ca. 1915–1930.
Silverplate. Sylvia and Charles Venable Collection.

that Gebelein did not wish to produce wares that were innovative in design or technique, but if he did, the reform movement did not encourage him to do so.[19]

Besides these reductive aesthetics, which did not promote the maintenance or acquisition of exceptional technical skill, the ideology of the arts and crafts movement was problematical for silversmiths in both the manufactory and small shop settings. As Leslie Bowman has pointed out,[20] the reformist goal of elevating the craftsman by eliminating the division of labor, while simultaneously producing high quality, handcrafted objects for the middle class, was at odds with the realities of the marketplace. More than in any other country in the world, silverware manufacturers in the United States had spent over a half century trying to provide quality goods to the bourgeoisie. And they were so successful that America was, by the early twentieth century, the largest producer and consumer of silverware in the world. The industry's enormous growth had been achieved, however, because machines did much of the basic preparatory work and because the division of labor allowed craftsmen to excel at their specialties, thereby becoming more efficient. The

purchase of raw materials in large quantities and the creation of national marketing systems further enabled manufacturers to produce and distribute silverware at competitive prices that many could afford. By calling for the abandonment of such highly organized production in favor of small shops in which only hand tools were used and a single craftsman was responsible for the creation of an object from start to finish, the arts and crafts movement doomed itself to failure. The cost of hand labor was simply too high and the production of small shops too low to compete in the marketplace.

Given these realities, it is not surprising that the ideas of the arts and crafts movement were compromised in the area of silverware. While the aesthetics of simplicity triumphed in many ways, the means of their realization were usually anything but revolutionary. True, some small shops did do most work by hand, but so too did large firms when required. Consequently, when arts and crafts ideology popularized the appreciation of hand-processed silverware, many manufacturers simply labeled their products as "Handmade" or "Hand-Wrought." Even though most of these objects were produced

FIG. 9.12. Hand mirror. Unger Brothers, Newark, N.J., ca. 1910–1920.
Sterling silver and enamel. The Mitchell Wolfson, Jr., Collection.

FIG. 9.13. Hand mirror. Arthur Nevill Kirk, Cranbrook Academy, Bloomfield Hills, Mich., ca. 1931.
Sterling silver, ivory, enamel, and semiprecious stones. Cranbrook Academy of Art Museum.

FIG. 9.14. Bowl. Kalo Shop, Chicago, Ill., ca. 1914–1918. Sterling silver. Dallas Museum of Art.

FIG. 9.15. Punch bowl, ladle, and tray. Robert Riddle Jarvie, Chicago, Ill., 1911.
Sterling silver. ©1991 The Art Institute of Chicago.

FIG. 9.16. Teapot. Shreve & Co., San Francisco, Cal., ca. 1911. Sterling silver and ivory. Dallas Museum of Art.

through a combination of mechanical and hand techniques, the image such labeling conjured up was a romantic and highly marketable one of forthright craftsmen lovingly creating silver objects, rather than of a busy manufactory. Tiffany's, for example, began marking certain wares in the arts and crafts taste as "SPECIAL HAND WORK" around 1907 (fig. 9.10).[21] Similarly, the Derby Silver Co. introduced a line of "Hand Beaten" wares, the bodies of which were spun or stamped (fig. 9.11). Decorative hammer marks were subsequently added as a surface finish. Unger Brothers achieved a similar effect in its toilet ware with hammer marks stamped directly onto the surface (fig. 9.12). Although the quality of design and execution is not as fine when compared to expensive handmade examples (fig. 9.13), the combination of hammer marks and an enameled boss was acceptable to middle-class consumers who could not afford more opulent versions. Many other firms used similar techniques. As late as 1928, for example, the Stieff Co. of Baltimore promoted its wares as "Stieff Hand-Wrought Sterling Silver," despite their highly chased surfaces being anything but reformist in nature. Stieff nevertheless invoked reform ideology to sell its products when it stated:

A GOOD SILVER SERVICE is one of a woman's most treasured possessions. Each occasion for its use brings with it that gratifying pride of ownership that time only serves to increase. As time goes on, its constant employment develops an ever increasing attachment—deeper and more intimate through years of constant association. Since this is true, since the silver service is so personal, so endeared to the user, the thought of using impersonal machine made silverware seems to be at variance with the very

spirit that lies in the silver service. Silver wrought by hand, however, seems to give just that touch, that expression of intimacy that every woman desires.

The House of Stieff, realizing this obligation to American woman-hood, has made every effort to combine the genius of the designer with the cunning and skill of the master craftsman in creating pieces of silver that leave nothing to be desired. Masterpieces of master workmen.[22]

Since virtually all firms maintained a stable of silversmiths who could raise and decorate wares by hand when necessary, labeling of this type was undoubtedly done to compete more effectively against smaller rival shops that sold their wares on the basis of their being handmade.

Along with appropriating arts and crafts rhetoric, manufacturers had no difficulty in adopting the aesthetics of reform. Certainly it is true that some firms, like the Kalo and Jarvie shops in Chicago (figs. 9.14–15),[23] appear to have consistently hand raised the relatively simple, unornamented shapes championed by the reformist. It is also true that the forms were well-suited for mechanically aided production. For example, the round shapes so often used in arts and crafts–style silver were ideal for spinning up on a lathe. The wares of Shreve & Co. of San Francisco illustrate this point. As a medium-sized producer of commercial wares, Shreve did not hesitate to adopt the simplified aesthetics of the reform style. Items such as its teapot (fig. 9.16) were primarily made on a lathe, with hammer marks added later. Even George Gebelein's small shop had a spinning lathe for producing less expensive lines, as did the Craft Shop of Marshall Field & Co. in Chicago.[24]

FIG. 9.17. Dish. Arts and Crafts Shop of Shreve, Crump & Low Co., Boston, Mass., 1902–1914. Sterling silver and stones. ©1991 The Art Institute of Chicago. This dish is patterned after examples by the English designer Charles Robert Ashbee.

When manufacturers adopted the arts and crafts taste for simple shapes, they also used hammer marks as a symbolic surface treatment. The fashion of leaving hammer marks on a piece of silver to give it a handmade appearance was popularized first by Tiffany & Co. in the late 1870s, as noted above. Throughout the 1880s, large quantities of "hammered" silverware were made in this country, and manufacturers perfected many techniques for applying such marks to silver, from painstakingly doing it by hand to quickly stamping it with a die and press. Thus, although the contemporary work of British designers like C. R. Ashbee and Archibald Knox (1864–1933) must have reinforced the practice (fig. 9.17), for American silverworkers and customers such surfaces were not new.[25] Rather, as arts and crafts rhetoric made handcrafted silver more popular, the fashion for hammer marks in this country simply took on greater significance, regardless of how they were actually created.

In the end, the great success of the arts and crafts movement in the United States was the widespread adoption of its aesthetics, rather than its ideology. The vast majority of silverware made in this style came from manufactories, not small craft shops. Hand production methods were simply not efficient enough to generate large output. Elenita C. Chickering, for example, estimates that during the peak year of 1915, Arthur Stone's busy shop produced only 200 objects. In the entire existence of the smithy from 1901 to 1937, probably no more than 5,000 objects were made. And Stone was a well-known craftsman who employed thirty-eight others to aid in production during these years.[26] Certainly craft shops that employed larger numbers of workers, such as Kalo in Chicago, may have had higher annual outputs, but handicraft shops were typically small-scale producers.

The Boston shop of George Gebelein, for example, employed an average of five to six workmen and three people in the office by the 1920s. Like Stone's shop, Gebelein's produced relatively few objects. Between April 1911 and April 1912, only 436 orders for all types of work, including making jewelry, repairing, cleaning, and engraving were taken.[27] Furthermore, during the same period Gebelein regularly received complaints about the high price of his pieces from the sixteen or so retailers who sold his products on consignment. In 1910, for example, the manager of New York's National Society of Craftsmen told him that "perhaps your prices are a little too high." In 1914 Gustav Stickley's New York retail shop informed Gebelein that it had only sold "the less expensive things," and none of his work. In 1915 the manager of the Schervee Art Shop in Worcester, Massachusetts, summed up the problem when he said of Gebelein's wares, "It is a beautiful line, but we find that it is a line that people will ask for, and it has to be talked up a great deal, as it is beyond a great many."[28] By 1917 the situation was evidently severe. During ten months of that year, Gebelein made only $903 profit on $11,000 in sales, including $6,177 in new silverware.[29] Given his low profit margin, it was probably for economic reasons that he acquired his own spinning lathe. Before this purchase, Gebelein contracted out his spinning. To cut production costs, he purchased ready-to-work sheets of silver and disc stock, as well as ivory and wooden parts. He also had much of the engraving and casting done outside the shop by specialists who could produce the work more cheaply. And finally, Gebelein found that he could make a sizable profit by selling antique and new English and American silverware.[30] Gebelein's efforts to increase his competitiveness in the marketplace through the use of machinery and subcontracted specialists appear to have been typical of most arts and crafts silversmithies. In 1903, for example, a reporter for the *Jewelers' Circular* visited the workshop of the Boston Handicraft Shop that prided itself on being one of the "only places in New England devoted to handicraft working in silver." According to the reporter, however, "A jeweler or silversmith who made the inspection expecting to find radical departures from modern methods might be disappointed." For even in this bastion of arts and craft ideology, both a power lathe and modern gas soldering equipment were employed. "We used modern implements whenever we can," explained the manager, "and whenever their use will not interfere with our purpose. The idea

FIG. 9.18. Coffee set. Arthur J. Stone, Gardner, Mass., designed 1914.
Sterling silver and ivory. Dallas Museum of Art.

that we do everything by hand is not entirely correct. . . . That would not be very sensible in this age. . . . at least individuality and real worth is our aim."[31]

The fact that small shops found it difficult to compete in the marketplace without using some modern production methods does not mean that their products were unimportant. In 1922, Hanna Tachau commented in *International Studio* on the seminal role of small shops in the reform movement when she asked:

> But can a master silversmith, single-handed, under present factory conditions, make a living? Perhaps not, but it has been proven that small groups of craftsmen, working harmoniously together, practicing economy of both time and material, are not only able to produce work that reveals a fine aesthetic sense, but can make this kind of endeavor pay. Through their courageous adherence to art ideals that the love of their craft compels, they have become a significant factor in bringing to the public consciousness the fact that art need not be the exclusive property of the few who have riches as well as culture, but at the same time is the rightful heritage of the humble.[32]

Once these craft shops had demonstrated that there was a market for reformist wares, however, it was bigger producers that made them in quantities large and cheap enough to actually reach the middle class. The medium-sized firm of Shreve & Co. in San Francisco, for example, used machinery whenever possible to produce relatively large quantities of wares in the arts and crafts taste, which often could undersell those from craft shops. And for firms like Tiffany's and Gorham, which had large staffs and thousands of customers, reformist aesthetics were simply adopted as yet another style. By producing some wares in the new taste, these firms hoped to appeal to that section of the market which did not respond to its more elaborate objects.

THE COLONIAL REVIVAL

The colonial revival was the most successful aspect of the reformist movement. Besides the large manufacturers working in the taste to a great extent by 1910, most of the guiding lights of the crafts movement also exploited the style, including Mary C. Knight, Katherine Pratt, Karl Leinonen, Frans Gyllenberg, Porter Blanchard, Clemens Friedell, George Gebelein, and Arthur Stone (fig. 9.18). Underlying the colonial revival's success was the fact that artifacts and designs from America's colonial and new republic periods were already familiar to the buying public. In many ways, the interest in colonial history and aesthetics was more a survival than a true revival. As family

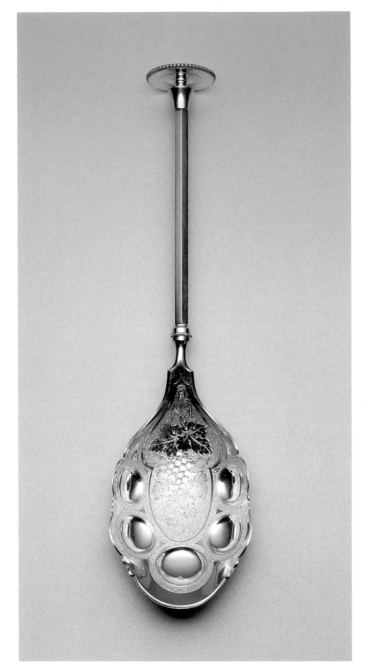

FIG. 9.19. *Old English* pattern serving spoon. Gorham Mfg. Co., Providence, R.I., ca. 1865–1875. Silver and silvergilt. Dallas Museum of Art.

heirlooms and patriotic symbols of American history, silverware made before 1840 had continually been revered by many. Consequently, manufacturers often were asked to fill out sets of objects that had survived only in part or had been divided through inheritance. In 1897, for example, the Philadelphia retailer Bailey, Banks & Biddle told potential customers that "Faithful reproduction of pieces to match old family heirlooms can always be procured of this Company."[33] Similarly, makers were willing to produce entirely new services based on earlier designs. A coffepot by Gale, North & Dominick and a serving spoon by Gorham, both from the 1860s, are fine examples of how earlier British and colonial American designs were still favored in some conservative circles during the mid nineteenth century (figs. 3.5, 9.19). Even patterns that bore no aesthetic relationship whatsoever with this country's colonial past could be associated with it. For example, an acorn-shaped tea and coffee set made in New York around 1850 was named the "Charter Oak" after the oak tree that stood in Hartford, Connecticut, until 1856 which figured prominently in the colonial history of the state (fig. 9.20).

The Centennial Exposition held in Philadelphia in 1876 was a great stimulus to the appreciation of colonial designs and artifacts. Through such romantic installations as a colonial-inspired "New England Kitchen," the Centennial built interest in America's artifactual past. This new appreciation was reflected in an 1876 Tiffany & Co. advertisement in *Harper's Weekly*, which stated that "to meet the prevailing taste T & CO. have revived the manufacture of hammered Silverware in the Old English Style, formerly made by them, and have also a pattern of Spoons and Forks in the style of the last century, to correspond."[34] Ten years later Tiffany's was even making silver in the seventeenth-century Dutch taste, in keeping with the colonial history of New York (fig. 9.21). During the 1880s, interest in America's early silverware grew among dealers and consumers thanks in part to articles such as "The Plate and Jewels of the Washingtons," which appeared in the *Jewelers' Weekly* in 1888, and the *Washington Centennial Loan Exhibition* held in 1889 at the New York Opera House. Reports of the exhibition note that it contained artifacts such as Edmund Randolph's cup and Benjamin Franklin's tea service. Interestingly, Gorham supported the exhibition by loaning objects from its corporate collection and by allowing an employee, John H. Buck, to curate the silver section.[35] In fact, the year before the exhibition, Gorham had published Buck's *Old Plate*, which listed for the first time the names of approximately 160 silversmiths who were active in America before 1800. The reason why Gorham took such an interest in this event and was collecting early American silverware was that in the mid 1880s the firm had introduced a line of sterling and plated goods in the colonial style, which it advertised through full-page layouts (ill. 9.1).[36] Undoubtedly, the firm felt that successful exhibitions could build public interest, which would translate into sales of its wares.

Thanks to efforts by Gorham and by a growing group of antiquarians, interest in colonial American silver was promoted by more publications and exhibitions during the 1890s

FIG. 9.20. Tea set. Charters, Cann & Dunn, maker, New York, N.Y.; Allcock & Allen, retailer,
New York, N.Y., ca. 1850. Coin silver and ivory. Charles Folk Collection.

and early twentieth century. For example, in 1893 there was a "small historical exhibit" of early American silverware at the Chicago world's fair and in the September 1896 issue of *Harper's New Monthly Magazine* Theodore S. Woolsey published "Old Silver," which presented many illustrations of early silver.[37] Ten years later, in 1906, the first major exhibition of American silver was held at the Museum of Fine Arts, Boston, and was soon followed by three others organized by New York's Metropolitan Museum of Art in 1907, 1909, and 1911. Another exhibition was shown at the Museum of Fine Arts, Boston, in 1911, and in 1913 the National Society of Colonial Dames of America supported the publication of E. Alfred Jones's massive *Old Silver of American Churches*.[38] By the time this study appeared, the colonial revival style dominated U.S. silverware design.

Why the country's colonial past so captivated American consumers is a multifaceted phenomenon that deserves much more scholarly attention. Nevertheless, certain major themes are apparent. First, the revitalization of interest, in the 1870s, in this country's early history was part of the contemporary predilection for exploring exotic and remote cultures. As discussed earlier, the 1870s saw designers and consumers turn to Russia, the Middle East, Renaissance Italy, and Japan, among others, for inspiration. Simultaneously, many in this country

were calling for an "American style" in the arts. Although silverware designers attempted to create a new style using imagery from North America's indigenous people, fauna, and flora, no national school ever emerged. By turning to their past, Americans could simultaneously satisfy their dual longing for exotic escapism and heightened nationalism.

By the late nineteenth century, contemporary Americans were removed by two full generations from the realities of life in the colonies. Severed from living memory, the past had become for many a mythical "Golden Age," a mental safe haven from the mounting pressures of an America caught in the grip of industrialization, urbanization, and massive immigration. In 1906, Alice Brown in her short story "The Silver Tea-Set" revealed how silver objects could act as bridges between the all too real present and the tranquil, perfect past of one's forefathers. In the story, the main character, Ann Barstow, owned a silver tea set, which her mother had given her. Constantly caressing and examining the heirloom, Ann is traumatized when it is stolen. Upon walking into the room where it had been, Ann realizes:

> A spot of brightness had gone out of it. The silver tea-set was not there. She hurried into the sitting-room, wild with hope that she might have set it away; but the place

FIG. 9.21. *Love Playing with Time* pattern serving spoon. Tiffany & Co., New York, N.Y., designed 1884, made ca. 1891–1902. Sterling silver. Dallas Museum of Art.

ILL. 9.1. Gorham Mfg. Co.'s colonial revival advertisement, 1886.

was empty. Ann went back into the kitchen, and sank down because her knees refused to hold her. Not once did she think of the value of what she had lost, but only as it linked the past to her own solitary days. The tea-set had been a kind of household deity, the memorial of her father's courage and her mother's happiness, a brighter sun of life than any that could rise again.

When the set was finally recovered, "Ann sat down before it and gathered it into her arms as if it were a child."[39] In 1913 Evelyn Marie Stuart, in an article entitled "Modern Modes in Silver," verbalized the connection between colonial revival designs and a vision of a better yet remote other world when she said of some colonial-style silverware: "About these pieces there is a feeling of the antique, so well does their nobility and dignified simplicity harmonize them with the best productions of an age when sham and haste were not."[40] Simultaneously, the "dignified simplicity" of colonial revival–style wares "harmonized" well with the realities of modern housekeeping. By 1910 servants were becoming increasingly hard to find and the relatively unadorned surfaces of these objects were easier to maintain, as were those in the arts and crafts and modernist tastes.

By the 1910s the colonial revival style dominated American design. For example, while specialized periodicals like Gustav Stickley's *Craftsman* promoted the use of "purist" arts and crafts–style homes and furnishings during the first two decades of the century, more general magazines like *House Beautiful* reveal that the colonial revival taste was far more prevalent in the period. With the exception of an occasional "craftsman" interior, those pictured in *House Beautiful* are overwhelmingly colonial revival in spirit and promoted as the antidote to the excesses of the 1880s.[41] In an article called "The Poor Taste of the Rich," an exotic Turkish room is juxtaposed with a colonial revival dining room. Even though the colonial room is not perfect, it is "excellent in many respects." The Turkish room, however, is said to be the "height of absurd decoration. . . . It is a villainous example of misspent riches. There is not one redeeming feature about the room. It is lacking in every essential that constitutes a successful interior."[42] For the successful colonial revival interior, the magazine advocated using appropriate silverware and collecting antiques, in advice columns and articles like "Rescued from the Junk-Shop" of 1904.[43] Advising its readers on the proper selection of tea services, *House Beautiful* noted, "Older patterns, once in vogue in our grandmothers' days, are in high favor" and "in buying new silver the housekeeper of 1908 will probably choose either the colonial, George III, or Queen Anne styles, or some modern design of good line and simple ornamentation."[44]

Always anxious to increase sales, silverware manufacturers added lines in the colonial revival style. Early examples in this taste were made between 1865 and 1885, but full hollowware lines and numerous flatware patterns did not appear until the late 1880s and 1890s. By the early twentieth century, the production of many firms was almost totally in this idiom. Besides the fact that an increasing number of consumers were enamored of colonial revival designs, manufacturers adopted and promoted the style for production reasons as well. The undecorated forms that typified the colonial revival and other variants of the arts and crafts movement were simply cheaper to make. Simultaneous with the early popularization of the reformist movement, the severe economic conditions of the 1890s were forcing producers to seek ways to reduce manufacturing costs. Because one of the main costs of a piece of silverware is labor, manufacturers attempted to eliminate as much handwork as possible on commercial lines. One way to do this was to make less complicated patterns. This industry-wide trend is documented by trade catalogues, photographic albums, and design drawings from every firm examined. For example, Whiting's day books, which contain miniature sketches of objects made between 1884 and 1923, clearly document this development (ills. 9.2–3). In the 1880s many of the objects were of irregular shape and elaborately decorated, thus requiring the creation of expensive dies or total fabrication by hand. By the late 1890s, most objects were much more regular in shape and plainer in decoration. By 1916, standardization was the rule, with manufacturers using a host of shallow, round forms that lent themselves to spinning and stamping.[45] If expensive decoration was wanted, it could simply be applied to these plainer forms.

However, by the 1910s decorative techniques like chasing and engraving, which were common before 1890 on commercial wares, appeared with much less frequency. But, since customers still wanted the opportunity to customize their purchases on occasion, manufacturers developed ways to accomplish this without requiring excessive handwork. In 1910, for example, the purchaser of a Gorham loving cup could choose from six generic sporting scenes printed on tissue paper. Rather than engrave a unique image on the ordered trophy, Gorham simply recorded the customer's selection and acid etched it onto the silver, thus cutting production costs. Wallace offered a similar service for trophies in the 1920s when its catalogues illustrated a small variety of cast ornaments that would "customize" a generic loving cup when soldered in place.[46] Forty years earlier, it would have been more common simply to chase the desired decoration onto such pieces. For domestic wares, similar solutions were used. On a colonial revival sauceboat made in 1916 by Gorham, for example, stamped, oval appliqués were soldered onto the rim rather than have the chaser who executed the less complicated floral motifs spend his valuable time doing the ovals (fig. 9.22).

There were also efforts to reduce the overall number of forms and patterns available. As noted earlier, by the turn of the century there were literally thousands of different hollow- and flatware patterns in production throughout the industry (fig. 9.23). The problem was especially chronic in the case of flatware. Always trying to outdo the competition, many firms added one or more new patterns annually. Between 1914 and 1924, for example, the nine companies that made up the Sterling Silversmiths Guild introduced 108 new designs in total, regardless of the fact that a single set of flatware dies for a given pattern was estimated to cost $30,000.[47] By 1926 this kind of investment had become such a burden on the industry that its representatives unanimously approved federal recommendations for the elimination of waste in sterling flatware production. Under the new guidelines a manufacturer could only introduce one new pattern every two years; produce no more than fifty-seven different types of utensils within each pattern; manufacture flatware in only two weights rather than three; and would refrain from supplying patterns after they had been discontinued for five years.[48] By agreeing to such voluntary rules, producers hoped to lessen competition and simplify the bewildering jungle of flatware patterns that had grown up since the 1870s.

Besides working with their competitors to reform the industry, producers also studied their own design process in search of ways to simplify it. In its 1923 report on Gorham, for example, Aldred & Co. noted that Gorham had invested in "hundreds of different shapes, sizes and patterns, many with only minute differences." It found fault with the design committee because it regularly approved the making of new designs in quantities as minute as six. Aldred pointed out that "it is quite impossible either to make or sell such items profitably." Instead, it recommended approving relatively few new designs and producing them in relatively large quantities so that some economy of scale could be achieved. Concerning the designers

ILL. 9.2. Page from Whiting Mfg. Co. day book, 1885. From left to right
the ledger notes design, date, order number, and title.

ILL. 9.3. Page from Whiting Mfg. Co. day book, 1916. From left to right
the ledger notes pattern and order number, title, date, and design.

FIG. 9.22. *Adam* pattern sauceboat and stand. Gorham Mfg. Co., maker, Providence, R.I.; Shreve, Crump & Low Co., retailer, Boston, Mass.; 1916. Sterling silver. Dallas Museum of Art.

themselves, the report recommended that Gorham reduce its staff of eighteen designers, "excluding those for special lines." According to Aldred, other firms by the early 1920s were functioning with as few as two or three designers. Furthermore, it was stated:

Under present practice, your designers go ahead, apparently untrammeled, conceiving and carrying through a great many designs. These are passed to the General Committee to consider which approves or rejects them. It is not unusual for the committee to consider 40 to 50 items in a single session. At least half are rejected. In the Providence plant alone, monthly expenses for designs, which are not carried to the point of a single sale average $3,500. With a consolidated, well-managed designing department, the designing would be directed either to things for which there is a known need, or, in the exceptional case, in a new creation. In either case, there would be intimate contact with the sales force so that no great amount of work would have to be discarded after being carried out at length. . . .

Sales should be the primary consideration, designing secondary to that. We think you had "the cart before the horse."[49]

The basic point that Gorham had too many designs in production and designers who did not know the needs of the market, was supported by data revealing that despite the numerous flatware patterns which the firm made, eleven of them accounted for fully 90 percent of flatware sales.

To rectify such problems, it was suggested that much of the variety in Gorham's lines be eliminated. For example, Gorham and its associated companies were to reduce the number of hollowware patterns to no more than forty tea sets, ten dinner sets, and twenty-five coffee sets. Furthermore, the greatest emphasis should be on "commercial" or inexpensive lines for which there was substantial demand from middle-class customers. And when more elaborate objects were produced, fewer preliminary drawings should be done and more of the overhead of the designing department should be added to the price of these wares.[50]

The ultimate development in this process of simplification and reorientation was the extensive test marketing of de-

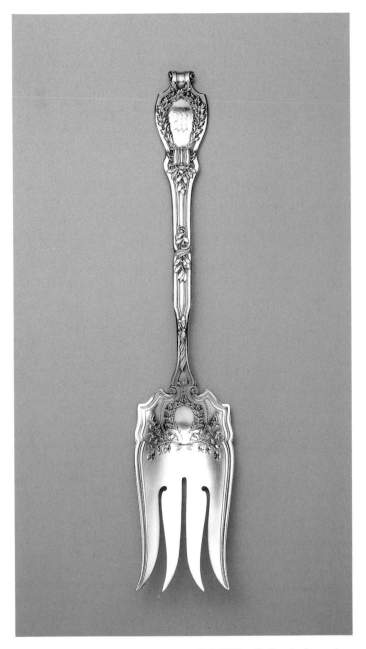

FIG. 9.23. *Madame DuBarry* pattern meat fork. William B. Durgin Co., maker, Concord, N.H.; Shreve, Crump & Low Co., retailer, Boston, Mass.; designed 1904. Sterling silver. Dallas Museum of Art.

signs. True, a crude form of market research had been practiced as early as the 1850s, when John Gorham made up a single object and sent photographs of it to retailers to see how many orders would come in. By the early twentieth century, however, sampling techniques had become much more sophisticated. A case in point was Oneida's flatware pattern *Bird of Paradise*. Originally, the handle motif of a griffin surrounded by scrollwork was lifted from the inlaid splat design on an early eighteenth-century English side chair. Following the creation of over 200 separate "spoon drawings," handmade samples were made. When the samples were test-marketed, however, it was found that "women did not like to mix animals with their eating," so a pair of love birds was substituted in place of the griffin. Once the test-marketing was successful, dies were cut and the new design put into production.[51]

As silverware firms increasingly tried to make their products more responsive to middle-class consumers' tastes and pocketbooks by simplifying designs and test-marketing, the role of the artist-designer was reduced in importance. Whereas before 1900 men like George Wilkinson, Edward C. Moore, William C. Codman, and Charles Osborne held exalted rank and power within their companys' hierarchies, their post–World War I counterparts held positions of lesser importance. Aldred & Co. reflected the shift from art to commerce when it told Gorham's management that it felt "designing should be directed by an executive, not an artist."[52]

The upsurge of interest in the arts and crafts movement in general, and the colonial revival in particular, during the precise period in which manufacturers were searching for ways to cut costs, was extremely fortuitous for producers. The circular and oval forms so common in reform aesthetics were ideal for spinning and die stamping, and close reliance on colonial prototypes meant that fewer forms and patterns had to be put into production, since early American silver did not have a wide variety of vessel forms or ornament. This was especially true when the selection was limited to original pieces made between 1730 and 1820, as was generally the case. Furthermore, a manufacturer could probably reduce the size of his design staff if he concentrated on colonial revival wares. Whereas the goal of design between 1875 and 1890 was innovation, the main thrust after 1890 was traditionalism. Consequently, designers had to "waste" less time on drawing and modeling original concepts, which might or might not prove useful to the company. Now a designer worked within the more efficient parameters of fewer forms and ornaments.

Having found a style that was not only popular with the public but instrumental in solving many of their production problems, manufacturers promoted the reformist taste, especially in its colonial revival form. In doing so, one of their major hurdles was reform ideology, which blamed the machine for the degradation of the worker and the destruction of good design. To combat this image of the evil machine, manufacturers took various stances. Some chose to downplay the machine's role by emphasizing the large amount of handwork still being done in silverware manufacturing. In 1917 Gorham gave potential customers a booklet patterned after a seventeenth-century treatise on silversmithing called *A Touchstone*. Using the same title, Gorham's book hypothesized what the English silversmith who authored the original in 1677 would say if he were to visit the firm's huge Elmwood plant in Providence. Following a tour, the specter was asked to comment on the differences between his seventeenth-century shop and Gorham's modern plant. He remarked that, except for the variation in scale, there was little difference between Gorham's plant and his old shop. As for the use of labor-saving machinery, he stated:

> Thus would we have done too in our time, had we but had men of mechanical skill and artifice sufficient to conceive and make such devices as I see here around me on every side. Yet is it apparent that these but aid in what we were wont to call the journeyman's portion of the work and that those experienced in the craft are still entrusted to fashion with their delicate tools all that goes to the final ornamenting of the silver-ware.[53]

A few years earlier, Towle had taken the opposite tack in an article entitled "The American Renaissance in Silversmithing: The Colonial Style," which appeared in 1912 in the *Fine Arts Journal*. Commenting on the central role of the machine in the silversmith's "ministrations to society," Towle's spokesman said, "It matters little how a piece is made if the spirit of true design is preserved in its fashioning. Mechanical means, which enable us to save both time and muscle, if they serve well and truly the intent of the master of design, are not only no hindrance to worthy production but a help to the wider cultivation of good taste, for through their economies even the humble home may possess real treasures. . . . machinery has become the handmaiden of his art."[54] The debate over hand versus machine production continued into the 1930s. During the trying economic times of the Great Depression, though, the balance tilted ever more toward mechanical processing.

The silverware industry also tried to market the colonial revival style as the epitome of good taste. In an editorial-style advertisement in the *Fine Arts Journal* of November 1913, a spokeswoman for the industry put forth this view when she said that "silverware today is far superior both in design and workmanship to that of a decade or more ago. . . . We may feel a just pride and a complete satisfaction in the fact that in all the length of this history nothing finer than our modern American silver or more eloquent of true and right principles has ever adorned the tables of kings."[55] Six years later, in 1919, another spokesperson for the silverware industry emphasized the correctness of contemporary designs by comparing them to those "of the depraved 'eighties.'" He said of the new age: "The era of ignorance and indifference was past—destined to take its place with the 'Dark Ages.' The meretricious and sham things of the 'eighties' no longer successfully masqueraded as 'artistic'. . . . A brief reminder of their nature is valuable as a contrast, to bring out the real significance of the present revival of good taste and esthetic sanity."[56] Perhaps the apex of this type of marketing was reached by the International Silver Co. in 1923. In a book that it distributed free of charge, International showed readers professionally decorated interiors studded with colonial revival silverware. Calling the objects "masterpieces of the classics," the firm claimed that "an ideal has been attained—the ideal of ultimate correctness in solid silver. These designs are no more for the passing day than the metal out of which they are wrought. Their beauty is ever reigning, transcending all whims of fashion. Their substance is ever-enduring, withstanding all hardships of use."[57]

To demonstrate graphically the "correctness" of their products, many manufacturers published evocative, multi-color advertisements that pictured romantic images of elite, eighteenth-century Americans. In 1919, for example, R. Wallace & Sons advertised two of its silverplated flatware patterns against a tranquil scene of elegantly clad and bewigged aristocrats strolling in a formal garden. The leading line of the copy read: "In this year of sensible Christmas giving, what could be more appropriate than beautiful, useful, enduring *Wallace Silver Plate!*" The same year, the American Silver Co. of Bristol, Connecticut, used an even more potent image to sell its *Somerset* pattern flatware (ill. 9.4). Positioned directly between a knife and fork in this advertisement is the image of a wealthy, White woman looking at a box of silver held by a Black boy. Two Black men hold her aloft in a sedan chair, while the White silversmith looks on.[58] For the many Americans who were becoming increasingly anxious about the swelling tide of immigrants from southern Europe and the thousands of African-Americans who were migrating north in search of work, such images must have been powerful indeed. Through them, manufacturers hoped that middle- and upper-class consumers, who were virtually all White, would purchase their colonial revival style wares as a means of transcending reality to find solace in America's mythic "Golden Age," where all was elegant and orderly, and where minorities knew their place and supported the dominant culture. Judging from the fact that the colonial revival taste remains to this day the most popular style for silverware, one must conclude that marketing it as the epitome of "good" taste and as a symbol of a purer, more "American" age still fulfills these desires while ameliorating the stresses of many who live in this country.

THE EXPERIMENT OF MODERNISM

Modernism in American silver design grew out of the reform movement that had given rise to the arts and crafts style. However, the core of the movement in the United States was British ideology, which was backward- rather than forward-looking in orientation. Nevertheless, some American silverware producers were influenced by more progressive ideas, which, while reformist in nature, were not as burdened by moralism. Influences from central European centers of contemporary design such as Berlin, Darmstadt, Munich, and Vienna, occasion-

ILL. 9.4. American Silver Co.'s *Somerset* pattern advertisement, 1919.

ally were felt in American products and advertising design. Most of the influences that relate closely to these sources were, not surprisingly, designed by central European immigrants, like Peter Müller-Munk (1904–1967). Coming to America in 1926, Müller-Munk designed a small number of handcrafted silver objects while working in New York City. Some examples, such as his tea set from around 1931 (fig. 9.24), are very Germanic in character, with a strong use of bold, geometric shapes and angular decoration.[59] Besides these immigrants, American manufacturers occasionally were influenced by central European design. Reed & Barton, for example, produced a few objects that were inspired by the work of Germans like Peter Behrens (1868–1940) and designers for the German Werkbund. Founded in 1907, the Werkbund was an association that encouraged leading manufacturers, designers, artists, and architects to work together. In 1912, the American Charles Dana organized an exhibition of Werkbund objects which toured the United States. It was through such exhibitions and contemporary periodicals, as well as through immigrant workers, that firms like Reed & Barton became familiar with this continental work.[60] The same is true of designs derived from Viennese prototypes. The products of the Wiener Werkstätte and its famous designers, such as Josef Hoffmann (1870–1956), were introduced to America through periodicals and the retail branch that the Werkstätte

maintained in New York City between 1922 and 1924.[61] Viennese influence, although not widespread, can be seen in some pieces of silver and graphic design. Occasionally, in the work of silversmith Marie Zimmermann (d. 1972), for example, an echo of Austrian influence is found. While not a copy of a central European prototype, her tureen-on-stand achieves the same balance between preciousness and boldness typically seen in Viennese metalwork (fig. 9.25). Here Zimmermann creates this contrast in part through the juxtaposition of a crystal finial and a wrought iron base. Zimmermann's composition is atypical, however. Overall, the impact of central European design on early twentieth-century American metalwork was not great. Denmark's influence was a different case.

On 19 May 1920, the front page of the *Jewelers' Weekly* proclaimed: "Like a breeze of fresh air there comes from far away Denmark some suggestions for silver design in their own and individual art in silverwork." According to the periodical, "There [had] been nothing particularly new in silverware for many years, so the Danish silver at least marks a change from that usually seen by Americans."[62] Given that the market was awash with colonial revival designs by 1920, many Americans must have found the "freshness" of Danish design appealing indeed. During the 1920s and 1930s, those consumers who wanted modernist silverware turned to Danish products in sizable numbers. By 1938, the United States was by far the largest consumer of Danish silverware, purchasing more than half that country's total production of sterling.[63] These Danish wares represented a full 60 percent of all dutiable (i.e., new) silver imported into the United States that year.[64]

The firm of Georg Jensen Sølvsmedie produced the vast majority of Danish silverware sold in America. Although Jensen (1866–1935) began work in 1904 in a small craft shop, his firm grew rapidly until it employed between 300 and 400 workmen in the mid 1930s. Furthermore, like many U.S. makers, it used labor-saving machines in forming objects and hand processes for decorating.[65] Nevertheless, Jensen was seen by many as the paragon of craftsmen. In 1924, *International Studio* quoted from Oscar Bensen's monograph on Jensen: "He has done infinitely more than any other individual artist to reestablish the happy conditions of craftsmanship in gold and silver that flourished individually before the blighting influence of the age of machinery."[66] Many American consumers liked Jensen's designs regardless of how they were actually produced. His products combined the clean lines and hammered surfaces of the arts and crafts movement with stylized floral motifs (fig. 9.26). Consequently, Georg Jensen has been able to maintain a showroom in New York City continuously since 1922, as well as a national distribution network, which has included, since the 1930s, numerous upscale department stores.

Besides being shown in retail outlets and exhibitions like *Swedish Contemporary Decorative Arts*, which was held at the Metropolitan Museum of Art in 1927, Scandinavian design was brought to American metalwork by numerous immigrants. In New York silversmiths like Peer Smed (1878–1943) who had

FIG. 9.24. Tea and coffee set. Peter Müller-Munk, New York, N.Y., ca. 1931.
Sterling silver and ivory. ©1994 The Metropolitan Museum of Art.

been trained in Denmark, produced exceptional objects in the "Jensen" taste (fig. 9.27). And in Chicago there were numerous Scandinavians at work. The Kalo Shop, for example, employed many of them in the production of its wares. Yet, at the Kalo Shop these foreigners were not allowed to influence design significantly. Rather, as a manager recalled, "[They'd] have to make it *our* way."[67] The process did not change until after 1940, when men like Danish-born Yngve Olsson and the Norwegian Daniel Pedersen took over ownership of the Kalo Shop. In other Chicago establishments the Scandinavian influence was felt earlier. Trained in Sweden, Julius Randahl, for example, produced numerous Jensenesque designs during the 1930s.[68] Another Swede, Knut Gustafson, also created silverware in the Scandinavian taste for his Chicago Silver Company, as did Norwegian-trained John Petterson, who had worked for Tiffany & Co. before starting the Petterson Studios in 1914.[69]

Of large-scale manufacturers, the most significant work in the Scandinavian taste was done by Gorham. As part of its 1920s reorganization, Gorham management decided to introduce a new modernist line. To design these wares, Gorham enticed the well-known Danish designer-silversmith Erik Magnussen (1884–1961) to come to Providence in 1925 (ill. 9.5).[70] Having studied art and chasing in Copenhagen and Berlin and having had exhibitions in Copenhagen, Berlin, Paris, and Rio de Janeiro, Magnussen was well known when he came to Amer-

ica. Consequently, at Gorham he was treated as an important personality, and given his own atelier away from the rest of the designers.

The earliest objects that Magnussen designed for Gorham were completely within the Danish idiom. In 1926 he designed a silver and ivory candy jar whose hand-hammered finish, double foot rim, and stylized plant motifs were closely related to the work of Georg Jensen (fig. 9.28). Within a year, however, he was designing much more radical pieces based on the "skyscraper" style popular in New York among a small, elite group of designers and wealthy consumers.[71] The quintessential example of these wares is his *Cubic* coffee set of 1927 (fig. 9.29). Based on cubist fine art developed by avant-garde painters like Pablo Picasso and Georges Braque earlier in the century, Magnussen's set is composed of colored, triangular facets. Evidently Gorham's management was impressed by the set, which Magnussen personally fabricated by hand, and decided to test it in New York to see what kind of market there might be for such artistic silverware (ill. 8.9). Although it received favorable reviews from the press—*The New York Times* even naming it *The Lights and Shadows of Manhattan* as if it were fine art—the general public found the set too bizarre. Gorham's advertising department quickly countered with trade literature saying that the set was never intended for public consumption. A 1928 pamphlet said:

FIG. 9.25. Tureen-on-stand. Marie Zimmermann, New York, N.Y., 1915.
Sterling silver, iron, and crystal. Private Collection.

FIG. 9.26. Compote. Johan Rohde, designer; Georg Jensen Sølvsmedie, maker, Copenhagen, Denmark; Neiman-Marcus, retailer, Dallas, Tex.; designed 1916, made ca. 1936. Sterling silver. Dallas Museum of Art.

Everyone quickly sensed the fact that the set was a significant contribution to modern art . . . but as for the fact that it was intended for exhibition not for daily use . . . that was harder to grasp . . . and soon the market saw a dozen undigested modifications of the set . . . offered as the last word in true American Applied Art. Erik Magnussen smiled to himself . . . he had long been busy on something more vital.[72]

What Magnussen had "been busy on" was a more conservative, cheaper-to-produce line of spun and stamped wares which Gorham named *The Modern American*. The firm told the public that "True art in silverware . . . true applied art in any medium . . . it must be good to look at . . . good to live with . . . it must not make us wince . . . it must soothe us and rest us and lift us up."[73] As before, however, the public did not respond to these modernist wares, even though they were widely promoted. Evidently the section of the market that wanted Scandinavian- or modernist-style objects found the cachet of buying imported Danish silverware by firms such as Jensen far more appealing, and avoided American products. As sales of his wares were poor, Magnussen left the firm in October 1929. Perhaps jealous of the special treatment Magnussen had been given, in 1930 Gorham's chief designer, William C. Codman

(son of William Christmas Codman), summed up Gorham's experiment in *An Illustrated History of Silverware Design*: "Recently a style so called 'Modern' has been introduced to the public, but it does not appear to have made much headway; and it only remains to be said that the fashion worthy of a place in succession to the best of the Georgian and Colonial periods has yet to be devised."[74]

The progress made by modernist silver design in America before World War II descended on the industry was sporadic at best. In many cases the finest objects produced in the taste were, as before, expensive luxury items made as single pieces or in minute quantities. For example, a splendid cigar humidor from 1925 with friezes depicting laborers, decorated in a style influenced by contemporary modernist painting and sculpture, appears to be unique, with few if any related pieces ever having been made (fig. 9.30). Limited production was especially true of most silver produced in this country in the French art deco style. Presented to U.S. designers and aesthetes at the 1925 exposition of applied arts in Paris, and in this country at exhibitions like the one held at the Metropolitan in New York during the late 1920s,[75] the art deco style influenced American silverware very little outside of the highest level (fig. 9.31). Nevertheless, a few exceptional objects were made in the taste during the late 1920s and 1930s. For its display at the 1939

FIG. 9.27. Pair of candlesticks. Peer Smed, New York, N.Y., 1934. Sterling silver.
William Hill Land & Cattle Co. Collection.

Chapter 9

world's fair in New York, for example, Tiffany & Co. created a small group of silverware, all in the art deco style. Included was a tea set (fig. 9.32). The set was costly and time-consuming to make and was apparently the only one ever produced. In fact, some of the pieces for the fair took so long to complete that they were not put on display there until 1940.[76] Except for a few objects such as these, the art deco taste had little influence on American silverware production in general.

Beyond the creation of small quantities of modernist handmade silver objects during the 1920s and 1930s, some designers and producers promoted the use of the machine and "machine" aesthetics as a means to bring modern design to the masses. In October 1929, for example, Peter Müller-Munk published "Machine—Hand" in *Creative Art*. He called for the development of silverware designs suited to the abilities of the machine, as opposed to ones that appeared handmade even though they were largely machine processed. He asked:

Why . . . do not our manufacturers try to improve upon their merchandise by adapting it to their machines, instead of doing the contrary?

We have heard and seen enough of the beauty of power houses, steel structures and all the implements of motors and furnaces to know that the machine is able to turn out a piece of beauty, but it is a fallacy to believe that it can replace or copy the work of the craftsman. The clearness of shape and the neatness of surface of a spun bowl is equal in aesthetic value to any hand-made piece and superior to its hand-wrought copy. If we could have designers who knew the machines which were to turn out their designs, and if these men would give the machine what it most longs for, we would really have achieved a new art resulting from the harmony of technique and object. The sharpness and chastity of the forms most easily spun or stamped in a die would take on a new impressive character, and we would discover that the frank admission of the machine's power surpasses by far the faked and childish semblance of the would-be hand-made product.[77]

The very next year, Gorham's chief designer, William C. Codman, stated a similar position from the point of view of the large-scale producer in an essay entitled "Art and Utility": "Hand-made work will always remain a privilege to be possessed by people with long purses . . . but there is no reason why good machine-made articles, in all their various grades, should not be marked by at least the same keen sense of fitness."[78] Following this advice, various manufacturers introduced lines of silverware in a machine aesthetic. To achieve the efficiency in production that they desired, producers designed objects which reflected the machine's ability to flatten, stamp, and spin metal extremely well.

ILL. 9.5. Erik Magnussen at Gorham Mfg. Co., ca. 1926.

While other firms like Bernard Rice's Sons (fig. 9.33) made some modernist wares, International Silver Co. and its subsidiaries worked most extensively in this mode. The Wilcox Silver Plate Co., for example, introduced an entire series of innovative tea sets in the late 1920s whose design was based on square and round shapes that could be produced mechanically for the most part (fig. 9.34). However, just because a design lends itself well to machine processing does not mean that it will be popular with the public. Although most of the items made by International Silver Co. and its subsidiaries were done in silverplate, thus putting them in reach of many consumers, they appear to have been made in relatively small quantities and are rarely seen on the market today. A coffee urn and tray designed by Eliel Saarinen and manufactured by the Wilcox Silver Plate Co. in 1934, for example, appears to be one of only a few made, though its constituent parts were suited to machine production, and it was part of the firm's regular line (fig. 9.35). Even Saarinen's sterling flatware pattern *Contempora* was not commercially successful, despite elaborate marketing efforts, including display in the exhibition *The Architect and the Industrial Arts: An Exhibition of Contemporary American Design* held in 1929 at the Metropolitan Museum of Art (fig. 9.36). In the end, silverware manufacturers discovered that while many Americans appreciated the slick surfaces and geometric shapes

FIG. 9.28. Candy jar. Erik Magnussen, designer; Gorham Mfg. Co., maker, Providence, R.I.; Spaulding & Co., retailer, Chicago, Ill.; 1926. Sterling silver and ivory. Dallas Museum of Art.

FIG. 9.29. *Cubic* pattern coffee set. Erik Magnussen, designer; Gorham Mfg. Co., maker, Providence, R.I.; 1927. Sterling silver and silvergilt. Museum of Art, Rhode Island School of Design.

FIG. 9.30. Cigar humidor. Tiffany & Co., New York, N.Y., 1925.
Sterling silver. Museum of Fine Arts, Houston.

of the machine taste in their cars and appliances, most preferred traditional styles in silverware.

In an attempt to maximize their products' success in the marketplace, many manufacturers tried to create designs and marketing campaigns that would appeal simultaneously to conservative and progressive customers. In 1929, the International Silver Co. advertised colonial revival– and modernist-style tea sets together, announcing "New Sophistication in keeping with fine old traditions of Silversmithing" (ill. 9.6). Besides being smaller in scale and thus suited to contemporary apartment dwelling, the wares were said to be "at once classic and modern." Although they were in fact radically new in form, the "New designs of International Silverplate [were] in no sense 'experimental.'"[79] Other producers attempted to achieve the same balance between the traditional and progressive. Oneida, for example, introduced a whole series of silverplated flatware patterns during the mid 1930s, which, while modernist in styling, were marketed as traditional in many ways. The *Berkeley Square* pattern, which was streamlined with a discreet border and a small, Jensenesque leaf motif on the handle, was not only given a traditional name but was compared in advertising material to the work of Paul Revere.[80] On 30 November 1936, Tiffany & Co. verbalized this dual strategy to its sales force in the following notice:

Tiffany & Co. are putting in stock today a new flatware pattern, which is in the modern trend of design but avoids the extreme squareness and angularity of many modernistic articles. Its classic simplicity will allow it to be used in harmony with period silver of the plainer styles as well as with silver of modern design. . . . The name Century has been chosen as the name that will always suggest the spirit of today, and also because in 1937 Tiffany & Co. will have their 100th anniversary.[81]

By designing objects that could be marketed as both traditional and progressive, and by advertising modernist pieces as traditional, and vice versa, manufacturers hoped to appeal to more than the relatively small group of Americans who genuinely appreciated modern design.

Beyond object design and advertising copy, this dual strategy was carried out in window and showroom displays. For example, in the late 1920s, when Gorham was promoting the modernist designs of Erik Magnussen, the firm demonstrated to its dealers how the new line could be mixed with colonial revival objects. In one demonstration, it even included hand tools and a series of partially raised silver pieces next to objects that were totally within the machine aesthetic (ill. 9.7). Over a decade later, around 1940, Tiffany & Co. achieved the same effect when it installed four dining room displays in its Fifth Avenue store (ill. 9.8) Two contained reproductions of eighteenth-century furniture and silverware. The others were very modern and contained the art deco–style silver that the firm had exhibited in the 1939 world's fair.[82] Even the Baltimore firm of Samuel Kirk & Son, which made highly traditional objects, used modernist graphic design to give its trade catalogues a contemporary look during the 1930s.[83]

Given the mixed nature of the messages sent out to customers by efforts such as these, it is hard to evaluate their success. Furthermore, the onset of the Great Depression caused

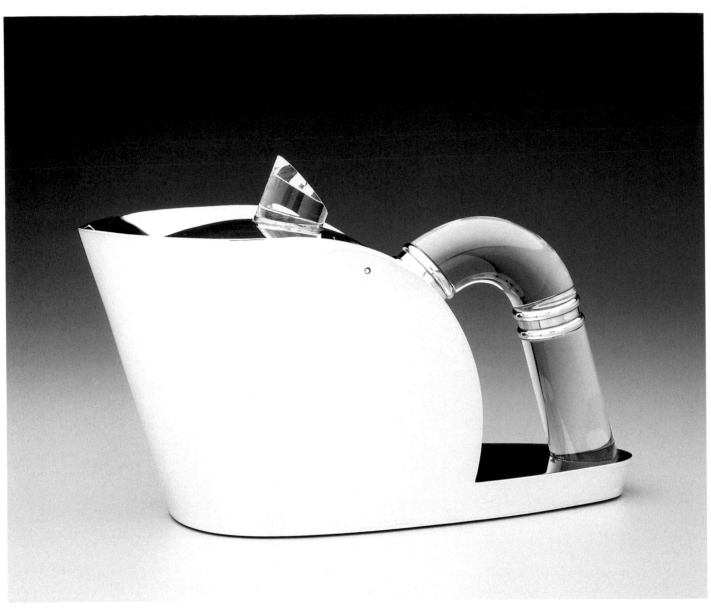

FIG. 9.31. Teapot. Jean Puiforcat, Paris, France, ca. 1935. Silver, silvergilt, and plastic.
Dallas Museum of Art.

FIG. 9.32. Tea set. Albert Barney, designer; Tiffany & Co., New York, N.Y.; 1939. Sterling silver, jade, and fibre. Denis Gallion and Daniel Morris / Historical Design Collection.

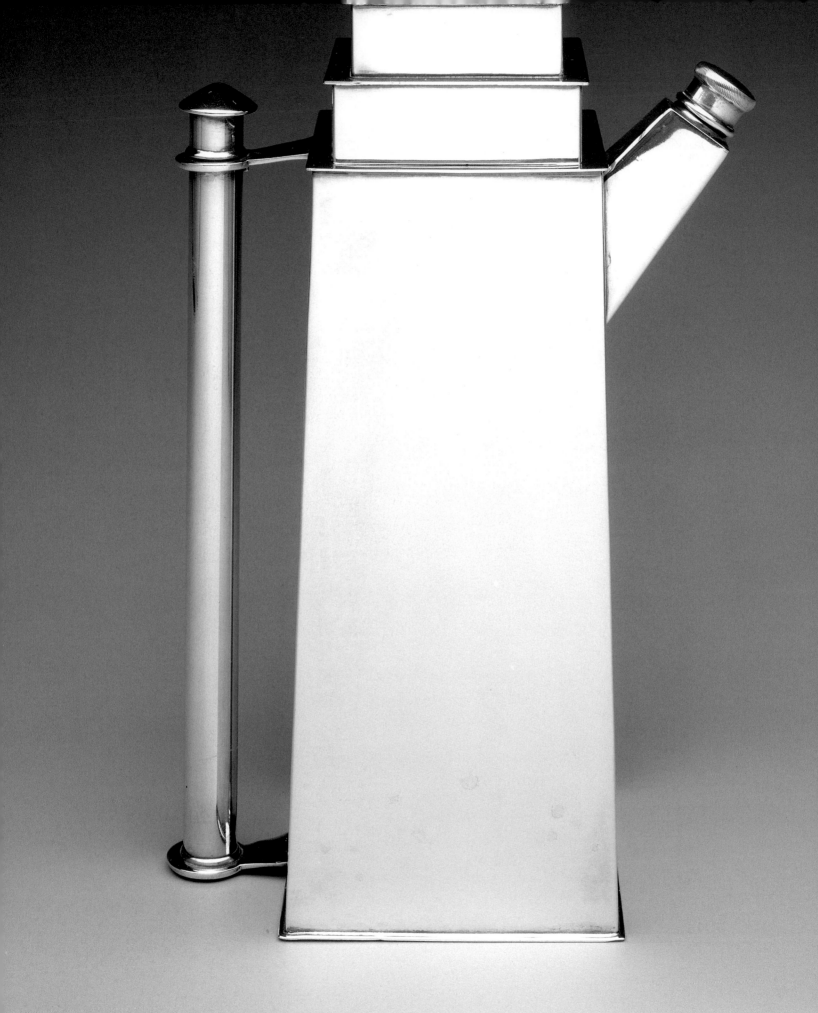

FACING PAGE: FIG. 9.33. *Skyscraper* pattern cocktail shaker. Louis W. Rice, designer; Bernard Rice's Sons, Inc., maker, New York, N.Y.; ca. 1930. Silverplate. William Hill Land & Cattle Co. Collection.

FIG. 9.34. Tea set. Jean G. Theobald, designer; Wilcox Silver Plate Co., maker, Meriden, Conn.; designed 1928. Silverplated pewter and wood. The Mitchell Wolfson, Jr., Collection.

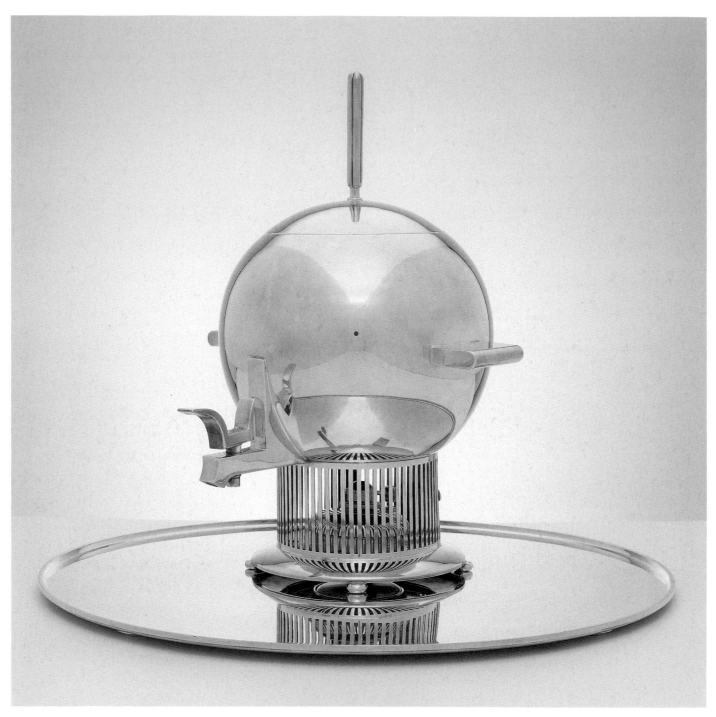

FIG. 9.35. Coffee urn and tray. Eliel Saarinen, designer; Wilcox Silver Plate Co., maker, Meriden, Conn.; designed 1934. Silverplate. Cranbrook Academy of Art Museum.

FIG. 9.36. *Contempora* pattern knife, spoon, and fork. Eliel Saarinen, designer; Reed & Barton, maker, Taunton, Mass.; designed ca. 1927–1928, made 1935. Sterling silver. Cranbrook Academy of Art Museum.

silver consumption to drop precipitously just as most modernist lines were introduced in the late 1920s and early 1930s. Yet, judging from the silverware that survives, it is clear that those who bought silver during this period preferred more traditional objects (fig. 9.37). Further weakening the modernist impulse in silver design was the widespread introduction of several important new materials that diverted attention from silver. Spun, stamped, cast, and extruded aluminum and chromed steel, for example, became increasingly popular during the 1930s with that segment of the market that appreciated modern design (figs. 9.38–39). Also, new plastic products that could be molded into virtually any shape and tinted in a wide range of colors attracted buyers (fig. 8.3). As consumers found that they could satisfy their urge for modernity through products in new and exciting, yet cheaper, materials, there was less need to do so through silver, which was not only expensive but perceived as more permanent. When one purchases silverware, especially sterling, it is usually with the intent of keeping it a lifetime and then passing it on to the next generation. Consequently, most consumers are reluctant to invest substantial amounts of income in silver made in an avant-garde style. By choosing something traditional, like the colonial revival style, one does not run the risk of being embarrassed while using the object during one's own lifetime, or of passing on to the children something that is completely out of fashion. Only silverplated flatware, with its relatively low cost and built-in obsolescence, seems to have mediated these concerns, because a sizable number of relatively modernist designs were produced during the 1930s and 1940s. But for most Americans, modernism was simply too risky to try during a stressful economic period, especially where something so symbolic and lasting as silver was concerned.

ILL. 9.6. International Silver Co.'s "New Sophistication" advertisement, 1929.

ILL. 9.7. Gorham Co. demonstration window display, ca. 1928.

Chapter 9

ILL. 9.8. Designs for table displays in Tiffany & Co.'s retail store in New York, ca. 1940.

FIG. 9.37. Pitcher. Gorham Mfg. Co., Providence, R.I., 1928. Sterling silver.
Museum of Art, Rhode Island School of Design.

FIG. 9.38. *Coronet* pattern coffee urn. Chase Brass & Copper Co., Waterbury, Conn., designed ca. 1930.
Chromeplate, plastic, and glass. Dallas Museum of Art.

FIG. 9.39. Thermos. Henry Dreyfuss, designer; American Thermos Bottle Co., maker, Norwich, Conn.; designed 1936. Aluminum, glass, enamel, rubber, and steel. Dallas Museum of Art.

1. Stuart 1912.

2. For an overview of art nouveau–style American objects, see Johnson 1979.

3. Rainwater 1975, 175–76, notes Dickinson as designer.

4. Hough 1990.

5. Bénédite 1900, 486.

6. Katzman 1978, 46, notes that the number of servants dropped from 1,830,000 in 1910 to 1,400,000 in 1920. Page 2288 notes that in 1870 there were 127 servants per 1,000 families as opposed to 67 per 1,000 in 1930.

7. This point is noted in Carpenter 1982, 221–27.

8. For two instances where it is associated with the art nouveau movement, see *Craftsman* 1905, 459, and Holbrook 1912, 113.

9. Tilden 1906, 243. Another writer who speaks proudly of *Martelé* is Moffitt 1899.

10. Stuart 1912, 581 and 583.

11. For studies of this movement as it pertains to America, see Kaplan 1987 and Bowman 1990.

12. Ruskin 1851, v. 2, p. 170. For an overview of the origins of the movement, see Bowman 1990, 17–30, and Kaplan 1987, 52–60.

13. For information on his visit to Chicago in 1900, see Darling 1977, 34.

14. For insight into how such relationships worked, see Brandt 1985.

15. For information on Friedell, see Morse 1986, 41–55, and Bowman 1990, 103. For information on Gebelein, see Leighton 1976. For information on Knight, Gyllenberg, and Leinonen, see Kaplan 1987, 272–75. For information on Stone, see Chickering 1981, 1986a, and 1986b.

16. Quoted in Chickering 1986a, 275.

17. Sam Hough provided information on the labor and cost involved in these objects; letter, Hough to Venable, 19 June 1991.

18. All information on Friedell taken from Morse 1986, 41–55. Quote taken from p. 46.

19. All information taken from Leighton 1976.

20. Bowman 1990, 33–42.

21. For information on this Tiffany & Co. line, see Kaplan 1987, 284–85.

22. Stieff 1928, 3.

23. For information on these shops, see Darling 1977, 45–61.

24. Leighton 1976, 75. For information on Marshall Field & Co., see Darling 1977, 74–75. The photo of the shop pictured in this source depicts spun "shells" on the workbenches.

25. For British-inspired examples, see Emery 1904.

26. Letter, Chickering to Venable, 11 Jan. 1993. Since there is only a partial listing of objects produced in the Stone shop, the 200 and 5,000 figures are an extrapolation from the partial card files kept by Mrs. Stone.

27. Gebelein 1911. During this period 441 orders were taken, but five were canceled.

28. Letter, National Society of Craftsmen to Gebelein, 17 May 1910, "N" letters; Letter, Gustav Stickley: The Craftsman to Gebelein, 11 Oct. 1914, "S" letters; and Letter, Schervee to Gebelein, 4 Dec. 1915, "S" letters, GCGA.

29. "Statement Showing the Profit and Loss. . . . ," 31 Dec. 1917, box 16, GCGA.

30. Gebelein appears to have purchased a lathe between 1916–18. Before that time one R. Dimes of Boston did much of his spinning. One Charles G. Ostrom of Boston supplied ivory and wooden parts ca. 1912–18. George E. Germer of Boston supplied designs for silverware and jewelry, as well as modeling and chasing, between 1912–22. Henry W. Langhan did engraving for Gebelein around 1911, while James Wilmot of Concord, N.H., was doing chasing. This information is all gathered from the Gebelein letter files at the GCGA.

31. "New England Handicraft Workers in Silver," *JCK* 46:25 (22 July 1903):73. I am indebted to Don Soeffing for bringing this source to my attention.

32. Tachau 1922, 413.

33. Bailey 1897, 4.

34. *HW* 20:1012 (20 May 1876):416.

35. "The Plate and Jewels of the Washingtons," *JW* 7:26 (25 Apr. 1888):61–66 and "Silverware in the Centennial Loan Exhibit," *JW* 8:2 (9 May 1889):49–52.

36. *JCK* 16:12 (Jan. 1886):xvi.

37. *HNMM* 93:556 (Sept. 1896):577–86. The 1893 exhibit is noted in Currier 1927, [1].

38. For information on the development of silver studies, see Ames 1989, 139–44.

39. Brown 1906, 709 and 715.

40. Stuart 1913, 693.

41. For representations of colonial interiors, see *HB* 17:2 (Jan. 1905):26–27; 18:5 (Oct. 1905):20–21; 23:2 (Jan. 1908):26–27; 13:5 (May 1908):168–72; and 26:5 (Oct. 1909):108–9.

42. *HB* 17:4 (Mar. 1905):26–27.

43. *HB* 15:5 (Apr. 1904):318–20; similar articles are "Coffee-Services," 23:4 (Mar. 1908):22–23; and "Table Decorations," 27:1 (Dec. 1909):6–8.

44. "Tea-Services," *HB* 23:2 (Jan. 1908):13.

45. Whiting 1884.

46. The Gorham etching patterns are in GA, Photographs, 2., III., b. Photo catalogue, 1926–27, p. L-2. The date of the page is 1 Aug. 1910. Estimates for the etchings range from $9 to $22.50. For the Wallace example, see Wallace 1921, 23.

47. *Elimination* 1926, 3.

48. *Ibid.,* 1–4.

49. Aldred 1923, 28.

50. *Ibid.*

51. Harold Franklin, "Portrait of a Pattern," *CJ* 2 (Mar. 1935):4–7.

52. *Ibid.,* 27.

53. Townsend 1917, 39–40.

54. Osgood 1912, 781–82.

55. Stuart 1913, 689 and 702.

56. Price 1919, IX and IV.

57. International 1923, 9–10.

58. *JCK* 78:1 (5 Feb. 1919):inside back cover and 133.

59. For information on Müller-Munk, see Davies 1983, 28.

60. For another example based on German ideas and for information on the influence of the Werkbund on American metalwork, see Kaplan 1987, 163.

61. There were a few exhibitions that included Viennese-inspired objects and interiors such as one designed by the Finnish-born architect Eliel Saarinen for a 1929 exhibition at the Metropolitan Museum of Art. For a picture of it, see Miller 1990, 25. For information of contemporary retail sources for Germanic objects, see Davies 1983, 84.

62. "A Word about Danish Silver," *JCK* 80:16 (19 May 1920):1.

63. Sixty-one percent by value and 56 percent by quantity.

64. *Silverware* 1940, 108 and 100.

65. *Ibid.,* 101.

66. Teevan 1924, 161.

67. Darling 1977, 53.

68. For examples, see *ibid.*, 87

69. *Ibid.*, 88–94.

70. All general information about Magnussen and his work at Gorham taken from Carpenter 1982, 256–64.

71. For an overview of the "Skyscraper" style, see Duncan 1986, 34–38.

72. Gorham 1928, n.p. The ellipses are in the original text.

73. *Ibid.*

74. Codman 1930, 72.

75. For information on the Metropolitan Museum of Art's exhibitions of art deco objects, see Miller 1990, 14–17.

76. TA, 1939 world's fair, letter to Craig Miller, 1 May 1981.

77. Müller-Munk 1929, 710–11.

78. Codman 1930, 5. For similar comments, see Price 1919, 10–11.

79. *JCK* 99:6 (5 Sept. 1929):72.

80. *CJ* 2 (Mar. 1935):5–7.

81. Notices 1932, 1 (30 Nov. 1936):71.

82. Drawing in TA, shelf 24/7, box A.

83. For an example, see Kirk 1931. The cover shows a colonial revival pitcher and goblet in a modernist layout.

CONCLUSION

Of the increasingly distant and foreign world of nineteenth- and early-twentieth-century America, only artifacts remain to illuminate its impotent, if not extinct, traditions. This past survives only in physical and intellectual creations. As for that world's silverware, it could be breathtakingly beautiful at its finest. Even without the reconstruction of a socioeconomic context, one can appreciate the silver's design and marvel at its technical virtuosity. Based solely on the quality and quantity of the objects the United States was producing by 1880, it can be argued that this country was the foremost contemporary creator of silverware in the world. But examined within the context of written and visual records left by both producers and consumers, American silverware made between 1840 and 1940 becomes more intelligible. One's appreciation relies less on the sheer beauty of its surface and more on the power of its history.

The development of a major silverware industry in the United States in the century following 1840 is indeed a story worth telling. At the onset, production was encouraged by the Tariff of 1842, which effectively drove foreign silverware from the American marketplace. With a secure market for their products, entrepreneurs took advantage of the situation by applying machine technology and the division of labor to the production of silverware. Master craftsmen were brought from Europe to train native apprentices, who in turn dominated the industry, with amazing results. By the 1870s the industry was led by firms in southern New England (including Gorham, Meriden Britannia, and Reed & Barton) and in New York City (including Tiffany's, Wendt, Whiting, and Wood & Hughes). The largest of these concerns employed hundreds of highly skilled individuals who performed much hand labor. Machinery executed only the most basic operations.

Between 1840 and 1875, professional designers entered the industry. Men such as George Wilkinson revolutionized American design in the 1860s, moving it away from the European-centered Gothic and rococo revivals to more original concepts based on classical motifs. Buoyed by the vibrant economy stimulated by the Civil War, American consumers not only accepted these new designs but came to view silver as a necessity in their dining and family rituals. As the market grew, producers expanded their distribution network and experimented with advertising.

The years between 1875 and World War I saw the U.S. silverware industry and market mature. Production was expanded by hiring additional workers and by constructing extensive and better organized manufactories, such as Gorham's Elmwood plant (1890) and Tiffany & Co.'s Forest Hill works (1894). To run these facilities, an entire level of professional managers emerged. During the recessions of the 1880s and 1890s, these managers sought ways to increase efficiency and cut costs. They instituted formal work rules, asked foremen to "drive" their workers harder, and experimented with the piecework system. Although these efforts were marred by occasional labor unrest, including the strikes of 1887 and 1902, production generally rose throughout the period. Nevertheless, factors such as price wars, inflation, and periodic recessions made the 1890s and early twentieth century a difficult era for silverware makers.

To sell their wares, producers intensified advertising efforts. Through trade catalogues and journals, world's fairs, elaborate showrooms, and the popular press, Americans were enticed to purchase silver in huge quantities. By the late nineteenth century, the United States led the world in the production and consumption of silverware. Silver was made in almost every form imaginable, from macaroni servers to sterling dressing tables. Because of the constant decline in the price of silver bullion between 1870 and 1915 and fierce competition, even lower middle-class households could afford some silverware by the 1890s.

In addition to leading in production and consumption of silverware, U.S. firms were arguably the most innovative in terms of design. Tiffany & Co.'s triumph with Japanese-inspired objects at the 1878 Paris world's fair first brought international acclaim to American work. Producing extraordinary wares in the moresque, Russian, beaux-arts, "American," and art nouveau styles, U.S. makers remained in the forefront into the early twentieth century. In fact, the quality of their best work was so high that it came to be seen as "fine" art by consumers. However, the reformist movements that gained momentum after 1895 brought an appreciation for simplified designs and emphasis on handwork. Although some examples in the arts and crafts, colonial revival, and modernist tastes that dominated between 1900 and 1940 were handmade—as the finest silverware had always been—most were not. The simple, unornamented shapes that characterize these styles were ideal for mechanical production. Nevertheless, manufacturers found it difficult to make a profit (except in the late 1920s) no matter how much they advertised. Although silverware sales recovered somewhat by the very late 1930s, World War II first brought rationing and then halted silver manufacture almost totally by 1944.

In many ways World War II was a watershed event for this country. For the silverware industry, the war marked the end of a decade of decline and the dawn of a new age in which silver objects were to play a much smaller part in American life. This change in attitude towards silver had begun with the popularization of reformist ideology that called for not only the simplification of aesthetics, but a simplification of one's life. Around the turn of the century a growing interest in "hygienic" environments that were easy to clean reinforced this shift. When the lush, dark interiors of the 1880s were replaced with sparer, lighter ones, the lifestyles and rituals that had created those earlier environments and made them meaningful were also transformed. In the case of silver, an increasing number of Americans did not just want simple objects that were easy to clean, but did not desire silver at all.

Even if one still wished to continue using silverware as before, "the servant problem" made that difficult. In 1924 the *International Studio* reported: "We have it, on the authority of an informed and admirable housewife, that an added reason for the decline in the use of silver in the home is the sheer inability to obtain servants capable of taking the proper care of household silver."[1] Servants were seen less and less in middle-class homes as U.S. immigration laws tightened and wages increased in the wake of World War I. Without the labor and skill of these countless individuals, most families could not maintain the households of the nineteenth century, which simply required too much manual labor to be run efficiently. Extremely long and elaborate dinners, popular between the Civil War and the First World War, consumed huge amounts of silverware, but without the requisite number of servants in the dining room and kitchen, they were no longer possible. True, as the nature of entertaining changed, activities like the cocktail party emerged and required new types of equipage that could be made of silver. Yet, rather than purchase silver cocktail shakers, hors d'oeuvres trays, candy dishes, cigarette boxes, and ashtrays, consumers often bought examples made of new materials like aluminum, chrome, or plastic. Simultaneously, collecting antique silver became increasingly popular among America's upper class, one of the industry's most important markets. After 1930, in fact, there was no duty on imported silverware made before 1830. Consequently, old silver pieces might actually have been less expensive than comparable modern ones.[2]

The advent and proliferation of bicycles, automobiles, telephones, and motion pictures pulled Americans away from the home. While home life was still important, it lost much of its significance. Consequently, the objects associated with the home declined in symbolic power. Silverware, for example, remained a fine wedding or Christmas gift; however, a young bride did not care so much about having flatware to properly serve everything from sardines to ice cream. By the late 1930s, the standard five-piece place setting and simplified serving sets had emerged, supplanting the large and complicated services of the late nineteenth century.

In the waning years of the twentieth century, silverware is even less of a necessity in our lives. Most Americans no longer have the attention span to appreciate extraordinary silver objects in daily life. In contrast to our nineteenth-century ancestors, we rush through our meals and cannot linger to enjoy chased salad servers or notice the "worm holes" cut into the silver leaves decorating a fruit plate. Similarly, exotic foods from every corner of the globe are available at almost any local grocery store. Because it has become commonplace in our society, we feel no need to celebrate food with silverware. And finally, many alternative materials, from stamped stainless steel to injection-molded plastic, have displaced silver because they are cheaper and nearly maintenance-free. The world that once created and understood such extraordinary objects has indeed vanished forever. Only the artifacts remain as records of that era's achievements and failures, the bearers of its messages and dreams to the future.

NOTES

1. Teevan 1924, 160.
2. *Silverware* 1940, 2.

REFERENCES

ABM 1906
"Commercial Palaces." *Architects' and Builders' Magazine* 7:5 n.s. (Feb. 1906):177–92.

AJ 1875a
"The Bryant Testimonial Vase." *Art Journal* 1 (May 1875, New York edition):145–49.

AJ 1875b
"American Art-work in Silver." *Art Journal* 1 (Dec. 1875, New York edition):371–74.

AJ 1876
"Contributions to the International Exhibition, Philadelphia." *Art Journal* 15 n.s. (1876, London edition):341–44.

Alden *vs.* Gorham 1867
"Augustus E. Alden *vs.* Gorham Mfg. Co." Circuit Court of the United States, District of Rhode Island, 16 Apr. 1867. A printed transcript of proceedings is in Rider Collection, Box 220, no. 12, John Hay Library, Brown University, Providence, R.I.

Aldred 1923
Aldred & Co. "The Silversmiths Company of New York, Gorham Manufacturing Company, and Affiliated Companies." New York: Aldred & Co., 1923. A typescript copy of this report is in GA, II. Corporate, 3. Financial, f. Appraisals and Inventories. A typescript called "Comments on Report of Aldred & Co." accompanies the report. References to this are cited as being in "Comments."

AM
Atlantic Monthly (Boston, 1875).

AM 1867
"Among the Workers in Silver." *Atlantic Monthly* 20:122 (Dec. 1867): 729–39.

Ames 1989
Kenneth L. Ames and Gerald W. R. Ward, eds. *Decorative Arts and Household Furnishings in America, 1650–1920: An Annotated Bibliography.* Winterthur, Del.: Winterthur Museum, 1989.

Articles 1865
Gorham Mfg. Co. "Articles of Agreement." 4 vols. Vol. 1 covers years 1865–71 and is for master workmen. Vol. 2 covers 1871–86. Vol. 3 covers 1876–77. Vol. 4 covers 1864–72. Vols. 2–4 are for apprentices. Located in GA, III. Personnel, 1. Articles of Agreement.

Audsley 1875
George A. Audsley and James L. Bowes. *Keramic Art of Japan.* London, 1875.

Bailey 1897
Bailey, Banks, & Biddle Co. Catalogue. Philadelphia, 1897. *TCAW* no. 1630.

Bailey 1908
Bailey, Banks, & Biddle Co. *Trophies.* Philadelphia, ca. 1908. *TCAW* no. 1631.

Ball, Black & Co. 1863
Ball, Black & Co. "Payroll Ledger, 1863–1902." 2 vols. GA, III. Personnel, 9. Acquired Companies, Black, Starr-Gorham.

Barta 1925
The Barta Press. *The Cataloging of Silverware: Suggestions for Exhibiting Silverware to the Best Advantage.* Boston, 1925. *TCAW* no. 3042.

Beckman 1975
Elizabeth D. Beckman. *Cincinnati Silversmiths, Jewelers, Watchmakers, and Clockmakers.* Cincinnati: B. B. & Co., 1975.

Bénédite 1900
L. Bénédite et al. *Exposition universelle de 1900: Les beaux-arts et les arts décoratifs.* Paris, 1900.

Bergengren 1915
Ralph Bergengren. "Apostles of Taste in Silver." *House Beautiful* 18 (June 1915):19–21.

Bigelow 1857
David Bigelow. *History of Prominent Mercantile and Manufacturing Firms of the United States.* Vol. 4. Boston, 1857.

Board 1868
Gorham Mfg. Co. "Minutes of the Board of Directors, 1868–1892." GA, II. Corporate, 2. Secretary.

Bolles 1879
Albert S. Bolles. *Industrial History of the United States.* New York, 1879.

Bouilhet 1912
Henri Bouilhet. *L'Orfèvrerie française aux XVIIIᵉ et XIXᵉ siècles.* 3 vols. Paris: H. Laurens, 1908–12. Vol. 3 (1912) covers the nineteenth century.

Bowman 1990
Leslie Greene Bowman. *American Arts and Crafts: Virtue in Design.* Los Angeles: Los Angeles County Museum of Art, 1990.

Bradbury 1912
Frederick Bradbury. *History of Old Sheffield Plate.* 1912. Reprint. Sheffield, England: J. W. Northend, 1969.

Brandt 1985
Beverly Kay Brandt. "Mutually Helpful Relations: Architects, Craftsmen, and the Society of Arts and Crafts, Boston." Ph.D. diss., Boston University, 1985.

British 1971
British Parliamentary Papers, Select Committee Reports and Other Papers on Silver and Gold Ware with Proceedings, Minutes of Evidence, Appendices, and Indices, 1817–94. Trade and Industry: Silver and Gold Wares. Vol. 2. Shannon, Ireland: Irish University Press, 1971. For "Report from the Select Committee on Gold and Silver (Hall Marking)" (31 July 1878), see 61ff. For the committee's second report (19 May 1879), see 329ff.

Brown 1906
Alice Brown. "The Silver Tea-Set." *Harper's New Monthly Magazine* 113:667 (Oct. 1906):707–15.

Burke 1986
Doreen Bolger Burke et al. *In Pursuit of Beauty: Americans and the Aesthetic Movement.* New York: Metropolitan Museum of Art, 1986.

Caccavale 1990
Ruth W. Caccavale. "From Imitation to Innovation: The Japanesque Silver of Tiffany and Company." Unpublished paper, 1990.

Carpenter 1978
Charles H. Carpenter, Jr., with Mary Grace Carpenter. *Tiffany Silver.* New York: Dodd, Mead, 1978.

Carpenter 1982
Charles H. Carpenter, Jr., *Gorham Silver, 1831–1981.* New York: Dodd, Mead, 1982.

Chandler 1977
Alfred D. Chandler, Jr., *The Visible Hand: The Managerial Revolution in American Business.* Cambridge: Harvard University Press, 1977.

Chickering 1981
Elenita C. Chickering. *Arthur J. Stone: Handwrought Silver, 1901–1937.* Boston: Boston Athenaeum, 1981.

Chickering 1986a
Elenita C. Chickering. "Arthur J. Stone, Silversmith." *Antiques* 129:1 (Jan. 1986):274–83.

Chickering 1986b
Elenita C. Chickering. "Arthur J. Stone's Silver Flatware 1901–1937." *Silver* 29:1 (Jan.–Feb. 1986):10–19.

Christie's
Christie, Manson, and Woods, Ltd. Auction catalogues cited are for the New York house.

Christofle 1991
Christofle: 150 ans d'art et de rêve [*Dossier de l'Art* 2 (July–Aug. 1991)]. The issue is entirely devoted to the history of Orfèvrerie Christofle.

CJ
Community Jeweler (Oneida, N.Y., 1934).

Coates 1891
Foster Coates. "How Delmonico Sets a Table." *Ladies' Home Journal* 8:12 (Nov. 1891):10.

Codman 1930
William Codman. *An Illustrated History of Silverware Design.* Providence: Gorham, 1930.

Collier 1886
Robert Laird Collier. *English Home Life.* Boston, 1886.

Colton 1846
Calvin Colton. *The Life and Times of Henry Clay.* 2 vols. New York, 1846.

CR 1842
"Statute II." *Congressional Record.* 27th Congress, Session II, Ch. 270 (1842):548–67.

Craftsman 1905
"Some Recent Examples of Gorham Silverware." *The Craftsman* 7:4 (Jan. 1905):447–59.

Craftsman 1906
"Artist and Silversmith—How One Man Worked to Be a Successful Designer." *The Craftsman* 10:2 (Nov. 1906):177–79.

Culme 1977
John Culme. *Nineteenth-Century Silver.* London and New York: Hamlyn Publishing Group for Century Life Books, 1977.

Csiksezentmihalyi 1981
Mihaly Csiksezentmihalyi and Eugene Rochberg-Halton. *The Meaning of Things: Symbols in the Development of the Self.* Cambridge: Cambridge University Press, 1981.

Currier 1927
Currier & Roby. *Annual Spring Exhibition.* New York, 1927. *TCAW* no. 3073.

Darcel 1867
Alfred Darcel. "Bronze et fonte modernes." *Gazette des beaux arts* 23 (1867):419–38.

Darling 1977
Sharon S. Darling. *Chicago Metalsmiths: An Illustrated History.* Chicago: Chicago Historical Society, 1977.

Davies 1983
Karen Davies. *At Home in Manhattan: Modern Decorative Arts, 1925 to the Depression.* New Haven: Yale University Art Gallery, 1983.

de Wolfe 1929
Elsie de Wolfe. *Correct Table Silver: Its Choice and Use.* Wallingford, Conn.: International Silver Co., 1929.

Directory 1884
Jeweler's Mercantile Agency. *Directory of Wholesale Dealers (Manufacturers & Jobbers) of Jewelry, Watches, Clocks, Diamonds & Precious Stones, Silver & Silver-Plated Ware- Etc. in the United States.* New York, 1884.

Dominy 1987
Arthur L. Dominy and Rudolph A. Morgenfruh. *Silver at Your Service.* Del Mar, Cal.: D & M Publishing, 1987.

Draper 1988
Elaine S. Draper. *The Wilkinson Family Story.* Vol. 1. Privately printed, [1988].

Draper 1990
Elaine S. Draper. "The Silver King." *Silver* 23:2 (Mar.–Apr. 1991):13–15.

Draper 1991
Elaine S. Draper. "The Wilkinson Influence." *Silver* 24:3 (May–June 1991):13–15.

Duncan 1986
Alastair Duncan. *American Art Deco.* New York: Harry N. Abrams, 1986.

EA
Elkington & Co. Archives, Victoria and Albert Museum, London. Housed in the National Archives of Art and Design, London.

Elimination 1926
United States Department of Commerce. *Elimination of Waste: Simplified Practice. Sterling Silver Flatware.* Washington, D.C.: Government Printing Office, 1926.

Elkington 1840
Elkington & Co. "Elkington & Co. Drawing Books." ca. 1840–90. Victoria and Albert Museum, London. Illustrated with drawings and some lithographs, this series of volumes contains images of Elkington wares from the founding of the firm.

Emery 1904
Elizabeth Emery. "Some Recent Work." *Arts and Crafts* 15:3 (Feb. 1903):132–39.

Fales 1916
Winnifred S. Fales. *The "R. Wallace" Book: Table Settings and Social Convention for Every Occasion.* Wallingford, Conn.: R. Wallace & Sons Mfg. Co., ca. 1916. Copy used is in the design library at the Gorham plant, Providence, R.I.

Falize 1878
[Lucien Falize.] "Exposition universelle. Les industries d'art au Champ de Mars. 1. Orfèvrerie et bijouterie." *Gazette des beaux arts* 18 (1878):217–55. This article was written under the pseudonym of M. Josse.

Falize 1883
[Lucien Falize.] "L'art japonais." *Revue des arts décoratifs* 3 (1882–83):353–63. This article was written under the pseudonym of M. Josse.

Farnum 1876
Alexander Farnum. *The Century Vase.* Providence, 1876.

Fels 1959
Rendigs Fels. *American Business Cycles, 1865–1897.* Chapel Hill: University of North Carolina Press, 1959.

Fennimore 1972
Donald L. Fennimore. "Thomas Fletcher and Sidney Gardiner: The Stylistic Development of Their Domestic Silver." *Antiques* 102:4 (Oct. 1972):642–49.

Finn 1976
Dallas Finn. "Japan at the Centennial." *Nineteenth Century* 2:3–4 (Autumn 1976):33–40.

Fowler 1863
Fowler and Wells. "Phrenological analysis of John Gorham." New York, 19 Mar. 1863. GA, I. Historical, 1. Gorham Family, File 15.

Fuessle 1929
Newton A. Fuessle. "Sterling Silver for Everybody: How the Cost of Sterling Silverware to the Public Is Being Reduced." *The Outlook* (29 June 1921). Copy used is an unpaginated offprint which was distributed by Gorham.

GA
Gorham Archives. John Hay Library, Brown University, Providence, R.I. Information following "GA" notation represents location within archives. Some items remain at the Gorham plant in Providence and are noted as such when necessary.

GCGA

George Christian Gebelein Archives. Henry Ford Museum & Greenfield Village, Dearborn, Mich. Although unsorted as yet, this source has a wealth of information on Gebelein and his shop.

Gebelein 1911

George Christian Gebelein. "Gebelein Day Book, 1911–1915." GCGA.

Gems 1877

Gems of The Centennial Exhibition. New York, 1877.

Getman 1966

Burrill M. Getman. "Charter for Gorham." A typescript copy dated 7 Dec. 1966 is in GA, I. Historical, 4. Histories Written about Gorham, File 22. Getman was a president of Gorham.

Gibb 1943

George Sweet Gibb. The Whitesmiths of Taunton: A History of Reed and Barton, 1824–1943. Cambridge: Harvard University Press, 1943. Reprint. New York: J. & J. Harper Editions, 1969. The reprint has a noteworthy introduction.

Gleason's

Gleason's Pictorial Drawing-Room Companion (New York, 1851).

Goodrich 1854

C. R. Goodrich and B. Spillman, eds. The World of Science, Art, and Industry Illustrated from Examples in the New York Exhibition, 1853–1854. New York, 1854.

Gordon 1982

David M. Gordon et al. Segmented Work, Divided Workers: The Historical Transformation of Labor in the United States. London: Cambridge University Press, 1982.

Gorham 1852

John Gorham. "Diary of a trip to England & France." 1852. GA, I. Historical, 1. Gorham Family, File 12.

Gorham 1860

John Gorham. "Diary of a trip to Europe." 1860. GA, I. Historical, 1. Gorham Family, File 12.

Gorham 1876

Gorham Mfg. Co. The Gorham Company's Exhibit of Solid Silver Ware of Sterling Purity, Centre of Main Building, Centennial Exhibition. New York, [1876]. Copy used is at Eleutherian Mills Historical Library, Greenville, Del.

Gorham 1879

Gorham Mfg. Co. "Hollowware Photobook." 1879. GA, Photographs, 2. Photobooks, III. Silver, b. Hollowware.

Gorham 1886

Gorham Mfg. Co. Catalogue of Sterling Silver and Silver Plated Wares of the Gorham Manufacturing Co. Including Examples of Their Productions in Other Metals. New York, Autumn 1886. Copy used is in the design library at the Gorham plant, Providence, R.I.

Gorham 1888

Gorham Mfg. Co. Catalogue of Sterling Silver and Silver Plated Wares of the Gorham Manufacturing Co. Including Examples of Their Productions in Other Metals. New York, Autumn 1888. Copy used is in the design library at the Gorham plant, Providence, R.I.

Gorham 1889

Gorham Mfg. Co. Choice Examples of Sterling Silver Ware. New York, Autumn 1889. Copy used is in the design library at the Gorham plant, Providence, R.I.

Gorham 1892

Gorham Mfg. Co. Women's Work at the Gorham Manufacturing Company, Silversmiths, Providence and New York. Providence, [1892].

Gorham 1893

John Gorham. "John Gorham's history." 1893. GA, I. Historical, 1. Gorham Family, File 18.

Gorham 1894

John Gorham. "John Gorham draft notes on the history of Gorham." 1894. GA, I. Historical, 1. Gorham Family, File 19.

Gorham 1899

Gorham Mfg. Co. "Hollowware Photobook." 1899. GA, Photographs, 2. Photobooks, III. Silver, b. Hollowware.

Gorham 1904

Gorham Mfg. Co. Catalogue of Sterling Silver Ware. New York, 1904. TCAW no. 3080.

Gorham 1906

Gorham Mfg. Co. Catalogue of Sterling Silver Ware. New York, 1906. TCAW no. 3079.

Gorham 1928

Gorham Mfg. Co. The Modern American. New York, 1928. Copy used is in the design library at the Gorham plant, Providence, R.I.

Gorham 1929

Gorham Mfg. Co. Prominent American Brides and the Silver Patterns They Have Chosen. Providence, ca. 1929. Copy used is in the design library at the Gorham plant, Providence, R.I.

Gorham 1932

Gorham Mfg. Co. "The Sales Manual and History of the Gorham Company." Providence, 1932. A typescript copy is in GA, I. Historical, 4. Histories Written about Gorham.

Gorham Mark 1918

Gorham Mfg. Co. The Gorham Mark. New York, ca. 1918.

Gorham Rules 1910

Gorham Mfg. Co. Rules and Regulations of the Gorham Mfg. Co. Providence, 1910. Copy used is in GA, III. Personnel, 6. Working Conditions.

Green 1983

Harvey Green. *The Light of the Home: An Intimate View of the Lives of Women in Victorian America*. New York: Pantheon Books, 1983.

Grogan 1911

Grogan & Co. *The Search for Beauty*. Pittsburgh, 1911. Copy used is in the design library at the Gorham plant, Providence, R.I.

Grover 1987

Kathryn Grover, ed. *Dining in America, 1850–1900*. Amherst: University of Massachusetts Press in association with the Strong Museum, 1987.

Guild 1929

Sterling Silversmiths Guild of America. *Sterling Silversmiths Guild Purchase Plan for the Retail Purchase of Sterling Out of Income*. 1929. Copy used is in the design library at the Gorham Plant, Providence, R.I.

Hayden 1982

Dolores Hayden. *The Grand Domestic Revolution: A History of Feminist Designs for American Homes, Neighborhoods, and Cities*. Cambridge: MIT Press, 1982.

Hazen 1839

Edward Hazen. *The Panorama of Professions and Trades; or Every Man's Book*. 1836. 2d ed. Philadelphia, 1839.

HB

House Beautiful (Chicago, 1896).

Heydt 1893

George F. Heydt. *A Glimpse of the Tiffany Exhibit, Chicago, 1893: Sketch of the House*. New York, 1893.

Historical 1950

"Historical Record." GA, I. Historical, 4. Histories Written about Gorham. This volume contains lists of important events and persons in Gorham's history. It also contains a graph showing sales, bullion melted, and number of employees. It seems to have been compiled around 1950 and was occasionally updated subsequently.

HNMM

Harper's New Monthly Magazine (New York, 1850).

HNMM 1868

"Silver and Silver Plate." *Harper's New Monthly Magazine* 37 (Sept. 1868):432–38.

Hogan 1977

Edmund P. Hogan. *An American Heritage: A Book about the International Silver Company*. Dallas: Taylor Publishing Co., 1977.

Holbrook 1912

John S. Holbrook. *Silver for the Dining Room: Selected Periods*. Cambridge, Mass.: [Harvard] University Press, 1912. This book was printed for Gorham.

Hood 1971

Graham Hood. *American Silver: A History of Style, 1650–1900*. New York: Praeger Publishers, 1971.

Hosley 1990

William Hosley. *The Japan Idea: Art and Life in Victorian America*. Hartford: Wadsworth Atheneum, 1990.

Hough 1990

Samuel J. Hough. "Service de Toilette, Martelé." *Silver* 23:6 (Nov.–Dec. 1990):24–26.

Household 1862

The Book of the Household; or Family Dictionary of Everything Connected with Housekeeping, and Domestic Medicine. London, [1862].

Howe 1976

Katherine S. Howe and David B. Warren. *The Gothic Revival Style in America, 1830–1970*. Houston: Museum of Fine Arts, 1976.

HW

Harper's Weekly (New York, 1857).

Hyde 1979

Lewis Hyde. *The Gift: Imagination and the Erotic Life of Property*. New York: Vintage Books, 1983.

Illustrated 1878

The [Art Journal's] Illustrated Catalogue of the Paris International Exhibition. London, 1878.

International 1923

International Silver Co. *Solid Silver in the Modern American Home, Showing the New Trends in Silver Usage as Developed by Modern Decorators*. Meriden, Conn., 1923.

IS

International Studio (New York and London, 1897).

IS 1906

"Recent Work in Objets d'Art and Artistic Jewellery by Paulding Farnham." *International Studio* 29 (Oct. 1906): 92–99.

ISA

International Silver Co. Archive, Meriden Historical Society, Meriden, Conn. This archive is in the process of being organized and is still difficult to use.

Japanese Commission 1876

Japanese Commission. *Official Catalogue of the Japanese Section, and Descriptive Notes on the Industry and Agriculture of Japan*. Philadelphia, 1876.

Japonisme 1988

Japonisme. Paris: Editions de la réunion des musées nationaux, 1988.

Jastram 1981

Roy W. Jastram. *Silver: The Restless Metal*. New York: John Wiley & Sons, 1981.

JCK
 Jewelers' Circular-Keystone (New York, 1869). In 1873 the Jewelers' Circular and Horological Review was founded through the merger of the American Horological Journal (1869) and the Jewelers' Circular (1870). In 1900 the periodical absorbed the Jewelers' Weekly followed by the Jewelers' Review two years later. In 1935 it absorbed the Keystone (Philadelphia, 1899–1935).

JFI
 Journal of the Franklin Institute (Philadelphia, 1826).

JM
 Jeweller and Metalworker (London, 1873).

JN
 Jewelry News (date and place of publication unknown).

Johnson 1979
 Diane C. Johnson. American Art Nouveau. New York: Harry N. Abrams, 1979.

JR
 Jewelers' Review (New York, 1887–1902).

JSW
 Jeweler, Silversmith and Watchmaker (Philadelphia and New York, 1876–78). The original title of this periodical was Jeweler, Silversmith, and American Art Journal. The only complete run known survives in the Cincinnati Public Library.

JW
 Jewelers' Weekly (New York, 1885–1900).

Kaplan 1987
 Wendy Kaplan et al. "The Art that is Life": The Arts and Crafts Movement in America, 1875–1920. Boston: Museum of Fine Arts, Boston, 1987.

Katzman 1978
 David M. Katzman. Seven Days a Week: Women and Domestic Service in Industrializing America. New York: Oxford University Press, 1978.

Kilbride 1988
 Richard J. Kilbride. Art Deco Chrome: The Chase Era. Greenwich, Conn.: Filigree Press, 1988.

Kirk 1931
 Samuel Kirk & Son. Sterling Silverware by Kirk. Baltimore, 1931. TCAW no. 3091.

Kornblith 1985
 Gary J. Kornblith. "The Craftsman as Industrialist: Jonas Chickering and the Transformation of American Piano Making." Business History Review 59 (1985):349–68.

Krantz 1894
 M. Camille Krantz. International Exposition of Chicago, 1893. Paris, 1894. This report was compiled by the Ministry of Commerce, Industries, Post, and Telegraphs. A typescript English translation is in GA, I. Historical, 5. Articles about Gorham, c. Exhibitions.

Leighton 1976
 Margaretha Gebelein Leighton. George Christian Gebelein, Boston Silversmith, 1878–1945. Boston: privately printed, 1976.

Levenstein 1988
 Harvey A. Levenstein. Revolution at the Table: The Transformation of the American Diet. New York and Oxford: Oxford University Press, 1988.

LHJ
 Ladies' Home Journal (Philadelphia, 1883).

McCabe 1877
 James D. McCabe. The Illustrated History of the Centennial Exhibition. Philadelphia, 1877.

McClinton 1968
 Katharine Morrison McClinton. Collecting American Nineteenth Century Silver. New York: Charles Scribner's Sons, 1968.

McCracken 1988
 Grant McCracken. Culture and Consumption: New Approaches to the Symbolic Character of Consumer Goods and Activities. Bloomington: Indiana University Press, 1988.

Maffett 1990
 Everett L. Maffett. Silver Banquet II: A Compendium on Railroad Dining Car Silver Serving Pieces. Eaton, Ohio: Silver Press, 1990.

Marchand 1985
 Roland Marchand. Advertising the American Dream: Making Way for Modernity, 1920–1940. Berkeley: University of California Press, 1985.

Mayall 1851
 Beard Mayall et al. Tallis's History and Description of the Crystal Palace and the Exhibition of the World's Industry in 1851. Vol. 1. London, 1851.

Meriden 1867
 Meriden Britannia Co. Heavily Electro Plated, Nickel, Silver, and White Metal Goods. West Meriden, Conn., 1867. TCAW no. 1664.

Meriden 1871
 Meriden Britannia Co. Illustrated Catalogue and Price List of Heavily Plated Goods. West Meriden, Conn., 1871. TCAW no. 3099.

Meriden 1873
 Meriden Britannia Co. Appendix to Price List of July 1st, 1871, of Heavily Plated Goods. West Meriden, Conn., 1873. TCAW no. 1666.

Meriden 1881
Meriden Britannia Co. *Electro Gold & Silver Plate*. West Meriden, Conn., 1881. *TCAW* no. 1668.

Meriden 1882
Meriden Britannia Co. *Electro Gold & Silver Plate*. West Meriden, Conn., 1882. Copy used is in ISA.

Meriden 1893
Meriden Britannia Co. Catalogue of Pavilion at the World's Columbian Exposition. West Meriden, Conn., 1893. *TCAW* no. 3097.

Meriden 1907
Meriden Britannia Co. *The Silver Standard, a Periodical of 1847. . . .* West Meriden, Conn., 1907. *TCAW* no. 3103.

Meriden 1910
Meriden Britannia Co. *Price List of 1847 Rogers Bros. Spoons, Forks, Knives, Etc.* West Meriden, Conn., ca. 1910. *TCAW* no. 1671.

Mesnard 1867
Jules Mesnard. *Les merveilles de l'exposition universelle de 1867.* Vol. 1. Paris, 1867.

Metropolitan 1907
C. H. "The Edward C. Moore Collection." *Metropolitan Museum of Art Bulletin* 2 (1907):105–6.

Middletown 1879
Middletown Plate Co. *Illustrated Catalogue and Price List of Fine Electro Plate on Hard White Metal.* Middletown, Conn., 1879.

Miller 1990
R. Craig Miller. *Modern Design in the Metropolitan Museum of Art, 1890–1990.* New York: Harry N. Abrams, 1990.

MJ
Manufacturing Jeweler (Providence, 1884).

Moffitt 1899
Charlotte Moffitt. "New Designs in Silver." *House Beautiful* 7:1 (Dec. 1899):55–58.

Morse 1986
Edward W. Morse, ed. *Silver in the Golden State: Images and Essays Celebrating the History and Art of Silver in California.* Oakland: Oakland Museum History Department, 1986.

Muller-Munk 1929
Peter Müller-Munk. "Machine—Hand." *Creative Art* 5:4 (Oct. 1929):709–12.

Naeve 1986
Milo M. Naeve and Lynn Springer Roberts. *A Decade of Decorative Arts: The Antiquarian Society of The Art Institute of Chicago.* Chicago: The Art Institute of Chicago, 1986.

Nelson 1946
Donald M. Nelson. *Arsenal of Democracy: The Story of American War Production.* New York: Harcourt, Brace and Co., 1946.

New York 1848
New York Mercantile Register, 1848–1849. New York, 1848.

New York 1854
New York Industrial Exhibition: General Report of the British Commissioners. London, 1854.

New York 1894
New York [State]. *Board of Managers, World's Columbian Exposition. Report . . . 1894.* Albany, 1894.

Norton 1877
Frank H. Norton, ed. *Frank Leslie's Illustrated Historical Register of the Centennial Exposition.* New York, 1877.

Notices 1932
Tiffany & Co. These two volumes of "Notices" contain memos sent to the sales staff by management. Vol. 1 covers the years 1932–42. Vol. 2 covers 1941–46. They are in TA.

NR 1878
"A Walk Through Tiffany's." *National Review* 4:1 (July 1878):11–28.

O'Connor 1988
Kathleen B. O'Connor, ed. *Nineteenth-Century American Silver: Report of a Yale-Smithsonian Material Culture Seminar at Yale University, 7–8 April 1988.* New Haven: Yale University, 1988.

Official 1851
Official Descriptive and Illustrated Catalogue. Great Exhibition of the Works of Industry of all Nations, 1851. Vol. 3. London, 1851.

Official 1889
Paris Universal Exposition 1889: Official Catalogue of the United States Exhibit. Paris, 1889.

Orfèvrerie 1862
Orfèvrerie Christofle. Catalogue. Paris, 1862.

Osborne Collection
Charles Osborne Collection. Located in the Winterthur Museum Library, this is the only known collection of Osborne drawings, photographs, and papers. Its main index number is 91x23.

Osgood 1876
Samuel Osgood. "The Bryant Vase." *Harpers' New Monthly Magazine* 53 (July 1876):245–52.

Osgood 1912
Albert Osgood. "The American Renaissance in Silversmithing: The Colonial Style." *Fine Arts Journal* 27 (Dec. 1912):775–88.

Parsell 1901

J. M. Parsell. "Tiffany & Co. Forest Hill Works. Statistics & Memo for Private Reference." ca. 1901. Although initially compiled around 1901, this volume contains financial information for the period 1870 to 1917. This exceptionally important source is in TA.

Pelletier 1918a

Le Roy Pelletier. *Are You Practicing False Patriotism?* New York: The Gorham Co., 1918. Copy used is in the design library at the Gorham plant, Providence, R.I.

Pelletier 1918b

Le Roy Pelletier. *Are Your Economics on Straight?* New York: The Gorham Co., 1918. Copy used is in the design library at the Gorham plant, Providence, R.I.

Penzer 1954

N. M. Penzer. *Paul Storr: the Last of the Goldsmiths.* Boston: Boston Book and Art Shop, 1954.

Percy 1878

Randolph T. Percy. "The American At Work, IV. Among the Silver-Platers." *Appletons' Journal* 5:31 n.s. (Dec. 1878): 482–94.

Peterson 1937

Florence Peterson. *Strikes in the United States, 1880–1936.* U.S. Department of Labor Bulletin no. 651. Washington, D.C.: Government Printing Office, 1938.

Petroski 1992

Henry Petroski. *The Evolution of Useful Things.* New York: Alfred A. Knopf, 1992.

Philadelphia 1976

Philadelphia: Three Centuries of American Art. Philadelphia: Philadelphia Museum of Art, 1976.

PHSHP 1976

Philadelphia Social History Project, University of Pennsylvania. The surviving, computerized census and city directory data for this now defunct project are stored at Van Pelt Library, University of Pennsylvania, Philadelphia.

Pickering 1878

Thomas R. Pickering. *Paris Universal Exposition 1878: Official Catalogue of the United States Exhibitors.* London, 1878.

Price 1919

C. Matlock Price. "The Art of Silversmithing in America." *International Studio* 69 (Nov. 1919):3–17.

Puig 1989

Francis J. Puig, Judith Banister, Gerald W. R. Ward, and David McFadden. *English and American Silver in the Collection of The Minneapolis Institute of Arts.* Minneapolis: Institute of Arts, 1989.

Purtell 1971

Joseph Purtell. *The Tiffany Touch.* New York: Random House, 1971.

RAD

Revue des arts décoratifs (Paris, 1880).

Rainwater 1968

Dorothy T. Rainwater and H. Ivan Rainwater. *American Silverplate.* Nashville, Tenn.: Everybody's Press, 1968.

Rainwater 1975

Dorothy T. Rainwater. *Encyclopedia of American Silver Manufacturers.* 2d ed. New York: Crown Publishers, 1975. First published in 1966, this book was republished with minor revisions in 1986 by Schiffer Publishing, West Chester, Pa.

Reed & Barton 1875

Reed & Barton. Catalogue. Taunton, Mass., 1875. *TCAW* no. 3106.

Reed & Barton 1877

Reed & Barton. *Illustrated Catalogue. . . .* Taunton, Mass., 1877. *TCAW* no. 1675.

Reed & Barton 1885

Reed & Barton. Catalogue. Taunton, Mass., 1885. *TCAW* no. 1676.

Report 1901

Report of the Commissioner-General for the United States to the International Universal Exhibition, Paris, 1900. Vol. 4. Washington, D.C.: Government Printing Office, 1901. Senate Document no. 232.

Reports 1880

Reports of the United States Commissioners to the Paris Universal Exposition, 1878. Vol. 1. Washington, D.C., 1880.

Reports 1889

Reports of Artisans selected by the Mansion House Committee to Visit the Paris Universal Exhibition, 1889. London, 1889.

Reports 1891

Reports of the United States Commissioners to the Universal Exposition of 1889 at Paris. Vol. 2. Washington, D.C., 1891.

R. G. Dun & Co.

R. G. Dun & Co. "Credit Ledgers." R. G. Dun & Co. Collection. Baker Library, Harvard University Graduate School, Harvard University, Cambridge.

Richards 1853

William C. Richards. *A Day in the New York Crystal Palace.* New York, 1853.

RISD 1985

A Handbook of the Museum of Art: Rhode Island School of Design. Providence: Rhode Island School of Design, 1985.

Roell 1989
    Craig H. Roell. *The Piano in America, 1890–1940*. Chapel Hill: University of North Carolina Press, 1989.

Royal 1910
    Royal Manufacturing Co. Catalogue. Detroit, ca. 1910. *TCAW* no. 1683.

Ruskin 1851
    John Ruskin. *The Stones of Venice*. Vol. 2. Boston, 1851.

Safford 1990
    Frances G. Safford and Ruth W. Caccavale. "E. J. Soligny, The Chaser of the Bryant Vase." *Antiques* 137:3 (Mar. 1990): 688–97.

St. Johnston 1886
    A. St. Johnston. "American Silver-Work." *Magazine of Art* 9 (1886):13–18.

Sandhurst 1876
    Phillip T. Sandhurst et al. *The Great Centennial Exhibition Critically Described and Illustrated*. Philadelphia, 1876.

Schlesinger 1946
    Arthur M. Schlesinger. *Learning How to Behave: A Historical Study of American Etiquette Books*. New York: Macmillan, 1946.

Scientific American 1877
    "The Manufacture of Silverware." *Scientific American* 36:19 (12 May 1877):290–91.

Scientific American 1879
    "American Industries, No. 22. The Manufacture of Silver-Plated Ware." *Scientific American* 41:19 (8 Nov. 1879):296.

Scranton 1991
    Philip Scranton. "Diversity in Diversity: Flexible Production and American Industrialization, 1870–1930." *Business History Review* 65 (1991):27–90.

Scrapbook 1891
    "Scrapbook 1891–1896." GA, I. Historical, 5. Articles about Gorham. This volume contains clippings about Gorham.

Scrapbooks
    Tiffany & Co. "Tiffany & Co. Scrapbooks." 8 vols. 1846–1900. These volumes were once paginated but have lost most of their numbers due to embrittlement. They are in TA.

Scribner's
    Scribner's Monthly (New York, 1870).

Scribner's 1874
    "The Silver Age." *Scribner's Monthly* 9:1 (Dec. 1874): 193–209.

Silver
    Silver Magazine (Whittier, Cal., 1968).

Silver 1902
    Silver and Plated Ware in Foreign Countries. Special Consular Reports, v. 23, part 2. Washington, D.C.: Government Printing Office, 1902. Government Document no. C 18.9:23/a.

Silverware 1940
    United States Tariff Commission. *Silverware, Solid and Plated*. Report no. 139, 2d s. Washington, D.C.: Government Printing Office, 1940. Government Document no. TC 1.9:139.

Snow 1935
    William G. Snow. "Early Silver Plating in America." *Metal Industry* 33:6 (June 1935):202–5.

Soeffing 1987
    D. Albert Soeffing. "Joseph Seymour." *Silver* 20:6 (Nov.–Dec. 1987):30–34.

Soeffing 1988
    D. Albert Soeffing. *Silver Medallion Flatware*. New York: New Books, 1988.

Soeffing 1991
    D. Albert Soeffing. "The New York City Gold and Silver Manufacturers' Petition of 1842." *Silver* 24:3 (May–June 1991):8–11.

Souvenir 1877
    Souvenir of the Centennial Exhibition. Philadelphia, 1877.

SPB
    Sotheby Parke Bernet, Inc., New York. All sales catalogues cited are for the New York house.

Steele 1877
    T. Steele & Son. *What Shall I Buy for a Present, A Manual*. Hartford, Conn., 1877. *TCAW* no. 1690.

Steward 1902
    W. Augustus Steward. "American Jewelry and Silversmith's Work, Seen by Foreign Eyes: Silversmithing." *Jewelers' Circular-Keystone* 44:1 (5 Feb. 1902):35.

Stieff 1928
    Stieff Company. *Stieff Hand-Wrought Sterling Silver*. Baltimore: Stieff Company, 1928.

Stokes 1990
    Jayne E. Stokes. *Sumptuous Surrounds: Silver Overlay on Ceramics and Glass. The Collection of Warren Gilson*. Milwaukee: Milwaukee Art Museum, 1990.

Strasser 1989
    Susan Strasser. *Satisfaction Guaranteed: The Making of the American Mass Market*. New York: Pantheon Books, 1989.

Stuart 1912
    Evelyn Marie Stuart. "The American Renaissance in Silversmithing." *Fine Arts Journal* 27 (Sept. 1912):571–84.

Stuart 1913

Evelyn Marie Stuart. "Modern Modes in Silver." *Fine Arts Journal* 29 (Nov. 1913):688–702.

Summary Volume 1913

"Summary Volume: Appraisal of Gorham Manufacturing Co." 1913. GA, II. Corporate, 3. Financial, f. Appraisals and Inventories.

TA

Tiffany & Co. Archives, Parsippany, N.J.

Tachau 1922

Hanna Tachau. "American Art in Silvercraft." *International Studio* 75 (Aug. 1922):412–15.

Taylor 1878

[Edwin C. Taylor]. "Silver in Art." *International Review* 5 (1878):241–46.

Taylor 1879a

Edwin C. Taylor. "An American Wedge." *International Review* 6 (1879):170–75.

Taylor 1879b

Edwin C. Taylor. "Metal Work of All Ages." *National Repository* 6 (Nov. 1879):393–407.

TCAW

Trade Catalogues at Winterthur. Part 1. Compiled by E. Richard McKinstry. New York: Garland Publishing, 1984. Part 2. Compiled by Eleanor McD. Thompson. Bethesda, Md.: Congressional Information Services, 1991. These guides index 3,233 trade catalogues at Winterthur Museum Library. A number cited after *TCAW* in an endnote or reference denotes the microfiche card for that particular trade catalogue.

Technical 1877

"Technical Manual of descriptions of processes and metallurgy." Providence, 1877–78. The manual contains information on processes used at Gorham and marginal comments on various processes used at Tiffany & Co. in the late 1870s. Sam Hough believes Frederic A. Jordan to be the author of the marginalia. The volume survives in GA, I. Historical, 13. Technical.

Teevan 1924

Bernard Teevan. "Georg Jensen's Silver." *International Studio* 80 (Nov. 1924):160–63.

Tiffany 1876

Tiffany & Co. *Loan Collection: A Retrospective Exhibit on Silver Presentation and Commemorative Pieces.* New York, 1876.

Tiffany 1893

Tiffany & Co. *Catalogue of Tiffany & Co.'s Exhibit, Manufacturers and Liberal Arts Building, World's Columbian Exposition, Chicago, 1893.* New York, 1893.

Tiffany Rules 1897

Tiffany & Co. *Tiffany & Co. Forest Hill Works. Rules.* Newark, N.J., 1897. Printed placard of rules in TA, Scrapbook of "Printed Matter," 6.

Tilden 1906

Henry C. Tilden. "Martelé, A New Distinctive School." *Brush and Pencil* 18:5 (May 1906):239–43.

Tomlinson 1858

Charles Tomlinson. *Illustrations of Useful Arts, Manufactures, and Trades.* London, 1858.

Townsend 1893

Horace Townsend. "American Silverwork." *American Architect and Building News* 41:915 (8 July 1893):26–27.

Townsend 1917

Horace Townsend. *A Touchstone for Silver.* New York: Gorham, 1917.

Townsend 1918

Horace Townsend. *Nicholas Heinzelman: The Man and The Artist.* New York: Gorham, 1918.

Trachtenberg 1982

Alan Trachtenberg. *The Incorporation of America: Culture and Society in the Gilded Age.* New York: Hill and Wang, 1982.

Tracy 1970

Berry B. Tracy et al. *Nineteenth-Century America: Furniture and Other Decorative Arts.* New York: Metropolitan Museum of Art, 1970.

Tufts 1888

James W. Tufts Co. Catalogue. Boston, 1888. *TCAW* no. 1692.

Tufts 1899

James W. Tufts Co. *Catalogue supplement.* Boston, 1899. *TCAW* no. 1695.

Turner 1972

Noel D. Turner. *American Silver Flatware, 1837–1910.* New York: A. S. Barnes, 1972.

Venable 1987

Charles L. Venable. "The Silverplated Ice Water Pitcher: An Image of Changing America, 1850–1900." *Material Culture* 19:1 (Spring 1987):39–48.

VF

Vanity Fair (New York, 1914).

Vinchon 1880

Marius Vinchon. "L'exposition moderne du métal à l'union centrale." *Gazette des beaux arts* 22, 2d s. (1880):425–47.

Wallace 1921

R. Wallace & Sons Mfg. Co. *Wallace Silver: Prize Cups and Trophies.* Wallingford, Conn., 1921. *TCAW* no. 3120.

Ward 1979
Barbara McLean Ward and Gerald W. R. Ward, eds. *Silver in American Life: Selections from the Mabel Brady Garvan and Other Collections at Yale University*. Boston: David R. Godine in association with the Yale University Art Gallery and the American Federation of Arts, 1979.

Ward 1986
Barbara McLean Ward. "Metalwares." In *The Great River: Arts & Society of the Connecticut Valley, 1635–1820*, ed. Gerald W. R. Ward and William N. Hosley, Jr., 273–77. Hartford, Conn.: Wadsworth Atheneum, 1986.

Ward 1987
Barbara McLean Ward. "Women's Property and Family Continuity in Eighteenth-Century Connecticut." In *Early American Probate Inventories*, ed. Peter Benes, 74–85. The Dublin Seminar for New England Folklife Annual Proceedings 1987. Boston: Boston University, 1987.

Wardle 1963
Patricia Wardle. *Victorian Silver and Silver-Plate*. New York: Thomas Nelson & Sons, 1963.

Warren 1987
David B. Warren, Katherine S. Howe, and Michael K. Brown. *Marks of Achievement: Four Centuries of American Presentation Silver*. New York: Harry N. Abrams for the Museum of Fine Arts, Houston, 1987.

Waters 1981
Deborah Dependahl Waters. "'The Workmanship of an American Artist': Philadelphia's Precious Metals Trades and Crafts, 1788–1832." Ph.D. diss., University of Delaware, 1981.

Webster 1845
Thomas Webster. *An Encyclopedia of Domestic Economy*. New York, 1845.

Weisberg 1975
Gabriel P. Weisberg et al. *Japonisme: Japanese Influence on French Art, 1854–1910*. Cleveland: Cleveland Museum of Art, 1975.

Whiting 1884
Whiting Mfg. Co. "Whiting Day Books." Vol. 1 covers 1884–98. Vol. 2 covers 1898–1918. These volumes are logs for special items made at Whiting during these years. They are in GA, XII. Acquired Companies, 14. Whiting.

Williams 1985
Susan Williams. *Savory Suppers & Fashionable Feasts: Dining in Victorian America*. New York: Pantheon Books in association with the Strong Museum, 1985.

Williamson 1944
Harold F. Williamson, ed. *The Growth of the American Economy*. New York: Prentice-Hall, 1944.

WJ
The Watchmaker & Jeweler (New York, 1869).

Zapata 1991a
Janet Zapata. "The Rediscovery of Paulding Farnham, Tiffany's Designer Extraordinaire, Part I: Jewelry." *Antiques* 139:3 (Mar. 1991):556–67.

Zapata 1991b
Janet Zapata. "The Rediscovery of Paulding Farnham, Tiffany's Designer Extraordinaire, Part II: Silver." *Antiques* 139:4 (Apr. 1991):718–29.

GLOSSARY

This glossary is drawn from the "Manufacturing Vocabulary" in Gorham Co., "The Sales Manual and History of the Gorham Company" (Providence, 1932):76–80. The manual was distributed to salesmen so that they would be conversant with the basic vocabulary and processes of silver making.

ANNEALING Process by which silver is softened through the application of heat.

APPLIED BONDS A cast or rolled wire border which is soldered to the article.

ASSAYING Process of determining the constituents of a metal and the quality of it.

BELTING Process of putting a flat, horizontal edge on the bowl of a spoon by applying it to an endless belt covered with Carborundum and glue.

BLANK Piece of flat sheet silver stock used in die stamping.

BLANKING Process by which the spoon and fork blanks are cut from the sheet metal.

BOBBING Process of removing file marks and scratches through the use of pumice and oil and a walrus hide buff.

BRIGHT FINISH A bright polish given to silver with different grades of rouge on cotton buff.

BRITANNIA METAL Metal that is 90 percent tin, 2 percent copper, and 8 percent antimony.

BRUSHING Process of removing file marks and scratches with pumice and oil on a hair brush.

BUFF A disc used in polishing which is made up of a number of pieces of cloth.

BURNISHING Process of polishing by rubbing a highly polished steel tool of bloodstone over the surface of the metal.

BUTLER FINISH A polish given to silver done with tripoli (siliceous rottenstone) polishing composition to produce a medium-bright finish.

CAST BORDER An applied border made of cast silver.

CASTING Process of pouring metal into a mold to reproduce the model from which the mold was made.

CHASING
1) Flat: process of decorating with a blunt tool by shaping the surface of the metal without raising it from the back.
2) Repoussé: process of decorating with a blunt tool by shaping the surface of the metal. The metal is raised from the back, leaving the ornament in bas-relief.

COIN SILVER Silver that is 900–1000 fine.

COLORING Process of polishing with rouge to give a bright finish.

CROSS ROLLING Process by which the bowl section of the blank is widened.

CUTTING DOWN Process by which bobbing marks are removed with tripoli composition before polishing.

DIE SINKING Process by which a design or pattern is cut out of a piece of steel to form a die.

DRAFTING Process of drawing metal into a tube shape with a plunger and die.

DRAWING Process of making wire by drawing silver through a circular hole.

DRIPPING Immersion of silver in a solution of sulphuric acid and water to remove the copper oxide obtained in annealing. A quick dip of nitric acid is sometimes used.

ELECTROPLATING Process of coating a base metal with gold, silver, or nickel by means of a cyanide solution and electricity.

EMBOSSING Process of ornamenting by stamping the metal with a die.

ENGRAVING Process of decorating by cutting away the metal with cutting tools.

ETCHING Process of ornamenting metal by eating it away with acid.

FACING Process of removing the flange or burr from the edge of a piece of metal by using a belt or wheel.

FINISHING Process of polishing silver.

FIRE A scale of copper oxide which forms on the silver during the process of annealing.

FRENCH FINISH A gray polish given to silver by means of buffing with a mixture of pumice and oil.

GERMAN SILVER A composition of copper, nickel, and zinc.

GILDING Process of depositing a coating of gold on a metal by means of a solution of gold cyanide and electricity.

GRADING Process of gauging the varying thicknesses of a metal spoon or fork to a mathematical scale.

GREASE BUFFING Process of greasing with pumice and oil for French finish.

INSERT Piece of sterling silver melted to the base of the bowl of standard plated spoons where heaviest wear will occur.

KNURLING Process of making borders or moldings on an article by rolling the design on the metal piece between two circular dies.

LACQUERING Process of coating silverware with cellulose lacquer.

LITHARGE A lead substance which is mixed with glycerin and used to fill the hollow handles of cutlery items.

MILLING Process of cutting away metal on a milling machine with revolving cutters.

NICKEL SILVER Base metal composed of copper, nickel, and zinc, often called German silver or white metal.

OXIDIZING Process of "setting out" a design on a piece of metal by dipping it into a solution of boiling water and sodium sulphide.

PIERCING Process of cutting away the metal with cutting dies or a saw.

PINCH ROLLING Process of lengthening the bowl of a spoon while it is still in the blank form.

PLANISHING Process of smoothing the surface of silver with a hammer.

PROFILING Process of removing the flange from the stamped halves of hollowware pieces.

ROLLED EDGE An edge of a hollowware piece rolled back to form a hollowware border.

ROLLED WIRE Wire or strip which is rolled between two circular dies and used for applied designs, borders, or moldings.

SATIN FINISH A matte finish obtained by picking up the surface of the metal like the nap on cloth, with a long-haired steel wire brush.

SCRATCH BRUSHING Process of applying a finish to silver plate with a wire brush.

SHEFFIELD PLATE Not made today. Originally it was made in Sheffield, England, by rolling sheets of silver over a copper base.

SLUSH MOLDING Process of molding white or Britannia metal handles, spouts, and tips.

SNARLING Process of raising the metal on hollowware pieces from behind in repoussé chasing.

SOLDERS
1) Silver solder: contains 50 percent or more silver. Melting point varies with quality of zinc which, with copper and silver, composes silver solder.
2) Hard solder: solder which has a high melting point.
3) Soft solder: solder which has lead in it. This solder is used with Britannia metal because of its low melting point.

SPINNING Process of shaping metal by forcing it over a form or chuck with a blunt steel tool while the metal and form are revolving on a lathe.

SPOT WELDING Process of welding the two halves of a knife handle together to ensure a close fit when soldering them.

STERLING Silver that is 925–1000 fine, copper being the alloy.

STONING Process of using pumice stones to remove scratch marks and other imperfections from flat silver pieces.

TINING Process of stamping out the tines of a fork with a cutting die.

TURNING Cutting away or cleaning up the metal with a cutting tool from a piece which is fitted over a form and revolved on a lathe.

BIOGRAPHIES OF SELECTED SILVER PRODUCERS AND RETAILERS

The following biographies are by D. Albert Soeffing except for that on Joseph Heinrich. Soeffing has spent over two decades researching the U.S. silverware industry and is working on a book concerning American silver makers before 1875. These entries do not represent every maker discussed in the text. Entries were included only when substantial new information which is not in other sources was available. For information on other makers please refer to Rainwater 1975, Gibb 1943, Hogan 1977, and Burke 1986. For information on Tiffany's and Gorham beyond that in this text, see Carpenter 1978 and 1982. Manufacturing marks are indicated in italics.

WILLIAM ADAMS, NEW YORK, N.Y.
WORKING 1829–1862

There is no doubt that William Adams (1801–ca. 1862) was a silversmith of great ability, as attested to by the urn presented to Henry Clay in 1845 (fig. 1.1). Adams was also active in politics and was acquainted with federal officials as early as 1841. In that year he received an order to create a silver mace for the House of Representatives to replace the original, destroyed in the War of 1812. In 1842 the silversmiths of New York City petitioned the Senate to press for an increase in the tariff on foreign gold and silver goods. The petition was presented through Henry Clay by a delegation of silversmiths who traveled to Washington. Several hundred signatures were collected on the document, but William Adams's is not among them. This seems peculiar, given that Adams not only produced the Clay presentation vase three years later, but knew Clay personally since "on the occasion of one of Henry Clay's visits to New York he received his friends at Adams' House." Further evidence of Adams's political activities may be found in the fact that he held the following offices in New York City: assistant alderman (1840–42), president of the board of aldermen (1842–43), alderman (1847–48), and commissioner of repairs and supplies (1850, 1852).

On 5 August 1896, the *Jewelers' Circular* reported that Adams trained with "Pierre Chicotree, a Frenchman." Although no listing of a silversmith with this name can be found, we may assume that Adams served with Peter Chitry, whose name was subject to many variant spellings. Peter and his brother Edward were born in France, and both became New York City silversmiths. Prior to their arrival, they resided on Santo Domingo, a French sugar island, fleeing to the United States after narrowly escaping the slaughter of the 1791 uprising. The two were the only members of their family to survive.

Adams produced large quantities of silver during his career, much of it of superior quality. For a number of years he was granted contracts by New York's American Institute to supply premiums for its annual exhibitions of manufactured goods.

ALLCOCK & ALLEN, NEW YORK, N.Y.
ALLCOCK (HUGH) & ALLEN (DAVID W.) 1847–1853
ALLCOCK, ALLEN & BONNEL (JONATHAN) 1853–1854

This was a short-lived firm. A rare broadside dated 7 April 1847 announces a May opening of John Warrin's Furnishing Warehouse at 341 Broadway. All manner of silverware is prominently advertised with the promise of "every style and pattern made to order on the most reasonable terms." On the same sheet is printed "H. Allcock's Card," which states: "Having engaged with Mr. John Warrin as superintendent of this establishment, I solicit the favor and patronage of my friends, and flatter myself that an acquaintance with the Wholesale and Retail business for upwards of 15 years will enable me to offer goods that, for style, quality, and moderate prices, cannot fail to give satisfaction to all who will favor me with their patronage."

Whether Warrin died or was bought out by the new partnership of Allcock & Allen is unknown. But something must have happened shortly after the April broadside, since Allcock & Allen was listed in the 1847 New York City Directory at the 341 Broadway address. The directory listings were generally compiled and completed by 1 July. In any event, the firm was located at the address until 1851. In that year it moved to 519 Broadway, where it remained until 1854. The store was prominently located, assuring it a portion of the carriage trade.

It is unlikely that silver bearing Allcock & Allen's retail mark was of the firm's own manufacture. In some cases, it is definitely known that such a silver mark was made by others. The broadside supports the suggestion that the business was only a retailer.

BAILEY & CO., PHILADELPHIA, PA.
BAILEY (JOSEPH T.) & KITCHEN (ANDREW B.) 1832–1848
BAILEY & CO. 1848–1878
BAILEY, BANKS & BIDDLE 1878–PRESENT

The original firm was founded by Joseph Trowbridge Bailey (d. 1853 or 1854) and Andrew B. Kitchen (d. 1840) and was located at 136 Chestnut Street. In 1840 Joseph's brother Eli Westcott Bailey, a New York City jeweler and importer hurt financially by the Panic of 1837, came to Philadelphia and entered the firm. The name continued as Bailey & Kitchen. When Joseph died, Eli became the senior partner of Bailey & Co. until he retired in 1867, remaining a special partner until 1889. He died at 90 in 1899, his obituary appearing in the *Jewelers' Circular* of 5 April of that year. The firm was located at the following addresses: 817 Chestnut Street (1857–68), 12th and Chestnut (1868–1904), 1218 Chestnut (1904–53), and 16th and Chestnut (1953–present).

Evidence gleaned from advertisements and industrial censuses indicates that Bailey & Co. did not enter into the manufacture of silverware until the early 1850s, probably 1852. Before that time, a vast proportion of its solid silver goods was produced by the firm of Taylor & Lawrie, a partnership of an Irishman and a Scotsman. Consequently, Bailey & Kitchen's retail mark is often accompanied by Taylor & Lawrie's pseudo-hallmarks consisting of an American eagle, a Scotch thistle, and an Irish harp. Evidence indicates that, when Bailey & Co. added silversmithing to its production of jewelry and extensive importation of fancy goods, another Irishman, George B. Sharp, ran the manufacturing portion of the establishment. During this period, the wares were usually marked with a sterling mark of *(lion) s (shield)*. This part of the business was discontinued about 1868, when the firm reverted to manufacturing jewelry and retailing silverware and fancy goods.

BALL, BLACK & CO., NEW YORK, N.Y.
BALL (HENRY), TOMPKINS (ERASTUS O.) & BLACK (WM.) 1839–1851
BALL, BLACK & CO. 1851–1874
BLACK, STARR & FROST 1874–1908
BLACK, STARR & FROST, INC. 1908–1929
BLACK, STARR & FROST-GORHAM, INC. 1929–1940
BLACK, STARR & GORHAM, INC. 1940–1962
BLACK, STARR & FROST, LTD. 1962–1990

This firm descended from the retail establishment of Frederick Marquand, who had been in business in New York since 1823. In 1833 the firm of Marquand & Co. included William Black and Henry Ball. In 1836 Erastus O. Tompkins and J. D. Williams were admitted to the firm, and in 1839 the name was changed to Ball, Tompkins & Black. In 1851 it became Ball, Black & Co. In 1852 Ebenezer Monroe became a partner.

There can be no doubt that Ball, Black & Co. was the leading jewelry house in the nation until it was overtaken by Tiffany & Co. From the beginning, it was entrusted with important commissions of jewelry and silverware. When the firm moved to its new building at 247 Broadway in 1848, it was equipped with some of the first large plate glass windows, perfect for the display of goods. In 1851 the company exhibited nineteen gold-sheathed swords of its design, made for the State of Illinois for presentation to the officers of the Illinois regiments who had served in the Mexican-American War. Such offerings received tremendous amounts of publicity for the time.

In 1859 Ball, Black & Co. purchased the lot at the southwest corner of Broadway and Prince Streets (565–67 Broadway) and erected a marble "palace" that opened in 1860 and still stands today. It was touted as the first completely fireproof building constructed in America. Its imported French plate glass windows were the largest in the country, and its steam driven elevator was a rarity. On 14 October 1860, the Prince of Wales visited the establishment under the guidance of William Ball. Before his departure, he placed orders for jewelry and silverware worth in excess of $12,000, a large sum for the time.

Ball, Black & Co. instituted the first modern safe deposit vault system in the country. The basement of the new building ran the full length of the premises and into areas under the surrounding pavement. Within was an area 50 feet long, 25 feet wide, and 16 feet high designated as a "safe" and surrounded by heavy bars of "chilled iron." The entrance had a massive door with a combination lock. For further safety, this enclosed area contained a smaller burglarproof vault "for the safekeeping of coin, diamonds and jewels of great value." It was attended at all times by a heavily armed group of six men. Reportedly, chests of plate and jewelry belonging to wealthy Southern families survived the Civil War inside the Ball, Black & Co. vault while all their other possessions were lost.

Enormous amounts of American-made silver were sold by the firm. It is reported that William Gale supplied goods for Marquand & Co. Nicholas Bogert and John Moore made silver tea sets and other hollowware for Ball, Tompkins & Black. The great designer and manufacturer of American "fancy" flatware patterns, Michael Gibney, had a special relationship with the firm which was continued after his death in 1860 by his son Francis. Many other noted American silversmiths produced for the store. But perhaps none is less known or more important than John R. Wendt, who relocated from Boston in order to occupy two floors of factory space in the 565–67 Broadway building. A billhead advertisement from the early Marquand years leads us to believe that the company may have produced some of its own silver. However, the successor firms, although prominent manufacturers of jewelry, only retailed silverware.

BEIDERHASE & CO., NEW YORK, N.Y.
COPELAND (ROBERT) & BEIDERHASE (BERNARD D.) 1851–1855
(LOCATION UNKNOWN) 1856–1859
BERNARD D. BEIDERHASE 1859–1860
EMPLOYEE OF JOHN R. WENDT 1861–186?
PARTNER IN JOHN R. WENDT & CO. 186?–1871
CAPITAL BEHIND WM. BOGERT & CO. 1866–1874
B. D. BEIDERHASE & CO. 1871–1874

Bernard Beiderhase (d. 1874) was a German immigrant who throughout his lifetime maintained strong ties to other German silversmiths working in the United States. The 1859–60

New York City directory lists Beiderhase as a chaser. As early as 1851 he was in partnership with Robert Copeland, running a modest-sized silverware manufactory. It is listed in the New York State Industrial Census of 1855 as having a capital of $5,000 and fabricating 6,000 ounces of silver per annum for an annual value of $10,000. By the early 1860s, he was employed in the shop of John R. Wendt. By 1866 he had an interest in the Wendt firm, along with Charles Witteck. Beiderhase was also wealthy enough to provide capital for the newly formed firm of Wm. Bogert & Co. between 1866 and 1874.

Beiderhase received design patents for at least six flatware patterns, the first being granted in 1868 when he was with Wendt & Co. Additionally, he and Witteck jointly held patents for the production of "satin" and "pearl" finishes. During 1873 and 1874, Beiderhase Co. was sued by Tiffany & Co. for patent infringements. The first action involved the patents held on satin and pearl finishes. Tiffany & Co. had purchased an earlier metal stippling patent and claimed exclusive right. The second action challenged Beiderhase's Design Patent no. 5,876 for a flatware pattern named *Bird*, stating that the design infringed on the *Japanese* pattern patented by Edward C. Moore. Tiffany & Co. prevailed in both legal actions, which resulted in injunctions and financial penalties against Beiderhase & Co.

WILLIAM BOGERT, ALBANY, NEWBURGH, AND NEW YORK, N.Y.
WORKING 1839–1881

William (d. 1881) was one of at least three silversmithing sons of Nicholas J. Bogert and the one who achieved the most prominence in the American silverware industry. Little is known of his early history. Even the year of his birth is not certain. Evidence suggests he is the "William Bogert, silversmith," working in Albany in the late 1830s and the early 1840s. From there he left to work in New York City with William Forbes, a member of the extensive Forbes silversmithing family. Because the Bogerts and the Forbes were tied together by marriage in at least two instances, and because William's father, Nicholas, had apprenticed with W. G. Forbes in earlier years, this move is not surprising. Furthermore, William Van Gilder Forbes, another of the Forbes family silversmiths, is buried in the Bogert family plot in St. Andrew's Cemetery, near Walden, New York.

By the mid 1850s Bogert relocated to Newburgh, New York, going into business with John Gordon, his brother-in-law and a former apprentice of his father. At the beginning there was another partner named Eaton. It is reported that the partnership was not particularly successful, and after a time, Bogert became the sole proprietor. Nevertheless, during this period he and his partners were producing items for some of the leading retail houses, including Ball, Black & Co.

Some of Bogert's most important work was undoubtedly done when he returned to New York City in 1866. Here he bought out the estate of Charles Grosjean, a leading silversmith who had produced heavily for Tiffany & Co. At this time his firm was styled William Bogert & Co., the "& Co." being Bernard D. Beiderhase. Beiderhase was a talented designer and

silversmith in his own right and was already a partner in the prominent firm of John R. Wendt & Co. Bogert assumed Grosjean's former role, producing exclusively for Tiffany & Co. and manufacturing expensive, high-end silverware. Often figural in style and generally heavy in weight, it frequently was decorated with exquisitely detailed castings (see fig. 6.12). In 1869 Tiffany & Co. formed its own silver works, and many of its former suppliers, including Bogert, were cast aside.

By the 1870s William had entered into partnership with one of the other giants of the New York City silversmithing scene—John Polhamus. Their relationship does not appear to have been a happy one, since Bogert later sued Polhamus. Polhamus died in 1877, shortly after judgment was entered against him. Bogert followed a few short years later, passing on Christmas Day, 1881. A curious memorial still exists—a four-sided, silver-tipped, brass-bodied, wooden-based pyramid—which bears the inscription "In Memory of William Bogert, a true friend and faithful artisan, whose work was excelled by no silversmith of his day. This model pyramid is a part of his work made shortly before his death December 25, 1881." This piece is in a private collection.

ZALMON BOSTWICK, NEW YORK, N.Y.
WORKING 1846–1852

A directory advertisement of 1847 indicates that Zalmon Bostwick (d. 1852) was "Successor to Thompson." While several Thompsons and Thomsons exist in the New York City listings, the one which best suits as predecessor is William Thomson, manufacturing silversmith, last found in 1844–45. Bostwick's first listing is in 1846–47. The working dates of the other possibilities eliminate them.

The Industrial Census of 1850 gives information for "E. Bostwick." This is certainly Zalmon. It lists his trade as silversmith and shows capital amounting to $3,000. Motive power was "hand," and he employed four men. The annual value of production amounted to $14,000 of silverware goods. From this census information and other advertisements, we know that Bostwick was producing flatware and hollowware and might be classified as a medium-sized producer.

Although he was manufacturing silverware a relatively short time—six years—a fair number of his silver pieces survive. From these it is evident that he was making sophisticated objects (see fig. 3.10).

BUTLER, MCCARTY & CO., PHILADELPHIA, PA.
BUTLER (FRANKLIN) & MCCARTY (EDWARD) 1849–1868
BUTLER, MCCARTY & CO. 1868–1876
MCCARTY & HURLBURT (HENRY O.) 1876–?

Information regarding this firm is scant. Franklin Butler, watchmaker and jeweler, appears in the Philadelphia directories as early as 1846. Edward McCarty is listed as a silversmith beginning in 1845. In 1849 or early 1850 the two entered into the partnership of Butler & McCarty for the purposes of retailing watches and jewelry and manufacturing silverware and small silver items. They appear in the Federal Industrial Census of

1850 as fabricating 9,000 ounces of silver per annum, resulting in the production of $13,500 worth of silverware and $4,500 worth of pencil cases and other items. The firm also produced thimbles, as indicated in an 1855 directory listing. The figures for the Industrial Census of 1860 show a firm approximately one-half its size of 1850. But, as a result of the economic boom caused by the Civil War, it had become considerably more prosperous by the mid 1860s. In 1868 the firm took in Henry O. Hurlburt, and became Butler, McCarty & Co. Evidence suggests the purpose was to add capital for expansion. Butler died in an accident in 1870, but the business was continued under the same name until 1 January 1876, when it became McCarty & Hurlburt.

J. E. CALDWELL & CO., PHILADELPHIA, PA.
JAMES E. CALDWELL 1839–1843
BENNETT & CALDWELL 1843–1848
J. E. CALDWELL & CO. 1848–?
J. E. CALDWELL CO. ?–PRESENT

James Emmett Caldwell (1813–1881) was born in Poughkeepsie, New York, where he was apprenticed to Peter P. Hayes at an early age. Under Hayes's tutelage he learned the jewelry trade and specialized as a watchmaker. One of his obituaries reports that, for a short time after completing his training, he was employed in New York City. By the mid 1830s Caldwell had arrived in Philadelphia, and in 1839 he went into business for himself. For a time he was in partnership with a Mr. Bennett. (There is some confusion as to the year of origin of the partnership; it may have started some years earlier than listed above.) From 1 May 1848 until May 1856, the "& Co." consisted of John C. Farr, who became a leading watchmaker and jeweler in Philadelphia. Thereafter, various other partners were admitted into the firm, resulting in several changes in the ownership through the years.

For a time the firm engaged in the manufacture of silver flatware and hollowware. The evidence for this assertion rests on a Caldwell advertisement of the early 1850s. Just how long this portion of the business was maintained is uncertain. It does not appear to have been a lengthy period, since by the end of the 1850s the word "manufacturer" in respect to silverware is dropped from advertisements. Other records indicate that for the greater portion of its history the company was a retailer, selling the goods of silver manufacturers or acting as agent to have goods made up on special order.

By the 1850s Caldwell's, with Bailey & Co. as its competitor, shared the patronage of the wealthy citizens and visitors of Philadelphia. In 1868, flush with the profits from the Civil War period, the firm erected a marble palace at 902 Chestnut Street. Within a couple of months of opening, it was totally gutted by fire as a result of burglars trying to blow up a safe. Losses exceeded $1 million. However, some of the safes still held their goods undamaged, and the firm was heavily insured. Within a few months it rebuilt at the same location and reopened to a profitable trade.

The firm reportedly initiated new business practices in Philadelphia. One of these was the "one-price system." Previously, prices had been variable and subject to bargaining. Additionally, Caldwell's joined the movement to conduct business during shorter and more regular hours. The store also implemented a policy in which salesmen waited in readiness to serve the customer and did not "push" a sale. This provided a gentleness and refinement that was uncommon enough to be worthy of comment in period documents.

Business locations for the firm were: 163 Chestnut Street (1839–44), 140 Chestnut (1844–58), 822 Chestnut (1858–68), 902 Chestnut (1868–1916), and Chestnut and Juniper (1916–present).

CHARTERS, CANN & DUNN, NEW YORK, N.Y.
CHARTERS (THOMAS, JR.), CANN (JOHN) &
DUNN (DAVID) 1848–1856
CANN & DUNN 1856–1860
JOHN CANN 1860–1863

As far as is known, the firm did not engage in the production of flatware. An advertisement for Cann & Dunn in the Brooklyn directory of 1858 states: "They will be prepared to fulfill, as usual, all orders from the Trade for Vases, Urns, Salvers, Pitchers, Tea and Coffee Services, Trumpets, Plates, Goblets, Cups, & c." Judging from earlier material, the former firm of Charters, Cann & Dunn manufactured much the same line of goods. This assertion is also supported by surviving examples, the firm's manufacturing mark not being found on flatware.

Cann & Dunn was a prominent firm distinguished for its quality. It was often responsible for silverware given as public presentations. Its manufacturing logo, still frequently found, is *(lion)* CC&D *(arm and hammer)*.

ALBERT COLES, NEW YORK, N.Y
WORKING 1835–1877

Albert Coles (1815–1885) was a major manufacturer of flatware. In addition, he produced numerous other forms, including cups, goblets, napkin rings, snuff and tobacco boxes, match boxes, portemonnaies, bouquet holders, children's rattles, nutmeg graters, and coffin plates. His business was steady and prosperous. Early on he specialized in fancy and hollow-handled knives with silver blades, such as those used for butter, tea, and dessert. The quality of his work in this area was acknowledged by the American Institute, which awarded him the gold medal for his knives in several annual exhibitions. Coles also sold his silver: he had a large retail establishment at the location of his factory at 4 and 6 Liberty Place. As so often was the case in the nineteenth century, members of Coles's family were allied with the trade. His son Albert L. was a silversmith with the firm. His daughter Mary C. married the wealthy heir of George W. Platt, refiner and jeweler, who owned the building which housed Coles's store and manufactory. His nephews Gilbert E. (Coles & Reynolds) and William L. (Coles & Vancourt) were trained in his factory and were in his employ at times during their careers.

Coles is sometimes found listed as Albert Cole. This is incorrect and undoubtedly stems from an erroneous city directory listing transcribed by earlier researchers. A genealogical search reveals that Albert's ancestor Robert arrived in Massachusetts Bay Colony in 1630 and that the family name has always included the *s*.

FRANCIS W. COOPER, NEW YORK, N.Y.
WORKING 1842–1891
COOPER (FRANCIS W.) & FISHER (RICHARD) 1858–1862

Francis Cooper was a small manufacturer of solid silverware; his products are seldom seen today. Nevertheless, he was a skillful workman whose goods were retailed by such houses as Ball, Black & Co. and Tiffany & Co. Judging from surviving examples, he specialized in fancy presentation goblets and cups and in ecclesiastical plate. He did, however, manufacture a wide range of hollowware and flatware. According to an 1876 advertisement, his product line included waiters, pitchers, tea sets, communion services, cups, napkins rings, ladles, spoons, and forks. Many of these wares probably bear only retailer marks and thus go unrecognized as Cooper's work.

For a few years he was in partnership with Richard Fisher. Cooper was the practical workman, while Fisher supplied the capital. Although Cooper was certainly old enough to retire, the termination of his business was hastened by a disastrous fire late in 1890.

SAMUEL T. CROSBY, BOSTON, MASS.
CROSBY & BROWN 1849–1853
SAMUEL T. CROSBY 1854–1859
SAMUEL T. CROSBY & CO. 1859–1861
CROSBY, HUNNEWELL & MORSE (HENRY D.) 1861–1864
CROSBY & MORSE 1864–1869
CROSBY, MORSE & FOSS (CHARLES M.) 1869–1875
CROSBY & FOSS 1875–?

A report of 1856 states that Samuel T. Crosby was the successor of Obadiah Rich, who retired and transferred his interest in the establishment in 1849. Rich and his successors were located at 69 Washington Street until 1861. Directory listings and advertisements indicate that the earlier firms manufactured silverware. But by the early 1860s, this status is at least partly, if not completely, in doubt. Later advertisements appear to be those of a general retail jeweler. In 1868 Crosby & Morse emphasized its expertise in fine diamonds, claiming to be "the only diamond cutters in the country," and several subsequent listings indexed the company under "Diamonds."

DOMINICK & HAFF, NEW YORK, N.Y.
GALE (WILLIAM), DOMINICK & HAFF 1870–1872
DOMINICK (HENRY BLANCHARD) & HAFF (LEROY B.) 1872–1928
ACQUIRED BY REED & BARTON 1928

This firm was heir to the famous silversmithing house of William Gale, and manufactured a full line of goods. An advertisement of 1877 states that they were "makers of wares in sterling silver, also fancy goods and novelties in silver, including bangles in endless variety of styles and prices, dime holders, dress holders, worsted holders, chatelaines, purses, bachelor's pin cushions, scarf pins, lace pins, belt buckles, combs, and c."

The firm's reputation for quality design and excellent execution is well deserved. Some of its "hammered" silver and appliqué work was among the best in the industry, much of it almost certainly custom ordered. Its flatware was held in the highest regard. In 1880 Dominick & Haff purchased the flatware dies of Adams & Shaw, which had earlier acquired the dies of the firm of J. R. Wendt & Co. and its successors. Many of these patterns were still active and popular even though they were nearly twenty years old. Additionally, the firm itself introduced substantial numbers of new patterns. Almost without exception, the designs are distinctive, the die work superior, and much of the output of substantial weight. After 1900 some advertisements state that Dominick & Haff's wares were "made in medium and heavy weights only."

WILLIAM B. DURGIN, CONCORD, N.H.
WILLIAM B. DURGIN 1853–1898
WILLIAM B. DURGIN CO. (INC.) 1898–1905
DURGIN DIVISION OF GORHAM AFTER 1905

At sixteen, William Durgin (1833–1905) left his home in the mountains of New Hampshire to seek employment in Boston. He initially tried to apprentice in the jewelry business, but was finally bound to Newell Harding to learn the art of the silversmith. Although he returned to work in New Hampshire upon completion of his term, his ties to Boston remained strong. Over time, he drew a number of skilled workmen from that city and marketed great amounts of his goods through Boston retailers, particularly Palmer & Batchelder.

Evidently New Hampshire afforded him significant opportunities. It was reported in an article appearing in the *Jewelers' Circular-Weekly* of 5 February 1919 that upon his return Durgin bought out both of the jewelers making silver spoons in Concord. Soon after, he bought the tools of another manufacturer in Claremont, New Hampshire, "thus giving himself a clear field in his native State." Although, with limited capital, he made but a modest start, his progress was rapid. By the 1860s his was a prosperous concern producing sophisticated, die-struck patterns. In time, it became one of the largest manufacturers of full lines of flatware and hollowware in the country and was known for the high quality of its goods, which were principally made for the trade.

During 1903 and 1904 the firm, expanding rapidly and pressed for space, constructed a massive new plant in Concord. By this time, it employed three hundred men and was using approximately 12,000 ounces of silver per week. Durgin is reported to have given enormous amounts of energy to the planning and construction of the new works. But in the next year, 1905, both he and his son, George F., died. The firm passed out of the Durgin family and was acquired by the Gorham Company.

FORD & TUPPER, NEW YORK, N.Y.
FORD (PATRICK), TUPPER (JONAS) & BEHAN (WILLIAM)
1866–1867
FORD & TUPPER 1867–1874
PATRICK FORD 1874–1881

Patrick Ford and William Behan had previously been in the employ of the Gale firm. Joining with Tupper, they operated a jewelry store at 609 Broadway, a prime location in the midst of the most prominent shopping area of the city. The bulk of their trade was in gold and silver goods, including silverplated wares. As far as is presently known, the firm did not manufacture flatware or hollowware but retailed the silver goods of others.

The Ford & Tupper retail stamp is commonly found, suggesting that, in its day, substantial sales were made through this house.

WILLIAM GALE, NEW YORK, N.Y.
GALE & STICKLER (JOHN) 1821–1823
JOHN L. & W. GALE 1825–1827
GALE & MOSELEY 1828–1833
GALE, WOOD (JACOB) & HUGHES (JOSEPH H.) 1833–1845
GALE & HAYDEN (NATHANIEL)* 1845–1849
WM. GALE, SON & CO. 1850–1853
WM. GALE & SON 1853–1859
GALE & WILLIS (JOHN R., SON-IN-LAW OF WILLIAM, SR.) 1859–1862
WM. GALE & SON 1862–1867
WILLIAM GALE, JR. & CO. 1867–1868
GALE, NORTH & DOMINICK 1868–1869
GALE & CORNING (EDWARD) 1869–1870
GALE, DOMINICK & HAFF 1870–1872
DOMINICK & HAFF 1872–1928

Billheads and advertising cards of this firm indicate that it was established in 1821 and was for a while perhaps the largest silverware manufacturer in the country. Evidence suggests that William Gale, Sr. (1799–1864), was related to silversmiths Jesse and John L. Gale, listed in the early nineteenth-century New York City directories. For example, cemetery records of the Gale family plot in Greenwood, Brooklyn, show a Jesse Gale who was relocated from a cemetery in the Bloomingdale area of New York City, as well as a John Lee Gale, presumably a son, who died at the age of 18 years and 4 months.

On 7 December 1826, William Gale, Sr., received a patent for roller dies which gave him leadership in the industry. His technique involved engraving patterns on steel rollers, which were then used to impress full designs on flatware. It rendered obsolete the older system of dies, similar to those used in a coining press, by creating a much less expensive and easier process for manufacturing ornamented spoons and forks. With such a product line, Gale was able to supply the likes of the prestigious Marquand & Co. of New York City and prominent jewelers in the South who catered to the southern elite. By the 1850s Gale was a wealthy man, having made money not only in the silverware business but also as a result of his ventures in the rapidly rising New York real estate market. By the time he died in 1867, his estate was valued at several hundred thousand dollars, a sum which would translate into many millions today.

William Gale, Jr. (1825–1885), carried on a prosperous business for some time after his father's retirement and death. The Federal Industrial Census of 1870 for the partnership of Gale & Corning reports an annual product of $120,000 and thirty-five employees—still a large operation, though somewhat diminished from earlier years. William Gale, Jr., died at Pittsford, Vermont.

*Nathaniel Hayden was in the silverware and jewelry business in New York City and Charleston, S.C., during the mid nineteenth century. While keeping some of his interests in the trade, he also established himself as a wealthy banker and broker.

JOSEPH HEINRICH, NEW YORK, N.Y., AND PARIS, FRANCE
JOSEPH HEINRICH, MOLDER 1880
JOSEPH HEINRICH, FINISHER 1885
JOSEPH HEINRICH'S 1897–CA. 1925

Joseph Heinrich was a prolific copperware maker who is virtually unknown today. In the 1880s he apparently worked as a metal molder and finisher in New York City and maintained residences at 644 East 11th Street (1880) and 606 East 11th Street (1885). Research by Margaret C. Caldwell indicates that between 1897 and the late 1920s, he was working in New York making copperware. After 1902 he maintained two locations, one at 948 Broadway (opposite the Flatiron Building) and another at 227 West 29th Street. The latter was probably a workshop and perhaps a wholesale showroom. In 1934 only Heinrich's home address is listed.

At the turn of the century, Joseph Heinrich's shop was apparently well known. Not only were his wares retailed by many prominent merchants, including Black, Starr & Frost; Cowell & Hubbard; Shreve, Crump & Low Co.; and Tiffany & Co., but Heinrich also advertised in *House Beautiful*. In the December 1907 issue (23:1, p. 49), for example, his firm's advertisement reads: "EXQUISITE CHAFING DISHES / The most complete and artistic stock of fine Chafing Dishes, Copper Table service and cooking utensils; Caseroles [*sic*] and Metal Dishes of every variety may be found in my new store. Shipment can be made for Christmas gifts, if ordered now. Write for circular and prices." Pictured is a rabbit chafing dish like that in fig. 9.3. Pitchers and egg coddlers were also made in this style. A wide variety of other copper and silver objects were produced, ranging from complex punch bowls (see fig. 6.68) to simple coffee services. Most Heinrich pieces bear only the mark COPPER & SILVER and a retailer's label or mark. Some also bear numbers denoting sizes. A few, however, are actually marked by Heinrich. A simple coffee set probably dating from the 1920s, in the author's collection, is impressed: JOS. HEINRICHS / PARIS + NEW YORK / PURE COPPER. A rabbit chafing dish with copper underplate and serving utensils belonging to Margaret Caldwell is marked: JOS. HEINRICHS / PARIS + NEW YORK and PURE COPPER / STERLING SILVER. The burner is stamped: PAT APPLIED FOR / PAR AUG 2, 1904 / MAGIC (in script). The patent refers to no. 766,618 for an improved fluid burner for chafing dishes. Although all the marks say "Heinrichs," his advertisements refer to "Heinrich's." At present nothing is known about his Paris operation.

JONES, BALL & POOR, BOSTON, MASS.
JOHN B. JONES 18?–1839
JONES, LOW & BALL 1839–1846
JONES, BALL & POOR 1846–1853
JONES, BALL & CO. 1853–1855
JONES, SHREVE, BROWN & CO. 1855–1857
SHREVE, BROWN & CO. 1857–1860
SHREVE, STANWOOD & CO. 1860–1869
SHREVE, CRUMP & LOW 1869–1888
SHREVE, CRUMP & LOW CO. 1888–PRESENT

In its early years this firm was a manufacturer of silverware. Just how and when it gave up this portion of its business and devoted itself solely to the retail trade is not precisely known. Judging from a chronological series of billheads, the change does not appear to have occurred before 1860. The firm's production was of high quality, and many of its goods were purchased by rich Bostonians. Jones, Ball & Co. was among the silverware "manufacturers" which exhibited at the 1853 New York Crystal Palace Exhibition, where its wares were described as "remarkable for their chaste style and for substantial workmanship."

KENNARD & JENKS, BOSTON, MASS.
LEWIS E. JENKS 1872–1876
KENNARD (EDWARD PARRY) & JENKS 1876–1879
KENNARD & CO. 1879–1880
SOLD TO THE GORHAM CO. 1880

Lewis Jenks had previously been in the employ of Bigelow Bros. & Kennard and its successor, Bigelow, Kennard & Co., retail jewelers. About 1872 he left, taking up the manufacture of fine silverware. In 1876 Edward Kennard joined the firm. Edward's father was Martin Parry Kennard, a wealthy and prominent Bostonian and a principal of the house of Bigelow, Kennard & Co. It is logical to conclude that his father's store sold some of the firm's products. In 1880 Gorham purchased Kennard & Co. and moved its tools and machinery to Providence.

PETER L. (LEWIS) KRIDER, PHILADELPHIA, PA.
WORKING 1851–1888
KRIDER (PETER L.) & BIDDLE (JOHN W.) 1858–1871
PETER L. KRIDER CO.
(AUGUST WEBER, PARTNER) 1888–1910

According to a trade journal obituary, Peter Krider (1821–1895) was born in Philadelphia and worked on a farm until he was fourteen. During the next six years he served an apprenticeship with John Curry, a local silversmith. For a period following, he worked at the factory of R. & W. Wilson until he was able to establish his own business in 1851. Besides producing large amounts of solid silver flatware and hollowware, Krider was also an important manufacturer of society and exposition medals which were struck in various metals, including gold, silver, and bronze. That this was a fair-sized firm is indicated by the Federal Industrial Censuses of 1860, 1870, and 1880 and a short description of the premises in *Philadelphia's Leading Industries* (1866). According to these sources, the business was well capitalized and employed as many as thirty-five skilled workmen. Its products were distributed over a wide geographical area, a large trade being conducted with Kentucky and the southern states at one time. Krider's reputation as a decent and upstanding businessman was so high that he was known in the trade as "Honest Peter."

JOHN CHANDLER MOORE, NEW YORK, N.Y.
WORKING 1832–1851

John Chandler Moore was born about 1803, and we can assume that he died about 1855, when he disappears from the directory listings. In the Population Census of 1850 for Kings County, Williamsburgh (Brooklyn), John C. Moore, silversmith, is reported to be forty-seven years of age and to have been born in New Jersey. His wife Margaret is forty-six; his sons Edward, John, and Thomas are twenty-three, thirteen, and seven, respectively; and his daughter Mary is sixteen. The rest of the family were all born in New York. In the same year the Industrial Census informs us that he was a fairly large manufacturer, having $8,000 in capital in the business, an annual product of $30,000, and twenty-two employees. From 1856 forward, the silverware firm is listed in directories as E. C. Moore. However, in 1860, the firm is still listed under John's name in the Industrial Census, where it is recorded as having capital of $60,000, an annual production value of $100,000, and fifty employees. It is odd that the census still listed the firm under his name, if he indeed had faded from the scene five years earlier. But it is not beyond one's imagination that the firm might have retained the old name in some capacity.

Moore played an important role in connection with the house of Tiffany & Co. Besides supplying Tiffany's with large quantities of silver, it is said that he made a special agreement with the company prior to his retirement in 1851. It is clear that Moore and his son Edward Chandler had special privileges with the retailer. But one should remember that until this silverware manufactory was acquired by Tiffany's in 1869, there were numerous other quality manufacturers who helped to fill the silver cases at Tiffany's, among them William Bogert, Henry Hebbard, and John Polhamus.

MORGAN MORGANS, JR., NEW YORK, N.Y.
MONTGOMERY & CO. (MORGAN MORGANS, JR.) 1877
MORGAN MORGANS, JR., 1878–1883
ACQUIRED BY GEORGE W. SHIEBLER 1883

Morgan Morgans, Jr., came from an affluent New York family, his father, Morgan Morgans, Sr., being a particularly prominent and wealthy man. Directory listings indicate that they owned a large foundry and produced hardware. In 1877 Morgans, Jr., provided the capital to buy the machinery, tools, fixtures, and stock of Albert Coles. He did this in partnership with Samuel Montgomery, one of Coles's salesmen, under the firm name Montgomery & Co. At the beginning of 1878 he assumed complete control. Morgans, Jr., held at least two design patents. One was for fire fenders, presumably designed for the use of the family foundry business. The other, no. 10,436 of 5 February 1878, was for a flatware pattern named *Cupid*. The pattern is usually assumed to be one made by Coles. This error no doubt occurred because Morgans continued to use Coles's identifying mark, consisting of *AC (eagle and head)*, as his own. However, the firm was not a financial success, and Morgans was forced to dispose of it in 1883. George W. Shiebler purchased the business and consolidated it with his rapidly growing silverware manufacturing operations.

AUGUSTUS ROGERS, NEW YORK, N.Y. AND BOSTON, MASS.

AUGUSTUS ROGERS (NEW YORK) 1830–1831
AUGUSTUS ROGERS (BOSTON) 1840–1852
ROGERS (AUGUSTUS) & WENDT (JOHN R.) 1853–1857
ROGERS, WENDT & LEMME (FERDINAND) 1857–1858
ROGERS, WENDT & CO. 1859
ROGERS, WENDT & WILKINSON 1860
AUGUSTUS ROGERS 1860–1871

A contemporary report, published in 1856, states that Rogers (d. 1871) established himself in Boston in 1840, after working for some years in New York. It also reports that Rogers & Wendt were "said to be the largest exclusive manufacturers of hollow silver-ware in Boston, and probably in the Union." Although employed by Rogers, Wendt did not own an interest until about 1853. By 1856 the partnership of Rogers & Wendt engaged about forty employees, a substantial number for the time, and "manufacture[d] every variety of hollow-ware, tea service, urns, pitchers, goblets, & c., from the plainest to the costliest and most highly ornamented." Around 1852 there also existed a partnership in the names of Rogers & Langdon (William G.); it became Rogers, Wendt & Langdon in 1856. Probably a separate enterprise devoted to the manufacture of watch cases, this firm was dissolved in 1857. Little is known of Langdon and Lemme or the roles they played in the businesses. In 1859 Wendt separated from Rogers and worked as an independent silversmith in Boston for a short while before relocating in New York City, where he had a special relationship with Ball, Black & Co. Rogers continued to work under his own name until his death in 1871.

JOSEPH SEYMOUR, SYRACUSE, N.Y.

JOSEPH SEYMOUR (PRE-SYRACUSE) 1835–1846
NORTON & SEYMOUR 1849–1853
NORTON, SEYMOUR & CO. 1854–1857
JOSEPH SEYMOUR & CO. 1857–1870
JOSEPH SEYMOUR & SON 1870–1879
JOSEPH SEYMOUR & SONS 1879
JOSEPH SEYMOUR & SONS CO. 1879–1898
JOSEPH SEYMOUR MFG. CO. 1898–1905

Evidence suggests that Joseph Seymour (1815–1887) was the most important factor in the growth of the Syracuse silver manufacturing industry. After serving an apprenticeship with his stepfather, Joseph Harper, he spent a period of time working in the large silver manufactory of the Rogers Brothers in Hartford, Connecticut. There he was exposed to the complexities of the latest machinery and the methods of mass production. The early years of his career are vague, but we know that in 1846 he arrived in Syracuse, having worked in New York City and Utica. In Syracuse he was employed to superintend the relatively new silver manufactory of Willard & Hawley. Seymour associated himself with Benjamin R. Norton, a local jeweler, to help build his own silverware manufacturing business. In 1854 they admitted David Hotchkiss to the firm and changed the name to Norton, Seymour & Co. From 1857 onward, Seymour had direct control of the business in which he held an interest. Like other Syracuse firms, Seymour's specialized in flatware production. Seymour held two design patents for spoonwork and one for flatware manufacturing.

After experiencing difficulty in the early 1890s, the firm was awarded the contract to produce the official souvenir spoon for the Pan-American Exposition of 1901. Contemporary sources estimated that the firm would produce over one million spoons for the event. Nevertheless, about 1905 it was forced to close.

GEORGE B. SHARP, PHILADELPHIA, PA.
WORKING 1850–1874

A short obituary relates that Sharp was born in Ireland in 1819 and immigrated to the United States while still young. Upon his arrival he apprenticed in the jewelery and silverware trade. He died in Philadelphia on 22 February 1904 of Bright's disease, a type of kidney failure. This was a common cause of death in the trade, being associated with exposure to mercury, cyanide, and related chemicals necessary to the manufacturing of jewelry and silverware.

Sharp first appears as an independent manufacturer in the 1850 Philadelphia directories and is associated with William Sharp, presumed to be a brother. They are listed twice in the 1850 Federal Industrial Census, once as a silver manufactory producing silverware to the value of $15,000 per annum and again as a jewelry manufactory producing $5,000 worth of product annually. In 1852 or 1853, Sharp entered into the exclusive employ of the great Philadelphia retail house Bailey & Co. He remained with it until the mid 1860s, when he resumed silverware manufacturing on his own.

Sharp is noted for the high quality of his production, much of which was retailed to the wealthy citizens of Philadelphia. A number of his innovative flatware patterns were granted design patents. He also produced silverware designed by his employee Augustus Conradt. The Federal Industrial Census of 1870 shows a well capitalized firm ($75,000) with an annual product of over $100,000 and forty-five employees. But in 1874, just a few years later, the firm failed, a victim of the Panic of 1873. There are some indications that Sharp continued in business on a limited basis as a jeweler and silversmith until he retired around 1880.

There is a serious error in the current literature regarding Sharp's manufacturing mark. His own mark is a pair of lions flanking and looking inward on the letter *s*. The mark sometimes attributed to him, which consists of *(lion) s (shield)*, is a sterling standard mark exclusive to the firm of Bailey & Co.

GEORGE W. SHIEBLER, NEW YORK, N.Y.
GEORGE W. SHIEBLER 1876–1891
GEORGE W. SHIEBLER & CO. (BROTHER WILLIAM)
1891–1910

George Shiebler (1846–1920) was born to a German immigrant family living in Baltimore, Maryland. His father, Andrew, and mother, Christine (née Fox), had several other children. Two older brothers, Andrew K. and William, also entered the New York jewelry and silverware trades and all achieved a great measure of success.

George received his early education in Washington, D.C., where he was, for a time, employed as a Western Union messenger. When still a young man he began working as a salesman in a jewelry manufacturing business which specialized in gold chains. Soon thereafter he became a junior partner, the firm becoming Hodenpyl, Tunnison & Shiebler. In 1876 he bought out the business of Coles & Reynolds and started to manufacture silverware. Within a few years he acquired the tools and dies of a number of older firms, including those of John Polhamus in 1877 and Morgan Morgans in 1883. Shiebler continued to manufacture their flatware patterns and product lines, and added many of his own. Soon he became one of the largest producers of flatware and novelties in the country. The firm also manufactured hollowware, although on a more limited basis, at its Brooklyn manufactory.

Shiebler was a designer of great note and originality. He was known as "a man of innate artistic ability and with a love of the beautiful which became so manifest in his product that his wares attained a distinct success." He held a number of design patents for flatware patterns and for souvenir spoons. And his idea to revive the use of "medallion work" in jewelry and silverware had so favorable an outcome that domestic as well as European producers soon copied him. His energy and artistry manifested themselves even in his large Park Slope mansion in Brooklyn, which he personally designed and decorated, incorporating many novel features for comfort and convenience. Shiebler was especially proud of the chute which led from the street to the refrigerator in the kitchen, through which ice was delivered daily.

In 1910 Shiebler dissolved his firm and retired as a manufacturer. What happened to the tools and dies of George W. Shiebler & Co. is uncertain. There are reports that Gorham purchased a number of them. At least one set of Shiebler's flatware dies, *American Beauty*, went to the Mauser Mfg. Co.

During his lifetime Shiebler contributed to many private and public organizations and served as both director and officer of the New York Jewelers' Association. Following the sale of his firm, he spent the last ten years of his life employed by Gorham. Shiebler is buried in Greenwood Cemetery, Brooklyn, New York.

TIFFT & WHITING, NEW YORK, N.Y.
TIFFT (ALBERT C.) & WHITING (WILLIAM DEAN) 1840–1853
WHITING & GOODING (& CO.) 1853–1858
WHITING, FESSENDEN (H.B.) & COWAN (WILLIAM M.)
1858–1859
TIFFT, WHITING & CO. 1859–1864
WHITING, COWAN & BOWEN (SIMEON) 1864–1866
WHITING MFG. CO. 1866–1924

The firm originated in 1840 as a jewelry manufacturer, but in 1847 commenced the manufacture of silverware at its works in North Attleboro, Massachusetts. W. D. Whiting, the younger partner, had apprenticed with the former firm of Draper & Tifft. In 1853 Tifft retired a wealthy man, selling out to Whiting. At this time the manufacture of jewelry was discontinued in favor of the exclusive production of flatware and hollowware. The firm continued to exist under various partnerships until Tifft reentered it in 1859. When he retired again in 1864, the firm took other partners until the reorganization of 1866, which formed the Whiting Mfg. Co. Reportedly, Tifft & Whiting took a "leading position" in the manufacture of silver tableware "through the application of improved machinery."

JAMES S. VANCOURT, NEW YORK, N.Y.
WORKING 1845–1861
COLES (WILLIAM L.) & VANCOURT 1848–1852

James S. Vancourt first appears in the New York City directory in 1845 as an independent silversmith at 4 Little Green Street. This site was adjacent to the silver manufactory of Albert Coles at 6 Little Green. Coles employed his nephew William L., who formed a partnership with Vancourt in 1848. The partners were "spoon makers," a term indicating the production of a general line of flatware. They specialized in hollow-handled knives, especially those used for butter, fruit, and dessert. A Vancourt advertisement from the mid 1850s states: "Butter, Fish, Fruit, Dessert & Pie Knives, Crumb Scrapers, Ice Cream Slicers, & c. on hand and made to order." The technical knowledge to produce hollow-handled knives was undoubtedly transferred to the firm through the shop of Albert Coles, who excelled in their production.

The manufacturing marks of the firms show close similarities to that of Albert Coles. Whereas Coles used *(eagle) AC (head)*, that of Coles & Vancourt is *(eagle) C&V (head)* and that of Vancourt *(eagle) V (head)*.* Such close ties suggest that Vancourt was apprenticed to or employed by Albert Coles before setting up his own business.

*This mark has been incorrectly attributed to George C. Vaughn of Buffalo, New York.

JOHN T. VANSANT, PHILADELPHIA, PA.
JOHN T. VANSANT MFG. CO. 1881–1884
JOHN T. VANSANT & BRO. 1884–1886
VANSANT SILVER CO., LTD. 1886–1892

The Vansant firms were relatively small. The succession of name changes was a result of financial difficulties which required complete reorganizations. The superintendent and manager of the Vansant Silver Co., Ltd., was Stephen E. Vansant. In 1892 the firm was acquired by Simons, Bro. & Co., another Philadelphia manufacturer prominent in the production of thimbles, cane heads, and novelties. An undated advertising card states that "Simons, Bro. & Co. desire to announce the addition to their business of the manufacturing of silver ware—solid & plated—lately carried on by the Vansant Man'f. Co. A large assortment of choice goods on hand and new and original designs constantly added to stock."

The firms' output included substantial amounts of flatware employing broad, bright-cut engraved patterns, as well as outstanding and unusual medallion work.

JAMES WATTS, PHILADELPHIA, PA.
JAMES WATTS 1832–1839
J. & W. (WILLIAM) WATTS 1839–1852
JAS. WATTS & CO. 1853–1859
WATTS (JAMES) & HARPER (HENRY) 1859–1862
JAMES WATTS 1862–1882
JAMES WATTS & SON (JAMES & JAMES W.) 1882–1887
JAMES WATTS (JAMES W.) 1887–?

Despite its lengthy manufacturing history in Philadelphia, scarcely anything is known about this firm. In general, it supplied silver to the retail trade and therefore did not maintain a high public profile. However, it is known that Watts was a native of Ireland. Although it does not appear in the Philadelphia directories until 1835, advertisements of the 1860s clearly state that the firm was established in 1832. The discrepancy of several years suggests that Watts might have taken over the business of another, the practice being to advertise a firm as having originated on the earliest date of its earliest predecessor.

Watts was a major mid-nineteenth-century silverware manufacturer, especially of flatware. The Federal Industrial Census of 1850 reports that he had a capital of $42,000, employed twenty-two people, and fabricated an annual product worth $60,400. By contrast, his listing in 1880 shows a capital of only $9,000 with six employees and an annual product of $16,000. His wares are marked with a horse over a chevron.

JOHN R. WENDT & CO., BOSTON, MASS. AND NEW YORK, N.Y.
ROGERS & WENDT 1853–1857
ROGERS, WENDT & LEMME 1857–1858
JOHN R. WENDT 1859–1860
ROGERS, WENDT & WILKINSON 1860
J. R. WENDT & CO. 1860–1871

Johann Rudolph Wendt (1826–1907) was born in Osnabrück, Germany. Early in 1842, at the age of fifteen, he was apprenticed to the Osnabrück master goldsmith Dietrich Heinrich Stadt II. Records indicate that he served his master with distinction. In 1847, after five years of training, Wendt made two repoussé silver salt cellars and a gold seal ring as evidence of his skills as *Meisterstücke* and was accepted into the Guild as a

journeyman. It appears that Wendt immigrated to the United States during the politically turbulent year 1848, since he disappears from the records of his native Osnabrück in this year and appears in America shortly thereafter.

In 1850 Wendt was listed in the Boston directories as a silver chaser. His success was rapid, for he was already in a silverware manufacturing partnership with Augustus Rogers by 1853. A contemporary report in *Leading Pursuits and Leading Men* (1856) mentions the Rogers & Wendt partnership and states: "Mr. J. R. Wendt, a German, [is] reputed to be one of the best designers and chasers in the art."

Wendt held patents for at least two design patterns for flatware. There are two others by "Rudolph Wendt," but it is uncertain whether they are by him or by a nephew or cousin employed by him. Additionally, in the *Digest of Assignments of Patents* (held in the National Archives and dated 4 December 1856) is a record of a proposed patent by John R. Wendt, assigned to John R. Wendt and Augustus Rogers "for the manufacture of Hollow Metallic Brads and Balls," presumably in silver. In 1856 Wendt was briefly involved in a firm titled Rogers, Wendt & Langdon, which manufactured watch cases. For a few months in 1859, Wendt took up manufacturing alone.

In January 1860 Augustus Rogers, John Wendt, and George Wilkinson formed a partnership for the purpose of supplying silverware to the prominent New York City retail house Ball, Black & Co. For reasons unknown the firm lasted only eight months. Wilkinson had been the chief designer for Gorham and returned to that position when things did not work out. However, Wendt moved forward on his own. The impressive Ball, Black & Co. building was completed in 1860, and Wendt occupied the fourth and fifth floors. It should be noted that John R. Wendt & Co. was a separate firm working on the premises, and although he had a special relationship with Ball, Black & Co., he was not a part of it.

The Federal Industrial Census of 1870 indicates a capital of just over $16,000 for the firm, which employed seven males and three females and had an annual production of $30,000. Additionally, it had an 8-horsepower steam engine and owned an impressive amount of machinery. These production figures are lower than one might expect, and there is evidence to suggest that Wendt might have understated them, or that they might have been listed incorrectly.

In 1871 the firm was sold to Wendt's partners Bernard D. Beiderhase and Charles Witteck. Little is known about the remainder of Wendt's life. His will, dated 28 June 1904, represented him to be a resident of Shaverstown, Staten Island, New York. Estate papers indicate, however, that he died in Germany in 1907. There is no mention of a wife or children, his heirs being sisters, sisters-in-law, and nieces, all residents of Germany.

For the greater part of his career, Wendt did not use a manufacturing mark, his pieces being marked only by the retailer. Consequently most pieces can only be attributed to him based on their style and on his work for Ball, Black & Co.

WHITING MFG. CO., NEW YORK, N.Y.
WORKING 1866–1924

The Whiting Mfg. Co. was formed in 1866 and was sucessor to Tifft & Whiting. The principals were William D. Whiting, president; William M. Cowan, vice-president; and Charles E. Buckley, treasurer. Later George E. Strong joined the firm. In 1869–70, the firm acquired the flatware dies of Michael Gibney and Henry Hebbard. These two manufacturers had produced some of the most elegant and popular silverware of the day. George E. Strong had had an interest in the Hebbard firm beginning in 1866. That he was a principal in Whiting by 1869 shows a linkage between the two companies. Evidence suggests that Hebbard & Co. was dissolved because of the loss of the Tiffany & Co. account, the Tiffany firm having purchased Edward Moore's large silverware manufacturing firm in 1869.

Whiting's factory was located in North Attleboro, Massachusetts, where it operated until a disastrous fire in 1875. At that point, F. Jones, a refiner from Newark, New Jersey, purchased the ruins, salvaged what machinery and dies it could, and removed all operations to New York City. The new establishment housed both commercial and manufacturing departments in a large double corner building at 692 and 694 Broadway, at Fourth Street, extending through to Lafayette Place. Charles Osborne was chief designer for the firm during two different periods and once held the position of vice-president. He received numerous patents, regular and design, for silver flatware and hollowware.

In 1924 the firm was sold to Gorham; a couple of years later, its equipment was moved to Providence, Rhode Island, to be merged into the Gorham operations.

WOOD & HUGHES, NEW YORK, N.Y.
GALE (WILLIAM, SR.), WOOD (JACOB)
& HUGHES (JOSEPH H.) 1833–1845
WOOD & HUGHES (JASPER W.) 1845–1899
GRAFF, WASHBOURNE & DUNN 1899–1961

Jacob Wood and Joseph Hughes left William Gale, Sr., in 1833. The Gale and the Wood & Hughes firms grew to be, for a time, the largest manufacturers of silverware in the country. The Industrial Census of the State of New York for 1855 reports that Wood & Hughes produced an annual product of $225,000 and employed 105 individuals.

An obituary for Henry Wood, who died in 1900, states that the original member of the firm of Gale, Wood & Hughes was Joseph H. Hughes. This is at variance with contemporary published sources, which list Jasper W. (1811–1864) as the individual. As for the firm of Wood & Hughes, Jasper's founding partner, Jacob, died in 1850 and Jasper himself retired in 1856. In subsequent years, others with some proprietary interest were Stephen T. Frapie, previously employed by the firm (admitted to partnership in 1850); Charles Wood, brother of Jacob (admitted prior to 1863); Henry Wood, brother of Jacob (admitted 1863); Charles H. Hughes (admitted prior to 1863); and Dixon G. Hughes, son of Jasper W. (admitted 1864).

The existence of the firm was seriously threatened by the outbreak of the Civil War. Wood & Hughes, like many other New York and Philadelphia firms, had a great many southern accounts which were suddenly uncollectible. Soon thereafter, however, the northern economic boom created by the Civil War enabled Wood & Hughes to survive and even prosper.

This firm produced a full line of table silverware, including numerous ornamental patterns of flatware. Many of these were patented by Charles F. Richers, who was likely chief designer during the 1860s and 1870s. A number of Wood & Hughes's flatware designs were also patented by Charles Witteck, who worked for them for a period following dissolution of the Beiderhase firm. In 1891 the Wood & Hughes building suffered a disastrous fire from which the company never fully recovered. The fire resulted in the "loss of records, models and patterns." In 1899 the partners made it known that they wished to sell out. At that time, Mr. Frost of Black, Starr & Frost suggested to Clarence A. Dunn that he, along with his other young friends, Charles Graff and William L. Washbourne, form a partnership to buy out Wood & Hughes. Frost assured them that his prestigious retail outlet wanted a special relationship with a good silverware manufacturer. This was evidently true since large amounts of Black, Starr & Frost silver bears the manufacturing logo of Graff, Washbourne & Dunn. Also, much of the silver retailed by Black, Starr & Frost shows stylistic evidence of having been produced in the Graff, Washbourne & Dunn shops, although it lacks the firm's manufacturing mark.

EXHIBITION CHECKLIST AND LIST OF ILLUSTRATIONS

All figure entries are for objects in the exhibition. Entries noted as illustrations are materials included in the catalogue only. Figures and illustrations are listed following the order of their appearance in the text. When known, individual photographers have been credited; otherwise, photographs are courtesy of the lending institution or archives. When possible, inscriptions have been recorded exactly as they appear on objects in terms of capitalization and line breakage. Marks are recorded as completely as possible, although the manner in which they appear (e.g., incuse or "in an oval") is not always noted due to inconsistencies in the information provided by lenders. When known, the specific type of silver used is noted (e.g., coin or sterling); if unknown, the material is simply listed as "silver." Unless otherwise stated, the prices of objects represent what it cost a maker to produce the piece plus profit, not the retail cost to the consumer, which could have been from 50 to 100 percent higher. Information on cost and labor for Gorham objects was provided by Samuel J. Hough. Debbie Morgan researched the Tiffany & Co. pieces. Please refer to the references when internal citations appear.

PART I FOUNDATIONS LAID, 1840–1875

Chapter 1
The Tariff of 1842 and the Reorganization of Production

Fig. 1.1
Covered urn. William Adams, New York, N.Y., 1845. Coin silver, h. 23½ in. (59.7 cm), w. 19 in. (48.3 cm), d. 11½ in. (29.2 cm). Marked: *William Adams / Manufacturer of Silverware / New York.* Inscribed: *Presented to Henry Clay by the gold & silver artisans of the city of New York / as a tribute of their respect for the faithful & patriotic manner in which he has discharged his high public trusts and Especially for his early and untiring advocacy of the protection to American industry / 1845 / Committee / Wm. Adams / Moses G. Baldwin / Alfred G. Peckhan / Edw. Y. Prime / Daniel Carpenter / David Dunn* and *Protection.* Collection of the Henry Clay Memorial Foundation, located at Ashland, The Henry Clay Estate, gift of Col. Robert Pepper Clay. Photo Tom Jenkins.

The basic shape of this urn is derived from ancient Greek *kraters.* Some decorative features, such as the eagle finial, also have antecedents in the ancient world. However, the curvilinear nature of the handles and most of the engraved decoration reflect the emergence of the rococo revival in the United States in the mid 1840s.

Ill. 1.1
Roller die. From *Scientific American* 1877, cover.

Fig. 1.2
Table caster. Edward Gleason, designer; Roswell Gleason & Sons, maker, Dorchester, Mass.; patented 1857. Silverplate, brass, and cut glass, h. 16⅛ in. (41 cm), diam. 9 in. (22.9 cm). Marked: *PATENTED DEC. 1 1857.* Dallas Museum of Art, gift of the 1992 Silver Supper, 1993.11.a–m. Photo Tom Jenkins.

When the knob at lower right is turned, the six central doors rotate open to reveal glass condiment bottles. The patent record (no. 18,740) for this design refers to it as both a "table caster" and a "revolving bottle-caster."

Fig. 1.3
Fish set. George B. Sharp, Philadelphia, Pa., ca. 1869–1873. Sterling silver, l. (slice) 10 in. (25.4 cm), w. 1¼ in. (3.2 cm). Slice marked: *(lion) S (lion) / PATENT 1866.* Inscribed: *M.* Dallas Museum of Art, The Charles R. Masling and John E. Furen Collection, gift of Mr. and Mrs. William Rubin, The Arthur A. Everts Co., and Arthur and Marie Berger by exchange, 1991. 101.11.1–2. Photo Tom Jenkins.

The 1866 date refers to patent no. 2,475 which Augustus Conradt, a Sharp employee, received for a flatware handle featuring the same central beaded bar as here. Sharp's own patent (no. 3,766) for the stork motif was not granted until 1869.

Ill. 1.2
John Gorham, ca. 1885. Courtesy Brown University Library.

Ill. 1.3
The Gorham Mfg. Co. plant on Steeple St., Providence, R.I., ca. 1885. Courtesy Brown University Library.

Ill. 1.4
Gorham Mfg. Co. advertisement, 1852. Courtesy Brown University Library.

The kettle from the *Chinese Service* is shown at bottom. The original printed source for this ad is unknown.

Ill. 1.5
Charles L. Tiffany, ca. 1890. Courtesy Tiffany & Co.

Fig. 1.4
Basket. Edward C. Moore, maker; Tiffany & Co., retailer, New York, N.Y.; ca. 1854–1855. Coin silver, h. 10½ in. (26.7 cm), w. 13 in. (33 cm), d. 9 in. (22.9 cm). Marked: *TIFFANY & CO. / M LATE M / TIFFANY, YOUNG, & ELLIS / 550 BROADWAY / 369*. Dallas Museum of Art, The Eugene and Margaret McDermott Fund, 1989.16. Photo Tom Jenkins.

Tiffany & Co.'s ledgers note that this basket was designed for either cake or grapes and cost $50 to manufacture. Originally it was one of a pair. Its rococo revival design features grape vines on the footrim, rim, and handle. Both form and ornament are similar to contemporary English baskets.

Ill. 1.6
Edward C. Moore, ca. 1885. Courtesy Tiffany & Co.

Fig. 1.5
Sugar sifter. Edward C. Moore, maker; Tiffany & Co., retailer, New York, N.Y.; ca. 1865. Sterling silver and silvergilt, l. 6½ in. (16.5 cm), w. 2 in. (5.1 cm). Marked: *TIFFANY & CO / QUALITY / 925–1000* and *M* and *725*. Dallas Museum of Art, The Charles R. Masling and John E. Furen Collection, gift of Mr. and Mrs. William Rubin, The Arthur A. Everts Co., and Arthur and Marie Berger by exchange, 1991.101.8. Photo Tom Jenkins.

Sifters such as this were used to sprinkle sugar over fruit and other foods. The cast handle is in the classical taste, featuring acanthus leaves and a ram's head.

Chapter 2
The Retail and Wholesale Trades

Ill. 2.1
Tiffany & Co. store on Union Square, New York, N.Y., ca. 1890. Courtesy Tiffany & Co.

Fig. 2.1
Transatlantic cable section. Tiffany & Co., New York, N.Y., ca. 1858. Steel and brass, l. 4 in. (10.2 cm), diam. ¾ in. (1.9 cm). Marked: *ATLANTIC TELEGRAPH CABLE / GUARANTEED BY / TIFFANY & CO. / BROADWAY. NEW YORK*. D. Albert Soeffing Collection. Photo Tom Jenkins.

A variety of cable souvenirs were made. This was probably the simplest.

Fig. 2.2
Sword hilt. Tiffany & Co., New York, N.Y., 1864. Sterling silver, silvergilt, and steel, l. 39 in. (98 cm). Scabbard marked: *TIFFANY & CO. / QUALITY / 925–1000 / M*. Inscribed: *Voted to Maj. Gen. W.S. Hancock at the Mississippi Valley Sanitary Fair, St. Louis, June 4, 1864* and *U.S.* Smithsonian Institution, National Museum of American History.

Winfield Scott Hancock (1824–1886) was a major Union general who distinguished himself at Gettysburg. The female figure holding a sword on the grip represents War. Decorating the pommel is an eagle, and on the knuckle guard is a figure of Victory holding a laurel wreath. The blade is decorated with the image of an infantry officer and man-at-arms.

Ill. 2.2
Tiffany & Co. merchandise shown at the 1867 Paris world's fair. Courtesy Tiffany & Co.

Fig. 2.3
Pitcher. Jones, Ball & Poor, Boston, Mass., ca. 1846. Coin silver, h. 11 in. (27.9 cm), w. 9 in. (22.9 cm), d. 7 in. (17.8 cm). Marked: *JONES, BALL & POOR / BOSTON / PURE COIN*. Inscribed: *A.W. HUBBARD*. D. Albert Soeffing Collection. Photo Tom Jenkins.

Pitchers of this type were exhibited by Jones, Ball & Poor's successor, Jones, Ball & Co., at the 1853 New York world's fair. Although this is a particularly elaborate example, the basic shape and similar cast elements were popular and appear on pitchers by other makers.

Ill. 2.3
Interior view of the Ball, Black & Co. store, 247 Broadway, New York, N.Y., in 1857. From Bigelow 1857, 139. Courtesy Winterthur Library: Printed Book and Periodical Collection.

This store was perhaps the first in the United States to have large plate-glass windows for the display of merchandise.

Ill. 2.4
Collins Service, ca. 1854. From Goodrich 1854, 107. Courtesy Private Collection.

This tea and coffee service was probably made in John C. Moore's shop. In 1851 it was presented to Edward K. Collins in appreciation of his establishing "an American Line of Transatlantic Steamers." The set was gold and valued at $5,000.

Fig. 2.4
Centerpiece. John C. Moore, maker; Tiffany & Co., retailer, New York, N.Y.; ca. 1851. Silver, silvergilt, and silverplated bronze, h. 23¾ in. (60.3 cm), diam. 16⅞ in. (42.9 cm). Marked: *TIFFANY & CO. / 271 Broadway / J.C.M.* Inscribed: *The / Albany City Bank / To / Watts Sherman / 1851*. The Preservation Society of Newport County, Newport, Rhode Island. Photo John W. Corbett.

Traditionally entitled *The Four Seasons,* this piece was exhibited at the 1853 New York world's fair as representing the ancient elements: earth, air, water, and fire. Furthermore, it has been suggested that the centerpiece was made in 1853 rather than 1851. But given that it is dated 1851, that John C. Moore retired in 1851, and that Tiffany's moved out of its showroom at 271 Broadway in 1853, it probably was indeed made in 1851. The style and placement of the figures are close to English examples.

Fig. 2.5
Pitcher. J. R. Wendt & Co., maker; Ball, Black & Co., retailer, New York, N.Y.; ca. 1866. Sterling silver, h. 12 in. (30.5 cm), w. 6 in. (15.2 cm), d. 5 in. (12.7 cm). Marked: *BALL, BLACK & CO. / 925/1000 / NEW YORK.* Inscribed: *J.L.E.S. / 1866.* Dallas Museum of Art, gift of the 1988 Dallas Symposium, Janet S. Slaton, Robert H. Hoy III, Dr. and Mrs. Kenneth M. Hamlett, Mr. and Mrs. Robert Curry, Mrs. Loren C. McCullar, Mr. and Mrs. Robert F. Venable, Mrs. James F. Jarrell, Jr., and the "Lot for a Little Fund," 1989.99. Photo Tom Jenkins.

This piece's shape is directly based on that of ancient wine pitchers called *oinochoe.* The two inset medallions featuring classical heads on lined backgrounds are characteristic of those cast by Wendt on documented flatware. The handle is decorated with a lion's head and skin.

Fig. 2.6
Detail of salad set. Attributed to J. R. Wendt & Co. (or successor), maker; Ball, Black & Co., retailer, New York, N.Y.; ca. 1866–1873. Sterling silver and silvergilt, l. (spoon) 12 in. (30.5 cm), w. 2¾ in. (6.9 cm). Marked: *BALL, BLACK & CO. / STERLING.* Inscribed: *S.* Dallas Museum of Art, The Stephen Vaughan Collection, gift of the 1991 Silver Supper, 1992. 7.11.1–2. Photo Tom Jenkins.

Because the Egyptian revival style fell from fashion in the first years of the 1870s, it is likely that this salad set was made by J. R. Wendt & Co., which was in business until 1871. However, Wendt's successor, B. D. Beiderhase & Co., could have produced it at the very end of the fashion. Other sets of the shape are known, but none with the same handle decoration. The female figure was probably meant to represent Cleopatra.

Ill. 2.5
View of silverware and jewelry district of lower Manhattan, ca. 1885. *Maiden Lane at Broadway,* J. J. Fogerty, publisher, New York, N.Y. Courtesy Museum of the City of New York, The J. Clarence Davies Collection, 29.100.2279.

Ill. 2.6
View of the Waltham Building, 1–5 Bond St., New York, N.Y., 1877. From *JCK* 8:3 (Apr. 1877):n.p. Courtesy Chilton Co.

Fig. 2.7
Tea and coffee set. George Wilkinson, designer; Gorham Mfg. Co., maker, Providence, R.I.; Starr & Marcus, retailer, New York, N.Y.; designed 1868, made 1870–1871. Sterling silver, ivory, and silvergilt, h. (coffeepot) 9 in. (22.9 cm), w. 9⅝ in. (24.4 cm), d. 5½ in. (14 cm). Coffeepot marked: *STARR & MARCUS / C* (date letter for 1870) */ STERLING / (lion) (anchor) G / 690 / 6½ PINTS.* Creamer and sugar bowl marked: *D* (date letter for 1871). Inscribed: *SAK.* Dallas Museum of Art, General Acquisitions Fund, 1988.135.1–5. Photo Tom Jenkins.

This model (no. 690) was originally introduced with only the five pieces seen here at a manufacturing cost of $162. By 1873 that cost had risen to $245. The same year a kettle-on-stand and an urn were added in the pattern. They cost $165 and $160 to make, respectively. A variety of engraved ornament was offered as well. This particular version is especially successful because the engraving features lotus blossoms, which complement the Egyptian-style winged sphinxes and masks.

Fig. 2.8
Kettle-on-stand. Augustus Rogers, Boston, Mass., ca. 1850. Coin silver and ivory, h. 15¾ in. (40 cm), diam. 10½ in. (26.7 cm). Marked: **A. ROGERS.* / BOSTON / PURE COIN A. ROGERS* (struck over another mark ending with) *& CO.* Inscribed: *MFW.* Dallas Museum of Art, gift of Mr. and Mrs. Willard E. Brown III, The Bolton Foundation, an anonymous donor, and the Decorative Arts Acquisition Fund, 1991.1.a–b. Photo Tom Jenkins.

Although Rogers's mark is struck over that of another, it is nevertheless felt that this kettle was made in his shop. Rogers did not sell retail and it is thus unlikely that his sizable shop bought and remarked ware by other makers for sale to the trade. It is possible that the piece was simply mismarked with a retailer's mark and subsequently corrected. The house seen on the side is believed to be that of the original owner. The repoussé, rococo revival–style decoration on the kettle's walls depicts exotic Asian landscapes and figures in a variety of pursuits.

Chapter 3
Influences and Innovation: Design

Fig. 3.1
Lady's pattern serving spoon and fish set. Attributed to George Wilkinson, designer; Gorham Mfg. Co., maker, Providence, R.I.; designed 1868. Sterling silver, l. (slice) 10 in. (25.4 cm), w. 3 in. (7.6 cm). Fish set marked: *(lion) (anchor) G PATENT 1868 STERLING.* Fish set inscribed: *J.G.* Dallas Museum of Art, The Charles R. Masling and John E. Furen Collection, gift of Mr. and Mrs. William Rubin, The Arthur A. Everts Co., and Arthur and Marie Berger by exchange, 1991.101.1.1–2, 1991.101.2. Photo Tom Jenkins.

The bold use of discs and bars in this pattern was especially innovative and is typical of Wilkinson's handling of form. Note the cast female hands complete with rings and lace cuffs.

Ill. 3.1
George Wilkinson, 1892. Portrait by F. A. Heller. Courtesy Brown University Library.

Fig. 3.2
Chafing dish. Attributed to George Wilkinson, designer; Gorham Mfg. Co., maker, Providence, R.I.; ca. 1865. Coin silver, h. 7⅝ in. (19.7 cm), w. 11½ in. (29.2 cm), d. 10¼ in. (26 cm). Marked: *(lion) (anchor) G / 150 / S & M* and *G484 / CH*. High Museum of Art, Atlanta, Ga. The Virginia Carroll Crawford Collection, 1982.305.

The original design for this model (no. 150) was for an ice cream stand, which was evidently adapted into a chafing dish as a custom order.

Fig. 3.3
Tea and coffee set. Attributed to J. R. Wendt & Co., maker; Ball, Black & Co., retailer, New York, N.Y.; ca. 1865–1871. Sterling silver and ivory, h. (coffeepot) 11¼ in. (28.6 cm), w. 8⅜ in. (21.3 cm), d. 5¾ in. (14.6 cm). Marked: *BALL, BLACK & CO / 925 / 1000 / NEW YORK*. Inscribed: *KML*. Dallas Museum of Art, gift of Mr. and Mrs. James R. McNab and Mrs. Albert Hill, 1988.43.1–5. Photo Tom Jenkins.

The waste bowl lacks the engraving found on the other pieces and has different legs. It was probably a later addition to the set. The central bands were not applied, but are repoussé. The lined background of the medallions are characteristic of Wendt's work.

Ill. 3.2
Meriden Britannia Co. tea and coffee set design no. 01660, 1867. From Meriden 1867, 13. Courtesy Winterthur Library: Printed Book and Periodical Collection.

Although the catalogue states that the manufactured version of this particular design had bases instead of feet, plated examples are known which are supported on feet. Solid silver versions are known from several makers, including Samuel T. Crosby of Boston.

Fig. 3.4
Pitcher. Koehler & Ritter, San Francisco, Cal., ca. 1870–1875. Silver, h. 11 in. (27.9 cm), w. 8 in. (20.3 cm), d. 6 in. (15.2 cm). Marked: *(castle) / S.F.CAL. S.F.CAL. / K & R*. Inscribed: *G*. Private Collection, San Antonio. Photo Tom Jenkins.

Gorham sold large amounts of silver in California and greatly influenced silver design there. This pitcher is similar to contemporary Gorham products in both style and quality. The gilt neck band is removable to facilitate cleaning.

Ill. 3.3
Frederick Elkington & Co. tankard design no. 13,468, 1872. From Elkington 1840, v. 9 (25 Oct. 1872):50. Courtesy The Board of Trustees of the Victoria & Albert Museum, V & A Picture Library.

This design is close to Gorham's designs of the early 1870s.

Fig. 3.5
Coffeepot with trivet from nine-piece tea and coffee set. Attributed to Gale, North & Dominick, maker; Ford & Tupper, retailer, New York, N.Y.; ca. 1869. Silver and ivory, h. (pot on trivet) 12 in. (30.5 cm), w. 9¾ in. (24.8 cm), d. 6¼ in. (15.9 cm). Marked: *FORD & TUPPER*. Dallas Museum of Art, The Helen Corbitt Irish Memorial Fund, 1989.21.1–2. Photo Tom Jenkins.

Although this piece was not marked by any of the Gale partnerships, it is virtually identical to several examples made by Gale and his son and therefore is attributable to their successor.

Ill. 3.4
Frederick Elkington & Co. kettle-on-stand design no. 10,513, 1867. From Elkington 1840, v. 7 (8 Feb. 1867):50. Courtesy The Board of Trustees of the Victoria & Albert Museum, V & A Picture Library.

Such Georgian revival designs were highly influential in both Great Britain and the United States.

Fig. 3.6
Two butter knives. Top: New York, N.Y., or New England, ca. 1850–1860. Bottom: Tifft & Whiting, New York, N.Y., ca. 1850–1860. Silver and agate, l. (bottom knife) 7½ in. (19.1 cm), w. ⅞ in. (3.4 cm). Marked: *(rooster) T & W (arm and hammer)*. Inscribed: *Bridges*. Top knife unmarked but inscribed *Marilla*. D. Albert Soeffing Collection. Photo Tom Jenkins.

This type of knife was directly based on British examples featuring agate handles. In this country they often were used as wedding gifts, as demonstrated by the engraved wedding ring and pair of doves on the unmarked example.

Fig. 3.7
Pair of dessert or fruit knives. Joseph Seymour & Co., Syracuse, N.Y., ca. 1865. Coin silver, l. 8 in. (20.3 cm), w. ⅞ in. (3.4 cm). Marked: *J. S. & CO*. Inscribed: *R*. D. Albert Soeffing Collection. Photo Tom Jenkins.

Although the geometric background patterns were created through engine turning, the rest of the decoration was hand engraved. Upon close comparison, variations are evident in the hand engraving.

Fig. 3.8
Detail of *Cottage* pattern ice cream server. Joseph Seymour & Co., Syracuse, N.Y., ca. 1865. Coin silver, l. 10⅞ in. (27.6 cm). Marked: *J S & CO*. D. Albert Soeffing Collection. Photo D. Albert Soeffing.

Engraved scenes were especially popular in Syracuse. This one features a woman feeding ice cream to a child. The geometric background pattern was mechanically engine turned.

Fig. 3.9
Spoon. James Watts, maker; Butler, McCarty & Co., retailer, Philadelphia, Pa.; ca. 1868–1876. Coin silver, l. 8½ in. (21.6 cm), w. 1¾ in. (4.4 cm). Marked: *COIN (horse over chevron) BUTLER McCARTY & Co.* Inscribed: *C.* Dallas Museum of Art, gift of Sylvia and Charles Venable in honor of Faith P. Bybee, 1992.288. Photo Tom Jenkins.

The eccentric profile of the handle and the engraved ornament are typical of Philadelphia work.

Fig. 3.10
Pitcher and goblet. Zalmon Bostwick, New York, N.Y., ca. 1845. Coin silver, h. (pitcher) 11 in. (27.9 cm), w. 8½ in. (21.6 cm), d. 5½ in. (14 cm). Pitcher marked: *Z Bostwick / NEW YORK.* Pitcher inscribed: *(Sampson crest) / S* and *John W. Livingston / to Joseph Sampson / 1845.* High Museum of Art, Atlanta, Ga., Virginia Carroll Crawford Collection, 1984.142.1–.2.

The pitcher's shape was copied directly from a contemporary English stoneware pitcher (see fig. 3.11). Only the complicated figures on the ceramic prototype were omitted. The matching pitcher and goblet are in the Brooklyn Museum.

Fig. 3.11
Pitcher. Charles Meigh Pottery, Hanley, Staffordshire, England; design registered 1842. Stoneware, h. 10½ in. (26.7 cm), w. 8⅜ in. (21.3 cm), d. 5⅝ in. (14.4 cm). Unmarked. Dallas Museum of Art, The Faith P. and Charles L. Bybee Collection, gift of Faith P. Bybee, 1986.48.

Besides Bostwick, the American Pottery Co., Jersey City, N.J., copied this pitcher. Ceramic tea sets were also available in this design, which features figures of the Apostles. Photo Lee Clockman.

Fig. 3.12
Gothic pattern dessert knife, sugar sifter, fork, and spoon. Gale & Hayden, New York, N.Y., patented 1847; knife dated 1852, fork 1853, and spoon 1848. Coin silver, l. (knife) 8⅛ in. (20.6 cm), w. ¾ in. (1.9 cm). Knife marked: *Church & Batterson / 1852 / (pellet) / G & S.* Inscribed: (knife) *J.M.,* (sifter) *SHJ,* (fork) *LTCS,* (spoon) *GEM.* Dallas Museum of Art, gift of Mr. and Mrs. Marshall Steves (knife) 1991.12; The Charles R. Masling and John E. Furen Collection, gift of Mr. and Mrs. William Rubin, The Arthur A. Everts Co., and Arthur and Marie Berger by exchange, 1991.101.14.1 3. Photo Tom Jenkins.

This pattern was patented (no. 150) by Gale & Hayden. Besides this version with crenellations, another without them was also patented and produced. Church & Batterson, who retailed the knife, were in partnership in Hartford, Connecticut, between 1851 and 1855.

Fig. 3.13. Flagon. Francis W. Cooper, New York, N.Y., ca. 1867. Silver and semiprecious stones, h. 10½ in. (26.7 cm), diam. 5⅛ in. (13 cm). Marked: *F.W. Cooper / Amity St N.Y.* Inscribed: *Barabas IRVINGTON / THE GIFT OF MATILDA WEBB WORGAN / ASCENSION - DAY A.D. 1867 / LAUS DEO.* The Carnegie Museum of Art, Pittsburgh, DuPuy Fund, 1987.6. Photo Tom Barr.

Several similarly shaped flagons are known. The surface ornament, however, varies among them. Currently it is unknown to which church this piece belonged.

Fig. 3.14
Tureen. Wm. Gale & Son, New York, N.Y., 1855. Silver and silverplate, h. 10¾ in. (27.3 cm), w. 15 in. (38.1 cm), d. 10¼ in. (26 cm). Marked: *Wm.GALE & SON / NEW-YORK / 1855 / WG&S.* Inscribed: *F.C.S.* Dallas Museum of Art, gift of the Friends of Decorative Arts, 1987.356.a–c. Photo Tom Jenkins.

During the 1850s, this design was considered extremely stylish by many. The fact that a similar Gale tureen was presented by the Chamber of Commerce and Merchants of New York City to Commodore Matthew C. Perry for his role in the 1854 treaty with Japan attests to this fact. That example is at the New-York Historical Society and another is in the Art Institute of Chicago (see Naeve 1986, 89–90). The Dallas example survives with its original silverplated liner.

Fig. 3.15
Pair of ewers. Samuel Kirk, Baltimore, Md., ca. 1835–1846. Coin silver, h. 16⅝ in. (42.2 cm), w. 9⅞ in. (25.1 cm), d. 6½ in. (16.5 cm). Marked: *S. KIRK / S.K. / 11 oz.* Inscribed: *GEA.* High Museum of Art, Atlanta, Ga., Virginia Carroll Crawford Collection, 1982.302.1–2. Photo David Zeiger.

On the sides are repoussé scenes featuring Asian figures and architecture. The fronts are decorated with dolphins spewing water, symbolizing the ewers' use as water pitchers.

Fig. 3.16
Coffee set. Samuel T. Crosby, Boston, Mass., ca. 1846. Coin silver and ivory, h. (pot) 13 in. (33 cm), w. 10½ in. (26.7 cm), d. 6 in. (15.2 cm). Milk jug marked: *S.T.CROSBY. / PURE COIN BOSTON / (eagle) (unidentified mark).* Inscribed: *EAW.* Philadelphia Museum of Art, gift of Sara Wadsworth Wood, 1980-70-1-5. Photo Eric Mitchell.

The neoclassical decorative scheme of these pieces features leaves in a scale pattern and snakes, both elements which appear in ancient Roman metalwork. The pineapple finials are derived from late-eighteenth-century American and British examples. The presence of a tea caddy and waste bowl suggests that the set originally included a teapot, now missing. The service was made for Emmaline Austin Wadsworth (d. 1885), daughter of Edwin Austin of Boston. She married William Wolcott Wadsworth (1810–1852) of Geneseo, New York, in 1846.

Fig. 3.17
Detail of centerpiece from *Pompeian* pattern dessert service. Albert Wilms, designer; Frederick Elkington & Co., maker, London and Birmingham, England; designed ca. 1862, made 1876. Sterling silver, silverplate, silvergilt, glass, and wood, h. (candelabrum) 28½ in. (72.4 cm), diam. 18 in. (45.8 cm); h. (plateau) 3½ in. (8.9 cm), diam. 15½ in. (39.4 cm). Candelabrum marked: *(Queen's head) (lion) FE (anchor) B.* Plateau marked: *E & and CO N* flanking *E & CO* (in shield). Dallas Museum of Art, gift of the Meadows Foundation, Inc., 1988.44.a–b. Photo Tom Jenkins.

The top of this centerpiece features seven candle sockets. A holder with a cut glass bowl fits into the central socket when desired. To use the piece as an epergne, small, cut glass bowls were originally available for insertion into the remaining sockets. The entire service consists of this centerpiece on plateau and four compotiers, the larger two of which sit on plateaus. This design was first exhibited at the 1862 London world's fair. As ill. 6.5 reveals, dessert services like this were in use in the United States.

Fig. 3.18
Fruit stand. Attributed to George Wilkinson, designer; Gorham Mfg. Co., maker, Providence, R.I.; designed 1866. Silver, h. 16¾ in. (42.6 cm), w. 13 in. (33 cm), d. 11 in. (27.9 cm). Marked: *164 / (lion) (anchor) G.* Inscribed: *R.* Dallas Museum of Art, The Charles R. Masling and John E. Furen Collection, gift of Mr. and Mrs. William Rubin, The Arthur A. Everts Co., and Arthur and Marie Berger by exchange, 1991. 101.17. Photo Tom Jenkins.

Gorham produced a series of fruit stands related to this example. Most were smaller and featured different cast elements on the bowl's rim, although the central female figure was often the same. In this example, the figure stands on a celestial sphere. The upper figures on this stand represent the gods Apollo and Vulcan as children. This model (no. 164) was well publicized by Gorham in a woodcut which it supplied to various publishers. The cut appears in *HNMM* 1868 and "American Silverware," *WJ* 1:4 (Dec. 1869):1.

Fig. 3.19
Punch bowl and pair of candelabra. Tiffany & Co., New York, N.Y., 1873. Sterling silver and silvergilt, h. (bowl) 16½ in. (41.9 cm), w. 26½ in. (67.3 cm); h. (candelabra) 30½ in. (77.4 cm). Bowl marked: *TIFFANY & CO. / 2379 / QUALITY / 925.1000 / M / 5200 / UNION SQUARE.* Candelabra marked: *TIFFANY & CO. / 3180 / QUALITY / 925.1000 / M / 5200 / UNION SQUARE.* Bowl inscribed: *The United States of America / Viscount d'Itajuba / His Majesty, The Emperor of Brazil / Article I of the Treaty Between the United States and Her Britannic Majesty / Concluded at Washington May 8, 1871, as a Mark of Their Appreciation of the / Dignity, Learning, Ability, and Impartiality with Which He Discharged His Arduous Duties at / Geneva.* © 1991 The Art Institute of Chi-

cago, gift of the Antiquarian Society through Mr. and Mrs. William Y. Hutchinson Fund, 1985.221.a–c. All rights reserved. Photo Kathleen Culbert-Aguilar, Chicago.

The United States commissioned three sets, including this, for presentation to the international commissioners who arbitrated U.S. grievances against Great Britain for its breach of neutrality during the Civil War. Besides punch bowls and candelabra, each service had a pair of wine coolers. In 1873 Tiffany's exhibited a service of this design at the Vienna world's fair. It may have produced additional sets for private customers.

Fig. 3.20
Detail of pastry server. Wood & Hughes, New York, N.Y., ca. 1860–1875. Sterling silver and silvergilt, l. 10⅝ in. (27 cm), w. 3¼ in. (8.3 cm). Marked: *STERLING / W & H.* Private Collection, San Antonio. Photo Tom Jenkins.

The serving portion is spade-shaped and is decorated with stippled work, neoclassical engraving, and gilding.

Fig. 3.21
Detail of ladle. Wood & Hughes, New York, N.Y., ca. 1860–1875. Coin silver, l. 15 in. (38.1 cm), w. 5 in. (12.7 cm). Marked: *W & H STERLING.* Inscribed: *VW.* Charles J. Robertson Collection. Photo Tom Jenkins.

Although not neoclassical in subject matter, the likeness of a contemporary woman with necklace and plumed hat is handled in a classical manner, being in high relief on a plain ground. The use of spheres and bars in the composition is characteristic of work from the 1860s and early 1870s.

Fig. 3.22
Pitcher. Wood & Hughes, New York, N.Y., ca. 1865–1875. Coin silver, h. 12 in. (30.5 cm), w. 8 in. (20.3 cm), d. 5⅝ in. (14.3 cm). Marked: *W & H / 900 / 1000.* Inscribed: *CMG.* William Hill Land & Cattle Co. Collection. Photo Tom Jenkins.

Innovative in shape and well executed, this pitcher reveals the high quality of many of this firm's products. The rim features a pharaoh's head, while on the side are medallions of a female. The use of an Egyptian revival element suggests that the piece was made between 1868 and 1873, when the style was most popular.

Fig. 3.23
Candelabrum (one of a pair). Frederick Elkington & Co., London and Birmingham, England, designed 1872. Goldplated bronze, h. 24½ in. (62.2 cm), w. 9⅛ in. (23.2 cm), d. 8⅝ in. (21.9 cm). Marked: *E & Co.* (in a shield surmounted by a crown) *M* and *8942 / 5470 / 4 / D.G.* Dallas Museum of Art, gift of Paul Zane Pilzer, Jeffery S. Juster, Mrs. John O'Boyle, and Mrs. Barron U. Kidd in honor of Alan M. May., 1990. 164.1.a–f. Photo Tom Jenkins.

Elkington was one of Europe's most important exponents of the Egyptian revival style, producing a wide variety of flat- and hollowware in the taste. As with this candelabrum, Elkington typically covered the surface of a form with dense Egyptian-inspired ornament. The "hieroglyphics" used here are not authentic and apparently convey no message. The drawings for this design note that the actual pieces were to be finished in "Gold Bronze No. 305." Because the Dallas examples are numbered three and four it is assumed they were once part of a set of at least four candelabra.

Fig. 3.24
Centerpiece. Dominick & Haff, maker, New York, N.Y.; Cowell & Hubbard Co., retailer, Cleveland, Ohio; ca. 1872–1875. Sterling silver and glass, h. 11 in. (27.9 cm), diam. 11⅞ in. (30.2 cm). Marked: *(blank date diamond) (circle) D.H.* and *STERLING H 88 X 15* and *THE COWELL & HUBBARD CO.* © 1991 The Art Institute of Chicago, Laura S. Matthews Fund, 1983.215. All rights reserved.

Dominick & Haff used the D.H. mark found on this piece into the 1880s. However, the Egyptian revival style, represented here by lotuses, sphinxes, and females with quail headdresses, quickly fell from favor after 1873. Consequently, it is unlikely that the centerpiece was made much after that date.

Fig. 3.25
Wine decanter set from the *Furber Service*. Attributed to George Wilkinson, designer; Gorham Mfg. Co., maker, Providence, R.I.; 1873. Sterling silver, silvergilt, and glass, h. 17½ in. (44.5 cm), w. 10 in. (24.5 cm), d. 9½ in. (24.1 cm). Stand marked: *105 / (lion) (anchor) G / STERLING / F.* Inscribed: *EIF.* Museum of Art, Rhode Island School of Design, gift of Textron, Inc., 1991.126.36.

On the sides of the stand are cast representations of a falcon wearing the double crown of Upper and Lower Egypt. In the ancient kingdom this symbol represented both the god Horus and divine kingship.

Fig. 3.26
Isis pattern fish set. Attributed to George Wilkinson, designer; Gorham Mfg. Co., maker, Providence, R.I.; William Wilson McGrew, retailer, Cincinnati, Ohio; designed 1871. Sterling silver and silvergilt, l. (slice) 12¾ in. (32.4 cm), w. 3¼ in. (8.1 cm). Marked: *(lion) (anchor) G STERLING W. WILSON MCGREW.* Inscribed: *From B. & H. S.* and *RF.* Dallas Museum of Art, The Stephen Vaughan Collection, gift of the 1991 Silver Supper, 1992.7.12.1–2. Photo Tom Jenkins.

The original leather box, labeled *WM. WILSON MCGREW / JEWELLER / & / SILVERSMITH / CINCINNATI,* survives for this example. The pattern was available only in serving pieces and a few hollowware items including napkin rings. This set reflects the options of pierced or engraved decoration that were available.

Fig. 3.27
Ladle. Attributed to George Wilkinson, designer; Gorham Mfg. Co., maker, Providence, R.I.; ca. 1870. Sterling silver and silvergilt, l. 12½ in. (31.8 cm), w. 3½ in. (8.9 cm), d. 3 in. (7.6 cm). Marked: *(lion) (anchor) G / STERLING.* Dallas Museum of Art, The Charles R. Masling and John E. Furen Collection, gift of Mr. and Mrs. William Rubin, The Arthur A. Everts Co., and Arthur and Marie Berger by exchange, 1991.101.6. Photo Tom Jenkins.

The combination of such a severe handle with finely detailed cast elements is typical of Wilkinson's designs. The two human forms are Egyptian-style servant figures called *ushapti.*

Ill. 3.5
Frederick Elkington & Co. water jug design no. 527, 1868. From Elkington 1840, v. 8 (27 May 1868). Courtesy The Board of Trustees of the Victoria & Albert Museum, V & A Picture Library.

The Tiffany's example which inspired this design is shown in ill. 2.2. Another Tiffany-derived pitcher design (no. 534) was done at Elkington's in December 1868.

PART II GLORY ACHIEVED, 1875–1915

Chapter 4
The Rise of the Manufactory
and the Division of Labor

Ill. 4.1
Views of the Tiffany & Co. manufactory, 53 and 55 Prince St., New York, N.Y., 1877. From *Scientific American* 1877, cover.

The images are: fig. 1, melting; fig. 2, rolling; fig. 3, flatware blanks; fig. 4, roller die; fig. 5, partially finished blank; fig. 6, die stamping; fig. 7, polishing; and fig. 8, finished pitcher.

Ill. 4.2
Views of the Reed & Barton manufactory, Taunton, Mass., 1879. From *Scientific American* 1879, cover.

The views are of casting (top left); burnishing (top right); plating (center); satin finishing (lower left); and soldering (lower right).

Ill. 4.3
The design studio at Tiffany & Co. manufactory, 53 and 55 Prince St., New York, N.Y., ca. 1885. Courtesy Tiffany & Co.

Note the large number of patterns in the room and the high quality of natural light.

Ill. 4.4
F. A. Heller in Gorham Mfg. Co. design studio, Elmwood manufactory, Providence, R.I., 1892. Courtesy Brown University Library.

Ill. 4.5
Images of spinning, snarling (repoussé chasing), and chasing, Tiffany & Co. Prince St. manufactory, 1877. From *Scientific American* 1877, 290.

Fig. 4.1
Coffeepot. Meriden Britannia Co., Meriden, Conn., and Rogers Smith & Co., New Haven, Conn., makers, ca. 1871. Silverplate and ivory, h. 11 in. (27.9 cm), w. 9¼ in. (23.5 cm), d. 5¼ in. (13.3 cm). Marked: *Rogers Smith & Co / New / Haven / Conn / 1884 / C*. Dallas Museum of Art, anonymous gift in honor of Charles R. Masling, 1988.83. Photo Tom Jenkins.

The pot's body was spun up over a chuck rotating on a lathe. Once it was formed and the chuck removed, the appendages were soldered on. Although this particular pot is marked only by Rogers Smith & Co., it appears that the undecorated body was made by Meriden Britannia. The model (no. 1,884) is illustrated in contemporary Meriden Britannia trade catalogues. It is also possible that Rogers Smith & Co. produced the pot under license from Meriden Britannia.

Fig. 4.2
Fish set. New York, N.Y., ca. 1865–1875. Sterling silver, l. (slice) 12 in. (30.5 cm), w. 3 in. (7.6 cm). Marked: *STERLING / PATENT*. Inscribed: *EJD*. Dallas Museum of Art, The Stephen Vaughan Collection, gift of the 1991 Silver Supper, 1992.7.10.1–2. Photo Tom Jenkins.

The set's handles were cast. Their Renaissance-inspired design and the eccentric blade and tine shapes are related to contemporary examples from central Europe. These shapes usually were used in conjunction with handle designs by John R. Wendt and Bernard D. Beiderhase. It is thus likely that this model was also made by one of them or possibly their successor firms, Renziehausen & Co. and Adams & Shaw Co. Apparently no part of this design was actually patented.

Fig. 4.3
Pitcher. Tiffany & Co., New York, N.Y., 1893. Sterling silver, h. 8½ in. (21.6 cm), w. 8 in. (20.3 cm), d. 7 in. (17.8 cm). Marked: *TIFFANY & CO. / 5465 MAKERS 4523 / STERLING SILVER / 925–1000/ M (1893 world's fair globe with T mark) / 6 PINTS*. Inscribed: *ARTHUR E. DELMHORST / In Affectionate Appreciation / of Many Years of Devoted Friendship / FRANCES A. GUTHERIE / 1906–1948*. Dallas Museum of Art, The Eugene and Margaret McDermott Fund, 1989. 2MCD. Photo Tom Jenkins.

The flowers on this piece were created through repoussé chasing. At least eleven different decorative schemes were used on the basic "gourd" shape seen here. This "chased chrysanthemums" version was ordered especially for the 1893 Chicago world's fair and cost the large sum of $593 to manufacture because of the complicated repoussé work. Other variations cost as little as $34, while the most expensive was $700. The basic shape was occasionally used for loving cups by adding another handle in place of the spout.

Ill. 4.6
Gorham Mfg. Co. black coffee set and tray no. A5535, by Nicholas Heinzelman, 1899. From Gorham 1899, 15. Courtesy Brown University Library.

The exceptionally fine chasing seen on this set is characteristic of Nicholas Heinzelman. His work is typically densely patterned and relatively flat.

Fig. 4.4
Fish set. James S. Vancourt, New York, N.Y., ca. 1852–1861. Coin silver, l. (slice) 11½ in. (29.2 cm), w. 2¼ in. (5.7 cm). Marked: *(eagle) V (head)*. Inscribed: *EAS*. D. Albert Soeffing Collection. Photo Tom Jenkins.

Except for the cut-out shape of the pieces, all the decoration was engraved. Fish and dolphins often appear on fish sets because they are symbolic of the objects' function.

Fig. 4.5
Water set from the *Furber Service*. Gorham Mfg. Co., Providence, R.I., 1878. Sterling silver and silvergilt, h. (pitcher) 6⅜ in. (16.2 cm), w. 7⅛ in. (18.1 cm), d. 4¼ in. (10.8 cm). Pitcher marked: *(lion) (anchor) G / STERLING / 936*. Cups also marked: *41*. Tray also marked: *A23 / K*. Tray inscribed: *EIF*. Museum of Art, Rhode Island School of Design, gift of Textron, Inc., 1993.126.48–50.

The water imagery on this set was hand engraved. It is part of a series of objects engraved in this style dating from about 1880.

Fig. 4.6
Fish set. Gorham Mfg. Co., Providence, R.I., ca. 1885. Sterling silver, l. (knife) 10⅜ in. (26.4 cm), w. 2⅜ in. (6 cm). Marked: *STERLING / (lion) (anchor) G / 150*. Private Collection, San Antonio. Photo Tom Jenkins.

The elaborate decoration on the blade and tines was done by acid etching. Similar models are known in which the fish are gilded.

Fig. 4.7
Salad set. Wood & Hughes, maker, New York, N.Y.; A. B. Griswold & Co., retailer, New Orleans, La.; ca. 1885–1895. Sterling silver, l. (spoon) 10 in. (25.4 cm), w. 3¾ in. (9.5 cm). Marked: *W & H STERLING* and *A.B. GRISWOLD & CO.* Inscribed: *CL*. Dallas Museum of Art, Stephen Vaughan Collection, gift of the Decorative Arts Guild of North Texas' 1993 Maryland Trip, 1993.51.1–2. Photo Tom Jenkins.

The lobster and crab were acid etched. However, the handles were hand forged. The busts were apparently struck with a hand-held die. George Shiebler introduced this Grecian-style work in 1882, and numerous firms here and abroad soon followed suit.

Ill. 4.7
Engine turning, ca. 1878. From Percy 1878, 489.

Ill. 4.8
Woman working in Gorham Mfg. Co.'s box-making department, Elmwood manufactory, ca. 1892. From Gorham 1892, pl. vii. Courtesy Brown University Library.

Ill. 4.9
View of Gorham Mfg. Co. products in their original boxes, 1879. From Gorham 1879, 137. Courtesy Brown University Library.

Fig. 4.8
Vase. La Pierre Mfg. Co., New York, N.Y., and Newark, N.J., ca. 1890–1910. Glass with silver overlay, h. 9 in. (22.9 cm), diam. 6½ in. (16.5 cm). Marked: *LAP* and *FL* (conjoined). Philadelphia Museum of Art, bequest of Mrs. James Alan Montgomery, 1990-55-44.

Silver overlay work was done on a wide variety of materials. Glass, as here, and ceramics were the most common. The curvilinear floral motif on this piece is an excellent example of art nouveau styling. La Pierre Mfg. Co. was an important producer of glass overlay. Founded in New York about 1888 and incorporated in Newark in 1895, the firm was acquired by International Silver Co. in 1929.

Fig. 4.9
Pastry or ice cream server in original box. J. E. Caldwell & Co., retailer, Philadelphia, Pa., ca. 1880. Sterling silver, l. 9 in. (22.9 cm), w. 4¾ in. (12.1 cm). Marked: *STERLING J.E. CALDWELL & CO.* Inscribed: *ANF / Nov. 3rd. / 1880.* Dallas Museum of Art, The Stephen Vaughan Collection, gift of the 1991 Silver Supper, 1992.7.3–4. Photo Tom Jenkins.

Although this piece has no maker's mark, it was probably made in Philadelphia, where firms like Peter L. Krider Co. were producing objects of such high quality. The bright-cut engraving on the serving area is in the Japanese taste.

Ill. 4.10
Selection of tags used to label and track stock as it moved through the Tiffany & Co. manufactory and retail store. Courtesy Tiffany & Co.

Chapter 5
At Home and Abroad: Marketing

Fig. 5.1
Goelet Schooner Cup. Whiting Mfg. Co., New York, N.Y., ca. 1891. Sterling silver, h. 21½ in. (54.6 cm), diam. 14¾ in. (37.5 cm). Marked: *WHITING MFG CO NEW YORK (lion holding W) STERLING 3676.* Inscribed: *Goelet Schooner Cup / 1891.* New York Yacht Club. Photo Helga Photo Studio.

It is likely that Whiting's chief designer, Charles Osborne, designed this piece. The swirling decoration of waves and seahorses is appropriate to the vase's use as the 1891 *Goelet Schooner Cup* and is in keeping with Osborne's work. Ogden Goelet, who funded this vase, was a major patron of the New York Yacht Club, and many of the Goelet prizes are extraordinary works of art. This example originally had a top surmounted by a female nude.

Ill. 5.1
The Gorham Co. Building, Broadway and 19th St., New York, N.Y., built 1884. From Gorham 1896, inside front cover. Courtesy Winterthur Library: Printed Book and Periodical Collection.

Ill. 5.2
The Gorham Co. Building, Fifth Ave. and 36th St., New York, N.Y., built 1904. From Gorham 1904. Courtesy Winterthur Library: Printed Book and Periodical Collection.

Ill. 5.3
The Meriden Britannia Co. showroom, Union Square, New York, N.Y., ca. 1887. From "A Chapter in the History of American Silver-Plated Ware," *JW* 4:12 (20 July 1887):1038. Courtesy New York Public Library.

Ill. 5.4
The Tiffany & Co. Building, Fifth Ave. and 37th St., New York, N.Y., built 1906. Courtesy Tiffany & Co. Archives, Tiffany & Co.

Ill. 5.5
Interior of the Tiffany & Co. Building, ca. 1906. Courtesy Tiffany & Co. Archives, Tiffany & Co.

Ill. 5.6
Interior of the T. Steele & Son store, Hartford, Conn., ca. 1877. From Steele 1877, 11. Courtesy Winterthur Library: Printed Book and Periodical Collection.

Ill. 5.7
B. & W. B. Smith advertisement, 1886. From *JW* 1:20 (17 Mar. 1886):978. Courtesy Chilton Co.

Ill. 5.8
Gorham Mfg. Co. advertisement, 1889. From *JCK* 20:6 (July 1889):18. Courtesy Gorham, Inc.

Fig. 5.2
Tape measures, needle cases, thimble cases, shuttle, thread winder, scissors, darning egg, and emery. Various makers, United States, ca. 1890–1910. Sterling silver, silverplate, wood, and fabric, h. (pig tape measure) 1 in. (2.54 cm), w. 2⅛ in. (5.4 cm), d. ½ in. (1.3 cm). Dallas Museum of Art, gift of Elizabeth Weaver, 1993.68. Photo Tom Jenkins.

Although many sewing tools are unmarked, several of these are stamped by Unger Brothers, Newark, New Jersey, who produced an extensive line of tools between 1900 and 1910.

Fig. 5.3
Cocktail shaker. United States, ca. 1915. Silverplate, brass, copper, and glass, h. 22½ in. (57.2 cm), diam. 4 in. (10.2 cm). Marked: *FAC-SIMILE EIGHTEEN POUNDER SHRAPNEL SHELL / PATENT APPLIED FOR IN AMERICA AND FOREIGN COUNTRIES.* The Mitchell Wolfson, Jr., Collection,

courtesy The Wolfsonian Foundation, Miami Beach, Fla., and Genoa, Italy, 87.634.20.7.1–2 a–b.

Although this example has no maker's mark, it is similar to a *Shrapnel Shell* cocktail shaker advertised by Gorham in 1915. Gorham's version was distributed with a booklet entitled *The Shrapnel and Other Cocktails.* The shaker's upper compartment is for mixing cocktails, and the bottom contains a set of four glasses with stand.

Fig. 5.4

Tilting ice water set. Meriden Britannia Co., Meriden, Conn., ca. 1872. Silverplate, ivory, and enamel, h. (pitcher on stand) 16½ in. (41.9 cm), w. 9⅜ in. (23.8 cm), d. 10½ in. (26.7 cm). Pitcher marked: *(circle with shield containing a scale)* (surrounded by) *MERIDEN / B. COMPANY / PATD JUNE 13, 1868 / PATD NOV. 3D, 1868 / 4* and *PATD MARCH 26, 1872* and *767.* Tray inscribed: *SK.* Dallas Museum of Art, gift of the Dallas Antiques and Fine Arts Society, 1994. Photo Tom Jenkins.

Tilting ice water pitchers were popular between 1865 and 1890. Having peaked in the mid 1880s, their popularity declined rapidly during the early 1890s as refrigeration made ice readily available throughout the country. The first examples, dating from the late 1850s and 1860s, were generally single pitchers. However, in the early 1870s pitchers were increasingly placed on stands and grouped into sets with trays, goblets, and waste bowls as here. Introduced around 1872, this is an early example of such a set. It is also noteworthy for its engraved decoration, which simulates wood grain. Such ornament was derived from Russian metalwork. Other decorative schemes were also available. A "tilting ice urn" of identical shape, but featuring floral engraving and a goat head instead of a polar bear, was advertised in 1873 as costing $36 wholesale when chased (Meriden 1873, 30).

To date, no patent corresponding to the 1872 date marked on this example has been found. However, the 3 November 1868 patent refers to no. 83,747, which Dennis C. Wilcox assigned to Meriden Britannia for the "Manufacture of Double Wall Ice Pitchers." The 13 June date may be a mistake since no corresponding patent is known. On 30 June 1868, however, Charles C. Foote assigned to Meriden his patent (no. 79,335) for an "Enameled Metallic Ice Pitcher."

Fig. 5.5

Left: *George Washington* pattern souvenir spoon. Davis & Galt, maker, Philadelphia, Pa.; M. W. Galt, Bro. & Co., designer and retailer, Washington, D.C.; designed 1889. Sterling silver with silvergilt, l. 6 in. (15.2 cm), w. 1⅛ in. (2.9 cm). Marked: *(fleur-de-lis) STERLING* and *M.W.GALT BRO. & CO.* Inscribed: *(crest)* and *BORN / 1732 / DIED / 1799.* D. Albert Soeffing Collection. Right: *Witch* pattern souvenir spoon. Seth Low, designer; Gorham Mfg. Co, maker, Providence, R.I.; Daniel Low & Co., retailer, Salem, Mass.; designed 1891. Sterling silver with silvergilt, l. 4¼ in. (10.8 cm), w. ⅞ in. (2.2 cm).

Marked: *DANIEL LOW / (lion) (anchor) G / STERLING.* Inscribed: *SALEM 1692* (in design) and *SBM.* Dallas Museum of Art, gift of Susan Mayfield Tribble, 1993.66. Photo Tom Jenkins.

The Washington model was the first souvenir spoon made in the United States. It was available in three forms: one with the bust in the bowl, one with a twist handle, and this version, which cost $4.50. The crest is that of the Washington family. A *Martha Washington* spoon was also available. The *Witch* spoon is credited with starting the national craze for collecting souvenir spoons. It was made in two versions. This example, the second, more elaborate one, was owned by Susan Beatrice Mayfield Atkins (1883–1926) of Dallas. Small in scale, this particular spoon was intended to be used for coffee; it cost $1.50, according to a 1908 catalogue.

Ill. 5.9

The Meriden Britannia Co. pavilion at the 1876 Philadelphia world's fair. From Norton 1877, 285. Courtesy Winterthur Library: Printed Book and Periodical Collection.

Fig. 5.6

Coffeepot. Attributed to Edward C. Moore, designer; Tiffany & Co., maker, New York, N.Y.; 1874. Sterling silver and ivory, h. 10½ in. (26.7 cm), w. 7 in. (17.8 cm), d. 5 in. (12.7 cm). Marked: *TIFFANY & CO. / 3633 / QUALITY / 925–1000 / M / 3410 / UNION SQUARE.* Inscribed: *C.* Dallas Museum of Art, gift of Mr. and Mrs. Jay Gillette by exchange, Mr. and Mrs. John H. Chiles, Mr. and Mrs. D. A. Berg, and Dr. and Mrs. Kenneth M. Hamlett, Jr., 1990.186. Photo Tom Jenkins.

Tiffany & Co. called the style of this pot "Indian." It also noted that the piece was commissioned by C. T. Cook, who was Tiffany & Co.'s treasurer at the time. The basic manufacturing cost of the pot was $72, plus an additional charge of $104 for chasing. It was apparently the only example ever made and was not part of a larger set.

Ill. 5.10

Part of the Tiffany & Co. exhibit at the 1876 Philadelphia world's fair. From "The Centennial," *HW* 20:1036 (4 Nov. 1876):888. Courtesy Winterthur Library: Printed Book and Periodical Collection.

The coffeepot is that shown in fig. 5.6.

Ill. 5.11

Century Vase, designed by George Wilkinson and Thomas Pairpoint for Gorham Mfg. Co., ca. 1876. Courtesy Brown University Library.

Made of sterling silver and measuring 50 by 62 in. (127 by 157 cm), this vase was valued at $25,000 in 1876. It took Gorham's silversmiths 17,900 man-hours to complete. Virtually every detail of the composition is symbolic of some aspect of American history. The American Indian and pioneer at lower center represent the first stages of civilization as understood by nineteenth-century historians. The two figural groups flanking the central urn depict the "Peaceable Kingdom" and the "Horrors of War." The central figure atop the vase, "America, as the presiding genius, a female figure elegantly and most gracefully draped, stands on a globe, with symbols of literature, science, and art at her feet, with outstretched arms, and holding branches of palm and laurel, emblems of success, and welcome, inviting Europe, Asia, and Africa to join with her in celebrating the triumphs of her Centennial year" (Farnum 1876, 10). By the 1930s, such ornate styling was in great disrepute and the vase was ordered melted down.

Fig. 5.7
Progress Vase. W. C. Beattie, designer; Reed & Barton, maker, Taunton, Mass.; ca. 1876. Sterling silver, h. 48 in. (122 cm), w. 50 in. (127 cm), d. 14 in. (35.6 cm). Marks unavailable. Inscribed: *XIX CENTURY / AMERICA / XV CENTURY / PROGRESS.* Reed & Barton, Inc., Collection.

The iconographic scheme of this piece depicts "the Progress of America from savage to civilized life, by a contrast in condition in the fifteenth and nineteenth centuries." In keeping with contemporary ideas concerning the uncivilized nature of Native Americans, the figural group on the right symbolizes the "primitive state of America" before Europeans arrived. The Aztec warrior astride a "wild" horse in a barren landscape reflects such beliefs. In contrast, the left-hand group shows "the genius of Columbia bearing the olive branch of Peace in one hand and the faces of just government in the other." The central vase "represents the present attainment of manufacturing gained under the peaceful dove with the olive leaf." The crowning figure of Liberty "is the inspiring genius by which the progress of the four centuries has been accomplished" (Reed & Barton 1875, n.p.). The vase's retail price was $7,500, but it apparently never sold and was retained by the firm.

Fig. 5.8
Punch bowl and ladle from the *Mackay Service*. Charles Grosjean, designer; Tiffany & Co., maker, New York, N.Y.; ca. 1878. Sterling silver and silvergilt, h. (bowl) 15½ in. (39.4 cm), diam. 23¼ in. (59 cm); l. (ladle) 21½ in. (55 cm). Bowl marked: *TIFFANY & CO. / 4885 MAKERS 5635 / STERLING-SILVER / 925–1000 / M.* Bowl inscribed: *MLM / (Hungerford coat-of-arms) / (crate nos. 297/8) / THIS BOWL IS FROM / THE SILVER SERVICE OF / MR. AND MRS. JOHN WILLIAM MACKAY WHICH CONSISTS OF ABOUT 1350 PIECES / WEIGHING 14,718 OUNCES / THIS SILVER WAS TAKEN FROM THE / COMSTOCK LODE AT VIRGINIA CITY / NEVADA / BY JOHN WILLIAM MACKAY / AND COMPLETED BY TIFFANY AND COMPANY / NEW YORK, N.Y. IN 1878 / PRESENTED TO ELLIN MACKAY BERLIN / BY HER BROTHER / JOHN WILLIAM MACKAY / JUNE 1949.* David M. Campbell Collection.

Although an article in the New York's *Evening Chronicle* (6 Aug. 1878) states that Charles Grosjean designed the *Mackay Service* and that Isidore Heydet and Henry Friebel were the lead workmen in its execution, Tiffany & Co.'s chief designer Edward C. Moore certainly influenced its creation. The style of its decoration and the presence of a Chinese dragon inside the bowl are closely related to Moore's work from the 1860s and early 1870s. This type of dense Asian-inspired ornament was referred to as both *Indian* and *Sou Chou*. In all, the *Mackay Service* consisted of 1,250 pieces and is said to have taken 200 men two years to complete. The chasing alone required forty highly skilled workers. The cost for the entire set was said to have been $125,000.

Fig. 5.9
Coffee set. Tiffany & Co., New York, N.Y., ca. 1878–1885. Sterling silver, copper, and ivory, h. (pot) 8½ in. (21.6 cm), w. 6½ in. (16.5 cm), d. 3⅞ in. (9.8 cm). Pot marked: *TIFFANY & CO. / 5362 M 1829 / STERLING SILVER / -AND- / OTHER-METALS / 942.* Hot milk jug and sugar bowl marked as above except for pattern, order, and hammering design numbers: *6409, 9789, 1476* and *5399, 9789, 1477,* respectively. Private Collection. Photo Tom Jenkins.

At least seven differently decorated versions of this coffeepot were produced, this being the most costly to make at $133. The milk jug was designed specifically to match the pot, while the sugar bowl shape originated with another set but was ornamented to match this one. The vessel shapes were in use until at least 1905.

Ill. 5.12
Facade of the American Section of Manufacturers, showing entrances to the Tiffany & Co. and Gorham Mfg. Co. displays at the 1893 World's Columbian Exposition. From New York 1894, opp. 88. Courtesy Winterthur Library: Printed Book and Periodical Collection.

The arched windows seen along each side were used for displaying silverware and jewelry.

Ill. 5.13
The Gorham Co. pavilion at the 1915 Pan American Exposition, San Francisco. Courtesy Brown University Library.

At the fair, silverware manufacturers were grouped together. The entrance on the right led to the Meriden Britannia Co. exhibit.

Ill. 5.14
Christopher Columbus, by Frédéric Auguste Bartholdi, 1893. Courtesy Brown University Library.

This silver original was melted down in the early twentieth century, but bronze versions survive.

Fig. 5.10
Nautilus Centerpiece. William C. Codman, designer; Gorham Mfg. Co., maker, Providence, R.I.; 1893. Sterling silver, silvergilt, shell, pearls, and semiprecious stones, h. 20 in. (51 cm), w.

15½ in. (39.4 cm), d. 12½ in. (31.8 cm). Marked: *(lion) (anchor) G / STERLING / 4700* (in oval) */ (1893 world's fair date mark).* Inscriptions: *LUDWIG VOGELSTEIN / UPON THE OCCA-SION OF HIS / FIFTIETH BIRTHDAY / WITH AFFECTION AND ESTEEM FROM / HIS FRIENDS AND ASSOCIATES OF / THE AMERICAN METAL COMPANY, LIMITED / FEB-RUARY 3, 1921.* Dallas Museum of Art, gift of the 1990 Silver Supper, 1990.176. Photo Tom Jenkins.

The beaux-arts style of this piece reflects the European training of Codman, who had recently become Gorham's chief designer. Although the centerpiece is directly based on Renaissance prototypes, the character of the work is wholly of its era. The theme is the birth of Venus. Borne aloft on gilt shells by her father Neptune, Venus holds up a nautilus shell, emblem of the sea. Atop the shell sits the figure Nike representing victory, a reference to the United States at the 1893 Chicago world's fair, for which the piece was made. Gorham was so pleased with the centerpiece that it reproduced the original design drawing in numerous books and pamphlets given away at the fair, and distributed the image to newspapers.

Fig. 5.11
Egyptian pattern coffeepot. Tiffany & Co., New York, N.Y., 1893. Sterling silver, enamel, ivory, and jade, h. 10 in. (24.5 cm), w. 6 in. (15.3 cm). Marked: *TIFFANY & Co / 11346 MAKERS 3797 / STERLING SILVER / 925–1000 / (1893 world's fair globe with T mark).* Inscription: *ABK.* The Carnegie Museum of Art, Pittsburgh, AODA Purchase Fund, 1983.16.2. Photo Tom Barr.

As reflected by the use of stylized lotuses and palm fronds, the decoration on this pot was called *Egyptian* by Tiffany's. Besides this model, single examples in the *Byzantine* and *Viking* styles were also made for display at the 1893 Chicago world's fair. Those versions were more expensive ($609 and $531, respectively) because they carried semiprecious stones. This particular example cost $290 to make.

Ill. 5.15
Magnolia Vase, designed by John T. Curran for Tiffany & Co., 1893. © 1980 The Metropolitan Museum of Art.

Standing 31 inches high, this vase is perhaps the most elaborate example of enameled silver ever made in the United States. When exhibited at the 1893 Chicago world's fair, the piece was highly acclaimed as purely American. The form was derived from the ceramics of the ancient Southwest, while the flowers and plants on the sides represent the north, south, east, and west of the United States. Because of the extreme difficulty of its execution, the vase had a retail price of $10,000 (50,000 francs), according to a French observer. The work is now in the Metropolitan Museum of Art.

Chapter 6
Consumption and Design

Ill. 6.1
Selection of flatware representing the wide variety of forms and designs made in the United States between 1860 and 1890. Dallas Museum of Art, from The Stephen Vaughan Collection and The Charles R. Masling and John E. Furen Collection. Photo Tom Jenkins.

Fig. 6.1
Part of Gorham Mfg. Co's *Furber Service,* on exhibition in 1992 at the Museum of Art, Rhode Island School of Design. Courtesy Museum of Art, Rhode Island School of Design.

The Furber commission was the largest one ever received by the Gorham Mfg. Co. Consisting of 740 pieces, the set was made between 1871 and 1879. The fact that Elvira Irwine Furber's monogram appears on most pieces suggests that the service may have been given to her by her parents following her marriage, or purchased by her with her own money. Besides the dessert service for twenty-four, the commission contains a wide variety of forms, including cruet stands, a wine decanter stand, a table bell, butter pats, vegetable dishes, trays, tureens, a celery vase, and an ice bowl. Large, fabric-lined packing crates accompany the service for storage.

Objects from the *Furber Service* included in the exhibition, but not reproduced individually in the catalogue, are listed below. All were made by Gorham and were the gift of Textron, Inc., to the Museum of Art, Rhode Island School of Design.

Two fruit plates, 1879. Sterling and silvergilt, diam. 8½ in. (21.6 cm); diam. 6 in. (15.2 cm). Marked: *(lion) (anchor) G / STER-LING / L.* 1991.126.63–64. The smaller plate may have been used to hold fruit pits.

Berry spoon, ca. 1879. Sterling silver and silvergilt, l. 6 in. (15.2 cm). Marked: *STERLING / (lion) (anchor) G.* 1991.126.71.

Ice cream spoon, ca. 1879. Sterling silver and silvergilt, l. 6¾ in. (17.1 cm). Marked: *(lion) (anchor) G / STERLING.* 1991. 126.70.

Melon fork, ca. 1879. Sterling silver and silvergilt, l. 6¾ in. (17.1 cm). Marked: *(lion) (anchor) G / STERLING / 100.* 1991.126.73.

Fruit knife, ca. 1879. Sterling silver, silvergilt, and bronze, l. 8 in. (20.3 cm). Marked: *STERLING / (lion) (anchor) G.* 1991. 126.74.

Pair of candelabra, 1879. Sterling and silvergilt, h. 34½ in. (87.6 cm), w. 16½ in. (41.9 cm), d. 16½ in. (41.9 cm). Marked: *Gorham & Co. / (lion) (anchor) G / STERLING / L / B92.* 1991.126.81.

Compote, 1872. Sterling and silvergilt, h. 10½ in. (26.7 cm), w. 14 in. (35.6 cm), d. 11 in. (27.9 cm). Marked: *(lion) (anchor) G / STERLING / E / 985.* 1991.126.27.

Cake basket, 1874. Sterling and silvergilt, h. 8 in. (20.3 cm), w. 10¼ in. (26 cm), d. 7 in. (17.8 cm). Marked: *(lion) (anchor) G / STERLING / G*. Inscribed: *EIF*. 1991.126.28.

Fig. 6.2
Ice spoon and cake knife. Gorham Mfg. Co., Providence, R.I., ca. 1870. Sterling silver and silvergilt, l. (spoon) 9⅝ in. (24.4 cm), w. 2½ in. (6.4 cm); l. (knife) 10 in. (24.5 cm), w. 1¼ in. (4 cm). Marked: *(lion) (anchor) G / STERLING*. Spoon inscribed: *W*. Dallas Museum of Art, The Stephen Vaughan Collection, gift of the 1991 Silver Supper, 1992.7.6, 1992.7.5. Photo Tom Jenkins.

These pieces are representative of the high quality of U.S. flatware design after the Civil War. Besides the fineness of the bright-cut, pierced, and applied decoration, the utensils are well engineered. The holes in the spoon's bowl allowed water to drip away before the ice was lifted out of its container, and the teeth on the back of the knife blade allowed the server to cut through a cake's icing neatly.

Fig. 6.3
Fruit or nut bowl (one of a pair) from the *Furber Service*. Gorham Mfg. Co., Providence, R.I., 1871. Sterling silver with silvergilt, h. 12¾ in. (32.4 cm), w. 18 in. (45.7 cm), d. 9¼ in. (23.5 cm). Marked: *(lion) (anchor) G / STERLING / 775 / D*. Inscribed: *EIF*. Museum of Art, Rhode Island School of Design, gift of Textron, Inc., 1991.126.25–26.

In keeping with their use, these bowls are supported by grape vines in which foxes and birds search for fruit. The female figure may be Ceres, goddess of the harvest. Gorham's records indicate that these were the only examples made. Because of their complexity each stand required around 300 hours to make at a wholesale cost of $427 apiece.

Fig. 6.4
Salad set. Gorham Mfg. Co., Providence, R.I., ca. 1880. Sterling silver and silvergilt, l. (spoon) 9¾ in. (24.8 cm), w. 2½ in. (15.9 cm). Marked: *(lion) (anchor) G / STERLING / 330*. Inscribed: *B*. Dallas Museum of Art, The Eugene and Margaret McDermott Fund, 1989.4.1–.2.MCD. Photo Tom Jenkins.

This pattern exists in several variations. Besides salad sets, macaroni servers with long tines at right angles to the bowl are known. Also, various casting patterns for the faux bamboo handles were used since differences exist among surviving examples.

Ill. 6.2
Candelabra on stands by Tiffany & Co., 1884. Private Collection. Photo courtesy Sotheby's.

Standing over 70 inches tall and weighing 3,033 troy ounces apiece, these pieces are some of the largest ever made by Tiffany & Co. Mary Jane Morgan, who ordered the pair, is known to have helped design some of the silver she purchased and may have influenced the creation of these candelabra. Although

the lavish use of leaves and flowers relates to Tiffany & Co.'s work in the Indian and Near Eastern tastes, these pieces were originally called *Roman*, probably in reference to the herm figures ornamenting their midsections. The original price of the pair was rumored to be between $24,000 and $40,000. When sold in 1886 they brought $8,100.

Fig. 6.5
Ice cream server. Gorham Mfg. Co., Providence, R.I., 1870. Sterling silver, l. 11 in. (27.9 cm), w. 3½ in. (8.9 cm). Marked: *8 / (lion) (anchor) G / STERLING / C*. Inscribed: *SAW*. Dallas Museum of Art, gift of the Tri Delta Charity Antiques Show in honor of Henry S. Coger, 1989.136. Photo Tom Jenkins.

This model closely relates to a series of salad spoons and forks, made in 1870 by Gorham, which have branches for handles and crabs at the top of the bowl. The lobes of the bowl on this spoon are sharp to facilitate cutting frozen ice cream or other hard foods.

Fig. 6.6
Butter pats from the *Furber Service*. Gorham Mfg. Co., Providence, R.I., 1879. Sterling silver and silvergilt, l. 3 in. (7.6 cm), w. 3 in. (7.6 cm). Marked: *(lion) (anchor) G / STERLING / L*. Some inscribed: *EIF*. Museum of Art, Rhode Island School of Design, gift of Textron, Inc., 1991.126.68.1–6.

Individual butter pats, like napkin rings and salt cellars, were widely used in nineteenth-century America and were made in a wide quality range. This set represents the pinnacle of the form. The pats are elaborately ornamented with engraving and gilding and are from a set of twenty-four.

Fig. 6.7
Tea set. Whiting Mfg. Co., New York, N.Y., ca. 1880–1890. Sterling silver, h. (pot) 5 in. (12.7 cm), w. 5 in. (12.7 cm), d. 3¾ in. (9.5 cm). Marked: *(lion holding W) / STERLING / 445*. Dallas Museum of Art, gift of Daniel Morris and Denis Gallion, 1991.30.1–3. Photo Tom Jenkins.

The decoration on this set is in the Persian taste and was achieved through flat chasing. If this design had been produced in large quantities, a similar effect could have been achieved through acid etching, which would have required less labor.

Fig. 6.8
Tea flatware. Gorham Mfg. Co., Providence, R.I., ca. 1879. Sterling silver and silvergilt, l. (knife) 7½ in. (10 cm), w. ⅞ in. (2.2 cm). Marked: *GORHAM / (lion) (anchor) G / STERLING 285*. Dallas Museum of Art, The Stephen Vaughan Collection, gift of the 1991 Silver Supper, 1992.7.9.1–3. Photo Tom Jenkins.

This highly innovative pattern (no. 285) was available only in specialty flatware. Besides tea ware, the other items were an ice cream knife, fish fork and knife, nut spoon and pick, pap spoon, crumb knife, and melon knife and fork. The bright-cut and silvergilt ornament on these examples were additions to the basic plain version.

Fig. 6.9
Tea caddy. George Wilkinson, designer; Gorham Mfg. Co., maker, Providence, R.I.; designed 1861. Coin silver, h. 6¾ in. (116 cm), w. 4½ in. (11.4 cm), d. 3 in. (7.6 cm). Marked: *(lion) (anchor) G / 20 / COIN.* Inscribed: *B.* Dallas Museum of Art, gift of The Dallas Antiques and Fine Arts Society, 1990.3. Photo Tom Jenkins.

This model was available plain or elaborately engraved as here. Excluding the unknown expense of the additional bright-cut decoration, the cost of the basic caddy was nearly $17 by 1868. The design, which juxtaposes elegant neoclassical ornamentation with a solid geometric form and areas of undecorated surfaces, is typical of Wilkinson's work.

Fig. 6.10
Coffeepot and tray. Gorham Mfg. Co., Providence, R.I., designed 1889, made 1891. Sterling silver and ivory, h. (pot) 10 in. (25.4 cm), w. 7¼ in. (18.4 cm), d. 4¼ in. (10.8 cm); w. (tray) 10 in. (25.4 cm), d. 10⅛ in. (25.7 cm). Marked: *(lion) (anchor) G / 2997 / STERLING / (1891 lion's head date mark) / 925.* Minneapolis Institute of Arts, gift of the Decorative Arts Council, 1985.106.1–2.

Despite their exceptionally high quality, this pot and tray appear to have been production pieces introduced in July 1889 at a manufacturing cost of $300 (Puig 1989, 301). In 1890 Gorham supplied an image of a virtually identical pot and tray to the *Jeweler's Circular* for reproduction (McClinton 1968, 82). The decoration features thistles, which were a popular motif during the 1880s and early 1890s (see fig. 6.58).

Fig. 6.11
Chocolate pot. John T. Vansant Mfg. Co., maker; Simons, Bro. & Co., retailer, Philadelphia, Pa.; ca. 1881–1884. Sterling silver and ivory, h. 7¾ in. (19.7 cm), w. 8 in. (20.3 cm), d. 4¼ in. (10.8 cm). Marked: *SIMONS BRO. & CO. / (horse head) V & Co (lion)* and *STERLING.* Inscribed: *MSC.* Mr. and Mrs. Alexander C. Speyer III Collection. Photo Tom Barr.

The style of this pot is characteristic of much silver made in the Delaware Valley during the nineteenth century. While repoussé floral decoration is usually associated with Baltimore, large amounts of it were used in Philadelphia in the late 1870s and 1880s.

Ill. 6.3
Diagram of *service à la russe,* 1862. From Orfèvrerie 1862: inside cover. Courtesy Orfèvrerie Christofle, Paris. Photo Studio Kollar.

Fig. 6.12
Bell. William Bogert & Co., New York, N.Y., ca. 1866–1875. Sterling silver, h. 12½ in. (31.8 cm), w. 6½ in. (16.5 cm), d. 5¾ in. (14.6 cm). Marked: *B ENG' STERLING B.* Dallas Museum of Art, lent by The Charles R. Masling and John E. Furen Collection, 126.1988. Photo Tom Jenkins.

This bell may have been part of a larger table service, because a closely related centerpiece by Bogert survives which features three neoclassical female figures, including the one of Ceres seen here.

Fig. 6.13
Fish set. Albert Coles, New York, N.Y., ca. 1865. Coin silver, l. (slice) 12½ in. (31.8 cm), w. 2½ in. (6.4 cm). Marked: *(eagle) AC (head).* Inscribed: *MS.* D. Albert Soeffing Collection. Photo Tom Jenkins.

The decoration on this set, combining the techniques of die stamping, engine turning, and hand engraving, is suited to the function of the pieces. Water-loving cattails and a dolphin appear on the handles, and the blade features a lake scene.

Fig. 6.14
Bird pattern macaroni server. B. D. Beiderhase & Co., New York, N.Y., patented 1872. Sterling silver and silvergilt, l. 10½ in. (26.7 cm), w. 2¾ in. (7 cm). Marked: *VALENTINE STERLING PATENT.* Inscribed: *Alice.* Private Collection, San Antonio. Photo Tom Jenkins.

The Boston jeweler Albert L. Lincoln of Lincoln & Foss received the first patent on a macaroni server in 1856 (no. 15,266). The example seen here relates to that early model in that its tines are arrayed along one edge as feathers on a bird's wing. The *Bird* pattern was a variant pattern featuring a series of different birds. It was so close to Tiffany & Co.'s *Japanese* (now *Audubon*) pattern that Tiffany & Co. sued Beiderhase for patent infringement and won. "Valentine" was probably a retailer.

Fig. 6.15
Hizen pattern berry spoon. Gorham Mfg. Co., Providence, R.I., ca. 1880. Sterling silver and silvergilt, l. 9 in. (22.9 cm), w. 3 in. (7.6 cm). Marked: *(lion) (anchor) G / STERLING.* Dallas Museum of Art, The Stephen Vaughan Collection, gift of the 1991 Silver Supper, 1992.7.7. Photo Tom Jenkins.

Hizen was one of Gorham's most overtly Asian patterns. This example features a dragon on the handle and a carp in the bowl. The name for this pattern may derive from a Japanese potter named Hizen who worked in the late nineteenth century (see ill. 6.11).

Fig. 6.16
Lobster pick. Frank W. Smith Co., Gardner, Mass., ca. 1910–1930. Sterling silver, l. 7½ in. (19.1 cm), w. ½ in. (1.3 cm). Marked: *(S lion moon logo) STERLING PAT APPL D FOR.* Dallas Museum of Art, The Stephen Vaughan Collection, gift of the Decorative Arts Guild of North Texas' 1993 Maryland Trip, 1993.55. Photo Tom Jenkins.

The lobster and seaweed on this pick are symbolic of its use. Both the tines and the concave end of the handle would be useful in removing the meat from a lobster shell. To date no patent is known for this design.

Fig. 6.17
Pair of asparagus tongs. Bailey & Co., Philadelphia, Pa., ca. 1865–1868. Sterling silver, l. 4½ in. (51.4 cm), 2⅞ in. (7.3 cm). Marked: *BAILEY & CO (star) / (lion) S (shield) (lion)*. Dallas Museum of Art, gift of Mr. and Mrs. Marshall Steves, 1991. 13.1–2. Photo Tom Jenkins.

This pair of tongs and their two mates, now in the Bayou Bend Collection, Houston, are the earliest known examples of American individual asparagus tongs. The mark of the lion and shield with an S appearing on these tongs is the sterling mark of Bailey & Co.

Fig. 6.18
Napkin ring. United States, ca. 1865. Silver, h. 1¾ in. (4.4 cm), w. 2¼ in. (5.7 cm), d. 1¾ in. (4.4 cm). Unmarked. Inscribed: *Adtlie*. D. Albert Soeffing Collection. Photo Tom Jenkins.

Although the use of napkin rings is considered by historians to have been a middle-class act, elaborate, expensive examples such as this were made for wealthy customers. However, in upper-class households they were probably used only for family meals, not formal dining. The whimsical fly on this example identified it and its napkin as belonging to a particular member of the family. Idiosyncratic decoration is common on napkin rings. The plainest types generally are numbered or have individuals' names engraved on them.

Fig. 6.19
Butter pick and sardine server. George W. Shiebler, New York, N.Y., ca. 1880–1890. Sterling silver and silvergilt, l. (server) 6½ in. (16.5 cm), w. 2⅛ in. (5.4 cm). Pick marked: *(winged S) / STERLING / 2784*. Server marked: *H.S.& CO. / (winged S) / STERLING / 2851*. Dallas Museum of Art, The Stephen Vaughan Collection, gift of the 1991 Silver Supper, 1992.7.2, 8. Photo Tom Jenkins.

Shiebler was famous for his innovative designs. With handles in the form of blades of grass and sardine- and root-shaped tines, these pieces reflect this originality. Known to collectors as the "Grass" pattern, it was evidently available only in special serving pieces.

Fig. 6.20
Child's table service. Tiffany & Co., New York, N.Y., 1905. Sterling silver and ivory, diam. (plate) 8 in. (20.3 cm); h. (porringer) 2 in. (5.1 cm), w. 8¾ in. (22.2 cm), d. 5½ in. (14 cm). Bowl and underplate marked: *TIFFANY & CO. / 15499 MAKERS 5947 / STERLING SILVER / 925–1000 / C*. Porringer and plate marked as others except for the pattern nos. *1550 2* and *1550 1*, respectively. All inscribed: *From James Stillman / April 5th 1907*. Underplate, porringer, and plate inscribed: *F.A.V.Jr*. The Chrysler Museum, gift of Frank A. Vanderlip, Jr., 1976.52.8–11. Photo Scott Wolff.

This set is a fine example of art nouveau design. The porringer illustrates the nursery rhyme "Tom Tom the Piper's Son"; the plate, "Little Red Riding Hood"; and the bowl and underplate, "Sing a Song of Sixpence." The service originally included a matching beaker and napkin ring. A knife, fork, and spoon were made to match the pattern as well. The cost to make the pieces seen here was $190.

Fig. 6.21
Cake plate. Shreve & Co., San Francisco, Cal., ca. 1911. Sterling silver, h. 1½ in. (3.8 cm), diam. 12 in. (30.5 cm). Marked: *S (bell) S / SHREVE & CO / STERLING / SAN FRANCISCO*. Inscribed: *ML* and *FROM / GRANDMA KILE / TO / BONNIE & BILLY / JUNE 21st 1911*. Dallas Museum of Art, gift of The Dallas Antiques and Fine Arts Society, 1988.33. Photo Lee Clockman.

The body of this piece was formed on a lathe. However, the addition of an engraved "strapwork" design complete with "rivets" gives this plate a medieval character popularized by the arts and crafts movement.

Fig. 6.22
Thimble in original box. United States; W. F. Robbins, retailer, Skowhegan, Maine; ca. 1875–1920. Silver and velvet, h. (box closed) 1⅞ in. (4.8 cm), w. 1⅛ in. (2.9 cm), d. 1⅛ in. (2.9 cm). Thimble marked: *12* and *Silver*. Box marked: *W.F. Robbins, / Skowhegan, Me*. Dallas Museum of Art, gift of Elizabeth Weaver, 1993.68. Photo Tom Jenkins.

Sewing equipment appears to have been especially popular during the nineteenth century as courting and engagement gifts. Numerous thimbles are engraved with the receiver's name. This example retains the original note which accompanied its presentation. It reads: "To my dear Mary whom I love the most of any girl."

Fig. 6.23
Fish set. Bailey & Co., Philadelphia, Pa., ca. 1860. Sterling silver, l. (slice) 12⅛ in. (30.8 cm), w. 2¼ in. (5.7 cm). Marked: *BAILY & CO. (lion) (lion) S (shield) (lion)*. Inscribed: *St. Valentine's Day / (two hearts with arrow) / 1860* and *CAB*. Private Collection, San Antonio. Photo Tom Jenkins.

The use of engine-turned decoration as seen here reached its peak of popularity between 1860 and 1875. Twist-turned handles were used by makers throughout the industry, including in upstate New York and the Midwest.

Ill. 6.4
The Bridesmaids' Dinner, New York, N.Y., 1905. Courtesy Collections of the Museum of the City of New York, The Byron Collection.

This party was given by Mrs. Eben Wright at her 10 West 53rd St. residence, for Miss Julia Lorillard Edgar, who married Richard H. Williams, Jr., on 25 April 1905.

Ill. 6.5
Dining room of the Leland Stanford house, San Francisco, Cal., 1874–1876. Courtesy Stanford University Archives. Photo Eadweard Muybridge.

With its high ceilings, wall-to-wall carpeting, chandeliers, and lavish sideboards, this dining room is representative of those found in wealthy households across the United States during the mid nineteenth century. During this period, silver hollowware was typically displayed throughout the dining room. The centerpiece on the table appears to be identical to that in fig. 3.17.

Ill. 6.6
Winter, from a Meriden Britannia Co. trade catalogue, 1881. From Meriden 1881, 13. Courtesy The Winterthur Library: Printed Book and Periodical Collection.

Fig. 6.24
Bryant Vase. James H. Whitehouse, designer; Tiffany & Co., maker, New York, N.Y.; 1875–1876. Sterling silver and gold, h. 33½ in. (85.1 cm), w. 14 in. (35.6 cm), d. 11 5/16 in. (28.7 cm). Marked: *TIFFANY & Co UNION SQUARE NEW YORK. DESIGN PATENT MAY 1875* and *TIFFANY & Co MAKERS.* Inscribed: *TRUTH CRUSHED TO EARTH SHALL RISE AGAIN.* Portrait medallion signed: *EJ (conjoined) S.* © 1989 The Metropolitan Museum of Art, gift of William Cullen Bryant, 1877, 77.9.

To reflect William Cullen Bryant's beliefs about nature and its importance in God's hierarchy, the vase is covered with flora and fauna. Also included are a medallion of "Poetry contemplating Nature," four biographical medallions and a portrait one, as well as images of a printing press and broken shackles (representing Bryant's abolitionist stance). Because of the complicated decoration, Eugene J. Soligny spent hundreds of hours chasing the vase. Consequently, the actual cost of the vase was double the $5,000 estimate. Perhaps to recoup some of its investment, Tiffany & Co. produced electrotyped copies for sale to the public, of which four are known to survive.

Ill. 6.7
Pages from a Gorham Mfg. Co. technical notebook, ca. 1877–1878. Courtesy Brown University.

This unpublished notebook is one of the most important documents on U.S. silversmithing to survive. Not only does it document numerous receipts for alloys and patinations in use at Gorham in the 1870s, but it provides technical and design information on Tiffany's as well. The book appears to have been written at Gorham, but it is annotated by Frederick A. Jordan, who worked at Tiffany's during the critical years of the late 1870s. Because of the importance of technical information to a producer, volumes such as this would have been available to only the most trusted employees. Generally they were kept by senior staff and stored in a vault.

Ill. 6.8
Charles Osborne at work, ca. 1900. Courtesy The Winterthur Library: Joseph Downs Collection of Manuscripts and Printed Ephemera.

Fig. 6.25
Serving fork and scoop. Whiting Mfg. Co., New York, N.Y., ca. 1875–1880. Sterling silver, l. (scoop) 9¾ in. (24.8 cm), w. 2½ in. (6.4 cm). Fork marked: *5A / STERLING.* Scoop marked: *(lion holding W) / STERLING / A.* Fork inscribed: *JCN.* Dallas Museum of Art (fork), The Charles R. Masling and John E. Furen Collection, gift of Mr. and Mrs. William Rubin, The Arthur A. Everts Co., and Arthur and Marie Berger by exchange, 1991.101.12; (scoop) gift of Nicholas Harris Gallery, 1991.5. Photo Tom Jenkins.

The exceptional nature of the design and casting of these pieces is representative of the extraordinary quality of which Whiting was capable. Although only these two designs are known to the author, a larger series of bird motifs may have been produced. The pheasant version exists as a salad set and as a macaroni server. The hummingbird scoop is the only example in this design known to the author. It is also the only Whiting bird piece with the Whiting mark; all the pheasant examples seen to date are unmarked.

Fig. 6.26
Goelet Schooner Prize. Whiting Mfg. Co., New York, N.Y., ca. 1882. Sterling silver, enamel, and glass, h. (pitcher) 12 5/8 in. (32.1 cm), w. 4 7/8 in. (12.4 cm); w. (tray) 18½ in. (47 cm), d. 14 in. (35.6 cm). Pitcher and tray marked: *(lion holding W) / STERLING / 1117.* Tray inscribed: *Schooner Prize / Presented By / Mr. Ogden Goelet. / To The / New York Yacht Club / Won By / Schooner Yacht Montauk / Samuel R. Platt, Owner / Newport R.I. Aug. 8th 1882.* © 1994 The Metropolitan Museum of Art, lent by Samuel Schwartz, 1972, L.1972.46.1–2.

Designed as the 1882 *Goelet Schooner Prize*, the set's ornament deals with the sea. A mermaid and dolphin are chased on the side of the pitcher. Seahorses and seaweed grace both pieces. The tray's corners are embellished with mermaid faces. Much of the plant life is highlighted with multicolored enamel in the style of Tiffany & Co. The bottom of the tray is a piece of etched glass.

Fig. 6.27
Ivory pattern jelly server. Charles Osborne, designer; Whiting Mfg. Co., maker, New York, N.Y.; designed 1890. Sterling silver, silvergilt, and ivory, l. 9¼ in. (23.5 cm), w. 2½ in. (6.4 cm). Marked: *(lion holding W) / STERLING / 2888.* Dallas Museum of Art, The Stephen Vaughan Collection, gift of the Dallas Antiques and Fine Arts Society, 1993.53. Photo Tom Jenkins.

Ivory, patented in 1891, was one of Whiting's most exceptional flatware patterns. The ivory handles were intended to fade from dark to light as here. At least twenty-four flatware pieces were available in the pattern, including a fried oyster server, lettuce fork, and ice cream slice.

Ill. 6.9
William Christmas Codman, ca. 1895. Courtesy Brown University Library.

Fig. 6.28
Cupid pattern fish set. Morgan Morgans, Jr., New York, N.Y., patented 1878. Sterling silver and silvergilt, l. (slice) 12 in. (30.5 cm), w. 2¾ in. (7 cm). Marked: *(eagle) AC (head)* and *STERLING / PAT. 1878.* Inscribed: *DT.* D. Albert Soeffing Collection. Photo Tom Jenkins.

The handles of these pieces are in a patented die-stamped pattern (no. 10,436). However, the elaborate engraving on the tines and blade is unusually eclectic in its mixture of motifs. When George Shiebler bought out Morgans in 1883 he continued to use the *Cupid* pattern.

Ill. 6.10
Helicon Vase, by Leonard Morel-Ladeuil for Frederick Elkington & Co., 1871. Courtesy Her Majesty Queen Elizabeth II.

The two recumbent female figures on the base represent Music and Poetry. The central vase is surmounted by two "genii," one holding Apollo's lyre. Escutcheons on the handles are engraved with the names of Homer, Shakespeare, Molière, Byron, Handel, Beethoven, Haydn, and Mozart. The silver vase was shown at international expositions in London (1872), Vienna (1873), and Philadelphia (1876).

Fig. 6.29
Neptune Epergne and plateau from the *Furber Service.* Attributed to Thomas Pairpoint, designer; Gorham Mfg. Co., maker, Providence, R.I.; 1872 and 1876. Sterling silver, silvergilt, and glass, h. (epergne) 26 in. (66 cm), w. 36 in. (91.4 cm), d. 21½ in. (54.6 cm). Epergne marked: *(lion) (anchor) G / STERLING / 965 / E* (date letter for 1872). Plateau marked: *STERLING / (lion) (anchor) G / GORHAM & CO / UNION SQUARE N.Y. / I* (date letter for 1876). Museum of Art, Rhode Island School of Design, gift of Textron, Inc. 1991.126.79.1, .80.

According to period accounts, the oblong bowls attached to the sides were for fruit, and the shells above for flowers. The crowning figure is of Aurora, goddess of morning, who carries a festoon of flowers in her hands. The relief plaques on the sides of the fruit bowls depict Love and Contentment. Seeing this piece at the 1876 Philadelphia world's fair, one reviewer felt it was highly original, representing "a happy departure from the ideas of the Renaissance, which have influenced largely the concepts of modern artists in silver" (Gems 1877, 13–14). This source illustrates the epergne on a different plateau, one ornamented with "flowers, buds, and tendrils." The present one, decorated with equestrian figures, is the largest of three in the *Furber Service,* but may not have been used with this epergne originally.

The creation of the epergne was a major project for Gorham. Calling it a "fruit stand," company records state that the piece weighed 400 troy ounces, valued at $540. There were special charges of $700 for executing drawings and models, as well as $200 to make a basemetal sample. About 600 hours of silversmithing time were lavished on the piece at a cost of $196. Cast-

ing required 120 hours ($66), chasing 627 hours ($375), and engraving 78 hours ($47). When finishing, gilding, and profit were added, the factory price was $2,999.70.

Fig. 6.30
Dewey Loving Cup. William C. Codman, designer; Gorham Mfg. Co., maker, Providence, R.I.; 1899. Sterling silver, silvergilt, enamel, and wood, h. 102 in. (259 cm). Marked: *(lion) (anchor) G / STERLING.* Inscribed: *THE DEWEY LOVING CUP / PRESENTED TO / TO THE CONQUERING ADMIRAL / BY SEVENTY THOUSAND / AMERICAN CITIZENS / AS A TRIBUTE / OF THEIR GRATITUDE.* Decorative and Industrial Arts Collection of the Chicago Historical Society, gift of George G. Dewey, 1934.77a–d. Photo Lynn Diane DeMarco.

Following his victory over the Spanish at the Battle of Manila Bay in 1898, Admiral George Dewey (1837–1917) became a great U.S. hero. To honor him upon his return to America, the *New York Journal* began a national campaign to collect dimes for the creation of a silver presentation piece. Codman, who designed the cup, filled the composition with references to U.S. imperialism and Dewey, including scenes of the Battle of Manila Bay, Dewey's home in Montpelier, Vermont, and the New York Dewey celebration at Grant's Tomb. The vase is surmounted by Victory holding Dewey's portrait. With the silver having been contributed, Gorham's cost of manufacturing the cup was $5,700.

Fig. 6.31
Wine cooler. Tiffany & Co., New York, N.Y., 1900. Sterling silver and copper, h. 12½ in. (31.8 cm), diam. 8⅝ in. (21.9 cm). Marked: *TIFFANY & Co. / 14478 MAKERS 3138 / STERLING SILVER / 925–1000 / T / 9 PINTS.* Inscribed: *MHD* and *EGR.* © 1992 The Art Institute of Chicago, Restricted gift of Mrs. Harold T. Martin, 1978.442. All rights reserved.

Despite a discrepancy between the time it was ordered and the date of the wedding, this piece may have been a wedding gift to Marcellus Harley Dodge (1881–1963) and Ethel Geraldine Rockefeller (1882–1973), whose initials it bears. Probably used as a wine cooler, it is listed as a "Love Cup" in Tiffany & Co.'s records. Its design is derived from antique metal and ceramic vases from southern Italy. They too feature scrolled handles and are sometimes decorated with grape vines and gadrooning. The dark center section is patinated copper. The manufacturing cost was $267.

When they married in 1907, the Dodges were said to be the richest young couple in the United States. He was the heir to and eventual chairman of the board of the Remington Arms Co., and she was the only daughter of William Rockefeller, brother of John D. Rockefeller. At age twenty-six, his fortune was estimated at $60 million and hers was even greater. The couple, and this wine cooler, resided on their estate, Giralda Farms, near Madison, New Jersey.

Fig. 6.32
Water jug and stand. Samuel Kirk & Son, Baltimore, Md., 1879. Silver, h. (jug) 13¼ in. (33.7 cm); diam. (stand) 8⅞ in. (22.6 cm). Marked: *S. Kirk & Son 11 oz.* Inscribed: *To Alexander Biddle from the children of his brother J. Williams Biddle as a token of their grateful recognition of his continuous services and devotion to their interests. Nov. 1879.* The Maryland Historical Society, Baltimore, gift from the Samuel Kirk Museum, 1984.80.13.1–2.

Following the untimely death of Jonathan Williams Biddle in 1856, his brother Alexander apparently took over the management of his nieces and nephews' business affairs. In 1879 the children honored their uncle, a prominent Philadelphia businessman, with this jug and stand as a token of their appreciation.

Fig. 6.33
Teapot from a three-piece set. Edward C. Moore, maker; Tiffany & Co., retailer, New York, N.Y.; 1867. Sterling silver, ivory, and silvergilt, h. 9½ in. (24.1 cm), d. 8 in. (20.3 cm), w. 8½ in. (21.6 cm). Marked: *TIFFANY & Co. / 1770 / M QUALITY 925/1000 M / 4189 / 550 BROADWAY.* Inscribed: *C.* Philadelphia Museum of Art, gift of the Friends of the Philadelphia Museum of Art, 1973-94-8-a.

The pot and the matching creamer and sugar bowl which were included in this exhibition reflect Edward C. Moore's fascination with moresque ornament during the 1860s. A set in the same pattern was sent to the 1867 Paris world's fair (see ill. 2.2). Four different decorative schemes were available on this shape, as well as a waste bowl and coffeepot.

Fig. 6.34
Coffee set. Tiffany & Co., New York, N.Y., 1902–1903. Sterling silver, silvergilt, enamel, ivory, and pearls, h. (pot) 9⅝ in. (24.4 cm); l. (tray) 17½ in. (44.5 cm). Pot, creamer, and bowl marked: *TIFFANY & CO. / 15313 MAKERS 5812 / STERLING/ 925–1000/ C.* Tray marked similarly except for pattern no. *15559.* Inscribed: *M.* The Masco Art Collection.

This set's elaborate Near Eastern decoration required extensive enameling, chasing, gilding, and the setting of pearls. Two similar sets were produced, one with semiprecious stones, the other with enamel.

Fig. 6.35
Four-Elephant Fruit Stand. Gorham Mfg. Co., Providence, R.I., 1881. Sterling silver and silvergilt, h. 10½ in. (26.7 cm), w. 40 in. (50.8 cm), d. 16 in. (40.6 cm). Marked: *(lion) (anchor) G STERLING N* (date letter for 1881) *1800.* Inscribed: *RA.* The Masco Art Collection.

This stand required nearly $1,500 and 900 man-hours to complete. Chasing alone took 511 hours, occupying two craftsmen for a month or more. Nevertheless, the stand was not a custom order. Apparently Gorham was willing to invest large amounts of capital and labor, gambling that the firm could sell

the piece. Only large, well-financed firms like Gorham could afford such a practice. Whether Gorham made other stands like this one is unknown. However, the molds for the elephants were used to form supports for a pair of candelabra exhibited at the 1889 Paris world's fair. Furthermore, the fruit stand must have sat on a mirrored plateau originally because the monogram is engraved in reverse on the underside of the base. When reflected in a mirror it reads properly.

Fig. 6.36
Flagon. Tiffany & Co., New York, N.Y., 1910. Sterling silver, silvergilt, ivory, and semiprecious stones, h. 23 in. (58.4 cm). Marks unavailable. Private Collection, courtesy Hoffman Gampetro Antiques. Photo courtesy Christie's.

Around the turn of the century, Tiffany's made a series of elaborate vessels from mounted tusks, some of which were exhibited at the 1900 Paris world's fair. With its stones and carving, this example is one of the most extraordinary. The manufacturing cost for it was $3,724. According to oral history, this flagon was given by the American Ambassador to France to the French Ambassador to the United States.

Fig. 6.37
Covered beaker. Tiffany & Co., New York, N.Y., ca. 1878. Sterling silver and moonstones, h. 10½ in. (26.7 cm), diam. 5⅛ in. (13 cm). Marked: *TIFFANY & CO. / 5201 MAKERS 8926 / STERLING SILVER / 925–1000 / M.* The Carnegie Museum of Art, AODA Purchase Fund, 1984.12.2.a,b. Photo Tom Barr.

The entwined snakes on the cover and center of this piece are derived from Celtic and Teutonic art.

Fig. 6.38
Beer pitcher. Bailey & Co., Philadelphia, Pa., ca. 1860–1868. Sterling silver, h. 9½ in. (24.1 cm), w. 9½ in. (24.1 cm), d. 6¾ in. (17.1 cm). Marked: *BAILEY & CO / (lion) (lion) / (lion) S (shield) / CHESTNUT ST PHILA.* Inscribed: *E.* Dallas Museum of Art, gift of the Professional Members League, 1993.17. Photo Tom Jenkins.

This pitcher's shape is taken from contemporary wooden prototypes. The use of hops and barley on the handle indicates that it was intended for beer.

Fig. 6.39
Coffeepot. Whiting Mfg. Co., New York, N.Y., ca. 1883. Sterling silver, ivory, and silvergilt, h. 9 in. (22.9 cm), w. 5½ in. (14 cm). Marked: *(lion holding W) / STERLING / 885.* Inscribed: *1858 / (crest reading FORTEM POSCE ANIMUM) / 1883.* Dallas Museum of Art, anonymous gift in honor of Mrs. Eugene McDermott, 1989.75. Photo Tom Jenkins.

This pot is part of a series of Whiting hollowware designs whose surfaces imitate textiles. It is particularly elaborate, having a "salvage edge" neck, "rope" handle, and "tied" collar. Originally, the vessel may have been a twenty-fifth wedding anniversary gift.

Fig. 6.40
Tray. Attributed to Kennard & Jenks, maker, Boston, Mass.; Bailey, Banks & Biddle, retailer, Philadelphia, Pa.; ca. 1878–1880. Sterling silver, w. 10 in. (24.5 cm), d. 10 in. (24.5 cm). Marked: *BAILEY, BANKS & BIDDLE / PHILADELPHIA* and *K STER-LING*. Mr. and Mrs. Alexander C. Speyer III Collection. Photo Tom Barr.

The *K* mark is believed to be that of Kennard & Jenks or perhaps that of its short-lived successor, Kennard & Co. Both firms appear to have specialized in such Russian-style pieces, and Gorham continued the production of them following its acquisition of the Boston firm in 1880. Besides the Russian prototypes, similar pieces also were made by other European firms, including Elkington and Christofle. Porcelain examples featuring napkins are also known and were occasionally mounted as cake plates by U.S. silverplate manufacturers.

Fig. 6.41
Pitcher. Tiffany & Co., New York, N.Y., 1875. Sterling silver and copper, h. 8⅛ in. (20.6 cm), w. 3¾ in. (9.4 cm). Marked: *TIFFANY & CO. / 4065 MAKERS 5392 / STERLING SILVER / 925–1000 / M*. Museum of Fine Arts, Boston, gift of Gideon F. T. Reed, 1877.61.

This pitcher is an early example of Tiffany & Co.'s niello work. The technique consists of inlaying another metal (in this case copper) into the silver body. The piece cost $120 to make. Tiffany's deemed this example important enough to show it at the 1876 Philadelphia world's fair, after which it was presented to the Museum of Fine Arts, Boston. The pitcher was the first piece of American silver to enter that collection.

Fig. 6.42
Pair of vases. Jomi Eisuke, Kyoto, Japan, ca. 1885. Bronze, copper, silver, and the Japanese alloys *shakudo, shibuichi,* and *sentoku,* h. 7¼ in. (18.4 cm). Marked: *(Jomi seal).* Dallas Museum of Art, Foundation for the Arts Collection, The John R. Young Collection, gift of M. Frances and John R. Young, 1993.86.3.1–.2.FA. Photo Tom Jenkins.

These vases are characteristic of the type of Japanese mixed-metal work which was seen by Americans and Europeans beginning in the mid nineteenth century. The techniques for producing such complicated inlaid and patinated surfaces were independently recreated in workshops at Tiffany's and Gorham in the 1870s and early 1880s.

Fig. 6.43
Tea kettle. Tiffany & Co., New York, N.Y., ca. 1879. Sterling silver and ivory, h. 12 in. (30.5 cm), w. 7½ in. (19.1 cm), d. 5½ in. (14 cm). Marked: *TIFFANY & Co. / 5335 MAKERS 233 / STERLING SILVER.* Inscribed: *L.M.* Dallas Museum of Art, gift of the Friends of Decorative Arts, 1988.61.a–b. Photo Tom Jenkins.

Plain versions of this body shape exist, but the engraved decoration on this example is believed to be unique. Called a "tea kettle" in Tiffany & Co.'s records, the piece was ordered to go with a sugar bowl and creamer (no. 4,676) of earlier design. The kettle cost $80 to make and was originally oxidized.

Fig. 6.44
Tray. Gorham Mfg. Co., Providence, R.I., 1881. Sterling silver, l. 12 in. (30.5 cm), w. 11 in. (30 cm). Marked: *(lion) (anchor) G / STERLING E42 / N / GORHAM & CO / H.* Dallas Museum of Art, Decorative Arts Acquisition Fund, 1993.10. Photo Tom Jenkins.

This piece was one of a series of special-order trays made in 1881. So that the marks would not damage the exceptionally fine chasing, they were engraved on the verso, not stamped.

Ill. 6.11
Ceramic plate by the Japanese potter Hizen, ca. 1875. From Audsley 1875, pl. 8. Courtesy Dallas Public Library.

Fig. 6.45
Punch bowl. Tiffany & Co., New York, N.Y., 1881. Sterling silver and silvergilt, h. 8 in. (20.3 cm), diam. 15⅞ in. (40.3 cm). Marked: *TIFFANY & CO. / 6310 MAKERS 2345 / STERLING SILVER / 925–1000 / 1438 / M / 8 QTS* and *Mr. and Mrs. / Alexander Blum / 1st Septr 1883.* Dallas Museum of Art, gift of Tiffany & Company, 1982.84. Photo David Wharton.

Apparently this is one of three bowls of this shape made. Whereas this design was achieved primarily through engraving and acid etching, one of the others had elaborate applied mounts. Here only the decorations on the base were applied. This version cost $72 to make.

Ill. 6.12
Tiffany & Co. hammering and mounting design for punch bowl no. 6,310, 1881. Courtesy Dallas Museum of Art. Photo Tom Jenkins.

This drawing is done in red and black ink on beige paper and measures 27 by 22 in. (68.5 by 56 cm). It illustrates how sophisticated were the design and production of the best U.S. silverware. Not only is the decorative scheme rendered in minute detail, but every insect and "spot" is identified by a casting or electrotyping number. In addition to a hammering and mounting design there would also have been a full-size drawing, showing the basic shape of the piece, which indicated the dies and lathe chucks to be used. The drawing was a gift of Tiffany & Company to the Dallas Museum of Art (acc. no. 1985.153). The white areas are paper repairs.

Fig. 6.46
Set of twelve fruit knives. Gorham Mfg. Co., Providence, R.I., ca. 1880. Silver, bronze, and gilding, l. (each) 7⅞ in. (20 cm), w. ⅞ in. (2.2 cm). Marked: *(lion) (anchor) G / STERLING / 5.* Dallas Museum of Art, The Lucy Ball Owsley Memorial Fund, Decorative Arts Acquisitions Fund, and funds from an anonymous donor, 1992.324.1–12. Photo Tom Jenkins.

Besides Gorham, other firms in the United States and Europe made flatware based on Japanese knives. Several English dessert sets are known, as is a luncheon set by Peter Krider of Philadelphia. However, Krider appears to have purchased the bronze handles from Gorham.

Fig. 6.47
Vase. Tiffany & Co., New York, N.Y., ca. 1877. Steel, sterling silver, and copper, h. 8⅝ in. (21.9 cm), diam. 3 in. (7.6 cm). Marked: *TIFFANY & CO. / 5045 MAKERS 114 / STERLING SILVER / AND / OTHER METALS / 141*. Inscribed: *F&BC*. Dallas Museum of Art, The Eugene and Margaret McDermott Fund, 1989.3.MCD. Photo Tom Jenkins.

This vase is part of a series Tiffany's produced using silver appliqués on a nonprecious metal body. Records indicate that the outer surface of this example is of rusted steel. Another version was of copper. On the back side are silver appliquéd polonia leaves and geometric cutouts. Except for the monogram, all the decoration is based on Japanese sources. The cylindrical form is copied from imported Japanese brushholders.

Fig. 6.48
Salad set. Whiting Mfg. Co., New York, N.Y., ca. 1880–1885. Sterling silver, silvergilt, and wood, l. (spoon) 11 in. (27.9 cm), w. 2 in. (5.1 cm). Marked: *(lion holding W) / STERLING / 11*. Dallas Museum of Art, anonymous gift, 1990.148.a–b. Photo Tom Jenkins.

This set is part of a series of Whiting salad servers featuring wooden handles with cast appliqués tacked to them with silver nails. The geometric designs carved in the wooden handles of these examples are traditional Japanese ones.

Fig. 6.49
Tray. Gorham Mfg. Co., Providence, R.I., 1883. Copper and silver, h. 1 in. (2.54 cm), w. 9¼ in. (23.5 cm), 8 in. (20.3 cm). Marked: *(anchor) / Y59 / P*. Dallas Museum of Art, Decorative Arts Acquisitions Fund, 1994.2. Photo Tom Jenkins.

This tray is part of a line of copperwares made by Gorham between 1881 and 1885. Many of the objects produced were masculine in nature, such as smoking sets, inkstands, ale mugs, and loving cups. Evidently the dark brown and red patinas given to these articles were felt to be particularly appropriate for men. This example features pine and cherry branches and a Japanese figure riding a yak.

Fig. 6.50
Vase. Tiffany & Co., New York, N.Y., 1893. Sterling silver, gold, and enamel, h. 13 in. (33 cm), diam. 5 in. (12.7 cm). Marked: *TIFFANY & CO. / 11225 T 3211 / (1893 world's fair globe mark)*. Inscribed: *FROM GEORGE AND MARGARET WESTINGHOUSE / XMAS 1897*. Mr. Jerome Rapoport and Ms. Susan Falk Collection. Photo courtesy Christie's.

Enameled pieces such as this represent the high point of the industry's attempt to introduce color into its products. Enamel work of this quality was extremely difficult, requiring the application of numerous powdered pigments and multiple firings to fuse them together. This example was shown at the 1893 Chicago world's fair and cost $563 to make.

Fig. 6.51
Cairo pattern ice cream slice. Gorham Mfg. Co., Providence, R.I., ca. 1884. Sterling silver, silvergilt, copper, gold, and other metals, l. 10 in. (25.4 cm), w. 2¼ in. (12.9 cm). Marked: *(lion) (anchor) G / STERLING AND OTHER METALS*. Dallas Museum of Art, gift of Phyllis Tucker in honor of Charles R. Masling, 1988.66. Photo Tom Jenkins.

When this pattern was first introduced it was called *Curio*, and only later was the name changed to *Cairo*. Evidently such flatware was so expensive that there was little demand for it, and consequently its production was very low.

Fig. 6.52
Clock. Tiffany & Co., New York, N.Y., ca. 1880. Sterling silver and *mokume*, h. 9 in. (22.9 cm), w. 9 in. (22.9 cm), d. 5¼ in. (13.3 cm). Marked: *TIFFANY & CO. / 6173 MAKERS [unavailable number] / STERLING-SILVER / -AND- / OTHER-METALS / 236*. Private Collection, courtesy Hoffman Gampetro Antiques. Photo courtesy Christie's.

This clock demonstrates the complicated nature of many of Tiffany & Co.'s mixed-metal creations. The original drawing reveals that the piece is constructed from approximately forty separate panels made from five different types of *mokume*. Each type is numbered individually.

Fig. 6.53
Coffeepot. Orfèvrerie Christofle, Paris, France, ca. 1880. Silver, ivory, and other metals, h. 5⅜ in. (13.5 cm). Marked: *CHRISTOFLE / No A27*. Musée Bouilhet-Christofle, Paris, M.870. Photo Studio Kollar.

This model is one of a series of vessels created by Christofle for exhibition at the *Exposition des Arts du Métal à Paris* at the *Union central des Arts Décoratifs* in 1880. While Christofle was unquestionably working in the Japanese taste before any American firm, this particular series was patterned after Tiffany & Co. wares shown at the 1878 Paris world's fair. Unlike Christofle's earlier wares, these copy Tiffany's use of silver and mixed metal appliqués on a hammered surface. Other forms in this style by the Paris firm include teapots, pitchers, and flatware.

Fig. 6.54
Cup and saucer. Orfèvrerie Christofle, Paris, France, ca. 1880. Silver and other metals, h. (cup) 2½ in. (6.4 cm); diam. (saucer) 4¾ in. (12.1 cm). Marked: *130 / CHRISTOFLE ORFEVRES / C (bee) C C (bee) C and (head)*. Mr. and Mrs. Alexander C. Speyer III Collection. Photo Tom Barr.

This cup and saucer are part of a group of Tiffany-style objects Christofle produced around 1880. The hammered surface and the nature of the colored appliqués are characteristic of these pieces.

Fig. 6.55
Tray. Pavel Ovchinnikov, Moscow, Russia, 1884. Silver and other metals, h. 7/8 in. (2.2 cm), w. 8½ in. (21.6 cm), d. 8½ in. (21.6 cm). Marked: *(Moscow mark) / OVCHINNIKOV* (in Russian) */ (B.C. over 1884) 84 A.* Mr. and Mrs. Alexander C. Speyer III Collection. Photo Tom Barr.

The Ovchinnikov workshop produced a group of objects which were near copies of Tiffany & Co. examples exhibited at the 1878 Paris world's fair. While some of these Russian wares are not of as high a standard technically as their prototypes, this tray comes very close to the Tiffany's original.

Fig. 6.56
Tête-à-tête set. James W. Tufts Co., Boston, Mass., ca. 1885. Silverplate and ivory, h. (pot) 4 in. (10.2 cm), w. 5¾ in. (14.6 cm), d. 3½ in. (8.89 cm). Marked: *JAMES W TUFTS / BOSTON WARRANTED / QUADRUPLE PLATE* (all in a circle) and *1900.* Wadsworth Atheneum, gift of the Collectors Council of the Wadsworth Atheneum, 1988.24. Photo Joseph Szaszfai.

In its 1888 catalogue Tufts Co. described this model (no. 1,900) as a tête-à-tête set. As a set the three pieces cost $10.50 wholesale; with a presentation case the cost was $15 (Tufts 1888, 117). The Japanese-style decoration was executed through bright-cutting and is of extremely high quality.

Ill. 6.13
The Sterling Co. advertisement, 1888. From *JCK* 19:9 (Oct. 1888):4. Courtesy Chilton Co.

Fig. 6.57
Tureen. George Gill, designer; Reed & Barton, maker, Taunton, Mass.; designed ca. 1873. Silverplate, h. 11 in. (27.9 cm), w. 12¾ in. (32.4 cm), d. 10 in. (25.4 cm). Marked: *MFD & PLATED BY / REED & BARTON / 2629 / G / DESIGN / PAT. AUG. 12 1873.* Dallas Museum of Art, The Faith P. and Charles L. Bybee Collection, gift of Faith P. Bybee in honor of Charles L. Venable, 1989.46.a–b. Photo Tom Jenkins.

The patent date marked on this tureen refers to no. 6,802. In 1873, George Gill of Taunton, Massachusetts, was granted this patent for the design of a tea service which incorporated the lion finial seen here. It was typical for firms to patent one design and then mark wares as patented if they incorporated any feature of that first design.

In 1877, Reed & Barton described this tureen (no. 2,629) as "satin chased" (Reed & Barton 1877, 62). The model was available in three sizes—12½, 16, and 20 pints—costs of $22, $24, and $27, respectively. The body and ornamental design were made in several other forms, including a six-piece tea and coffee set ($60) and an urn ($34). The decoration of all these pieces is an eclectic mixture of Asian motifs. The lion finial is derived from Assyrian art, while the diaper pattern and chrysanthemums on the legs come from Japanese sources. The design remained in production during the 1870s, but apparently was discontinued in the early 1880s.

Fig. 6.58
Stand. Charles Parker Co. and Meriden Britannia Co., Meriden, Conn., ca. 1885. Brass, marble, silverplate, and other metallic platings, h. 33¼ in. (84.5 cm), w. 11¾ in. (29.8 cm), d. 11¼ in. (29.8 cm). Labeled: *The Chas. Parker Co. / Meriden, Conn. / Manufacturers of / Artistic Bronze Goods.* Dallas Museum of Art, gift of Idelle and Leon Rabin in honor of Judy Nix, 1989.9. Photo Tom Jenkins.

Exactly what each of the Meriden firms contributed to this stand is unknown. While it is labeled by Parker, Meriden Britannia advertised lamps and stands in the 1880s which incorporated the same side panels. A centerpiece using the figural panel is visible in the Meriden showroom in ill. 5.3. Presumably one company made them and the other simply purchased the elements as needed.

Fig. 6.59
Fruit plate. Gorham Mfg. Co., Providence, R.I., 1881. Sterling silver, silvergilt, and copper, h. 2½ in. (6.4 cm), diam. 12 in. (30.5 cm). Marked: *(lion) (anchor) G / STERLING / AND OTHER METALS / C24 / N* (date letter for 1881) and *(French duty marks).* Dallas Museum of Art, The Eugene and Margaret McDermott Fund, 1989.6.MCD. Photo Tom Jenkins.

This custom ordered plate is one of three types made by Gorham in 1880 and 1881. One features apple branches in blossom; another, branches supporting a spider web; and this version, branches in full fruit. Because of the complicated applied decoration, the plates were expensive, costing $150 to make. At some point in its history the plate was exported to France and was stamped with French duty marks.

Fig. 6.60
Narragansett pattern berry spoon. Gorham Mfg. Co., Providence, R.I., designed 1884. Sterling silver and silvergilt, l. 9¾ in. (24.8 cm), w. 3¼ in. (8.3 cm). Marked: *STERLING (lion) (anchor) G.* Dallas Museum of Art, gift of Loyd Taylor and Paxton Gremillion, 1991.76. Photo Tom Jenkins.

This pattern features shells and sealife characteristic of Narragansett Bay off the cost of Rhode Island. The elements are so accurate that many of them probably were cast from actual objects. There were eleven serving pieces made in the pattern: fish fork and knife; salad fork and spoon; oyster fork; sugar, jelly, preserve and berry spoons; and soup and gravy ladles. Gorham occasionally made hollowware with the same applied ornament, and Whiting made repoussé salad plates and bowls with similar shell decoration.

Fig. 6.61
Dish and spoon. Wood & Hughes, New York, N.Y., ca. 1880–1890 (dish); Gorham Mfg. Co., Providence, R.I., ca. 1885–1890 (spoon). Sterling silver and silvergilt, h. (dish) 1½ in. (3.8 cm), w. 6¾ in. (17.1 cm), d. 4⅛ in. (10.5 cm); l. (spoon) 6 in. (15.2 cm), w. 1¼ in. (3.2 cm). Dish marked: *189 / W & H / STERLING.* Spoon marked: *(lion) (anchor) G STERLING 765.*

Dallas Museum of Art, The Charles R. Masling and John E. Furen Collection, gift of Mr. and Mrs. William Rubin, The Arthur A. Everts Co., and Arthur and Marie Berger by exchange, 1991.101.5, 20. Photo Tom Jenkins.

Numerous firms made shell-shaped objects in the 1880s. Gorham, for example, made nut and salt dishes, as well as spoons such as this one.

Fig. 6.62

Venetian pattern nut bowl. Simpson, Hall, Miller & Co., Meriden, Conn., ca. 1887. Silverplate, h. 9 in. (22.9 cm), w. 6½ in. (16.5 cm), d. 6½ in. (16.5 cm). Marked in a circle: *SIMPSON, MILLER, HALL & CO / QUADRUPLE / PLATE* and 64. Meriden Historical Society, Inc.

Although called "Venetian" by the maker, the style of this bowl is derived from Japanese art. The hammered surface and the cherry branch, insects, and "cracked ice" motifs all come from Asian sources.

Ill. 6.14

Indian Chief, by Meriden Britannia Co., designed ca. 1876. From Meriden 1882, 286. Courtesy Meriden Historical Society, Inc.

This figure and its mate, *Indian Squaw*, were exhibited at the 1876 Philadelphia world's fair. They stood approximately 16 inches high, continued to be made into the 1880s, and were occasionally included as decorative elements on centerpieces. The silverplated *Chief* (no. 6,400) cost $50 and the *Squaw* (no. 6,300) $45 when finished in "old silver, gold inlaid" (Meriden 1882, 286). The examples lent by the Meriden Historical Society were not available for photography at the time of publication but were included in the exhibition.

Fig. 6.63

Cigar humidor. Robert Francis Hunter, artist; Tiffany & Co., maker, New York, N.Y.; 1889. Sterling silver, h. 9¼ in. (23.5 cm), w. 12¾ in. (32.4 cm), d. 8⅛ in. (20.6 cm). Marked: *TIFFANY & Co. / 10185 M 5702 / STERLING SILVER*. Inscribed: *Presented to / Lionel Walter de Rothschild / by / August Belmont / New York, June 1889*. Dallas Museum of Art, Foundation for the Arts Collection, Mrs. John B. O'Hara Fund, 1993.69.1–3. Photo Tom Jenkins.

Etched onto the box are Robert Hunter's scenes of the outdoor pursuits of lacrosse, tobogganing, baseball, bronco busting, duck hunting, trotter horse racing, ice boat racing, and buffalo hunting. The nature of the scenes was meant to appeal to Lionel de Rothschild, who was one of Britain's great naturalists. Belmont, the Rothschilds' U.S. representative, gave the box to Lionel upon his graduation from Cambridge. The piece's original traveling case, made of California laurel and leather, survives, along with the sketches for the sporting scenes. The box cost $511 to make.

Fig. 6.64

Pitcher. Gorham Mfg. Co., Providence, R.I., 1885. Sterling silver, h. 10 in. (25.4 cm), w. 7¼ in. (18.4 cm), d. 4½ in. (11.4 cm). Marked: *(lion) G (anchor) / STERLING / 1295 / (boar's head*, date mark for 1885*)*. Museum of Fine Arts, Boston, Edwin E. Jack Fund, 1983.331.

Gorham's records indicate that this model (no. 1,295) was virtually all hand raised, requiring 55 hours of silversmithing ($19). Chasing the snakes' scales took 86 hours ($43), while casting the heads took one and one-half hours (87 cents). The net factory price was $160.

Fig. 6.65

Pueblo pattern vase. Tiffany & Co., New York, N.Y., 1893. Sterling silver, copper, enamel, and rubies, h. 2½ in. (6.35 cm), diam. 4 in. (10.2 cm). Marked: *TIFFANY & CO. / 11181 T 3169 / STERLING / (1893 world's fair globe and T mark)*. Inscribed: *Souvenir of America from Nellie*. William Hill Land & Cattle Co. Collection. Photo Tom Jenkins.

This vase was exhibited at the 1893 Chicago world's fair. It is closely related to those designed by Paulding Farnham for the 1900 Paris world's fair and may have been designed by him. Four differently decorated versions were made at a manufacturing cost of from $18 to $54. One of the others was called *Aztec*.

Fig. 6.66

Vase. Paulding Farnham, designer; Tiffany & Co., maker, New York, N.Y.; 1900. Sterling silver, copper, and turquoise, h. 7½ in. (19.1 cm), diam. 8¾ in. (22.2 cm). Marked: *TIFFANY & Co. / 13362 MAKERS 3 / STERLING SILVER / OTHER METALS / 8½ PINTS / (peacock and feather marks*, for 1900 and 1901 World's Fairs*)*. High Museum of Art, Atlanta, Ga., Virginia Carroll Crawford Collection, 1984.170.

This is one of a series of three bowls based on Native American objects which Farnham designed for display at the 1900 Paris and 1901 Buffalo world's fairs. This example is patterned after a Hupa Indian basket and is set with Arizona turquoise. The zigzag pattern was achieved by inlaying copper into the silver body. The manufacturing cost of the piece was $613.

Fig. 6.67

Cigar humidor from the *U.S.S. New Mexico Service*. Tiffany & Co., New York, N.Y., 1918. Sterling silver and enamel, h. 5½ in. (14 cm), w. 10¾ in. (27.2 cm), d. 7½ in. (19.1 cm). Marked: *TIFFANY & CO. / MAKERS / 01419 / STERLING SILVER / 925–1000 / M*. Palace of the Governors, Museum of New Mexico. Photo Arthur Taylor.

This piece is based on the famous pueblo in Taos, New Mexico. In all, the *U.S.S. New Mexico Service* contained more than forty pieces of hollowware. Details such as the ladder, chili peppers, and cactus are highlighted with enamels.

Fig. 6.68
Bowl and tray from a punch set. Attributed to Joseph Heinrich, maker, New York, N.Y., and Paris, France; Shreve, Crump & Low Co., retailer, Boston, Mass.; ca. 1900–1915. Copper, silver, silvergilt, bone, and stone, h. (bowl) 15 in. (38.1 cm), w. 24 in. (61 cm), d. 19¼ in. (48.9 cm); h. (tray) 3½ in. (8.9 cm), w. 32⅜ in. (82.2 cm), d. 29 in. (73.7 cm). Tray marked: *SHREVE CRUMP & LOW Co / BOSTON, MASS. / COPPER & SILVER.* © 1994 The Metropolitan Museum of Art, lent by Gloria Manney, 1987, L.1987.36.1–2.

The rest of this set consists of a ladle, cups, and a pair of pitchers. Like the bowl and tray, the other pieces are decorated with silver, bone, and stone ornaments symbolizing the American West. Joseph Heinrich was New York's premier maker of innovative copperwares. Although a few of his pieces bear his name, most only read *COPPER & SILVER* and have a retailer's mark or label.

Fig. 6.69
Ice bowl and spoon. Gorham Mfg. Co., maker, Providence, R.I.; Galt Bros. & Co., retailer, Washington, D.C.; designed 1870, made 1871. Sterling silver, h. (bowl) 7 in. (17.8 cm), w. 10¾ in. (27.3 cm), d. 6¾ in. (17.1 cm); l. (spoon) 11¼ in. (28.6 cm), w. 2¼ in. (5.7 cm). Bowl marked: *(lion) (anchor) G / 125 / STERLING / D* (date letter for 1871). Spoon marked: *63 / STERLING / (lion) (anchor) G.* Bowl inscribed: *M.W. Galt Bros. & Co. Washington, D.C.* Dallas Museum of Art, The Eugene and Margaret McDermott Fund, 1989.5.1–2. Photo Tom Jenkins.

This model was perhaps Gorham's most popular ice bowl and was in production until at least the mid 1880s. The manufacturing costs of the bowl and spoon were $82 and $8, respectively. The bowl was cast in two halves, onto which the icicles were soldered. The bears are secured with wing nuts.

PART III RESTRUCTURE AND REFORM, 1885–1940

Chapter 7
The Drive for Efficiency: Production

Ill. 7.1
The Tiffany & Co. Prince St. manufactory, New York, N.Y., ca. 1878. From Percy 1878.

Ill. 7.2
The George W. Shiebler manufactory, Underhill and St. Mark's Ave., Brooklyn, N.Y., 1889. From *JCK* 20:2 (Mar. 1889):131. Courtesy Chilton Co.

Ill. 7.3
The Hays Building, 21 and 23 Maiden Ln., New York, N.Y., built 1892. From *JCK* 24:13 (27 Apr. 1892):21. Courtesy Chilton Co.

Ill. 7.4
The Meriden Britannia Co. manufactory, Meriden, Conn., ca. 1882. Courtesy International Silver Co. Archives, Meriden Historical Society, Inc.

Ill. 7.5
The Gorham Mfg. Co. Elmwood manufactory, Providence, R.I., ca. 1890. From Gorham 1893, n.p. Courtesy Brown University Library.

Ill. 7.6
Drop presses in Gorham Mfg. Co. preparatory room, Elmwood manufactory, Providence, R.I., ca. 1890. Courtesy Brown University Library.

Note the use of both upper and side windows, as well as electric fixtures, to ensure ample light. Active dies are conveniently stored near the presses. The worker in the foreground is waiting to anneal silver pieces with a torch between pressings. The room was 205 by 80 feet in size.

Ill. 7.7
The Tiffany & Co. Forest Hill manufactory, Newark, N.J., ca. 1915. Courtesy Tiffany & Co.

Ill. 7.8
First-floor layout of the Tiffany & Co. Forest Hill manufactory, Newark, N.J., ca. 1901. From Parsell 1901, n.p. Courtesy Tiffany & Co.

Ill. 7.9
Second-floor layout of the Tiffany & Co. Forest Hill manufactory, Newark, N.J., ca. 1901. From Parsell 1901, n.p. Courtesy Tiffany & Co.

Fig. 7.1
Comanche Cup. Tiffany & Co., New York, N.Y., 1873. Sterling silver, h. 16 in. (40.1 cm), w. 23¼ in. (59.1 cm). Marked: *TIFFANY & CO. / 2867 / QUALITY / 925–1000 / M / 586 / UNION SQUARE.* Inscribed: *RB / FROM / L.J.P. / JANY 1ST 1874* and *EJ* (conjoined) *S.* The Masco Art Collection.

This trophy was awarded to Robert Bonner, publisher of the New York *Ledger.* Appropriately for horse racing, the design features a "Comanche Indian" riding a steed in full flight. The signed relief plaques around the base are the work of Eugene Soligny, Tiffany & Co.'s master chaser of the period. However, it is not clear whether he chased the horse and rider. The total manufacturing cost of the trophy was $960, including $720 for "patterns" and $240 for chasing. Interestingly, August Belmont, who commissioned the prize, was not billed for it until the end of 1876 and received a discount for being a good customer.

Ill. 7.10
Silversmith's Hall, 860 Broadway, New York, N.Y., built 1892. From *JCK* 24:12 (20 Apr. 1892):21. Courtesy Chilton Co.

Edward Holbrook, ca. 1910. Courtesy Brown University Library.

Chapter 8
Boosting Sales and Cutting Costs: Marketing

Fig. 8.1

Martelé dessert plate and *Grape* pattern salt dish and pepper shaker. William C. Codman, designer; Gorham Mfg. Co., maker, Providence, R.I.; 1905. Silver, diam. (plate) 10½ in. (26.7 cm); h. (shaker) 4¾ in. (12.1 cm); diam. (dish) 2⅞ in. (2.22 cm). Plate marked: *Martelé / (eagle) / (lion) (anchor) G / .9584 / RHS.* Dish and shaker marked: *(lion) (anchor) G.* Dish also marked: *A4961;* shaker also marked: *A4960.* Plate inscribed: *MFL.* Dallas Museum of Art, The Charles R. Masling and John E. Furen Collection, gift of Mr. and Mrs. William Rubin, The Arthur A. Everts Co., and Arthur and Marie Berger by exchange, 1991.101.22, 1991.101.21.1–2.a–b.

The salt dish and pepper shaker are good examples of patterns which were designed to complement the *Martelé* line but were not part of it. The plate was originally part of a large set. Because of the amount of time chaser Ernest W. Register (b. 1861) spent on the decoration, each plate cost $60 to make, probably retailing for over $100 apiece. The salt dish and pepper shaker were also expensive, selling for $24 a pair. The *Grape* pattern was introduced in 1905 and included other forms such as a tea set and caddy.

Ill. 8.1

Tiffany & Co. exhibit in the House of Jewels, 1939 New York world's fair. Courtesy Tiffany & Co. The art deco tea set in the foreground is seen in fig. 9.32.

Ill. 8.2

International Silver Co.'s advertisement for *20th Century* pattern silverware, 1938. From *Hotel Management* 34:3 (Sept. 1938):5. Courtesy International Silver Co. Archives, Meriden Historical Society, Inc., and the Detroit Public Library.

For other examples of advertisements and trade catalogues featuring silverware for railways, see Maffett 1990 and Dominy 1987.

Fig. 8.2

Serving spoon. William C. Codman, designer; Gorham Mfg. Co., maker, Providence, R.I.; ca. 1895–1900. Sterling silver and silvergilt, l. 8⅞ in. (22.5 cm), w. 3¾ in. (9.5 cm). Marked: *H86 / (lion) (anchor) G / STERLING.* Dallas Museum of Art, The Stephen Vaughan Collection, gift of the Dallas Antiques and Fine Arts Society, 1993.54.

This spoon is part of an art nouveau line of flatware designed to harmonize with *Martelé.* However, because Gorham cast the pieces in this series, the flatware was cheaper than hand-wrought examples.

Ill. 8.3

Elsie de Wolfe, ca. 1929. From de Wolfe 1929, n.p. Courtesy International Silver Co. Archives, Meriden Historical Society, Inc., and Stephen Vaughan.

Ill. 8.4

Gorham Mfg. Co.'s "Smartest Brides" advertisement, 1929. From *VF* 32:3 (May 1929):101. Courtesy The Texas/Dallas History and Archives Division, Dallas Public Library, and Gorham, Inc.

Booklets of the "Smartest Brides" were also produced throughout the United States.

Ill. 8.5

Gorham Mfg. Co.'s "Without Being Extravagant . . ." advertisement, 1930. From *VF* 34:3 (May 1930):87. Courtesy The Texas/Dallas History and Archives Division, Dallas Public Library, and Gorham, Inc.

Edward Steichen did the photography for all the advertisements in this series.

Ill. 8.6

International Silver Co.'s *Silhouette* advertisement, 1929. From *JCK* 99:6 (5 Sept. 1929):76. Courtesy Chilton Co., and International Silver Co. Archives, Meriden Historical Society, Inc.

Fig. 8.3

De Luxe Gift Box. Oneida Ltd., Oneida, N.Y., designed 1934. Plastic, h. 1½ in. (3.81 cm), w. 6¾ in. (9.5 cm), d. 3¼ in. (8.3 cm). Marked: *COMMUNITY.* Rusty Venable Collection. Photo Tom Jenkins.

Oneida introduced such boxes to boost sales of its *Community Plate* line of medium-priced silverplated flatware. The case's base was "done in a luxurious effect of hand-carved Ebony" and was fitted with covers of "Old Ivory," "Chinese Lacquer Red," and "Green Jade" (*CJ* 1 [Sept. 1934]:2, 22–23, and 27). Each originally contained a paper liner to support up to six pieces of flatware and a slot on the lid's underside for a disposable label. When the silverware, lining, and label were removed, the box could serve a variety of uses.

Ill. 8.7

Oneida's "Crystal Cases" advertisement, 1936. From *CJ* 3 (Oct. 1936):2. Courtesy Oneida Ltd. All rights reserved.

Ill. 8.8

Michigan Store Fixture Co.'s "30 Stores Now Under Way!" advertisement, 1929. From *JCK* 99:7 (12 Sept. 1929):25. Courtesy Chilton Co.

Ill. 8.9

Gorham Co. demonstration window display, ca. 1928. Courtesy Brown University Library. The coffee set pictured is that in fig. 9.29.

Ill. 8.10
A Gorham Co. employee, Mrs. Grace Robinson, demonstrating table setting at the New York or Boston store, ca. 1925. Courtesy Brown University Library.

The seated woman is Mrs. Lillian Lunn of Columbia University.

Fig. 8.4
Part of a coffee set. Black, Starr & Frost-Gorham, Inc., retailer, New York, N.Y., 1936. 14k gold, ivory, and porcelain, h. (pot) 11⅞ in. (30.2 cm); l. (tray) 17½ in. (44.5 cm). Marked: *(eagle) / BLACK, STARR & FROST / 7914 / 14 KT*, plus other order numbers on various pieces. Tray inscribed: *JAHIL / 1886 1936* and *"Their kind hearts and true Christian Characters / have made their lives joyous, and the world more beautiful for others." / for / Dear Father and Mother / on their / Golden Wedding Anniversary / Nov 3rd 1936 / from Percy and Jean* (simulated signatures). Other pieces variously inscribed. Museum of the City of New York, bequest of Percy L. Hance, 1975.156.17–21. Photo John Parnell.

These pieces are part of a large, boxed service for twelve. The porcelain cup liners are by Lenox. The colonial revival style of this design is typical of most work in precious metals from the 1920s and 1930s. John Atkinson Hance was a senior partner in the stock brokerage firm of Jesup & Lamont. His wife was Irene Louise Plume.

Chapter 9
Art and Commerce: Design

Fig. 9.1
New Art pattern salad set. William B. Durgin Co., maker, Concord, N.H.; Shreve, Crump & Low Co., retailer, Boston, Mass.; designed 1904. Sterling silver, l. (spoon) 9¾ in. (24.8 cm), w. 3⅛ in. (7.9 cm). Marked: *D STERLING Shreve, Crump & Low Co.* Inscribed: *FHL*. Dallas Museum of Art, The Stephen Vaughan Collection, gift of the 1992 Silver Supper and Mr. and Mrs. John H. Chiles, 1993.57.1–2. Photo Tom Jenkins.

New Art was a variant pattern only made in serving pieces. Different flowers appeared on various pieces. This design is very close to the Durgin pattern *Iris*.

Fig. 9.2
Decanter. William B. Durgin Co., Concord, N.H., and T. G. Hawkes & Co., Corning, N.Y., ca. 1900. Sterling silver, silver-gilt, and cut glass, h. 12⅝ in. (32.1 cm), w. 6½ in. (16.5 cm), d. 6 in. (15.2 cm). Marked: *D STERLING*, Norwest Corporation, Minneapolis.

Cut glass mounted in silver was at its height of popularity between 1890 and 1915. This example, with its fluid art nouveau styling, is especially successful. The model was available ungilded. Hawkes & Co. supplied many silver producers with glass for mounting.

Fig. 9.3
Chafing dish. Joseph Heinrich, maker, New York, N.Y., and Paris, France; Cowell & Hubbard Co., retailer, Cleveland, Ohio; ca. 1900–1915. Copper, silver, and wood, h. 11¼ in. (28.6 cm), w. 21¼ in. (54 cm), d. 14¾ in. (37.5 cm). Marked: *COPPER & SILVER / 4*. Labeled: *THE COWELL & HUBBARD CO.* Dallas Museum of Art, gift of the Alvin and Lucy Owsley Foundation and memorial funds in memory of Constance Owsley Garrett, 1989.14.a–c. Photo Tom Jenkins.

This extremely popular chafing dish model was retailed through many prominent jewelry stores across the United States. Cast rabbits were also used on egg coddlers and pitchers.

Fig. 9.4
Ash tray and cigarette case. Unger Brothers, Newark, N.J., ca. 1900–1910. Sterling silver, l. (tray) 6½ in. (16.5 cm), w. 3½ in. (8.9 cm). Marked: *UB* (conjoined) *STERLING 925 UB* (conjoined). Case inscribed: *CY*. Dallas Museum of Art, The Charles R. Masling and John E. Furen Collection, gift of Mr. and Mrs. William Rubin, The Arthur A. Everts Co., and Arthur and Marie Berger by exchange, 1991.101.15–16. Photo Tom Jenkins.

Unger Brothers produced some of the most provocative art nouveau designs in the United States. The images of a partially nude female and a woman smoking would have been considered risqué by many Americans. Nevertheless, the firm made an extensive line of such stamped wares. It is possible they were intended for male consumers.

Fig. 9.5
Pair of *Martelé* vases. William C. Codman, designer; Gorham Mfg. Co., maker, Providence, R.I.; 1899. Silver, h. 18¼ in. (46.4 cm), diam. 7½ in. (19.1 cm). Marked: *(eagle) (lion) (anchor) G / 950–1000 FINE / 1477* (in oval) and *(sickle*, date mark for 1899*)*. Inscribed: *JS*. Dallas Museum of Art, The Oberod Collection, anonymous gift, 1991.33.1–2. Photo Tom Jenkins.

Because of the 130 hours required to chase each one, these vases cost Gorham the large sum of $300 apiece to make. A series of related examples was made for consideration for display at the 1900 Paris world's fair. This pair features irises and tulips.

Fig. 9.6
Martelé dressing table and stool. William C. Codman, designer; Gorham Mfg. Co., maker, Providence, R.I.; 1899–1900. Silver, glass, fabric, and ivory, h. (table) 58½ in. (149 cm), w. 37½ in. (95.3 cm), d. 21 in. (53 cm). Table and stool marked: *Martelé / (eagle) / (lion) (anchor) G / 950–1000 fine*. Table also marked: *2117* (in oval). Stool also marked: same as above except for: *3709* (in an oval) / *(sickle*, date mark for 1899*)*. Private Collection, courtesy Hoffman Gampetro Antiques. Photo courtesy Sotheby's.

This table and stool, along with the dressing set which originally accompanied them, were the most extraordinary objects created by Gorham for the 1900 Paris world's fair. To ensure success, Gorham had its best workers execute the pieces. Head designer Codman did the designs that featured symbols reflecting the times of day when the table would be used—Aurora for morning and an owl for night. Lead silversmith Joseph E. Straker oversaw the piece's construction, and the firm's best chaser, Robert Bain, executed the most difficult decoration. Following the Paris fair, the pieces were purchased by Boston millionaire Thomas W. Lawson.

Fig. 9.7
Martelé pitcher. William C. Codman, designer; Gorham Mfg. Co., maker, Providence, R.I.; Spaulding & Co., retailer, Chicago, Ill.; 1909. Silver, h. 10 in. (25.4 cm), w. 8½ in. (21.6 cm), d. 5¾ in. (14.6 cm). Marked: *Martelé / (eagle) / (lion) (anchor) G / .9584 / PCX / SPAULDING & CO / CHICAGO.* Dallas Museum of Art, The Oberod Collection, anonymous gift, 1991.32. Photo Tom Jenkins.

Even though this piece is relatively plain, the chaser Christopher Clissold spent nearly a week executing the decoration. The pitcher's costing record notes "Martelé - new style" in reference to the less complicated nature of these later *Martelé* examples. Apparently the pitcher originally sat upon a small, rectangular salver.

Fig. 9.8
Martelé candelabrum (one of a pair). William C. Codman, designer; Gorham Mfg. Co., maker, Providence, R.I.; 1905. Silver, h. 18⅜ in. (46.7 cm), w. 16 in. (40.1 cm), d. 16 in. (40.1 cm). Marked: *Martelé / (eagle) / (lion) (anchor) G / .9584 / RHH.* Dallas Museum of Art, The Oberod Collection, anonymous gift, 1991.34.1–2. Photo Tom Jenkins.

Called an "Electrolier" by Gorham, this piece originally must have had electrical fittings for light bulbs which slipped into the candle sockets. Evidently this arrangement was not successful since the fittings do not survive. Besides the electrical attachments, candlesticks were originally part of this very expensive order. The candelabra alone cost $525 apiece to make, primarily because of the nearly 600 hours that Clemens Friedell took to chase the pair. The ornament Friedell chased is in the form of poppy flowers, leaves, and seed pods.

Fig. 9.9
Covered cup. George Christian Gebelein, Boston, Mass., ca. 1915–1930. Sterling silver, h. 4⅛ in. (10.5 cm), w. 8 in. (20.3 cm), d. 4½ in. (11.4 cm). Marked: *GEBELEIN.* Dallas Museum of Art, 20th-Century Design Fund, 1993.8.1–2. Photo Tom Jenkins.

This cup is directly based on British and American silver from the late seventeenth century. It may even be an exact copy. When placed under the cup, the lid becomes a stand.

Fig. 9.10
Pitcher. Tiffany & Co., New York, N.Y., 1909. Sterling silver, h. 8⅛ in. (20.6 cm), w. 9¼ in. (23.5 cm), d. 5¾ in. (14.6 cm).

Marked: *TIFFANY & Co. / 17580 MAKERS 6535 / STERLING SILVER / 925–1000 / M* and *SPECIAL HAND WORK / 5½ PINTS.* William Hill Land & Cattle Co. Collection. Photo Tom Jenkins.

Tiffany & Co.'s "special hand work" line apparently was not a great commercial success and is extremely rare today. The faceted surface of this pitcher was created by bending the silver, not soldering panels together. The rim around the inside of the lip was added for extra strength.

Fig. 9.11
Pitcher. Derby Silver Co., Derby, Conn., ca. 1915–1930. Silverplate, h. 6¼ in. (15.9 cm), w. 8⅝ in. (21.9 cm), d. 6 in. (15.2 cm). Marked: *W.M. Mounts / DERBY S. P. CO. INTERNATIONAL S. CO.* (in D-shaped reserve) / *HAND BEATEN.* Sylvia and Charles Venable Collection. Photo Tom Jenkins.

Although marked as if it were hand raised, this pitcher was mechanically formed. The hammer marks were added later to make it more competitive against handmade arts and crafts–style silver. W. M. Mounts was probably a retailer.

Fig. 9.12
Hand mirror. Unger Brothers, Newark, N.J., ca. 1910–1920. Sterling silver and enamel, l. 11½ in. (29.2 cm), w. 6¼ in. (15.9 cm). Marked: *STERLING / UB* (conjoined) *925 FINE / CROSS.* The Mitchell Wolfson, Jr., Collection, courtesy The Wolfsonian Foundation, Miami Beach, Fla., and Genoa, Italy, 1990.1271.

This mirror is made of two die-stamped halves soldered together. The "hammer marks" were produced during stamping, not by hand.

Fig. 9.13
Hand mirror. Arthur Nevill Kirk, Cranbrook Academy, Bloomfield Hills, Mich., ca. 1931. Sterling silver, ivory, enamel, and semiprecious stones, l. 10 in. (25.4 cm), w. 5½ in. (14 cm). Unmarked. Cranbrook Academy of Art Museum, gift of Henry Scripps Booth, 1987.61. Photo R. H. Hensleigh.

As he did with all his pieces, Kirk produced this mirror through meticulous handwork. The result was a unique object of great expense. Kirk was especially skilled at enameling silver, as demonstrated by the central decoration. This mirror was commissioned by Henry Scripps Booth, the son of Cranbrook's founders George and Ellen Booth, for his wife Carolyn.

Fig. 9.14
Bowl. Kalo Shop, Chicago, Ill., ca. 1914–1918. Sterling silver, h. 4¼ in. (10.8 cm), diam. 11¼ in. (28.6 cm). Marked: *HAND WROUGHT / AT / THE KALO SHOPS / CHICAGO AND NEW YORK / 4L.* Dallas Museum of Art, anonymous gift, 1991.22. Photo Tom Jenkins.

This bowl is part of a small group of bowls and trays which combine the shapes of circle and square. Typically, Kalo bowls are circular throughout. This one was made during the brief period when Kalo maintained a retail shop in New York, as well as in Chicago.

Fig. 9.15
Punch bowl, ladle, and tray. Robert Riddle Jarvie, Chicago, Ill., 1911. Sterling silver, h. (bowl) 10⅛ in. (25.7 cm), diam. 15½ in. (39.4 cm); diam. (tray) 20¾ in. (52.7 cm). Marked: *Jarvie / Chicago / STERLING.* Bowl inscribed: *PRESENTED TO JOHN J. HATTSTAEDT BY THE FACULTY OF THE AMERICAN CONSERVATORY OF MUSIC ON THE TWENTY-FIFTH ANNIVERSARY OF ITS FOUNDATION 1886–1911.* © 1991 The Art Institute of Chicago, gift of Mr. and Mrs. John R. Hattstaedt in memory of his father, John J. Hattstaedt, 1974.293a–c. All rights reserved.

Greatly influenced by the Chicago Prairie School of architecture in its design, this punch set is possibly Jarvie's most ambitious object. Because his production was extremely low, Jarvie silver is rare today.

Fig. 9.16
Teapot. Shreve & Co., San Francisco, Cal., ca. 1911. Sterling silver and ivory, h. 7¼ in. (18.4 cm), diam. 7 in. (17.8 cm). Marked: *S (bell) S / SHREVE & Co / STERLING / SAN FRANCISCO* and *2 PINTS / 3309.* Inscribed: *FEB. 15, 1911.* Dallas Museum of Art, Foundation for the Arts Collection, gift of Mrs. Alfred L. Bromberg and Mr. and Mrs. Barton C. English, 1990.2.a–b.FA. Photo Tom Jenkins.

The lathe-turned shape of this pot was based on Japanese porcelain prototypes. This model was available with a stand and burner.

Fig. 9.17
Dish. Arts and Crafts Shop of Shreve, Crump & Low Co., Boston, Mass., 1902–1914. Sterling silver and stones, h. 2¼ in. (5.7 cm), w. 11½ in. (29.2 cm), d. 4¼ in. (10.7 cm). Marked: *SHREVE, CRUMP / & LOW CO. / STERLING* and *(eagle).* Inscribed: *RLA.* © 1991 The Art Institute of Chicago, Mr. and Mrs. Robert A. Kubicek Fund, 1981.206. All rights reserved. Photo Robert Hashimoto.

This dish is directly patterned after examples by the English designer Charles Robert Ashbee, some of which were imported into the United States during the period. The form was also widely known through printed sources.

Fig. 9.18
Coffee set. Arthur J. Stone, Gardner, Mass., designed 1914. Sterling silver and ivory, h. (coffeepot) 8¾ in. (22.2 cm), w. 6½ in. (16.5 cm), d. 4 in. (10.2 cm); l. (tray) 16¾ in. (42.5 cm), w. 11⅜ in. (28.9 cm). Pot marked: *STERLING / (A.STONE with hammer) / H.* Inscribed: *LWJ.* Dallas Museum of Art, 20th-Century Design Fund, 1993.9.1–4. Photo Tom Jenkins.

Based on eighteenth-century American examples, this design was featured in Bergengren 1915, 21. The marks (*H* on the pot and basket, *C* on creamer, and *T* on the tray) indicate that

Stone's craftsmen Arthur L. Hartwell, David Carlson, and Herbert A. Taylor made pieces for the set. The handles of the sugar bowl and creamer are pierced.

Fig. 9.19
Old English pattern serving spoon. Gorham Mfg. Co., Providence, R.I., ca. 1865–1875. Silver and silvergilt, l. 9½ in. (24.3 cm), w. 2½ in. (6.4 cm). Unmarked. Inscribed: *MEP.* Dallas Museum of Art, The Stephen Vaughan Collection, gift of the 1991 Silver Supper, 1991.7.3. Photo Tom Jenkins.

This is one of Gorham's earliest colonial revival patterns. The handle is directly based on English "seal-top" spoons. The bowl with its elaborate engraving is not, however. Wood & Hughes made flatware with similar handles.

Fig. 9.20
Tea set. Charters, Cann & Dunn, maker, New York, N.Y.; Allcock & Allen, retailer, New York, N.Y., ca. 1850. Coin silver and ivory, h. (urn) 17 in. (43.2 cm), w. 11½ in. (29.2 cm), d. 11¼ in. (28.6 cm). Marked: *ALLCOCK & ALLEN / (eagle and shield) CC&D (arm and hammer) / NY.* Inscribed: *WEBBER.* Charles Folk Collection. Photo Tom Jenkins.

This is one of the earliest examples of acorn-shaped silverware. The quality of design on this example is extremely high, with various parts of an oak tree being used in interesting and successful ways. During the 1850s and 1860s, such designs were often called *Charter Oak.* Sets were made in silverplate, as well.

Fig. 9.21
Love Playing with Time pattern serving spoon. Tiffany & Co., New York, N.Y., designed 1884, made ca. 1891–1902. Sterling silver, l. 11⅞ in. (30.2 cm), w. 3½ in. (8.9 cm). Marked: *TIFFANY & CO. / STERLING / T / 619.* Dallas Museum of Art, gift of Mr. and Mrs. Richard E. Gutman, 1991.100.1. Photo Tom Jenkins.

This spoon depicts *Love Playing with Time* and was part of a series of seven baroque-style spoons introduced in 1884. The series was based on seventeenth-century Dutch examples. The back of the bowl has an extended "rat tail" and acid-etched foliate decoration. The ring allowed the spoon to be displayed on the wall when not in use. This pattern cost $18 to make and was available with gilding for an additional charge.

Ill. 9.1
Gorham Mfg. Co.'s colonial revival advertisement, 1886. From *JCK* 16:12 (Jan. 1886):xvi. Courtesy Gorham, Inc.

Note the colonial revival nature of both the architecture and the silverware.

Ill. 9.2
Page from Whiting Mfg. Co. day book, 1885. From Whiting 1884, v. 1, n.p. Courtesy Brown University Library.

From left to right the ledger notes design, date, order number, and title.

Ill. 9.3
Page from Whiting Mfg. Co. day book, 1916. From Whiting 1884, v. 2, n.p. Courtesy Brown University Library.

From left to right the ledger notes pattern and order number, title, date, and design.

Fig. 9.22
Adam pattern sauceboat and stand. Gorham Mfg. Co., maker, Providence, R.I.; Shreve, Crump & Low Co., retailer, Boston, Mass.; 1916. Sterling silver, h. (boat) 5 in. (12.7 cm), w. 7 in. (17.8 cm), d. 3½ in. (8.9 cm); l. (stand) 8 in. (20.3 cm), w. 5½ in. (14 cm). Boat marked: *(lion) (anchor) G / STERLING / A9968 / (bear, date mark for 1916)* and *SHREVE, CRUMP & LOW CO.* Stand identically marked except for *A9969*. Dallas Museum of Art, The Stephen Vaughan Collection, gift of the 1992 Silver Supper, 1993.56.a–b. Photo Tom Jenkins.

The shape of the sauceboat is based on eighteenth-century American and British examples. The decoration is also patterned after neoclassical pieces, but is much less exact. The pieces were made to match the *Adam* pattern tea set (no. A9951). Introduced in 1916, the boat and stand were available through the 1920s. Volatility in the economy caused by WWI and the 1921 recession made the prices of these pieces fluctuate radically. When introduced in 1916 the boat's wholesale cost was $59. By September 1917 it cost $79 and then rose to $108 by the end of 1919. The recession resulted in falling prices and the boat's cost was reduced to $64. However, in 1922 the piece became a special order item at a wholesale price of $140. In October 1929 the price was $150 which meant that the boat alone retailed for around $250. The tray cost an additional $75 wholesale ($135 retail). The set took 85 hours to make.

Fig. 9.23
Madame DuBarry pattern meat fork. William B. Durgin Co., maker, Concord, N.H.; Shreve, Crump & Low Co., retailer, Boston, Mass.; designed 1904. Sterling silver, l. 9⅜ in. (23.8 cm), w. 1¾ in. (4.4 cm). Marked: *D STERLING Shreve Crump & Low.* Inscribed: *W.* Dallas Museum of Art, The Stephen Vaughan Collection, gift of the Dallas Antiques and Fine Arts Society, 1993.52. Photo Tom Jenkins.

Although loosely based on eighteenth-century French flatware, this pattern is closer to contemporary beaux-arts designs. A full range of flatware was available in this pattern.

Ill. 9.4
American Silver Co.'s *Somerset* pattern advertisement, 1919. From *JCK* 78:1 (5 Feb. 1919):133. Courtesy Chilton Co.

Fig. 9.24
Tea and coffee set. Peter Müller-Munk, New York, N.Y., ca. 1931. Sterling silver and ivory, h. (kettle) 10 in. (24.5 cm); l. (tray) 24¾ in. (62.9 cm). Marked: *P (in circle) PETER MULLER-MUNK HANDWROUGHT STERLING SILVER 925/ 1000 STERLING.* © 1994 The Metropolitan Museum of Art, gift of Mr. and Mrs. Herbert J. Isenburger, 1978.439.1–5.

The design of this set reflects Müller-Munk's Germanic training. Its severe form and ornament are close to examples made between 1900 and 1945 in design centers like Munich, Berlin, and Vienna.

Fig. 9.25
Tureen-on-stand. Marie Zimmermann, New York, N.Y., 1915. Sterling silver, iron, and crystal, h. 16 in. (40.6 cm), diam. 11¼ in. (28.6 cm). Marked: *Marie Zimmermann (in script) / FINE SILVER / Maker (in script) / no. 1479–1915 / (logo).* Private Collection. Photo courtesy Sotheby's.

This tureen is one of Zimmermann's most exceptional pieces. The character of the hammered surface and the use of low relief ornament is related to contemporary Viennese work. The iron stand demonstrates Zimmermann's ability to work in a variety of metals, including copper.

Fig. 9.26
Compote. Johan Rohde, designer; Georg Jensen Sølvsmedie, maker, Copenhagen, Denmark; Neiman-Marcus, retailer, Dallas, Tex.; designed 1916, made ca. 1936. Sterling silver, h. 8 in. (20.3 cm), diam. 11 in. (27.9 cm). Marked: *GEORG JENSEN / JR (conjoined) / 925S / STERLING DENMARK / 196.* Dallas Museum of Art, gift of Herbert Marcus, 1936.1.

This piece is typical of the majority of Jensen silver sold in the United States. While more elaborate examples were made, Americans tended to prefer simple designs.

Fig. 9.27
Pair of candlesticks. Peer Smed, New York, N.Y., 1934. Sterling silver, h. 17 in. (43.2 cm), diam. 6½ in. (16.5 cm). Marked: *1934 / PEER SMED / STERLING.* William Hill Land & Cattle Co. Collection. Photo Tom Jenkins.

The use of a hammered surface and leaves is typical of Scandinavian-inspired silverwork. Like many of his contemporaries, Smed seems to have found it hard to compete against Jensen's products and thus produced relatively little work.

Fig. 9.28
Candy jar. Erik Magnussen, designer; Gorham Mfg. Co., maker, Providence, R.I.; Spaulding & Co., retailer, Chicago, Ill.; 1926. Sterling silver and ivory, h. 8¾ in. (22.2 cm), diam. 6⅝ in. (16.8 cm). Marked: *GORHAM / (lion) (anchor) G / STERLING / EHH* and *MADE FOR SPAULDING & COMPANY / EM.* Dallas Museum of Art, gift in memory of Ethyl Carradine Kurth, 1990.230.a–b. Photo Tom Jenkins.

Besides handmade wares such as this example, Magnussen also designed a line of stamped and spun wares for Gorham. This piece was called a candy jar by Gorham.

Ill. 9.5
Erik Magnussen at Gorham Mfg. Co, ca. 1926. Courtesy Brown University Library.

By showing the artist contemplating his work placed on a ped-estal like sculpture, this photograph linked Magnussen's de-signs for Gorham with fine art.

Fig. 9.29
Cubic pattern coffee set. Erik Magnussen, designer; Gorham Mfg. Co., maker, Providence, R.I.; 1927. Sterling silver and silvergilt, h. (pot) 9¾ in. (24.8 cm), w. 9⅛ in. (23.2 cm), d. 4 in. (10.2 cm); l. (tray) 22 in. (55.1 cm), w. 13⅝ in. (34.6 cm). Marked: *GORHAM / EM / (lion) (anchor) G / 28 / STERLING / DESIGNED AND EXECUTED BY ERIK MAGNUSSEN / 1927.* Museum of Art, Rhode Island School of Design, gift of Textron, Inc., 1991.126.488.1–4.

This set was not only radical in its design but extremely difficult to make. It was constructed from panels which were patinated or gilded to enhance the cubist composition. Other *Cubic* pattern objects were also created, including a salad set and com-pote.

Fig. 9.30
Cigar humidor. Tiffany & Co., New York, N.Y., 1925. Sterling silver, h. 8⅝ in. (21.9 cm), w. 14⅜ in. (36.6 cm), d. 10¼ in. (26 cm). Marked: *TIFFANY & Co. / MAKERS / 39944 / STER-LING SILVER / 925–1000 / M.* Inscribed: *CML* and *TO CARL M LOBE PRESIDENT OF THE AMERICAN METAL COM-PANY LIMITED ON THE OCCASION OF HIS FIFTIETH BIRTHDAY FROM HIS ASSOCIATES SEPTEMBER 28 1925.* Museum of Fine Arts, Houston, gift of "One Great Night in November," 1987.267.

The style of the relief panels is closely related to some contem-porary painting which used strongly silhouetted figures and depicted scenes of workers. While this style in painting reached its height of popularity in the United States during the 1930s, it was seldom used in silverwork. Cigar humidors and related smoking equipment were objects frequently presented to men (see fig. 6.63).

Fig. 9.31
Teapot. Jean Puiforcat, Paris, France, ca. 1935. Silver, silvergilt, and plastic, h. 5½ in. (14 cm), w. 9 in. (22.9 cm), d. 3 in. (7.6 cm). Marked: *EP / JEAN PUIFORCAT / (head).* Dallas Mu-seum of Art, gift of Puiforcat Corporation, 1985.161.

In its slick surface and bold design, this pot is representative of the best French art deco design. It is also interesting as an early use of lucite plastic.

Fig. 9.32
Tea set. Albert Barney, designer; Tiffany & Co., New York, N.Y.; 1939. Sterling silver, jade, and fiber, h. (kettle) 13⅞ in. (35.2 cm); l. (tray) 24½ in. (62.2 cm), w. 14 in. (35.6 cm). Pot marked: *TIFFANY & Co. / TIFFANY & Co. / MAKERS / STERLING SILVER / 22647 / M* and *2 PINTS.* Inscribed: *MSR.* Denis Gallion and Daniel Morris / Historical Design Collection, New York City.

The geometric shapes and plain surfaces of this set reflect strong French influence. Designed for display at the 1939 New York world's fair, the set's retail value was $2,200 (see ill. 8.1).

Fig. 9.33
Skyscraper pattern cocktail shaker. Louis W. Rice, designer; Bernard Rice's Sons, Inc., maker, New York, N.Y.; ca. 1930. Silverplate, h. 11⅛ in. (28.3 cm), w. 7⅜ in. (18.7 cm), d. 4⅛ in. (10.5 cm). Marked: *SKY / SCRAPER / DES. PAT. / PENDING / APOLLO / E.P.N.S. / MADE IN U.S.A. BY / BERNARD RICE'S SONS, INC. / 5267.* William Hill Land & Cattle Co. Collection. Photo Tom Jenkins.

The skyscraper was an icon of modernist America and was used in a variety of applied arts. Since the cocktail was also identified with the United States, it is not surprising that the two im-ages were combined here. The *Skyscraper* pattern was part of the *Apollo Studio* line, which also included tea sets, pitchers, and dressing sets.

Fig. 9.34
Tea set. Jean G. Theobald, designer; Wilcox Silver Plate Co., maker, Meriden, Conn.; designed 1928. Silverplated pewter and wood, h. 4 in. (10.2 cm), w. 8½ in. (21.6 cm), d. 7 in. (17.8 cm). Marked: *WILCOX S. P. CO. / INTERNATIONAL S. CO. (in D-shaped reserve with crossed hammers in center) / 7036.* The Mitchell Wolfson, Jr., Collection, courtesy The Wolfsonian Foundation, Miami Beach, Fla., and Genoa, Italy, 1983.9.7.1–4.

This set is one of three radical tea set designs commissioned by International Silver for production by Wilcox in the late 1920s. As seen in ill. 9.6, this model was marketed as being "Compact to fit into the scheme of daily living." Its patent (no. 76,564) refers to it as a "Table Set."

Fig. 9.35
Coffee urn and tray. Eliel Saarinen, designer; Wilcox Silver Plate Co., maker, Meriden, Conn.; designed 1934. Silverplate, h. (urn) 14¼ in. (36.2 cm); diam. (tray) 18 in. (45.7 cm). Urn and tray marked: *WILCOX S. P. CO. / EPNS / INTERNATIONAL S. CO. / N5873 / TS.* Cranbrook Academy of Art Museum, 1935.8a–b. Photo R. H. Hensleigh.

The prototype for this piece was unveiled in the exhibition *Con-temporary American Industrial Arts* at the Metropolitan Mu-seum of Art in 1934. Although it was included as a "line" item in trade literature and several variations seem to exist, the model was evidently not commercially successful. With a capacity of twenty-six cups, the urn (no. 5,873) listed for $80 and the tray (no. 5,875) cost $30.

Fig. 9.36
Contempora pattern knife, spoon, and fork. Eliel Saarinen, designer; Reed & Barton, maker, Taunton, Mass.; designed ca. 1927–1928, made 1935. Sterling silver, l. (knife) 8⅝ in. (21.9 cm). Fork and spoon marked: *STERLING (rectangle, circle, dia-mond) R.* Knife blade marked: *MIRRORSTEEL STAINLESS.*

Knife handle marked: *STERLING HANDLE*. Cranbrook Academy of Art Museum, 1935.41a–c. Photo R. H. Hensleigh.

This pattern was originally designed for Dominick & Haff, but was transferred to Reed & Barton when it acquired that firm in 1928. The pattern's sales campaign touted it as "Expressing in Sterling Silver, The Spirit of American Life and Art." Advertising material also noted that "Saarinen's creation was the subject of intense interest and artistic acclaim" at "an exhibition of original sterling patterns, typifying the best in contemporary design, recently held at the Metropolitan Museum of Art in New York City." The show was *The Architect and the Industrial Arts: An Exhibition of Contemporary American Design*, held in 1929. In spite of the publicity, *Contempora* was not commercially successful and it was removed from production in 1936.

Ill. 9.6
International Silver Co.'s "New Sophistication" advertisement, 1929. From *VF* 32:3 (May 1929):113. Courtesy International Silver Co. Archives, Meriden Historical Society, Inc.

Ill. 9.7
Gorham Co. demonstration window display, ca. 1928. Courtesy Brown University Library.

Note the combination of modernist and colonial revival wares, as well as hammers and unfinished objects to emphasize the handmade nature of the pieces.

Ill. 9.8
Designs for table displays in Tiffany & Co.'s retail store in New York, ca. 1940. Courtesy Tiffany & Co.

These renderings document how Tiffany & Co. tried to appeal to avant garde and conservative consumers simultaneously.

Fig. 9.37
Pitcher. Gorham Mfg. Co., Providence, R.I., 1928. Sterling silver, h. 11 in. (28 cm), w. 9⅜ in. (23.8 cm), d. 5½ in. (14 cm). Marked: *GORHAM / (lion) (anchor) G / STERLING / NFQ / (sheaf of wheat, date mark for 1928) / REPRODUCTION*. Museum of Art, Rhode Island School of Design, gift of Textron, Inc., 1991.126.189.

As marked on its bottom, this pitcher is based directly on an antique example. Besides marking wares "REPRODUCTION," Gorham also marked some "XIX CENTURY HEIRLOOM." This particular piece is patterned after a seventeenth-century Spanish prototype. Objects in the Spanish taste were especially appealing to individuals participating in the colonial Spanish revival. This movement was strongest in Florida, the Southwest, and California.

Fig. 9.38
Coronet pattern coffee urn. Chase Brass & Copper Co., Waterbury, Conn., designed ca. 1930. Chromeplate, plastic, and glass, h. 12 in. (30.5 cm), w. 10¼ in. (26 cm), d. 10 in. (25.4 cm). Marked: *CHASE BRASS & COPPER CO. / (centaur) / WATTS HIGH 900 WATTS LOW 100 / MODEL 17088 VOLTS 110–120 A.C.-D.C.* Dallas Museum of Art, gift of David T. Owsley, 1990.222.1.a–c. Photo Tom Jenkins.

The use of chromeplate and white plastic gives this urn an appearance similar to silver and ivory, but at much lower cost. In 1938 this urn (no. 17,088) retailed for $19.95 and an entire set (no. 90,121), consisting of urn, creamer, sugar, and tray, cost $28.95. Consequently, these models were relatively popular, as was the rest of Chase's *Specialty* line. In promoting the *Coronet* urn Chase's catalogue said: "When many cups of coffee are needed for meals, buffet parties, bridge and club meetings, this beautiful percolating urn will make 18 cupfuls. And with the percolating basket removed, it will store an additional 7 cupfuls, and serve 25 people" (Kilbride 1988, 47).

Fig. 9.39
Thermos. Henry Dreyfuss, designer; American Thermos Bottle Co., maker, Norwich, Conn.; designed 1936. Aluminum, glass, enamel, rubber, and steel, h. 7¼ in. (18.4 cm), w. 7½ in. (19.1 cm), d. 5¼ in. (13.3 cm). Marked: *THE AMERICAN THERMOS BOTTLE CO. / THE ONLY / THERMOS / REG. U.S. PAT. OFFICE / NO. 549 / VACUUM BOTTLE / DESIGNED BY / HENRY DREYFUSS* (in script) */ NORWICH, CONN. U.S.A.* Dallas Museum of Art, gift of David T. Owsley through the Owsley Alconda Foundation, 1994. Photo Tom Jenkins.

This thermos (model no. 549) was available in several sizes and is typical of the new types of materials and streamlined designs introduced in the 1930s. The inner glass thermos bottle is enclosed in an aluminum and enameled steel shell. Some firms, like Gorham, had introduced lines of aluminum wares earlier, but it was in the 1930s that the metal was first used extensively. Here the material is given a "machine" aesthetic through bold geometric shaping and a brushed surface. After World War II, stamped and spun aluminum table ware became increasingly popular.

The presence of the designer's name in facsimile script on this object is important. Henry Dreyfuss (1903–1972) was one of this country's most famous industrial designers during the second quarter of the twentieth century. By marking its wares with his name, the manufacturer hoped to increase sales to consumers who desired "designer" products.

INDEX